The scientific study of mental disorder is progressing rapidly because of new discoveries in molecular genetics, cognitive processes, neurochemistry, and neuroanatomy. The study of mental disorder has evolved from a primarily descriptive discipline into a mature science with strong biological underpinnings that incorporates social and developmental data. *Psychopathology: The Evolving Science of Mental Disorder* combines these fields of research to present a comprehensive picture of current research on psychosis.

In this timely volume honoring Professor Philip Holzman, distinguished investigators from varied fields present new findings from their laboratories, as well as perspectives on areas of rapid growth and change. The editors also provide thoughtful overviews of four major themes in psychopathology research: brain mechanisms, development, thinking, and genetics.

Psychopathology

Philip S. Holzman. Photo copyright © Martha Stewart. Used by permission.

Psychopathology

The evolving science of mental disorder

Edited by

Steven Matthysse
McLean Hospital
Harvard Medical School

Deborah L. Levy
McLean Hospital
Harvard Medical School

Jerome Kagan
Harvard University

Francine M. Benes
McLean Hospital
Harvard Medical School

CAMBRIDGE
UNIVERSITY PRESS

Published by the Press Syndicate of the University of Cambridge
The Pitt Building, Trumpington Street, Cambridge CB2 1RP
40 West 20th Street, New York, NY 10011-4211, USA
10 Stamford Road, Oakleigh, Melbourne 3166, Australia

First published 1996

Printed in the United States of America

Supported by the Schizophrenia Research Program of Scottish Rite Freemasonry,
Northern Masonic Jurisdiction

Library of Congress Cataloging-in-Publication Data

Psychopathology : the evolving science of mental disorder / edited by
Steven Matthysse . . . [et al.].

p.   cm.

Includes index.

ISBN 0-521-44469-1 (hc)

1. Schizophrenia.
[DNLM: 1. Schizophrenia.   2. Psychopathology.   WM 203 P97358
1995]
RC514.P71879   1996
616.89′82 – dc20
DNLM/DLC
for Library of Congress   95-12354
                                                                CIP

A catalog record for this book is available from the British Library.

ISBN 0-521-44469-1 Hardback

To Professor Philip Holzman
Master of the art of psychological experimentation

Contents

Development

Thinking

Response and reflections

Contributors

Francine M. Benes
Laboratory for Structural
Neuroscience
Mailman Research Center
McLean Hospital
115 Mill Street
Belmont, MA 02178

Roger Brown
William James Hall
Harvard University
22 Kirkland Street
Cambridge, MA 02138

Jean P. Chapman
Department of Psychology
University of Wisconsin-Madison
1202 West Johnson Street
Madison, WI 53706

Loren J. Chapman
Department of Psychology
University of Wisconsin-Madison
1202 West Johnson Street
Madison, WI 53706

Dante Cicchetti
Mount Hope Center
187 Edinburgh Street
Rochester, NY 14608

L. Erlenmeyer-Kimling
Psychiatric Institute, Annex,
3rd Floor
722 West 168th Street
New York, NY 10032

Norman Garmezy
5115 Lakeridge Road
Edina, MN 55436

Patricia Goldman-Rakic
Section of Neurobiology
SHM C303
Yale University School of
Medicine
333 Cedar Street
New Haven, CT 06510

Philip S. Holzman
William James Hall
Harvard University
33 Kirkland Street
Cambridge, MA 02138

Jerome Kagan
William James Hall
Harvard University
33 Kirkland Street
Cambridge, MA 02138

Seymour S. Kety
National Institutes of Health
10 Center Drive, Room 4C110
MSC 1366
Bethesda, MD 20892

Kenneth K. Kidd
Yale University School of
Medicine
333 Cedar Street
New Haven, CT 06510

Einar Kringlen
Psykiatrisk Klinikk
Blindernvn, 85
Postboks 85
Vinderen, 0319 Oslo
Norway

Deborah L. Levy
Psychology Research Laboratory
Wyman Building
McLean Hospital
115 Mill Street
Belmont, MA 02178

Brendan A. Maher
William James Hall
Harvard University
33 Kirkland Street
Cambridge, MA 02138

Steven Matthysse
Psychology Research Laboratory
Wyman Building
McLean Hospital
115 Mill Street
Belmont, MA 02178

Allan F. Mirsky
National Institutes of Health
10 Center Drive, Room 4C110
MSC 1366
Bethesda, MD 20892

Gillian O'Driscoll
Department of Psychology
Stewart Biological Science Building
205 Dr. Penfield Avenue
Montreal, Quebec
Canada H3A 1B1

Sohee Park
Department of Psychology and
Institute for Neuroscience
Northwestern University
2029 Sheridan Road
Evanston, IL 60208

Josef Parnas
Department of Psychiatry
Hvidovre Hospital
Brøndbyøstervej 160
2650 Hvidovre
Denmark

Anne Sereno
Center for Molecular and
Behavioral Neuroscience
Rutgers University
Aidekman Research Center
University Heights
197 University Avenue
Newark, NJ 07102

Martha E. Shenton
Department of Psychiatry – 116A
VAMC – Brockton
940 Belmont Street
Brockton, MA 02401

Herbert E. Spohn
Menninger Foundation
PO Box 829
Topeka, KS 66601

Sheldon H. White
William James Hall
Harvard University
33 Kirkland Street
Cambridge, MA 02138

Preface

From his first research study ("The schematizing process: Perceptual attitudes and personality qualities in sensitivity to change") to his latest ("The functional neuroanatomy of antisaccade eye movements investigated with positron emission tomography"), Philip Holzman has explored experimental psychopathology with a depth and breadth unequalled in our time. His studies of smooth pursuit eye movement dysfunction, and its connections with thought disorder and genetics, are known to every student of the field. The evolution of his work parallels the evolution of the science of mental disorder – reaching ever more deeply downward into biological mechanisms – but it retains an upward glance, at the phenomena of psychopathology, that the field sometimes forgets in its reductionistic zeal. To be fully informative about schizophrenia, Dr. Holzman has written, "phenomena should be explored which point, Janus-like, in two directions at once: they should be tied to the psychology of schizophrenia, and at the same time related to known processes in the brain." For abundant scholarly reasons, and other reasons that words cannot express, we celebrate our colleague Philip Holzman at mid-career, as he leaves lectern and mortarboard behind to pursue his research full-time.

We also celebrate the sixtieth year of the Schizophrenia Research Program of Scottish Rite Freemasonry, whose Benevolent Foundation supported the preparation of this book, as it has supported more than 500 research projects in its distinguished history. The Scottish Rite program began before the founding of the National Institutes of Health, as Masonic bodies sought a charity that would "be unique," "have widespread benefit to all humanity," and "be within our means." It has retained a central role in schizophrenia research, by focusing on creative ideas in their early stages, when they are yet too novel to attract conventional funding. The Scottish Rite has persisted over these 60 years, despite the attractiveness of other, more visible, charities, because – in the words of one of its leaders – "money wisely spent for research produces benefits that work for all people for all time."

Finally, in this volume on *Psychopathology: The Evolving Science of Mental Disorder* we celebrate the coming of age of our field. The chapters that follow – divided into "brain mechanisms," "development," "thinking," and "genetics" – show plainly that psychopathology has joined the ranks of the mature sciences, both in the canons of scientific evidence and in the ingenuity of experimental design. The leaders of the field are gathered here, some to report new results, some to share their mature vision; the reader is invited to join the feast.

Steven Matthysse

Brain mechanisms

1

Editor's introduction: From controversy to connectivity

Francine M. Benes

> In medicine and in natural science, it is in general the rule that only the positive findings prove something, but that negative results often only state that we are not able as yet to achieve the positive.
> From "The Problem of the Anatomy of Schizophrenia," by Spielmeyer (1930)

In the early part of this century, brain imaging and histopathologic strategies were used extensively to investigate whether there is a neuroanatomic substrate to schizophrenia. Today, it is well known to those who study schizophrenia that these investigations yielded inconsistent findings and ultimately gave rise to a controversy that has been without precedent in the field of neuroscience. In its most essential form, the dispute regarding a structural defect in schizophrenia rested on the dichotomy between the view that schizophrenia is a neurodegenerative disorder and the opposing one, that it is not due to an organic problem. The implication of the latter viewpoint was that schizophrenia is a "functional" entity in which there are no objective changes in the structural integrity of the brain. Those supporting the idea that schizophrenia is a brain disorder were consigned to an historic tomb where no respectable scientists of that era would dare to be found.

As Spielmeyer's quote at the beginning of this section implies, the belief that a structural defect is present in the brains of schizophrenics was less remarkable than the contrary belief, that there is no anatomic substrate to schizophrenia. By supporting the latter possibility, the nay-sayers proved nothing about schizophrenia. The inability of early investigators to demonstrate convincingly either positive *or* negative findings in the brains of schizophrenic subjects can now be understood in the context of the limited techniques available to address such a complex question. From today's perspective, one cannot have confidence in data (a) not derived by quantitative techniques, (b) not acquired under blind conditions, (c) not based on the diagnosis of the schizophrenic cases using validated criteria, and (d) often not having a normal control group for comparison. Even if these design considerations had been routinely incorporated into histopathologic study designs of that period, the investigations conducted during the first half of this century would still have been futile because the analytic approaches employed were not sensitive enough to reveal subtle changes in connectivity (Benes, 1988).

Chapters 2 through 6 of this section describe sophisticated technological approaches that are now being routinely applied to the study of schizophrenia. In the field of brain imaging, magnetic resonance technology can now routinely attain a level of spatial resolution that is orders of magnitude greater than that provided by pneumoencephalography. This improved anatomic resolution, particularly when combined with functional imaging capabilities, will eventually allow investigators to establish meaningful relationships between cognitive processes and specific anatomic regions of interest, and will help to characterize the *macroanatomic circuitry* affected in schizophrenia.

In recent years, many different cortical and subcortical brain regions have been implicated in the pathophysiology of schizophrenia. By using a combination of behavioral, electrophysiological and ultrastructural analyses, basic neuroscientists are beginning to identify the intrinsic circuitry present within key corticolimbic regions of rodent and primate brain and are using such information to begin modelling different aspects of the schizophrenic syndrome. In postmortem research, recently developed molecular probes have made it possible to begin analyzing the neural circuitry involved in higher cognitive function. By using receptor binding autoradiography, immunocytochemistry, and *in situ* hybridization, investigators are comparing findings in normal and schizophrenic subjects and are attempting to solve the conundrum as to how thinking becomes disordered in schizophrenia.

Two particularly important innovations have enabled the neuroscience community to respond to the challenge posed by Spielmeyer (1930). The first came in 1972, when Ewald Weibel demonstrated that three-dimensional biological structures can be expressed and quantified using mathematical equations. With the development of stereomorphometry as a field, structural images, once evaluated subjectively, could now be analyzed with standardized approaches to both sampling and measurement. It soon became apparent, however, that enormous amounts of primary microscopic data could be obtained with stereomorphometric approaches. In fact, the greater the amount of data collected, the more reliable would be the answer obtained. Ironically, stereomorphometry created an entirely new problem for neuroscientists, one for which the solution would require massive database management capabilities. Computer-assisted technology for quantifying, storing, and statistically analyzing neuroanatomical information has been a critical advance for the field of neuroscience in general, and for the study of schizophrenia in particular. Today, it is routinely possible for investigators studying this disorder to collect extremely large amounts of data, often from digitized images, and, using sophisticated statistical software, to "number crunch" this information so that meaningful comparisons can be made. Twenty years ago, it would have been virtually impossible for a neuroscientist to complete a morphometric analysis of regional volume or cell counts using the manual methods available prior to computerization. Today, however, computer-assisted technology is routinely applied to the study of the human brain and, together with stereomorphometric principles, it is a *sine qua non* for histopathologic studies of schizophrenia.

Even with computer assistance, stereomorphometric analysis remains a highly labor-intensive, time-consuming undertaking, one that still tries the endurance and persistence of those who use it. During Spielmeyer's period, neuroscientists were probably as hardworking and dedicated as those who study schizophrenia today. Unlike this current generation of schizophrenia researchers, Spielmeyer's colleagues had neither stereomorphometry nor computer-assisted analysis available to them, and could not have imagined the directions that studies of the central nervous system would be taking in the final decades of the twentieth century.

The chapters in this section illustrate in different ways how the technological advances of stereomorphometry and computer-assisted analysis have become common denominators in studies of schizophrenia, whether they are performed ante- or postmortem, and whether they employ *in vivo* imaging or postmortem microscopy. Thus far, the most significant advance in our understanding of the pathophysiology of schizophrenia is that it is due not to a neurodegenerative process but, rather, to subtle changes of neural circuitry in key regions of the corticolimbic system. Using computer-assisted stereomorphometry, this field is beginning to define the discrete aspects of faulty wiring present in subjects with schizophrenia and, in so doing, is moving from uninformed controversy toward a detailed understanding of altered connectivity in schizophrenia. We can now appreciate that Spielmeyer showed not only insight, but also prescience when he recognized that the ignorance of his time could be cured only by scientific advances not available during his lifetime, perhaps advances he himself might have imagined. There is now reason to feel optimistic about our prospects for defining the alterations in neural circuitry that are present in individuals who suffer from schizophrenia.

References

Benes, F. M. Post-mortem structural analyses of schizophrenic brain. Study designs and the interpretation of data. *Psychiat. Develop.* 1988; 6:213–226.

Benes, F. M. Post-mortem correlates of brain imaging findings in schizophrenia. *Harvard Review of Psychiatry.* 1993; 1.

Spielmeyer, W. The problem of the anatomy of schizophrenia. *J. Nerv. Ment. Dis.* 1930; 72:241–244.

Weibel, E. R. *Stereological Methods. Practical Methods for Biological Morphometry.* New York: Academic Press. 1979; 1.

2

The functional parcellation of dorsolateral prefrontal cortex and the heterogeneous facets of schizophrenia

Patricia Goldman-Rakic

Introduction

Neuropsychological evidence and clinical observations have repeatedly, directly or indirectly, implicated the prefrontal cortex as a site of dysfunction in schizophrenia – based on the similarity of impairments observed in demented patients and those with frontal lobe damage (e.g., Farkas et al., 1984; Levin, 1984a, 1984b; Weinberger et al., 1986; Goldman-Rakic, 1987, 1991). Although such findings have significantly advanced the empirical support for the "frontal-lobe" hypothesis, countless other results in the literature leave considerable room for doubt about any singular explanation for this heterogeneous disorder. Whatever the status of prefrontal involvement in schizophrenia, basic studies of its structure and function have provided support for two major conclusions: Prefrontal cortex is specialized to direct or guide behavior by internalized representations of facts, events and other memoranda (Goldman-Rakic, 1987), and prefrontal cortex carries out its functions through interactions within a complex distributed network of reciprocating pathways (Goldman-Rakic, 1988a, 1988b; Selemon and Goldman-Rakic, 1988; Goldman-Rakic et al., 1993).

It has been argued elsewhere that guiding behavior by representations – ideas and concepts – normally requires working memory and that schizophrenic thought disorder could involve a breakdown in this basic capacity for "on line" processing (Goldman-Rakic, 1987; 1991). This framework incorporates the traditional views of prefrontal association cortex as the area of the brain essential for executive (Luria, 1966; Shallice, 1982), conceptual (Goldstein, 1949) and temporal integration (Fuster, 1980; Ingvar, 1980; Milner et al., 1985) but proposes a unifying theoretical foundation, cellular mechanisms and modular functional architecture out of which such complex functions as comprehension, reasoning and intentionality could emerge. If, as we have argued, the prefrontal cortex is the node in a circuit where internalized schemata, symbolic representations and ideas from long-term memory are brought to bear on ongoing events, it is not difficult to imagine that a defect in this node or in any other that feeds into it, could lead to scrambled language and disordered thinking. In our view, it is conceivable that thought disorder and behavioral disorganization may be reducible to an impairment of the operational mechanism(s) by which symbolic representations are both accessed from long-term memory and held "in mind" to guide behavior in the absence of instructive stimuli in the outside world. Basic studies of the prefrontal cortex would be central to understanding this mechanism.

This chapter reviews recent evidence from experimental research with nonhuman primates that links specific regions of prefrontal cortex to specific functions shown to be defective in schizophrenics – smooth pursuit tracking, Wisconsin Card Sort Test and delayed-response performance. Although these tasks are formally quite dissimilar, we have argued that each requires working memory to one degree or other and I believe it is this feature that makes them both vulnerable to prefrontal damage in humans and markers of prefrontal dysfunction in patients suffering from schizophrenia and/or other dementias. If the working memory demand in neuropsychological tests and in human cognition generally can be shown to be the common nexus of vulnerability in a disease such as schizophrenia, this functional thread should lead to improvement in diagnosis and possibly in treatments. Further, to the extent that specific deficits associated with schizophrenia (or any other dementia) are also associated with specific regions of the prefrontal cortex, where working memory functions are most developed, the frontally lesioned monkey may provide an important animal model of schizophrenia.

It follows that tasks designed to tap working memory will be (1) impaired in schizophrenic subjects; (2) dissociable from sensory-guided performance; and (3) correlated with their clinical symptoms. Further, prefrontal cortex of schizophrenic patients might be expected to exhibit pathophysiological changes at some stage of the illness. Nevertheless, the view that schizophrenic thought disorder is defective regulation of behavior by current internalized schemata or symbolic representations and information from long-term storage focuses attention on defective *processing* rather than on abnormal content or abnormal structure. Ultimately, we will need to address the extent to which thought disorder expressed by patients in their daily lives can be related to the variety of impairments exhibited in psychologically more delimited performance designed to test working memory processes.

The definition of working memory

Working memory is a concept developed by cognitive psychologists to refer to a distinct operation required for cognition, namely, the ability to update and/or bring information to mind from long-term memory and/or to integrate incoming information for the purpose of making an informed decision, judgment or response (Baddeley, 1986). As explained by Baddeley, the transient and active memory system referred to here as "working memory" evolved from the older concept, "short-term" memory. Working memory can be distinguished operationally from canonical or associative memory by several formal criteria: (i) its short duration; (ii) its limited capacity, and, I contend (iii), its neural substrate (Goldman-Rakic, 1987).

Most formal neuropsychological tasks have components of both associative and working memory. For present purposes, I suggest that a test can be judged as tapping working memory if its performance depends upon: (1) instructions, calculations, i.e., any information that *is not present in the environment* at the time of response choices and/or (2) requires *updating of current and/or past information on a moment-to-moment basis.* The classical delayed-response tasks used extensively in animal research are prime examples of tasks that tax a subject's ability to hold information "in mind" for a short period of time because correct performance on such tasks is memory-guided rather than sensory-guided and their correct execution requires constant updating of the relevant information; a habitual or stereotyped pattern of responding will lead to error as contingencies change from trial to trial or, in real life, moment-to-moment. The relevant memorandum in spatial delayed-response tasks is the location or direction of an object. The relevant memorandum in the Wisconsin Card Sort Test (WCST) is a categorical representation of the attributes of an object (e.g., its color or shape). Few tests are pure tests of working memory and so their effectiveness as tests of psychological dysfunction will depend on their loading upon these factors.

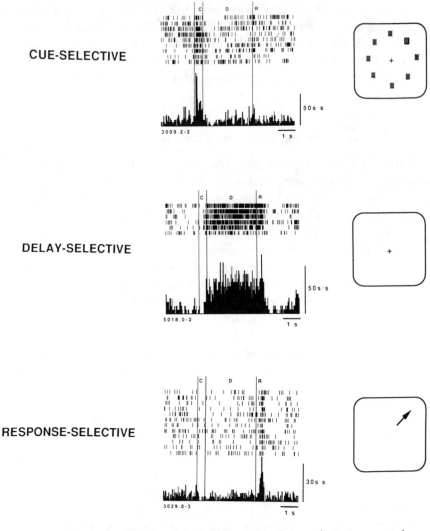

Figure 2.1. This figure displays from top to bottom the main events of an oculomotor delayed-response task and the three principal types of neurons – cue-selective, delay-selective and response-related – that can be recorded from area 46 in the dorsolateral cortex during the performance of the oculomotor delayed-response task. The cue-selective type of cell registers the incoming sensory cue (indicated by the darker square) with a brief phasic response; the delay-selective neuron is tonically activated after the cue disappears and remains activated until a response is initiated at the end of the delay; the response-related neuron displays a phasic response in relation to the eye movement either before the motion is initiated (pre-saccadic) or after it is completed (post-saccadic). Most neurons recorded in prefrontal cortex are directionally tuned and exhibit their most robust response only for stimuli of a particular direction. Many cells have compound

Oculomotor and manual delayed-response tasks

Studies in nonhuman primates

Delayed response. Monkeys are capable of remembering briefly presented visuospatial information over short delays – in the classical spatial delayed-response tasks (for review, see Goldman-Rakic, 1987; Fuster, 1989) as well as in the more demanding 8-item oculomotor version of that task (Funahashi et al., 1989). The ability of monkeys to retain in working memory an item of spatial information is not unlike the capacity of a human to remember a seven-digit phone number, the name of the individual just introduced, or the last hand in a bridge game. As is well established, lesions of the dorsolateral prefrontal cortex produce marked impairments on spatial delayed-response and delayed-alternation tasks and the cortical focus for these deficits is the principal sulcus (or Walker's area 46). Importantly, equally large lesions elsewhere in the parietal or temporal lobes or in other portions of prefrontal cortex fail to produce consistent or profound deficits on these tasks even though these areas of the cortex are connected with the prefrontal areas and are activated during the performance of working memory tasks (Friedman and Goldman-Rakic, 1988, 1994). Thus, many areas of the cortex contribute to performance of complex tasks but few are specialized for the *working memory component* of the performance.

Studies in this laboratory have employed an oculomotor delayed-response (ODR) paradigm to study the physiology of working memory in the rhesus monkey (Funahashi et al., 1989, 1990, 1991, 1993a). The modification of this task employed by Park and Holzman (1992; see below and elsewhere in this volume) is similar in all essential details to that used by Funahashi et al. (1989). As depicted in Figure 2.1, in the nonhuman version of the paradigm, the monkey is required to fixate a central point at the center of a TV monitor during all phases of the trial. In experiments with nonhuman primates, the

Caption to Figure 2.1. *(cont.)*
responses, i.e., show combinations of cue-, delay- and response-related activation. The three types of neurons with common directional "fields" may be interconnected within a columnar unit of cortex. The response of a given cell appears to be the same trial after trial as observed from the pattern of activation in the rasters displaying activity on the individual trials from which the cell's average response is derived.

requirement of fixation, particularly during the delay, prevents the animal from anticipatory responses that would obviate the delay and hence the memory requirement in the task. In the case of the nonhuman primates, the animals are trained to fixate by a method of approximation training after implantation of a Teflon-coated coil under the conjunctiva of one eye. Eye movements are monitored by a computer which keeps a running record of the initial position of the eye, eye movements during the delay period and the latency and end point of the saccade at the end of the delay. Once fixation training is completed, the monkeys are trained in a sequence of steps to maintain fixation when target stimuli are presented in various positions in the visual field; generally eight target locations corresponding to the four cardinal and four diagonal axes are used. On any given trial, a target appears for 500 msec followed by a delay period of 3–5 seconds during which the TV monitor is blank except for the fixation point. At the end of the delay, the fixation point disappears, signaling the monkey to move its eyes to the location in which the target had appeared only seconds before. Single unit analysis of neurons in the area of the principal sulcus has revealed three principal types of neurons that constitute the main elements of a prefrontal working memory circuit – neurons that register the stimulus to be recalled (Funahashi et al., 1990), neurons that retain the information on line (Funahashi et al., 1989) and neurons that use the information to guide the timing and/or direction of an appropriate response (Funahashi et al., 1991). Finally, as shown in Figure 2.2, a partial lesion of the dorsolateral prefrontal cortex in one hemisphere can disrupt performance on the oculomotor delayed-response task, particularly under conditions of memory guidance; the same lesion has little or no effect on the accuracy, timing or velocity of eye movements when eye movements of identical direction and amplitude are sensory-guided, i.e., elicited by external, cues. Similarly dramatic results have been obtained in monkeys using cryogenic depression to produce reversible inactivation of prefrontal areas (Chafee and Goldman-Rakic, unpublished observations). The parallel results obtained in rhesus monkeys with prefrontal lesions and those described by Park and Holzman in schizophrenics (see below) provide important evidence for the selective involvement of prefrontal cortex in the processing deficits of schizophrenics.

The role of the dorsolateral prefrontal cortex in working memory is strongly supported by consistent results from numerous experimental

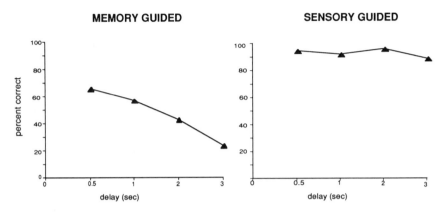

Figure 2.2. The performance of a monkey given a unilateral prefrontal lesion on the oculomotor delayed-response tasks (memory-guided, left graph) and on the sensory-guided control task (right), in which the cue remains on during the delay and is present when the response is made. The monkey is impaired in a delay-dependent manner on the memory-guided version of the task, and performs well at all delays on the sensory-guided version of the task. Note the similarity to the results obtained with schizophrenic patients on these tasks by Park and Holzman.

approaches. In normal monkeys performing manual versions of the delayed-response task, portions of the principal sulcus are activated nearly 20% over its level of involvement in associative memory tasks (Friedman and Goldman-Rakic, 1994) and similar findings have been replicated with the ODR version of the task (Friedman et al., in preparation). Additionally, performance on manual (Goldman and Rosvold, 1970; Goldman et al., 1971; Passingham, 1975) and, as shown above, on oculomotor (Funahashi et al., 1991) delayed-response tasks, is selectively impaired by surgical removal of the principal sulcus as well as by experimental depletion of catecholamines (Brozoski et al., 1979) or pharmacological blockade of dopamine D1 receptors (Sawaguchi and Goldman-Rakic, 1991) or reversible cooling of this area (Alexander and Goldman, 1978; Chaffee and Goldman-Rakic, in preparation). Importantly, none of these treatments applied to the principal sulcal area of prefrontal cortex alter associative memory, i.e., performance on tasks such as visual discrimination where stimulus–response associations are fixed and unchanging. Likewise, none of these treatments impair sensory-guided performance, as when stimuli remain in view during delay periods of delayed-response tasks and the monkey has only to defer its response to a visible cue until the end of the delay. Thus, studies employing electrophysiological measurements, and/or pharmacological, surgical or reversible lesions of prefrontal circuits establish a strong dependence of spatial delayed-response performance, whether in a manual or an oculomotor format, on the integrity of prefrontal circuits.

Smooth pursuit eye tracking. It has long been supposed that the smooth pursuit eye tracking deficit reflected a dysfunction of that part of the prefrontal cortex known as the frontal eye field (FEF) (Levin, 1984a). However, smooth pursuit deficits had not before been demonstrated following lesions of this region in nonhuman primates. More often, the FEF had been explored for its role in saccadic eye movements, and numerous studies have documented neuronal activities related to the saccadic system in monkeys (Bruce and Goldberg, 1984). Now, work from Bruce's laboratory has obtained unambiguous behavioral and electrophysiological evidence for the involvement of the FEF region of prefrontal cortex in smooth pursuit tracking (MacAvoy et al., 1991). Using surgical ablation, microstimulation and neuronal recording, Bruce and colleagues discovered that a buried region of cortex in the ventral bank of the arcuate sulcus was a smooth pursuit field located within the traditional and larger FEF which mediates saccadic eye movements. Neurons in this ventral area responded in association with the smooth pursuit eye movements, and lesions of this region produced smooth pursuit eye tracking deficits that resembled those observed in schizophrenic patients. Further, microstimulation in the same area produced low velocity smoothly continuous eye tracking during prolonged stimulation. As described in MacAvoy et al. (1991), before a frontal eye field lesion, monkeys were able to track with a high smooth pursuit gain, whereas after a lesion of the FEF that included the depth of the arcuate sulcus, the gain of their eye tracking was diminished and the animals had to use large catch-up saccades to keep on track, similar to the deficit exhibited by schizophrenics. Similar to schizophrenics, the monkeys' optokinetic following was normal, showing that the deficit cannot be attributed to a motor problem.

Studies of human subjects: Schizophrenic patients and healthy controls

In Chapter 3 of this volume, Park and O'Driscoll report tests of schizophrenic patients on a modified version of the oculomotor task employed in studies of lesioned rhesus monkeys (Funahashi et al., 1989). In this task the target is presented only for 300 msec, and two delays – 5 and 30 sec – were employed. The investigators also required their human subjects to perform a distracter task during the delay. This is an essential modification to prevent the transformation of the spatial memorandum to a verbal mediator, e.g., "the 2 o'clock position." Verbal mediators would obviate the visuospatial character of the memory as well as bridge the delay. Schizophrenics were impaired both on the visuospatial ODR task and in a haptic version of the task; and their performance was spared on the sensory-guided version of the task. The deficit observed in the patients was most prominent on the memory-guided tasks with much slighter impairments on the sensory task. This pattern of results represents a remarkable correspondence between the findings in patients and those obtained repeatedly in monkeys with prefrontal lesions.

To date, there has been little information on the localization of dysfunction in schizophrenics performing delayed-response tasks, although such information should be forthcoming. However, imaging studies have begun to address both the involvement of the prefrontal cortex in working memory and the particular areas activated in normal human performance. In a recent study, Jonides et al. (1993) employed a task of spatial working memory modeled on the oculomotor paradigm described above. Instead of individual items, the stimulus was an array of three dots randomly positioned on an imaginary circle centered on the fixation spot. The stimuli were presented for 200 msec and the delay lasted 3 seconds. At the end of the delay, a probe circle appeared on the screen and the subject pressed a response button to register whether the circle was centered on a previously presented dot or not. Thus, the subject had to keep in mind the stimulus array or the individual positions of three dots. The Talairach coordinate system used to localize the cortical areas engaged by this task isolated Brodmann area 47 in the prefrontal cortex, Brodmann area 40 in the posterior parietal cortex, Brodmann area 19 in the occipital lobe and Brodmann area 6 in the prefrontal cortex. All of the activated areas were in the right hemisphere. The findings provide evidence for the proposed role of prefrontal cortex in working memory and extend previous evidence for a network organization of areas that support this function (Goldman-Rakic, 1987, 1988a, 1988b). However, the localization of the task is dubious on several grounds. Area 47 is not known to be involved in spatial function; it is not apparently homologous to area 46 in the monkey although its cytoarchitecture needs to be examined in this regard. The fact that area 47 is activated in positron emission tomographic (PET) studies when subjects perform word generation tasks suggests the possibility that the subjects in the Jonides et al. (1993) study may have solved the task through verbal mediation and lowered demand on spatial memory. The studies in the nonhuman primate have the advantage for cortical localization of spatial working memory in that verbal mediation can be ruled out as a confounding factor.

Another relevant PET study is that of Petrides et al. (1993a, 1993b), who imaged normal subjects as they were required to remember the order of objects previously selected. Area 46 and adjacent area 9 were activated in this task, which requires memory of both location and object features. Andreasen et al. (1992) used single photon emission computed tomography (SPECT) to study blood flow in normal subjects and schizophrenic patients. In that study, blood flow was increased in area 9. The localization of specific cytoarchitectonic regions in these studies must be interpreted cautiously, but together with other results, they emphasize how common is the activation of dorsolateral prefrontal areas in tasks tapping working memory.

More exact correspondence in the localization of spatial working memory function across human and nonhuman primates has been achieved by a recent experiment at Yale employing the method of functional magnetic resonance imaging (McCarthy et al., 1993). Functional MRI offers high spatial resolution in individual subjects. In this study, subjects had to judge whether a current stimulus (irregular and unnameable shape) was in the same or different location on a TV monitor compared to a stimulus presented two trials back in a sequence of presentations that occurred every 1.7 seconds. This task, like the oculomotor delayed-response paradigm used with monkeys, places considerable demand upon spatial working memory in that it requires the subjects to keep a running record of incoming stimuli. Significant activation above control conditions was found in area 46. The area of activation corresponds closely to that recently mapped cytoarchitectonically by us in human postmortem brains as area 46 (Rajkowska and Goldman-Rakic, 1994a, 1994b) and to area 46 in the nonhuman primate, where memory cells are located and where lesions cause disruption in spatial working memory tasks.

It seems clear from these new studies in human subjects with and without the diagnosis of schizophrenia that there is an emerging consensus on the role of prefrontal cortex in spatial working memory function, and that neurobiological studies of the dorsolateral prefrontal areas in nonhuman primates can provide a solid animal model for examination of the neural mechanisms that may be compromised in schizophrenic dementia.

The anti-saccade tasks

Studies in nonhuman primates

Rhesus monkeys have recently also been studied on anti-saccade tasks, and similar tests have been used with patients suffering frontal lobe damage (Guitton et al., 1985). Our study (Funahashi et al., 1993a) was designed to examine the activity of the same neuron in the dorsolateral prefrontal cortex during conventional oculomotor delayed-response trials, in which monkeys made memory-guided saccades toward a remembered location (standard ODR task), compared to anti-saccade trials, i.e., trials requiring saccades in the *opposite* direction, away from the location of the remembered stimulus (anti-saccade, AS-ODR) (Figure 2.3). On anti-saccade trials, the monkeys learned to override the prepotent tendency to look in the direction of the remembered visual stimulus. We could thus examine the role of neurons when a given response must be programmed and also when the same response must be inhibited to determine whether these opponent functions are mediated by the same or different neurons. Many schemes of prefrontal organization that have treated the executive and inhibitory roles of prefrontal cortex as separable functions (Mishkin, 1964; Fuster, 1980) would predict that pro-saccade and anti-saccade trials represent different tasks, different functions, and different cortical areas.

Contrary to these expectations, the findings obtained in our laboratory (Funahashi et al., 1993b) and illustrated in Figure 2.3 show a prefrontal neuron whose increased firing in the delay encodes the location of a visual stimulus, *independent* of the direction of the impending saccade. First, the unit responded within 98 msec to the onset of the visual stimulus only when it appeared on the right. Second, stimulus offset triggered increased firing in the delay, again selectively when the visual stimulus to be remembered was on the right (Figure 2.3A, left and right). Third, and most relevant for the memory code, on the anti-saccade trials neuronal activity was enhanced in the delay only when the stimulus was on the right although the saccade was

A. ODR task

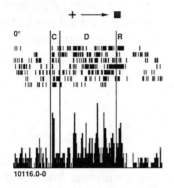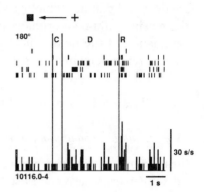

B. AS-ODR task (correct trials)

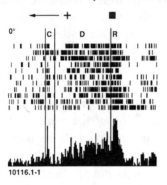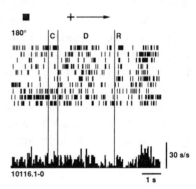

C. AS-ODR task (error trials)

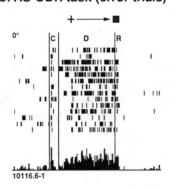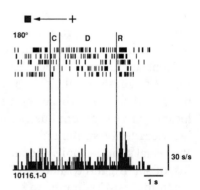

Figure 2.3. This figure illustrates a prefrontal neuron whose increased firing in the delay encodes the location of the visual stimulus, independent of the direction of the saccade. First, the unit responded within 98 msec to the onset of the visual stimulus only when it appeared on the right. Second,

directed to the left (Figure 2.3B, left). Finally, on AS-ODR *error* trials, neuronal activity in the delay was again in accord with the rightward stimulus when the monkey mistakenly directed its saccades *toward* the target (Figure 2.3C, right). Thus, the activity of this neuron in the delay was keyed to the direction of the stimulus and not to the direction of the impending saccade, whether that saccade was correct or incorrect and whether it was toward or away from the original stimulus. A similar pattern of stimulus dependence was found in the delay period activity of 68% of neurons located in the principal sulcus. The preponderance of cue-dependent delay neurons in this area constitutes strong evidence of a prefrontal specialization for ideational processing that *does not rely* on a motor code and is not mediated by motor signals. However, it should be emphasized that some prefrontal neurons do encode the direction of the motor response in the delay interval, independent of cue location, and these neurons represent approximately 25% of the population studied. Similar *motor* coding neurons have been reported in the frontal eye fields, the posterior parietal cortex, the supplementary motor cortex and the neostriatum

Caption to Figure 2.3. *(cont.)*
stimulus offset triggered increased firing in the delay, again selectively when the visual stimulus to be remembered was on the right (cf. Figure 2.2A, left and right). Third, and most relevant for the memory code, on the anti-saccade trials neuronal activity was enhanced in the delay only when the stimulus was on the right although the saccade was directed to the left (Figure 2.2B, left), and additionally, was preceded by a pre-saccadic burst an average of 53 sec before *leftward* saccades. Finally, on AS-ODR *error* trials, neuronal activity in the delay was again in accord with the rightward stimulus when the monkey mistakenly directed its saccades *toward* the target (Figure 2.2C, right). Thus, the activity of this neuron in the delay was keyed to the direction of the stimulus and not to that of the impending saccade, whether that saccade was correct or incorrect and whether it was toward or away from the original stimulus. A similar pattern of stimulus-dependence was found in the delay period activity in approximately two-thirds of the prefrontal neurons studied. The preponderance of cue-dependent delay neurons in this area constitutes strong evidence of a prefrontal specialization for ideational processing that does not rely on a motor code and is not mediated by motor signals. These studies provide firm evidence for a memory process working on a representation of a stimulus when that stimulus is no longer present. Further, they show that representational memory of a past event can negate as well as proscribe an impending response. Thus, disruption of the working memory mechanism through injury or disease could explain many phenomena of disinhibition, i.e., release of unwanted or inappropriate responses. (From Funahashi, Chafee, and Goldman-Rakic, 1993)

and superior colliculus (reviewed in Goldman-Rakic et al., 1992). The prefrontal region from which our recordings were made has connections to all of these structures (Goldman and Nauta, 1976; Selemon and Goldman-Rakic, 1985, 1988; Cavada and Goldman-Rakic, 1989; Bates and Goldman-Rakic, 1993), and could through these connections participate in the timing and/or direction of response output.

Working memory as characterized in studies of human cognition is more than a passive storage device but also a workspace for manipulation of symbolic representations (Carpenter and Just, 1988). Such a workspace may be needed to perform the delayed anti-saccade task in monkeys because this task requires a mental inversion analogous to processes engaged in humans performing an anti-saccade task, the Stroop Test or Wisconsin Card Sort Test. In these tasks, as in AS-ODR, habitual, usually sensory-driven, responses must be inhibited and less potent, usually instruction-guided, alternative responses selected. Loss of cue-coding prefrontal neurons may explain why damage to prefrontal cortex commonly results not only in the absence of a correct response but perseveration and disinhibition of the competing habitual responses presumably mediated by other regions of the brain. As described below, schizophrenic patients have been shown to be impaired on a variety of anti-saccade tasks. If these deficits reflect the operation of working memory mechanisms residing in prefrontal cortex, as seems reasonable, understanding the neural mechanism subserving delayed-response function in nonhuman primates could hold clues to cognitive dysfunction in mental illness as well.

Studies in schizophrenic patients and healthy human subjects

Impairments on anti-saccade paradigms have been demonstrated both in patients with large frontal lobe lesions (Guitton et al., 1985; Pierrot-Deseilligny et al., 1991), and in patients suffering from schizophrenia (Fukushima et al., 1988; Thaker et al., 1989; Sweeney et al., 1991; O'Driscoll et al., 1995). These studies have all shown that patients make more errors than normals do when required to move their eyes opposite to the direction in which a spatial stimulus is located. None of these tasks employed delays between the cue and anti-response as recently reported in monkeys (Funahashi et al., 1993b); it is reasonable to expect that introducing such a delay would exacerbate the deficits of schizophrenic patients. The anti-saccade studies show that schizophrenic patients have difficulty overriding stimulus-driven responses to guide their responses by instructions, providing yet another example of memory-guided performance deficits and a common denominator among schizophrenic patients, patients with frontal damage and nonhuman primates with permanent or reversible prefrontal lesions.

The role of the frontal eye field in the control of both saccadic and smooth pursuit eye movements in humans is well established. Saccadic eye movements have been studied in the control of both sensory-guided (Guitton et al., 1985) and memory-guided (Pierrot-Deseilligny et al., 1991) saccades. Both studies concluded that the FEF was central to the deficits observed, in line with the experiments in rhesus monkey (MacAvoy et al., 1991; Funahashi et al., 1993b). In addition, when area 46 was included in the cortical injury suffered by patients, impairments were observed in memory-guided saccades, also in line with the experimental findings in monkey.

Several studies have now imaged the normal human brain during the performance of anti-saccade tasks. O'Driscoll et al. (1995), using PET, found activation of the prefrontal eye field region of the dorsolateral prefrontal cortex, the posterior parietal cortex and the supplementary motor area in normal subjects performing sensory-guided anti-saccades. In this study, the FEF and posterior parietal areas were sites of increased blood flow during performance of the conventional saccade ("pro-saccade") task as well. Blood flow was not elevated in area 46 and this result is exactly what would be expected based on studies in nonhuman primates. Similar results, i.e., increased perfusion of FEF but not area 46, were also obtained by Paus et al., who used a central stimulus and a 200 msec gap between stimulus offset and the anti-saccade response (Paus et al., 1993). The frontal eye field region would be expected to have a preeminent role in sensory-guided pro- and anti-saccade tasks; and only when a clear *memory* component is enforced, as with the introduction of a significant delay, would area 46 be predicted to become substantially engaged. This expectation from our model was confirmed in a recent study by Sweeney et al. (in press). Blood flow to area 46 was increased bilaterally during performance by normal subjects of both conventional and anti-saccade versions of an oculomotor delayed-response task which employed delays of 2 seconds and this area was not activated during sensory-guided saccades.

The Wisconsin Card Sort Test and other nonspatial tasks

Studies in nonhuman primates

Working memory has been demonstrated in more than one knowledge domain and, as we shall see, in more than one area of the prefrontal cortex. The multiplicity of special purpose working memory domains is a principle that we derived from both functional and anatomical findings in nonhuman primates. The principle can be summarized as follows: informational domain, not process, is mapped across prefrontal cortex. In other words, the mechanisms for working memory are essentially replicated in different areas within prefrontal cortex; however, each area will process different types of information. Direct evidence for this view has recently been obtained in our laboratory from studies of nonspatial memory, i.e., memory for the features or attributes of objects rather than memory for the location of objects (Wilson et al., 1993). Recordings were obtained from neurons in areas 12 and 45 of Walker on the inferior convexity region in monkeys trained to perform delayed-response tasks in which spatial *or* feature memoranda had to be recalled on independent, randomly interwoven trials. Both spatial and feature trials required exactly the same eye movements at the end of the delay, but differed in the nature of the mnemonic representation that guided those responses.

Our major finding is that most of the inferior convexity neurons encoded the features of the stimulus rather than their locations. An example of one such neuron is shown in Figure 2.4. It was activated during the delay period whenever the monkey was recalling a particular pattern requiring a delayed response to the right. Importantly, the same neurons did not respond above baseline during the delay preceding an identical rightward response on trials with spatial cues. Neurons exhibiting selective neuronal activity during recall for the location of stimuli were rarely observed in this region, appearing instead in the dorsolateral cortical regions where spatial processing has been localized in previous studies (Funahashi et al., 1989). These results provide strong evidence that information about objects may be processed separately from those dedicated to the analysis of spatial location and vice versa. Thus, spatial and object processing are dissociable at both the cortical area level and the single neuron level. The

A. Face Memoranda

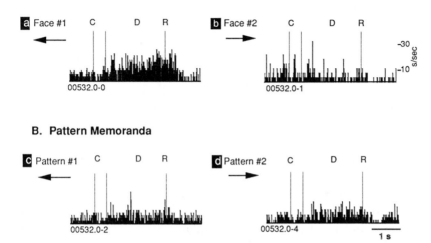

B. Pattern Memoranda

Figure 2.4. The neuron shown was recorded as a monkey performed a working memory task in which the memoranda were the pictures of monkey faces on half the trials and a pair of objects on the remaining trials. The neuron shown in this figure was activated in the delay when the stimulus to be recalled was a particular face (*a*, left panel); but not for a different face (*b*, right panel). The same neuron was not differentially activated by the recall of patterned cues (*c* & *d*, lower panels). This result illustrates that prefrontal neurons can code selective aspects of (or selected images in) working memory. Arrows indicate direction of response for a given memorandum. (Modified from Wilson, O. Scalaidhe, and Goldman-Rakic, 1993)

inferior convexity lying adjacent to the principal sulcus and arcuate region appears to be a region containing specialized circuits for recalling the attributes of stimuli and holding them in short-term memory – thus processing nonspatial information in a manner analogous to the mechanism by which the nearby principal sulcus mediates memory of spatial information. These results establish that more than one working memory domain exists in the prefrontal cortex. The finding that the prefrontal cortex contains a second general area with working memory functions supports my prediction that prefrontal areas are specialized for working memory function and that at least some of its subdivisions represent different informational domains rather than different processes (Goldman-Rakic, 1987).

Studies in schizophrenic patients and healthy human subjects

The Wisconsin Card Sort Test is commonly employed as a diagnostic instrument for assessment of prefrontal involvement in patients suffering brain injury. The design of this instrument resembles the object discrimination reversal tasks used at Wisconsin by Harlow to test monkeys. In this task, the subject is asked to sort a deck of cards which bear stimuli that vary in number, color and shape (Grant and Berg, 1948). As each card in the stack comes up, the subject has to match it to a set of reference cards on the basis of one dimension that is arbitrarily selected by the experimenter (e.g., color). The experimenter then informs the subject if he or she is "right" or "wrong" and the patient tries to get as many correct matches as possible. After the subject achieves a specified number of consecutive correct matches, the sorting principle is shifted without warning, e.g., to shape or number and the patients must modify their responses accordingly. The impairment expressed by patients with prefrontal damage is a difficulty in switching categories in the WCST and perseverating incorrect choices long after they have ceased to be correct. Patients with right or left hemisphere prefrontal damage exhibit difficulty in switching from one category to another.

We have postulated that a working memory component is present in the Wisconsin Card Sort Test (Goldman-Rakic, 1987). Although the relevant features of the stimuli (color, size, shape) are all present in the environment at the time of response, they contain no information about the correct response – it must be provided from representational memory – in this case, the instruction or concept, "color," "shape," "number" guides the response choice. The use of a higher order representational system (concept color, shape) to guide response choice is deficient in patients with frontal lesions and in schizophrenic patients. Further, we have argued that the inability to keep the concept or category in mind increases the patient's reliance on external cues and on associative conditioning whereby each instance of a color that was previously reinforced is repeated until a conditional response repertoire based on stimulus-response association principles is built up. According to this view, switching categories poses a problem precisely because the patient has no deficit in associative learning, has learned the discrimination task well and the tendency to respond associatively or reflexively must be extinguished.

Likewise, monkeys and patients with prefrontal lesions perform as do normals on associative tasks like visual discrimination problems because the prefrontal cortex is not essential for such behavior. The Wisconsin Card Sort Test deficit has been attributed specifically to dysfunction in the dorsolateral prefrontal cortex (Milner, 1963, 1964; Weinberger et al., 1986). On the basis of the studies in nonhuman primates discussed above (Wilson et al., 1993), we can surmise that dysfunction of dorsolateral areas 12 and 45 may be the relevant component of dorsolateral prefrontal cortex that is the focus of the impairment in patients with larger frontal lobe lesions.

Schizophrenics are impaired on the Wisconsin Card Sort Test (Berman et al., 1986; Weinberger et al., 1986), a test that is diagnostic of prefrontal cortex injury. Weinberger et al. were the first to assess blood flow during the performance of the Wisconsin Card Sort Test. Blood flow to the prefrontal cortex of schizophrenics was decreased in an "at rest" condition; but more importantly, perfusion of the dorsolateral prefrontal cortex was impaired in the schizophrenics relative to controls during the performance of the sorting task. Furthermore, prefrontal cerebral blood flow in patients correlates positively with performance on the WCST.

Patients with prefrontal lesions are also impaired on tasks in which they must keep track of the recency or order of their previous responses (Milner et al., 1985; Petrides and Milner, 1982) as well as project sequences of future responses on "look-ahead" puzzles like the Tower of London Test (Shallice, 1982). In the latter task, as mentioned, a goal has to be decomposed into subgoals and the subgoals must be tackled in the correct order. The Tower of London requires the planning and sequencing of a series of "moves," i.e., reorganization of multiple disks on one peg to achieve a reordering of these objects on another peg following the rule that no larger disk should be placed upon a smaller disk. The planning in this task thus requires mental transformations in space and time as well as compliance with instructions. This task shares some important processing demands with the Wisconsin Card Sort Test and a reliance on a working memory component. In the Tower of London task, working memory components are strongly evident because both planning and reference to instructions are quintessentially the manipulation of mental representations. Very recently, SPECT imaging of schizophrenics performing the Tower of London Test have further amplified the

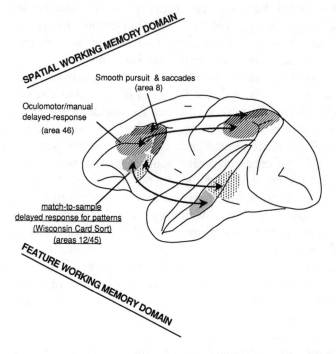

Figure 2.5. Diagram summarizing the functional divisions of the dorsolateral prefrontal cortex that can be linked to deficits observed in schizophrenic patients. Large regions of prefrontal cortex remain as yet uncharted with respect to specific deficits that can be related to symptoms of schizophrenic dementia. The findings summarized here provide evidence for the nonhuman primate as a model system for analysis of thought and affective disorders in humans.

evidence for prefrontal involvement in schizophrenia (Andreasen et al., 1992). Neuroleptic-free patients expressed hypofrontality during performance of the Tower of London task and their prefrontal perfusion was correlated with the prominence of negative symptoms. Interestingly, the area of prefrontal cortex was medial rather than lateral and probably involved area 9 as defined in Figure 2.5.

Summary

The literature on cognitive deficits in schizophrenia supports the conclusion that schizophrenic patients are consistently impaired on tests which invoke working memory and further supports clinical observations on the similarity between patients with prefrontal damage and those with schizophrenia. It is perhaps noteworthy that many tasks used with nonhuman primates have proven useful in the study of human patients, and vice versa. Among these are object reversal (Harlow, 1959), and delayed-alternation and anti-saccade tasks (Guitton et al., 1985). Self-ordering tasks first studied in humans (Petrides and Milner, 1982) have been implemented in monkeys and shown to be dependent on areas 9 and 46 (Petrides, 1991). All of these tasks have strong working memory components and their cross-species generality in itself provides support for the nonhuman primate as a model of human cognition. Furthermore, the specific deficits can be produced by selective lesions in distinctly different subareas of the dorsolateral prefrontal cortex. As summarized in Figure 2.5, considerable evidence suggests that spatial processing in rhesus monkey may be carried out in a dorsolateral subdivision of the prefrontal cortex, principally Walker's area 46; nonspatial processing in areas 12 and 45 on the inferior convexity; and eye tracking associated principally with area 8. It follows that dysfunction in one of these areas could be the pathophysiological basis of the corresponding deficit in schizophrenics and that the heterogeneity of dysfunction in individual patients may be related to extent and number of prefrontal areas that are compromised.

Given the functional evidence for prefrontal dysfunction in schizophrenics, it is important to assess the integrity of its cells and circuits in humans suffering with schizophrenia. We have begun to examine the dorsolateral prefrontal cortex in postmortem studies (Selemon et al., 1993; Selemon et al., in preparation) as have others (Benes et al., 1992; Akbarian et al., 1993). All of these studies point to a pathological change in the dorsolateral regions of schizophrenics. The description of these structural deficits is beyond the scope of the present review, but it is relevant to mention their existence.

We cannot say whether knowledge of the prefrontal cortical contribution to the psychopathology of schizophrenia holds any promise for treatment of this disorder or its prevention. It does seem reasonable, however, that insight into the processing mechanisms of schizophrenics could provide a key to remediation by rehabilitative training in habits and/or routines or structured use of artificial memory devices for overcoming the loss of an updating mechanism in the thought process. This possibility sounds fairly remote, but is challenging nonetheless for the scientist so inclined to pursue them. At a more feasible level, it should be possible to use working memory capacity as a marker in future linkage studies designed to analyze the genetic factor in this disease. Certainly a wide-view lens on prefrontal circuitry and its ultrastructure, neurotransmitter complement and mechanisms of development can help focus development of effective drugs for pharmacotherapy. Unquestionably, animal models are essential for the understanding of the neurobiology of cognition and its dissolution in the major mental disorders.

References

Akbarian, S., Bunney, W. E. Jr., Potkin, S. G., Wigal, S. B., Hagman, J. O., Sandman, C. A., and Jones, E. G. (1993) Altered distribution of nicotinamide-adenine dinucleotide phosphate-diaphorase cells in frontal lobe of schizophrenics implies disturbances of cortical development. *Arch. Gen. Psychiatry* 50:169–177.

Alexander, G. E., and Goldman, P. S. (1978) Functional development of the dorsolateral prefrontal cortex: an analysis utilizing reversible cryogenic depression. *Brain Res.* 143:233–249.

Andreasen, N. C., Rezai, K., Alliger, R., Swayze, V. W. II, Flaum, M., Kirchner, P., Cohen, G., and O'Leary, D. S. (1992) Hypofrontality in neuroleptic-naive patients and in patients with chronic schizophrenia: Assessment with xenon 133 single-photon emission computed tomography and the Tower of London. *Arch. Gen. Psychiatry* 49:943–958.

Baddeley, A. (1986) *Working Memory.* London: Oxford University Press.

Bates, J. F., and Goldman-Rakic, P. S. (1993) Prefrontal connections of medial motor areas in the rhesus monkey. *J. Comp. Neurol.* 335:1–18.

Benes, F. M., Sorensen, I., Vincent, S. L., Bird, E. D., and Sathi, M. (1992) Increased density of glutamate-immunoreactive vertical processes in superficial laminae in cingulate cortex of schizophrenic brain. *Cereb. Cortex* 2:503–512.

Berman, K. F., Zec, R. F., and Weinberger, D. R. (1986) Physiological dysfunction of dorsolateral prefrontal cortex in schizophrenia: 2. Regional cerebral blood flow (rCBF) evidence. *Arch. Gen. Psychiatry* 43:126–135.

Brozoski, T., Brown, R. M., Rosvold, H. E., and Goldman, P. S. (1979) Cognitive deficit caused by regional depletion of dopamine in prefrontal cortex of rhesus monkey. *Science* 205:929–932.

Bruce, C. J., and Goldberg, M. E. (1984) Physiology of the frontal eye fields. *Trends in Neurosci.* 7:436–441.

Buchsbaum, M. S., DeLisi, L. E., and Holcomb, H. H. (1984) Anteroposterior gradients in cerebral glucose use in schizophrenia and affective disorders. *Arch. Gen. Psychiatry.* 41:1159–1166.

Carpenter, P. A., and Just, M. A. (1988) The role of working memory in language comprehension. In D. Klahr and K. Kotovsky, eds., *Complex Information Processing: The Impact of Herbert A. Simon.* Hillsdale, NJ: Erlbaum.

Cavada, C., and Goldman-Rakic, P. S. (1989) Posterior parietal cortex in rhesus monkey: II. Evidence for segretated corticocortical networks linking sensory and limbic areas with the frontal lobe. *J. Comp. Neurol.* 287:422–445.

Farkas, T., Wolf, A. P., Jaeger, J., Brodie, J. D., Christman, D. R., Fowler, J. S. (1984) Regional brain glucose metabolism in chronic schizophrenia. *Arch. Gen. Psychiatry* 41:293–300.

Friedman, H. R. and Goldman-Rakic, P. S. (1988) Activation of the hippocampus and dentate gyrus by working memory: A 2-deoxyglucose study of behaving rhesus monkeys. *J. Neuroscience* 8:4693–4706.

Friedman, H. R., and Goldman-Rakic, P. S. (1994) Coactivation of prefrontal cortex and inferior parietal cortex in working memory tasks revealed by 2DG functional mapping in the rhesus monkey. *J. Neurosci.*

Fukushima, J., Fukushima, K., Chiba, T., Tanaka, S., Yamashita, I. and Kato, M. (1988) Disturbances of voluntary control of saccadic eye movements in schizophrenic patients. *Biolog. Psychiatry* 23:670–677.

Funahashi, S., Bruce, C. J., and Goldman-Rakic, P. S. (1989) Mnemonic coding of visual space in the monkey's dorsolateral prefrontal cortex. *J. Neurophysiol.* 61:331–349.

Funahashi, S., Bruce, C. J., and Goldman-Rakic, P. S. (1990) Visuospatial coding in primate prefrontal neurons revealed by oculomotor paradigms. *J. Neurophysiol.* 63:814–831.

Funahashi, S., Bruce, C. J., and Goldman-Rakic, P. S. (1991) Neuronal activity related to saccadic eye movements in the monkey's dorsolateral prefrontal cortex. *J. Neurophysiol.* 65:1464–1483.

Funahashi, S., Bruce, C. J., and Goldman-Rakic, P. S. (1993a) Dorsolateral prefrontal lesions and oculomotor delayed-response performance: Evidence for mnemonic "scotomas." *J. Neurosci.* 13:1479–1497.

Funahashi, S., Chafee, M. V., and Goldman-Rakic, P. S. (1993b) Prefrontal neuronal activity in rhesus monkeys performing a delayed anti-saccade task. *Nature* 365:753–756.

Fuster, J. M. (1980) *The Prefrontal Cortex.* New York: Raven Press.

Fuster, J. M. (1989) *The Prefrontal Cortex,* 2nd ed. New York: Raven Press, p. 255.

Goldman, P. S., and Nauta, W.J.H. (1976) Autoradiographic demonstration of a projection from prefrontal association cortex to the superior colliculus in the rhesus monkey. *Brain Res.* 116:145–149.

Goldman, P. S., and Rosvold, H. E. (1970) Localization of function within the dorsolateral prefrontal cortex of the rhesus monkey. *Exp. Neurol.* 27:291–304.

Goldman, P. S., Rosvold, H. E., Vest, B., and Galkin, T. W. (1971) Analysis of the delayed alternation deficit produced by dorsolateral prefrontal lesions in the rhesus monkey. *J. Comp. Physiol. Psychol.* 77:212–220.

Goldman-Rakic, P. S. (1987). Circuitry of the prefrontal cortex and the regulation of behavior by representational knowledge. In F. Plum and V. Mountcastle, eds., *Handbook of Physiology*, vol. 5, p. 373. Bethesda, MD: American Physiological Society.

Goldman-Rakic, P. S. (1988a) Topography of cognition: Parallel distributed networks in primate association cortex. *Ann. Rev. Neurosci.* 11:137–156.

Goldman-Rakic, P. S. (1988b) Changing concepts of cortical connectivity: Parallel distributed cortical networks. In P. Rakic and W. Singer, eds., *Neurobiology of Neocortex* (Chicester Dahlem Konferenzen), p. 177. New York: Wiley.

Goldman-Rakic, P. S. (1991) Prefrontal cortical dysfunction in schizophrenia: The relevance of working memory. In B. J. Carroll and J. E. Barrett, eds., *Psychopathology and the Brain* (American Psychopathological Association), pp. 1–23. New York: Raven Press.

Goldman-Rakic, P. S., Bates, J. F., and Chafee, M. (1992) The prefrontal cortex and internally generated motor acts. *Current Opinion in Neurobiology* 2:830–835.

Goldman-Rakic, P. S., Chafee, M., and Friedman, H. (1993) Allocation of function in distributed circuits. In T. Ono, L. R. Squire, M. E. Raichle, D. I. Perrett, and M. Fukuda, eds., *Brain Mechanisms of Perception and Memory: From Neuron to Behavior*, pt. IV, ch. 26, pp. 445–456. New York: Oxford University Press.

Goldstein, K. (1949) Frontal lobotomy and impairment of abstract attitude. *J. Nerv. Ment. Dis.* 110:93–111.

Grant, D. A., and Berg, E. A. (1948) A behavioral analysis of degree of reinforcement and ease of shifting to new responses in a Weigl-type card-sorting problem. *J. Exp. Psychol.* 38:404–411.

Guitton, D., Buchtel, H. A., and Douglas, R. M. (1985) Frontal lobe lesions in man cause difficulties in suppressing reflexive glances and in generating goal-directed saccades. *Exp. Brain Res.* 58:455–472.

Harlow, H. F. (1959) The development of learning in the rhesus monkey. *Amer. Scientist* 47:459–479.

Ingvar, D. H. (1980) Abnormal distribution of cerebral activity in chronic schizophrenia: A neurophysiological interpretation. In C. Baxter and T.

Melnechuk, eds., *Perspectives in Schizophrenia*, p. 107. New York: Raven Press.

Jonides, J., Smith, E. E., Koeppe, R. A., Awh, E., Minoshima, S., and Mintun, M. A. (1993) Spatial working memory in humans as revealed by PET. *Nature* 363:623–625.

Levin, S. (1984a) Frontal lobe dysfunctions in schizophrenia. I. Eye movement impairments. *J. Psychiat. Res.* 18:27–55.

Levin, S. (1984b) Frontal lobe dysfunctions in schizophrenia. II. Impairments of psychological and brain functions. *J. Psychiat. Res.* 18:57–72.

Luria, A. R. (1966) *Higher Cortical Functions in Man.* New York: Basic Books.

MacAvoy, M. G., Bruce, C. J., and Gottlieb, J. P. (1991) Smooth pursuit eye movement representation in the primate frontal eye field. *Cereb. Cortex* 1:95–102.

McCarthy, G., Blamire, A. M., Nobre, A. C., Puce, A., Hyder, F., Bloch, G., Phelps, E., Rothman, P., Goldman-Rakic, P. S., and Shulman, R. G. (1993) Functional magnetic resonance imaging during a spatial working memory task in humans. *Soc. Neurosci. Abstr.* 19:790.

Milner, B. (1963) Effects of different brain lesions on card sorting. *Arch. Neurol.* 9:100–110.

Milner, B. (1964) Some effects of frontal lobectomy in man. In J. M. Warren and K. Akert, eds., *The Frontal Granular Cortex and Behavior*, p. 313. New York: McGraw-Hill.

Milner, B., Petrides, M., and Smith, M. L. (1985) Frontal lobes and the temporal organization of memory. *Human Neurobiology* 4:137–142.

Mishkin, M. (1964) Perseveration of central sets after frontal lesions in monkeys. In J. M. Warren and K. Akert, eds., *The Frontal Granular Cortex and Behavior*, p. 219. New York: McGraw-Hill.

O'Driscoll, G. A., Alpert, N. M., Matthysse, S. W., Levy, D. L., Rauch, S. L., and Holzman, P. S. (1995) The functional neuroanatomy of antisaccade eye movements investigated with positron emission tomography. *Proc. Nat. Acad. Sci.* 92:925–929.

Park, S., and Holzman, P. S. (1992) Schizophrenics show spatial working memory deficits. *Arch. Gen. Psychiat.* 49:975–982.

Paus, T., Petrides, M., Evans, A. C. and Meyer, E. (1993) Role of the human anterior cingulate cortex in the control of oculomotor, manual and speech responses: A positron emission tomography study. *J. Neurophysiol.* 70:453–469.

Passingham, R. (1975) Delayed matching after selective prefrontal lesions in monkeys (Macaca mulatta). *Brain Res.* 92:89–102.

Petrides, M. (1991) Functional specialization within the dorsolateral frontal cortex for serial order memory. *Proc. R. Soc. Lond. B. Biol. Soc.* 246: 299–306.

Petrides, M., Alivisatos, B., Evans, A. C., and Meyer, E. (1993a) Dissociation of human mid-dorsolateral from posterior dorsolateral frontal cortex in memory processing. *Proc. Natl. Acad. Sci. USA* 90:873–877.

Petrides, M., Alivisatos, B., Meyer, E., and Evans, A. C. (1993b) Functional activation of the human frontal cortex during the performance of verbal working memory tasks. *Proc. Natl. Acad. Sci. USA* 90:878–882.

Petrides, M., and Milner, B. (1982) Deficits on subject-ordered tasks after frontal- and temporal-lobe lesions in man. *Neuropsychologia* 20:249–262.

Pierrot-Deseilligny, C., Rivaud, S., Gaymard, B., and Agid, Y. (1991) Cortical control of memory-guided saccades in man. *Exp. Brain Res.* 83:607–617.

Rajkowska, G., and Goldman-Rakic, P. S. (1994a) Cytoarchitectonic definition of prefrontal areas in the normal human cortex: I. Remapping of areas 9 and 46 using quantitative criteria. *Cereb. Cortex.*

Rajkowska, G., and Goldman-Rakic, P. S. (1994b) Cytoarchitectonic definition of prefrontal areas in the normal human cortex: II. Variability in locations of areas 9 and 46 and relationship to the Talairach coordinate system. *Cereb. Cortex.*

Sawaguchi, T., and Goldman-Rakic, P. S. (1991) D1 dopamine receptors in prefrontal cortex: involvement in working memory. *Science* 251:947–950.

Selemon, L. D., and Goldman-Rakic, P. S. (1985) Longitudinal topography and interdigitation of corticostriatal projections in the rhesus monkey. *J. Neurosci.* 5:776–794.

Selemon, L. D., and Goldman-Rakic, P. S. (1988). Common cortical and subcortical target areas of the dorsolateral prefrontal and posterior parietal cortices in the rhesus monkey: A double label study of distributed neural networks. *J. Neurosci.* 8:4049–4068.

Selemon, L. D., Rajkowska, G., and Goldman-Rakic, P. S. (1993) Cytologic abnormalities in area 9 of the schizophrenic cortex. *Soc. Neurosci. Abstr.* 19:200.

Shallice, T. (1982) Specific impairments in planning. *Phil. Trans. R. Soc. Lond. B.* 298:199–209.

Sweeney, J. A., Haas, G. L., Carl, J. R., and Keshavan, M. (1991) Oculomotor dysfunctions in schizophrenia. *Soc. Neurosci. Abstr.* 17:861.

Sweeney, J. A., Mintun, M. A., Kwee, S., Wiseman, M. B., Brown, D. L., Rosenberg, D. R., and Carl, J. R. (in press) A positron emission tomography study of voluntary saccadic eye movements and spatial working memory. *J. Neurophysiol.*

Thaker, G., Kirkpatrick, B., Buchanan, R. W., Ellsbery, R., Lahti, A., and Tamminga, C. (1989) Oculomotor abnormalities and their clinical correlates in schizophrenia. *Psychopharmacol. Bull.* 25:491–497.

Weinberger, D. R., Berman, K. F., and Zec, R. F. (1986) Physiological dysfunction of dorsolateral prefrontal cortex in schizophrenia: I. Regional cerebral blood flow (rCBF) evidence. *Arch. Gen Psychiatry* 43:114–125.

Wilson, F. A. W., O Scalaidhe, S. P., and Goldman-Rakic, P. S. (1993) Dissociation of object and spatial processing domains in primate prefrontal cortex. *Science* 260:1955–1958.

3

Components of working memory deficit in schizophrenia

Sohee Park and Gillian O'Driscoll

Introduction

In this chapter, we focus on the working memory deficit of schizophrenic patients, as assessed by delayed-response tasks. The relevance of delayed-response performance to schizophrenia has already been extensively documented by Goldman-Rakic (1987, 1991; see also Chapter 2, this volume). A typical delayed-response task involves the presentation of a stimulus, followed by a delay period and the subsequent presentation of a small set of alternative choices. Although the delayed-response task is a simple procedure, it involves a variety of cognitive functions. In order to succeed, the target stimulus or, to be more specific, the context-relevant attribute of the stimulus, must be encoded (e.g., spatial location). This information is maintained in working memory during the delay period. Then, a motor command must be successfully executed in order to elicit a response, which may involve voluntary control over the motor system. The delayed-response task is not dependent on recognition memory because at the response stage, there is no external cue in the response environment.

Deficits in delayed-response task performance remain one of the best-documented symptoms of prefrontal damage (e.g., Jacobsen, 1935; Kojima et al., 1982). Lesions in the principal sulcus impair performance on delayed-response tasks in monkeys (e.g., Blum, 1952; Goldman and Rosvold, 1970; Gross and Weiskrantz, 1964). Humans with dorsolateral prefrontal lesions show analogous deficits on tasks that require a delayed response (e.g., Oscar-Berman, 1975; Freedman and Oscar-Berman, 1986; Lewinsohn et al., 1972).

Both animals and humans with prefrontal lesions are excessively distractible and tend to be susceptible to irrelevant stimuli. They rely heavily on external cues to guide behavior even when these cues are not reliable (Bartus and Levere, 1977; Lhermitte, 1986; Lhermitte et al., 1986). When patients with lesions in the frontal lobes are asked to perform cognitive tasks that deal with well-rehearsed information, they perform adequately, but when the task demands context-relevant modification of strategies, these patients experience enormous difficulty. They may continue to rely on previously successful but now irrelevant responses, or allow momentary external influences to override internal goals. Perseverative tendencies, distractibility, rigidity and inability to regulate behavior according to context are some of the major symptoms of frontal lobe damage (Luria, 1966; Fuster, 1980; Petrides and Milner, 1982; Shallice, 1982; Duncan, 1986) and these deficits extend to the social sphere. Similarities in neuropsychological and social profiles have led many investigators to suggest that frontal lobe deficits may be responsible for some of the most profound symptoms of schizophrenia (see, e.g., Kraepelin, 1919; Levin, 1984a, 1984b; Goldman-Rakic, 1991; also Goldman-Rakic, Chapter 3, this volume). In turn, distractibility, rigidity, loss of goal-directedness and other related dysfunctions have been explained as problems of the *central executive* system or *working memory* by neuropsychologists and cognitive psychologists.

Cognitive models of central executive system and working memory

Our discussion of working memory will be limited to the context of a simple delayed-response problem, and therefore we will not attempt to address the question of general capacity of the *central executive system* (see Just and Carpenter, 1992). Baddeley's working memory model (1986) consists of the central executive system, which is subserved by modality-specific subsystems such as the *verbal articulatory loop* for phonological–auditory input and the *visuospatial sketchpad* for visuospatial input. The verbal articulatory loop is a phonological input store that can hold auditory information via rehearsal processes and thereby keep it temporarily. This is the process involved, for example, when one repeats a phone number in mind while searching for a pen. The visuospatial sketchpad is an input store that maintains and manipulates visuospatial images. These subsystems are closely tied to sensory systems, and a recent imaging study shows that the supramarginal gyrus and Broca's area are implicated in the verbal articulatory loop (Paulescu et al., 1993). In Baddeley's model, the central executive deploys attentional resources, selects control processes and strategies, and coordinates information flow from the subsystems. The function of working memory is to hold information in the conscious realm until it can be used to guide behavior or be transferred to the knowledge storage system, which may be conceptualized as the long-term memory or the reference memory (Baddeley, 1986; Roitblat, 1987). The articulatory and the visuospatial sketchpad systems can hold on to information for long delays through rehearsal or visuospatial mnemonic strategies.

Similarly, Shallice (1988) postulates the existence of a *supervisory attentional system* that is needed when *controlled* processing is required to override *automatic* routine processes or motor programs. According to Shiffrin and Schneider (1977), automatic processes arise as a result of extended practice on a task. Once a skill is mastered (or a motor program formed), it becomes an automatic process gaining direct access to long-term memory and occurring outside the conscious realm. Hence, automatic processes can be carried out in parallel. In contrast, controlled processing makes heavy demands on central processing capacity and takes place in the conscious realm. The *supervisory attentional* system monitors the internal and external context in order to modulate the outputs of independent schema-like action modules that oversee routine responses (i.e., automatic processes).

A dysfunctional supervisory attentional system or central executive would result in little or no deficit when the environment is stable and only routine responses are required. However, in novel situations, where new responses are demanded of the organism, an impaired central executive would be associated with a noticeable decrement in performance, even when the sensory or the motor components required to carry out the new tasks are intact. These are the kinds of situations in which frontal and schizophrenic patients fail. Thus, studies of these populations should be able to differentiate performance deficits related to sensory or motor problems from those related to deficits in central executive or working memory. The latter deficits should be observable regardless of the input and output modalities of the paradigm.

Working memory deficit of schizophrenic patients

Park and Holzman (1992, 1993) found that schizophrenic patients are impaired in making memory-guided eye movements and hand movements in the absence of a sensory deficit. The tasks employed were modelled after the oculomotor delayed-response tasks that were used to investigate spatial working memory function in rhesus monkeys (see Goldman-Rakic, Chapter 3, this volume). Figure 3.1 illustrates the oculomotor delayed-response tasks used in the Park and Holzman studies. Schizophrenic patients were less accurate than normal controls and bipolar patients in this task. To rule out the possibility that this deficit may have been due to a sensorimotor problem, a control task was included that was identical to the memory task except that the target never disappeared. The subject was simply required to make an eye movement to a visible target after the delay period. Schizophrenic patients performed as well as the control subjects on the sensorimotor control task. The authors interpreted these results as evidence of a deficit in working memory that was similar to the deficits displayed by monkeys with dorsolateral prefrontal (DLPFC) lesions (Funahashi et al., 1989, 1990, 1993).

On a recognition memory task, the target is present at the response stage and the subject must select the target from a number of alternatives. In a recall task, the target is not present at the response stage. Recognition memory is not involved in spatial delayed-response performance, because at the response stage of the task, there is no external cue in the response environment. Schizophrenic patients have been reported to have impaired free recall but intact recognition memory (Koh and Petersen, 1978). This pattern of deficits is similar to that observed in frontal lobe patients who are prone to "forgetting to remember" (Hecaen and Albert, 1978). Spared recognition coupled with impaired recall is also typical of patients with diseases that involve reduced dopaminergic activity – for example, Parkinson's disease (e.g., Taylor et al., 1986). Recognition memory is believed to be dependent on a neural circuit that includes the hippocampus, amygdala, medial thalamus, nucleus basalis and orbital frontal areas (Mishkin and Bach-evalier, 1983), whereas free recall is thought to involve the prefrontal cortex (Taylor et al., 1986).

There is also some *indirect* evidence for the role of the frontal system in the working memory deficit of schizophrenic patients. Neuropsy-

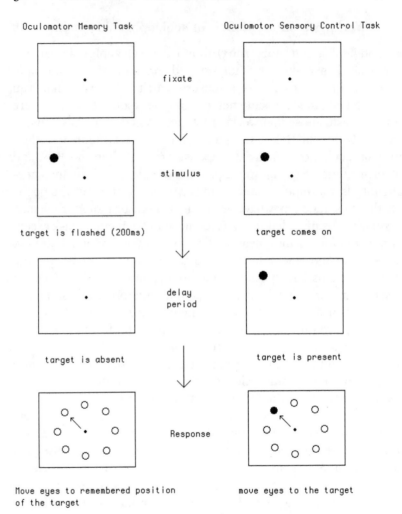

Figure 3.1. Oculomotor delayed-response tasks

chological tests of frontal lobe function were conducted in the same subjects who completed the oculomotor delayed-response task above (Park, 1991). There was a significant correlation between working memory accuracy and number of errors on the Wisconsin Card Sort Test ($r = -.54$, $p < .001$) when all subjects were examined (Park, 1991; Park and Holzman, 1991). This is not surprising since normal subjects perform well both on the WCST and on the oculomotor delayed-response task. But the same association was also observed within the schizophrenic group; there was a significant correlation between the accuracy of oculomotor delayed-response performance and both the total number of errors ($r = -.82, p < .005$) and the number of perseverative errors ($r = -.73, p < .02$) on the WCST (Park, 1991; Park and Holzman, 1991). Overall, those patients who made more errors on WCST performed less accurately on the delayed-response task. Working memory performance and failure to maintain set on the WCST are also associated in schizotypic college students (Park et al., 1995).

In contrast to their performance on the WCST, these schizophrenic patients were not impaired on the verbal fluency task (FAS), another neuropsychological test of frontal lobe function, compared with normals and bipolars ($F(2,33) = 1.25, p > 0.25$), and delayed-response performance was not correlated with performance on the verbal fluency task. WCST performance may be mediated by DLPFC (e.g., Milner, 1963; Weinberger et al., 1986), whereas the verbal fluency task may involve the orbitofrontal system (Kolb and Wishaw, 1985). However, the anatomical specificity of these two neuropsychological tests is still open to debate and therefore interpretation of the localizing significance of the above results must be made with caution.*

Another line of indirect evidence implicating possible frontal dysfunction in the delayed-response deficit of schizophrenic patients is obtained from their eye tracking data. There was an association between performance on the oculomotor delayed-response task and smooth pursuit eye tracking within the schizophrenic population (Park and Holzman, 1993) and in the healthy relatives of schizophrenic patients (Park et al., 1993). That is, subjects with smooth pursuit eye movement (SPEM) dysfunction had poorer accuracy on the delayed-response task. SPEM impairment in schizophrenic patients has been suggested to involve dysfunctional frontal eye fields (Levin, 1984a, 1984b). Indeed, SPEM dysfunction is associated with impaired performance on neuropsychological tests of frontal functions (Katsanis and Iacono, 1991), suggesting that perhaps an intact frontal system may be important for both working memory and SPEM. Again, the precise nature of this association is open to debate.

We have discussed how some cognitive features of schizophrenia and frontal lobe patients may be conceptualized as dysfunctions of the

---

* On this point, see also Chapter 5, by Deborah L. Levy, this volume – Eds.

central executive system. Although the delayed-response task is a simple procedure, successful performance may depend on these functional components:

1. Mental representation of goal or sequence
2. Maintenance of target representation during the delay period
3. Inhibition of competing, irrelevant stimuli
4. Initiation and execution of an appropriate motor response

Failure to facilitate any of these hypothetical components may lead to an overall deficit in goal-directedness. Therefore, it is necessary to analyze global behavioral descriptions into cognitively and neuro-biologically meaningful components in order to uncover which functional components pose difficulties for schizophrenic patients and why.

Mental representation of goal or sequence

The ability to formulate the goal of the delayed-response task does not seem to be responsible for the schizophrenic patients' deficit, since subjects were unimpaired on the sensorimotor control task, which made the same sequential demands on the patient as the memory-guided task.

Maintenance of target representation during the delay period

Maintenance of the target representation during the delay may have posed difficulties for the subjects. It is helpful to examine neuro-physiological data from the primate oculomotor delayed-response studies to formulate our hypotheses on how this might occur. There are neurons in the principal sulcus (area 46) of rhesus monkeys that increase firing *only* during the delay period (e.g., Funahashi et al., 1989, 1990, 1993). Moreover, there is a correlation between cell activity and the performance of the monkey. Funahashi et al. (1989, 1990, 1993) suggest that spatial working memory in rhesus monkeys is mediated by the "memory fields" that are encoded and maintained by the neurons in the principal sulcus. Thus, spatial representation in working memory in the monkey is thought to be maintained by a significant increase in neuronal activity in specific areas in the principal sulcus. In the case of working memory failure, the interruption of cell firing for a variety of reasons probably leads to loss of information.

The working memory deficit displayed by schizophrenic patients is not likely to be the result of a specific, localized, structural lesion in the principal sulcus. Schizophrenic patients make equal numbers of errors in both visual hemifields and in all quadrants (Park, 1991; Park and Holzman, 1992), indicating that the problem is distributed over the entire visual field. This result contrasts with data from animal lesion studies. Funahashi et al. (1993) observed mnemonic "scotomas" in the visual field specific to the site of the lesion in the monkey.

Recent theoretical and experimental work on how the dopamine system may affect working memory leads us to some interesting hypotheses. Cohen and Servan-Schreiber's neural network model (1992) of schizophrenic symptoms predicts that a decrease in dopamine gain at each unit (not necessarily neurons) may lead to a loss of context-relevant processing. Experimental manipulations with dopamine show that dopamine antagonists disrupt oculomotor delayed-response performance in rhesus monkeys (Sawaguchi and Goldman-Rakic, 1991) and dopamine agonists increase accuracy of delayed-response performance in humans (Luciana et al., 1992). Thus, one way of thinking about the working memory deficit involves the idea of reduced activity of neurons. The cells themselves may not be able to increase firing, or even if an increase in the cell activity is achieved, direct (e.g., by electrocortical stimulation) or indirect (e.g., by sudden external stimuli) interruptions may occur. Susceptibility to disruption, rather than static disruption, is possible. What kind of internal or external activity can disrupt cell firing and target representation maintenance? Introduction of concurrent tasks during the delay period has little or no effect on performance of the working memory task, as long as such tasks are not performed within the same modality; for example, a digit span task does not interfere with spatial working memory maintenance (see Baddeley, 1986). Even if the tasks are performed within the same sensory modality, they do not interfere if they are sufficiently separated in levels of processing; for example, neither caloric or rotatory-induced nystagmus (involuntary smooth eye movement) disrupts spatial working memory, whereas tracking a moving target (voluntary smooth eye movement) results in a marked decrement in spatial working memory performance (see Baddeley, 1986).

In a pilot study of the delayed-response task, it was found that most subjects (both controls and patients) performed the task by developing idiosyncratic mnemonic strategies – for example by assigning numbers to each target position or using fingers to record the target position (Yesutis, 1990). In other words, working memory was not utilized because the answer was coded externally, in much the same way as if the target position had been written down on a piece of paper. The results from the pilot study of working memory showed that schizophrenic patients were less accurate than the normal controls. However, the difference observed could have been the result of more efficient use of external mnemonic strategies by normal controls. For this reason, a concurrent but noninterfering task was introduced during the delay period, obliging all subjects to engage in the same mental activity (Park and Holzman, 1992, 1993). These concurrent tasks had the additional benefit of ensuring that all subjects fixated on the center of the screen during the delay. The concurrent tasks, number subtraction and category switching did not disrupt delayed-response performance but they prevented subjects from engaging in external mnemonic strategies in a pilot study (Park, 1991). Thus, schizophrenic patients' deficits in delayed response cannot be ascribed to the superior mnemonic strategies of normals, or to interference by the concurrent tasks themselves.

Inhibition of competing, irrelevant stimuli

Although schizophrenic patients performed less accurately than the control groups, it was not clear whether the problem lay in the maintenance of spatial information in working memory or with failed inhibition of competing responses. Konorski and Lawicka (1964) reported that prefrontal-lesioned dogs made numerous perseverative errors in a 3-choice delayed-response task, but these dogs always corrected their errors by subsequently choosing the correct position. This pattern of results suggests that in these animals, maintenance of spatial representation during the delay was not the main problem. They seemed unable to inhibit competing, previously reinforced responses. In the delayed-response task, schizophrenic patients made perseverative errors, whereas normals and bipolars rarely did. In order to disentangle the errors due to a failure to maintain spatial representation and those due to disinhibition of competing responses, we analyzed the types of errors made by subjects in a previous study by Park and Holzman (1993). That is, all errors were examined to see if *subsequent* attempts to move eyes to the remembered position of the target were successful. In addition to the subjects reported, two more

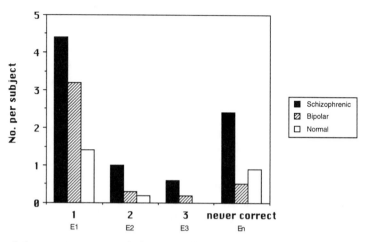

Figure 3.2. Frequency of corrected errors per subject. The X-axis represents the number of incorrect guesses made by subjects before they chose the correct position. E1 means there was 1 error before the correct choice was made. E2 means there were 2 errors before the correct choice was made. E3 means there were 3 incorrect guesses before the correct choice was made. En means the subject never got to the correct position within the time limit of 10 seconds. The Y-axis represents the mean number of errors made per subject.

schizophrenic patients who met the recruiting criteria were tested. Figure 3.2 shows the frequency of errors made per subject before the correct position was finally chosen. It can be seen that schizophrenic patients *do* correct errors, after the first unsuccessful attempt, usually on the second try. Sometimes schizophrenic patients make errors apparently because they are unable to inhibit irrelevant responses, but when they are given another chance, often they are then able to choose the correct target. Therefore, the initial errors seem to be caused by temporary disinhibition. However, it can also be seen that there are some errors which are *never* corrected, suggesting a possible failure to maintain spatial representation of the target. Thus, schizophrenic patients seem to be susceptible both to interference from competing response tendencies, leading to a faulty initiated choice, and to a maintenance failure of the target representation, as evidenced by the presence of *never-corrected* errors.

We examined the group differences in the number of errors that were corrected after one unsuccessful attempt (E_1) and those that are never corrected (E_n). Schizophrenic patients made significantly more E_1 errors per subject than normal controls ($F(1,59) = 22.0$, $p < 0.0001$) and bipolars ($F(1,27) = 5.3$, $p < 0.03$). They also made more E_n errors than normals ($F(1,59) = 8.0$, $p < 0.007$) and bipolars ($F(1,27) = 7.8$, $p < 0.01$). Figure 2 illustrates the error analysis.

Interference from competing response tendencies is commonly observed in animals and humans with lesions in the frontal lobes (see, e.g., Goldberg and Bilder, 1985; Stamm, 1985). Indeed, there seems to be an association between delayed-response performance and some neuropsychological tests of frontal lobe functions. Performance on the oculomtor and haptic delayed-response tasks correlated significantly with perseverative errors on the WCST (Park, 1991; Park and Holzman, 1991). In addition, Park and Holzman (1993) found an association between eye tracking performance and accuracy on the oculomotor working memory task in schizophrenic patients. The smooth pursuit eye tracking dysfunction in schizophrenic patients has been suggested to involve deficits in the frontal eye fields (Levin, 1984a,b).

We now examine whether there is a difference between those patients with normal SPEM and those with impaired eye tracking in the *types* of delayed-response task errors made. In the normal control group, eye tracking was not associated with error types. We did not compute the correlation for the bipolar patients because they were all receiving lithium, which impairs smooth pursuit eye tracking (Levy et al., 1985). Within the schizophrenic group (lithium-free), the number of never-corrected errors per subject (i.e., those errors that probably arise from maintenance failure) was significantly correlated with smooth pursuit eye tracking performance ($r = -.49$, $p < .05$). Thus, schizophrenic patients with impaired SPEM tend to make more of these *never-corrected* errors than do the schizophrenic patients with normal eye tracking. On the other hand, the number of errors that was corrected after one unsuccessful attempt (i.e., those errors that probably arise from interference due to competing response tendencies) was not correlated with eye tracking ($r = .32$, $p > .10$), suggesting that schizophrenic patients with both good eye tracking and bad eye tracking were susceptible to interference from irrelevant stimuli. Therefore, in schizophrenic patients, a disruption in the process responsible for maintaining information during the delay period of the oculomotor delayed-response task seems to be associated with impaired eye tracking performance, but inhibition of competing, irrelevant stimuli is unrelated to eye tracking performance.

Initiation and execution of motor response

In our experiments, delays in initiating responses can be observed in the response times. Schizophrenic patients were significantly slower than bipolar patients and normal controls on the memory-guided eye movement task, although they were not slower than the bipolar patients on the sensory control task (Park and Holzman, 1992, 1993). The execution of appropriate motor responses was often impeded by incorrect eye movements, which were later corrected, as discussed in the preceding section.

Future directions

It is important to note that we still do not know what disrupts the maintenance of information during the delay. Although we can rule out concurrent tasks during the delay, we cannot rule out the possibility that other distracting influences may interfere with maintenance. Stamm (1985) summarized electrocortical stimulation studies, in which the principal sulcus was stimulated during the delayed-response task. Correct performance in the monkey was disrupted *only* if the electrocortical stimulation to principal sulcus occurred during the early period of the delay (less than 2 seconds) or at the end of the cue presentation. This finding remained stable with different delay periods and with changing the hand of response. At present, Park and colleagues in Zurich are investigating the temporal parameters of working memory in schizophrenic patients. It is already known that schizophrenic patients make more errors than normals overall, but their susceptibility to distracting stimuli may also differ from normals across the delay period. Such a difference may lead us to understand more about how performance on working memory tasks can be disrupted.

In addition to the temporal parameter, the spatial properties of distracting stimuli are being studied in schizophrenic patients, patients with focal cerebral lesions and normal controls. Since the target position is thought to be spatially coded and maintained by specific cells in the principal sulcus in rhesus monkeys (e.g., Funahashi et al. 1989, 1990, 1993), the spatial relation between the target stimulus and the distracting stimulus may be an important factor in determining susceptibility to working memory deficits. In the oculomotor delayed-response paradigm, the distracting stimulus is introduced unexpectedly during the delay period and the distance, intensity and similarity to the target stimulus are varied systematically. A parallel neurophysiological study in animals that can document cell activities during the interrupted delay period as a function of different properties of the distractor is much needed. Information on the differing efficacy of various parameters of the distractor may provide clues as to how maintenance of representation in working memory may be disrupted.

In this chapter, we have attempted to unravel what processes underlie the working memory deficit in schizophrenic patients. Judging from their pattern of errors, it seems unlikely that any one process alone is responsible for the observed delayed-response deficit. We find that there are at least two different types of errors and that only the *never-corrected* errors are associated with the SPEM deficit in schizophrenic patients. On the other hand, those errors generated by interference from competing stimuli seem to be independent of eye tracking dysfunction. It is possible that separate neuroanatomical systems are mediating these different types of errors (for example, the dorsolateral system versus the orbitofrontal system), but future studies are necessary to address this issue. Finally, we need to clarify what these errors mean in the context of specific schizophrenic symptoms.

Animal models of schizophrenia have been extremely enlightening and influential in guiding us toward formulating more lucid hypotheses. Now we need to be able to go one step further in order to integrate our findings with the clinical realities of schizophrenia. Systematic studies of working memory may help elucidate neurophysiological mechanisms and psychological processes involved in some of the cardinal symptoms of schizophrenia.

Acknowledgments

This work was supported in part by the NARSAD Young Investigator Award, a Human Frontiers of Science Long Term Fellowship and Swiss National Science Foundation Grant to Sohee Park. We are grateful to our mentors, Philip Holzman, Deborah Levy and Steven Matthysse, for their encouragement, patience and perennial intellectual support. In addition, we thank Jeanyung Chey and Janet Levoff.

References

Baddeley, A. (1986) *Working memory.* New York: Oxford University Press.

Bartus, R. T, and Levere, T. E. (1977) Frontal decortication in rhesus monkeys: A test of interference hypothesis. *Brain Res.* 119:133–148.

Berman, K. F., Gold, J., Randolph, C., Jones, D. W., Berg, G. W., Goldberg, T. E., Carlson, R. E., and Weinberger, D. R. (1990) Studies of frontal lobe functions with positron emission tomography and regional cerebral blood flow. *J. of Nuclear Medicine. Proceedings of the 37th Annual Meeting,* 750.

Blum, R. A. (1952) Effects of subtotal lesions of frontal granular cortex on delayed reaction in monkeys. *AMA Arch. Neurol. Psychiatry* 67:375–386.

Cohen, J. D., and Servan-Schreiber, D. (1992). Context, cortex and dopamine: A connectionist approach to behavior and biology in schizophrenia. *Psychological Review.* 99(1): 45–77.

Duncan, J. (1986) Disorganization of behaviour after frontal lobe damage. *Cognitive Neuropsychology* 3:271–290.

Freedman, M., and Oscar-Berman, M. (1986) Bilateral frontal lobe disease and selective delayed-response deficits in humans. *Behav. Neurosci.* 100:337–342.

Funahashi, S., Bruce, C. J., and Goldman-Rakic, P. S. (1989) Mnemonic coding of visual cortex in the monkey's dorsolateral prefrontal cortex. *Journal of Neurophysiology,* 61(2): 331–348.

Funahashi, S., Bruce, C. J., and Goldman-Rakic, P. S. (1990) Visuospatial coding in primate prefrontal neurons revealed by oculomtor paradigms. *Journal of Neurophysiology* 63: 814–831.

Funahashi, S., Bruce, C. J., and Goldman-Rakic, P. S. (1993) Dorsolateral prefrontal lesion and oculomotor delayed response performance: Evidence for mnemonic "scotomas." *J. Neuroscience* 13(4): 1479–1497.

Fuster, J. M. (1980) *The prefrontal cortex: Anatomy, physiology and neuropsychology of the frontal lobes.* New York: Raven Press.

Goldberg, E., and Bilder, R. (1985) The frontal lobes and hierarchical organization of cognitive control. In E. Perecman, ed., *The frontal lobes revisited.* Hillsdale, NJ: LEA.

Goldman, P. S., and Rosvold, H. E. (1970) Localization of function within the dorsolateral prefrontal cortex of the rhesus monkey. *Exp. Neurol.* 27:291–304.

Goldman-Rakic, P. S. (1987) Circuitry of primate prefrontal cortex and regulation of behavior by representational knowledge. In F. Plum and

V. Mountcastle, eds., *Handbook of physiology – The nervous system V.* Bethesda, MD: American Physiological Society.

Goldman-Rakic, P. S. (1991) Prefrontal cortical dysfunction in schizophrenia: The relevance of working memory. In B. Carroll, ed., *Psychopathology and the brain.* New York: Raven Press.

Gross, C. G., and Weiskrantz, L. (1964) Some changes in behaviour produced by lateral frontal lesion in the macaque. In J. M. Warren and K. Akert, eds., *Frontal granular cortex and behavior.* New York: McGraw-Hill.

Hecaen, H., and Albert, M. (1978) *Human Neuropsychology.* New York: Wiley.

Jacobsen, C. F. (1936) Studies of cerebral functions in primates: I. The functions of the frontal association areas in monkeys. *Comparative Psychology Monographs* 13:3–60.

Just, M. A., and Carpenter, P. A. (1992) A capacity theory of comprehension: Individual differences in working memory. *Psychological Review* 99(1): 122–149.

Katsanis, J., and Iacono, W. G. (1991) Clinical, neuropsychological and brain structural correlates of smooth pursuit eye tracking performance in chronic schizophrenia. *J. Abnormal Psychology* 100(4): 526–534.

Koh, C., and Petersen, A. R. (1978) Recognition memory of schizophrenic patients. *J. Abnormal Psychology* 87:303–313.

Kojima, S., Kojima, M., and Goldman-Rakic (1982) Operant behavioral analysis of memory loss in monkeys with prefrontal lesions. *Brain Res.* 248:51–59.

Kolb, B., and Wishaw, I. Q. (1985) *Fundamentals of human neuropsychology.* 2nd ed. New York: Freeman.

Konorski, J., and Lawicka, W. (1964) Analyses of errors by prefrontal animals on the delayed-response test. In J. M. Warren and K. Akert, eds., *The frontal granular cortex and behavior.* New York: McGraw-Hill.

Kraepelin, E. (1919) *Dementia Praecox,* translated by R. M. Barclay (1971). Edinburgh: Livingstone.

Levin, S. (1984a) Frontal lobe dysfunctions in schizophrenia – I. Eye movement impairments. *Journal of Psychiatric Research* 18(1): 27–55.

Levin, S. (1984b) Frontal lobe dysfunctions in schizophrenia – II. Impairments of psychological brain functions. *Journal of Psychiatric Research* 18(1): 57–72.

Levy, D. L., Dorus, E., Shaughnessy, R., Yasillo, N. J., Pandey, G. N., Janicak, P. G., Gibbons, R. D., Gaviria, M., and Davis, J. M. (1985) Pharmacological evidence for specific pursuit dysfunction to schizophrenia: Lithium carbonate associated abnormal pursuit. *Archives of General Psychiatry* 42: 335–341.

Lewinsohn, P. M., Zieler, J. L., Libet, L. Eyeberg, S., and Nielson, G. (1972) Short-term memory; a comparison between frontal and nonfrontal right and left hemisphere brain-damaged patients. *J. Comp. Physiol. Psy.* 81:248–255.

Lhermitte, F. (1986) Human autonomy and the frontal lobes. II. Patient behavior in complex and social situations. "The environmental dependency syndrome." *Ann. Neurol.* 19:335–343.

Lhermitte, F., Pillon, B., and Serdaru, M. (1986). Human autonomy and the frontal lobes. I. Imitation and utilization behavior: A neuropsychological study of 75 patients. *Ann. Neurol.* 19: 326–334.

Luciana, M., Depue, R. A., Arbisi, P., and Leon, A. (1992) Facilitation of working memory in humans by a D2 dopamine receptor agonist. *Journal of Cognitive Neuroscience* 4(1): 58–68.

Luria, A. R. (1966) *Higher cortical function in man.* New York: Basic Books.

Luria, A. R. (1973) The frontal lobes and regulation of behavior. In K. Pribram and A. R. Luria, eds., *Psychophysiology of the frontal lobes.* New York: Academic Press.

Milner, B. (1963) Effects of different brain lesions on card sorting. *Archives of Neurology* 9:100–110.

Mishkin, M., and Bachevalier, J. (1983) Object recognition impaired by ventromedial but not dorsolateral prefrontal cortical lesions in monkeys. *Soc. Neurosci. Abstr.* 9:29.

Oscar-Berman, M. (1975) The effects of dorsolateral-frontal and ventrolateral-orbitofrontal lesions on spatial discrimination learning and delayed response in two modalities. *Neuropsychologia.* 13:237–246.

Park, S. (1991) The role of prefrontal cortex in spatial working memory deficits of schizophrenic patients. Doctoral Disseration. Harvard University.

Park, S., and Holzman, P. S. (1991) The role of prefrontal cortex in spatial working memory deficits of schizophrenic patients. *Schizophrenia Research,* 4(3), abstracts supp.

Park, S., and Holzman, P. S. (1992) Schizophrenics show working memory deficits. *Arch. Gen. Psychiatry* 49:975–982.

Park, S., and Holzman, P. S. (1993). Association of working memory deficit and eye tracking dysfunction in schizophrenia. *Schizophrenia Research* 11:55–61.

Park, S., Holzman, P. S., and Lenzenweger, M. L. (1995) Individual difference in spatial working memory in relation to schizotypy. *Journal of Abnormal Psychology* 104(2): 355–364.

Park, S., Holzman, P. S., and Levy, D. L. (1993) Spatial working memory deficit in the relatives of schizophrenic patients is associated with their smooth pursuit eye tracking performance. *Schizophrenia Research* 9(2): 184.

Paulescu, E., Frith, C. D., and Frackowiak, R.S.J. (1993) The neural components of working memory. *Nature* 362: 342–345.

Petrides, M., and Milner, B. (1982) Deficits on subject-ordered tasks after frontal and temporal lobe lesions in man. *Neuropsychologia* 20:249–262.

Roitblat, H. L. (1987). *Introduction to comparative cognition.* New York: Freeman.

Sawaguchi, T., and Goldman-Rakic, P. S. (1991) D1 Dopamine receptors in prefrontal cortex: Involvement in working memory. *Science* 251: 947–950.

Shallice, T. (1982) Specific impairments of planning. *Phil. Trans. Royal Soc. Lon. B.*, 199–209.

Shallice, T. (1988) *From neuropsychology to mental structures.* Cambridge University Press.

Shiffrin, R. M., and Schneider, W. (1977) Controlled and automatic human information processing II. *Psychological Review* 84:127–190.

Stamm, J. S. (1985) The riddle of the monkey's delayed response deficit has been solved. In E. Perecman, ed., *The frontal lobes revisited.* Hillsdale, NJ: LEA.

Taylor, A. E., Saint-Cyr, J. A., and Lang, A. E. (1986) Parkinson's disease, cognitive changes in relations to treatment response. *Brain* 110:35–51.

Weinberger, D. R., Berman, K. F., and Zec, R. F. (1986) Physiologic dysfunction of dorsolateral prefrontal cortex in schizophrenia. I. regional cerebral blood flow evidence. *Arch. Gen. Psychiatry* 43:114–124.

Yesutis, J. (1990) Spatial memory and schizophrenia. Unpublished senior thesis, Harvard University.

4

Temporal lobe structural abnormalities in schizophrenia: A selective review and presentation of new magnetic resonance findings

Martha E. Shenton

> It seemed not improbable that cortical centres which are last organized, which are the most highly evolved and voluntary and which are supposed to be localized in the left side of the brain, might suffer first in insanity.
> Crichton-Browne (1879), p. 42

I. Introduction

Schizophrenia is a major mental illness that affects 1% of the general population and is extremely costly to the patient, family, and larger community. Unfortunately, its etiology is as yet unknown, and for this reason it is categorized as a "functional" psychosis rather than an "organic" psychosis, a category which implies that it arises from no known structural or pathological alteration of the brain. The role of brain dysfunction, however, in the etiology of schizophrenia seems likely in light of recent brain structural and functional studies, and has been suspected since Kraepelin (1919/1971) and Bleuler (1911/1950) first delineated the syndrome(s). Kraepelin, in fact, believed that the symptoms of schizophrenia, which he called Dementia Praecox, would ultimately be linked to abnormalities in both the frontal and temporal lobes. He believed that the frontal lobes were responsible for the disruption in reasoning so clearly evident in schizophrenia, while the temporal lobes were responsible for auditory hallucinations and delusions. Other workers at the close of the nineteenth century, such as Crichton-Browne, quoted above, as well as Alzheimer (1897), Kahlbaum (1874), and Hecker (1871) also believed that to understand the etiology of severe mental illnesses, such as schizophrenia, an understanding of the brain was necessary. Consequently, this period in the history of psychopathology was marked by intense activity both in the classification of psychiatric disorders as well as in the investigation of neuroanatomical abnormalities in postmortem brains.

Early evidence supporting the notion that the symptoms of schizophrenia could be explained by a brain dysfunction came from *qualitative* studies that tended to show increased lateral ventricles (e.g., Hecker, 1871), and widespread changes in neocortex, generally not associated with gliosis (e.g., Alzheimer, 1897). Later findings from autopsy and pneumoencephalography studies (e.g., Southard, 1910, 1915; Jacobi and Winkler, 1927; Haug, 1962) suggested increased lateral ventricles in schizophrenia as well as tissue loss in the region of the superior temporal gyrus of the temporal lobe (Southard, 1915). Moreover, Jacobi and Winkler's study was particularly instrumental in supporting Kraepelin's (1919) speculation that schizophrenia resulted from damage to both the temporal and frontal lobes. These researchers reported a link between hallucinosis and temporal lobe damage, and a link between intellectual deficits and frontal lobe damage.

Careful, methodologically controlled postmortem studies, however, often led to negative findings (e.g., Dunlap, 1924; 1928; Spielmeyer, 1930; Rowland and Mettler, 1949), and results became more controversial as concerns were raised about possible methodological artifacts. (See Seidman, 1983, and Kirch and Weinberger, 1986, for a more complete review of these early studies.) Conflicting findings in these early reports led to some skepticism, and as early as 1924, Dunlap concluded that there were no abnormalities observed in postmortem studies of schizophrenia that could not also be found in normal controls. He further criticized the early studies for not demonstrating consistent, reliable indicators of brain dysfunction. The focus of biological research thus began to shift away from structural studies of the brain to neurochemical studies. As interest in the efficacy of structural research waned, Plum (1972) meted the final blow when he stated that "schizophrenia is the graveyard of neuropathologists." Further investigations of brain abnormalities in schizophrenia were thus discouraged and the conclusions drawn from better controlled studies led to the conviction that neurological changes were not confirmed in the brains of schizophrenic patients.

All of the earlier positive findings were thus forgotten, discarded, or abandoned. And, while some researchers continued to theorize about the importance of brain abnormalities in schizophrenia (e.g., MacLean, 1952; Kety, 1959; Stevens, 1973; Torrey and Peterson,

1974), it was not until 1976, with the emerging technology of computed tomography (CT), that interest was rekindled by a CT study of schizophrenic patients reported by Johnstone and co-workers. In that study enlarged lateral ventricles were observed in patients with schizophrenia, confirming earlier pneumoencephalography studies (e.g., Jacobi and Winkler, 1927; Haug, 1962). This one study, which called attention to a new window for viewing the brain, has now led to more than 100 studies (see review in Shelton and Weinberger, 1986), most of which (75%) have reported increased lateral ventricles in schizophrenic patients even though fewer than 10% of the CT scans have been interpreted as abnormal by a clinical neuroradiologist.

The current explosion of studies has continued with both the newer technology of magnetic resonance (MR) imaging studies (the first schizophrenia study was conducted by Smith et al., 1984), and with more recent postmortem studies (beginning with Scheibel and Kovelman, 1979, 1981). These newer studies, based on more reliably diagnosed patients (e.g., using DSM-III and DSM-III-R criteria, APA, 1980, 1987) and more advanced, *quantitative* techniques for measurement, have demonstrated that brain abnormalities can be clearly delineated in schizophrenia.

This chapter focuses on the evidence for temporal lobe structural abnormalities in schizophrenia. We have chosen to review temporal lobe studies because evidence has amassed to suggest a strong relationship between abnormalities in this region of the brain and schizophrenia. We review both postmortem and structural MR studies which suggest that morphometric abnormalities in the brains of schizophrenic patients show a selectivity to temporal lobe structures, especially the limbic system, and which are especially pronounced on the left. We will not, however, review the literature on laterality studies in schizophrenia. We focus instead on the recent data that have amassed to suggest left-sided are greater than right-sided abnormalities in temporal lobe brain structures in schizophrenia. We will also review MR temporal lobe findings recently reported by our group (Shenton et al., 1990, 1991, 1992). The evidence that will be presented is consonant with reports of functional abnormalities in event-related potentials (Faux et al., 1990; McCarley et al., 1991), with positron emission tomography (PET) studies (e.g., DeLisi et al., 1989; Wiesel et al., 1987), with studies of attentional processes (Posner et al., 1988), and with general hypotheses that left > right hemisphere abnormalities may represent a fundamental genetic/

developmental abnormality in schizophrenia (Crichton-Browne, 1879; Southard, 1915; Flor-Henry, 1969; Crow et al., 1989; Crow, 1990a, 1990b).

We further emphasize at the outset that although evidence is presented suggesting the importance of temporal lobe abnormalities in the pathophysiology of schizophrenia, this in no way implies that neuroanatomical abnormalities that are localized to temporal and medial temporal lobe structures are isolated and not linked to other abnormalities in the brain. It is, in fact, well known that the temporal lobe is densely connected with other brain areas, that brain function depends upon interconnectivity, and that a focus on the temporal lobe should not imply that other brain areas, such as the frontal lobe, may not be critically involved in schizophrenic pathology. On the contrary, the brain can be viewed as an integrated network of neural systems with "reciprocally connected neocortical areas (i.e., prefrontal, temporal, and inferior parietal cortex) that have links with interconnected structures of the limbic system (e.g., hippocampus, amygdala, and septum) which in turn are closely connected with the hypothalamus and the brainstem (including the reticular activating system), all of which have cortical connections, especially to prefrontal cortex" (Zec and Weinberger, 1986, p. 194). Additionally, areas in the frontal lobe, such as the cingulate gyrus, have reciprocal connections with the hippocampus in the anterior portion, and the cingulate is also connected with dorsolateral prefrontal and orbitofrontal cortex (Pandya et al., 1981), as well as with Brodmann areas 9 and 10 (Vogt and Pandya, 1987; Vogt et al., 1987), regions shown to be functionally affected in schizophrenia (Weinberger, 1986). Moreover, the prefrontal cortex has direct and indirect connections with the amygdala (Fuster, 1980), hippocampus, and parahippocampal gyrus (Goldman-Rakic et al., 1984), and regions in the posterior superior temporal gyrus of the temporal lobe are connected through projections to the prefrontal cortex (Brodmann's area 46) and to the premotor cortex (Brodmann's area 8) in the frontal lobes (e.g., Pandya and Seltzer, 1982). Thus damage to one part of the brain, such as in the temporal lobe, may be related to damage to an interconnected network that is not proximal but nonetheless importantly linked.

It is within this context that we present a growing body of evidence suggesting the importance of temporal lobe abnormalities, particularly pronounced on the left, and their role in schizophrenia. First, there will be a brief overview of the anatomy and functions that characterize the temporal lobe, which will include a short synopsis of the component parts of the temporal lobe and what is known today regarding their role in memory, emotion, and cognition. A brief review of human studies showing damage to temporal lobe structures and their relationship to psychoses will also be provided, followed by a more detailed review of postmortem and imaging studies indicating medial temporal and temporal lobe structural abnormalities in schizophrenia. Next, data from a recent MR study conducted in our laboratory (Shenton et al., 1992) will be presented that demonstrate a strong association between temporal lobe abnormalities and the presence of thought disorder in schizophrenia. We conclude with a synthesis of the findings in schizophrenia along with some comments and speculations regarding the role of temporal lobe abnormalities in the etiology of schizophrenia.

II. The anatomy and function of the temporal lobes: A brief synopsis

It is useful to provide an overview of temporal lobe anatomy and function since this region of the brain has figured importantly in recent schizophrenia investigations. Listed below are the major subdivisions within the temporal lobe (see also Figure 4.1), followed by detailed descriptions of the temporal lobe, including the superior temporal gyrus and medial temporal lobe structures (hippocampus, amygdala, and parahippocampal gyrus).

Superior Temporal Gyrus (STG)

1. Primary and secondary (associative) auditory cortex are located in the STG and are important for the initial analysis of auditory information.
2. Language-related areas are generally lateralized to the left STG in both right- and left-handed individuals. These areas are located in the posterior region of the STG, and include the planum temporale, a region that has long been implicated as a biological substrate of language.

Middle and Inferior Gyri

1. These areas are linked to the further processing of sensory information, including auditory and visual stimuli. Specific neurons in these regions may also be responsive to complex species-specific features such as faces.

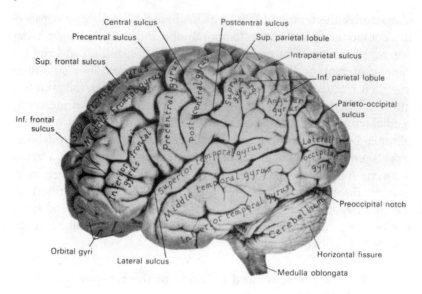

Figure 4.1. Photograph of the lateral view of the brain. (From Carpenter and Sutin, 1983, *Human Neuroanatomy,* courtesy Williams & Wilkins.)

Medial Temporal Lobe Structures

1. The hippocampus and adjacent entorhinal cortex (part of the parahippocampal gyrus) are involved in the laying down and retrieval of long-term memory via interconnections with neocortical (gray matter) regions in the brain. Cognitive memory functions also tend to be lateralized, as, for example, verbal memories, which are likely stored in the left STG even though the initial stages of analysis and consolidation may have begun in the hippocampus.
2. The function of the amygdala is less well understood, although it is thought to be involved in the emotional aspects of memory, learning, and cognition and may provide the emotional valence that facilitates the coding of memories.

The temporal lobe

The human brain weighs approximately 1,400 grams and comprises 2% of the total body weight (Carpenter, 1991). The sulcogyral pattern of the brain has been used to separate the cerebrum into six lobes: frontal, temporal, parietal, occipital, insular, and limbic (though neither the insular nor limbic lobes are true lobes since they represent a synthesis of marginal portions of several lobes). The temporal lobe lies inferior to the lateral, or sylvian, sulcus and is bounded posteriorly by the occipital and parietal lobes (see Figure 4.1). Along the surface of the temporal lobe there are three parallel convolutions, the superior, middle, and inferior gyri (see Figure 4.1). The superior temporal sulcus is parallel to the lateral, or sylvian, sulcus, and it terminates posteriorly with the angular gyrus. The fusiform, occipitotemporal gyrus, and parahippocampal gyri are located on the inferior surface of the temporal lobe (not shown) while the transverse gyri of Heschl (see Figure 4.2) are located on the superior surface of the temporal lobe (seen only spreading open the sylvian fissure and lifting up the frontal lobe). The parahippocampal gyrus and the medial protrusion of the uncus are separated from the occipitotemporal gyrus by the collateral sulcus. Within the STG, along the longitudinal axis, lies the hippocampus and adjacent amygdala. The parahippocampal gyrus lies medial and lateral to the amygdala-hippocampal formation. Figure 4.3 shows a coronal 1.5-mm slice which delineates these medial temporal and neocortical structures.

All of these latter structures, the amygdala, hippocampus, and parahippocampal gyrus, are medial temporal lobe structures which are part of the limbic system, a region in the medial part of the brain that includes parts of the temporal, frontal, parietal, and occipital lobes and is concerned with emotion. The limbic system, or limbic lobe, was labelled as such by MacLean (1952) and is based on earlier work by Papez (1937), who described a loop that consisted of structures important to attention, cognition, and emotional responses in humans. These regions have also figured importantly in studies of schizophrenia, as demonstrated by postmortem studies of the cingulate gyrus (e.g., Benes and Bird, 1987; Benes et al., 1992)* as well as MR *in vivo* studies of medial temporal lobe structures in schizophrenia (discussed in Sections IV through VI).

Main functional subdivisions within the temporal lobe

Superior temporal gyrus. Along the surface of the STG, and posteriorly, Heschl's transverse gyri can be seen. Figure 4.2 shows the superior surface of the temporal lobe, including a view of Heschl's

---

* See also Chapter 1, by Francine M. Benes, this volume – Eds.

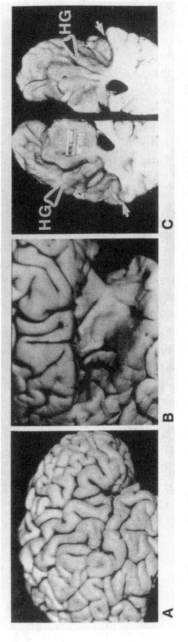

Figure 4.2. A: Photograph of lateral surface of the brain; B: Spreading of the Sylvian fissure to expose the superior surface of the superior temporal gyrus; C: Slice showing the asymmetry of the superior surface of the temporal lobes. The planum temporale are defined anteriorly by Heshl's gyrus (HG) and posteriorly by the posterior margin of the Sylvian fissure (white arrows). (Adapted from LeMay, 1992, *AJNR*, 13:493–504.)

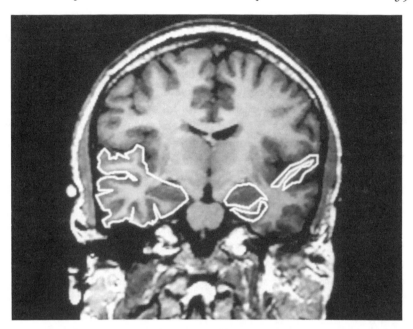

Figure 4.3. Coronal 1.5-mm slice showing medial temporal and neocortical structures. The region bordering the Sylvian fissure is the superior temporal gyrus (left side of patient is right side for viewer). The almond-shaped region in the medial portion of the temporal lobe is the amygdala and the region demarcated beneath is the parahippocampal gyrus. The whole temporal lobe is also outlined. (From Shenton et al., 1992, courtesy *The New Engl. J. Med.*)

gyri and, posteriorly, a flattened region known as the planum temporale. Heschl's gyri, usually numbering two but sometimes only one, are thought to subserve primary auditory processing while Wernicke's area (Brodmann's areas 41 and 42), including the planum temporale, on the lateral surface of the left STG, are thought to subserve reading and language comprehension (Wernicke, 1874; Penfield and Roberts, 1959).

Damage to the left cerebral hemisphere, in the *posterior* part of the temporal cortex in humans, can result in aphasia. This is because it is this hemisphere that tends to be dominant for language, in both left- and right-handed individuals (DaMasio, 1992). Damage in the posterior region can result in a form of aphasia where speech is fluent but there may be paraphasic substitutions (verbal or semantic) in which one word, or even nonexistent words (neologisms), may be produced in place of other words more appropriate to a given sentence construction. Often these patients also show impaired comprehension of spoken language (Benson and Geschwind, 1987). Left anterior temporal resections, in contrast, result in recent verbal memory deficits (Ojemann and Dodrill, 1985) while electrical stimulation on the left posterior STG results in disordered thinking (Haglund et al., 1992), as well as complex auditory hallucinations such as the experience of "memories" of voices or complex sounds such as songs (Penfield and Perot, 1963). Verbal memory deficits, disordered thought, and auditory hallucinations are important clinical symptoms in schizophrenia and thus make this brain region of particular interest to psychopathologists.

Several lines of evidence further implicate the *left* STG and surrounding cortex in the processing of auditory stimuli and language, as well as in verbal memory. For example, more recent studies have used extracellular recording and PET in human subjects to map the function of these temporal lobe areas. Extracellular recordings in the temporal lobe of epileptic patients, done during reading, naming, and verbal memory tasks, have shown that neurons in the STG, and surrounding cortex, were responsive during speech (both overt and silent), naming, and reading (Ojemann et al., 1988). Some neurons were also responsive during a verbal memory task, and, of this group, a differential response was observed for the storage vs retrieval of memory tasks. Moreover, areas in the temporal cortex, when stimulated, disrupted the performance of tasks such as object naming, reading, recent verbal memory, and phoneme identification (Ojemann, 1991), suggesting that these areas contain at least part of the neural substrate for such functions. Changes in regional cerebral blood flow have also been measured by PET studies of humans during word processing tasks, and these studies have demonstrated that the posterior STG, or Wernicke's area, was activated during tasks involving both word comprehension and retrieval of information from memory (Wise et al., 1991). Evidence from aphasia studies also suggests the importance of the posterior STG to language functioning (DaMasio, 1992).

The superior temporal gyrus, a multimodal sensory convergence area of the brain, may also be important to the focusing of attention (Pandya and Yeterian, 1985). Mirsky and co-workers (1991) have further suggested that the STG, as well as the inferior parietal cortices and the corpus striatum, are important to the focus-execute functions of attention.* This heuristic model may prove important to schizophrenia research, particularly since focusing of attention on relevant environmental stimuli is one area in which schizophrenic patients show marked difficulty and the STG may be an important component of this cognitively impaired system in schizophrenia.

Finally, it is of interest to note that early autopsy studies done by Southard (1910, 1915) at the turn of the century showed that in an examination of 25 cases of schizophrenia, a large number of patients with auditory hallucinations showed "suprasylvian atrophy" with the entire *left* sylvian fissure atrophied, including a "withering away" of the *left* STG. He also noted an unusual arrangement in the convolutions of the sulcogyral pattern in the left temporal lobe and concluded that there was striking evidence for temporal lobe involvement in schizophrenia. This latter finding, of disordered sulcogyral pattern in the left temporal lobe, has also been observed more recently in postmortem studies of schizophrenia (Jakob and Beckmann, 1986; Bruton et al., 1990) and will be discussed in detail in section IV.

Taken as a whole, these findings suggest that the *left* STG contains areas that subserve not only primary auditory functions but also language functions, including verbal memory. These areas contain the neural substrates underlying word comprehension and verbal memory, as well as other language functions such as naming. Moreover, these functions seem to be clearly lateralized to the left hemisphere. Geschwind and Levitsky (1968), and later Galaburda and co-workers (Galaburda, 1984; Galaburda et al., 1987), have further localized some aspects of language processing to the planum temporale on the left, a flat region just lateral to Heschl's gyrus, which is often larger on the left by a factor of 10. This region is clearly visible in Figure 4.2. The increased size of the planum temporale in the left temporal lobe has also been observed in postmortem analyses of fetuses (Witelson and Pallie, 1973) and in postmortem analyses of adults and infants (Wada et al., 1975). There is also evidence that choline-acetyltransferase (ChAT) activity is increased in the left STG, particularly in the region of the planum temporale (Amaducci et al., 1981), suggesting neurochemical correlates of hemispheric specialization for this region of the brain. Additionally, Chi and co-workers (1977) have noted an earlier cortical folding of the gyri and sulci in the right temporal lobe, as opposed to the left, suggesting that slowly develop-

---

* See also Chapter 17, by Allan Mirsky, this volume – Eds.

ing structures in the brain, such as the left planum temporale, may be more vulnerable to disrupting influences (i.e., as noted in dyslexia – Galaburda and Kemper, 1979).

Thus the regions on the left seem to represent, at least in part, the neural substrates of language and communication that are present prior to birth and that lag in development behind the right hemisphere (last trimester of fetal development). Crow (1990a, 1990b) has hypothesized that such temporal lobe asymmetries may be a key to understanding the etiology of schizophrenia. He further suggests that schizophrenia may be associated with a cerebral dominance gene. This remains speculative at this time, although recent data suggesting left STG abnormalities in schizophrenia are quite exciting as they demonstrate a strong relationship between the clinical symptoms of auditory hallucinations (Barta et al., 1990) and thought disorder (Shenton et al., 1992) with reduced volume in the *left* STG (see section V).

Medial temporal lobe structures: The hippocampus, amygdala, and parahippocampal gyrus. The hippocampus, amygdala, and parahippocampal gyrus are located in the medial portion of the temporal lobe (see Figure 4.3). The amygdala and hippocampal structures lie within and run parallel to the STG, as does the parahippocampal gyrus, although this structure is located in the most medial aspect of the temporal lobe.

    a. Hippocampus. The hippocampus, once thought to be related primarily to olfactory function, is now thought to be important to specific memory functions such as declarative, or knowledge-based, aspects of memory. Accordingly, damage or resection of the temporal lobe, which includes the hippocampus, is seen to result in an anterograde amnesia on memory tasks involving free recall or recognition (Milner, 1972; Scoville and Milner, 1957; Corkin, 1984), but no impaired performance on other memory tasks such as priming (where cues are given to aid the recall of material previously presented), and skill learning (Milner, 1962; Corkin, 1965; 1968; see Cohen, 1984, for a review). The temporal lobe amnesic patient H.M., who has been studied through a period of many years, exhibited deficits in the delayed recall of virtually all types of information (see Corkin, 1984, for a review).

The function of the hippocampus has also been lateralized to some extent in humans. Epileptic patients with unilateral hippocampal re-moval show different patterns of impaired memory function depend-ing on the side of removal. More specifically, patients with left hippo-campal excision show deficits on verbal memory tasks (Frisk and Milner, 1990), while patients with right hippocampal excision show deficits on tasks involving recall of spatial or visual stimuli (Smith and Milner, 1981; Jones-Gotman, 1986; Smith, 1988). Additionally, the hippocampal functions may subserve time-limited aspects of memory that are gradually restructured and reorganized into permanent mem-ory, probably in the neocortex (Squire, 1992). Thus the hippocampus participates in the storage and/or consolidation and retrieval of spe-cific aspects of memory for a time after learning, but the hippocampus is not the ultimate storage for long-term memory (Squire, 1992). Long-term memory is thought, instead, to be stored, at least in part, in the higher order association areas that process the stimuli, areas such as the inferotemporal cortex for visual information, and the left STG for verbal information (Penfield and Perot, 1963; Mishkin et al., 1984; Zola-Morgan et al., 1986; Ojemann et al., 1988; Ojemann 1991; Squire, 1992).

Damage to the hippocampus, either directly or indirectly through connections with it, can therefore lead to a disruption in memory and, if this damage is on the left, can lead to disruptions in verbal memory and/or to the storage and retrieval of verbal information laid down in neocortex. Such findings are particularly relevant to more recent findings of hippocampal damage in schizophrenia (see sections IV and V) and may be important to understanding some of the clinical manifestations of this disorder such as formal thought disorder, which if often evaluated by investigating the verbal productions of schizo-phrenic patients (e.g., Johnston and Holzman, 1979).

b. Parahippocampal gyrus. The parahippocampal gyrus serves as the major input–output pathway between the hippocampus and cortical association areas. More specifically, the entorhinal cortex re-ceives a large input from the hippocampus and, in turn, gives rise to a major outflow to "the entire cortical mantle" (Swanson and Köhler, 1986). Input areas to the parahippocampal gyrus also include: "orbit-ofrontal, medial frontal, and dorsolateral prefrontal cortices, cingulate gyrus cortices, rostral insula, retrosplenial cortex, olfactory and peri-amygdaloid cortices, rostral superior temporal gyrus, superior tempo-ral sulcus, presubicular cortices, perirhinal cortex, and caudal portions of the parahippocampal gyrus" (Arnold et al., 1991, p. 629). The entorhinal cortex of the parahippocampal gyrus is also the main route in which cortical information enters the hippocampal circuit (Insausti et al., 1987) although the subiculum and presubiculum subregions of the hippocampus are also major relays to the hippocampus proper and the prefrontal cortex sends two different projections to the hippocampal formation that terminate in the presubiculum (Goldman-Rakic et al., 1984). The inference that can be drawn here, nonetheless, is that cortical input to the entorhinal cortex generally involves higher order polysensory information that is presumably highly elaborated and multimodal as it enters the hippocampal circuit.

In summary then, since the parahippocampal gyrus serves as a major gateway from the hippocampus to many other regions of the brain, and since it receives input from many regions of the brain, damage here can lead to many cognitive deficits including deficits in memory storage or retrieval from other areas of the brain, because of a disconnection between the hippocampus and other cortical areas. For example, monkeys with parahippocampal damage show the same pattern of memory impairment on at least one memory task as do monkeys with circumscribed hippocampal lesions (Zola-Morgan et al., 1989). Such findings may also be relevant to schizophrenia (see sections IV and V).

c. Amygdala. The amygdala, whose function is less well understood, is thought to be important in selecting sensory information, in interrelating highly processed cortical input, and in imparting an emotional valence to aspects of learning and memory (Gloor, 1986). Early work investigating this structure showed that damage to the amygdala resulted in passive, withdrawn animals, while stimulation of this structure resulted in rage or fright responses (Klüver and Bucy, 1939). This structure, therefore, has come to be viewed as subserving the emotional import given to stimuli.

Summary

The STG, amygdala, hippocampus, and parahippocampal gyrus are highly interconnected anatomically. That is, the STG has direct connections to both the amygdala and the parahippocampal gyrus (Amaral et al., 1983), and parts of the parahippocampal gyrus, including areas such as the entorhinal cortex, provide a major gateway between the hippocampus and other cortical areas. Additionally, the entorhinal cortex projects directly to the hippocampus (Witter and Amaral, 1991), which in turn projects to the entorhinal cortex via the subiculum (for a review, see Rosene and Van Hoesen, 1987), and the hippocampus and amygdala are reciprocally connected, with the amygdala projecting directly to the entorhinal cortex (Saunders et al., 1988). A direct connection from dorsolateral prefrontal cortex has also been found to project to part of the parahippocampal gyrus (Rakic and Nowakowski, 1981) and the rostral superior temporal cortex is directly connected to entorhinal cortex (Amaral et al., 1983). These regions also appear to be functionally important for associative links in memory (e.g., Penfield and Perot, 1963; Sanghera et al., 1979; Ojemann et al., 1988; Squire and Zola-Morgan, 1991; Witter and Amaral, 1991).

Anatomical and functional evidence thus suggest that the hippocampus, parahippocampal gyrus, amygdala, and STG are anatomically as well as functionally related. Moreover, the functions of the hippocampus appear to be lateralized and, on the left side, the hippocampus, via the parahippocampal gyrus, may be important for the initial stages of processing verbal information that is later consolidated as verbal memory and stored, at least in part, in the left STG (Squire and Zola-Morgan, 1991). Since this region is important to the processing of both auditory and language information, it is likely important to schizophrenia, as is illustrated in sections IV and V, where we review the evidence for left temporal lobe abnormalities in schizophrenia.

III. Relationship of temporal lobe damage to psychoses

Damage to the temporal lobes in humans by brain trauma, stroke, or epilepsy affects memory, affect, and/or cognition, and epileptogenic foci in the *left* temporal lobe are strongly associated with schizophrenic-like psychoses (Jackson, 1888; Hillbom, 1951; Mulder and Daly, 1952; Penfield and Jasper, 1954; Hill, 1962; Pond, 1962; Davidson and Bagley, 1969; Flor-Henry, 1969; Trimble and Perez, 1982; Roberts et al., 1990). In fact, when psychosis is present it most often occurs when damage is in the left but not right temporal lobe.

More recently, Trimble and Perez (1982) have noted that the rate of schizophrenia is 5–10% in epileptic populations (compared to 1%

in the general population), and that 11 out of 16 patients with temporal lobe epilepsy examined by them met the diagnostic criteria for schizophrenia. Trimble (1990) has further noted that the subgroup of patients with epileptic foci in the left temporal lobe tend to develop schizophrenia-like symptoms characterized primarily by Schneiderian "first rank" symptoms (i.e., disruptions in thought and language processes and/or auditory hallucinations). On the basis of these observations, Trimble has suggested that such symptoms be viewed as signifiers of temporal lobe pathology, in the dominant (usually left) hemisphere, rather than as pathognomonic for schizophrenia.

These findings, though circumstantial, underscore the importance of left temporal lobe foci and their association with psychotic symptoms, an association which may, in turn, be important to understanding the pathophysiology of schizophrenia.

IV. Findings of temporal lobe abnormalities from recent postmortem studies

Recent advances in biological and psychological measures in schizophrenia now afford an opportunity for a rapprochement of these levels of analysis that will lead to a richer understanding of this disorder. Here, we review postmortem findings of temporal lobe changes in schizophrenia, changes hypothesized by both Southard (1910; 1915) and Kraepelin (1919/1971) to underlie the psychological symptoms of hallucinations and delusions so frequently observed in this disorder. Following this, a review of magnetic resonance (MR) temporal lobe findings in schizophrenia is presented, including data from a recent study in our laboratory that documents an association between structural changes in the temporal lobe and clinical symptoms in schizophrenia.

Table 4.1 provides a survey of 22 postmortem studies conducted since 1979 that have examined the temporal lobe in schizophrenic patients. Both the volumes and the cytoarchitectonics of limbic system structures such as the amygdala, hippocampus, and parahippocampal gyrus have been examined, as well as the temporal horns of the lateral ventricles, which are in close apposition to these medial temporal lobe structures. In addition, the sulcogyral pattern of the temporal lobe has been examined and this information is also included in Table 4.1.

Overall, as can be seen in this table, and in the recent review by Roberts and Bruton (1990), there is now strong and convergent post-mortem evidence supporting temporal lobe structural changes in schizophrenia. Furthermore, while there are exceptions, the data in Table 4.1 clearly indicate that the temporal lobe changes in schizophrenia tend to be lateralized to the left in right-handed individuals, a finding that will be echoed in the MR structural studies (reported below). (Parenthetically, the small number of exceptions noted in Table 4.1 is most likely due to sampling differences. For example, Bruton et al. [1990] and Heckers et al. [1990] used both older patients and controls [mean age > 60 years]; advanced age itself may result in brain changes that obscure other more subtle differences between groups. Altshuler et al. [1987] included in her sample patients with prefrontal lobotomies or leukotomies. It is important to note, however, that even these studies were not entirely negative: Bruton et al. [1990] reported sulcogyral pattern abnormalities in the temporal lobe, Heckers et al. [1990] noted the greatest increase in the left temporal horns of the lateral ventricles in schizophrenic patients, and Altshuler et al. [1987] observed that the most impaired schizophrenics showed cellular disarray in pyramidal cells in the hippocampus or shape differences [Altshuler et al., 1990] in the hippocampus [see Table 4.1].)

Since most of the tissue reductions reported have not been accompanied by gliosis (e.g., Roberts et al., 1986, 1987; Falkai et al., 1988a), which would suggest an insult or trauma to the brain, many researchers (e.g., Crow, 1990a, 1990b) have interpreted these findings as reflecting a neurodevelopmental origin. At present, however, it is not yet known whether the etiology of the observed abnormalities is related: (1) to treatment (less likely); (2) to a progressive disorder (e.g., Nasrallah et al., 1986, and Woods et al., 1990, suggest that an increase in lateral ventricles over time in schizophrenics reflects a progressive disorder); (3) to a static disorder (e.g., Pillowsky et al., 1988, and Vita et al., 1988, suggest that there is no change in lateral ventricle size over time in schizophrenic patients and that the insult to the brain is thus static); or (4) to a neurodevelopmental disorder that in some cases is progressive while in other cases is not. We do, however, believe that the capability to test these hypotheses is at hand with sensitive, quantitative volumetric analyses that have just recently been achieved with new *in vivo* tools. One particularly important tool for addressing these questions, by examining *in vivo* brains longi-

Table 4.1. *Temporal lobe structural alterations in schizophrenia*

Authors	Subject Characteristics	Temporal lobe measures	Findings (SZ compared with NCL)
Scheibel & Kovelman, 1979 (Abstract)	15 SZ. (Ratings not blind to Diagnosis). 15 NCL	HIPP pyramidal-cell orientation/density.	Pyramidal cell disarray in CA1-CA3.
Scheibel & Kovelman, 1981	8 Paranoid SZ.	Same as above.	Same as above.
Kovelman & Scheibel, 1984	10 SZ (M); 49.6 yr. 8 Non-SZ; 50.8 yr.	HIPP of left hemispheres only.	Pyramidal cell disarray in left anterior & middle HIPP.
Bogerts, 1984; Bogerts et al., 1985	13 SZ (3 M/7 F); 41 yr.; Duration=10 yr. (No ECT/insulin Rx). 9 NCL (6 M/3 F); 53 yr.	Left hemisphere only; Vogt collection (1928-1953). Volumes: limbic system structures & basal ganglia.	↓ Volume amygdala, HIPP, PHG, & pallidum internum. No differences br.wt.
Brown et al., 1986	41 SZ (24 M/17 F); 66.6 yr. 29 AFF (12 M/17 F); 68 yr. 16 ALZ (9 M/7 F); 78.9 yr. 7 Huntington's (6 M/1 F); 72.4 yr.	Vogt collection (1956-1978); no leukotomy pts. Br.wt.; planimetric measures: TH, LAT VENT & PHG.	6% ↓ br.wt., 11% ↓ thickness left PHG, 19% ↑ LAT VENT, 97% ↑ TH.
Falkai et al., 1986	13 SZ (2 M/11 F) 43.4 yr; duration=9 yr. 11 NCL (7 M/4 F);42.6 yr.	Vogt collection (1928-1960); left hemispheres only. Volume pyramidal /glial cell counts CA1-CA4 of HIPP.	↓ Left HIPP volume. ↓ #pyramidal cells CA1 -CA4, mostly in paranoid-hallucinosis SZs.
Jakob and Beckmann, 1986	64 SZ (25 M/39 F); 61 yr, duration=14 yr. 10 Non-SZ (8 M/2 F); 61.7 yr. (7 oligophrenics, 2 organic, 1 pers. disorder).	Ratings not blind to diagnosis; qualitative/quantitative measures TL, cyto-architectonic measures entorhinal PHG.	42 SZs: ↑ vertical sulco-gyral pattern in left TL. 22 SZs:heteropic displacement of left entorhinal neurons.
Roberts et al., 1986	5 SZ (1 M/4 F); 39.2 yr; Ss/Bogerts 1985. 7 NCL (4 M/3 F); 50.9 yr. 5 Huntington's (1 M/4 F); 54.2 yr.	Vogt collection (1928-1953); left hemisphere only. Computer densitometry of GFAP*.	No gliosis in TL.
Colter et al., 1987	17 SZ. (subset of Brown et al., 1986). 11 AFF "	Area measures of HIPP (also dorsal part) & PHG (gyral, white, & sulcal parts).	Gyral part PHG↓, 23% ↓ white & 41% ↓ gray matter.
Roberts et al., 1987	18 SZ (14 M/4 F); 54.9 yr. 12 NCL (9 M/3 F); 69.2 yr. 8 AFF (4 M/4 F); 67.3 yr.	Vogt collection (1956-1978); gliosis TL, examined using GFAP*. Ss/Brown 1986.	No gliosis observed.
Altshuler et al., 1987	7 SZ (3 M/4 F); 50.3 yr. (n=5 ECT; n=4 prefrontal lobotomy; n=3 leukotomy). 6 NCL (2 M/4 F);46.5 yr.;2=Parkinson's	Yakovlev collection. Pyramidal-cell orientation in HIPP.	No differences, but most impaired SZs showed >disarray.
Falkai et al., 1988-a	13 SZ (2 M/11 F); 43.4 yr. 11 NCL (7 M/4 F);42.6 yr.(Ss/Falkai 1986)	Vogt collection (1928-1960); all left hemisphere except 2. Entorhinal region.	Volume of entorhinal region ↓ with no ↑ glial cells.

Study	Subjects	Methods	Findings
Christison et al., 1989	17 SZ (11 M/6 F);45 yr.(n=16leukotomies). 14 Leukotomy CTL; (7 M/7 F); 44 yr. 18 Nonlobotomy CTL;(7 M/11 F);50 yr.	Yakovlev collection (1930-1972); computerized morphometric analysis size/shape CA1 in mid-HIPP.	No differences CA1 region of middle HIPP.
Crow et al., 1989	41 SZ (22 M/19 F); Ss/Bruton, 1990. 53 NCL (30 M/23 F). 30 ALZ.	Brains collected 1978-1985; right/left hemispheres available. LAT VENT & gliosis examined.	LAT VENT↑ in left TH (not seen in ALZ patients=bilateral↑).
Jakob & Beckmann, 1989	76 SZ (age range 27-78 years). 16 NCL (sex/age matched to patients).	Qualitative analysis of sulco-gyral pattern of TL.	56/76 SZs abnormalities/deviations sulco-gyral pattern, mainly in left TL.
Jeste & Lohr, 1989	13 SZ (7 M/6 F); 44 yr.(all=leukotomies; n=9 ECT treatment). 9 Non-SZ (4 M/5 F); 57 yr.(all= leukotomies; n=4 ECT treatment). 16 NCL (8 M/8 F); 48 yr.	Yakovlev collection; right/left HIPP examined using semi-automated planimetric measurements.	Volume of pyramidal cells↓ in CA1-CA4. Greatest↓ in the left CA4.
Altshuler et al., 1990	12 SZ (9 M/3 F); 50 yr. 17 Suicides (11 M/6 F); 35 yr. 10 NCL (8 M/2 F); 43 yr.	Brains/NIMH. Cases=gliosis excluded; left/right hemispheres/same patients not available. Area measures:PHG/HIPP.	Bilateral PHG↓ (differ from NCLs -not suicides-on right). No HIPP↓, but shape differences in both structures for SZs.
Bruton et al., 1990	56 SZ M= 67.7 yr./F=78.8 yr. 56 NCL (age/sex matched); M=65.7 yr./F=78.4.	8 SZs not included, e.g., leukotomy. Area measures; qualitative for sulco-gyral pattern.	44% SZs focal pathologies 21% NCLs. Calcification of HIPP, sulco-gyral pattern abnormality in TL, 2.9%↓ (right), & 5.1%↓ (left) in br.wt. in SZs.
Heckers et al., 1990	20 SZ (9 M/11 F); 63.7 yr. 20 Patients with no Psychiatric history (9 M/11 F); 64.3 yr.	17 left/13 rt. hemispheres available each group; 8 SZs/7 NCLs excluded. Volumes: amygdala, HIPP, 3 horns of LAT VENT.	No differences in volume of amygdala or HIPP; bilateral↑ in LAT VENT (not significant) with greatest↑ in left THs.
Arnold et al., 1991	6 SZ (3 M/3 F); 23 to 88 yr. (All prefrontal lobotomies or leukotomies). 16 NCL (7 M/9 F); 33-80 yr.	Yakovlev collection; all of entorhinal cortex examined.	Abnormalities rostral & intermediate parts of entorhinal, including: invaginations in surface, disruption of cell layers, & displacement of neurons.
Benes et al., 1991	14 SZ [7=with no mood disturbance (53.4 yr.); 7=with mood disturbance (48.7 yr.)]. 9 NCL 59.4 yr.	Cross-sections of posterior HIPP from the Human Brain Tissue Resource Center, McLean Hospital. Morphometric analyses.	↓ pyramidal neuron size in SZ for all CA sectors of HIPP (> CA4); ↓ # of pyramidal cells in CA 1 in SZ w/out mood disturbance.

Table 4.1. (cont.)

Conrad et al, 1991	11 SZ (M; n=9 paranoid, n=1 catatonic; n=2 seizures; n=1 metastasized cancer to brain; n=1 ECT); 53 yr. 7 NCL (M); 50.7 yr.	Brains from West Los Angeles VAMC; right hemispheres only; orientation of pyramidal cells in anterior, middle, & posterior HIPP.	↑Disorganization of pyramidal cells in the right HIPP.

Key: SZ=schizophrenic; NCL=normal control; AFF=affective disorder; ALZ=alzheimer disease; M=male; F=female; PHG=parahippocampal gyrus; TL=temporal lobe; HIPP=hippocampus; LAT VENT=lateral ventricles; TH=temporal horn; "x" yr.=mean age; duration=mean duration of illness; br. wt.=brain weight.

*Glial fibrillary acid protein, a marker of astrocytes.

tudinally, in first episode patients, and in high-risk populations – not possible in postmortem analyses – is MR imaging, which we review below.

V. Findings of temporal lobe structural abnormalities from recent MRI studies

MR imaging as a new tool for the in vivo *investigation of the brain*

It is important, before reviewing MR temporal lobe studies in schizophrenia, to recognize the advance in technology that MR imaging offers for viewing the brain. MR imaging was first introduced into the field of radiology in the 1980s, with the first visualization of a human hand in 1982, and then later a human brain. It is therefore a tool that has only recently been explored for its usefulness in documenting brain alterations. It offers many advantages over computerized tomography (CT) scans, including: (1) it does not use radiation, thereby allowing multiple scans and repeated measures to evaluate the course of brain changes; (2) gray and white matter can be clearly delineated, which is not possible with CT; (3) imaging can be done in any plane, which is particularly advantageous for studies of the temporal lobe because the coronal plane offers the best visualization of the temporal lobe (Squire and Zola-Morgan, 1991; Jack et al., 1988, 1989); and (4) MRI does not have the problem of "bone hardening" artifact that makes CT studies of the temporal lobe particularly problematic.

The ability to maximize this new imaging tool, however, has only just begun. That is, it is only recently that the technology to extract objective, quantitative information from *in vivo* magnetic resonance images has become available. For example, many early imaging studies, including some more recent MR studies (see Table 4.2), did not optimize the information potentially available in MR images but instead used a small number of very thick (i.e., 1 cm) slices to make inferences about differences in brain structures between normal controls and schizophrenics. Additionally, many of the MR measurement analyses, except for just a few of the most recent studies, used low field strength magnets (i.e., less than 1.5 tesla), slice thickness has often been greater than 5 mm, and all too often measurements have relied upon relatively crude and imprecise methodologies, such as one-dimensional linear and two-dimensional planimetric analyses of

Table 4.2. MR imaging studies of temporal lobe structures in schizophrenia

Author	Subject Characteristics	Imaging Parameters	Temporal Lobe Measures	Findings
DeLisi et al., 1988	24 SZ (14 M/10 F); 11 sets/sibs + 2 unrelated cases; 31.9 yr. 18 NCL (11 M/7 F); 35.4 yr. (Families with 2 or > SZ).	0.5 tesla scanner: 12 1-cm, contiguous coronal slices.	Planimetric measurements on 2 slices: HIPP, amygdala, & PHG.	Amygdala-HIPP & PHG, as a whole, ↓bilaterally. Left anterior/posterior amygdala-HIPP trend ↓(p=.11/.09); PHG (right) trend ↓(p=.09).
Kelsoe et al., 1988	27 SZ (22 M/5 F) 29 yr; (22 rt-handed, 2 left, 1 unknown; duration=8.4 yr. 14 NCL (10 M/4 F) 31 yr. 13 rt-handed, 1 left.	0.5 tesla scanner: 12-13 1-cm, contiguous coronal slices.	Area/volume measures: TL, amygdala -HIPP, LAT VENT, prefrontal cortex, caudate, & globus pallidus-putamen area. (Ratings not blind to diagnosis).	↑LAT VENT (mostly left), 73% ↑3rd ventricle.
Rossi et al., 1989	15 SZ (M); 26.7 yr. rt-handed; duration=4.26 yr. 11 NCL (M) 28.3 yr. rt-handed.	0.5 tesla scanner: 8-mm, contiguous coronal slices.	Linear/area measurements of TL made by a radiologist.	Bilateral↓ in TLs significant only the left. Right TL > than left in both SZs & NCLs.
Suddath et al., 1989	17 SZ (10 M/7 F); 30.6 yr. 17 NCL (10 M/7 F); 33.2 yr.	0.5 tesla scanner: 12 1-cm, contiguous coronal slices.	3-4 slices used to define prefontal lobe; 6-8 used to define TL. Loats computerized image analysis to sum area measures.	15%↓ right TL, 18%↓ right TL gray matter, & 21%↓ left TL gray matter. No volume↓ in TL white matter or in prefrontal gray/white matter; the amygdala/anterior HIPP↓. Bilateral↓ LAT VENT, correlated left TL gray↓.
Coffman et al., 1989	36 SZ (M). 14 NCL (M); matched for age	1.4 tesla scanner: 2 5-mm coronal slices.	Right & left TL area measures made from 2 slices.	Strong trend for left TL↓. Right minus left difference score also >.
Johnstone et al., 1989	21 SZ (15 M/6 F); 36 yr. duration=at least 5 yrs. 20 Bipolars (12 M/8 F); M=35 yr./F=42.5 yr. 21 NCL (16 M/5 F); M=32.9 yr. /F=39 yr.	0.15 tesla scanner: 6-10 8-mm coronal slices.	TL & LAT VENT measured on slice > area for each structure. (Subjects not matched for SES).	Left TL↓ than right (reverse true for NCLs & bipolars). M SZs ↑LAT VENT > in TH & 30% difference in LAT VENT between good & poor outcome SZs.
Rossi et al., 1990	17 SZ (10 M/7 F); 24.5 yr. rt-handed; duration=4.4 yrs; (relapsing, noninstitutionalized sample). 13 NCL (10 M/3 F); 27.8 yr. rt-handed; matched for education level.	0.5 tesla scanner: 7-8 8-mm, contiguous coronal slices.	Linear/area measures by a radiologist on slice showing largest extent of TL.	No differences in VBR noted but SZs ↓left temporal lobes.

Barta et al., 1990	15 SZ (M); 30.6 yr. (living in community at time of testing); 13 rt-handed, 2 left-handed. 15 NCL (M); 30.7 yr. (14 rt-handed, 1 left-handed; (matched for education & SES).	1.5 tesla scanner: 9 3-mm coronal slices of TL. 5 mm axial slices of whole brain.	TL, amygdala, STG, 3rd VENT, control regions, & whole brain measured by summing volume over 2 slices for amygdala, 3=STG, 9=TL, 2=3rd VENT, 1=control regions, & 5=whole brain.	Left amygdala 8%↓, STG 11%↓. TL was not ↓ in SZs, but there was a trend for right TL↓.
Bogerts et al., 1990	34 SZ (22 M/12 F); 25 yr. education=13.6; 1st episode patients. 25 NCL (15 M/10 F); 28.2 yr.	1.0 tesla scanner: 63 3.1-mm, contiguous coronal slices of the whole brain.	HIPP/amygdala measured as 1 structure divided in 2 at mammilary bodies. TH of LAT VENT divided into anterior/ posterior. TL was measured; semi-automated computer mensuration.	20% ↓ Left HIPP (posterior) & total (left & right), 9%↓ amygdala-HIPP in M SZs. 9%↓ Right TL in M SZs. 40%↑ Left anterior TH in M SZs & 15%↑ Left total TH in M SZs & 32%↑ in F SZs.
Schwarzkopf et al., 1990 (Abstract)	36 SZ (M) Ss were categorized as (+) or (-) family history.	T1 wt. MR scans.	Measures left/right VBR & 3rd VENT.	Left VBR & 3rd VENT↑ in sporadic (non-familial) SZs.
Suddath et al., 1990	15 M SZ Twins Discordant for SZ; (8 M/7 F pairs); 32.4 yr.; duration=10.5 yrs.	1.5 tesla scanner: 30 5-mm, contiguous coronal slices (15 cm of brain covered).	Area measures summed for volume of prefrontal & TL. 6 slices used to measure amygdala, anterior HIPP, 3rd VENT, & THs & body of LAT VENT.	Total volume left TL gray matter↓ in SZ twins. No differences noted for white matter, prefrontal, or right TL (gray or white matter). Bilateral HIPP area/volume↓ (> left). LAT VENT↑.
Dauphinais et al., 1990	12 sib pairs (15 M/13 F); 32.4 yr.; SZ or SZAFF; duration=12.8 yrs. 21 NCL (12 M/9 F); 36.5 yr.	0.5 tesla scanner: 12 10-mm, contiguous coronal slices.	Area measures of TL, LAT VENT, TH of LAT VENT, & amygdala-HIPP.	Bilateral↓ TL & ↑LAT VENT (> left TH).
Degreef et al., 1990	25 SZ; first episode. 17 NCL (sex/age matched).	T1 wt. MR scans. 3.1 mm contiguous coronal slices.	Measured frontal, occipital, TH (anterior /posterior) LAT VENT, 3rd & 4th VENTs.	20%↑ in 3rd VENT, 20%↑ in frontal horns (32% left/20% right), 34%↑ left LAT VENT, 25%↑ left occipital horn, & 17%↑ left TH. Anterior part of TH↑30% on left.
DeLisi et al., 1991	30 SZ; first episode; 23 M/7 F; 22 rt-handed; 32.7 yr. 15 SZ; chronic; 27.3 yr. 9 M/6 F; 12 rt-handed. 20 NCL; neurology patients, 18 rt-handed;28.7 yr./12M/8F	1.5 tesla scanner: 30 coronal, 5 mm slices (2 mm gaps). 20 axial, 5 mm slices.	Measured total brain, LAT VENT, TL. (missing posterior part), & amygdala- HIPP, PHG, caudate & lentiform nuclei. Measures traced & then summed.	Chronic SZs & 1st episode ↑LAT VENT (> on left) but chronic SZs ↑LAT VENT than 1st episode. Only chronic SZs ↓TL (> on left).

Table 4.2. (cont.)

Young et al., 1991	31 SZ; 24 M/7 F; 29.3 yr. rt-handed; duration=6 yrs. 33 NCL; 25 M/8 F; 28.3 yr. rt-handed.	0.08 tesla scanner; 10, 12-mm coronal slices.	Measures traced from digitized images: TL, amygdala-HIPP, PHG, caudate nucleus, LAT & 3rd VENT.	No ratio measures differed. Left TL↓ both groups. Left amygdala↓ in NCLs, but not in SZs. Left PHG↓ in SZs, but not NCLs. (+)symptoms correlated ↑VBR.
Rossi et al., 1991	16 BP; 47 yr. rt-handed. 10 SZ; 28.6 yr. rt-handed.	0.5 tesla scanner; 15 5 mm (2 mm gap), coronal slices.	Measured area in left & right TL from 5 coronal slices. Analyses co-varied for age differences between groups.	When 5 area measurements totalled, SZs ↓ left & right TL. Both groups ↑right than left TL.
Shenton et al., 1991	12 SZ (M); 40 yr. rt-handed; duration=10 yrs. 10 NCL (M); 40 yr. rt-handed.	1.5 tesla scanner; 5 mm axial slices of a 120 mm slab of the brain.	Computerized image processing to make volume measurements of whole intraventricular system.	No differences mean LAT VENT, but NCLs showed left > right LAT VENT asymmetry not seen in SZs. Deviation from (Left > Right) correlated ↑thought disorder.
Jernigan et al., 1991	42 SZ (28 M/14 F); 30 yr. duration=10 years. 24 NCL (19 M/5 F); 32.2 yr.	1.5 tesla scanner; Axial slices of whole brain. 5 mm axial slices (2.5 mm gap).	Image analysis used to calculate volumes. Regions measured: subcortical gray matter, ventricles, & cortical gray matter.	No volume differences in VENTs of SZs but volume ↓ in mesial TL regions: amygdala, HIPP, & PHG. Volume of the lenticular nuclei↑ in SZs with an earlier age of onset.
Swayze et al., 1992	54 SZ (36 M/18 F); M=32.3 yr. /F=35.4 yr. 5 left-handed, 1 mixed, 48 rt. 48 BP (29 M/19 F); M=33.4 yr. /F=34.6 yr. 5 left-handed, 4 mixed, 39 rt. 47 NCL (28 M/19 F); 43 rt-handed, 4 mixed.	0.5 tesla scanner; 8 1-cm, coronal slices.	Planimetric measurements 3-4 slices of TL, caudate, putamen, amygdala, & HIPP.	Right TL↑ than left for all except BPs. No differences in HIPP, amygdala, or TL measures. ↑Putamen &, to a < extent, ↑caudate, in M SZs (authors state similar to Jernigan's findings).
Williamson et al., 1992	24 SZ (22 M/2 F); 36.8 yr. rt-handed; duration=14 yrs. 10 NCL (9 M/1 F); 32 yr. 9 rt-handed, 1 left-handed.	1.5 tesla scanner; 13 5-mm, coronal slices (5 mm gap).	Left & right frontal regions, temporal regions, & VENT measured (latter rated on 3-point scale). T1/T2 relaxation times.	↑T2 values left frontal white matter, & left temporal cortex & white matter, & left lenticular nucleus. ↑T1 values left frontal white matter, left temporal cortex & left temporal white matter, & in left lenticular nucleus.

74

DeLisi et al., 1992	50 Schizophreniform/acute SZAFF (32 M/18 F); 26.2 yr. 28 Schizophreniform/acute SZAFF; 15 M/13 F; 27 yr. 34 NCL; 18 M/15 F; 28 yr.	1.5 tesla scanner: 5 mm axial slices (2 mm gap) of whole brain.	Measures drawn & volumes summed over slices. Left & right hemispheres, TL, frontal lobes, & LAT VENT.	Women ↓right/left hemispheres. In both sexes, regardless of diagnosis, ↑right hemisphere. Schizophreniforms no ↑LAT VENT compared to NCLs. At 2 year follow-up, those with ↑LAT VENT at onset had poorer outcome (measured by #of hospitalizations). Of 24 patients at follow-up, 20% ↑LAT VENT & 20% ↓. Trend for left LAT VENT↑ in schizophreniform /acute SZAFF patients.
Zipursky et al., 1992	22 SZ (M); 34.1 yr. rt-handed; duration=11.3 yrs. 20 NCL; M; 36.2 yr. rt-handed.	1.5 tesla scanner: 3.5 cm slab of brain imaged; 7 5-mm slices (2.5 mm gap).	7 consecutive, 5 mm, axial slices used to segment brain: gray matter, white matter, & CSF. Intracranial volume, LAT VENT & 3rd VENT, subcortex/total cortex assessed.	Gray matter volume ↓ widespread: in frontal, temporal, & occipital regions (not in parietal region).
Shenton et al., 1992	15 SZ (M); 37 yr. rt-handed; duration=15.8 yrs. 15 NCL (M); 37 yr. rt-handed; matched age/SES.	1.5 tesla scanner: 54 3-mm interleaved (no gaps) axial slices of whole brain; 124 1.5-mm interleaved (no gaps) coronal slices of whole brain.	Volume of whole brain (gray & white matter) & CSF using automated computerized image processing; semi-automated methods for TL, amygdala-HIPP, PHG, STG.	↓Gray matter volume: 19% ↓left anterior amygdala-HIPP, 13% ↓left PHG, & 15%↓left STG. Left STG volume correlated with TDI (r=-0.81, p=0.001). No volume ↓ in overall brain or TL.

Key: SZ=schizophrenic; NCL=normal control; AFF=affective disorder; BP=Bipolar; M=male; F=female; PHG=parahippocampal gyrus; TL=temporal lobe; VBR=ventricular brain ratio; STG=superior temporal gyrus; LAT VENT=lateral ventricles; "x" yr.=mean age; duration=mean duration of illness; TH=temporal horns; M=male; F=female; "x" age=mean age; duration="x" =mean duration of illness.

+ This table reviews MR studies evaluating temporal lobe structures in SZ and it includes studies that have reported asymmetries in the lateral ventricles as well. In some cases information came from a published abstract and is therefore less complete with respect to MR imaging parameters. In addition, extensive information regarding MR parameters of regions outside the temporal lobe are not included since the major focus is upon temporal lobe findings in SZ. When the table does not specify "whole brain", whole brain was not measured in the study. [Parts of this table were adapted for a *Harvard Rev. of Psychiatry* article (McCarley et al., 1993-b).]

selected cross sections of anatomy. Such measurements have not only proven to be less than accurate, but they have also not taken full advantage of the information contained in MR images (Wyper et al., 1979; Filipek et al., 1988; Pfefferbaum et al., 1990).

The technology to extract objective, quantitative information from MR scans using multivariate image processing techniques, however, had to await improvements in the signal to noise ratio of MR scanners (see Gerig et al., 1989, 1990, and Höhne et al., 1990, for a more complete discussion). This limitation has most recently been solved by sophisticated hardware and software that have improved signal intensity variations, called "shading artifact," which relate to both radio frequency and magnetic field inhomogeneities (Kohn et al., 1991). With such improvements in image quality due to high spatial resolution magnets, and with the adaptation of multichannel methods used in remote sensing in satellite images (Vannier et al., 1985), as well as methods adapted from computer vision research (e.g., Marr, 1982; Gerig et al., 1989; Höhne et al., 1990), for the first time it is possible to access new information about morphology and tissue characteristics of the brain from *in vivo* images.

This new approach for extracting information, brought about by new image processing technology, not only exploits more fully information contained in MR scans, but also, as previously stated, offers more precise and accurate measurements. These factors have been particularly important to schizophrenia, where brain abnormalities are often more subtle and therefore harder to detect, than for other pathophysiological diseases, and where, consequently, precise and accurate measurements become that much more important. Our laboratory has applied these newly developed MR imaging techniques to high spatial resolution MR images in order to quantify *in vivo* differences between the brains of normal controls and patients afflicted with schizophrenia. These data will be presented, following a review of MR temporal lobe studies in schizophrenia, in order to provide an example of what new image-processing techniques offer future studies in this field.

Review of temporal lobe MR imaging studies in schizophrenia

Table 4.2 summarizes 24 MRI studies of temporal lobe structures in schizophrenia, including asymmetry findings in the size of the lateral ventricles. We first comment on the studies measuring temporal lobe volume, where differences in measurement technique, as well as in subject populations, may account for differing findings. Three studies have reported no differences in temporal lobe size between normals and schizophrenics (Barta et al., 1990; Shenton et al., 1992; Swayze et al., 1992), five studies have reported left temporal lobe reduction in schizophrenia (Coffman et al., 1989; Johnstone et al., 1989; Rossi et al., 1989, 1990; DeLisi et al., 1991), one study has reported gray matter reduction in the left temporal lobe (Suddath et al., 1990), three studies have reported bilateral reduction in the temporal lobe (Suddath et al., 1989; Dauphinais et al., 1990; Rossi et al., 1991 – compared to bipolars), and one study has reported right temporal lobe reduction in schizophrenia (Bogerts et al., 1990 – male first episode patients). The three studies that have examined most, or all, of the temporal lobe have reported: (1) the right temporal lobe is smaller in male first episode patients (Bogerts et al., 1990); (2) no differences between chronic, positive symptom, male schizophrenics and normal controls (Shenton et al., 1992); and, (3) left temporal lobe gray matter reduction in schizophrenic twins compared to well co-twins (Suddath et al., 1990). It is clear that future studies examining the whole temporal lobe in homogeneous, well-defined patient groups are needed; at present it is uncertain which subgroups of schizophrenic patients have temporal lobe volume reductions.

The data from MR studies of medial temporal lobe volume in schizophrenia are much more consistent and, in general, are in agreement with findings from postmortem studies. More specifically, as is clearly evident from Table 4.2, volume reductions have been consistently reported in medial temporal lobe structures, including the hippocampus-amygdala and parahippocampal gyrus (e.g., Besson et al., 1987; DeLisi et al., 1988; Suddath et al., 1989, 1990; Barta et al., 1990; Bogerts et al., 1990; Jernigan et al., 1991; Shenton et al., 1992). Only one MR study has reported no differences between normal controls and schizophrenics on hippocampal and amygdala measures (Swayze et al., 1992). Additionally, most of the MR studies reviewed in Table 4.2 show a more pronounced reduction on the left for anterior amygdala-hippocampus measures and, to a lesser extent, for the parahippocampal gyrus. Moreover, two studies (Barta et al., 1990; Shenton et al., 1992) have examined, and reported, a reduction in tissue in the left superior temporal gyrus (STG) in schizophrenic patients. This structure, as previously mentioned, and as will be discussed in detail below, is of particular interest because it may be related to the occurrence of both auditory hallucinations and thought disorder, cardinal symptoms of schizophrenia.

Included in Table 4.2 are also MR studies of asymmetries in the lateral ventricles. These studies are included because they provide information regarding the temporal, or inferior, horn of the lateral ventricles, a region surrounding medial temporal lobe structures. These data, taken together, suggest that an increase in the lateral ventricles, particularly in the left temporal horn region, may be indicative of tissue reduction in surrounding areas in the medial temporal lobe. These findings are particularly exciting because they are consistent with postmortem findings of Brown and co-workers (1986), who reported an overall increase of 19% in the lateral ventricles of schizophrenics compared to normal controls but a 97% increase in the temporal horns of the lateral ventricles (examined only left hemispheres). Crow and co-workers (1989), who examined both left and right hemispheres, also observed temporal horn enlargement in postmortem brains of schizophrenic patients that was most pronounced on the left. The enlarged temporal horns may be more specific to schizophrenia then enlarged lateral ventricles, which are seen in several neurological disorders. The specificity of the increase of cerebrospinal fluid (CSF) to the left temporal horn may reflect replacement of surrounding medial temporal lobe tissue by CSF.

In summary, MR studies of temporal lobe structures in schizophrenia suggest that the amygdala-hippocampal complex, particularly the anterior portion, is reduced in schizophrenics compared to normal controls and this reduction is most clearly seen on the left. The parahippocampal gyrus is also reduced in schizophrenics, frequently bilaterally, with left > right reduction. In addition, two studies from independent laboratories (Barta et al., 1990; Shenton et al., 1992) have suggested a reduction in tissue in the left STG thus confirming, though less dramatically so, Southard's anecdotal description (1910, 1915) of a "withering away" of the left STG in schizophrenia.

MR study from our laboratory illustrating temporal lobe pathology

Our laboratory has applied newly developed MR image processing to high spatial resolution MR images in order to quantify *in vivo* differences between the brains of schizophrenics and normal control subjects. To illustrate the findings and techniques, we present some recent data from an MR study of whole brain gray matter, white matter, and CSF, and more localized temporal lobe structures in schizophrenia (Shenton et al., 1992).

Our group's focus on the temporal lobe in schizophrenia was based on our early P300 evoked potential data (Morstyn et al., 1983; Shenton et al., 1989a; Faux et al., 1990) and a subsequent CT study, which showed an association between left sylvian fissure enlargement and positive symptoms (McCarley et al., 1989). We followed up on this CT study with an MRI investigation of temporal lobe abnormalities and their association with thought disorder (Shenton et al., 1992) and evoked potential abnormalities (McCarley et al., 1993a). Subjects for the MR study were 15 male, right-handed, chronic, predominantly positive symptom patients recruited from the Brockton Veterans Affairs Medical Center, and 15 age- , sex- , and handedness-matched normal controls. The mean age of the patients was 37 and mean duration of illness was 15.8 years. Normal controls were recruited from newspaper advertisements and they, as well as their first-degree relatives, were free of major mental disorder. All subjects were screened for disease factors that might affect brain MR including substance abuse or addiction and neurological illness.

With respect to measurement of clinical symptomatology, it is important to emphasize that the growing sensitivity and sophistication of clinical measures has paralleled the growing use of sophisticated hardware technology (such as MRI), and, in our opinion, has been equally necessary and important for advances in the field of psychopathology research. Our study therefore employed clinical instruments that we, and others, have found to be both reliable and strongly related to the clinical symptoms of schizophrenia. We evaluated patients' clinical symptoms for behavioral excesses such as hallucinations and delusions, and formal thought disorder, using the Scale for the Assessment of Positive Symptoms (Andreasen, 1984). We also evaluated patients for behavioral deficits, including anhedonia, alogia, and flat affect, using the Scale for the Assessment of Negative Symptoms (Andreasen, 1981). Based on the classification of these two scales, our patients were rated as showing predominantly positive symptoms (11/15), although four patients showed a mixed symptom picture, and no study patient was characterized as having predominantly negative symptoms.

As a sensitive and robust instrument to assess a wide range of formal thought disorder, we used the Thought Disorder Index (TDI), developed by Johnston and Holzman (1979), and later revised by Solovay, Shenton, and co-workers (1986). This instrument uses subjects' responses to Rorschach cards as a way of eliciting speech samples that can then be reliably scored for numerous categories of formal thought disorder, including bizarre word usage, neologisms, looseness, fragmentation, etc. The TDI has been shown to be reliable, it can readily discriminate between thought disorders present in schizophrenic and affective patients (Solovay et al., 1987), and it is sensitive enough to measure low levels of thought disorder in the relatives of psychotic patients, even though the relatives carry no psychiatric diagnosis (Shenton et al., 1989b).

The TDI total score can also be used as a comprehensive summary measure of thought disorder. We have found this measure to be indispensable for correlations with both structural (Shenton et al., 1992) and functional biological measures (P300 – Shenton et al., 1989a; McCarley et al., 1993b). The mean score for our recent study patients was 60.4, ranging from 1.7 to 214 (normals score average 5 or under).

The MR scans were obtained from a 1.5 tesla magnet and the whole brain was scanned using two different acquisitions: one axial acquisition (3-mm contiguous slices) that was used for the computerized image processing, and one acquisition done using three-dimensional Fourier-transform (3DFT) spoiled-gradient-recalled acquisition (SPGR) and reformatted in the coronal plane as 1.5-mm contiguous slices through the entire brain. The latter acquisition was included because it afforded excellent gray and white matter contrast of temporal lobe structures. The voxel (volume of pixel) dimensions were: 0.975 × 0.975 × 3 for the axial acquisition, and 0.975 × 0.975 × 1.5 for the coronal acquisition.

Image processing was done in order to segment whole brain into gray matter, white matter, and CSF using computerized algorithms (see Shenton et al., 1992; Cline et al., 1987, 1988, 1990, 1991; Kikinis et al., 1990, 1992), whereas regional definitions in the temporal lobe were done using a cursor to define the temporal lobe structures, on multiple slices, including the amygdala-hippocampal complex, the parahippocampal gyrus, and the STG (for a more complete description of the landmarks used, see Shenton et al., 1992). All measurements were done without knowledge of diagnosis or other clinical or evoked potential measures in the study.

The analysis showed that there were no significant mean differences between the two groups on any of the whole brain measures (white matter, gray matter, CSF-subarachnoidal or intraventricular). There was, however, a difference in the variance for the lateral ventricles in which schizophrenics showed an increase in the size range of the lateral ventricles compared to normal controls, which was more pronounced on the left. This finding is consistent with the literature showing increased lateral ventricles in schizophrenia (reviewed in Shelton and Weinberger, 1986). There was also a significant increase in size for the temporal horn subdivisions of both lateral ventricles, with left temporal horn enlargement (180%) being greater than right (74%). Absence of global changes in cortical gray matter is consistent with the findings of Jernigan et al. (1991), who, like our study, examined the entire brain and used automated segmentation techniques. Zipursky et al. (1992) found an overall decrease in cortical gray matter in a study which had gaps in slices and relied on interpolated volumes (see Table 4.2).

We next examined more local regions of interest within the temporal lobe which showed quite dramatic tissue reductions in schizophrenics compared to normal controls. While no statistically significant differences were noted in the overall volume of the temporal lobe, we observed statistically significant reductions in gray matter regions of interest (ROI) including: left amygdala-hippocampal (19%), left parahippocampal gyrus (13%, also 8% on the right), and left STG (15%). Figure 4.4 shows a schizophrenic patient with tissue loss in the amygdala-hippocampus and parahippocampal gyrus on the left (viewer's right), as well as a decrease in tissue in left STG (compare this to Figure 4.3 of these same regions for a normal control). Note also the increase in CSF in the sylvian fissure region. Figure 4.5A shows the strong separation of schizophrenic and normal control subjects on the volume of the posterior portion of the left STG, the portion of the STG that contains the planum temporale; note that 8 of the 15 schizophrenic patients have volumes less than any of the normal controls.

This localized temporal lobe pathology was consistent with MR cross-sectional (area) measurements of the anterior amygdala-hippocampal complex (e.g., DeLisi et al., 1988; Barta et al., 1990; Suddath et al., 1990; Young et al., 1991) and the parahippocampal gyrus (Young et al., 1991), as well as with postmortem studies reporting tissue reductions in the hippocampus and the parahippocampal gyrus (e.g., Bogerts 1984; Bogerts et al., 1985; Brown et al., 1986;

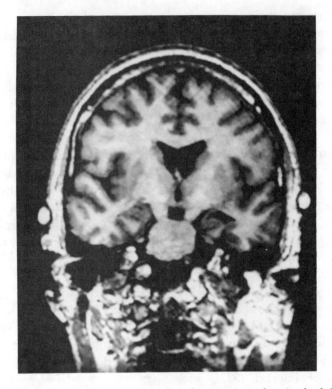

Figure 4.4. Coronal 1.5-mm slice showing tissue loss in the left sylvian fissure (viewer's right), left superior temporal gyrus, and a black CSF filled region within the left amygdala. (From Shenton et al., 1992, courtesy *The New Engl. J. Med.*)

Colter et al., 1987; Jeste and Lohr, 1989), and cellular disarray in the left anterior and middle hippocampus (Kovelman and Scheibel, 1984) and the entorhinal cortex (Jakob and Beckmann, 1989; Arnold et al., 1991).

An important clinicopathological correlate was also observed between left posterior STG volume reduction and an increase in the amount of thought disorder ($r = -.81$). This relationship is clearly evident in Figure 4.5 *B*, which shows that as thought disorder increases, there is a concomitant decrease in the tissue in the *left* posterior STG. This finding confirmed Bleuler's (1911/1950) prediction that thought disorder, the primary symptom of schizophrenia, would ultimately be linked to a brain disorder.

We thought this finding especially intriguing because the posterior

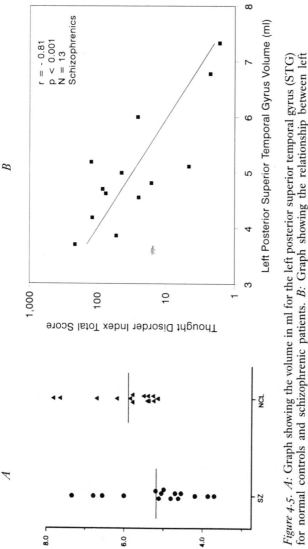

Figure 4.5. A: Graph showing the volume in ml for the left posterior superior temporal gyrus (STG) for normal controls and schizophrenic patients. *B*: Graph showing the relationship between left posterior STG and thought disorder in schizophrenic patients. (Adapted from Shenton et al., 1992, *The New Engl. J. Med.*, 327:604–612)

portion of the STG includes Heschl's gyrus and the planum temporale, regions long implicated as neuroanatomical substrates of language (Penfield and Perot, 1963; Geschwind and Levitsky, 1968; Galaburda, 1984; Galaburda et al., 1987; Ojemann et al., 1988; Steinmetz et al., 1989; Ojemann, 1991). This finding is also noteworthy in light of work done by Barta and co-workers (1990, 1992). These investigators reported an association between auditory hallucinations and volume reductions in a more anterior portion of the STG (the first description of STG *volume* abnormalities in schizophrenia), and this group has recently confirmed our finding of a thought disorder–left posterior STG association, thus further linking the left STG with positive symptoms of schizophrenia. Further, we note that Southard's (1910, 1915) early work had suggested that schizophrenic patients with auditory hallucinations were more likely to have tissue reduction in the left STG. More recently, Haglund and co-workers' (1992) stimulation of the left posterior STG in seizure disorder patients undergoing neurosurgery led to disordered, jumbled thoughts. Finally, we note the relative specificity of our MR findings, since they were not accompanied by reductions in overall gray matter, white matter, or CSF. These volume reductions in STG and medial temporal lobe structures were also highly intercorrelated in the schizophrenic group, but not the normal control group, suggesting that there may be damage to a network of neuroanatomical connections, a point whose significance is discussed below.

VI. Summary

We began this chapter by citing a quotation from Crichton-Browne (1879), who suggested that the most highly evolved functions of the brain, more lateralized to the left hemisphere, might be most affected in psychosis. We then presented evidence that we think strongly suggests that medial temporal lobe structures, including the amygdala-hippocampal complex and parahippocampal gyrus, as well as neocortical STG, represent an interconnected neural network that is functionally important for associative links in memory (e.g., Penfield and Perot, 1963; Amaral et al., 1983; Rosene and Van Hoesen, 1987; Ojemann et al., 1988; Saunders et al., 1988; Squire and Zola-Morgan, 1991; Witter and Amaral, 1991), and which may be damaged in schizophrenia. We think that these tissue reductions are not only highly interconnected and lateralized to the left temporal lobe, but they also call attention to the verbal, communicative, and auditory associative memory functions that are quite specific to these areas. More specifically, there are now several lines of evidence, alluded to earlier in this review, which suggest that the hippocampus is important in gating memory storage and retrieval, with the long-term storage of information occurring at neocortical sites in response to input arising from the hippocampus (Squire, 1992). The STG is important for auditory associative memory (Penfield and Perot, 1963; Ojemann et al., 1988), including verbal memory on the left, and we speculate that the abnormalities in this interconnected network, which includes links to medial temporal lobe structures as well as to frontal lobe cortices, may result in both physiological (P300; McCarley et al., 1993a), and clinical disturbances in the form of auditory hallucinations (Barta et al., 1990), and thought disorder (Shenton et al., 1992, 1993).

For auditory stimuli, such as the auditory event related P300 potential, the memory system of "updating," i.e., attending to novel stimuli and constantly updating what is novel and what is not (Donchin, 1979), might involve the medial temporal-STG system. This would then suggest that reduced left temporal P300 amplitude in schizophrenics would be correlated with reductions in these structures [as shown by a recent study by McCarley et al. (1993a)], as well as be related to memory tasks involving verbal memory, which preliminary data by Nestor, from our group, have shown (Nestor et al., 1992). Additionally, we might expect thought disorder to be related to structural damage to this interconnected network, as reported by us (Shenton et al., 1992), since this region of the brain includes the planum temporale, and damage might result in an inability to establish or maintain a proper gradient of strength of associational linkages for verbal material. Moreover, since these regions (medial temporal lobe structures, and neocortical STG) are highly interconnected anatomically and functionally (see section II), it is quite possible that damage to this interconnected network affects a number of functions, including: storage and retrieval of verbal information, auditory associative memory, verbal memory, and language-related functions where there is a disruption in the strength of associative links that results in thought disorder and, as described by Bleuler (1911/1950), "incidental" linkages. More research is needed to delineate further these brain–behavior linkages in order to understand better the pathophysiology of schizophrenia.

Acknowledgments

I want to thank Robert McCarley and Ron Kikinis for their continued collaboration on all aspects of the MR studies; Cynthia Wible for help with understanding neural connections with temporal lobe structures; Robert Bilder, Brian O'Donnell, and Margaret Niznikiewicz for their critical review on sections of this manuscript; and Lisa Kaplan, Lloyd Smith, Sue Law, and Marie Fairbanks for their assistance in organizing and locating the references.

Work on this paper was supported by NIMH KO2 MH 01110, NIMH R29 MH 50747, The Scottish Rite Foundation, and the Theodore and Vada Stanley Foundation.

References

Altshuler, L. L., A. Conrad, J. A. Kovelman, and A. Scheibel. 1987. Hippo-campal pyramidal cell orientation in schizophrenia. *Arch Gen. Psychiatry* 44:1094–1098.

Altshuler, L. L., M. F. Casanova, T. E. Goldberg, and J. E. Kleinman. 1990. The hippocampus and parahippocampus in schizophrenic, suicide, and control brains. *Arch Gen. Psychiatry* 47:1029–1034.

Alzheimer, A. 1897. Beitrage zur pathologischen anatomie der hirnrinde und zur anatomischen grundlage einiger psychosen. *Monatsschrift für Psychiarie und Neurologie* 2:82–119.

Amaducci, L., S. Sorbi, A. Albanese, and G. Gainotti, 1981. Choline acetyltransferase (Chat) activity differs in right and left human temporal lobes. *Neurol.* 31:799–805.

Amaral, D. G., R. Insansti, and W. M. Cowan. 1983. Evidence for a direct projection from superior temporal gyrus to the entorhinal cortex in the monkey. *Brain Res.* 275:263–277.

American Psychiatric Association, Committee on Nomenclature and Statistics. *Diagnostic and Statistical Manual of Mental Disorders*, 3rd ed. 1980. Washington D.C.: American Psychiatric Association.

American Psychiatric Association, Committee on Nomenclature and Statistics. *Diagnostic and Statistical Manual of Mental Disorders*, 3rd ed., revised). 1987. Washington D.C.: American Psychiatric Association.

Andreasen, N. C. 1981. *Scale for the Assessment of Negative Symptoms (SANS)*. Iowa City: Department of Psychiatry, University of Iowa College of Medicine.

Andreasen, N. C. 1984. *Scale for the Assessment of Positive Symptoms (SAPS)*. Iowa City: Department of Psychiatry, University of Iowa College of Medicine.

Arnold, S. E., B. T. Hyman, G. W. Van Hoesen, and A. Damasio. 1991.

Some cytoarchitectural abnormalities of the entorhinal cortex in schizophrenia. *Arch. Gen. Psychiatry* 48:625–632.

Barta, P. E., G. D. Pearlson, R. E. Powers, S. S. Richards, and L. E. Tune. 1990. Auditory hallucinations and smaller superior temporal gyral volume in schizophrenia. *Am. J. Psychiatry* 147:1457–1462.

Barta, P. E., G. D. Pearlson, R. E. Powers, R. Menon, S. Richards, and L. E. Tune. 1992. Temporal lobe in schizophrenia. *APA New Res. Abstr.* 146.

Benes, F. M., and E. D. Bird. 1987. An analysis of the arrangement of neurons in the cingulate cortex of schizophrenic patients. *Arch. Gen. Psychiatry* 44:608–616.

Benes, F. M., I. Sorensen, and E. D. Bird. 1991. Reduced neuronal size in posterior hippocampus of schizophrenic patients. *Schizophr. Bull.* 17(4): 597–608.

Benes, F. M., S. V. Vincent, G. Alsterberg, E. D. Bird, and J. P. SanGiovanni. 1992. Increased GABA$_a$ receptor binding in superficial layers of cingulate cortex in schizophrenics. *J. Neurosci.* 12(3): 924–929.

Benson, D. F., and N. Geschwind. 1987. Aphasia and related disorders: A clinical approach. In *Principles of behavioral neurology*, ed. M. Mesulam, pp. 193–238. Philadelphia: F. A. Davis.

Besson, J.A.O., F. M. Corrigan, G. R. Cherryman, and F. W. Smith. 1987. Nuclear magnetic resonance brain imaging in chronic schizophrenia. *Br. J. Psychiatry* 150:161–163.

Bleuler, E. 1911/1950. *Dementia praecox or the group of schizophrenias*, H. Zinkin, trans. New York: International Universities Press.

Bogerts, B. 1984. Zur neuropathologie der schizophrenien. *Fortschritte der Neurologie Psychiatrie* 52:428–437.

Bogerts, B., E. Meertz, and R. Schonfeldt-Bausch. 1985. Basal ganglia and limbic system pathology in schizophrenia: A morphometric study of brain volume and shrinkage. *Arch Gen. Psychiatry* 42:784–791.

Bogerts, B., M. Ashtari, G. Degreef, J. M. Alvir, R. M. Bilder, and J. A. Lieberman. 1990. Reduced temporal limbic structure volumes on magnetic resonance images in first episode schizophrenia. *Psychiatr. Res: Neuroimaging* 35:1–13.

Brown, R., N. Colter, J.A.N. Corsellis, T. J. Crow, C. D. Frith, R. Jagoe, E. C. Johnstone, and L. Marsh. 1986. Postmortem evidence of structural changes in schizophrenia. *Arch Gen. Psychiatry* 43:36–42.

Bruton, C. J., T. J. Crow, C. D. Frith, E. C. Johnstone, D.G.C. Owens, and G. W. Roberts. 1990. Schizophrenia and the brain: A prospective clinico-neuropathological study. *Psychol. Med.* 20:285–304.

Carpenter, M. B. 1991. *Core text of neuroanatomy*, 4th ed. Baltimore: Williams & Wilkins.

Chi, J. G., E. C. Dooling, and F. H. Gilles. 1977. Gyral development of the human brain. *Ann Neurol.* 1:86–93.

Christison, G. W., M. F. Casanova, D. R. Weinberger, R. Rawlings, and J. E. Kleinman. 1989. A quantitative investigation of hippocampal pyramidal cell size, shape, and variability of orientation in schizophrenia. *Arch. Gen. Psychiatry* 46:1027–1032.

Cline, H. E., C. L. Dumoulin, H. R. Hart, W. E. Lorensen, and S. Ludke. 1987. 3D reconstruction of the brain from magnetic resonance images using a connectivity algorithm. *Magn. Reson. Imaging* 5:345–352.

Cline, H. E., W. E. Lorensen, S. Ludke, C. R. Crawford, and B. C. Teeter. 1988. Two algorithms for the three-dimensional reconstruction of tomograms. *Med. Phys.* 15:320–327.

Cline, H. E., W. E. Lorensen, R. Kikinis, and F. A. Jolesz. 1990. Three-dimensional segmentation of MR images of the head using probability and connectivity. *J. Comput. Assist. Tomogr.* 14(6): 1037–1045.

Cline, H. E., W. E. Lorensen, S. P. Souza, F. A. Jolesz, R. Kikinis, G. Gerig, and T. E. Kennedy. 1991. 3D surface rendering: MR images of the brain and its vasculature. *J. Comput. Assist. Tomogr.* 15(2): 344–355.

Coffman, J. A., S. B. Schwarzkopf, S. C. Olson, M. W. Torello, R. A. Bornstein, and H. A. Nasrallah. 1989. Temporal lobe asymmetry in schizophrenics demonstrated by coronal MRI brain scans. *Schizophr. Res.* 2:117.

Cohen, N. J. 1984. Preserved learning capacity in amnesia: Evidence for multiple memory systems. In *Neuropsychology of memory*, ed. L. R. Squire and N. Butters, pp. 83–103. New York: Guilford Press.

Colter, N., S. Battal, T. J. Crow, E. C. Johnstone, R. Brown, and C. Bruton. 1987. White matter reduction in the parahippocampal gyrus of patients with schizophrenia. *Arch Gen. Psychiatry* 44:1023.

Conrad, A. J., T. Abebe, R. Austin, S. Forsythe, and A. B. Scheibel. 1991. Hippocampal pyramidal cell disarray in schizophrenia as a bilateral phenomenon. *Arch Gen. Psychiatry* 48:413–417.

Corkin, S. 1965. Tactually-guided maze learning in man: Effects of unilateral cortical excisions and bilateral hippocampal lesions. *Neuropsychologia* 3:339–351.

Corkin, S. 1968. Acquisition of motor skill after bilateral medial temporal lobe excision. *Neuropsychologia* 6:225–264.

Corkin, S. 1984. Lasting consequences of bilateral medial temporal lobectomy: Clinical course and experimental findings in H. M. *Seminars in Neurol.* 4:249–259.

Crichton-Browne, J. 1879. On the weight of the brain and its component parts in the insane. *Brain* 2:42–67.

Crow, T. J. The continuum of psychosis and its genetic origins: The sixty-fifth Maudsley lecture. 1990(a). *Br. J. Psychiatry* 156:788–797.

Crow, T. J. 1990(b). Temporal lobe asymmetry as the key to the etiology of schizophrenia. *Schizophr. Bull.* 16:433–443.

Crow, T. J., J. Ball, S. Bloom, R. Brown, C. J. Bruton, N. Colter, C. D. Frith, E. C. Johnstone, D.G.C. Owens, and G. W. Roberts. 1989. Schizophrenia as an anomaly of development of cerebral asymmetry: A postmortem study and a proposal concerning the genetic basis of the disease. *Arch Gen. Psychiatry* 46:1145–1150.

DaMasio, A. R. 1992. Aphasia. *N. Engl. J. Med.* 326:531–539.

Dauphinais, D., L. E. DeLisi, T. J. Crow, K. Alexandropoulos, N. Colter, I. Tuma, and E. S. Gershon. 1990. Reduction in temporal lobe size in siblings with schizophrenia: A magnetic resonance imaging study. *Psychiatr. Res.: Neuroimaging* 35:137–147.

Davidson, K., and C. R. Bagley. 1969. Schizophrenia-like psychoses associated with organic disorders of the central nervous system: A review of the literature. *Br. J. Psychiatry* (special publication No. 4):113–184.

Degreef, G., B. Bogerts, M. Ashtari, and J. Lieberman. 1990. Ventricular system morphology in first episode schizophrenia: A volumetric study of ventricular subdivisions on MRI. *Schizophr. Res.* 3:18.

DeLisi, L. E., D. Dauphinais, and E. S. Gershon. 1988. Perinatal complications and reduced size of brain limbic structures in familial schizophrenia. *Schizophr. Bull.* 14:185–191.

DeLisi, L. E. M. S. Buchsbaum, H. H. Holcomb, K. C. Langston, A. C. King, R. Kessler, D. Pickar, W. T. Carpenter, J. M. Morihisa Jr., R. Margolin, and D. R. Weinberger. 1989. Increased temporal lobe glucose use in chronic schizophrenic patients. *Biol. Psychiatry* 25:835–851.

DeLisi, L. E., A. L. Hoff, J. E. Schwartz, G. W. Shields, S. N. Halthore, S. M. Gupta, F. A. Henn, and A. K. Anand. 1991. Brain morphology in first-episode schizophrenic-like psychotic patients: A quantitative magnetic resonance imaging study. *Biol. Psychiatry* 29:159–175.

DeLisi, L. E., P. Stritzke, R. Riordan, V. Holan, A. Boccio, M. Kushner, J. McClelland, O. Van Eyl, A. K. Anand. 1992. The timing of brain morphological changes in schizophrenia and their relationship to clinical outcome. *Biol. Psychiatry* 31:241–254.

Donchin, E. 1979. Event-related potentials: A tool in the study of human information processing. In *Evoked brain potentials and behavior*, ed. H. Begleiter, pp. 13–88. New York: Plenum Press.

Dunlap, C. B. 1924. Dementia praecox: Some preliminary observations on brains from carefully selected cases, and a consideration of certain sources of error. *Am. J. Psychiatry* 80(3): 403–421.

Dunlap, C. B. 1928. Pathology of the brain in schizophrenia. *Assoc. for Res. in Nerv. and Ment. Dis. Proceedings* 5:371–383.

Falkai, P., and B. Bogerts. 1986. Cell loss in the hippocampus of schizophrenics. *Eur. Arch. Psychiatr. Neurol. Sci.* 236:154–161.

Falkai, P., B. Bogerts, and M. Rozumek. 1988(a). Limbic pathology in schizophrenia: The entorhinal region – a morphometric study. *Biol. Psychiatry* 24:515–521.

Falkai, P., B. Bogerts, G. W. Roberts, and T. J. Crow. 1988(b). Measurements of the alpha-cell-migration in the entorhinal region: A marker for the developmental disturbances in schizophrenia? *Schizophr. Res.* 1:157–158.

Faux, S. F., M. E. Shenton, R. W. McCarley, P. G. Nestor, B. Marcy, and A. Ludwig. 1990. Preservation of P300 event-related potential topographic asymmetries in schizophrenia with use of either linked-ear or nose reference sites. *Electroencephalogr. Clin. Neurophysiol.* 75:378–391.

Filipek, P. A., D. N. Kennedy, V. S. Caviness Jr., S. L. Rossnick, T. A. Spraggins, and P. M. Starewicz. 1988. Magnetic resonance imaging-based brain morphometry: Development and application to normal subjects. *Ann Neurol.* 25:61–67.

Flor-Henry, P. 1969. Psychosis and temporal lobe epilepsy: A controlled investigation. *Epilepsia* 10:363–395.

Frisk, V., and B. Milner. 1990. The role of the left hippocampal region in the acquisition and retention of story content. *Neuropsychologia* 28(4): 349–359.

Fuster, J. M. 1980. *The prefrontal cortex: Anatomy, physiology, and neuropsychology of the frontal lobe* (2nd ed.). New York: Raven Press.

Galaburda, A. M. 1984. Anatomical asymmetry. In *Cerebral dominance: The biological foundations,* ed. N. Geschwind and A. M. Galaburda, pp. 11–25. Cambridge, MA: Harvard University Press.

Galaburda, A. M., and T. L. Kemper. 1979. Cytoarchitectonic abnormalities in developmental dyslexia: A case study. *Ann. Neurol.* 6:94–100.

Galaburda, A. M., J. Corsiglia, G. D. Rosen, and G. F. Sherman. 1987. Planum temporale asymmetry, reappraisal since Geschwind and Levitsky. *Neuropsychologia* 25:853–868.

Gerig, G., W. Kuoni, R. Kikinis, and O. Kübler. 1989. Medical imaging and computer vision: An integrated approach for diagnosis and planning. In: *Proc. II DAGM Symposium on Computer Vision.* Hamburg.

Gerig, G., R. Kikinis, and O. Kübler. 1990. Significant improvement of MR image data quality using anisotropic diffusion filtering. *Technical Report BIWI-TR-124.* Communication Technology Laboratory, Image Science Division, ETH-Zurich, Switzerland.

Geschwind, N., and W. Levitsky. 1968. Human brain: Left-right asymmetries in the temporal speech region. *Science* 161:186–187.

Gloor, P. 1986. The role of the human limbic system in perception, memory and affect. In *The limbic system,* ed. B. K. Doane and K. E. Livingston. New York: Raven Press.

Goldman-Rakic, P. S., L. D. Selemon, and M. L. Schwartz. 1984. Dual pathways connecting the dorsolateral prefrontal cortex with the hippocampal formation and parahippocampal cortex in the rhesus monkey. *Neurosc.* 12:719–743.

Haglund, M. M., G. A. Ojemann, and D. W. Hochman. 1992. Optical imaging of epileptiform and functional activity in human cerebral cortex. *Nature* 358(6388): 668–671.

Haug, J. O. 1962. Pneumoencephalographic studies in mental disease. *Acta. Psychiatr. Scand.* 38(Suppl. 165): 11–104.

Hecker, E. 1871. Die Hebephrenic. *Arch. patholiche Anat. und für Physiol. Klinische Medicin* 52:394–429.

Heckers, S., H. Heinsen, Y. Heinsen, and H. Beckmann. 1990. Morphometry of the parahippocampal gyrus in schizophrenics and controls: Some anatomical considerations. *J. Neural. Transm.* 80:151–155.

Hill, D. 1962. The schizophrenia-like psychoses of epilepsy, discussion. *Proc. R. Soc. Med.* 55:315–316.

Hillbom, E. 1951. Schizophrenia-like psychoses after brain trauma. *Acta Psychiatr. and Neurol. Scand.* 60:36–47.

Höhne, K. H., M. Bomans, A. Pommert, M. Riemer, V. Tiede, and G. Wiebecke. 1990. Rendering tomographic volume data: Adequacy of methods of different modalities and organs. In *NATO ASI Series Vol. F60: 3D Imaging in medicine,* ed. K. H. Höhne, H. Fuchs, and S. M. Pizer, pp. 197–227. Berlin: Springer-Verlag.

Insausti, R., D. G. Amaral, and W. M. Cowan. 1987. The entorhinal cortex of the monkey: II. Cortical afferents. *J. Comp. Neurol.* 15:264(3): 356–395.

Jack, C. R., D. G. Gehring, F. W. Sharbrough, J. P. Felmlee, G. Forbes, V. S. Hench, and A. R. Zinsmeister. 1988. Temporal lobe volume measurement from MR images: Accuracy and left-right asymmetry in normal persons. *J. Comput. Assist. Tomogr.* 12:21–29.

Jack, C. R., C. K. Twomey, A. R. Zinsmeister, F. W. Sharbrough, R. C. Petersen, and G. D. Cascino. 1989. Anterior temporal lobes and hippocampal formations: Normative volumetric measurements from MR images in young adults. *Radiology* 172:549–554.

Jackson, J. H. 1888. Remarks on the diagnosis and treatment of the diseases of the brain. *Br. Med. Journal* 2(59): 111.

Jacobi, W., and H. Winkler. 1927. Encephalographische studien an chronisch schizophrenen. *Archiv. für Psychiatrie und Nervenkrankheiten* 81: 299–332.

Jakob, H., and H. Beckmann. 1986. Prenatal developmental disturbances in the limbic allocortex in schizophrenics. *J. Neural. Transm.* 65:303–326.

Jakob, H., and H. Beckmann. 1989. Gross and histological criteria for developmental disorders in brains of schizophrenics. *J. R. Soc. Med.* 82:466–469.

Jernigan, T. L., S. Zisook, R. K. Heaton, J. T. Moranville, J. R. Hesselink,

and D. Braff. 1991. Magnetic resonance imaging abnormalities in len-
ticular nuclei and cerebral cortex in schizophrenia. *Arch. Gen. Psychiatry*
48:881–890.

Jeste, D. V., and J. B. Lohr. 1989. Hippocampal pathologic findings in
schizophrenia: A morphometric study. *Arch. Gen. Psychiatry* 46:1019–
1024.

Johnston, M. H., and P. S. Holzman. 1979. *Assessing schizophrenic thinking.*
San Francisco: Jossey-Bass.

Johnstone, E. C., T. J. Crow, C. D. Frith, and J. Husband. 1976. Cerebral
ventricular size and cognitive impairment in chronic schizophrenia.
Lancet ii:924–926.

Johnstone, E. C., D.G.C. Owens, T. J. Crow, C. D. Frith, K. Alexandropolis,
G. Bydder, and N. Colter. 1989. Temporal lobe structure as determined by nuclear magnetic resonance in schizophrenics and bipolar
affective disorder. *J. Neurol. Neurosurg. Psychiatry* 52:736–741.

Jones-Gotman, M. 1986. Right hippocampal excision impairs learning and
recall of a list of abstract designs. *Neuropsychologia* 24:659–670.

Kahlbaum, K. 1874. *Die Katatonie oder der Spannungsirresein.* Berlin: Hirsh-
wald.

Kelsoe, J. R., J. L. Cadet, D. Pickar, and D. R. Weinberger. 1988. Quantitative neuroanatomy in schizophrenia: A controlled magnetic resonance
imaging study. *Arch. Gen. Psychiatry* 45:533–541.

Kety, S. S. 1959. Biochemical theories of schizophrenia. *Science* 129:1528–
1532.

Kikinis, R., F. A. Jolesz, G. Gerig, T. Sandor, H. E. Cline, W. E. Lorensen,
M. Halle, and S. A. Benton. 1990. 3D morphometric and morphometric information derived from clinical brain MR images. In *NATO
ASI Series Vol. F60: 3D Imaging in medicine,* ed. K. H. Hohne, H. Fuchs,
and S. M. Pizer, pp. 441–454. Berlin: Springer-Verlag.

Kikinis, R., M. E. Shenton, F. A. Jolesz, G. Gerig, J. Martin, M. Anderson,
D. Metcalf, C.R.G. Guttmann, R. W. McCarley, W. E. Lorensen, and
H. E. Cline. 1992. Routine quantitative MRI-based analysis of brain
and fluid spaces. *Magn. Res. Imaging* 2:619–629.

Kirch, D. G., and D. R. Weinberger. 1986. Anatomical neuropathology in
schizophrenia: Post-mortem findings. In *Handbook of schizophrenia, Vol.
I: The neurology of schizophrenia,* ed. H. A. Nasrallah and D. R. Weinberger, pp. 325–348. New York: Elsevier.

Klüver, H., and P. C. Bucy. 1939. Preliminary analysis of the temporal lobe
in monkeys. *Arch. Neurol Psychiatry* 42:979–1000.

Kohn, M. I., N. K. Tanna, G. T. Herman, S. M. Resnick, P. D. Mosley,
R. E. Gur, A. Alavi, R. A. Zimmerman, and R. C. Gur. 1991. Analysis
of brain and cerebrospinal fluid volumes with MR imaging. *Radiology*
178:115–122.

Kovelman, J. A., and A. B. Scheibel. 1984. A neurohistological correlate of schizophrenia. *Biol. Psychiatry* 191:1601–1621.

Kraepelin, E. 1919/1971. *Dementia praecox and paraphrenia*. Edinburgh: Livingstone, 1919. Translated (1971) by R. M. Barclay and G. M. Robertson. New York: R. E. Krieger.

LeMay, M. 1992. Left-right dissymmetry, handedness. *AJNR*. 13:493–504.

MacLean, P. D. 1952. Some psychiatric implications of physiological studies on frontotemporal portion of limbic system (visceral brain). *Electroencephalogr. Clin. Neurophysiol.* 4:407–418.

Marr, D. 1982. *Vision.* New York: Freeman.

McCarley, R. W., S. F. Faux, M. E. Shenton, M. LeMay, M. Cane, R. Ballinger, and F. W. Duffy. 1989. CT abnormalities in schizophrenia: A preliminary study of their correlations with P300/P200 electrophysiological features and positive/negative symptoms. *Arch. Gen. Psychiatry* 46:698–708.

McCarley, R. W., S. F. Faux, M. E. Shenton, P. G. Nestor, and J. Adams. 1991. Event-related potentials in schizophrenia: Their biological and clinical correlates and a new model of schizophrenic pathophysiology. *Schizophr. Res.* 4:209–231.

McCarley, R. W., M. E. Shenton, B. F. O'Donnell, S. F. Faux, R. Kikinis, P. G. Nestor, and F. A. Jolesz. 1993(a). Auditory P300 abnormalities and left posterior superior temporal gyrus volume reduction in schizophrenia. *Arch. Gen. Psychiatry* 50:190–197.

McCarley, R. W., M. E. Shenton, B. F. O'Donnell, and P. G. Nestor. 1993(b). Uniting Kraepelin and Bleuler: The psychology of schizophrenia and the biology of temporal lobe abnormalities. *Harvard Rev. Psychiatry* 1:36–56.

Milner, B. 1962. Les troubles de la memoire accompagnant des lesions hippocampiques bilaterales. [Memory impairment associated with bilateral hippocampal lesions.] *Physiologie de l'hippocampe*, pp. 257–272. Paris: Centre National de la Recherche Scientifique.

Milner, B. 1972. Disorders of learning and memory after temporal lobe lesions in man. *Clin. Neurosurg.* 19:421–466.

Mirsky, A. F., B. J. Anthony, C. C. Duncan, M. B. Ahearn, and S. G. Kellam. 1991. Analysis of the elements of attention: A neuropsychological approach. *Neuropsychol. Rev.* 2:109–145.

Mishkin, M., B. Malamut, and J. Bachevalier. 1984. Memories and habits: Two neural systems. In *Neurobiology of learning and memory*, ed. G. Lynch, J. L. McGaugh, and N. M. Weinberger, pp. 65–77. New York: Guilford Press.

Morstyn, R., F. H. Duffy, and R. W. McCarley. 1983. Altered P300 topography in schizophrenia. *Arch. Gen. Psychiatry* 62:203–208.

Mulder, D. W., and D. Daly. 1952. Psychiatric symptoms associated with lesion of the temporal lobe. *JAMA* 150:173–176.

Nasrallah, H. A., S. C. Olson, M. McCalley-Whitters, S. Chapman, and C. G. Jacoby. 1986. Cerebral ventricular enlargement in schizophrenia. *Arch Gen. Psychiatry* 43:157–159.

Nestor, P. G., S. F. Faux, R. W. McCarley, V. Penhune, M. E. Shenton, S. D. Pollak, and S. F. Sands. 1992. Attentional cues in chronic schizophrenia: Abnormal disengagement of attention. *J. Ab. Psychol.* 101(4): 682–689.

Ojemann, G. A. 1991. Cortical organization of language. *J. Neurosci.* 11(8):2281–2287.

Ojemann, G. A., and C. B. Dodrill. 1985. Verbal memory deficits after left temporal lobectomy for epilepsy. *J. Neurosurg.* 62:101–107.

Ojemann, G. A., O. Creutzfeldt, E. Lettich, and M. Haglund. 1988. Neuronal activity in human lateral temporal cortex related to short-term verbal memory, naming and reading. *Brain* 111:1383–1403.

Pandya, D. N., G. W. Van Hoesen, and M. M. Mesulam. 1981. Efferent connections of the cingulate gyrus in the rhesus monkey. *Exp. Brain Res.* 42:319–330.

Pandya, D. N., and B. Seltzer. 1982. Association areas of the cerebral cortex. *Trends Neurosci.* 5:386–390.

Pandya, D. N., and E. H. Yeterian. 1985. Architecture and connection of cortical association areas. In *Cerebral cortex: Association and auditory cortices*, vol. 4., ed. A. Peters and E. G. Jones, pp. 3–61. New York: Plenum.

Papez, J. W. 1937. A proposed mechanism of emotion. *Arch Neurol.* 38: 725–743.

Penfield, W., and H. Jasper. 1954. *Epilepsy and the functional anatomy of the human brain.* Boston: Little, Brown.

Penfield, W., and L. Roberts. 1959. *Speech and brain mechanisms.* Princeton: Princeton University Press.

Penfield, W., and P. Perot. 1963. The brain's record of auditory and visual experience: A final summary and discussion. *Brain* 86(Part 4): 596–695.

Pfefferbaum, A., K. O. Lim, M. Rosenbloom, and R. B. Zipursky. 1990. Brain magnetic resonance imaging: Approaches for investigating schizophrenia. *Schizophr. Bull.* 16:453–476.

Pillowsky, B., D. M. Juliano, L. B. Bigelow, and D. R. Weinberger. 1988. Stability of CT scan findings in schizophrenia: Results of an 8 year follow-up study. *J. Neurol. Neurosurg. Psychiatry* 51:209–213.

Plum, F. 1972. Prospects for research on schizophrenia. 3. Neuropsychology. Neuropathological Findings. *Neurosci. Res. Program Bull.* 10:384–388.

Pond, D. A. 1962. The schizophrenia-like psychoses of epilepsy, discussion. *Proc. R. Soc. Med.* 55:316.

Posner, M. I., T. S. Early, E. Reiman, P. J. Pardo, and M. Dhawan. 1988. Asymmetries in hemispheric control of attention in schizophrenia. *Arch. Gen. Psychiatry* 45:814–821.

Rakic, P., and R. S. Nowakowski. 1981. The time of origin of neurons in the hippocampal region of the rhesus monkey. *J. Comp. Neurol.* 196:99–128.

Roberts, G. W., and C. J. Bruton. 1990. Annotation notes from the graveyard: Neuropathology and schizophrenia. *Neuropath. and Appl. Neurobiology* 16:3–16.

Roberts, G. W., N. Colter, R. Lofthouse, B. Bogerts, M. Zech, and T. J. Crow. 1986. Gliosis in schizophrenia: A survey. *Biol. Psychiatry* 21:1043–1050.

Roberts, G. W., N. Colter, R. Lofthouse, E. C. Johnstone, and T. J. Crow. 1987. Is there gliosis in schizophrenia? Investigation of the temporal lobe. *Biol. Psychiatry* 22:1459–1468.

Roberts, G. W., D. J. Done, C. J. Bruton, and T. J. Crow. 1990. A "mock up" of schizophrenia: Temporal epilepsy and schizophrenia-like psychosis. *Biol. Psychiatry* 28:127–143.

Rosene, D. L., and G. W. Van Hoesen. 1987. The hippocampal formation of the primate brain: A review of some comparative aspects of cytoarchitecture and connections. In *Cerebral cortex*, vol 6., ed. E. G. Jones and A. Peters, pp. 345–456. New York: Plenum.

Rossi, A., P. Stratta, L. D'Albenzio, A. Tartaro, G. Schiazza, D. di Michele, S. Ceccoli, and M. Casacchia. 1989. Reduced temporal lobe area in schizophrenia by magnetic resonance imaging: Preliminary evidence. *Psychiatr. Res.* 29:261–263.

Rossi, A., P. Stratta, L. D'Albenzio, A. Tartaro, G. Schiazza, V. di Michele, F. Bolino, and M. Casacchia. 1990. Reduced temporal lobe areas in schizophrenia: Preliminary evidences from a controlled multiplanar magnetic resonance imaging study. *Biol. Psychiatry* 27:61–68.

Rossi, A., P. Stratta, V. di Michele, M. Gallucci, A. Splendianai, S. de Cataldo, and M. Casacchia. 1991. Temporal lobe structure by magnetic resonance in bipolar affective disorders and schizophrenia. *J. Aff. Dis.* 21:19–22.

Rowland, L. P., and F. A. Mettler. 1949. Cell concentration and laminar thickness of frontal cortex of psychotic patients. *J. Comp. Neurol.* 90:255–280.

Sanghera, M. K., E. T. Rolls, and A. Roper-Hall. 1979. Visual responses of neurons in the dorsolateral amygdala of the alert monkey. *Exp. Neurol.* 63:610–626.

Saunders, R. C., D. L. Rosene, and G. W. Van Hoesen. 1988. Comparison of the efferents of the amygdala and the hippocampal formation in the rhesus monkey: II. Reciprocal and non-reciprocal connections. *J. Comp. Neurol.* 271:185–207.

Scheibel, A. B., and J. A. Kovelman. 1979. Dendritic disarray in the hippo-campus of paranoid schizophrenia. Abstract and poster session. Presented at the *Annual Meeting of the Society of Biological Psychiatry.*

Scheibel, A. B., and J. A. Kovelman. 1981. Disorientation of the hippocam-pal pyramidal cell and its processes in the schizophrenic patient. *Biol. Psychiatry* 16:101–102.

Schwartzkopf, S. B., H. A. Nasrallah, S. C. Olson, and J. A. Coffman. 1990a. A factor analytic study of ventriculomegaly in schizophrenia: An MRI study. *Schizophr. Res.* 3(abstract): 18.

Schwartzkopf, S. B., S. C. Olson, J. A. Coffman, and H. A. Nasrallah. 1990b. Third and lateral ventricular volumes in schizophrenia: Support for progressive enlargement of both structures. *Psychopharm. Bull.* 25(3): 385–391.

Scoville, W. B., and B. Milner. 1957. Loss of recent memory after bilateral hippocampal lesions. *J. Neurol. Neurosurg. Psychiatry* 20:11–21.

Seidman, L. J. 1983. Schizophrenia and brain dysfunction: An integration of recent neurodiagnostic findings. *Psychol. Bull.* 94(2): 195–238.

Shelton, R. C., and D. R. Weinberger. 1986. X-ray computerized tomogra-phy studies in schizophrenia: A review and synthesis. In *Handbook of schizophrenia: Volume I: The neurology of schizophrenia,* ed. H. A. Nas-rallah and D. R. Weinberger, pp. 207–250. New York: Elsevier.

Shenton, M. E., S. F. Faux, R. W. McCarley, R. Ballinger, M. W. Coleman, M. W. Torello, and F. W. Duffy. 1989(a). Correlations between abnor-mal auditory P300 and positive symptoms in schizophrenia. *Biol. Psychi-atry* 25:710–716.

Shenton, M. E., M. R. Solovay, M. W. Coleman, H. Gale, and P. S. Holz-man. 1988(b). Thought disorder in the relatives of psychotic patients. *Arch. Gen. Psychiatry* 46:897–901.

Shenton, M. E., R. Kikinis, R. W. McCarley, T. Sandor, D. Metcalf, and F. A. Jolesz. 1990. MRI in SZ: Computer aided measures of brain & CSF. *APA New Res. Abstr.* 300.

Shenton, M. E., R. Kikinis, R. W. McCarley, D. Metcalf, J. Tieman, and F. A. Jolesz. 1991. Application of automated MRI volumetric measure-ment techniques to the ventricular system in schizophrenics and normal controls. *Schizophr. Res.* 5:103–113.

Shenton, M. E., R. Kikinis, F. A. Jolesz, S. D. Pollak, M. LeMay, C. G. Wible, H. Hokama, J. Martin, D. Metcalf, M. W. Coleman, and R. W. McCarley. 1992. Abnormalities of the left temporal lobe and thought disorder in schizophrenia: A quantitative magnetic resonance imaging study. *N. Engl. J. Med.* 327:604–612.

Shenton, M. E., B. F. O'Donnell, P. G. Nestor, C. G. Wible, R. Kikinis, S. F. Faux, S. D. Pollak, F. A. Jolesz, and R. W. McCarley. 1993. Temporal lobe abnormalities in a patient with schizophrenia who has word-finding difficulty: Use of high-resolution magnetic resonance imaging and auditory P300 event-related potentials. *Harvard Rev. Psychiatry* 1:110–117.

Smith, M. L. 1988. Recall of spatial location by the amnesic patient HM. *Brain Cogn.* 7:178–183.

Smith, M. L., and B. Milner. 1981. The role of the right hippocampus in the recall of spatial location. *Neuropsychologia* 19(6): 781–793.

Smith, R. C., M. Calderon, G. K. Ravichandran, J. Largen, G. Vroulis, A. Shvartsburd, J. Gordon, and J. C. Schoolar. 1984. Nuclear magnetic resonance in schizophrenia: A preliminary study. *Psychiatr. Res.* 12:137–147.

Solovay, M. R., M. E. Shenton, C. Gasperetti, M. W. Coleman, E. Kestnbaum, J. T. Carpenter, and P. S. Holzman. 1986. Scoring manual for the thought disorder index (revised version). *Schizophr. Bull.* 12:483–496.

Solovay, M. R., M. E. Shenton, and P. S. Holzman. 1987. Comparative studies of thought disorder: I. Mania and schizophrenia. *Arch Gen. Psychiatry* 44(1): 13–20.

Southard, E. E. 1910. A study of the dementia praecox group in the light of certain cases showing anomalies of scleroses in particular brain regions. *Am. J. Insanity* 67:119–176.

Southard, E. E. 1915. On the topographic distribution of cortex lesions and anomalies in dementia praecox with some account of their functional significance. *Am. J. Insanity* 71:603–671.

Spielmeyer, W. 1930. The problem of the anatomy of schizophrenia. *J. Nerv. Ment. Dis.* 72:241–244.

Squire, L. R. 1992. Memory and the hippocampus: A synthesis from findings with rats, monkeys, and humans. *Psychol. Bull.* 99(2): 195–231.

Squire, L. R., and S. Zola-Morgan. 1991. The medial temporal lobe memory system. *Science* 253:1380–1386.

Steinmetz, H., J. Rademacher, Y. Huang, H. Hefter, K. Zilles, A. Thron, and H. J. Freund. 1989. Cerebral asymmetry: MR planimetry of the human planum temporale. *J. Comput. Assist. Tomogr.* 13(6): 996–1005.

Stevens, J. R. 1973. An anatomy of schizophrenia? *Arch. Gen. Psychiatry* 29: 177–189.

Suddath, R. L., M. F. Casanova, T. E. Goldberg, D. G. Daniel, J. R. Kelsoe, and D. R. Weinberger. 1989. Temporal lobe pathology in schizophrenia: A quantitative magnetic resonance imaging study. *Am. J. Psychiatry* 146(4): 464–472.

Suddath, R. L., G. W. Christison, E. F. Torrey, M. F. Casanova, and D. R.

Weinberger. 1990. Anatomical abnormalities in the brains of monozygotic twins discordant for schizophrenia. *N. Eng. J. Med.* 322: 789–794.

Swanson, L. W., and C. Köhler. 1986. Anatomical evidence for direct projections from the entorhinal area to the entire cortical mantle in the rat. *J. Neurosci.* 6(10): 3010–3023.

Swayze, V. W., N. C. Andreasen, R. J. Alliger, W.T.C. Yuh, and J. C. Ehrhardt. 1992. Subcortical and temporal structures in affective disorder and schizophrenia: A magnetic resonance imaging study. *Biol. Psychiatry* 31:221–240.

Torrey, E. F., and M. R. Peterson. 1974. Schizophrenia and the limbic system. *Lancet* 2:942–946.

Trimble, M. R. 1990. First-rank symptoms of Schneider: A new perspective. *Br. J. Psychiatry* 156:195–200.

Trimble, M. R., and M. M. Perez. 1982. The phenomenology of the chronic psychoses of epilepsy. *Adv. Biol. Psychiatry* 8:98–105.

Vannier, M. W., R. L. Butterfield, D. Jordan, W. A. Murphy, R. G. Levitt, and M. Gado. 1985. Multispectral analysis of magnetic resonance images. *Radiology* 154:221–224.

Vita, A., E. Sacchetti, G. Valvassori, and C. L. Cazzullo. 1988. Brain morphology in schizophrenia: A 2- to 5-year CT scan follow-up study. *Acta. Psychiatr. Scan.* 78(5): 618–621.

Vogt, B. A., and D. N. Pandya. 1987. Cingulate cortex of the rhesus monkey: II. Cortical afferents. *J. Comp. Neurol.* 262:271–289.

Vogt, B. A., D. N. Pandya, and D. L. Rosene. 1987. Cingulate cortex of the rhesus monkey: I. Cytoarchitecture and thalamic afferents. *J. Comp. Neurol.* 262:256–270.

Wada, J. A., R. Clarke, and A. Hamm. 1975. Cerebral hemispheric asymmetry in humans. *Arch Neurol.* 32:239–246.

Weinberger, D. R. 1986. The pathogenesis: A neurodevelopmental theory. In *Handbook of schizophrenia: Volume I: The neurology of schizophrenia*, ed. H. A. Nasrallah and D. R. Weinberger, pp. 397–406. New York: Elsevier.

Wernicke, C. 1874. *Der aphasische symptomenkomplex.* Breslau: Cohen & Weigart.

Wiesel, F. A., G. Wik, I. Sjögren, G. Blomqvist, T. Greitz, and S. Stone-Elander. 1987. Regional brain glucose metabolism in drug free schizophrenic patients and clinical correlates. *Acta. Psychiatr. Scan.* 76:628–641.

Williamson, P., D. Pez, H. Merskey, S. Morrison, S. Karlik, D. Drost, T. Carr, P. Conlon. 1992. Frontal, temporal, and striatal proton relaxation times in schizophrenic patients and normal comparison subjects. *Am. J. Psychiatry* 149(4): 549–551.

Wise, R., F. Chollet, U. Hadar, K. Friston, E. Hoffner, and R. Frackowiak. 1991. Distribution of cortical neural networks involved in word comprehension and word retrieval. *Brain* 114:1803–1817.

Witelson, S. F., and W. Pallie. 1973. Left hemisphere specialization for language in the newborn: Neuroanatomical evidence of asymmetry. *Brain* 96:641–646.

Witter, M. P., and D. G. Amaral. 1991. Entorhinal cortex of the monkey: V. Projections to the dentate gyrus, hippocampus, and subicular complex. *J. Comp. Neurol.* 307:437–459.

Woods, B. T., D. Yurgelun-Todd, F. M. Benes, F. R. Frankenburg, H. G. Pope Jr., and J. McSparren. 1990. Progressive ventricular enlargement in schizophrenia: Comparison to bipolar affective disorder and correlation with clinical course. *Biol. Psychiatry* 27:341–352.

Wyper, D. F., J. D. Pickard, and M. Matheson. 1979. Accuracy of ventricular volume estimation. *J. Neurol. Neurosurg. Psychiatry* 42:345–350.

Young, A. H., D.H.R. Blackwood, H. Roxborough, J. K. McQueen, M. J. Martin, and D. Kean. 1991. A magnetic resonance imaging study of schizophrenia: Brain structure and clinical symptoms. *Br. J. Psychiatry* 158:158–164.

Zec, R. F., and D. R. Weinberger. 1986. Brain areas implicated in schizophrenia: A selective overview. In *Handbook of schizophrenia: Vol. I: The neurology of schizophrenia*, ed. H. A. Nasrallah and D. R. Weinberger, pp. 175–206. New York: Elsevier.

Zipursky, R. B., K. O. Lim, E. V. Sullivan, B. W. Brown, and A. Pfefferbaum. 1992. Widespread cerebral gray matter volume deficits in schizophrenia. *Arch. Gen. Psychiatry* 49:195–205.

Zola-Morgan, S., L. R. Squire, and D. G. Amaral. 1986. Human amnesia and the medial temporal region: Enduring memory impairment following a bilateral lesion limited to field CA1 of the hippocampus. *J. Neurosci.* 6:2950–2967.

Zola-Morgan, S., L. R. Squire, D. G. Amaral, and W. A. Suzuki, 1989. Lesions of perirhinal and parahippocampal cortex that spare the amygdala and hippocampal formation produce severe memory impairment. *J. Neurosci.* 9(12): 4355–4370.

5

Location, location, location: The pathway from behavior to brain locus in schizophrenia

Deborah L. Levy

Introduction

The brain sciences and advances in imaging technology draw the psychopathologist into the search for neuroanatomical loci for the major symptoms and behavioral abnormalities of mental diseases. But the pathway from symptom and behavior to brain area is not as simple as it may first appear. This chapter calls attention to some of the methodological errors that threaten to subvert our efforts. Some of these errors result from prematurely leaping to brain localization from very complex behaviors. Others reflect flawed extrapolations from established brain–behavior relations to as yet unestablished relations. Although the focus is on schizophrenia, the principles apply to the investigation of any disease process.

Historical context[1]

Scientific methodology has advanced considerably since Gall inferred that the characteristic of acquisitiveness was linked to a particularly prominent bump on the heads of pickpockets. Witness the fact that although there are numerous contemporary reports of memory disturbances in schizophrenics, there have been (thankfully) no attempts to look for corresponding bumps. The crudeness of Gall's theory of phrenology, reflected in its failure to employ experimental methods (no control groups, no "blind") and in his fallacious causal reasoning, had enormous influence on scientific receptivity to ideas about the relation between behavior and the brain in the early and middle nineteenth century. Perhaps as a backlash against the nonempirical origins of Gall's phrenological speculations, prevailing scientific sentiment spurned attempts to localize behaviors in specific brain areas and continued to endorse Flourens' notion that mental functions and behavior had no specific brain correlates. But to sustain this position required that scientists minimize the significance of a growing body of sound empirical evidence supporting brain localization of function long after its continued dismissal could be plausibly justified. The repudiation of the specific ideas associated with Gall's phrenology thus energized a wholesale rejection of all ideas regarding localization, even those for which there was substantial evidence of legitimacy.

The history of "cerebral localization" is punctuated with ironies, one of which is the ignominious fate suffered by Gall himself in the annals of the history of science. His discredited theory of phrenology has virtually eclipsed awareness of his scholarly anatomic expositions and appreciation of his preeminent role in empirically demonstrating the involvement of different parts of the brain in the regulation of behavior. It is even more ironic that his theory of phrenology, which, it is said (Head, 1926), originated in Gall's attempts to accommodate his personal distress at being surpassed by fellow students with better memory (which he thought was related to having large, protruding eyes), dwarfed the impact of his other work, which was grounded in solid intellectual accomplishment. Head (1926, 2, 4–5) described the magnitude of this paradox in writing of Gall's scientific legacy: "We habitually think of him with derision, as a quack who deduced character from the external conformation of the skull . . . But it is to this man that we are really indebted for the ideas we now hold of the relation of the constituent parts of the nervous system to one another . . . [Gall] introduced an entirely new method of approaching the structure and functions of the nervous system . . ."

Broca's discovery of the "speech center" is another chapter in the story of brain localization. This event is widely regarded as one of the truly powerful proofs of a causal relation between damage to a discrete region of the brain and impaired function, and, by implication, that specific parts of the brain, not the brain as an undifferentiated unit, mediate the performance of specific behaviors. Like Gall's claims, Broca's findings met with a controversial reception. But Broca's observations provided more acceptable evidence in favor of localized brain involvement in the regulation of behavior, perhaps because they could be readily subjected to empirical scrutiny.

In 1861, Broca was asked to examine a patient who presented

himself for treatment of a gangrenous limb. He found that the patient had an even more compelling symptom: he had not spoken for two decades, with the occasional exception of grunting a single mono-syllabic word, "tan." He also had a hemiplegia on his right side. In Broca's view, he was intellectually unimpaired and otherwise physi-cally normal. The patient died five days later and Broca's autopsy of the brain revealed a lesion in the opercular portion of the left inferior (third) frontal gyrus (subsequently designated as Brodmann area 44).[2] During the next two years Broca encountered other patients in whom the symptom of verbal aphasia invariably accompanied damage to this same part of the brain (Broca, 1863). Yet, despite the consistency of this pattern of brain damage, Broca was restrained about localizing the "speech center" to any specific area, or even to the left hemi-sphere: "Thus, here are eight cases where the lesions are located in the posterior third of the third frontal convolution. This number seems to me sufficient to give strong *presumptions*. And, most remark-ably, for all these patients the lesion occurred on the left side. *I do not dare draw conclusions and I wait for new facts*" (Broca, 1863, 202; italics added).

Based on data from a series of patients, Broca eventually did con-clude that the left third frontal gyrus was necessary for the articulation of speech. But then a patient of Charcot's proved to be an exception. Charcot's patient, like those of Broca and others, could not speak and had a right hemiplegia, but an autopsy revealed no lesion at the expected site, although this patient did have other damage located in the left hemisphere. A string of exceptions to the pattern described by Broca eventually followed. Today such exceptions are more likely to be considered statistical "outliers," or laid at the altar of "hetero-geneity," than grounds for reconsidering the interpretation of the original data.

Some 40 years later Pierre Marie (1906a) demonstrated that "Broca's area" can be destroyed without producing aphasia,[3] indicat-ing that more than one area of the brain must be involved in the production of language. Of course, it is now known that Broca's area, Wernicke's area, and the arcuate fasciculus are essential for the pro-duction of language, and that Broca's aphasia is actually associated with symptoms that are more complicated than the mere articulation of speech; they include sympathetic and facial apraxia, syntactic alex-ia, reading comprehension and writing impairment, and right hemiplegia (Benson and Geschwind, 1986). Indeed, there is yet another ironic twist: a focal lesion in "Broca's area" does not produce the symptoms of what is now known as "Broca's aphasia," or even a necessarily lasting impairment in language articulation; and the syndrome of "Broca's aphasia" involves a lesion that is not confined to "Broca's area" (Head, 1926; Mohr et al., 1978).

Another ironic complexity in this story is that Broca's original autopsy contained the very data that led to these revisions. He had, in fact, described far more extensive damage than a focal lesion of the third frontal gyrus, but it was only this latter finding that he considered to be etiologically significant. Broca believed that the more extensive damage was a consequence of the patient's general central nervous system deterioration and could not have been responsible for the original symptom of aphasia. According to Head (1926) Broca's emphasis on the association between the *focal* site of a lesion and specific kinds of symptoms was a direct outgrowth of, again ironically, his intellectual allegiances to the principles of localization contained in the theory of phrenology. Bouilland, a Gallist and a senior contemporary of Broca's, was so emphatically committed to the localization of speech in the frontal lobes that he never developed Broca's circumspection. As Head (1926) remarked, "As he [Bouilland] lived to a remarkable age and reached a position of great power in the medical world, he was always able to insist upon this view, whenever the question arose" (Head, 1926, 135–136).

These examples from the early history of our understanding of the aphasias were chosen to illustrate that ideas, even contradictory ones, can persist as scientific dogma, long after evidence of their insufficiency has been adduced. In the past the notion that the regulation of specific behaviors is localized in distinct parts of the brain has been as emphatically dismissed as it has been vigorously endorsed. The many ironies in these brief historical vignettes reflect common trends in the history of science: the tension between a prevailing viewpoint and the actual data, the irrational nature of resistance to new interpretations, and the ambivalent reception of data that depart from expectation.

The purpose of this discussion is not to reopen the historical debate over *whether* there are localized brain correlates of behavior, although this chapter is certainly relevant to that debate. Rather, its purpose is to note certain parallels between that debate and a contemporary trend that draws inferences about localized brain dysfunction from the behavior of schizophrenics. Such a discussion is particularly timely as efforts to localize the deviant behaviors of schizophrenics to specific brain regions take on renewed but unexamined enthusiasm.

Schizophrenia and the brain

There is general agreement that the profound disturbances in thinking, cognitive organization, perception, attention, information processing, motivation, reasoning, and affect regulation that accompany schizophrenia must indicate that something is wrong in the brain. Identifying the nature and location of these brain dysfunctions, however, poses a special challenge to psychopathology researchers. On the one hand, postmortem studies of brain tissue and structural imaging of the brain in living schizophrenics have yielded no shortage of positive findings. Some brain regions, such as the lateral ventricles, are comparatively large in schizophrenics (Johnstone et al., 1976); some, such as limbic temporal structures, are comparatively small (Bogerts et al., 1990); and others, such as the splenium of the corpus callosum, show anomalies of normal sexual dimorphism (Lewine et al., 1990). Cytoarchitectonic abnormalities (Benes et al., 1986; Jakob and Beckmann, 1986; Benes and Bird, 1987), localized volumetric reductions (Bogerts et al., 1985; Pakkenberg, 1990), cell disorientation (Kovelman and Scheibel, 1984), and alterations in receptor densities (Seeman et al., 1984) and brain neurochemistry (Reynolds, 1989) all have been reported as neuropathologic processes in schizophrenia.

On the other hand, the "clinical anatomic" method, which has proved to be so powerful in behavioral neurology, has not been equally successful in revealing the neuroanatomic correlates of the many disturbances in *behavior* associated with schizophrenia. In the behavioral neurology paradigm, as in experimentally induced lesions in animals, a focal lesion in a particular area of the brain often produces a unique cluster of behavioral symptoms, signs, and functional deficits with such reliability as to be pathognomonic of the site of the lesion. Broca's aphasia, described above, is but one of many possible examples. Or the behavioral consequences of focal damage may show topographic specificity to a particular neural network without exclusively implicating only one brain area in that network. For example, the symptom of unilateral neglect can result from a lesion in the thalamus, lateral prefrontal cortex, cingulate gyrus, striatum, or posterior parietal cortex, all of which make up an interconnecting brain network (Mesulam, 1981). Localization within the network requires information about the nature of other associated deficits (Weintraub and Mesulam, 1986). In the examples of Broca's aphasia and unilateral neglect, the links between brain and behavior – or between locus of function and loss of function – are direct: they logically lead to two inferences: (1) the normal performance of now impaired functions depended on the intactness of now afflicted areas, and (2) the undamaged parts of the brain are unable to perform the compromised behaviors.

In contrast to focal neurological disorders and brain damage of adult onset, the functional impairments and symptoms associated with schizophrenia have eluded ready extrapolation to particular brain systems. For example, no alteration in the morphology of the temporal lobe or the auditory cortex reliably corresponds to the symptom of auditory hallucinations. Nor are the blunted affect and amotivation so characteristic of chronic schizophrenia accompanied by an *identifiable* lesion in the frontal lobes. Unlike well-characterized neurological syndromes, the signs and symptoms of schizophrenia have not as yet been associated with a particular gross regional brain abnormality, are not diagnostically conclusive, do not occur in all patients, and are not specific to schizophrenia. Indeed, no one brain region has been exclusively implicated and the same pattern of morphological aberration is not found in all patients. Many patients show no detectable indications of brain structural abnormality. The inverse association between left posterior superior temporal gyrus size and amount of thought disorder (Shenton et al., 1992) is a rare exception to the more common pattern that the *clinical symptoms* of schizophrenia have no direct, consistent correlate in abnormal brain structure.

The paucity of such direct correlates between the behaviors of schizophrenics and abnormal brain morphology may reflect more about the adequacy of existing methodologies to detect such relations than whether they exist. It would be premature to rule out the possibility that discrete alterations at the synaptic level or focal pathology that is beyond the level of resolution currently available to researchers may eventually be detected and be associated with specific symptoms and signs of schizophrenia.

Behavioral impairment as a guide to brain dysfunction in schizophrenia

Since particular symptoms of schizophrenia have not been shown to be a direct expression of focal brain pathology (as it is generally defined for neurological conditions, such as tumors, infarctions, and traumatic injuries), the assessment of laboratory behaviors has become a major source of inferences about altered brain processes. But this route also leads through hazardous terrain. One remnant of the clinical anatomic method in current experimental psychopathology research is the tendency to infer similar pathophysiology when schizophrenics show behaviors and performance deficits *like* those seen in patients with specific neurological disorders. Deducing such connections between behavior and the brain can valuably capitalize on the power of human pattern recognition to detect similarities and differences. Certain psychotic symptoms shown by patients with focal lesions of the central nervous system *do* resemble the manifestations of psychosis in schizophrenics (Davison, 1983). Some of the performance deficits shown by patients with frontal lobe syndromes and basal ganglia disorders on neuropsychological and ocular motor tests *do* resemble those of schizophrenics. The amotivation, withdrawal, and affective blunting associated with frontal lobe syndromes *do* resemble the "negative symptoms" of schizophrenia.

Such resemblances in behavior compellingly tempt the investigator to make inferences about brain substrata, just as dissimilarities pull for the interpretation of underlying differences. But reasoning by analogy can be a precarious undertaking, because resemblances do not necessarily indicate equivalence any more than correlations indicate causes. One of the hazards of predicative thinking (the Virgin Mary is a woman, I am a woman, therefore I am the Virgin Mary) is the compromise of empirical logic (see Von Domarus, 1951). Some of the symptoms of schizophrenia are *like* those of some organic disorders, but schizophrenia *is* not those organic disorders. The performance of schizophrenics on a test may be impaired *like* that of a particular group of neurological patients, but schizophrenics do not therefore *have* that neurological disorder. Equally important, dissimilarities do not automatically indicate underlying differences. The varied clinical expressions of syphilis were once assumed to reflect different diseases until the discovery that the spirochete causes all of the symptoms (Hoch, 1972).

Reasoning by analogy is particularly likely to lead to flawed conclusions in relation to schizophrenia. The use of behavioral measures assumes that there is a known and relatively static relation between performance and *ability:* better performance reflects better ability and poor performance reflects impaired ability. For the purpose of linking behavior to the brain, a premium is placed on performance *deficits.* Interpreting the meaning of differences in performance is complicated, however, because schizophrenics perform poorly on most tasks. And the more difficult the task, the more likely it is that schizophrenics will perform worse than a comparison group. Because of such a "generalized deficit" in functioning, the mere demonstration of poor performance does not automatically connote differential ability or differential deficit (Chapman and Chapman, 1973, 1978). Similarly, because schizophrenics perform poorly on so many tasks, commonly observed deficits are likely to be highly correlated with each other, simply because they occur frequently in schizophrenics, but not necessarily because they are causally related to each other or reflect a common underlying etiologic process or a specific brain disturbance.

Neuropsychological and ocular motor functioning: An illustration

Neuropsychological and ocular motor tests have recently become popular sources of experimental data about performance deficits in schizophrenic patients. Such deficits are routinely interpreted to be indices of the functional integrity of various parts of the brain. The use of these tests provides a sharp focus for discussing some of the issues related to interpreting the meaning of poor performance in schizophrenics. Tests of "frontal" functioning warrant particular prominence in such a discussion for two reasons. First, poor performance on these tests has become increasingly influential as support for inferences about "frontal dysfunction" in schizophrenia. Second, "frontal tests," and the frontal lobes themselves, have certain special characteristics that increase the likelihood of falsely inferring "frontal dysfunctions" as the basis of performance decrements that are actually referable to other explanations, as discussed below.

The context in which neuropsychological and ocular motor tests were developed merits brief comment. These tests were designed to be used for examining specific clinical populations with specific central nervous system (CNS) conditions; they were not developed to function as *generic* indicators of localized brain dysfunction in any population to which they are administered. That is, their usefulness as clinical tools is based on their convergent and discriminant validity in well-characterized *adult neurological* populations; certain tests are differentially sensitive to damage in specific brain regions, or the regions to which they connect, and are relatively insensitive to focal damage at other sites. Certain other tests are sensitive to diffuse brain damage. The interpretive value of tests that have a degree of sensitivity and specificity for adult-onset brain compromise remains uncertain in relation to schizophrenia, where the brain pathology is not obviously unifocal and the pattern of findings suggests an onset prior to the completion of brain development (Benes et al., 1986; Falkai and Bogerts, 1986; Jakob and Beckmann, 1986; Weinberger, 1987; Murray and Lewis, 1988).

Schizophrenia is one of many conditions in which the alterations in brain structure and/or cytoarchitecture are both subtle and multifocal. Autism, for example, is associated with a wide range of cerebral cortical malformations, yet there is no single pathognomonic abnormality and no topographic specificity (Piven et al., 1990). Down syndrome also shows no obvious geographical specificity in its cytoarchitectural changes (Ross et al., 1984). Such multifocal diseases are not restricted to early development, for even Alzheimer's disease, once thought to involve localized disruption of the cytoarchitecture of the prefrontal cortex and hippocampus, is now known to involve diffuse pathology (Rogers and Morrison, 1985).

The fact that particular tests are sensitive to compromised functioning of specific brain regions is often interpreted to mean that poor performance in any population is pathognomonic of localized damage or regionally selective "dysfunction." But in good clinical practice extensive neuropsychological and ocular motor test batteries are employed to identify patterns of intact and impaired functions in patients with structural brain disease, and these patterns are then related to regional or network loci (Weintraub and Mesulam, 1986; Goldberg and Bilder, 1987; Leigh and Zee, 1991). Lesion location is not inferred from performance on a single test, because the sensitivity of any particular test may be high, but specificity may be far lower. For example, a frontal lobe syndrome is neither a sufficient nor a necessary condition for poor performance on the Wisconsin Card Sorting Test (WCST) (Heaton, 1981). While some frontal patients show performance deficits on the WCST (Milner, 1964; Drewe, 1974; Robinson et al., 1980; Anderson et al., 1991), other frontal lobe patients do not (Grafman et al., 1990; Anderson et al., 1991). Moreover, neurological patients without frontal lobe involvement may also perform poorly on this test (Drewe, 1974; Hermann et al., 1988; Grafman et al., 1990; Anderson et al., 1991), as may many patents with diffuse brain damage (Robinson et al., 1980). In fact, poor performance is not even dependent on the presence of neurological damage. Of 34 normal individuals tested on the WCST by Morice et al. (1990), 47.1% met the criterion suggested by Heaton (1981) for "focal frontal involvement" and 52.9% exceeded the threshold for "brain damage." Obviously, poor performance on the WCST cannot be equated with *having* a frontal lobe syndrome or even a frontal lobe dysfunction, any more than normal performance automatically connotes the absence of pathology at this site. Some of the implications of this kind of ambiguity for research on schizophrenia are pursued in the section on behavioral complexity below.

The frontal lobes are particularly likely to be the object of erroneous (i.e., false positive) inferences about regionally selective deficits (Goldberg and Bilder, 1987; Robbins, 1990; David, 1992). Both localized damage elsewhere in the brain and diffuse brain pathology are more apt to "masquerade as frontal pathology," to use Goldberg and Bilder's phrase, because of the extensive connections between frontal regions and other parts of the brain, the intricacy of the behaviors in which the frontal lobes play a role, and its relatively late phylogenetic development (Goldberg and Bilder, 1987).

Tests of frontal lobe function also tend to be difficult ones to perform compared with tests that tap the functional integrity of other brain regions. The greater difficulty of frontal tasks is particularly relevant to schizophrenia, because it increases the probability that poor performance will be detected, but leaves unclear whether selectively impaired performance is referable to differences among tests in difficulty level or to differential impairment of the functions assessed by these tests. One aspect of the greater difficulty of frontal tests is their behavioral complexity, a point to which we turn in the next section.

Behavioral complexity

Many of the tasks on which schizophrenics perform poorly, and which have become the basis for inferences about regionally selective brain dysfunction, are behaviorally complex. A single task frequently requires several operations (e.g., inhibiting one behavior while execut-ing another) that may involve several different spheres of behavior (e.g., cognitive, memory, motor), and that may, in addition, vary among themselves in difficulty. Many neuropsychological tests (e.g., WCST, Stroop) and many ocular motor tasks (see below) on which the performance of schizophrenics is "impaired" have several simul-taneous task demands. Which of the behaviors required to accomplish the task is responsible for the poor performance of schizophrenics? Both schizophrenics and individuals from other groups, such as pa-tients with frontal lobe lesions, may show impaired performance on a task, but the specific behaviors responsible for the poor performance may be different in each group.

The examples of anti-saccades and fixation

For illustrative purposes, consider the ocular motor tests of "anti-saccades" and a simplified derivative, a task requiring the inhibition of reflexive saccades to novel peripheral stimuli during visual fixation. In the anti-saccade paradigm, the subject is required to inhibit a saccade to a peripheral target light and to make a saccade to a point equidis-tant from center, but in the opposite periphery, where there is no target. Thus, if a light comes on 10 degrees to the left, the subject should make a saccade only to an imaginary point 10 degrees to the right.* This task requires the virtually simultaneous inhibition of a reflexive saccade and the production of a voluntary saccade, involving at least six operations: (1) detecting a peripheral target, (2) inhibiting a reflexive saccade to the peripheral target light, (3) estimating the location of the peripheral target light without looking at it, (4) initiat-ing a non-visually elicited saccade (i.e., to an unmarked location), (5) estimating the distance to the unmarked location, and (6) executing an accurate saccade to this location. In the fixation task, the subject is required to look at a target located straight ahead and to inhibit reflexive saccades to intermittently appearing peripheral target lights. The two tasks share the behavioral requirement of inhibiting a motor response to the peripheral light, but differ with respect to the require-ment of the ensuing motor task: in the fixation task, to inhibit all eye movements (that is, to fixate), and in the anti-saccade task, to make an eye movement to the location in the periphery opposite that of the

---

* See Figure 18.3 in Chapter 18, by Anne Sereno, this volume – Eds.

stimulus light. Errors in performance on both tasks are typically measured by the frequency of reflexive saccades to the peripheral target light, sometimes also termed a measure of "distractibility."

Schizophrenia researchers have been drawn to these tests of distractibility for one of two reasons: the explicit rationale was either to test schizophrenics on a measure of frontal dysfunction *or* to test schizophrenics on a measure of "basal ganglia dysfunction." The meaning ascribed to the results – in terms of localized brain dysfunction – has consistently matched the original rationale for choosing the task. The poorer performance of schizophrenics on the anti-saccade task (Fukushima et al., 1988, 1990; Thaker et al., 1989; Rosse et al., 1993) and on the reflexive saccade inhibition task (Paus, 1991) has been interpreted by all of these investigators as support for frontal dysfunction, confirming the original rationale, except for Thaker and colleagues (1989), who favored the interpretation of basal ganglia dysfunction, again, in keeping with the purpose of the study.

Although these tests are sensitive to disorders at both sites, they are not specific to either one, a consideration that has been largely neglected in both the choice of test and the interpretation of data on schizophrenics. High rates of reflexive saccades during the anti-saccade task can occur in patients with frontal lobe lesions, particularly involving dorsolateral (Guitton et al., 1985; Pierrot-Deseilligny et al., 1991) and mesial portions of the prefrontal cortex (Guitton et al., 1985), but this is not invariably the case (Guitton et al., 1985; Sharpe et al., 1985). Anti-saccade deficits are also found in patients with progressive supranuclear palsy (Pierrot-Deseilligny et al., 1989) and Alzheimer's disease (Fletcher and Sharpe, 1986). High rates of reflexive saccades to peripheral stimuli during a fixation task occur in patients with Huntington's disease (Leigh et al., 1983) and in patients with lesions of the ventrolateral and medial portions of the frontal lobe, but not in patients with dorsolateral frontal lesions (Paus et al., 1991).

The behavioral complexity of these tasks makes it difficult to determine whether schizophrenics and various groups of neurological patients actually show the *same* performance "impairment." The error measure is given the same name, to be sure, and the data are interpreted as if such ambiguity were not present, but is the performance of schizophrenics really as similar to that of certain groups of neurological patients as interpretation would suggest? Before considering some specific examples, it is useful to make explicit just what is reported to be "abnormal" about the performance of schizophrenics: they make more frequent reflexive saccades to a peripheral target *before* making a correct anti-saccade than do normal individuals; or they make more frequent reflexive saccades to a peripheral target when they should be fixating.

Contrary to widespread belief, schizophrenics do not show the same behavioral deficit on an anti-saccade task that Guitton et al. (1985) described in patients with unilateral dorsolateral-mesial prefrontal lesions. Nor, in fact, do Huntington's patients or most Alzheimer's patients. Not only did Guitton et al.'s patients have difficulty suppressing reflexive saccades, they were virtually *unable* to make anti-saccades. Guitton et al. (1985) reported that anti-saccades were "rarely" generated spontaneously by these patients, whether or not they were preceded by a reflexive saccade. Moreover, when an anti-saccade was made, it was typically *visually* triggered by the appearance of a target at the location to which the anti-saccade should have been made. Such visually triggered eye movements are reflexive saccades, not anti-saccades. In addition, those anti-saccades that were spontaneously made were hypometric – they recentered the eye – but an "anti-saccade" to the correct location was not made until, again, it was visually elicited by a target that appeared in the correct location. The specific similarity in performance between these frontal patients and schizophrenics, Huntington's, and most Alzheimer's patients is a high rate of reflexive saccades. Inability to generate an anti-saccade at all,[4] hypometric anti-saccades and failure to correct anti-saccade errors have not been described in these latter groups, although all of them are commonly described as showing the same *generic* behavioral impairment.

In contrast to these obvious dissimilarities in anti-saccade performance between schizophrenics and the frontal lobe lesion patients of Guitton et al. (1985), the schizophrenics studied by Paus (1991) *seem*, at first glance, to show exactly the same kind of behavioral deficit as the ventrolateral prefrontal patients studied by Paus et al. (1991) during two simple fixation tasks. One fixation task used in the Paus studies required the subject to look at a "meaningless stimulus" central fixation target and "not outside" a frame around it. Both schizophrenics and ventrolateral prefrontal patients made more reflexive glances to an intermittently appearing peripheral target while performing this task than did normal individuals. On another fixation task, subjects were required to classify the shape of a central target as either a wild or a domesticated animal, but no instructions were given about where to look. On this task also, a peripheral target appeared intermittently, but neither patient group differed from normal individuals in number of reflexive glances. All subjects made more reflexive saccades in the second condition, but only the controls made significantly more than they had in the first condition.

A cursory reading of these two studies suggests a strong behavioral similarity between schizophrenics and patients with a ventrolateral prefrontal lesion, a similarity that was interpreted by Paus (1991) as support for "frontal lobe dysfunction" in schizophrenics. Both the strength of the behavioral similarity and the validity of the finding of reflexive saccade disinhibition in either group are weakened by the fact that *the subjects were never told that peripheral stimuli would flash intermittently and that they were not to look at them.* In addition, no data were presented on the 29/40 trials involving only fixation (no peripheral stimuli appeared). Performance during this pure fixation task would have helped to determine whether increased saccadic distractibility also occurs during a less behaviorally complex task than one requiring *both* fixation and inhibition of reflexive saccades. Such a comparison would be relevant to conclusions regarding "the high task-specific distractibility of schizophrenics." Huntington's patients, for example, show impairments in fixation stability even in the absence of peripheral targets (Avanzini et al., 1979; Leigh et al., 1983), and make reflexive saccades even after having been explicitly told *not* to look at peripheral targets (Leigh et al., 1983).

The two conditions – fixation alone and fixation while inhibiting reflexive saccades – are examples of the kind of hierarchy of behaviors that could help to parse the specific components of the more behaviorally elaborate anti-saccade task. Each of the simpler tasks is one step more complex than the preceding one, yet each task decomposes another feature of the behavior required to perform an anti-saccade. These two conditions do not completely decompose the many behavioral requirements of performing an anti-saccade that were listed above, but each alone can help to identify a specific behavior that must be intact to perform an anti-saccade, and that could be responsible for impaired performance.

Because behavioral complexity makes it difficult to determine the specific impairments responsible for performance deficits and then to deduce their significance for localized brain involvement in relation to schizophrenia, alternative strategies that rely less on complex behaviors are needed. The next section addresses the merits of two neglected approaches: 1) the potential value of examining normal behaviors, and 2) the decomposition of the components of complex behaviors into operationally discrete, or "parsed" behaviors (see also chapter by Steven Matthysse, in this volume), illustrated in the context of functional brain imaging.

Changing conceptual orientation: New experimental paradigms

The value of studying normal behaviors

The behaviors that attract the attention of psychopathology researchers are those that are "abnormal" in some way. Implicit in the priority given to abnormal behaviors – and the resulting neglect of normal behaviors – are two related assumptions: (1) abnormal behavior is the most, if not the only, informative indicator of abnormal brain processes, and (2) normal behavior signifies a structurally and/or functionally intact brain.

The potential value of normal behavior in elucidating brain *dys*-function in schizophrenia may at first seem counterintuitive. There are, however, several experimental advantages offered by studying normal behavior. Tasks that schizophrenics perform normally are not susceptible to the interpretive uncertainties associated with generalized poor performance, task difficulty, side effects of psychotropic medication, or the influence of psychotic state. In particular, normal behavior bypasses the ambiguities that surround the distinction between competence on the one hand, and performance on the other hand, when the identification of abnormal behavior is *performance-based*. This rationale for attending to the normal performance of schizophrenics is similar to that underlying the value of studying non-psychotic first-degree relatives of schizophrenics (Holzman and Matthysse, 1990) and nonpsychotic schizotypes (Holzman et al., 1995).

Although schizophrenics as a group frequently perform worse than normal individuals as a group, substantial proportions of schizophrenics perform as well as normal individuals on most tasks. For example, on a simple tracking task, about half of schizophrenics show an impairment of smooth pursuit eye movements, but the other half show normal pursuit (Holzman et al., 1974). Focusing exclusively on the nature of the impairment responsible for eye tracking *dys*function addresses the performance deficit of one subgroup but ignores the behavior of the subgroup with normal eye tracking. Only data on the patients who perform normally can address whether the process by which normal eye tracking is accomplished is the same in schizophrenics as it is in nonschizophrenics.

The study of normal behavior also breaks the conceptual monopoly that the clinical anatomic method has exerted over the kinds of behaviors deemed important in relation to the brain. In particular, an overvaluation of compromised behavior excludes *dis*cordances between brain integrity and behavioral competence from the experimental repertoire and, by extension, from the way we think about schizophrenia or other severe mental disorders. Indeed, there is abundant evidence that normal behavior can occur in the absence of normal brain structure. Consider a few examples. "Functional resilience" is preserved in monkeys for years despite prenatal resection of the dorsolateral prefrontal cortex (Goldman and Galkin, 1978). In contrast to the effects of surgical transection of the corpus callosum in adulthood, congenital agenesis of the corpus callosum does not prevent interhemispheric communication (Sperry, 1968). Patients with dorsolateral frontal lobectomies perform normally on the WCST one year after surgery (Rosvold and Mirsky, 1964). Chemical and surgical lesions disrupt specific features of oculomotor behavior, but only transiently (Wurtz and Goldberg, 1972; Schiller et al., 1980; Newsome and Wurtz, 1988). Even genes that affect brain development can cause malformations in the nervous system, but leave behaviors completely or relatively uncompromised (Wahlsten, 1982).

The value of operationally discrete behaviors

Functional brain imaging is a method of examining the relation between behavior and functional activation of various brain regions. Differences among brain regions in functional activation, or neuronal activity, are reflected in differences in blood flow, glucose utilization, or oxygen consumption. Thus, the more functionally active a brain region is, the higher the blood flow in that region and the greater the oxygen and glucose utilization. Two of the most widely used functional brain imaging methods in schizophrenia research are the[133] Xenon inhalation technique of measuring regional cerebral blood flow using single-photon emission computed tomography, and glucose or O_2 metabolism using positron emission tomography (PET).

Two intrinsically uninterpretable rationales have generally guided the choice of task in functional brain imaging studies of schizophrenics. In the first, a task is chosen *because* schizophrenics perform it poorly; the Continuous Performance Test (CPT), for example, has been used in this context (Buchsbaum et al., 1992). Although the stated aim of such a study is to identify patterns of regional brain metabolism that distinguish schizophrenics from normal individuals, metabolic correlates of group differences in task proficiency are as parsimonious an explanation as the different disease states.

In the second, a task is chosen because it is expected to place a selective information processing "load" on a particular region of theoretical interest to the question of brain dysfunction in schizophrenia. That is, the functional integrity of a certain region of the brain is putatively linked to performing the task. The WCST has been used in this context as a test that specifically activates the dorsolateral prefrontal cortex (see Weinberger and Berman, 1988). Implicit in this approach is the erroneous assumption that a "functional area" of the brain is a "task area" (Petersen and Fiez, 1993).

A functional area of the brain is not a task area; there is no 'tennis forehand area' . . . Likewise, no area of the brain is devoted to a very complex function; 'attention' or 'language' is not localized in a particular Brodmann area or lobe. Any task or 'function' utilizes a complex and distributed set of brain areas.

The areas involved in performing a particular task are distributed in different locations in the brain, but the processing involved in task performance is not diffusely distributed among them. Each area makes a specific contribution to the performance of the task, and the contribution is determined by where the area resides within its richly connected parallel, distributed hierarchy. . . . The difficult but exciting job to which PET studies contribute is the identification of specific sets of computations with particular areas of the brain . . . no single experiment or image provides compelling evidence at this level of analysis. (Petersen and Fiez 1993, 513–514; italics added)

Moreover, even if performing a specific task activated only one brain region, which is not true of the WCST (Metz et al., 1987), as long as schizophrenic and normal individuals differ in performance on that task, it is virtually impossible to determine whether metabolic differences between the groups reflect an abnormality in any brain region (an exception to this injunction is described below). That is, we would not know whether a brain region was not activated because the patients were doing the task poorly, or whether the patients were performing poorly because a specific brain region was not sufficiently activated.

In both of these paradigms schizophrenics are typically performing a *different behavior* than are normal individuals* – that is, they are performing the task substantially worse. Differences in patterns of regional metabolism are to be expected when groups are not engaged in the same behavior. Indeed, as the discussion below illustrates, even minor changes in very simple elementary behaviors result in very marked changes in patterns of regional activation.

In light of the discussion above, one might conclude that the ideal task for studying metabolic correlates of behavior is one on which all subjects are engaged in the same behavior. This is one possible "solution" to the interpretive problem of differential performance: match schizophrenic and normal individuals for equivalent levels of proficiency on a task and see whether *equivalent* performance is associated with *different* patterns of regional metabolism in the two groups. Although such an approach is preferable to comparisons of disparate performance on complex tasks, it is nevertheless an imperfect solution when the task is multifaceted and requires several different and complex cognitive operations, because the specific behavior associated with any group differences in regional metabolism remains obscure.

Comparing groups that differ in proficiency does not automatically preclude useful or interpretable results. One reason that metabolic studies of schizophrenics have been especially troublesome to interpret is that the direction of group differences in performance parallels the group differences in regional metabolism: worse performance was associated with lower metabolism. Had the two variables been dissociated, for example, normal or elevated regional metabolism coinciding with worse performance, or lower metabolism in one region accompanied by increased activation in another area, the results would have been much more intriguing (Matthysse, 1986). However, the results would have been interpretable in terms of specific brain–behavior relationships *only* if one could identify the specific behavioral or cognitive process being examined in relation to pattern of regional brain activation.

Contrast this conventional approach to the study of regional brain

* See also Chapter 19, by Brendan Maher, this volume – Eds.

metabolism and behavior in schizophrenics with the very different method used in studies of functional correlates of behavior in normal individuals. This strategy, pioneered by Posner et al. (1988) and Petersen et al. (1989), explicitly recognizes both the complexity of behavior and the need to decompose the operations required to perform even simple behaviors.

The experimental design utilized in this approach has two critical features that immediately distinguish it from the conventional design used in studies of schizophrenics: (1) the requirement of sustained repetition of discrete cognitive or motor operations, and (2) the use of successively more complex behavior, each of which includes all critical features of the previous condition except for the single behavior that distinguishes the current condition. Because each condition serves as a control for the next, which differs in only one way, *the cognitive or motor operation required for a specific behavior can be isolated, and the brain areas that are activated by this specific behavior can be identified* by subtracting regional metabolism in a pair of successive conditions.

The method, as well as the nature of the tasks required to activate the dorsolateral prefrontal cortex, can be illustrated by the series of conditions used by Petersen et al. (1989) to study the processing of single words. They compared the PET scans of normal individuals engaged in each of the following actions: visually fixating on a point, observing a word at the same location as the fixation point, reading the word (a noun) aloud, and providing a "semantically appropriate verb" for the noun. Activation of the dorsolateral prefrontal cortex occurred only in the last condition, which also activated the anterior cingulate. Frith et al. (1991) used a similar design involving a series of sensorimotor tasks (lifting whichever of two fingers is touched by the examiner, lifting the finger that is not touched by the examiner, lifting one of the two fingers at random). Again, activation of the dorsolateral prefrontal cortex and anterior cingulate occurred only in the last condition.

These metabolic studies of normal individuals and recent work using echo-planar magnetic resonance imaging (McCarthy et al., 1993) demonstrate that it is possible to activate selective regions of the brain, including the prefrontal cortex, using operationally discrete tasks. The simplicity of these behaviors stands in marked contrast to the behavioral complexity of tasks like the CPT and the WCST. Such complex tasks are, in fact, not necessary to test functional activation of the prefrontal cortex.

The use of such operationally discrete tasks would be beneficial not only in metabolic studies concerned with the frontal lobes, but also in examining its interactions with other parts of the brain. Reduced blood flow in frontal regions has been widely reported in schizophrenics and interpreted as evidence of "frontal dysfunction" (see Weinberger and Berman, 1988). Yet decreased frontal blood flow does not usually reflect primary pathology at this site, or even frontal pathology at all. Changes in frontal metabolism secondary to probable deafferentation occur in pathological states in which the primary structural and metabolic abnormalities are located elsewhere in the brain. This is the case for progressive supranuclear palsy (D'Antona et al., 1985; Goffinet et al., 1989), even though the metabolically aberrant frontal region is structurally intact. Similarly, hypofrontality accompanies coma in patients with no frontal pathology and is part of a diffuse reduction in blood flow; the condition completely reverses when consciousness is regained (Deutsch, 1992). Thus, reduced frontal blood flow may be most informative as a clue that metabolic or structural pathology is present in *nonfrontal* regions.

Conclusion

The psychotic symptoms and the many behavioral abnormalities shown by schizophrenics tempt investigators to search for locations in the brain that could account for them. The superficial similarities between schizophrenics and various neurological populations in performance deficits, and in some symptoms, encourage the inference that the conditions are congruent. Such facile conclusions often ignore the glaring dissimilarities in performance and symptoms and emerge from data based on faulty experimental designs. Such paradigms have disproportionately claimed our scientific attention and interfered with rigorous scrutiny and judicious interpretation. Their most detrimental and insidious consequence, however, is constraint on new ideas and new paradigms for testing them.

The elusiveness of definitive answers to questions of brain localization undoubtedly reflects the complexity of the problems. For this reason it is especially important that we expand the arena of behavior that claims our interest and diversify our methods of studying it. It is timely to reconsider which specific behaviors are the most informative in brain–behavior studies of schizophrenia, how they can be most advantageously studied, and what assumptions guide the choice of the paradigms that we adopt. Such a reorientation might usefully include the study of normal behaviors. Above all, it must emphasize identifiable, operationally discrete behaviors and encourage the development of new approaches if we are ever to unravel how the mysteries of schizophrenia have remained so effectively hidden in the brain.

Ever since interest in the question was first aroused, the phenomena of aphasia have been presented for investigation in the same forms and under identical conditions; there has been no change in the problem to be solved. Every generation has examined the manifestations afresh, armed with different general conceptions and dominated by prejudices arising from the ideas of the day. The knowledge transmitted to subsequent workers in the field has thus been a mixture of theory and fact, and it has frequently happened that the theory has survived, whilst the new observations have been forgotten. . . . *The world clings to theories, for they are easier to remember, can be reproduced with effect and lead to a clarity of exposition foreign to a description of the crude experimental facts. There is in consequence a tendency to carry over the conceptions of one age on to the observations of the next. New wine is poured into old bottles with disastrous results.* [italics added]

The persistent tendency to localise a centre for normal speech in the frontal convolutions is one of the most striking examples of the influence of a theory, deduced from certain a priori considerations, upon observations of an entirely different character. (Head, 1926, 134–135)

Substitute the word "schizophrenia" for "aphasia," and Henry Head's summary of the evolution of understanding about the nature and causes of the aphasias might well have been written about the schizophrenias. Head (1926) considered Gall, Broca, Marie, Wernicke, and many others "victims of the philosophical fallacy of their day." Shall we break free of the philosophical fallacy of *our* day?

Acknowledgments

The author thanks Larry Abel, Francine Benes, Robert Bilder, Elizabeth Dorus, Philip Holzman, Clara Lajonchere, Mark Lenzenweger, Richard Lipton, Steven Matthysse, John Metz, Alfred Pope, Herbert Spohn, and Nicholas Yasillo for helpful comments on the manuscript and Christine Waternaux for translating Broca (1863). Supported in part by USPHS grants MH49487, MH31340, MH31154, MH44876.

Notes

1. Secondary source material: Head, 1926; Boring, 1929; Muller-Freienfels, 1935.

2. See Marie, 1906b, for some different opinions about the postmortem findings on Broca's first two cases.
3. A recent PET study (Petersen et al., 1989) showed that "Broca's area" is not specialized for speech per se; opening and closing the mouth and moving the tongue without speaking activate Broca's area.
4. Patients with severe Alzheimer's disease also fail to make anti-saccades (i.e., they fail to correct reflexive saccades to the target), probably because of task incomprehension (Abel et al., 1993).

References

Abel, L. A., H. Piroozi, H. C. Hendrie, and R. D. Yee. 1993. Effects of Alzheimer's disease on saccadic performance under different task demands. *Investigative Ophthalmology and Visual Science* 34:1136.

Anderson, S. W., H. Damasio, R. D. Jones, and D. Tranel. 1991. Wisconsin Card Sorting Test performance as a measure of frontal lobe damage. *Journal of Clinical and Experimental Neuropsychology* 13:909–922.

Avanzini, G., F. Girotti, T. Caraceni, and R. Spreafico. 1979. Oculomotor disorders in Huntington's chorea. *Journal of Neurology, Neurosurgery, and Psychiatry* 42:581–589.

Benes, F. M., and E. D. Bird. 1987. An analysis of the arrangement of neurons in the cingulate cortex of schizophrenic patients. *Archives of General Psychiatry* 44:608–616.

Benes, F. M., B. Davidson, and E. D. Bird. 1986. Quantitative cytoarchitectural studies of the cerebral cortex of schizophrenics. *Archives of General Psychiatry* 43:31–35.

Benson, D. F., and N. Geschwind. 1986. Aphasia and related disorders: A clinical approach. In *Principles of Behavioral Neurology*, edited by M.-M. Mesulam, pp. 193–238. Philadelphia: F.A. Davis.

Bogerts, B., E. Meertz, and R. Schonfeldt-Bausch. 1985. Basal ganglia and limbic system pathology in schizophrenia: A morphometric study of brain volume and shrinkage. *Archives of General Psychiatry* 42:784–791.

Bogerts, B., M. Ashtari, G. Degreef, J. Alvir, R. M. Bilder, and J. A. Lieberman. 1990. Reduced temporal limbic structure volumes on magnetic resonance images in first episode schizophrenia. *Psychiatry Research* 35:1–13.

Boring, E. G. 1929. *A History of Experimental Psychology.* New York: D. Appleton-Century.

Broca, P. 1863. Localisation des fonctions cerebrales – siège du language articule. *Bulletins et Memoires de la Société de Anthropologie de Paris* 4:200–204.

Buchsbaum, M. S., R. J. Haier, S. G. Potkin, K. Nuechterlein, H. S. Bracha, M. Katz, J. Lohr, J. Wu, S. Lottenberg, P. A. Jerabek, M. Trenary, R.

Tafalla, C. Reynolds, and W. E. Bunney, Jr. 1992. Frontostriatal disorder of cerebral metabolism in never-medicated schizophrenics. *Archives of General Psychiatry* 49:935–942.

Chapman, L. J., and J. P. Chapman. 1973. *Disordered Thought in Schizophrenia.* New York: Appleton-Century-Crofts.

Chapman, L. J., and Chapman, J. P. 1978. The measurement of differential deficit. *Journal of Psychiatric Research* 14:303–311.

D'Antona, R., J. C. Baron, Y. Samson, M. Serdaru, F. Viader, Y. Agid, and J. Cambier. 1985. Subcortical dementia: Frontal cortex hypometabolism detected by positron emission tomography in patients with progressive supranuclear palsy. *Brain* 108:785–799.

David, A. S., 1992. Frontal lobology – Psychiatry's new pseudoscience. *British Journal of Psychiatry* 161:244–248.

Davison, K. 1983. Schizophrenia-like psychoses associated with organic cerebral disorders: A review. *Psychiatric Developments* 1:1–34.

Deutsch, G. 1992. The nonspecificity of frontal dysfunction in disease and altered states: Cortical blood flow evidence. *Neuropsychiatry, Neuropsychology and Behavioral Neurology* 5:301–307.

Drewe, E. A. 1974. The effect of type and area of brain lesions on Wisconsin Card Sorting Test performance. *Cortex* 10:159–170.

Falkai, P., and B. Bogerts. 1986. Cell loss in the hippocampus of schizophrenics. *European Archives of Psychiatry and Neurological Sciences* 236: 154–161.

Fletcher, W. A., and J. A. Sharpe. 1986. Saccadic eye movement dysfunction in Alzheimer's disease. *Annals of Neurology* 20:464–471.

Frith, C. D., K. J. Friston, P. F. Liddle, and R.S.J. Frackowiak. 1991. Willed action and the prefrontal cortex in man: A study with PET. *Proceedings of the Royal Society London,* Ser. B 244:241–246.

Fukushima, J., K. Fukushima, T. Chiba, S. Tanaka, I. Yamashita, and M. Kato. 1988. Disturbances of voluntary saccadic eye movements in schizophrenic patients. *Biological Psychiatry* 23:670–677.

Fukushima, J., N. Morita, K. Fukushima, T. Chiba, S. Tanaka, and I. Yamashita. 1990. Voluntary control of saccadic eye movements in patients with schizophrenic and affective disorders. *Journal of Psychiatric Research* 24:9–24.

Goffinet, A. M., A. G. De Volder, C. Gillain, D. Rectem, A. Bol, C. Michel, M. Cogneau, D. Labar, and C. Laterre. 1989. Positron tomography demonstrates frontal lobe hypometabolism in progressive supranuclear palsy. *Annals of Neurology* 25:131–139.

Goldberg, E., and R. M. Bilder, Jr. 1987. The frontal lobes and hierarchical organization of cognitive control. In *The Frontal Lobes Revisited,* edited by E. Perecman, pp. 159–187. Hillsdale, NJ: Lawrence Erlbaum.

Goldman, P., and T. Galkin. 1978. Prenatal removal of frontal association cortex in the fetal rhesus monkey: Anatomical and functional consequences in postnatal life. *Brain Research* 152:451–484.

Grafman, J., B. Jonas, and A. Salazar. 1990. Wisconsin Card Sorting Test performance based on location and size of neuroanatomical lesion in Vietnam veterans with penetrating head injury. *Perceptual and Motor Skills* 71:1120–1122.

Guitton, D., H. A. Buchtel, and R. M. Douglas. 1985. Frontal lobe lesions in man cause difficulties in suppressing reflexive glances and in generating goal-directed saccades. *Experimental Brain Research* 58:455–472.

Head, H. 1926. *Aphasia and Kindred Disorders of Speech.* Vol. 1. New York: Cambridge University Press.

Heaton, R. K. 1981. *Wisconsin Card Sorting Test Manual.* Odessa, FL: Psychological Assessment Resources.

Hermann, B. P., A. R. Wyler, and E. T. Richey. 1988. Wisconsin Card Sorting Test performance in patients with complex partial seizures of temporal lobe origin. *Journal of Clinical and Experimental Neuropsychology* 10:467–476.

Hoch, P. 1972. General paresis. In *Differential Diagnosis in Clinical Psychiatry. The Lecture of Paul H. Hoch*, edited by M. O. Strahl and N.D.C. Lewis, pp. 228–257. New York: Science House.

Holzman, P. S., and S. Matthysse. 1990. The genetics of schizophrenia: A review. *Psychological Science* 1:279–286.

Holzman, P. S., L. R. Proctor, D. L. Levy, N. J. Yasillo, H. Y. Meltzer, and S. W. Hurt. 1974. Eye-tracking dysfunctions in schizophrenic patients and their relatives. *Archives of General Psychiatry* 31:143–151.

Holzman, P. S., M. Coleman, M. F. Lenzenweger, D. L. Levy, S. Matthysse, G. O'Driscoll, and S. Park. 1995. Relation between antisaccadic eye movements, working memory deficits and thought disorder and schizotypal traits. In: *Schizotypal Personality*, edited by A. Raine, T. Lencz, and S. A. Mednick. Orlando, FL: Academic Press.

Jakob, J., and H. Beckmann. 1986. Prenatal developmental disturbances in the limbic allocortex in schizophrenics. *Journal of Neural Transmission* 65:303–326.

Johnstone, E. C., C. D. Frith, T. J. Crow, E. J. Husband, and L. Kreel. 1976. Cerebral ventricular size and cognitive impairment in chronic schizophrenia. *Lancet* 2:924–926.

Kovelman, J. A., and A. B. Scheibel. 1984. A neurohistological correlate of schizophrenia. *Biological Psychiatry* 19:1601–1621.

Leigh, R. J., and D. S. Zee. 1991. *The Neurology of Eye Movements.* Philadelphia: F. A. Davis.

Leigh, R. J., S. A. Newman, S. E. Folstein, A. G. Lasker, and B. A. Jensen. 1983. Abnormal ocular motor control in Huntington's disease. *Neurology* 33:1268–1275.

Lewine, R. J., L. Gulley, S. Risch, R. Jewart, and J. L. Houpt. 1990. Sexual dimorphism, brain morphology, and schizophrenia. *Schizophrenia Bulletin* 16:195–203.

Marie, P. 1906a. La troisième circonvolution frontale gauche ne joue aucun role special dans la fonction du langage. *Semaine Medicale* 26 (23 May):241–247.

Marie, P. 1906b. L'aphasie de 1861 a 1866. *Semaine Medicale* 26 (28 Nov.):565–571.

Matthysse, S. 1986. The art of questioning oracles. *McLean Hospital Journal* 11:65–71.

McCarthy, G., A. M. Blamire, D. L. Rothman, R. Gruetter, and R. G. Shulman. 1993. Echo-planar magnetic resonance imaging studies of frontal cortex activation during word generation in humans. *Proceedings of the National Academy of Sciences* 90:4952–4956.

Mesulam, M.-M. 1981. A cortical network for directed attention and unilateral neglect. *Annals of Neurology* 10:309–325.

Metz, J. T., N. J. Yasillo, and M. Cooper. 1987. Cerebral metabolism and EEG: Relations to cognitive task. *Society for Neuroscience Abstracts* 13:1413.

Milner, B. 1964. Some effects of frontal lobectomy in man. In *The Frontal Granular Cortex and Behavior*, edited by J. M. Warren and K. Akert, pp. 313–331. New York: McGraw-Hill.

Mohr, J. P., M. S. Pessin, S. Finkelstein, H. H. Funkenstein, G. W. Duncan, and K. R. Davis. 1978. Broca aphasia: Pathologic and clinical. *Neurology* 28:311–324.

Morice, R. 1990. Cognitive inflexibility and pre-frontal dysfunction in schizophrenia and mania. *British Journal of Psychiatry* 157:50–54.

Muller-Freienfels, R. 1935. *The Evolution of Modern Psychology.* New Haven: Yale University Press.

Murray, R. M., and S. W. Lewis. 1988. Is schizophrenia a neurodevelopmental disorder? *British Medical Journal* 285:681–682.

Newsome, W. T., and R. H. Wurtz. 1988. Probing visual cortical function with discrete chemical lesions. *Trends in Neuroscience* 11:394–400.

Pakkenberg, B. 1990. Pronounced reduction in total neuron number in mediodorsal thalamic nucleus and nucleus accumbens in schizophrenics. *Archives of General Psychiatry* 47:1023–1028.

Paus, T. 1991. Two modes of central gaze fixation maintenance and oculomotor distractibility in schizophrenics. *Schizophrenia Research* 5:145–152.

Paus, T., M. Kalina, L. Patockova, Y. Angerova, R. Cerny, P. Mecir, J. Bauer, and P. Krabec. 1991. Medial vs lateral frontal lobe lesions and differential impairment of central-gaze fixation maintenance in man. *Brain* 114:2051–2067.

Petersen, S. E., and J. A. Fiez. 1993. The processing of single words studied with positron emission tomography. *Annual Review of Neuroscience* 16:509–530.

Petersen, S. E., P. T. Fox, M. I. Posner, M. Mintun, and M. E. Raichle. 1989. Positron emission tomographic studies of the processing of single words. *Journal of Cognitive Neuroscience* 1:153–170.

Pierrot-Deseilligny, C., S. Rivaud, B. Pillon, E. Fournier, and Y. Agid. 1989. Lateral visually-guided saccades in Progressive Supranuclear Palsy. *Brain* 112:471–487.

Pierrot-Deseilligny, C., S. Rivaud, B. Gaymard, and Y. Agid. 1991. Cortical control of reflexive visually-guided saccades. *Brain* 114:1473–1485.

Piven, J., M. L. Berthier, S. E. Starkstein, E. Nehme, G. Pearlson, and S. E. Folstein. 1990. Magnetic resonance imaging evidence for a defect of cerebral cortical development in autism. *American Journal of Psychiatry* 147:734–739.

Posner, M. I., S. E. Petersen, P. T. Fox, and M. E. Raichle. 1988. Localization of cognitive functions in the human brain. *Science* 240:1627–1631.

Reynolds, G. P. 1989. Beyond the dopamine hypothesis: The neurochemical pathology of schizophrenia. *British Journal of Psychiatry* 155:305–316.

Robbins, T. W. 1990. The case for frontostriatal dysfunction in schizophrenia. *Schizophrenia Bulletin* 16:391–402.

Robinson, A. L., R. K. Heaton, R.A.W. Lehman, and D. W. Stilson. 1980. The utility of the Wisconsin Card Sorting Test in detecting and localizing frontal lobe lesions. *Journal of Consulting and Clinical Psychology* 48:605–614.

Rogers, J., and J. H. Morrison. 1985. Quantitative morphology and regional and laminar distributions of senile plaques in Alzheimer's disease. *Journal of Neuroscience* 5:2801–2808.

Ross, M. H., A. M. Galaburda, and T. L. Kemper. 1984. Down's syndrome: Is there a decreased population of neurons? *Neurology* 34:909–916.

Rosse, R. B., B. L. Schwartz, S. Y. Kim, and S. I. Deutsch. 1993. Correlation between antisaccade and Wisconsin Card Sorting Test performance in schizophrenia. *American Journal of Psychiatry* 150:333–335.

Rosvold, H. E., and A. F. Mirsky. 1964. Unpublished data described by Rosvold in the discussion of Milner, B. 1964. In *The Frontal Granular Cortex and Behavior,* edited by J. M. Warren and K. Akert, p. 332. New York: McGraw-Hill.

Schiller, P. H., S. D. True, and J. L. Conway. 1980. Deficits in eye movements following frontal eye-field and superior colliculus ablation. *Journal of Neurophysiology* 44:1175–1189.

Seeman, P., C. Ulpian, C. Bergeron, P. Riederer, K. Jellinger, E. Gabriel, G. P. Reynolds, and W. W. Tourtellotte. 1984. Bimodal distribution of dopamine receptor densities in brains of schizophrenics. *Science* 225:728–731.

Sharpe, J. A., R. L. Bondar, and W. A. Fletcher. 1985. Contralateral gaze deviation after frontal lobe haemorrhage. *Journal of Neurology, Neurosurgery, and Psychiatry* 48:86–88.

Shenton, M. E., R. Kikinis, F. A. Jolesz, S. D. Pollak, M. LeMay, C. G. Wible, H. Hokama, J. Martin, D. Metcalf, M. Coleman, and R. W. McCarley. 1992. Abnormalities of the left temporal lobe and thought disorder in schizophrenia: A quantitative magnetic resonance imaging study. *New England Journal of Medicine* 327:604–612.

Sperry, R. W. 1968. Plasticity of neuronal maturation. *Developmental Biology* Suppl 2:306–327.

Thaker, G. K., J. A. Nguyen, and C. A. Tamminga. 1989. Increased saccadic distractibility in tardive dyskinesia: Functional evidence for subcortical GABA dysfunction. *Biological Psychiatry* 25:49–59.

Von Domarus, E. 1951. The specific laws of logic in schizophrenia. In *Language and Thought in Schizophrenia*, edited by J. S. Kasanin, pp. 104–114. Berkeley: University of California Press.

Wahlsten, D. 1982. Genes with incomplete penetrance and the analysis of brain development. In *Genetics of the Brain*, edited by I. Lieblich, pp. 367–391. Amsterdam: Elsevier Biomedical Press.

Weinberger, D. R. 1987. Implications of normal brain development for the pathogenesis of schizophrenia. *Archives of General Psychiatry* 44:660–669.

Weinberger, D. R., and K. F. Berman. 1988. Speculation on the meaning of cerebral metabolic hypofrontality in schizophrenia. *Schizophrenia Bulletin* 14:157–168.

Weintraub, S., and M.-M. Mesulam. 1986. Mental state assessment of young and elderly adults in behavioral neurology. In *Principles of Behavioral Neurology*, edited by M.-M. Mesulam, pp. 71–123. Philadelphia: F. A. Davis.

Wurtz, R. H., and M. E. Goldberg. 1972. Activity of superior colliculus in behaving monkey. IV. Effects of lesions on eye movements. *Journal of Neurophysiology* 35:587–596.

6

The defects of affect and attention in schizophrenia: A possible neuroanatomical substrate

Francine M. Benes

Where *affect* is lacking, there will also be lacking the drive to pursue the external and internal processes, to direct the path of the senses and the thoughts, i.e. active *attention* will be lacking.
Bleuler, 1950

Introduction

Two of the "core" defects found in schizophrenia are disturbances in affective experience and attention. On the one hand, schizophrenics commonly report having no emotions, other than the occasional experience of anger, leading some to describe themselves as feeling "dead" or "numb." On the other hand, an attentional defect seen early in the course of the illness (McGhie and Chapman, 1963) involves a loss of selectivity or "overinclusiveness" (Detre and Jarecki, 1968) that is believed to involve a loss of a central filter mechanism (Cameron, 1938). Although both affective experience and attention are essential to normal functioning, the basic neurophysiology of these functions have not been extensively investigated and consequently are not well-understood aspects of behavior. It is important to understand more about the ways in which emotional expression and selective attention are centrally processed, because such insights may provide some clues regarding the pathophysiology of schizophrenia. The concurrence of affective and attentional disturbances in this disorder may suggest that these two aspects of normal behavior are processed through similar or overlapping circuits. In this regard, it is noteworthy that some investigators believe there is a "parallelism in the integrity of attention and emotion" and that both may require an interplay between associative cortical regions and the limbic system (Mesulam and Geschwind, 1978).

According to William James (1884), an emotion is a bodily response involving a "feeling" that occurs in response to an idea. In contrast, the "central" hypothesis of emotion (Cannon, 1929/1970) has extended this idea by suggesting that the visceral component of emotion is merely a nonspecific autonomic response, while the ideational part is necessary to give it a context (Schacter, 1971). This hypothesis predicts that a significant part of every emotion is mediated through portions of the nervous system that process visceral information, while the meaning or context of the emotion is derived from cognitive activity that is processed at more central levels. To accomplish an integration of these two separate levels of response, it would be necessary to have some requisite interconnections throughout the central nervous system. Evidence suggests that the integrative mechanism present in the central nervous system for this purpose is tightly linked, so much so that even mimicking a facial expression associated with a particular emotion will result in the appropriate affective tone and autonomic responses (Ekman et al., 1983; Levenson et al., 1990). One brain area that may serve to integrate the conceptual and visceral components of emotional responses is the cingulate gyrus, a region having extensive connections with *both* associative neocortex and the limbic system (Papez, 1937). Concerning the current discussion, it is noteworthy that the anterior cingulate cortex has also been postulated to play an integral role in attentional responses as well (Baleydier and Maugierre, 1980), making it a likely region through which the link between attention and affect may be established (Mesulam and Geschwind, 1978). Thus, on theoretical grounds, the anterior cingulate region may also contribute to the disturbances of both affect and attention in schizophrenia described by Bleuler (1952).

In the discussion that follows, the experimental and clinical evidence suggesting that the anterior portion of the cingulate cortex plays a role in both emotional experience and attentional responses will be reviewed. Following this discussion, the idea that alterations of these functions might be related to abnormal processing in the anterior cingulate cortex of patients with schizophrenia is considered. Toward this end, recent histopathological findings in the anterior cingulate region in schizophrenic brain will be described. Based on these findings, a model to conceptualize how altered circuits within this region might contribute to disturbances in affective experience and attention will be presented.

The role of the anterior cingulate cortex in affect and attention

When Papez (1937) first suggested that the integration of higher cognitive functions with emotion might occur in cingulate gyrus, he could not have known that the specific connections he proposed for this mechanism were probably insufficient to explain such a complex phenomenon. The original connections described by Papez included the cingulum bundle outflow to the hippocampal formation, the fornical projection from the hippocampal formation to the mammillary body, a relay from this latter region to the anterior thalamic nucleus and, finally, a projection from there back to the cingulate cortex. Not surprisingly, the general function that Papez formulated for the cingulate gyrus still seems valid, and the connection pathways he defined are still universally accepted. Even so, studies of the anterior cingulate region over the past several decades have revealed a far more complex set of connections through which affective experience can be integrated with thought processes within this region. The anterior cingulate cortex has circuitry that plays a direct role in mediating not only emotional expression, but also attentional responses (Neafsey et al., 1993). Recent studies have defined a *ventral* portion of the anterior cingulate region that is believed to subsume a major role in the modulation of visceral motor and sensory activity and a *dorsal* division that is thought to be involved in controlling movement of the head and eyes during attentional responses (Neafsey et al., 1993). The connections for each of these subdivisions of the anterior cingulate region are described separately below.

The ventral division of the anterior cingulate cortex

The ventral portion of the anterior cingulate (VAC) region engages in a complex array of both cortical and subcortical connections. It receives an input from the dorsomedial nucleus of the thalamus and also receives afferents from the paraventricular and parataenial nuclei, phylogenetically older midline thalamic structures. From these latter areas, it receives an indirect relay of nociceptive pain information originating from the spinothalamic tracts (Vogt et al., 1993). The ventral anterior cingulate cortex also receives extensive inputs from many different limbic areas. For example, direct inputs to this region arise from the CA1 sector and subiculum of the hippocampal formation (Terreberry, 1985; Ruit and Neafsey, 1990; Van Groen and Wyss, 1990), the basolateral nucleus of the amygdala (Terreberry, 1985; Kitai and Kitai, 1990; Zeng and Stuesse, 1991), the lateral hypothalamus (Saper, 1985) and insular cortex (Saper, 1985; Kushel and Van der Kooy, 1988; Allen et al., 1991; Zeng and Stuesse, 1991). It also receives basal forebrain inputs from the nucleus accumbens and olfactory tubercle (Groenewegen et al., 1990).

In addition to its connection with these limbic forebrain regions, the role of VAC in integrating emotional activity at the cortical level is given even stronger support by the occurrence of direct sensory relays from the nucleus solitarius located at upper medullary and lower pontine levels of the brain stem (Van der Kooy et al., 1982; Terreberry and Neafsey, 1983). Through this nucleus, virtually all general visceral afferent information from the peripheral autonomic nervous system can potentially be integrated with higher cognitive functions mediated in associative neocortex by providing the anterior cingulate region with information regarding the status of the heart, lungs, gastrointestinal tract, bladder, and rectum. Similarly, the viscerosensory relays from virtually all the blood vessels of the body are also processed through this nucleus and can be potentially relayed to the ventral anterior cingulate cortex.

The efferent outflow from ventral portions of the anterior cingulate region parallels its afferent inputs to nuclei involved either directly or indirectly in visceral autonomic control. For example, the periaqueductal gray (Domesick, 1969; Beckstead, 1979; Wyss and Sripanidkulchai, 1984; Hurley et al., 1991), nucleus solitarius, dorsal vagal motor nucleus (cranial parasympathetic neurons), nucleus ambiguus (Van der Kooy et al., 1982; Terreberry and Neafsey, 1983; Hurley et al., 1991) and intermediolateral cell column of the spinal cord (preganglionic sympathetic neurons), all receive direct projections from the anterior cingulate region. Together, these important subcortical regions regulate preganglionic outflow of both the sympathetic and parasympathetic nervous system, as well as the special visceral efferent flow to the branchiometric muscles of the larynx and pharynx. As a result of a complex system of afferent and efferent relays, the anterior cingulate cortex is potentially capable of participating in complex visceral responses, through *direct* corticobulbar and corticospinal projections. Taking together the visceromotor and viscerosensory relays of the ventral anterior cingulate region, it is pos-

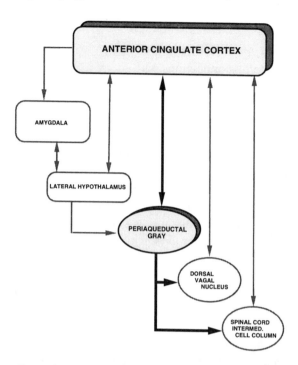

Figure 6.1. Connections of the ventral anterior cingulate cortex related to affective integration. A schematic diagram showing the connections of the *ventral* portion of the anterior cingulate gyrus thought to be involved in the processing of affective experience. As the diagram indicates, this cortical area has extensive reciprocal connections with many subcortical regions, such as the amygdala, lateral hypothalamus, periaqueductal gray, dorsal vagal motor nucleus (parasympathetic neurons) and the intermediolateral cell column of the spinal cord (sympathetic, preganglionic neurons, involved in the mediation of visceromotor and viscerosensory responses). The latter two areas are directly involved in the regulation of almost all parasympathetic and sympathetic responses, respectively, that occur in the thorax and abdomen. The outflow from the anterior cingulate region to the periaqueductal gray results in an inhibitory effect on the response to a noxious stimulus.

sible to conceptualize how the "feeling" component of emotion is integrated at the cortical level. In a state of fear, tachycardia, peripheral vasoconstriction, pupillary dilatation, and gastrointestinal motility could theoretically be modulated through this brain area. Alternatively, in a state of satisfaction, slowing of the heart rate, vasodilatation, and relaxation of the abdominal viscera can also be mediated and/or integrated through the ventral anterior cingulate cortex via its known connections (see Figure 6.1).

Dorsal anterior cingulate cortex

Like its ventral portion, the dorsal aspect of the anterior cingulate gyrus also has complex connections with many different regions, including the dorsomedial nucleus of the thalamus (Groenewegen, 1988; Groenewegen et al., 1990). Unlike the ventral anterior cingulate cortex, the latter nucleus is the only source of thalamic afferents to the dorsal division. Through the dorsomedial nucleus, the dorsal anterior cingulate region receives *indirect* inputs from the globus pallidus and substantia nigra pars reticulata, two key components of the extrapyramidal motor system. It is also connected with brain regions involved in oculomotor and visual processing, including indirect visual inputs from the superior colliculus via the dorsomedial thalamic nucleus and direct reciprocal relays with associative visual cortex. The outflow of the dorsal portion of anterior cingulate cortex carries impulses to several locations, including the dorsolateral quadrant of the periaqueductal gray, the superior colliculus, and the brain stem reticular formation (Domesick, 1969; Leonard, 1969; Beckstead, 1979; Wyss and Sripanidkulchai, 1984). The connectivity of the cingulate gyrus with the superior colliculus and visual association cortex forms possible channels through which attentional responses are mediated.

It seems reasonable to speculate that the connections of the dorsal anterior cingulate region with the visual cortex and the superior colliculus are well-suited to play a key role in attentional responses (Figure 6.2). The fact that this brain area also relays with the periaqueductal gray might further suggest that limbically related behaviors might play some role in the attentional responses associated with the dorsal division of the anterior cingulate cortex. As discussed below, the periaqueductal gray is believed to be pivotally involved in the "medial pain system" (Vogt et al., 1993).

Functional considerations of the anterior cingulate cortex

The functions of the ventral and dorsal portions of the anterior cingulate cortex deduced from the anatomic relationships just described have received further support from stimulation and ablation studies in rodents and primates and observations in human subjects. These findings are reviewed below for both the affective behaviors and at-

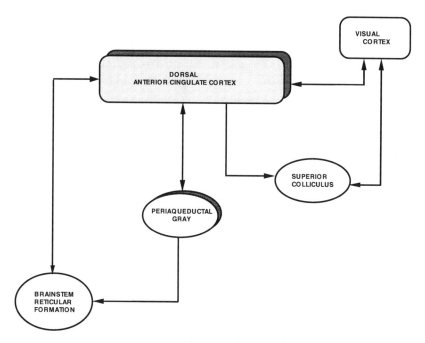

Figure 6.2. Connections of the dorsal anterior cingulate cortex related to selective attention. A schematic diagram showing the connections of the *dorsal* portion of the anterior cingulate gyrus thought to play a role in selective attention. As the diagram indicates, this region has extensive connections with the visual cortex, superior colliculus, periaqueductal gray and brain stem reticular formation. The loop of connections with the visual cortex and superior colliculus probably play an important role in coordinating the movement of the eyes toward an object of interest, while the connections with the periaqueductal gray and reticular formation may integrate such responses with visceromotor responses.

tentional responses attributed to the ventral and dorsal subdivisions, respectively, of the anterior cingulate regions (Neafsey et al., 1993).

Visceral and affective responses

Electrical stimulation of the cingulate region in monkeys is associated with a variety of visceromotor responses including lid opening, pupillary dilatation, respiratory movements, cardiovascular changes, piloerection (Kaada et al., 1940; Smith, 1945; Anand and Dua, 1956), and changes in facial expression (Smith, 1945). Interestingly, a decrease of affective responsiveness was noted in monkeys receiving extensive ablations of the cingulate gyrus (Ward, 1948). In cats, dilated pupils, bizarre posturing, and even "personality" changes, including inappropriate purring or growling without provocation, have been observed with cingulate lesions (Kennard, 1955). In human subjects, bilateral infarction of the cingulate gyrus has been associated with behavioral changes, such as docility and indifference (Laplane et al., 1981). This diminished emotional responsiveness may be similar to the anergia and blunted affect seen in schizophrenia (Damasio and Van Hoesen, 1983). Individuals with cingulate infarctions have also been described as developing a syndrome called *akinetic mutism*, a unique state in which an affected individual neither speaks nor moves. In this neurological equivalent of catatonia, subjects report having no "feelings" and, in their absence, losing the desire to speak or move (Damasio and Van Hoesen, 1983). Akinetic mutism illustrates the integral coupling of affect with motivation, and the loss of volition seen in patients with this syndrome may occur as a result of a diminished outflow from the cingulate area to the prefrontal cortex (Benes, 1993). Although most individuals with cingulate infarctions eventually recover, some have been left with permanent and disabling personality changes. In humans with documented seizure activity arising from the cingulate cortex (Devinsky and Luciano, 1993), emotional stimulation is a frequent precipitant of ictal activity (Mazars, 1970), and the majority of such patients exhibit limbically related features such as temper tantrums and organic psychoses (Mazars, 1970). In one reported case, a child with cingulate seizures was noted to run toward her mother during ictal episodes (Geier et al., 1977).

Attentional responses

Electrical stimulation of the anterior cingulate region in laboratory animals is associated with orienting movements of the head and eyes (Hall and Lindholm, 1974; Sinnamon and Galer, 1984; Neafsey et al., 1986), similar to those seen during attentional responses. In monkeys, lesions of the anterior cingulate region result in arrest of motor activity (Smith, 1945; Dunsmore and Lennox, 1950) and neglect of surrounding objects, even cage mates (Glees et al., 1950). In these animals, the neglect observed can be so profound that lesioned animals may walk into and even over other monkeys. A similar neglect syndrome has also been reported in cats with cingulate lesions (Kennard, 1955). In human subjects, bilateral infarction of the cingulate gyri is associated with a lack of attentiveness to the surrounding environment (Laplane et al., 1981). When subjects are asked to select a relevant semantic target without actually performing the act of saying a word, activation of cerebral blood flow in the anterior cingulate cortex, but not the supplementary motor area, is observed (Posner et al., 1988). Interestingly, there is a much greater change in blood flow in this region when the task involves choosing from *many* potential targets, rather than a few. When a target is detected, there appears to be a strong interference that reduces the likelihood of detecting a simultaneous target (Posner et al., 1988). The attentional responses associated with metabolic activation of the anterior cingulate area are particularly striking during semantic processing of words. Although activation of the anterior cingulate region is observed, this target detection system is probably mediated by the supplementary motor area. These two regions have been termed the "anterior attention system" (Posner et al., 1988); however, there is also a "posterior attention system" involving the parietal and occipital areas that is thought to play a role in pattern recognition rather than in target detection (Posner and Peterson, 1990).

When normal human subjects perform a Stroop attentional conflict paradigm, a robust activation of the anterior cingulate region is found (Pardo et al., 1990); however, when schizophrenic subjects perform the same task, the response to targets is much slower, particularly in the right visual field. Overall, schizophrenic subjects show attentional defects similar to those observed in individuals with left hemispheric lesions (Posner et al., 1988). It is noteworthy that abnormalities of smooth pursuit eye movements have also been observed in both schizophrenic subjects and their first-degree relatives (Holzman et al., 1988). The defects of conjugate eye movements described in schizophrenia could theoretically involve reciprocal connections between the cingulate cortex and front eye field 8, but direct connections between these regions have not been found (Benes, 1993). Such behavioral responses also may be more likely to involve connections of the anterior cingulate region with the visual cortex, superior colliculus (see above), and possibly even the supplementary motor area.

The interplay between affect and attention

Because schizophrenia commonly involves abnormalities of both affect and attention, a common pathophysiological mechanism could be localized in both the dorsal and ventral divisions of the anterior cingulate cortex. While the anterior cingulate region seems to play a key role in both affective and attentional functions, these behaviors are not exclusively processed in this region. For example, human subjects with lesions of the frontal or parietal regions also show both neglect syndromes and affective disturbances (Mesulam and Geschwind, 1978), although, as discussed above, the parietal area is part of the "posterior attention system" involved in pattern recognition (Posner and Peterson, 1990). Although attentional and affective disturbances can occur with lesions of other cortical areas, the anterior cingulate region is the only cortical area having direct subcortical connections that can play an integral role in the mediation of both attentional and affective responses. In conceptualizing this dual specialization of the anterior cingulate cortex, we can image that a subject who is attending to a stimulus will do so in proportion to the intensity of an associated affective response. In other words, if we have strong feelings about something, we are more apt to take note of it.

The pivotal role of the anterior cingulate cortex in mediating affect and attention probably emerged in the course of phylogenesis. As reptiles evolved into mammalian forms, a distinctive behavioral adaptation, separation behaviors with respect to young offspring, also appeared (MacLean, 1985). In rodents, specific ultrasonic vocalizations are emitted by pups during separation and are audible to their mothers. Once a mother hears such a vocalization, she will attempt to find and retrieve the displaced pup. It can be argued that the dual mediation of target detection and affective responsiveness by the cingulate gyrus is particularly adaptive for separation behavior because the perception of losing an offspring by a mother gives rise to not only a selective attentional response, but also a fear reaction. Both of these behaviors contribute to the retrieval of the pup. While the cingulate gyrus has evolved in parallel with the appearance of maternal protection of young mammals, this region has probably come to play a much broader role in integrating emotional responses with other cortically mediated behaviors requiring detection of specific targets (see above).

Findings in the anterior cingulate cortex in schizophrenia

Several recent studies have reported that there are significant histopathologic changes in the anterior cingulate cortex of schizophrenic brain. The first in this series of investigations demonstrated reductions in the density of neurons in the prefrontal, anterior cingulate and primary motor cortex of a schizophrenic group (Benes et al., 1986). The cingulate area showed the least difference between normal and schizophrenic subjects; however, a subsequent study suggested that more robust differences might be present in a particular neuronal subtype. Using a standard cell counting approach, a reduction in the density of nonpyramidal (interneurons), but not pyramidal neurons (projection cells) was observed in the anterior cingulate cortex of schizophrenic subjects when compared to normal controls (Benes et al., 1991). The differences in the density of interneurons occurred in most laminae, but layer II showed the most striking changes. Although there are many different types of interneurons in the cortex, gamma aminobutyric acid (GABA)-ergic inhibitory cells are most common and are functionally of greatest importance to normal cortical integration (Jones, 1987). If GABAergic neurons were indeed missing in schizophrenics, this might give rise to a compensatory up-regulation of $GABA_A$ receptor binding activity in the anterior cingulate region of individuals with schizophrenia, particularly in layer II, where the reduction in the density of interneurons was greatest.

To test the hypothesis of upregulated $GABA_A$ activity, a high resolution technique for localizing receptor binding activity on individual neuronal cell bodies (Young and Kuhar, 1979) was adapted to human postmortem cortex (Benes et al., 1989). As hypothesized, a marked increase of specific $GABA_A$ receptor binding was observed in the anterior cingulate region of schizophrenic subjects (Benes et al., 1992b). Consistent with the cell counting results, neuronal cell bodies in layer II of this region showed the greatest increase, with the binding activity being 84% higher in schizophrenics than in normal controls ($p = .001$). It is noteworthy that neither the reduced density of interneurons (Benes et al., 1991) nor the increased $GABA_A$ receptor binding (Benes et al., 1992b) appeared to be related to the effects of neuroleptic drug exposure, because young schizophrenics with either minimal or no exposure to these agents had findings similar to those for older drug-treated patients.

In a parallel series of studies, it appeared that a second abnormality might also be present within the anterior cingulate region of schizophrenics. One such study had suggested that clusters of neurons identified in layer II of this region might be smaller in size and separated by wider distances in schizophrenic patients (Benes and Bird, 1987). Prompted by the report that bundles of associative axons course vertically toward layer I of primate prefrontal cortex (Goldman-Rakic, 1981), the cluster data seemed to fit best a model in which increased numbers of vertical axons were envisioned as filling the space between neuronal aggregates in layer II as they course toward layer I of schizophrenic subjects. To test the hypothesis that schizophrenics might have larger bundles of vertical axons filling the wider spaces in layer II, an immunocytochemical method for localizing the neurofila-ment protein 200k (NFP200) subunit of cytoskeletal proteins in axons of human postmortem cortex was developed (Majocha et al., 1985). Using this method to compare the density of both vertical and horizon-tal axons in normal and schizophrenic subjects, the results suggested that patients with schizophrenia might indeed have a higher density of vertical, but not horizontal, axons in the anterior cingulate region (Benes et al., 1987). The vertical orientation of these fibers and their localization in superficial laminae was consistent with the idea that the fibers showing increases in schizophrenics might be associative af-ferents to the cingulate region. In a follow-up study using the same technique, an increase of vertical axons was again found in the cingu-late, but not the prefrontal, area of schizophrenics (Benes, 1993).

More recently, monoclonal antibodies raised against a glutamate-glutaraldehyde conjugate have been used to visualize vertical pro-cesses in superficial laminae of the anterior cingulate cortex. With this approach, it was found that the density of glutamate-containing verti-cal fibers with a small caliber (axons) was markedly increased (78%; $p = .0025$) in schizophrenic subjects when compared to normal con-trols (Benes et al., 1992a). Glutamate-immunoreactive fibers with a large calibre, presumably apical dendrites of pyramidal neurons, showed only a slightly higher density in the patient group. No increase of these fibers was found in the prefrontal area of schizophrenics (see above). As noted for the density of interneurons and specific $GABA_A$ receptor binding (see above), young schizophrenics with little or no neuroleptic exposure showed a similar increase in the density of glutamate-immunoreactive axons.

An integrative model for the anterior cingulate in schizophrenia

The microscopic studies of the anterior cingulate cortex of schizo-phrenics described above have suggested that there may be two separate defects affecting the circuitry of this region. On the one hand, there may be a reduction of inhibitory activity, while on the other, there may be an increase of excitatory inputs to superficial laminae. Both changes would be associated with an increase of pyramidal cell firing not only in layer II, but in deeper laminae as well, because of the considerable vertical integration that occurs within all cortical regions. For this latter reason, it is likely that alterations in layers I and II will produce secondary changes in layer V and, to a lesser extent, in layer VI. As Figure 6.3 shows, there are three different ways in which vertical intracortical integration would be affected within the anterior cingulate region as well as the prefrontal area with which it is extensively interconnected (refer to Figure 6.3: Normal circuit).

1. Ascending associative afferents course toward layer I (Figure 6.3–1A), where they form excitatory axospinous connections with apical dendrites of pyramidal neurons from both superficial and deep laminae (Conti et al., 1988). Some corticocortical axons that travel in a rostrocaudal direction originate in layer V (Galaburda and Pandya, 1983).
2. Pyramidal neurons in layers II, III, and VI of the anterior cingulate region all send apical dendrites in a straight vertical course toward layer I, where they receive afferent input from other cortical areas, intralaminar thalamic nuclei, and brain stem monoaminergic systems (Figure 6.3–2).
3. Pyramidal cells in layers II and III give off collateral axons (Figure 6.3–3) in layer V (Valverde, 1985). All of these cells are affected by inhibitory interneurons within layer II, either through axosomatic synapses on pyramidal cell bodies in layer II itself, or through axodendritic synapses on apical dendrites of pyramidal cells in deeper laminae (Figure 6.3–4).

Together, these three different types of vertical connectivity help ensure that the activities of various layers are functionally integrated by coordinating the outflow of activity from pyramidal neurons at different levels. It is noteworthy that there is a basic dichotomy regarding the termination sites for pyramidal neurons in the superficial and deep laminae. Pyramidal neurons in layers II and III project preferentially to other cortical areas, while those in layers V and VI send axons predominantly to subcortical sites (Jones, 1984). With regard to deeper laminae, pyramidal cells in layer VI generally project to the thalamus, while those in layer V send an efferent flow to the

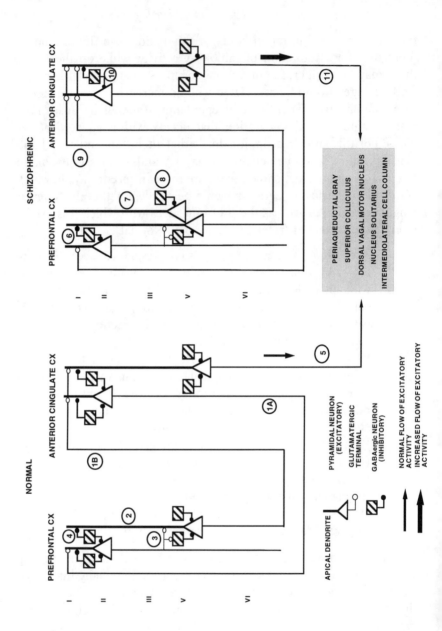

NORMAL

ANTERIOR CINGULATE CX

PREFRONTAL CX

ANTERIOR CINGULATE CX

PREFRONTAL CX

I

II

III

V

VI

PERIAQUEDUCTAL GRAY
SUPERIOR COLLICULUS
DORSAL VAGAL MOTOR NUCLEUS
NUCLEUS SOLITARIUS
INTERMEDIOLATERAL CELL COLUMN

APICAL DENDRITE

PYRAMIDAL NEURON
(EXCITATORY)

GLUTAMATERGIC
TERMINAL

GABAergic NEURON
(INHIBITORY)

NORMAL FLOW OF EXCITATORY
ACTIVITY

INCREASED FLOW OF EXCITATORY
ACTIVITY

Figure 6.3. Model for alterations of anterior cingulate connectivity in schizophrenia. A model diagram showing a set of connections between the prefrontal and anterior cingulate cortices of normal and schizophrenic brain.

Normal Circuit: Refer to appropriate numbers in diagram and below.
1. Pyramidal neurons in superficial (II and III) laminae send glutamatergic axons downward in a vertical direction to exit and course toward other cortical regions.
   A. An associative fiber from the anterior cingulate region is shown traveling in a *caudorostral* direction to the prefrontal area where it then courses vertically toward layer I.
   B. Some pyramidal neurons in layer V of the prefrontal area probably send axons in a *rostrocaudal* direction toward the anterior cingulate cortex.
2. Pyramidal neurons in layers II, III (not shown), and V send long apical dendrites vertically toward layer I.
3. Some pyramidal cells in layer II give off collateral branches in layer V, where they may interact with other pyramidal cells and/or GABAergic interneurons.
4. GABAergic neurons in layer II form axosomatic inhibitory synapses with pyramidal neurons in layer II, but also form inhibitory synapses with apical dendrites of pyramidal cells from many different laminae, including layer V.
5. Pyramidal neurons in layer V of the anterior cingulate cortex send a descending outflow to subcortical limbic regions including the periaqueductal gray, superior colliculus, dorsal vagal motor nucleus, nucleus solitarius, and intermediolateral cell column.

Schizophrenic Circuit: The same basic elements as described above for normals are depicted as being present in schizophrenics; however, there are two basic differences in the distribution of these intrinsic elements with respect to one another.
6. The proposed reduction of GABAergic interneurons in layer II of the prefrontal cortex would result in diminished inhibitory effects on pyramidal neurons in layer II and apical dendrites in layer I.
7. The increased number of pyramidal neurons in layer V of the prefrontal area would also send an increased complement of apical dendrites up to layer I.
8. Interneurons were not found to be diminished in number in layer V of the prefrontal cortex, but preliminary studies are showing that GABA$_A$ receptor binding is nevertheless increased significantly. If pyramidal cells are increased in number (see #7), but the number of interneurons is unchanged, there could be a *relative* decrease in inhibitory input to the pyramidal neurons of layer V.
9. Associative fibers originating in layer V of the prefrontal cortex travel in a rostrocaudal direction toward layer I of the anterior cingulate region, but there are more pyramidal cells in this lamina (Benes et al., 1992a) and therefore more glutamatergic fibers (Benes et al., 1992a).

(*Continued on next page*)

141

Caption to Figure 6.3. *(cont.)*

10. There is a decreased density of interneurons (Benes et al., 1991) and increased $GABA_A$ receptor binding activity (Benes et al., 1992b) in layer II of both the prefrontal and anterior cingulate region of schizophrenics. The putative decrease of GABAergic neurons in layer II would result in diminished inhibitory influences exerted on pyramidal cell bodies in layer II and apical dendrites of pyramidal cells in superficial and deep laminae.

11. The changes described in #6–10 above would give rise to a net increase in firing of pyramidal cells in layer V of the prefrontal cortex to layer I of the anterior cingulate region. The latter would produce excitation of apical dendrites from pyramidal neurons in layer II and V. The decrease of inhibitory activity in layer II of the anterior cingulate region would contribute further to this increase of firing for pyramidal cells in layers II and V. Moreover, the firing of layer II pyramidal cells would in turn generate collateral excitation in layer V.

Recent evidence suggests that there may be a reduction of GABAergic inhibitory activity in layer II, but not layer V, of the anterior cingulate cortex (Benes et al., 1991; 1992b). This would result in diminished inhibitory influences exerted on (a) pyramidal cell bodies in layer II and (b) distal apical dendrites of pyramidal cells in layers II and V. In layer V of the prefrontal area, while there is no reduction in the number of inhibitory interneurons (#8), an increase in the density of pyramidal cells (#8) has been found (Benes et al., 1991), resulting in a *relative* decrease in the overall amount of inhibitory influence exerted on layer V pyramidal cells. The outflow of associative activity from the prefrontal to the anterior cingulate cortex (#9) of schizophrenic brain would be increased by an overall increase in the number of such axons passing toward layer I, but also by the relative decrease of inhibitory influence exerted on these same cells. Overall, these changes would increase the firing of pyramidal cells in layers II and V of the anterior cingulate cortex and produce changes in both affective and attentional responses mediated through its connections with the amygdala, lateral hypothalamus, periaqueductal gray, superior colliculus, dorsal vagal nucleus, intermediolateral cell column, and nucleus solitarius (see text for details).

corpus striatum, superior colliculus, and brain stem (Jones, 1984). In the visual cortex, pyramidal neurons of layer V are particularly apt to send axons to the superior colliculus (Sefton et al., 1981) as part of a loop that integrates visual information with conjugate eye movements. In the cingulate cortex, layer V pyramidal cells are probably the principal source of efferent flow to subcortical loci, such as the amygdala, nucleus accumbens, lateral hypothalamus, periaqueductal gray, nucleus ambiguus, dorsal vagal nucleus, nucleus solitarius, and the intermediolateral cell column of the spinal cord (Figure 6.3–5). It is important to note that some corticocortical fibers, particularly those that travel in a rostrocaudal direction, originate in layer V (Galaburda and Pandya, 1983; see Figure 6.3–1B).

Implications for the anterior cingulate cortex of schizophrenics

As noted above, the defects that have been detected in the anterior cingulate region of schizophrenic subjects are most striking in superficial laminae; however, with the vertical integration that normally occurs in the cortex, it is likely that functional alterations are transmitted to deeper laminae, particularly layer V (see Figure 6.3). Inhibitory basket neurons located in layer II form axosomatic synapses with pyramidal cell bodies within layer II itself (Figure 6.3–6), but also form axodendritic synapses with distal dendritic branches of pyramidal cells (Figure 6.3–4), (Vogt, 1991). Since pyramidal neurons in layer V, like those in layers II and III, send apical dendrites toward layer I (Valverde, 1985), it is likely that most of these cells are affected by a decrease in the activity of GABAergic interneurons in layer II (Figure 6.3–10). Moreover, one study showed a paradoxical increase in the density of pyramidal neurons in layer V of the prefrontal cortex of schizophrenia (Benes et al., 1991), while other preliminary data are showing an upregulation of $GABA_A$ receptor binding activity (unpublished data) on an otherwise unchanged number of nonpyramidal cells (Benes et al., 1991). These later findings might suggest that there is a *relative* decrease of GABAergic input to the pyramidal neurons in layer V of the prefrontal area of schizophrenics (Figure 6.3–8) which would further promote the firing of the latter cells. Since some pyramidal neurons of layer V of this region give off associative axons that travel in a rostrocaudal direction (Galaburda and Pandya, 1983, p. 197), there could be an increased excitatory influence on the apical dendrites of pyramidal neurons from layers II,

III, and V found in layer I of the anterior cingulate cortex of schizophrenics (Figure 6.3–9). Taken together, a reduction in inhibitory
activity arising from a loss of GABAergic neurons in layer II and an
increased associative input to layer I could result in increased firing of
pyramidal neurons, not only in this layer but also in layer V.

Overall, the decreased inhibitory activity and increased excitatory
activity postulated to occur in superficial laminae of the anterior cingulate cortex in schizophrenics would likely influence the efferent
outflow not only from pyramidal neurons of layers II and III to other
cortical areas, but also from those in layer V to the various subcortical
regions in which they terminate.

Behavioral implications

The findings in the anterior cingulate cortex described above raise
some important questions concerning the pathophysiology of schizophrenia. The model in Figure 6.3 predicts that schizophrenics would
have excessive excitatory outflow from the anterior cingulate region to
subcortical centers that mediate autonomic responses involved in affective experience. To conceptualize the impact of the proposed
change, it is useful to consider the primary motor system for which
corticospinal fibers originating from pyramidal neurons in layer V
project directly to alpha motor neurons in the spinal cord anterior
gray and produce excitatory responses (Preston and Whitlock, 1961).
This descending system also interacts with inhibitory interneurons
involved in the regulation of motor neuron activity at spinal levels
(Jankowska et al., 1976). While the physiological influences of corticobulbar and corticospinal fibers arising from the anterior cingulate
region have not as yet been defined as clearly as those for the motor
cortex, it is reasonable to assume, for the sake of this discussion, that
some similarities in these relationships might exist. If so, then it might
be assumed that an increased outflow of activity from pyramidal neurons in layer V of the anterior cingulate cortex might hypothetically
result in an intensified autonomic response in visceral end organs.
This possibility, however, seems contrary to the situation observed in
schizophrenics, where there is usually a reduction or absence of visceral sensations. One way to explain this potential discrepancy is by
postulating that the illness might involve an increased outflow of
glutamatergic activity to brain stem and spinal levels, but one that
eventually causes an excitotoxic injury to postsynaptic neurons. Such

a mechanism could theoretically eliminate neurons needed for the relay of visceral information and could account for the loss of affective experience in individuals with schizophrenia. An argument against this idea, however, is that schizophrenic patients who recover from their illness, like some treated with the atypical antipsychotic agent clozapine, can experience the return of the visceral component to emotional experience (personal observation). Such a clinical phenomenon might suggest that the circuitry needed for the integration of visceral information with cognitive processes remains intact while being subjected to a chronic inhibitory influence. At first glance, this idea seems to be contrary to the speculative model presented here.

Let's assume for the moment that the proposed increase of outflow from the anterior cingulate region to brain stem and/or spinal levels might paradoxically play a role in inhibiting, rather than exciting, visceral sensations associated with emotion. A precedent for this idea can be found in the medial pain system in which the cingulate cortex plays an integral role (Vogt, 1993). This system mediates "affective responses to noxious stimuli" via the relay of spinothalamic activity through midline and intralaminar nuclei to the anterior cingulate cortex (Vogt et al., 1993). The relay of stimuli concerned with pain travels from the thalamus to layer I of the anterior cingulate region (Vogt et al., 1993) where it can cause an excitation of pyramidal neurons in cortical layers II, III, and V (see above). Since pyramidal cells in layer V in turn project to the periaqueductal gray of the midbrain (Figure 6.3–11) (Neafsey et al., 1993), they are able to send excitatory impulses to a subcortical limbic region which is known to exert potent descending inhibitory influences through an enkephalin-mediated mechanism (LeBars et al., 1979). The periaqueductal gray has extensive connections with both the hypothalamus and the brain stem reticular formation, regions through which significant modulatory influences on visceromotor and viscerosensory activity emanate. Thus, it is quite conceivable that stimulation of outflow from the anterior cingulate region to the periaqueductal gray could inhibit not only autonomic responses associated with a noxious stimulus, but also those that occur in the setting of other emotional experiences.

In rodent experiments in which noxious stimulation was used to excite neurons in the periaqueductal gray, the simultaneous stimulation of the medial prefrontal area, a homologue of the anterior cingulate region, abolished the response to noxious stimulation (Vogt et al., 1993). If such a paradigm could be applied to human brain, an increased flow of excitatory activity from pyramidal neurons in layer V of the anterior cingulate cortex to the periaqueductal gray (Figure 6.3–11) could be responsible for a tonic inhibition of visceral responses modulated through the latter region. In this setting, the subcortical limbic circuitry downstream from the anterior cingulate region could essentially be intact in a schizophrenic. This model could potentially explain how an individual who has not experienced affect consciously for many years might be able to do so when a descending excitatory influence on an inhibitory mechanism is eliminated.

A similar model may perhaps be applied to the attentional deficits seen in schizophrenia. Although the central mechanisms involved in attention are not well understood, it is likely that conjugate eye movements of both a voluntary and involuntary nature play a key role in attentional responses.* Toward this end, layer V pyramidal neurons of the anterior cingulate that project to the superior colliculus (Figure 6.3–11) may play a role in conjugate eye movements that occur during attentional responses. Interestingly, a defect in smooth pursuit eye movements described in schizophrenic subjects and their first-degree relatives (Holzman et al., 1988) could involve such a mechanism. Accordingly, a general increase of pyramidal neuron outflow from layer V of the anterior cingulate region to the superior colliculus could conceivably result in abnormal tracking of moving objects.

Conclusions

This chapter has discussed a conceptual framework for understanding how affective responses and selective attention might be rendered abnormal by alterations of intrinsic circuits within the anterior cingulate cortex of schizophrenics. Both these functions are mediated through the ventral and dorsal divisions, respectively, of this region and involve a complex outflow of activity to many different subcortical regions throughout the central nervous system. While only one brain region implicated in this disorder has been primarily discussed here, it is likely that schizophrenia involves intrinsic alterations in many other cortical, and possibly even subcortical, regions as well. A detailed understanding of the organization of intrinsic cortical circuits and their interactions with distal projection sites in normal and

---

* See Chapter 18, by Anne Sereno, this volume – Eds.

schizophrenic brain will contribute significantly to our understanding of this complex disorder.

References

Allen, G. V., Saper, C. B., Hurley, K. M., and Cechetto, D. F. 1991. Organization of visceral and limbic connections in the insular cortex of the rat. *J. Comp. Neurol.* 311:1–16.

Anand, B. K., and Dua, S. 1956. Circulatory and respiratory changes induced by electrical stimulation of the limbic system (visceral brain). *J. Neurophysiol.* 19:393–400.

Baleydier, C., and Maugiere, F. 1980. The duality of the cingulate gyrus in monkey. Neuroanatomical study and functional hypothesis. *Brain* 103:525–554.

Beckstead, R. M. 1979. An autoradiographic examination of corticortical and subcortical projections of the mediodorsal-projection (prefrontal) cortex in the rat. *J. Comp. Neurol.* 184:43–62.

Benes, F. M. 1989. Myelination of cortical-hippocampal relays during late adolescence: Anatomical correlates to the onset of schizophrenia. *Schizophrenia Bulletin* 15:585–594.

Benes, F. M. 1993. The relationship of cingulate cortex to schizophrenia. In B. A. Vogt, and M. Gabriel, eds., *The Neurobiology of Cingulate Cortex and Limbic Thalamus.* Boston: Birkhauser.

Benes, F. M., and Bird, E. D. 1987. An analysis of the arrangement of neurons in the cingulate cortex of schizophrenic patients. *Arch. Gen. Psychiat.* 44:608–616.

Benes, F. M., Davidson, J., and Bird, E. D. 1986. Quantitative cytoarchitectural studies of cerebral cortex of schizophrenics. *Arch. Gen. Psychiat.* 43:31–35.

Benes, F. M., Majocha, R., Bird, E. D., Marrotta, C. A. 1987. Increased vertical axon numbers in cingulate cortex of schizophrenics. *Arch. Gen. Psychiat.* 44:1017–1021.

Benes, F. M., Vincent, S. L., and SanGiovanni, J. P. 1989. High resolution imaging of receptor binding in analyzing neuropsychiatric diseases. *Biotechniques* 7:970–979.

Benes, F. M., McSparren, J., Bird, E. D., Vincent, S. L., and SanGiovanni, J. P. 1991. Deficits in small interneurons in prefrontal and anterior cingulate cortex of schizophrenic and schizoaffective patients. *Arch. Gen. Psychiat.* 48:996–1001.

Benes, F. M., Sorensen, I., Vincent, S. L., Bird, E. D., and Sathi, M. 1992a. Increased density of glutamate-immunoreactive vertical processes in superficial laminae in cingulate cortex of schizophrenic brain. *Cerebral Cortex* 2:503–512.

Benes, F. M., Vincent, S. L., Alsterberg, G., Bird, E. D., and SanGiovanni, J. P. 1992b. Increased GABA-A receptor binding in superficial layers of cingulate cortex in schizophrenics. *J. Neurosci.* 12:924–929.

Bleuler, E. 1952. *Dementia Praecox or the Group of Schizophrenias.* New York: International Press.

Cameron, N. 1938. Reasoning, regression and communication in schizophrenics. *Psychol. Monogr.* 50:1–33.

Cannon, W. B. 1929/1970. *Bodily Changes in Pain, Hunger, Fear and Rage. An Account of Recent Researchers into the Function of Emotional Excitement.* 2nd ed. College Park, MD: McGrath.

Conti, F., Fabri, M., and Manzoni, T. 1988. Glutamate-positive corticocortical neurons in the somatic sensory areas I and II of cats. *J. Neurosci.* 8:2948–2960.

Damasio, A. R., and Van Hoeson, G. W. 1983. Emotional disturbances associated with focal lesions of the limbic frontal lobe. In *Neuropsychology of Human Emotion*, K. M. Heilman and P. Satz, eds. New York: Guilford Press, pp. 85–110.

Detre, T. P., and Jarecki, H. G. 1971. *Modern Psychiatric Treatment.* Philadelphia: Lippincott, pp. 108–116.

Devinsky, O., and Luciano, D. 1993. The contribution of cingulate cortex to human behavior. In *The Neurobiology of Cingulate Cortex and Limbic Thalamus*, B. A. Vogt and M. Gabriel, eds. Boston: Birkhauser.

Domesick, V. B. 1969. Projections from the cingulate cortex in the rat. *Brain Res.* 12:296–230.

Dunsmore, R. H., and Lennox, M. A. 1950. Stimulation and strychnization of supracallosal anterior cingulate gyrus. *J. Neurophysiol.* 13:207–213.

Ekman, P., Levenson, R. W., and Friesen, W. V. 1983. Autonomic nervous system activity distinguishes among emotions. *Science* 221:1208–1210.

Galaburda, A. M., and Pandya, D. N. 1983. The intrinsic architectonic and connectional organization of the superior temporal region of the rhesus monkey. *J. Comp. Neurol.* 221:169–184.

Geier, S., Bancaud, J., Talairach, J., Bonis, A., Szikla, G., and Enjelvin, M. 1977. The seizures of frontal lobe epilepsy. A study of clinical manifestations. *Neurology* 27:951–958.

Glees, P., Cole, J., Whitty, W. M., and Cairns, H. 1950. The effects of lesions in the cingula gyrus and adjacent areas in monkeys. *J. Neurol. Neurosurg.* 13:178–190.

Goldman-Rakic, P. 1981. Development and plasticity of primate frontal association cortex. In *The Organization of the Cerebral Cortex*, F. O. Smith, ed. Cambridge: MIT Press, pp. 69–100.

Groenewegen, H. J. 1988. Organization of the afferent connections of the mediodorsal thalamic nucleus in the rat, related to the mediodorsal-prefrontal topography. *Neuroscience* 24:379–431.

Groenewegen, H. J., Berendse, H. W., Wolters, J. G., and Lohman, A.H.M.

1990. The anatomical relationship of the prefrontal cortex with the striopallidal system, the thalamus and the amygdala: Evidence for a parallel organization. In *The Prefrontal Cortex: Its Structure, Function and Pathology*, H.B.M. Uylings, C. G. Van Eden, J.P.C. De Bruin, M. A. Comer, and M.G.P. Feenstra, eds. Amsterdam: Elsevier; also published in *Progress in Brain Research* 85:147–166.

Hall, R. D., and Lindholm, E. P. 1974. Organization of motor and somatosensory neocortex in the albino rat. *Brain Res.* 66:23–38.

Holzman, P. S., Kringlen, E., Matthysse, S., Flanagan, S., Lipton, R., Cramer, G., Levin, S., Lange, K., and Levy, D. L. 1988. A single dominant gene can account for eye tracking dysfunctions and schizophrenia in offspring of discordant twins. *Arch. Gen. Psychiat.* 45:641–647.

Hurley, K. M., Herbert, H., Moga, M. M., and Saper, C. B. 1991. Efferent projections of the infralimbic cortex of the rat. *J. Comp. Neurol.* 308:249–276.

Jankowska, E., Padel, Y., and Tanaka, R. 1976. Disynaptic inhibition of spinal motoneurones from the motor cortex in monkey. *J. Physiol* 258:467–487.

Jones, E. G. 1984. Laminar distribution of cortical efferent cells. In *Cerebral Cortex*, A. Peters and E. G. Jones, eds. New York: Plenum, pp. 521–548.

Jones, E. G. 1987. GABA-peptide neurons in primate cerebral cortex. *J. Mind Behav.* 8:519–536.

Kaada, B. R., Pribram, K. H., and Epstein, J. A. 1940. Respiratory and vascular responses in monkeys from temporal pole, insula, orbital surface and cingulate gyrus. *J. Neurophysiol.* 12:347–356.

Kennard, M. A. 1955. The cingulate gyrus in relation to consciousness. *J. Nerv. Ment. Dis.* 121:34–39.

Kita, J., and Kitai, S. T. 1990. Amygdaloid projection to the frontal cortex and striatum of the rat. *J. Comp. Neurol.* 298:40–49.

Kushel, L. A., and Van der Kooy, D. 1988. Visceral cortex: integration of the mucosal senses with limbic information in the rat agranular insular cortex. *J. Comp. Neurol.* 270:39–54.

Laplane, D., Degos, J. D., Baulac, M., and Gray, F. 1981. Bilateral infarction of the anterior cingulate gyrus and of the fornices. *J. Neurol. Sci.* 51:289–300.

LeBars, D., Dickenson, A. H., and Besson, J. M. 1979. Diffuse noxious inhibitory controls (DNIC). I. Effects on dorsal horn convergent neurones in the rat. *Pain* 6:283–327.

Leonard, C. M. 1969. The prefrontal cortex of the rat. I. Cortical projection of the mediodorsal nucleus. II. Efferent connections. *Brain Res.* 12:321–343.

Levenson, R. W., Ekman, P., and Friesen, W. V. 1990. Voluntary facial action generates emotion-specific autonomic nervous system activity. *Psychophysiology* 27:363–384.

MacLean, P. D. 1985. Brain evolution relating to family, play and the separation cell. *Arch. Gen. Psychiat.* 42:405–417.

Majocha, R., Marotta, C., and Benes, F. 1985. Immunostaining of neurofilament protein in human post-mortem cortex. A sensitive and specific approach to the pattern analysis of human cortical cytoarchitecture. *Canad. J. Biochem.* 63:577–584.

Mazars, G. 1970. Criteria for identifying cingulate epilepsies. *Epilepsia* 11:41–47.

McGhie, A., and Chapman, J. 1961. Disorders of attention and perception in early schizophrenia. *Brit. J. Med. Psychol.* 34:103–116.

Mesulam, M.-M., and Geschwind, N. 1978. On the possible role of neocortex and its limbic connections in the process of attention and schizophrenia: Clinical cases of in attention in man and experimental anatomy in monkey. *J. Psychiat. Res.* 14:249–259.

Neafsey, E. J., Bold, E. L., Hass, G., Hurley-Gius, K. M., Quirk, G., Sievert, C. F., and Terreberry, R. R. 1986. The organization of the rat motor cortex: A microstimulation mapping study. *Brain Res. Rev.* 11:77–96.

Neafsey, E. J., Terreberry, R. R., Hurley, K. M., Ruit, K. G., and Frysztak, R. J. 1993. Anterior cingulate cortex in rodents: Connections, visceral control functions and implications for emotion. In B. A. Vogt, and M. Gabriel, eds., *The Neurobiology of Cingulate Cortex and Limbic Thalamus.* Boston: Birkhauser.

Papez, J. W. 1937. A proposed mechanism of emotion. *Arch. Neurol. Psychiat.* 38:725–743.

Pardo, J. V., Pardo, P. J., Janer, K. W., and Raichle, M. E. 1990. The anterior cingulate cortex mediates processing selection in the Stroop attentional conflict paradigm. *Proc. Natl. Acad. Sci., U.S.A.* 87:256–259.

Posner, M. K., Early, T. S., Reisman, E., Pardo, P. J., and Dhawan, M. 1988. Asymmetries in hemispheric control of attention in schizophrenia. *Arch. Gen. Psychiat.* 45:814–821.

Posner, M. I., and Peterson, S. E. 1990. The attention system of the human brain. *Ann. Rev. Neurosci.* 13:25–42.

Preston, J. B., and Whitlock, D. G. 1961. Intracellular potentials recorded from motoneurons following precentral gyrus stimulus in primate. *J. Neurophysiol.* 1961; 24:91–100.

Ruit, K. G., and Neafsey, E. J. 1990. Hippocampal input to a "visceral motor" corticobulbar pathway: an anatomical and electrophysiological study in the rat. *Exp. Brain Res.* 82:60–616.

Saper, C. B. 1985. Organization of cerebral cortical afferent systems in the rat. II. Hypothalamocortical projections. *J. Comp. Neurol.* 210:163–173.

Schacter, S. 1971. *Emotion, Obesity and Crime.* New York: Academic Press.

Sefton, A. J., McKay-Sim, A., Baur, L. A., and Cottee, L. J. 1981. Cortical projection to visual centers in the rat: An HRP study. *Brain Res.* 215:1–13.

Sinnamon, H. M., and Galer, B. S. 1984. Head movements elicited by electrical stimulation of the anteromedial cortex of the rat. *Physiol. Behav.* 33:185–190.

Smith, W. D. 1945. The functional significance of the rostral cingula cortex as revealed by its responses to electrical excitation. *J. Neurophysiol.* 8:241–255.

Terreberry, R. T. 1985. An anatomical and physiological investigation of the infralimbic region of the rat medial frontal cortex. Doctoral dissertation, University of Chicago.

Terreberry, R. R., and Neafsey, E. J. 1983. Rat medial frontal cortex: A visceral motor region with a direct projection to the solitary nucleus. *Brain Res.* 278:245–249.

Valverde, F. 1985. The organizing principle of primary visual cortex in the monkey. In *Cerebral Cortex,* vol. 3, A. Peters and E. G. Jones, eds. New York: Plenum Press, pp. 207–258.

Van der Kooy, D., McGinty, J. F., Koda, L. Y., Gerfen, C. R., and Bloom, F. E. 1982. Visceral cortex: Direct connections from prefrontal cortex to the solitary nucleus in the rat. *Neurosci. Lett.* 33:123–127.

Van Groen, T., and Wyss, J. M. 1990. Extrinsic projections from area CA1 of the rat hippocampus: Olfactory, cortical, subcortical and bilateral hippocampal formation projections. *J. Comp. Neurol.* 302:215–258.

Vogt, B. A. 1991. The role of layer I in cortical function. In *Cerebral Cortex* vol. 9, A. Peters and E. G. Jones, eds. New York: Plenum Press, pp. 49–80.

Vogt, B. A., Sikes, R., and Vogt, L. 1993. Anterior cingulate cortex and the medial pain system. In *The Neurobiology of Cingulate Cortex and Limbic Thalamus,* B. A. Vogt and M. Gabriel, eds. Boston: Birkhauser, pp. 313–344.

Ward, A. A. 1948. The cingula gyrus: Area 24. *J. Neurophysiol.* 11:13–23.

Wyss, J. M., and Sripanidkulchai, K. 1984. The topography of the mesencephalic and pontine projections from the cingulate cortex of the rat. *Brain Res.* 293:1–15.

Young, W. S., and Kuhar, M. J. 1979. A new method for receptor autoradiography: (3H) opioid receptors in rat brain. *Brain Res.* 179:225–270.

Zeng, D., and Stuesse, S. L. 1991. Morphological heterogeneity within the cingulate cortex in rat: A horseradish peroxidase transport study. *Brain Res.*

Development

7

Editor's introduction: Methods in the developmental study of madness

Jerome Kagan

The history of scientific disciplines is marked by one or more theoretical transformations that were made possible by the introduction of novel sources of evidence. Physics provides the best examples. The invention of apparatus that permitted measurements of the varied energy profiles emitted by different forms of matter motivated the creation of quantum mechanics and new conception of both the infinitesimal space of the atom and the near infinite expanse of the cosmos. The invention of the amplifier, electrode, and chemical stains for neurons provided surprising information about the brain that required concepts very different from those used by nineteenth-century scholars.

Developmental psychology and the psychology of personality have not often enjoyed the extraordinary advantages of new sources of evidence. The primary data in most studies of the development of personality and pathology remain verbal replies, spoken in interviews or written on questionnaires, that rely on the nontechnical language of everyday conversation. The use of physiological data, direct behavioral observations, or performance on specialized laboratory procedures is relatively rare in developmental studies. Even in psychiatric nosology, referential meanings of diagnostic categories are usually restricted to phenomenological information. The concept *social phobia*, for example, means that a patient has told a clinician that he experiences severe discomfort when he has to meet new people, avoids such social situations as much as possible, and, in addition, is unhappy with this aspect of his life.

Some readers may wonder why this state of affairs is a problem. What other evidence should a clinician use to diagnose social phobia, or a developmental psychologist use to categorize anxious children?

The problem with relying on such a restricted base of information is that each category consists of a heterogeneous group of individuals who have arrived at their symptom or personality profile through a varied combination of life histories and biological vulnerabilities. Discovery of these subtypes would enrich understanding of personality development and personality disorders, just as in nosology it would presumably lead to more effective treatment for each of the subcategories within the larger group. One can interpret the fact that a particular drug treatment helps only a proportion of anxious (or depressed) patients to mean that the diagnostic category is etiologically heterogeneous.

An analogy to infectious diseases may be helpful. The etiologies of malaria, influenza, tuberculosis, cholera, and hepatitis are relatively well understood. Each disease is a qualitative category defined by a distinct profile of consciously experienced symptoms together with features (signs) that cannot be detected from the patient's report of symptoms. The verbal reports of patients with any one of these diseases often include references to feelings of fatigue, fluctuations of body temperature, headache, muscular pain, diarrhea, or loss of appetite. A physician who did not know the fundamental causes of the disease – a situation analogous to the current state of affairs in the diagnosis of anxiety disorder or depression – would be forced to rely on the patient's reports and would probably invent categories like fatigue syndrome or fever syndrome. This is exactly what ancient physicians did. However, fatigue can accompany any one of the five infectious diseases; hence, the addition of other evidence is necessary in order to arrive at a more exact diagnosis. Most patients who complain of fatigue have neither malaria nor hepatitis. If the analogy between infectious diseases and current personality disorders is appropriate, patients who report high anxiety belong to a variety of different etiological groups. Supplementary evidence must be gathered in order to discover them.

Our laboratory has been following several longitudinal samples of children from infancy to late childhood. Only a proportion of older children who are described by their parents as extremely shy and fearful show the temperamental characteristics of high sympathetic arousal early in life, extreme fearfulness in the first two years, and low level of smiling and laughter when interacting with unfamiliar adults. The remaining children do not show these characteristics. These children belong to a qualitatively different group.* If developmental psychologists gathered physiological data or other laboratory measurements, in addition to parental reports, they probably would make more meaningful classifications.

A reasonable reply to this critique is that scientists have not yet invented laboratory procedures that could provide the new clarifying evidence. There is no agreement on which procedures should be added to the traditional corpus of information. Although it is true that psychiatrists and psychologists do not possess methods as sensitive as a blood test for the malarial parasite, some procedures are beginning to offer initial promise.

Consider the possible utility of three procedures that could aid in the classification of anxious subjects. First, impaired recall memory is a frequent characteristic of children or adults who are experiencing anxiety. Subjects who report anxiety but do not show impairment of recall memory are potentially different from those who do show the impairment. That fact provides an initial clue to a useful categorization.

Second, the Stroop interference procedure is potentially useful. Some veterans of the Vietnam War with post-traumatic stress disorder showed delayed response times in naming the colors of words that are symbolic of war. Thus, subjects who report anxiety but do not show interference to symbols representing possible sources of anxiety are potentially different from those who do show interference.

Finally, the central nucleus of the amygdala is necessary for display of potentiated startle which, in humans, is measured by the latency and magnitude of the blink reflex to a bright light or a loud sound that is preceded by a threatening picture. Subjects who report anxiety but do not show potentiation of the blink reflex to varied threatening scenes are potentially different from those who do. It is likely that tests of recall memory, Stroop interference, and potentiated startle would be useful supplements to the diagnostic interview in differentiating among subjects who report high anxiety, just as a blood test differentiates among patients who report extreme fatigue.

One important reason why additional evidence will be helpful is that the English language is not very good at making fine distinctions in either the intensity or the quality of emotions like anxiety, fear, or

---

* See also Chapter 12, by Jerome Kagan, this volume – Eds.

sadness. The English language has many more words to distinguish among closely related colors or shapes than words that differentiate among shades of the same feeling state. Perhaps that is because the visceral information from heart, gut, and muscles that is one important basis for emotional states does not synapse on the basolateral area of the amygdala, whereas visual and auditory information do. It is the basolateral area that communicates directly with the cerebral cortex. The observer has to infer the intensity and quality of psychic anguish from the subject's limited vocabulary. Because these verbal descriptions of emotional states are usually unable to capture fine distinctions in a category of feeling, they are like the view of a highway from an airplane that distinguishes automobiles from trees but cannot discriminate among the various brands of cars.

The restricted basis for classification also affects research strategy, and conclusions about the heritability of personality and psychiatric categories. Almost all research on the heritability of anxiety and depression uses only patient reports to arrive at standard diagnostic classifications. Scientists perform elegant statistical analyses on these data to arrive at estimates of the variance attributable to genes and to the environment for each diagnostic category. However, if the self-reports are, as we claim, analogous to reports of fatigue, the heritability coefficients apply to symptoms with varied etiologies and are not estimates of the heritability of the more fundamental traits.

To illustrate, suppose that a patient's report of feeling anxious with strangers is analogous to a complaint of fatigue. The intensity and chronicity of reported fatigue will depend on whether the patient was exposed to a pathogen for malaria, cholera, or hepatitis, the competence of the patient's immune system, and regimens of diet and rest. A study of fatigue in twins would probably find greater similarity between monozygotic (MZ) than between dizygotic (DZ) twins and scientists would conclude that fatigue was heritable. But that fact would not tell investigators about the heritability of the underlying causes of the fatigue.

MZ twins are more likely than DZ twins to be together in varied circumstances, to have similar diets and regimens, have similar risks of exposure to a pathogen, and, in addition, to have more similar immune resistance to infection. If the only data available are reports of fatigue, scientists will not be able to assign accurate estimates of the differential variance attributable to genes and environment.

A similar conclusion applies to anxiety and depression when the only data are self-reports of symptoms. Many scientists who study the heritability of pathology make three assumptions in order to implement the most popular mathematical analyses. First, MZ and DZ twins are presumed to be similar with respect to exposure to environmental influences relevant for the disorder. However, it is likely that MZ twins believe they are inherently more similar to each other compared with DZ twins. Thus, if one sibling learns that her MZ sister is feeling extremely anxious, that knowledge is likely to cause the second member of the twin pair to brood about her own level of anxiety and to conclude that she, too, is feeling anxious. This degree of similarity in affect states is not easily assignable to either shared or unshared environmental influences for it is due to a private belief held by the sibling. If MZ twins believe they are more similar to each other than DZ twins, the equal environmental assumption is flawed.

Second, each diagnostic category, or dichotomous trait, is usually assumed to rest on a latent, continuous liability to illness that is normally distributed in the population. The complaint of feeling anxious may be normally distributed, but it is far less obvious that vulnerability to an excitable limbic system – a possible basis for some anxiety disorders – is normally distributed. Our research suggests that only 20% of healthy infants are born with low thresholds of excitability in the amygdala and its projections.

Finally, most heritability analyses assume, first, that the effects of genes and environment are linearly additive and, second, that there is no interaction between these two influences. These assumptions are obviously incorrect for the fatigue that accompanies malaria. Some African-Americans inherit a sickled red blood cell that protects them against the malarial infection. Most Caucasians do not inherit this trait and, as a result, Caucasians are more likely to contract malaria if they live in a tropical climate, but unlikely to do so if they live in North America. There is an obvious interaction between genes for sickled red blood cells and environmental exposure to the malarial parasite, and neither the genes nor the parasite are normally distributed. Further, the genes for sickling and exposure to the pathogen are not linearly additive.

Similarly, it is unlikely that the vulnerability to the autonomic surge that is characteristic of patients with panic disorder, perhaps due to a specific neurochemistry in the medulla, is normally distributed in the population. It is more likely that a threshold of excitability must be passed before the autonomic surge will be felt in consciousness.

A related problem with current heritability estimates of environmental variance is that they are given in the absence of any direct, valid measures of the environment. The variance assigned to the environment is inferred, indirectly, from the differences between the correlations for MZ and DZ twins. The difference between MZ and DZ twins in reports of fatigue could not provide a valid estimate of the contribution of the environment to a malarial infection, because the reports are influenced, first by the personal criteria used to decide when one is feeling tired, as well as by regimens of diet, rest, differential life stress, and the competence of the individual's immune system to deal with the pathogen. The difference in the magnitude of the correlations between MZ and DZ twins is unable to separate the variance associated with each of the factors. Given these problems, it is unlikely that the currently popular statistical analysis applied to twin and sibling data can discover the degree of heritability of the more basic categories of personality disorder and mental illness in a given population.

It is hoped that the next cohort of investigators will expand the sources of evidence used in the study of personality development and deviance, and gather direct information on the environment, so that more informative conclusions about the role of experience in psychopathology can be declared. The chapters in this section make a substantial beginning.

8

Developmental psychopathology: From attribution toward information

Sheldon H. White

As we generally conceive of developmental psychopathology, it encompasses a number of more or less discrete and clearly defined disabilities of behavior, just as is the case for adult psychopathology. On the one side, children manifest disabilities coming from a clear and distinct physical source; the disabilities are of a kind most likely to be found in all times and cultures. On the other side, developmental psychopathology includes problems of disturbance and maladjustment that arise from the peculiar situation of children and youth growing up in twentieth-century American society. While one can, in the abstract, easily characterize these two broad sources of childhood problems, it is still no easy matter to confront a particular child in trouble and to find causes, sources, and points of address for that trouble.

During the twentieth century, theory and practice in developmental psychopathology have moved steadily away from the "disease model" framework and toward transactional models that address the stresses and risks entailed in the growing child's adjustment to family, school, peers, and community. We deal in this chapter with only the first slow, awkward steps in the development of a body of American conceptions and understanding of childhood psychopathology – from the turn of the century, when any and all problems of children might be attributed to the dark shadow of degeneracy, to the early 1930s, when the beginnings of significant research on children began to give a less dogmatic, more informed, more complex and more confusing picture of children and their problems. Research is not supposed to build confusion, of course. It is supposed to find pattern and order and, if we are to believe some of the more lyrical accounts, elegant simplicities in nature. Sometimes research brings us toward beautifully simple formulae. Sometimes, if the phenomena being addressed are complicated, research can be useful by helping us to respect that complexity.

It is my assumption that the development of an organized, coherent, cooperative research program is a much more sustained and fumbling process than historical stories generally make it out to be. It takes a while for individuals to commit themselves to the imagined possibility of a research program, to find resources, to obtain social support and cooperation, to hit upon interesting methods and problems, to build a body of methodology, and gradually to build an agreed-upon collective representation of what-we-are-all-doing-here-together. What goes on looks like the growth of knowledge as it is envisaged in Donald Campbell's (1988) evolutionary epistemology. *After* a scientific group has solved its early organizational problems, the collectivity achieves a coherent representation of itself and the individuals within become able to see themselves as sharing an ideal past and ideal future. Members can then construe their shared goals, responsibilities, and scientific possibilities by tracing a path between the two. Now a scientific history exists, wedded to the group's vision of the human meaning of its enterprise. The history and the vision are part of the same intellectual construction; change one and you change the other. This kind of mature vision of the history of developmental psychopathology is to be found in an excellent recent article by Cicchetti (1990). In this chapter, I try to trace through some of the prehistory that made possible the development of that vision.

That person-in-situation disorders form an important component of childhood psychopathology is not unlike the situation in adult psychopathology. In the nineteenth century, changing patterns of occupation and social life in the United States and England brought forth a sea of middle-class physical and mental disabilities variously named "nervous breakdown," "nervous collapse," "shattered nerves," "neurasthenia," "nervous weakness," "neurosis," and "functional nervous disorder" (Lutz, 1991; Oppenheim, 1991). Beard, Mitchell, and other nineteenth-century neurologists argued that social mobility was a significant factor in bringing on such disorders. Drawing upon anthropological writings (Van Gennep, 1961; Turner, 1969), Lutz (1991) has argued that "American nervousness" gave middle-class Americans a "ritual space," a moratorium, freeing nineteenth-century men and women from normal social demands and expectations while they moved from one social position to another. During the twentieth century, every effort has been made to differentiate "American nervousness" into a set of clear and distinct diagnostic categories, but at present the question of an exact taxonomy of adult mental disorders still remains troublesome (e.g., Wakefield, 1992).

All the difficulties adults face are shared, and in certain respects compounded, in the case of children. For adults, attributions of psychopathology are usually founded on presenting disabilities or symptoms. But many behaviors or conditions of small children that are not obviously pathological are nevertheless characterized that way because adults see in them the seeds of future disturbance. Without a doubt, there is real meaning to the notion of predisposing or risk factors in childhood. Yet longitudinal, birth-to-maturity studies of a kind that would allow us to make reasonably solid predictive inferences from childhood circumstances are a novelty of the past few decades.

Historically, American efforts to provide services for children in trouble have not awaited – could not wait for – the discoveries of exact categorizations, sufficient research, or good theory. Toward the end of the nineteenth century, services and professions for children grew in number and kind. Broad, speculative theories arose about *why* all these troubled children were to be found and *why* the needs for service were rising all around. Research programs arose, through surprisingly slow and awkward maneuvering, and through such programs psychologists and psychiatrists struggled to reconcile their conceptions and their practices.

The nineteenth century was, in many respects, a time of considerable change in the pattern of paths, choices, and expectations American society set before growing children. Child labor was, slowly and with difficulty, reduced. More and more children experienced more and more years of schooling. Problems of children were recognized, and all during the nineteenth century services and agencies were being established – orphan asylums, foster care, juvenile courts, homes for the insane, the epileptic, the retarded, the deaf, the blind. The introductory sections of Bremner's (1971) documentary history of children and youth in America offer useful brief essays describing the rising tide of institutional growth. With the new agencies there came new adult occupations dedicated to work with children, new voices in the public arena speaking for children, and a new politics. The "whole child professions" were coming into existence and, at a national level, what is sometimes called "the Children's Cause." The establishment of developmental psychology in universities was part of this movement. The new developmental psychologists participated in the renegotiations of the social contracts among parents, schools, professionals, and government (Siegel and White, 1982; White, 1990) and they provided "philosophies" for educational and therapeutic programs (White and Buka, 1987; White, 1991).

Wiebe (1967) has described the broad reorganization of American society that took place near the turn of this century. The social change brought with it new conceptions of the essential and the ideal in child development, new supports for some age-old problems of children and families, and a rising tide of efforts to cope with problems of children and families that were created or exacerbated by the social change. Services directed toward childhood psychopathology came in as part of all this. There were many actors and agencies. We can identify: (1) In the latter part of the nineteenth century, new institutions for retarded, insane, epileptic, and handicapped children; (2) in the same period, the growth of medical specialties of pediatrics and psychiatry; (3) between 1880 and 1920, the passage of compulsory education laws in all the American states, the emergence of problems of educational retardation and handicap, and the establishment of psychological clinics and special education programs for them; (4) a heightened public concern about juvenile delinquency and, in the 1890s, the establishment of juvenile courts connected to new facilities for diagnosis and treatment; (5) the organization of a first form of developmental psychology in the 1890s and, shortly after, the emergence of a first form of clinical psychology directed toward children; (6) Clifford Beers's founding of the Mental Hygiene Movement in 1906 and, a few years later, following the ideas of Adolf Meyer and the work of William Healy, the formation of the Child Guidance Movement; (7) social reformers (many of the most important ones female) and foundations, pushing, sustaining, and directing programs for child welfare and social reform; and (8) psychoanalysis, not an important influence on American psychology and psychiatry immediately after Freud's 1909 visit, but remaining on the American scene and, after a time, playing a more and more central role in the framing of diagnostic and therapeutic approaches to children's problems.

None of this was absolutely unique to the United States. The industrialized nations marched together, watching one another, in their approaches to health, education, and welfare. In Britain, a similar constellation of forces participated in the development of child psychiatry (Von Gontard, 1988).

G. Stanley Hall's perspective

G. Stanley Hall's writings give us some sense of what all this social change looked like to someone living in the middle of them. Hall led the first American efforts to establish a developmental psychology. He used a systematic program of questionnaire studies to put forward a broad evolutionary theory of child development (White, 1990). As president of Clark University, Hall was a public figure and became more and more involved with the people and institutions dealing with distressed children in American society. Conventional histories of psychology usually picture Hall as an experimental psychologist who moved over into child study, but the evidence is clear that Hall had clinical interests from the beginning of his work as a psychologist. While Hall sat in this country's first chair of psychology at Johns Hopkins, something most psychologists know about, he also served for a time as superintendent of Bayview Hospital for the Insane in the Baltimore area, something very few psychologists seem to know about. When Hall went from Hopkins to Clark University as president, he found Adolf Meyer in Worcester beside him. The two men were friends and collaborators. Clark's Psychology Department was generally understood as a haven for budding psychologists who had clinical interests. In a recent book about child clinics, Helen Witmer (1986) remarks, "There were present . . . in Clark University in the nineties most of the elements of what later grew into the mental hygiene movement."

Hall had begun child study with the belief that the scientific study of child development could guide parents, teachers, and others concerned with the care and education of children. He was one of many at the turn of the century who believed that university-based research and scholarship could guide society. Hall had the opportunity to play a leading role in the building of the modern research university and slowly, standing before the public in his roles as university president and spokesman for scientific child psychology, Hall met his clientele and became aware of its size, diversity, manifold needs, and fervor. Hall convened social welfare conferences at Clark University in 1909 and 1910 (Hall, 1910a, 1910b). At the 1909 conference, he announced the establishment of a Children's Institute, intended to establish a permanent connection between Clark and practical work on child welfare. Rosenzweig (1992) has recently argued that Hall's celebrated invitation to Sigmund Freud and his associates to attend the Clark twentieth-anniversary celebrations in 1909 was part of his effort to place Clark University in the leadership of American welfare work.

Theodate Smith headed the Children's Institute's correspondence department, and her job was to build a picture of the contemporary agencies, professions, and services directing themselves toward children's needs and problems (Diehl, 1991). After extensive reading and correspondence, Smith (1910) found 70 kinds of institution or service directed toward 10 categories of client or problem. Hall reproduces Smith's list (with minor editorial changes) in his 1911 *Educational Problems* and discusses them in two lengthy chapters. One chapter, "Special Child-Welfare Agencies Outside the School," deals with organizations that seek to relieve or moderate evils already existing; the other, "Preventive and Constructive Movements," discusses associations directed toward preventive work. Hall's version of the Smith survey is reproduced in Table 8.1 and is worth a little examination.

The Smith–Hall survey helps us understand the categorizations and goals governing American efforts to deal with children's problems at the turn of this century. Looking at the survey in one way, we can estimate what adults thought the diversity of problems and risks were. Looking at the survey in another way, we can see the conglomerate of institutions, agencies, and "whole child professions" arising to address them. Note that the first three groups of services in Table 8.1 are directed toward defective, delinquent, and dependent children. These were the traditional targets of charities and corrections at that time. Like many of his contemporaries, Hall was pessimistic about what such services might offer to society in the long run. In his view, the spectrum of institutions and services is ominous, a sign of difficult and conceivably intractable societal problems:

Now the worst of this whole sad business is that we are not sure that we are abating many of these evils, and, indeed, most of them seem to be increasing not only absolutely, but relatively to the increase of our population, despite all this labor and expense. . . . Now, if there is a regular percentage of increase in the cases needing treatment by the above agencies, an increase not due merely to better methods of enumeration, and if we cannot stop it, an eighth-grade boy can figure out the number of years it will take for the whole nation to become a hospital and all the morally, mentally, and physically well will have to devote themselves to caring for those born short, arrested, or perverted. This leads me to my first point, which is that we must not interfere too much with natural selection in the human field. If the rate of increase of the best children diminishes and that of the worst increases, the destiny of our land is sealed and our people are doomed to inevitable decay and ultimate extinction. These three Big Ds we deal with, the defectives, delinquents, and dependents, the great Biologos or spirit of life would designate or describe by another adjective big D [most likely Degeneracy] not fit to print or speak, for they are a fearful drag upon our civilization. (Hall, 1911, II, p. 77)

Degeneracy as a source of psychopathology and social problems

Hall understood degeneracy to be a serious, many-faceted source of a good many of the ills of American society, and eugenics to be a major hope of social redemption.[1] He was not alone in this concern. A contemporary *Encyclopedia of Social Reform* (Bliss and Binder, 1908) discussed degeneracy as a possible limiting condition for social reforms:

We . . . consider in this article the causes which tend to lower individual ability and to produce that individual degeneration which makes the individual lower than the norm (de, from, and genus, class or norm), unfitted to play his normal part in life. . . . All forms of unfittedness for life are more or less connected, and pass by degrees from the slightest unfittedness to the extremes of vice, intemperance, and disease. (p. 367)

The article goes on to quote Morel (1857), who is said to have first clearly defined degeneracy. "The clearest notion we can form of degeneracy is to regard it as a morbid deviation from an original type. This deviation, even if at the outset it was ever so slight, contained transmissible elements of such a nature that any one bearing in him the germs becomes more and more incapable of fulfilling his functions in the world; and mental progress, already checked in his own person, finds itself menaced also in his descendants" (p. 367). Morel, writing a year or two before Darwin first published his theory of evolution, conceived of degeneration as a deviation from a primitive perfect type of humankind under the influence of intoxications, bad environments, diseases, moral defects, early insults, or congenital factors.

Table 8.1. *Theodate Smith and G. Stanley Hall: Institutions and services for children in 1911*

Defective Children:
    Institutions for the Blind.
    Institutions for the Deaf (public and private).
    Institutions for the Feeble-Minded (public and private).
    Institutions for Speech Defects.
    Psychological Clinics.

Delinquent Children:
    Big Brothers Movement.
    Institutions for Delinquent Boys.
    Institutions for Delinquent Girls.
    Help for Girls Who Have Gone Wrong.
    Juvenile Courts.
    Psychopathic Institute (Chicago).
    Probation Work.
    Truant Schools.

Dependent and Needy Children:
    Associated Charities.
    Children's Aid Societies (placing-out system).
    Day Nurseries.
    Industrial Schools and Homes.
    Infant Asylums.
    Orphanages.

Hygienic Agencies:
    Fresh-Air Work.
    Milk Commissions and Depots.
    Public Baths and Gymnasiums.
    Society for the Prevention of Tuberculosis.

Moral and Religious Training:
    Church Clubs and Guilds.
    Institutional Churches.
    International Committee on Moral Training.
    Missionary Work.
    New England Watch and Ward Society.
    Purity Associations.
    Society for Ethical Culture.
    Societies for Moral Prophylaxis.
    Sunday Schools.
    Temperance Work.
    Y. M. C. A. (Junior Clubs).
    Y. W. C. A. (Junior Clubs).

Protective Associations:
    Censory Boards for Moving Pictures, etc.
    Consumers' League.
    Child-Labor Committee.

Table 8.1. *(cont.)*

      Humane Societies.
      Juvenile Protective Associations.
      Protective Associations for Girls.
      Societies for the Prevention of Crime.
      Societies for the Prevention of Cruelty to Children.
      Society for the Prevention of Vice (New York).

Recreation:
      Boys' Camps.
      Boys' Clubs.
      Boy Scouts.
      Boyville.
      Children's Libraries.
      Children's Theater.
      Girls' Clubs.
      Park Commissions.
      Playground Associations.
      Shut-In Societies.
      Story-Tellers' League.
      Vacation Schools.

Child-Welfare Movements Connected with Schools:
      Kindergartens.
      Medical Inspection in Schools.
      Open-Air Schools.
      Parents' and Teachers' Associations.
      Public Education Associations.
      School Nurses.
      Teachers' Clubs.

Relief for Sick Children:
      Children's Hospitals.
      Diet Kitchens.
      Dispensaries.
      District Nurses.
      Free Dental Associations.
      Fresh-Air and Convalescent Homes.
      Institutions for Crippled Children.
      Institutions for Nervous and Epileptic Children.

General Welfare Associations:
      Mothers' Congress and Clubs.
      Children's Bureaus.
      Children's Institute (Clark University).
      Child-Welfare Conferences.
      Child-Welfare Exhibit (New York).
      Child-Welfare Survey (Worcester).
      Civic Leagues.
      Stamp-Savings System, Penny Savings, etc.
      Relief and Aid Societies.
      Women's Clubs.

Hall's evolutionary conception of degeneracy was an overlay on another understanding. Another, older conception of degeneracy posed it as an outgrowth of bad living and working conditions:

Degeneracy theory, which was widely accepted by psychiatrists and neurologists between 1860 and 1910, assumed that living things acquired and modified their characteristics in response to their environments, and that these changes were then passed on to their offspring. Unhealthy environments, for example, city slums, or unsound habits of living such as heavy drinking, were believed to produce weakened individuals with morbid predispositions. If the noxious environments and habits were not corrected, symptoms became more severe in each succeeding generation. Nervous temperament in the first generation evolved into emotional disorders in the second, to pauperism, waywardness, or criminality in the third, and finally, to idiocy and extinction in the fourth and last stage of degeneration.

Degeneracy theorists, in contrast to eugenicists, were most concerned with improving social conditions and training persons to live in healthier ways. They, along with many other nineteenth-century commentators, blamed the characteristics of the urban poor on the slum conditions created by modern industrial capitalism, rather than on the innate biological make-up of the poor. To put it more simply, eugenicists believed that people made slums while degeneracy theorists believed that slums made people. (Gelb, 1990, p. 243)[2]

After Darwin, an evolutionary understanding of degeneracy grew. Adolf Meyer (1895–1896/1951), the leading American psychiatrist at the beginning of this century, looked back at the preevolutionary understanding in these terms:

Grown up in the Darwinian movement, we can hardly realize the primitive meaning of the general expression degeneration, as used by the writers who first introduced it. Morel speaks of the existence of a primitive perfect type of the human race; he calls it the master work and sum of creation. . . . Degeneration is for him a pathological deviation from this biblical primitive type, a degradation of the progeny. . . . The originally perfect man has [now] been swept away by the doctrine of evolution. . . . The perfect man of the new school is he who is as free as possible from the characteristic features of phylogenetically less mature types. Everything that reminded strongly of possible ancestors of a lower degree was stamped with the term atavism. (Meyer, 1895–1896/1951, p. 256)

After Darwin, degeneracy was atavistic, a throwback to a less-evolved form of humanity. On the one hand, degeneracy was used to explain the existence of people at the margins of social competence: the dependents, defectives, and delinquents. But self-supporting, intelligent, and law-abiding adults might be judged as degenerate also.

Some early writers, such as Max Nordau in Germany and Cesare Lombroso in Italy, concentrated on higher-order degenerates, men of considerable ability and eminence who nonetheless showed degeneracy through physical and mental stigmata. Nordau had argued that higher-order degenerates dwelling on the borderline between reason and madness showed themselves through physical stigmata such as deformities, stunted growth, or bodily asymmetry and mental stigmata such as lack of moral sense or moral proportion, egoism, impulsiveness, emotionalism, despondency, fear, a tendency toward absent-mindedness, doubts, and curious surmisings as to the causes of the universe, mysticism, and so on.

In his book *The Man of Genius*, the physician Cesare Lombroso (1910/1984) called genius "a degenerative psychosis of the epileptoid group" (p. 359) and listed the signs of degeneration commonly found in men of genius as : (1) smallness of body; (2) "rickets" – to which he associates being rachitic, lame, hunchbacked, or clubfooted; (3) pallor; (4) emaciation; (5) a cretin-like physiognomy; (6) lesions of the head and brain; (7) stammering; (8) left-handedness; (9) sterility; (10) unlikeness to parents; (11) precocity; (12) delayed development; (13) misoneism [dislike of novelty]; (14) vagabondage; (15) unconsciousness and instinctiveness; (16) somnambulism; (17) genius in inspiration [insights or ideas appearing in sudden bursts of illumination]; (18) contrast, intermittence, double personality; (19) stupidity; (20) hyperaesthesia [great sensitivity or sensibility]; (21) peraesthesia [apparent or intermittent anaesthesia]; (22) amnesia [absentmindedness; the ability to become totally absorbed in an activity]; (23) originality; and (24) fondness for special words. Lombroso's inferences about genius-as-degeneracy seem to have been drawn from unsystematic readings of great quantities of biographies of men of eminence. He felt he also saw forms of neurosis and mental alienation in many of those biographies – also chorea and epilepsy; melancholy; megalomania; *folie du doute* [great, crippling hesitancy and some other symptoms seeming akin to obsessive-compulsiveness]; alcoholism; hallucinations; and "moral insanity" [a term much used by psychiatrists in the late nineteenth century, as a supposed source of criminality and lack of feeling or concern for others].[3]

Pedigree studies of pathology

There was something old and something new in late-nineteenth-century conceptions of degeneracy. What was old was the aristocratic idea that there are well-born people and ill-born people. It is the destiny of the well-born people to create the culture, make the laws, and impose them upon the ill-born people; the ill-born people are destined to be regulated and controlled by the well-born people. What was new was the idea that the differentiation between the well-born and ill-born could be understood in terms of biological evolution.

People saw degeneracy as amorphous, apt to express itself in any and all kinds of pernicious symptomatology, and thus able to offer an umbrella explanation of any and all kinds of character flaws or bad behavior. "Degenerates" near the turn of the century had the kind of ubiquity, evil agency, and demonic force possessed by "Communists" in the 1940s and 1950s and "drug pushers" in the 1990s. Supporting this wide-ranging view were pedigree studies seeming to show that diverse kinds of human eminence and quality ran in families, on the one side, and all sorts of viciousness and infirmity showed familial linkages on the other. While Francis Galton (1869/1887, 1874) was publishing his pedigree studies of hereditary genius,[4] Richard Dugdale (1877/1891) published his pedigree study of criminals. Dugdale had been appointed by the New York Prison Association to visit 13 of the state's county jails, and he was struck by the fact that a number of the prison inmates were relatives. He made a genealogical study of a New York State family, the "Jukes" family, showing that one could trace across seven generations and 709 family members streaks of pauperism, illegitimacy, disease, harlotry, prostitution, assault, and thievery.[5]

Although Dugdale's interpretations of his data respected both genetic and environmental causes of crime and disorder, most of his audience fixated on the genetic component. *The Jukes* was widely read as a sermon on the consequences of inferior breeding. Social welfare literature in the nineteenth century often referred to the study in that way, and a series of genealogical studies of the family trees of dependents, delinquents, and defectives that followed it (Danielson and Davenport, 1912; Estabrook and Davenport, 1912; Goddard, 1912) were interpreted in that way. By far the best known was Henry Goddard's (1912) study of the ancestry of a mildly retarded girl, Deborah, at the Institute for Backward Children at Vineland. An ancestor of Deborah's, "Martin Kallikak, Sr.,"[6] had had an illegitimate son with a feebleminded tavern worker, and among the 480 descendants of that union Goddard claimed to find much retardation, dissolution, and disease. Martin had "straightened up and married a respectable girl of good family" and from that union there were 496 direct descendants, all but three of whom Goddard felt had normal or superior intelligence. Goddard argued that low intelligence was a major source of crime and social disorder, and argued for segregation of the retarded – separating them from the breeding population – or sterilization.[7]

The eugenics movement

As most people talked about degeneracy at the turn of this century, the problems it presented to the social order had to be dealt with by eugenic measures – procedures that would identify the well-born and the ill-born, and social programs that would encourage more production of offspring among the well-born and less production among the ill-born.

Now observations of everyday life were linked to a completely evolutionistic vision of degeneracy. Experiences and statistics seemed to picture a social system going awry. Evolutionary biology could be read to say that a looming menace lay behind the signs. G. Stanley Hall's interpretation of his survey of programs for defective, dependent, and delinquent children, quoted above, indicates exactly the deep concern that many Americans felt when so many things seemed to be going wrong in American society. Hall was, all things considered, relatively moderate.

In 1893, Henry M. Boies, a member of the Pennsylvania Board of Public Charities and the State Committee on Lunacy, wrote *Prisoners and Paupers*, in which he reported that between 1850 and 1890 the criminal population had increased 445 percent. Supposed causes of this great upsurge were the freeing of the slaves, immigration, intemperance, and the high fertility of criminal classes. Boies suggested that some people are genetically programmed to be criminals, and reminded his readers that "like begets like" (Reilly, 1991, pp. 9–17). The 1890 census showed that the proportion of idiocy and imbecility had increased in the American population. This kind of statistical increase might have reflected a rising supply of diagnostic and therapeutic facilities; to some, it reinforced fears that the feebleminded, uninhibited, and sensual were incredibly fertile.

Changing institutional and political arrangements reflected these growing concerns. In 1880, the Association of Medical Officers of American Institutions for Idiotic and Feeble-minded Persons changed emphasis from training feebleminded people for participation in everyday life to locking them away in institutions for the rest of their lives (especially females of childbearing age) (Reilly, 1991, p. 14). The Michigan legislature passed a law calling for the castration of all inmates of the Michigan Home for the Feeble-Minded and Epileptic, and of all persons convicted of a felony for the third time. Some proposed extending the law to include individuals committing rape or engaging in perverse sexual activity. There were a number of convergent arguments; a concern for the harmful effects of masturbation,[8] an interest in making inmates more docile, and eugenic considerations (Flood, 1899).

When IQ tests came along, they were (with remarkable ease) accepted as a technology for scientifically differentiating the well-born from the ill-born. Francis Galton in England had tried to create exactly that kind of technology in the Anthropometric Laboratory he established in 1884. But Galton's procedures, put forth as a program of mental testing in the United States by James McKeen Cattell (1890), never proved to be practical. What *were* practical were the alternative tests of Alfred Binet and Theophile Simon in 1905 and 1908. Americans used the Binet and Simon tests, taking them to be Galton's technology. Binet protested against the "brutal pessimism" and "deplorable verdicts" of those who argued that intelligence is a single, hereditarily fixed entity, and he wrote a book two years before his death setting forth a "mental orthopedics" offering exercises designed to raise the intelligence of children (Mann, 1979). But the protests were of no avail. To a remarkable extent, American psychologists co-opted the Binet and Simon instrument for what they saw as the right and proper purpose of an intelligence test, the scientific identification of genius and degeneracy.[9]

In 1916, Lewis M. Terman published the first Stanford–Binet test of intelligence, an enlarged version of the Binet–Simon instrument, standardized on 2,300 American children. Discussing the uses of his test, Terman lists first uses associated with the detection and control of the ill-born. The Stanford–Binet test will: (1) allow for rational placement of retarded school children in special classes; (2) locate the feebleminded and bring them under the surveillance and protection of society. "This will ultimately result in curtailing the reproduction of feeble-mindedness and in the elimination of an enormous amount of crime, pauperism, and industrial inefficiency" (p. 7); and (3) reduce

Table 8.2. *Goddard: Estimates of feeblemindedness in reformatories and institutions for delinquents*

Institution	Percent defective
St. Cloud Minnesota Reformatory	54
Rahway Reformatory, New Jersey (Binet)	46
Bedford Reformatory, New York – under 11 years	80
Lancaster, Massachusetts (girls' reformatory)	60
Lancaster, Massachusetts, 50 paroled girls	82
Lyman School for Boys, Westboro, Massachusetts	28
Pentonville, Illinois, Juveniles	40
Massachusetts Reformatory, Concord	52
Newark, New Jersey, Juvenile Court	66
Elmira Reformatory	70
Geneva, Illinois (Binet)	89
Ohio Boys School (Binet)	70
Ohio Girls School (Binet)	70
Virginia, 3 Reformatories (Binet)	79
New Jersey State Home for Girls	75
Glen Mills Schools, Pennsylvania, Girls' Department	72

delinquency because, Terman says, there is a close association between feeblemindedness and delinquency.[10]

Presumably, Goddard had demonstrated that close association. In 1914, Goddard (1914/1926) reported data that seemed to show that the feebleminded made up an extraordinarily high proportion of inmates of juvenile reformatories and institutions for delinquents (Table 8.2). A version of the Binet instrument had been used in some of these studies, and Goddard reported with some concern that the better the testing instrument the higher the proportion of feeblemindedness it seemed to yield.

In the first decade of this century, some American psychologists thought they had their hands on a scientific instrument that would differentiate the ill-born from the well-born. Psychologists were not the originators of the concept of degeneracy, nor were they the leading scientific sponsors of programs directed toward its control – not at the very beginning, at any rate. American interventions to control the reproduction of the ill-born began in the first decade of this century, just at the time when Binet and Simon were producing their instruments of 1905 and 1908 in France.

Between 1907 and 1912 Indiana, California, New Jersey, Iowa, and Washington passed laws for the sterilization of the feebleminded, the insane, and criminals (Kamin, 1974, pp. 10–11). By 1928, 21 states had enacted such laws. Reilly (1991, pp. 48–49) estimates that a minimum of 3,233 people were sterilized under these authorizations.[11] Between 1914 and 1917, 30 American states enacted new marriage laws or amended older ones. Marriages of idiots and the insane were voidable in three-quarters of the statutes; other states restricted marriages between individuals who were seen as unable to make contracts, or for eugenic reasons (Kevles, 1985). Connected to the eugenic arguments were, of course, immigration laws intended to favor some American subgroups over others. In 1921, Congress passed an emergency immigration restriction act. Immigration from any European country was limited to 3% of the foreign-born of that country in the 1910 census. In the 1924 Immigration Act, quotas were based on the 1890 census. The 1921 and 1924 enactments were designed to favor immigration from Northern Europe.

Charles B. Davenport, who had taught zoology at Harvard and Chicago, set up a Department of Experimental Evolution at Cold Spring Harbor, began collecting family pedigrees, and led a campaign to increase public awareness of eugenic issues and receptiveness to appropriate policies (Davenport, 1911; Kevles, 1985, pp. 144ff.). It is difficult in the 1990s to recapture the hopes and fears eugenic arguments aroused in Americans in the 1920s. "Fitter Families" competitions were held in the "human stock" sections of state fairs. A brochure says: "The time has come when the science of human husbandry must be developed, based on the principles now followed by scientific agriculture, if the better elements of our civilization are to dominate or even survive." Families entering such competitions had to provide information about the health and well-being of their ancestors, with individual members taking a medical examination and an intelligence test. At the 1924 Kansas Free Fair, winning families in three categories – small, average, and large – received a Governor's Fitter Family Trophy, presented by Governor Jonathan Davis, and "Grade A Individuals" won a Capper Medal, named for U.S. Senator Arthur Capper (Kevles, 1985, pp. 61–62).[12]

Hamilton's (1914) review article gives a good sense of what American eugenicism looked like to its proponents at the crest of its scientific influence. There were facts and there was fervor. The fervor lived on for a while. A book written by the Chicago lawyer D. A. Orebaugh in 1929 – *Crime, Degeneracy, and Immigration* – rehearsed the dangers of degeneracy. Degenerates, Orebaugh argued, are not simply the palpably weak and abnormal – idiots, imbeciles, morons, and the like. There are "higher degenerates" whose "higher mental attributes are quite often manifested in literary, artistic and philosophical works of unusual brilliance, but characterized by a want of logical coherence, a lack of balanced judgment and a predilection for the symbolic, the mystical, the bizarre, the esoteric and not infrequently by the erotic." Orebaugh cited as examples of this type Oscar Wilde, Maurice Maeterlinck, Friedrich Nietzsche, Walt Whitman, Edgar Allen Poe, and the contemporary school of Cubist painters.

Between the higher and lower degenerates lies a wide field made up in descending order of near geniuses, brilliant erratics, ne'er-do-wells, epileptics, infantiles , cranks, neurasthenics, neurotics, melancholics, lopsided and single tracked mentalities, paranoid personalities, drug addicts, alcoholics, prostitutes, sexual perverts and inverts, hoboes, bums, morons, monomaniacs, the feeble-minded, imbeciles, idiots and the definitely insane.[13] Truly a vast and motley aggregation of irresponsibles peculiarly susceptible to evil suggestion, distinguished by their congenital inability to fit into the social scheme, from whom our criminals of all types and grades are recruited. They and the problem they present require to be handled with wisdom and firmness by the normal-minded and responsible elements of society. (p. 40)

Orebaugh argued that therapeutically oriented efforts tend to preserve the ill-born, allow or encourage their proliferation, and lead ultimately toward harm for humankind:

Civilization, so-called, particularly in America, has taken out of nature's hands the selection of human materials for the perpetuation of the race, and as a consequence degeneracy, both latent and obvious, has been nurtured and amplified out of its usual ratio to the sane and normal. Nature's methods through a doubtful if not mistaken philanthropy have been reversed or counteracted. The most extraordinary efforts have been expended in the preservation not of the fittest, but of the unfit – the weakling, the defective, the degenerate. By the spread of hygienic knowledge and the multiplication of hospitals, infirmaries, orphan asylums, alms houses and other charitable institutions the propagation and preservation of these have been encouraged and assured – all at the expense of the normal and intelligent classes and with dubious appreciation on the part of the beneficiaries. A vicious circle made up of inferior and decadent humanity has been established whose periphery grows and expands in geometrical ratio, while the numbers of the fit, due to a lesser birthrate, steadily diminish. (pp. 40–41)

Orebaugh attributes to the growth of degeneracy, as by-products, a number of visible signs of decline in the quality of American life: "Yellow Journalism," the disintegration of parental authority, the waning of school discipline, the exaggeration of sex, the growth of American preoccupations with sport and amusements, inebriety and drug addiction, political corruption, the coddling of criminals, and disrespect for law.

Very much in the spirit of Orebaugh's book was a book by the well-known psychologist Carl Murchison (1926), *Criminal Intelligence*, which must set some sort of record for the generation of Draconian public policy recommendations from ambiguous data. Murchison collected Army Alpha test scores for a number of prison populations in the Midwest. His volume presents table after table of data, each table interpreted with admirable circumspection. So interpreted, the tables reveal a variety of murky and hardly very conclusive trends. In the end, with no visible chain of inference, Murchison launches into an attack on "the prevailing fallacy of maternalism" and recommends the abolition of the jury system; uniform punishment for the insane, the feebleminded, and the young; the abolition of release on bond, indeterminate sentences, and parole; and the provision that the third penitentiary conviction carry a death sentence.

There was something more to the early writing about degeneracy and eugenics than simply the development and defense of a scientific program, or what one might think of as lively and heated disputation commonly found between proponents and opponents of a theoretical program. Feelings ran high. The people singled out for discussion – the dependents, defectives, and delinquents – were Others to almost all the discussants, members of what were sometimes called "the dangerous classes" in the preceding century. On occasion, the speculative scientific discussion spilled over into argumentative scientific justifications of assault and murder.

American drumbeating for eugenics died down gradually in the early decades of this century, in part because a growing body of clinical experience and research work challenged the thin web of facts and assumptions on which the movement rested. One indicator of the shifting currents of thought was changes in approach toward the institutionalization of the feebleminded. The first institutions for "idiots" and "cretins" were built following pioneering efforts by Séguin in

France and Guggenbuhl in Switzerland, and reflected a belief that in such institutions appropriate programs for the children could bring about remediation and education. After Darwin, there was more and more belief that institutional inmates – not only the retarded, but the criminal and the insane – were degenerate, and now the institutions were seen as places to confine people who would degrade society (Von Gontard, 1988). In the 1910s, the tide began to turn again. In 1914, Walter Fernald in Massachusetts initiated a program to train feeble-minded youth and to lead them toward industrial jobs. By 1920, 75% of state schools in the United States were placing inmates in industrial occupations (Shea, 1980).

Part of what diminished American interest in eugenicism, perhaps, was the fact that Americans could watch the German nation carrying their very similar eugenicist thinking to horrifying conclusions. Despite the various American legislative enactments permitting castration and sterilization, the actual use of these procedures was limited in the United States because again and again it was found that many Americans wouldn't stand for them. Reilly (1991, p. 97) estimates that 38,087 sterilizations of institutionalized persons were performed in the United States over a period of 34 years. When the Germans passed a sterilization law under the newly elected National Socialists in 1933, they sterilized 150,000 people in the next 18 months. There are charges that the Nazis sterilized 3.5 million people between 1933 and 1945, but records have been destroyed and we will never exactly know (Reilly, 1991, pp. 106–110). But in Germany, of course, sterilization was only the edge of the wedge. The Germans murdered their retarded and insane through programs of involuntary "euthanasia" and proceeded to the Holocaust, all on articulated eugenic grounds, supported and justified by a good many physicians and scientists (Kevles, 1985; Lifton, 1986; Müller-Hill, 1988; Kater, 1989; Lerner, 1992).

Early research on children and their problems

At the very beginning, American psychology was an upper-middle-class enterprise situated in universities serving a managerial and professional clientele, in an era when the rich and the poor stood much farther apart, geographically and psychologically, than they do today. One sign of this distance was the importance of the settlement house movement in the late 1800s and the early 1900s. Settlement houses were places in which well-to-do young people came to live for a while, where they organized family and community services and could see the life of the poor close around them. The first settlement house was Toynbee Hall in England, set in London's East End when that vast region was mysterious and slightly frightening to the well-to-do of the city. Forty years before the founding of Toynbee Hall, an inspector of schools had said: The inner life of the classes below us in society is never penetrated by us. We are profoundly ignorant of the spring of public opinion, the elements of thought and the principles of action among them – these things which we recognize at once as constituting our own social life (Briggs and McCartney, 1984, p. 21). Sir Walter Besant, who often lectured at Toynbee Hall, wrote about the East End: "Perhaps the strangest thing of all is this: in a city of two millions of people there are no hotels; that means, of course, that there are no visitors" (Briggs and McCartney, 1984, p. 20). The Reverend Samuel Thomas Barnett, founder of Toynbee House, hoped to bring young Oxford and Cambridge undergraduates into this terra incognita, saying: "He who has, even for a month, shared the life of the poor, can never rest again in his old thoughts" (Briggs and McCartney, 1984, p. 5).

The settlement houses looked like domestic secular missions at a time when overseas religious missions were still quite numerous. Nowadays, the settlement houses look like significant nuclei of modern social science and the agencies and institutions of the welfare state. Jane Addams founded the first American settlement house, in Chicago in 1889, modeling it after Toynbee Hall. Hull House organized services for the poor and it was also, like Toynbee Hall, a center for research on the life of the poor of the West End around it (Residents of Hull-House, 1895). John Dewey and George Herbert Mead of the University of Chicago were frequent visitors to Hull House, and there seems little question that the brilliant beginnings of social science at the University of Chicago owed much to the earlier Hull House maps and papers.

Former residents of Hull House became leaders in the building of the American welfare state in the early decades of the twentieth century (Muncy, 1991). Jane Addams herself was a prominent and admired figure. Newspaper readers in 1913 voted her the second "most useful" American – after Thomas Edison, but before Andrew Carnegie and Theodore Roosevelt. Not surprisingly, the idealistic young flocked to service in settlement houses. Feuer (1969, p. 339) remarks: "By 1911, it is estimated, 2,500 residents and up to 15,000 volunteers were involved in 413 settlements – the majority of them young college graduates. The percentage of the involved American studentry was far higher in the settlement movement than in the Peace Corps a half-century later."

What American psychologists had to overcome in their consideration of childhood psychopathology was social distance, a lack of firsthand familiarity with the lives of children in trouble. Within the confines of a fast-moving academic career, G. Stanley Hall did what he could to acquire some concrete knowledge about children's problems. While he was at Johns Hopkins, he had served for a time as superintendent of the Bay View Asylum and later, as we have seen, he worked with Theodate Smith toward a detailed and differentiated picture of children in trouble in American society. Being unfamiliar with particularities, he swept the generality of dependents, defectives, and delinquents together under the vague menacing rubric of degeneracy. Clinical work and research work, coming along in the first decades of this century, complicated this simple picture.

Two streams of relatively coherent and organized research on children are to be found in the early decades of this century – the one a clinically based, idiographic, characterological program of studies on children with problems, associated with the mental hygiene and child guidance movements, the other a nomothetic study of developmental sequences, norms, and standards of child development that came to be housed in the institutes and centers of the child development movement. Both streams were begun by individuals living in the intellectual climate of degenerationist and eugenic arguments and, to a degree, subscribing to them. Both streams gradually built a more complex picture of developmental psychopathology and child development.

Clinical studies of children's problems

Lightner Witmer opened a clinic at the University of Pennsylvania in 1896 in which he proposed to practice "psychological orthogenics." Witmer seems to have begun clinical psychology in America and to have provided the first clinical facility opened specifically for children (Smith, 1914; Reisman, 1991). The clinic was reasonably successful in the terms by which most people define success; it was long-lived (Levine and Wishner, 1977) and widely imitated. In 1914, J. E. Wallace Wallin found 70 psychoeducational clinics following in Witmer's footsteps (Chapman, 1988). Yet Witmer and his work have received curiously little recognition. Possibly this was because his work was psychoeducational, directed toward the child in the school rather than the broader body of childhood problems parents and the community have to deal with. Possibly, some of the lack of recognition reflected Witmer's personality. He was a complicated, prickly man who put colleagues off. Levine and Levine (1992, p. 29ff.) offer an excellent discussion of Lightner Witmer and his influence.

Hunter's (1927) account traces the very early growth of medically based clinical facilities for children in trouble – picturing their origin, first, as "psychopathic institutes" attached to courts and serving to mediate the adjustments of the criminal law embodied in the juvenile courts system – subsequently, as child guidance clinics, serving as generalized mental health facilities.[14] The first such institute was the Chicago Juvenile Psychopathic Institute directed by William Healy; the second in 1912 was the outpatient department of the Boston Psychopathic Hospital directed by E. E. Southard; the third in 1913 was the Henry Phipps Psychiatric Clinic at Johns Hopkins under Adolf Meyer; and fourth was Boston's Judge Baker Child Guidance Center, which opened in 1917 with William Healy moving to serve as director. These four clinics rather rapidly worked out elements of a system of treatment which, with generous support from the Commonwealth Fund,[15] was then replicated over and over to form the basis of a nationwide system of 60 child guidance centers by 1942.[16] Horn's (1989) history of child guidance nicely traces through some of the evolutionary process:

The Chicago Institute and Judge Baker were the first facilities designed exclusively for children and for the treatment of juvenile delinquents in particular. By 1921, these provided models of the use of psychiatrist and psychologist as a clinical team and of psychiatric treatment through juvenile courts. Boston Psychopathic and Henry Phipps introduced psychiatric social workers into the clinic team and served the whole community instead of just the juvenile court. Child guidance clinics were based on these models, but the new facilities were novel in their exclusive reliance on the so-called dynamic psychiatry and in their broad integration into their local communities' services for children. (p. 57)

William Healy: Characterology and mental analysis

As director of the very first Psychopathic Institute, attached to the Juvenile Court of the City of Chicago, the young neurologist William

Healy pursued investigations of criminality – focusing his attention on youthful delinquency because of his feeling that adolescence was a strategic point both of origin and of therapeutic access for a great deal of nonyouthful criminality.[17] Healy was supported by a distinguished group of Chicago citizens. Julia Lathrop had played a significant part in organizing Healy's Institute and served as first president of the Institute until she left Chicago to become chief of the newly established Children's Bureau in Washington. An early resident of Hull House, Lathrop was one of a remarkable group of women who would play a leading role in American social reform efforts in the early decades of the twentieth century (Muncy, 1991). James Angell, George Herbert Mead, and Adolf Meyer served on Healy's advisory council, and Jane Addams on his executive committee.

Healy began his work with the generally prevalent assumption that inborn defectiveness was an important source of criminal behavior. Five years studying individual delinquents changed his mind. "Out of deep consideration of hard-won facts this work is produced," he says in opening his report of the work (Healy, 1915/1969, p. 3). An elaborate system of data collection for each case is reviewed – including family history, developmental history, history of the individual's environment, indications of mental and moral development, anthropometry, medical examination – with emphasis on the neurological and psychiatric, psychological testing, and the nature of the individual's delinquency. Procedures for each case included a diagnostic summary, provision for follow-up records, and some subsidiary records. What this thorough, detailed, and patient investigation of delinquents on a case-by-case basis amounted to, he said, may be termed *characterology*. "As students of character, we are dealing with the motives and driving forces of human conduct and, since conduct is directly a product of mental life, we immediately become involved in individual and differential psychology."

Healy's conclusions based upon detailed diagnostic workups of several hundred cases are terse and pointed.

About "born criminals": "The subject of born criminals, which found a main place in a criminology which discussed offenders by putting them in large general classes, can be disposed of by us in a few words. When we come to study cases more fully, we see no reason for maintaining any general notion that there is a class properly designated as born criminals" (Healy, 1915, p. 781).

About moral imbecility (a mainstay of nineteenth-century psychiatric characterizations of criminality): "When we began our work there was no point on which we expected more positive data than on moral imbecility. But our findings have turned out to be negative. We have been constantly on the look-out for a moral imbecile, that is, a person not subnormal and otherwise intact in mental powers, who shows himself devoid of moral feeling. We have not found one" (Healy, 1915, p. 783).[18]

In a later discussion of misconduct and mental conflict Healy (1917) describes the variety of youthful misbehaviors he has confronted:

General troublesomeness and mischief making, including destructiveness; stubbornness, obstinacy, chronic willfulness; truancy; remaining out over night and running away from home; vagrancy; stealing, including patholog-ical stealing . . . ; obtaining money by false representations; forgery, exhibi-tion of bad temper; general violent behavior; deliberate malicious mischief and violence; sexual offenses; cruelty – sadistic offenses; self-injury of the nature of masochistic offenses; injury to others, or attempt to injure." (p. 12)

The understanding of these misbehaviors is to be given by research using a developmental approach:

Concrete findings, rather than theories, have gradually formed the frame-work of our ideas concerning the relationship of mental conflicts to miscon-duct. . . . I would emphasize the most fundamental of facts concerning this subject, namely, that the use of the genetic method opens the way, as nothing else does, to the most formidable attacks upon misconduct. (p. 15)

The general method he uses, Healy says, is usually spoken of as *psychoanalysis* or *the psychoanalytic movement*, but he concedes that he does not follow the strict practices or theories of Freud. A reasonable name for his method, he says in his 1917 book, is *mental analysis*, which he defines thusly: "Mental analysis is a name given to the method of using the memory to penetrate into the former experiences of mental life" (p. 20).[19] The bulk of Healy's book is given to brief discussions of 40 youths brought before the court and reconstructions of the circumstances of their lives that brought them to the problem. He considers in the end, briefly, the question of whether all of these cases may be said to reflect a peculiar constitution of the children involved, heredity, or congenital predispositions. Once more, gently but determinedly, he tugs away from the imputations of the degenera-tionists. In the long run, Healy would turn toward psychoanalysis and co-write a volume on it (Healy et al., 1931).

Reducing the "menace of the feebleminded"

Directly, by careful study of the patterns of behavior of individual delinquents, and indirectly, by challenging some of the broad eugenicist arguments, Healy and other workers in child guidance and mental hygiene redirected American thought about feeblemindedness and social deviance. The findings of Goddard's 1914 survey, noted earlier (see Table 8.2), had been prominent in establishing public beliefs about the danger of the feebleminded to American society. A physician writing in *Mental Hygiene* recalls:

There was a time, a few years ago, when one could explain anything by just saying "feebleminded." It was a wonderful explanation because it seemed to solve so many difficulties. If a child stole, he was feebleminded; if murder was committed, the murderer was feebleminded; if a child did not want to go to school, he must be feebleminded; and if he did go to school and exhibit unpleasant behavior, surely he must be feebleminded. Feeblemindedness was a sufficient explanation of all these things. (Wile, 1926, quoted in Shea [1980], p. 138)

But were the reformatories and jails really brimming with defectives? The Goddard findings had their supporters. But Healy and Bronner reported on 500 delinquent boys and girls at the detention home of the Chicago Psychopathic Institute, finding that only about 10% of them were feebleminded. Subsequently, they studied 2,000 offenders who came before the Chicago Juvenile Courts between 1909 and 1915 and a second sample of 2,000 offenders who came before the Boston courts from 1917 to 1923. Only 13.5% of them were feebleminded (Bronner, 1914; Healy and Bronner, 1926). A remarkable reversal was under way. Study after study pursued the question of the incidence of feeblemindedness and as they did so the observed percentages dropped. Between 1910 and 1914 a median incidence of 50% feeblemindedness was reported for delinquent populations; between 1915 and 1919, 28%; between 1920 and 1924, 21%; and between 1925 and 1928, 20% (Shea, 1980, p. 194). In the end, the incidence of feeblemindedness in prisons and reformatories was found, again and again, to fall within the range of the general population.[20]

If research workers of the early decades of the twentieth century could effectively deflate the "menace of the feebleminded" in the United States, they were less successful in putting forth alternative hypotheses about the meaning of delinquency. Psychoanalysis became popular among American mental health workers in the 1940s and 1950s, I would guess, because mental health workers, like Healy, felt that it offered something like a reasonable intellectual frame for their work. They were encouraged in such use because able exponents of psychoanalysis came to the United States in the 1930s and 1940s, driven here by events in Europe. It would take a substantial amount of research work on normal patterns of child development, its range and variations, before the beginnings of a postpsychoanalytic framework for childhood psychopathology could emerge.

Research programs of the early 1930s

There were two movements in the early 1930s. The psychoanalysis Freud had put forth in his 1909 lectures began to win professional acceptance. As clinical encounters with children wore away the degeneracy thesis, what moved into its place was a growing acceptance of the psychoanalytic model as something that might be useful for understanding and dealing with disturbed children's behaviors. Neither the theory nor the therapeutic approach of orthodox Freudian psychoanalysis was built for children, of course. Clinicians such as William Healy established quasi-psychoanalytic practices. Followers of Freud led by Anna Freud and Melanie Klein put forth theories and practices to initiate what would become in time a large body of work on the psychoanalytic study of the child.[21]

The second movement was more ponderous and slow moving. A second systematic study of children and their development got under way. G. Stanley Hall's questionnaire research program at Clark was, effectively, completed by 1904. Hall sought to establish a Children's Institute at Clark University a few years later, but it was short-lived (Diehl, 1991). A few years later, a more enduring set of institutes and centers began to appear and a second wave of research in developmental psychology got under way. There was a fortuitous conjunction. In 1917, the Iowa state legislature appropriated funds for the establishment of the Iowa Child Welfare Research Station, and in 1918 the Laura Spelman Rockefeller Memorial was established, directed toward projects serving the welfare of women and children. Beardsley Ruml was appointed director. Trained as a psychologist at the University of Chicago, Ruml brought to the foundation a hope shared by a number of American philanthropoids in the 1920s – that the social sciences could be developed to serve as resources for the betterment of social and political conditions of American life.

Under Ruml, Lawrence K. Frank in 1923 began to support a series of child welfare research institutes. He began support to Teachers' College in 1924, Toronto and Minnesota in 1924, Cornell in 1926, and Berkeley in 1927. Frank arrived by the late 1920s at a $600,000-a-year program of subsidies to 30 different agencies and institutions. Some of the support was for research centers (including, interestingly, the Institut Jean-Jacques Rousseau in Geneva, housing the young Jean Piaget in the early stages of his career).

A second wave of research on child development got going in the 1930s. Neither Hall's social-biological theory of child development nor his questionnaire method was sustained. The new researchers on child development began, so to speak, at the beginning. Two new journals were established: *Child Development*, associated with the child development institutes, and the *American Journal of Orthopsychiatry*, serving as an outlet for a growing number of child guidance centers. The journal in which G. Stanley Hall had once published his questionnaire studies, the *Pedagogical Seminary*, continued to appear but it was now largely a vehicle for mainstream psychologists and it had a new name, the *Journal of Genetic Psychology*. No large theory or ideology informed any of these journals. Curiously, this was a time when theories were being set forth in Europe – those of Heinz Werner, Jean Piaget, and L. S. Vygotsky – that would later have a large influence on American developmental psychology. The three American journals traveled light theoretically. They shared a broad belief in biological, maturational mechanisms as forming the backbone of the phenomena of child development.

No one program of research governs *Child Development* between 1930 and 1934. The contents of the journal seem to reveal a number of small collective projects – groups of 10 or more papers directed toward a common scientific or practical objective. Some papers attempt to scale or measure positive features of child development or dimensions of individual differences. These projects are oriented toward tests and measurements. There are studies of better or worse preschool practices, and of the effects of preschooling on children. A good many papers seek to establish norms and sequences of aspects of physical growth, perception, emotional development, or intellectual development. And there are papers directed toward methods and methodology. The work is descriptive and normative. *Child Develop-ment* seems to be at the beginning of an effort to observe and measure the range of the typical in children's development. From such obser-vations, an empirical footing for definitions of psychopathology might be established in time.

During the same 5-year period, the papers of the *Journal of Genetic Psychology* are somewhat less tentative. Again, there are many small projects. A number of scientific interests and projects run beside each other. Some are projects reflected in the pages of *Child Development*, and some are different. *Child Development*'s papers on preschooling are replaced by papers reporting on experimental studies of learning. We are near the historic beginning of the learning theory movement, though the research in the *Journal of Genetic Psychology* is mostly quite atheoretical. Studies of children are largely directed by the intellec-tual framework of traditional comparative psychology. Papers on ani-mal development are mingled among the papers on children, and from time to time there are papers comparing children's development to that of animals. Neither *Child Development* nor the *Journal of Genetic Psychology* pays much attention to childhood psychopathology. Those journals are interested, at best, in the boundaries of the normative and the typical. The *American Journal of Orthopsychiatry* in the same years does deal with psychopathology, of course, but surprisingly little with questions of classification or causation. Much of that journal is given over to the professional roles, activities, and experiences of the people of the child guidance centers – psychiatrists, psychologists, social workers. Where observations of children appear, they are given in case material as taken from the treatment experience. The theoret-ical orientation is loosely psychoanalytic because, of course, neither the patients that are being seen in the child guidance centers nor the therapies that are directed toward them correspond to the clinical encounters from which Freud built classical psychoanalysis.

The hundreds of articles in the 1930s reflect the beginnings of what will be a long, slow growth. The flamboyant images of psycho-pathology set forth at the turn of the century have disappeared. They have been submerged in the details of the many little pieces of "nor-mal science" to be found in the journals of the 1930s. As has often been remarked, there is no large vision of childhood or child develop-ment to be found in those journals. They are "dull." Yet there is a collective empiricism and a body of shared methods and methodology and in time there will arise from this work meaningful new understandings of children's problems and their sources.

Notes

1. Hall was an ardent eugenicist. An enthusiastic article in one of his journals (Hamilton, 1914) probably gives a good reflection of his views.
2. Jordan (1993) gives an excellent history of this older conception of degeneracy as it emerged in England. The concept of degeneracy began not in theory but in everyday observations. People thought they saw degeneration among the working people around them. For example, Peter Gaskell wrote in his *The Manufacturing Population of England* [London: Baldwin and Craddock, 1833] "Any man who has stood at twelve o'clock at the single narrow door-way, which serves as the place of exit for the hands employed in the cotton-mills, must acknowledge, that an uglier set of men and women, of boys and girls, taken them in the mass, it would be impossible to congregate in a smaller compass. Their complexion is sallow and pallid – with a peculiar flatness of feature, caused by the want of a proper quantity of adipose substance to cushion out the cheeks. Their stature low – the average height of four hundred men, measured at different times, and different places, being five feet six inches. Their limbs slender, and playing badly and ungracefully. A very general bowing of the legs. Great numbers of girls and women walking lamely or awkwardly, with raised chests and spinal flexures. Nearly all have flat feet . . ." (Quoted in Jordan, 1993, p. 9).
3. Note that a peculiar tug-of-war about geniuses was taking place near the turn of this century, with men such as Lombroso terming them degenerates while others such as Francis Galton considered them to be in the advance guard of human evolution. Lewis Terman's longitudinal study of highly intelligent California children in the twentieth century seems to have been an attempt to settle this argument once and for all. Terman obviously favored Galton's position.
4. Galton (1869/1887) argued that the selection of men according to their status and reputations is reasonably equivalent to the selection of men according to their natural gifts. Beginning with lists of distinguished lord chancellors, judges, statesmen and premiers, commanders, literary men, men of science, poets, musicians, painters, divines, Senior Classics at Cambridge, oarsmen, and wrestlers, Galton looked for eminent family members. Of 977 eminent men, 415 (42%) had eminent relatives, leading Galton to conclude that great human ability "breeds true." Subsequently, Galton and Schuster (1906) began with a discussion of "noteworthiness" and an argument that being noteworthy

is an index of ability. Letters were sent to 467 members of the Royal Society and 207 of them sent back usable replies. There was a substantial number of noteworthy relatives.

5. In contrast to some contemporary studies of genetic factors in behavior, Dugdale's pedigree studies led him to conclude that the environment is ultimately the controlling factor for criminal behavior. "From the above considerations, the logical induction seems to be, that environment is the ultimate controlling factor in determining careers, placing heredity itself as an organized result of invariable environment. The permanence of ancestral types is only another demonstration of the fixity of the environment within limits which necessitate the development of typal characteristics" (Dugdale, 1877/1891, p. 66). To control crime, Dugdale recommends differentiated systems of incarceration for different kinds of criminals, education, and improved upbringing. "Thus public health and infant education conforming, in general plan, to Froebel's Kindergarten school, are the two legs upon which the general morality of the future must travel" (p. 119).

6. Greek: *kalos* = "good," *kakos* = "bad."

7. Goddard's integrity has been questioned because the photographs he used in his account of the Kallikaks were retouched. But Fancher (1987) has pointed out that such retouching may have been fairly common at that time and not necessarily deceptive or malign in intent.

8. Von Gontard (1988) writes about a variety of drastic methods used by British physicians to try to reduce masturbation in the 19th century. Bremner (1971, Vol. 2, pp. 855–856) quotes from a report of F. Hoyt Pilcher, Superintendent of the Asylum for Idiotic and Imbecile Youth in Topeka, Kansas, who castrated 11 inmates who were confirmed masterbators. "Five parents only have visited the institution since those operations were performed, and after observing the marked improvements in the boys above mentioned, gave me a written request to operate on their boys at my earliest convenience, and I believe that every parent in the state of Kansas who has children here, and having their welfare at heart, as I believe they nearly all have, would, after examining into the condition of those boys operated on, and observing the improvement in their condition, request the same treatment extended to their boys."

9. Interestingly, French usages of intelligence testing during the first four decades of this century were quite different from American usages (Schneider, 1992).

10. The remainder of the uses listed by Terman were to: (4) help the schools to recognize, and to respond appropriately to, children of superior intelligence; (5) assist in assigning children to appropriate school

grades; (6) help determine vocational fitness; and (7) serve as a standard for research on the factors determining educability and mental development.

11. Reilly's book is very carefully done and his quantitative estimate is, by far, the lowest I have seen in a half-dozen sources.

12. Ten years earlier, Hamilton (1914) had reported somewhat skeptically on an earlier effort. "Several thousand infants have been weighed, measured, mentally tested, scored by points and classified as to fitness at the *baby health contests* held in some 40 states during the last three years. The standardising score-cards are still crude, the method of measuring arbitrary, the mental testing largely amateurish and of little scientific value. Linking the contests with cattle-shows has hardly been a factor in their favor. Some of them have been unhygienic and hard on the babies. As an index to the rise of the curve of interest in babyhood, and as a pioneer effort to attract attention to the child-welfare aspect of Eugenics, however, they may not have been held in vain" (p. 36).

13. Turn-of-the-century degenerationist writings tended to set forth near-lyrical listings of the despicable and contemptible. On November 30, 1901, Arthur R. T. Wylie at Clark University sent out a questionnaire on SUB-NORMAL CHILDREN AND YOUTH which begins: "It is desired by means of this syllabus to gain material for the study of the bad and troublesome children of school and family life, those who have reached their limit in school, and those limited in only one line, the runaways, the vagrants, spendthrifts, dudes, hoboes, hoodlums, religious fanatics, sensualists, sentimentalists, vicious and impulsive characters, impulsive masturbators, the ne'er-do-wells, the gilded youth and those who gave early promise but dropped into a humble station which they just managed to fill." In 1911, Vinnie Hicks established a clinic in the Oakland Schools and began examining children with IQ tests. She found 365 who were "subnormal" and claimed that isolating them – "the absent, the tardy, the sickly, the unruly, the liars, thieves and cowards" would free the teacher to work with the normal children (Chapman, 1988, p. 58).

14. Historical chapters in Witmer (1986) are useful in giving a somewhat more extended picture of early origins. She describes (p. 41ff) several precursor efforts directed toward early treatment and prevention of mental disorder.

15. To a remarkable extent, the dominant research movements on children in the 1920s and 1930s were supported – and, to a degree, shaped – by private foundations. The Laura Spelman Rockefeller Foundation sustained the child development movement housed in the child welfare institutes and centers, with publications centering on the journal *Child*

Development. The Commonwealth Fund gave generous support to the organization of the child guidance movement, with publications centering in the *American Journal of Orthopsychiatry.* In that era, foundations gave broad, diversified support for child welfare programs and policy (Coffman, 1936).

16. There were some other forms of treatment centers for children that did not grow. Douglas Thom of the Boston Psychopathic Hospital had introduced "habit clinics" services for normal preschool children with behavior problems and by the 1920s there were 12 of them, 10 in Massachusetts and 2 in Missouri. These clinics offered instruction in child rearing to parents whose children's problems were judged to come from wrong habits.

17. In a series of eight theses, with admirable clarity and logic, Healy (1915/1969, pp. 11–12) sets forth his rationale for approaching crime through a study of the situations of youth.

18. Healy would later regret the very designation of his program: "Rather imbued with the notion, then fairly prevalent among neurologists and psychiatrists, that serious antisocial behavior betokened something pathological in the offender, we quite wrongfully, as I see it now, christened our infant "The Juvenile Psychopathic Institute" (Lowrey, 1948, p. 19). And indeed, when Healy left Chicago to head the Judge Baker Child Guidance Center in Boston, his institute was renamed the Institute for Juvenile Research.

19. Witmer (1986, pp. 8ff) argues that in the early years of this century there were three main groups of American psychiatrists interested in psychological questions: (1) followers of Freud such as William A. White, Ely Jelliffe, and A. A. Brill; (2) Morton Prince and Boris Sidis, who had developed ideas somewhat similar to those of Freud; and (3) a group led by Adolf Meyer, who was much less theoretical, who emphasized "common sense," and who was very much interested in prevention, habit training, and reeducation. Like most of his contemporaries, more likely than not, William Healy followed Meyer while keeping an eye on Freud.

20. This historic phenomenon of an apparent sharp decline of the observed incidence of feeblemindedness in prisons and reformatories remains surprising. Possibly, sentencing practices may have been changing. We know that there have been fads in the use of psychiatric diagnostic categories. Goldstein (1987) documents the rise and fall of *monomania* in nineteenth-century France, followed by a later rise and fall of *hysteria.*

21. Young-Bruehl (1988, pp. 156ff.) gives a good account of the beginnings of child analysis in Vienna in the 1920s, its growth, and its transplanting with the Freuds to England in the late 1930s.

References

Bliss, W.D.P., and Binder, R. M. (Eds.) (1908). *Encyclopedia of social reform.* New York: Funk & Wagnalls.

Bremner, R. H. (1971). *Children and youth in America: A documentary history* (3 vols.). Cambridge, MA: Harvard University Press.

Briggs, A., and McCartney, A. (1984). *Toynbee Hall: The first hundred years.* London: Routledge & Kegan Paul.

Bronner, A. F. (1914). A research on the proportion of mental defectives among delinquents. *Journal of Criminal Law and Criminology, 5,* 566.

Campbell, Donald T. (1988). *Methodology and epistemology for social science: Selected papers.* Chicago: University of Chicago Press.

Cattell, J. McK. (1890). Mental tests and measurements. *Mind, 15,* 373–380.

Chapman, P. D. (1988). *Schools as sorters: Lewis M. Terman, applied psychology, and the intelligence testing movement, 1890–1930.* New York: New York University Press.

Cicchetti, D. (1990). An historical perspective on the discipline of developmental psychopathology. In J. Rolf, A. S. Masten, D. Cichetti, K. H. Neuchterlein, and S. Weintraub (Eds.), *Risk and protective factors in the development of psychopathology* (pp. 2–28). Cambridge University Press.

Coffman, H. C. (1936). *American foundations: A study of their role in the child welfare movement.* New York: The General Board of the Young Men's Christian Association.

Danielson, F. H., and Davenport, C. B. (1912). *The hill folk: Report on a rural community of hereditary defectives.* Cold Spring Harbor, NY: Eugenics Record Office.

Davenport, C. B. (1911). *Heredity in relation to eugenics.* New York: Henry Holt.

Dawson, G. E. (1896). Study of youthful degeneracy. *Pedagogical Seminary, 4,* 221–258.

Diehl, S. A. (1991). Theodate Smith and Amy Tanner: Child savers of Clark University. *Journal of Genetic Psychology, 152,* 273–287.

Dugdale, R. L. (1891). "The Jukes": A study in crime, pauperism, disease and heredity, also further studies of criminals. New York: Putnam. (Originally published 1877)

Estabrook, A. E., and Davenport, C. B. (1912). *The Nam family: A study in cacogenics.* Cold Spring Harbor, NY: Eugenics Record Office.

Fancher, R. E. (1987). Henry Goddard and the Kallikak family photographs: "Conscious skullduggery" or "Whig history"? *American Psychologist, 42,* 585–590.

Feuer, Lewis S. (1969). *The conflict of generations: The character and significance of student movements.* New York: Basic Books.

Flood, E. (1898). Notes on the castration of idiot children. *American Journal of Psychology, 10,* 296–301.

Galton, F. (1874). *English men of science.* London: Macmillan.

Galton, F. (1887). *Hereditary genius: An inquiry into its laws and consequences.* New York: Appleton. (Originally published 1869)

Galton, F., and Schuster, E. (1906). *Noteworthy families (modern science): An index to kinships in near degrees between persons whose achievements are honourable, and have been publicly recorded.* London: John Murray.

Gelb, Steven A. (1990). Degeneracy theory, eugenics, and family studies (Review of Rafter, Nicole Hahn [1988]. *White trash: The eugenic family studies, 1877–1919.* Boston: Northeastern University Press). *Journal of the History of the Behavioral Sciences, 26,* 242–246.

Goddard, H. H. (1912). *The Kallikak family: A study in the heredity of feeble-mindedness.* New York: Macmillan.

Goddard, H. H. (1926). *Feeble-mindedness: Its causes and consequences.* New York: Macmillan. (Originally published 1914)

Goldstein, J. (1987). *Console and classify: The French psychiatric profession in the nineteenth century.* Cambridge University Press.

Hall, G. S., et al. (1910a). *Proceedings of the Child Conference for Research and Welfare,* I, 1909. New York: G. E. Stechert.

Hall, G. S., et al. (1910b). *Proceedings of the Child Conference for Research and Welfare,* 2, 1910.

Hall, G. S. (1911). *Educational problems,* Vol. II. New York: Appleton.

Hamilton, A. E. (1914). Eugenics. *Pedagogical Seminary, XXI,* 28–61.

Healy, W. (1917). *Mental conflicts and misconduct.* Boston: Little, Brown.

Healy, W. (1969). *The individual delinquent: A text-book of diagnosis and prognosis for all concerned in understanding offenders.* Montclair, NJ: Patterson Smith. (Originally published 1915)

Healy, W., and Bronner, A. (1926). *Delinquents and criminals: Their making and unmaking.* New York: Macmillan.

Healy, W., Bronner, A. F., and Bowers, A. M. (1931). *The structure and meaning of psychoanalysis.* New York: Knopf.

Horn, M. (1989). *Before it's too late: The child guidance movement in the United States, 1922–1945.* Philadelphia: Temple University Press.

Hunter, J. D. (1927). The history and development of institutes for the study of children. In J. Addams et al., *The child, the clinic and the court* (pp. 204–214). New York: New Republic.

Jordan, T. E. (1993). *The degeneracy crisis and Victorian youth.* Albany: State University of New York Press.

Kamin, L. J. (1974). *The science and politics of I.Q.* Potomac, MD: Erlbaum.

Kater, M. H. (1989). *Doctors under Hitler.* Chapel Hill: University of North Carolina Press.

Kevles, Daniel J. (1985). *In the name of eugenics: Genetics and the uses of human heredity.* New York: Knopf.

Lerner, R. M. (1992). *Final solutions: Biology, prejudice, and genocide.* University Park: Pennsylvania State University Press.

Levine, M., and Levine, A. (1992). *Helping children: A social history.* New York: Oxford University Press.

Levine, M., and Wishner, J. (1977). The case records of the psychological clinic at the University of Pennsylvania (1896–1961). *Journal of the History of the Behavioral Sciences, 13,* 59–66.

Lifton, R. J. (1986). *The Nazi doctors: Medical killing and the psychology of genocide.* New York: Basic Books.

Lombroso, Cesare (1984). *The man of genius.* New York: Garland. (Original work published 1910)

Lowrey, L. G. (Ed.) (1948). *Orthopsychiatry, 1923–1948: Retrospect and prospect.* New York: American Orthopsychiatric Association.

Lutz, Tom (1991). *American nervousness, 1903: An anecdotal history.* Ithaca: Cornell University Press.

Mann, L. (1979). *On the trail of process: A historical perspective on cognitive processes and their training.* New York: Grune & Stratton.

Meyer, A. (1951). A review of the signs of degeneration and of methods of registration. *The collected papers of Adolf Meyer: Vol. II. Psychiatry.* (E. E. Winters, Ed.) (pp. 256–272). Baltimore: The Johns Hopkins University Press. (Original work published 1895–1896)

Morel (1857). *Traité des dégénérescences physiques intellectuelles et morales de l'espèce humaine et des causes qui produisant ces variétés maladives.* Paris: Balliere.

Müller-Hill, B. (1988). *Murderous science: Elimination by scientific selection of Jews, Gypsies, and others, Germany 1933–1945* (trans. George A. Fraser). Oxford: Oxford University Press.

Muncy, R. (1991). *Creating a female dominion in social reform, 1890–1935.* New York: Oxford University Press.

Murchison, C. (1926). *Criminal intelligence.* Worcester, MA: Clark University.

Oppenheim, J. (1991). *"Shattered nerves": Doctors, patients, and depression in Victorian England.* New York: Oxford University.

Orebaugh, D. A. (1929). *Crime, degeneracy and immigration: Their interrelations and interreactions.* Boston: Richard G. Badger.

Reilly, P. R. (1991). *The surgical solution: A history of involuntary sterilization in the United States.* Baltimore: Johns Hopkins University Press.

Reisman, J. M. (1991). *A history of clinical psychology.* (2nd ed.) New York: Hemisphere.

Residents of Hull-House: A social settlement (at 335 South Halsted Street,

Chicago, Ill.) (1895). *Hull-house maps and papers: A presentation of nationalities and waves in a congested district of Chicago, together with comments and essays on problems growing out of the social conditions.* New York: Thomas Y. Crowell.

Rosenzweig, S. (1992). *Freud, Jung, and Hall the king-maker: The historic expedition to America (1909).* Seattle: Hogrefe & Huber.

Schneider, W. H. (1992). After Binet: French intelligence testing, 1900–1940. *Journal of the History of the Behavioral Sciences, XXVIII,* pp. 111–132.

Shea, C. M. (1980). The ideology of mental health and the emergence of the therapeutic liberal state: The American mental hygiene movement, 1900–1930. Unpublished Ph.D. thesis, University of Illinois at Urbana–Champaign.

Siegel, A. W., and White, S. H. (1982). The child study movement: Early growth and development of the symbolized child. *Advances in Child Behavior and Development, 17,* 233–285.

Smith, T. L. (1910). II. Correspondence Department of the Children's Institute. *Pedagogical Seminary, 17,* 176–182.

Smith, T. L. (1914). The development of psychological clinics in the United States. *Pedagogical Seminary, 21,* 143–153.

Stevenson, George S., and Smith, Geddes (1934). *Child guidance clinics, a quarter century of development.* New York: The Commonwealth Fund.

Terman, Lewis M. (1916). *The measurement of intelligence: An explanation of and a complete guide for the use of the Stanford revision and extension of the Binet Simon Intelligence Scale.* Boston: Houghton Mifflin.

Turner, Victor W. (1969). *The ritual process: Structure and anti-structure.* The Lewis Henry Morgan Lectures, 1966. Chicago, Aldine.

Van Gennep, Arnold (1961). *The rites of passage.* Chicago: University of Chicago Press.

Von Gontard, A. (1988). The development of child psychiatry in 19th century Britain. *Journal of Child Psychology and Psychiatry, 29,* 569–588.

Wakefield, Jerome C. (1992). The concept of mental disorder: On the boundary between biological facts and social values. *American Psychologist, 3,* 373–388.

White, S. H. (1990). Child Study at Clark University: 1894–1904. *Journal of the History of the Behavioral Sciences, 26,* 131–150.

White, S. H. (1991). Three visions of educational psychology. In L. Tolchinsky-Landsmann (Ed.), *Culture, schooling, and psychological development* (pp. 1–38). Norwood, NJ: Ablex.

White, S. H. (1992). G. Stanley Hall: From philosophy to developmental psychology. *Developmental Psychology, 28,* 25–34.

White, S. H., and Buka, S. (1987). Early education: Programs, traditions, and policies. In E. Z. Rothkopf (Ed.), *Review of Research in Education,*

Vol. 14 (pp. 43–91). Washington, DC: American Educational Research Association.

Wiebe, R. H. (1967). *The search for order: 1877–1920*. Westport, CT: Greenwood Press.

Wile, I. S. (1926). The relation of intelligence to behavior. *Mental Hygiene, 10*, 68.

Witmer, H. L. (1986). *Psychiatric clinics for children*. New York: Garland.

Young-Bruehl, E. (1988). *Anna Freud*. New York: Summit Books.

Comments on Sheldon H. White's chapter

Philip S. Holzman

The progress from "attribution to information" can be traced in the area of adult psychopathology as well. Throughout the ages people with psychological illnesses came to the attention not only of physicians, but of witch-hunters, jailers, and protectors of society's morality. As noted in a remarkable appendix to *The Vital Balance* (Menninger et al., 1985), scattered through ancient Sumerian and Egyptian texts which date back to about 2500 B.C. are references to depressions and hysterical symptoms. And in the system of medicine in ancient India, the Ayur-Veda, about 1400 B.C., a kind of diagnostic dictionary was assembled on the basis of seven kinds of demonic possession. The symptoms of such conditions as psychosis, melancholia, obsessionality, or intoxication, for example, have been recognized from the beginnings of recorded history. It is not so much their recognition and description but their interpretation and significance that has shifted over time.

Naming, designating, and distinguishing these conditions is the activity of diagnosis. But the act of assigning names to conditions can itself introduce a valence that has made for much suffering over the ages. Just as with children, diagnosis as name-calling has been the occasion for burning at the stake, asphyxiation in the gas chamber, ostracism from society, or excuse from responsibility. It is not the scientific enterprise of designation and classification that produces these excesses, but the attributive activities of the interpreters. Even in our enlightened contemporary era, a vice-presidential candidate was forced to withdraw from a campaign because he had once been treated for a depressive illness. Karl Menninger, one of the few who recognized the distinction between attribution and information, stated:

I don't agree that [schizophrenia] should be given the designation of a disease as if it were a thing . . . which only a few unfortunate, stupid, or otherwise unlucky individuals happen to get. . . . It hurts the individual. The individual so labeled is no longer a troubled individual. . . . He is regarded now as belonging to a special class of people to be treated, perhaps to be feared, to be scorned, to be pitied, to be avoided – always to be degraded, always to be suspect in regard to his predictability, in regard to his adaptability, and in regard to his competence. Objectively and subjectively he is stigmatized even if he ceases to have any of the symptoms upon which the original labeling was established. (Menninger, 1973, p. 192)

References

Menninger, K. (1973). *Sparks,* ed. L. Freeman. New York: Crowell.
Menninger, K., Mayman, M., and Pruyser, P. (1985). *The Vital Balance: The Life Process in Mental Health and Illness.* Gloucester, MA: Peter Smith.

9

A paradoxical partnership: Some historical and contemporary referents linking adult schizophreniform disorder and resilient children under stress

Norman Garmezy

Introduction

It seems paradoxical to suggest that a possible linkage may exist between adult schizophreniform disorder on the one hand and resilience in children exposed to highly disadvantaged circumstances. It is paradoxical in view of the great disparities which are so evident when contrasting the two groups: the wide age difference; the marked variations in developmental course; the striking differences in adaptability at different points in the life course, particularly the efficacious behaviors that are often characteristic of resilient children; the variation in prognoses and the likely disparities in long-term outcomes; and the marked differences in the origins and magnitude of scientific inquiry focused on each group. Particularly striking is the time period in which each group first became an object of description and inquiry. "Madness" was the original designate for the incorporative conception of schizophrenia, its study extending back to the seventeenth century. By contrast the study of resilience in children is largely a product of the closing decades of the twentieth century. Nevertheless, there exist ties whereby the contributions of a segment of a broader canvas of schizophrenia research has resulted in the identification of factors in a subset of schizophreniform patients that appear to parallel attributes of children (and possibly those of selective adults as well) who exhibit patterns of resilient behavior.

But first a disclaimer. It is necessary to make clear to the reader at the outset that the linkages to be described are essentially manifest competencies in the life course of seemingly vulnerable adults as well as in the lives of many disadvantaged and/or markedly stressed children. For both, outcomes often appear to be positive despite the stressors to which the two groups have been exposed. Thus the dual comparisons contained in this chapter are largely based on substantive *empirical* findings and are not intended to be perceived as precursors of an effort at a causal modeling either of schizophrenia or of adaptive functioning in children under stress.

To turn to the issue of possible parallel attributes in these two divergent groups, two contents seem applicable. The first derives from an expanding but as yet limited literature that emphasizes the power of summated chronic adversities that may affect the developmental histories of at-risk children as well as their resilient adult counterparts (Garmezy and Masten, 1991). The second also plays a role in the prediction of positive and negative outcomes in children's adaptation and possibly in schizophreniform adults. This focus is on early competencies and their potential subsequent influences on normative in contrast to non-normative behavioral development. In the study of psychopathology, such differences tap, in part, the historical distinction between what was once termed *process* and *reactive schizophrenia*. There remain tracings of these differences in risk and protectiveness from early historical treatises on the description of schizophrenia.

Early notations of risk factors in the context of "schizophrenia"

In 1672 Thomas Willis published his *Two Discourses Concerning the Soul of Brutes Which Is That of the Vital and Sensitive in Man*. The first discourse was *physiological;* the second was *pathological,* and focused on *hysteria, melancholia* (or depression), and *madness* (later to be designated, in turn, initially as dementia praecox, and subsequently schizophrenia).

Of "madness," Willis wrote:

. . . if in Melancholy, the Brain and Animal Spirits are said to be darkened with fume, and a thick obscurity; In Madness, they seem to be all as it were of an open burning or flame . . . three things are almost common to all: viz. First, that their Phantasies or Imaginations are perpetually busied with a storm of impetuous thoughts. . . . Secondly, that their notions or conceptions are either innocuous, or represented to them under a false or erroneous image. Thirdly, to their Delirium is most often joyned Audaciousness and Fury. (Hunter and Macalpine, 1963, pp. 190–191)

Then, turning to the treatment to be accorded such patients, Willis urged that given

the raging of the Spirits . . . things are to be administer'd as it were for the suppression or extinction of a flame raging above measure. Therefore let the diet be slender and not delicate, their clothing course, their beds hard, and their handling severe and rigid. . . In inveterate and habitual Madness the sick seldom submit to any Medical Cure; but such being placed in Bedlam, or an Hospital for Mad people, by the ordinary discipline of the place, either at length return to themselves, or else they are kept from being hurt, either to themselves or to others. (p. 192)

From this early-seventeenth-century commentary to the first decades of the twentieth century one witnesses the beginning of a transformation from the description of schizophrenic behavior to the positing of potential risk factors that emphasize genetic predisposition, often accompanied by a nod to environmental effects, particularly those that reflect familial–behavioral elements.

An example of this transition can be perceived in Kraepelin's treatise (1919) on *Dementia Praecox and Paraphrenia* [schizophrenia]. As I noted in an earlier article (Garmezy, 1978), this important volume provides a masterly 250-page description of the phenomenology of schizophrenia. Then in a final chapter, only four pages in length and entitled "How to Combat It," Kraepelin comments on environmental risk elements, their effects and the modes of avoidance of such negative circumstances. In 199 words Kraepelin introduces his conception of children at risk for schizophrenia and the modes for combating specific negative factors that could serve to potentiate the disease.

In children of such characteristics as we so very frequently find in the previous history of dementia praecox one might think of an attempt at prophylaxis especially if the malady had been already observed in the parents or brothers and sisters. Whether it is possible in such circumstances to ward off the outbreak of the threatening disease, we do not know. But in any case it will be advisable to promote to the utmost of one's power general bodily development and to avoid one-sided training in brain work, as it may well be assumed that a vigorous body grown up under natural conditions will be in a better position to overcome the danger that a child exposed to the influences of effeminacy, of poverty, and of exact routine, and especially of city education. Childhood spent in the country with plenty of open air, bodily exercise, escalation beginning late without ambitious aims, and simple food would be the principal points to keep in view. Meyer, who regards dementia praecox essentially as the effect of unfavorable influences of life and education of personalities with abnormal dispositions hopes by all these measures to be able to prevent the development of the malady. (p. 253)

This paragraph, filled with conjectures, can be viewed as an early forebear of aspects of schizophrenia research that began to appear some half a century later. This took form in the emergence of multiple research programs devoted to the study of *children at risk for schizophrenia*, with risk typically defined by the manifestation of psychiatric disorder in a parent. The results of multiple research programs conducted from the early 1950s onward have been superbly catalogued and described in ongoing investigations. These have been summarized by an international core of research investigators in a volume entitled *Children at Risk for Schizophrenia: A Longitudinal Perspective* (Watt et al., 1984).

Kraepelin's suggestions have proved to be surprisingly accurate. Three elements cited by him suggested some of the forerunners of results that were obtained, decades later, in the studies of children presumed to be vulnerable to schizophrenia: (1) the marked familial genetic predisposition to the disorder evidenced by his focus on children of schizophrenic parents (". . . especially if the malady had already been observed in the parents or brothers and sisters"); (2) a combinatorial pattern of genetic and environmental stressors that prepared psychiatry for the emergence of diathesis-stress theories focused on the joint power of predisposition and potentiator. These indicators included overideational behavior, inadequate or misidentified gender identification, disordered cognitions, overly exact routine, social isolation, compulsive behaviors; and (3) low socioeconomic status and poverty. Clearly these three components are not wholly independent of each other. Thus, genetic components may foster specific negative behavioral patterns, which in turn influence an individual's sociocultural disadvantaged status. Similarly, multiple and prolonged stressors associated with poverty may provide seed ground for potentiating a psychotic breakdown.

The impact of poverty and lower social class status received prominence as a risk factor for psychopathology during an era in which many sociologists and anthropologists were deeply involved with psychiatrists in studying sociocultural factors influencing psychopathology (Bastide, 1972; Dunham, 1959; Eaton, 1986; Hollingshead and Redlich, 1958; Langner and Michael, 1963; Linton, 1956; Srole et al., 1962). The large-scale departure of sociologists from the mental illness scene has resulted in an attenuation of interest in social factors that may influence manifestations of major mental disorders. In turn, this has led to a decrease in efforts to initiate a broad band of systematic interventions that were earlier focused on environmental change as advocated by Adolf Meyer (Lief, 1948).

Kraepelin's commentary on the potential significance of studying children at risk via early identification followed by an active intervention deserves added recognition in the light of the growth of interest that has been focused on the recent emergence of a field of study now identified as *developmental psychopathology*. Its prime emphasis is on the investigation of social, behavioral, and biological development, and the processes and mechanisms that influence behavior change (Cicchetti, 1989; Cicchetti and Toth, 1991, 1992; Lewis and Miller, 1990; Luthar, 1993; Rolf et al., 1990; Rutter, 1980; Sroufe and Rutter, 1984; Zigler and Glick, 1986).*

This developmental emphasis too had its early counterpart in the contributions of Eugen Bleuler. Manfred Bleuler (1986), illustrious son of an illustrious father, described E. Bleuler's contributions in providing an early appreciation of the critical issues of development that were markedly needed (then as well as now) to supplement the more evident preoccupation with diagnosis.

In a historical survey that provided an introduction and an overview for a *Handbook of Studies of Schizophrenia* (Burrows et al., 1986), Bleuler wrote of his father's clinical commitments, later to become his own. Referring to his father's early years as a psychiatrist M. Bleuler wrote:

As Director of a county Hospital . . . from 1886 to 1898 he was all day long with his patients, worked with them on clinical farms and in workshops, went for walks with them, play-acted with them. He was eager to arrive at an understanding of their speech and behaviour from comparing it with their life experience. He was impressed by the contradiction in their cognitive and emotional life and designated it as an overwhelming ambitendency. At the same time he became aware how preoccupation with their psychodynamic difficulties was a source of retiring from contact with others, of an overwhelming autism as he described it:

Becoming acquainted with the psychodynamics of a schizophrenic he understood the sense of the psychotic symptoms – but he felt that the actual origin of the psychosis was still to be discovered. In spite of this he had learned to appreciate the value of psychotherapeutic and psychosocial care for the patient. (M. Bleuler, 1986, p. 2)

---

*See also Chapter 11, by Dante Cicchetti, this volume – Eds.

M. Bleuler – in referring to his own studies, which dealt both with endocrinological studies of patients, and, of current importance, with the evolution of his own developmental perspective – reported a broadening of his research interests that focused on the descriptive content of his patients' lives.

The other main part of my studies concerned the development of the personalities and of the psychosis of schizophrenics over decades together with the influences on course and outcome (for instance the familial and the therapeutic influences . . .).

How can one understand the tragic turn from a cruel inner development which is not psychotic to the psychosis? We observe the endeavor of the future schizophrenic to overcome his inner disharmonies and the disharmonies of the outer world he lives in, his urge for confrontation of his autistic thinking with logic and reality becoming more and more cruel. His development reaches a threshold, a point of no return. From now on the patient gives up his attempts to adapt his inner contradictory life to reality and his attempts to harmonize it. Having this point of no return in his development behind him he has become psychotic, schizophrenic. This is not a theory, this is the formulation of what we perceive during psychotherapy of future or actual schizophrenics. Such a formulation facilitates our understanding the patient. It brings him nearer to us. It frees us from the cruel feeling that he is no longer one of us, that he had become an alien, one with whom we have nothing in common. (pp. 4–5)

The expansion of risk research in schizophrenia

Thus, three giants of psychiatry were forerunners of developmental aspects of schizophrenia that were to appear almost half a century later in research on the emergence of children *at risk* for schizophrenia as determined by the manifest mental disorder of the parent(s). A portion of the recent history of the study of children at risk for schizophrenia is in order.

The formal founding of a Consortium for Risk Research in Schizophrenia occurred in May 1973, with early support provided by the National Institute of Mental Health (NIMH). Its contemporary impetus came from the pioneering longitudinal research program conducted by Mednick and Schulsinger (1968) in Denmark focused on children born to schizophrenic parents. A little more than a decade later the volume reviewing the results of the multiple studies initiated by the Consortium teams appeared and Professor Bleuler, who had been adopted unanimously as the Consortium's godfather, was invited to write the foreword. In his preface he noted the uniqueness of the

structure and contents of a research organization that took all participating programs under its tent and the potential significance that
could accrue from both the focus and the database of the group. But
he also issued some warnings of "inherent dangers" in the research
quest: (1) that it was possible that no specific pathogens would be
found to be decisive in the etiology of schizophrenia (or of the affective disorders); (2) that the research efforts of the Consortium members, were it to focus too readily on objective, counting measures,
could lose sight of some of the "human qualities" that are basic to
many schizophrenic patients; and (3) that the research focus may
sidestep the search for ways of helping patients via active interventions.

Bleuler doubted that his third concern would be actualized, and in
this prediction his judgment proved to be accurate. The Consortium
never lost its humane concern for the well-being of the children and
their families.

Bleuler wrote of another emergent research problem that warranted exploration, namely to "seek to establish which conditions
allow children at risk to remain well and which lead them into illness."
This descriptive referent has now taken root within the research
movement identified with developmental psychopathology as the specific study area of adaptive children under stress (Sroufe and Rutter,
1984).

Referring to the Consortium's efforts to investigate the development and outcomes for children at risk for schizophrenia, Bleuler
wrote:

> I would not have dreamed what has become reality today, namely that a
> collaboration among so many investigators could come about, extending
> across the boundaries of professional disciplines, of theoretical persuasions,
> and of nations in a common effort that can reach fruition only after many
> years. . . . In short, the longitudinal investigation – lasting decades – of the
> fate of children at risk for psychosis is a task of gigantic scope well worth the
> great investment required. (p. xvii)

Reflecting back on the past two decades during which the Consortium operated, I have been struck by the role this important entryway
played in fostering a developmental psychopathology of schizophrenia. The research literature of adult schizophrenia provided numerous hypotheses and methods worthy of investigations of children
and adolescents born to schizophrenic parents as well as of children

reared in families marked by other types of parental psychiatric disorders.

In an early publication (Garmezy, 1975) I reproduced a list of the various methods, variables, and investigative contents that marked a portion of the collective Consortium's efforts. The composited variables occupied six printed pages. Despite their evident diversity, each variable had some reasonable rationale that warranted its exploratory usage in contrasting three groups of children: (1) those who were potentially at risk for schizophrenia, (2) those who were at risk for other psychiatric disorders, and (3) normal control children.

To cite merely a few, the range of experimental procedures included clinical and neuropsychological assessments, measures of information processing, attentional and vigilance tasks, Piagetian tasks, neurological studies, school evaluations, electrophysiology measures, visual motor tasks, studies of arousal, autonomic and vestibular functions, competence measures, cognitive styles, infant temperament data, mother-infant interaction, birth and obstetrical data, school records, biochemical measures, catecholamine metabolism assays, family process variables, and so forth.

The effort was extensive, the goal clearly evident: to seek out areas that could be considered valid early indicators of "risk" as reflected in pre-illness deviations from an adaptive and normative mode. The extensiveness of the multivariables that were investigated was one indication, then as well as now, of the uncertainty that surrounded potential contents that might prove promising in studies of children at risk for schizophrenia. The effort had the effect of expanding the range of potential *risk factors* without delimiting areas of exploration of more traditional variables that would presumably reflect elements suggested by the important contributions provided by clinical epidemiology.

In a chapter of a volume sponsored by the European Scientific Foundation's Network on Longitudinal Studies of Individual Development (Garmezy, 1993), I pointed to the breadth and depth of these early multiple programs, perceiving them as a current and complementary advance in conjunction with the tabular genetic studies of an earlier and current era that have provided rates for the occurrence of schizophrenia in offspring of schizophrenic parentage. I noted that the focus on discriminating variables may, in time, move us closer to the critical issue of discovering those processes and mechanisms that underlie resistance or capitulation factors to disorder in high-risk offspring. Were these developmental studies of adaptation of at-risk children to be joined to future advances in the molecular genetics of schizophrenia, it would represent a collaborative pairing necessary to provide, in time, an enhanced understanding of cases in which the at-risk status of some children is actualized into disorder, in contrast to other risk cases in which anticipated disordered outcomes remain unfulfilled.

There is another potential core of studies, set for the near future, that will further enhance our understanding of genetic risk, actualized or nonactualized. These will follow when the ultimate genetic breakthrough in schizophrenia is realized. Once available, there will follow a hoped-for reversal in the order of investigative primacy, with developmental studies of offspring who are bearers versus nonbearers of the genetic diathesis. It will not be surprising, given contemporary genetic scientific advances, to discover that other variables – familial, neuropsychological, biological, biochemical, psychological, sociocultural, and the like – may provide complementary clues needed to sharpen our understanding of actualized and nonactualized schizophrenia outcomes despite the critical genetic presence that reflects the potential vulnerability to the disease.

The rise of developmental psychopathology

The recent emergence of developmental psychopathology provides a supportive framework with its origins in a multiple parentage that includes, among other sciences, normative developmental psychology, developmental biology, genetics, and experimental and clinical psychopathology. A definition of its boundaries has been provided by Sroufe and Rutter (1984) in a seminal article on the domain of developmental psychopathology:

> The very name for the discipline provides a starting point for defining the scope and particular quality of this field. First, it is concerned with development and is therefore closely wedded to the whole of developmental psychology. The methods, theories, and perspectives of developmental psychology are important tools of inquiry. Second, the focus is on pathology, that is developmental deviations. Developmental psychopathology may be defined as *the study of the origins and course of individual patterns of behavioral maladaptation,* whatever the age of onset, whatever the causes, whatever the transformations in behavioral manifestation, and however complex the course of the developmental pattern may be. (p. 18)

The distinction, Sroufe and Rutter noted, between developmental psychopathology and clinical psychopathology resided in the research enterprise that marks the former. From the standpoint of this goal, the origins and time course of mental disorders are of critical importance to the developmental psychopathologist, as are the behavioral and biological transformations that occur at different points in development. Comparisons with normative behavior at these crucial points in development constitute the heartland of research from a developmental–psychopathological viewpoint.

Both typicality and atypicality are of particular interest in this research orientation. Who are the at-risk persons? What are their behavioral and biological patterns over time? What are the potentiating events for disorder when it occurs? Who among those defined to be at-risk individuals fail to manifest a disorder in comparison with those who do? Who, seemingly not at all viewed as at-risk candidates, develop psychopathology somewhere along the developmental trail? And, above all, what *factors, processes,* and *mechanisms* operate to produce seemingly unanticipated outcomes as well as those that follow a predictable course?

These latter points emphasize a basic goal of risk research – the investigation of those "risk" and "protective" factors that may be uniquely characteristic of some subsets of adaptive individuals, but not of others. Intensive study of such subsets of cases at crucial points in development will in time foster our knowledge of stabilizing and destabilizing elements in children's lives. But the critical research effort will be focused on identifying the processes that underlie behavioral and biological changes that make significant contributions to the emergence of pathology.

Eisenberg (1977) has written in a similar vein in his significant article on development as a unifying concept in psychiatry. The developmental process, he notes, begins with information encoded in the genome, but its phenotypic expression is modulated by environmental variables at each stage of development, including the intrauterine world of the fetus and the nature of the birth process itself. Eisenberg's environmental variables are the great stressors of contemporary society: disorganized homes, lack of environmental stimulation, failure of mother–child bonding, poor housing, community disorganization, and so on. Unfortunately, these stressors tend to cohere, heightening the probability of serious negative consequences for those exposed to multiple deprivations.

Multiple stressors and their consequences
for children's adaptation

What are the effects imposed upon children subjected to such dire multiple stressors? One of the first studies to support the cumulative impact of disadvantaging factors was reported by Rutter (1979). He selected six variables that reflected chronic familial adversities: (1) severe marital discord; (2) low social status; (3) overcrowding or large family size; (4) paternal criminality; (5) maternal psychiatric disorder; and (6) placement of a child in the care of local authority. The findings were strongly supportive of the interelatedness of cumulative disadvantage and manifest child psychiatric disorder. Zero or a single adversity provided no indication of behavioral disorder; two risk factors increased the probability of disorder fourfold; however, with four or more factors in evidence, manifest psychiatric disorder in offspring rose to 21%.

Research by Kolvin and his associates focused, in a similar fashion, on delinquent behavior in a research program identified as the Newcastle Families Longitudinal Study. These investigators, too, reported a comparable relationship between children's exposure to a number of chronic adversities and negative outcomes (Kolvin et al., 1988). The detrimental effects of exposure to cumulative stressors revealed a marked interrelatedness of multiple stressors with serious delinquent behavior exhibited by the offspring: a single stressor provided a 29% rate of later criminality; two stressors increased the rate to 69%. Interestingly, as deprivation accelerated, so did the delinquency rate; when it decreased, criminality rates declined.

Delinquency or generalized psychiatric disorders, however, are not the sole offshoots of cumulative stressors. Schizophrenia and its transmission offer a superb study that utilized a process model to explain an aspect of the development of the disorder in the offspring of schizophrenic mothers (Hans and Marcus, 1987; Marcus et al., 1987). A major study, conducted in Israel, was part of an NIMH–Jerusalem collaborative investigation of children deemed to be at risk for schizophrenia on the basis of maternal schizophrenia. David Rosenthal was the creative investigator who initiated the project; subsequently, Allan Mirsky carried it forward with the collaboration of a team of able Israeli and NIMH investigators.*

---

*See also Chapter 17, by Allan Mirsky, this volume – Eds.

Two groups of mothers and their offspring were studied: one group was drawn from a city population; the other consisted of members housed in kibbutz settings. The at-risk sample included almost all kibbutz children who lived in Israel and who had a schizophrenic parent (primarily mothers) living in the kibbutz. The matched control children were chosen among the classmates of each index child. Matching criteria for the at-risk and comparison groups included educational setting, age, ethnic origin, family size, parental educational level, and parental cultural level (Marcus et al., 1987).

Four risk factors were the focal elements that were hypothesized to be related to the offspring's probability of developing schizophrenia or a schizoid personality disorder.

The decision-tree model for the development of schizophrenia is presented in Figure 9.1. The four sequential cumulative risk factors were (1) a family history of schizophrenia; (2) early neurobehavioral signs in the child that may have reflected a constitutional deficit; (3) a stressful family environment marked by poor parenting behavior; and (4) poor social adjustment as reflected in the child's social withdrawal or antisocial behavior in the community.

Examination of the Marcus et al. (1987) data indicates that "yes" responses to all four negative variables provided 7 of the 9 cases that showed a marked breakdown into schizophrenia or its border states. In other cases, protective factors may have interceded to negate the risk elements. In suggesting such factors Marcus et al. have indicated the following possibilities: a "well-integrated central nervous system," a "structured nondemanding environment," "appropriate maternal parenting behaviors," and "positive social adjustment as a child." Such factors are inferential but they are on the important path that may indicate the operation of protective factors, internal and external, that influence escape from severe mental disorder despite the presence of risk elements.

Another study of the potential effects of cumulated risk is the *Rochester Longitudinal Study*, begun in 1970, which focused on the development of a sample of children selected because of maternal psychopathology. Included within the cohorts were schizophrenic parents and other forms of disordered states as well as normal groups of parents, varying in social class status, ethnicity, and race. The availability of a countywide psychiatric register enabled investigators to utilize data on socioeconomic status (SES), race, age, marital status, and obstetrical history together with the inclusion not solely of

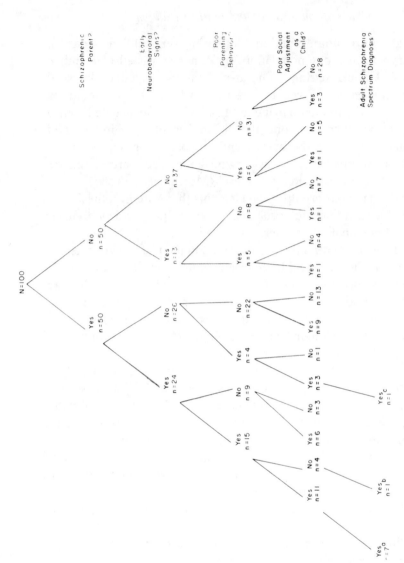

Figure 9.1. Decision-tree model for development of schizophrenia: Application to Israeli high-risk study.

Breakdown cases marked "a" = 1 residual-type schizophrenia, 3 paranoid schizophrenia, 2 schizoid personality disorders, and 1 mixed spectrum disorder. Breakdown case marked "b" = 1 residual-type schizophrenia. Breakdown case marked "c" = 1 schizoid personality disorder with dysthymic disorder.

schizophrenic mothers but of mothers presenting other psychiatric symptoms as well. The Rochester County register afforded the collaborating investigators the opportunity to catalogue presenting symptoms and diagnoses other than schizophrenia. Maternal diagnoses were initially based on (the then in use) DSM-II criteria; subsequently DSM-III criteria have confirmed the earlier diagnoses. The diagnoses included six groups of mothers: "schizophrenia, schizophrenia spectrum, neurotic depression, personality disorders, other neuroses and situational reactions" (Sameroff et al., 1982). The schizophrenia spectrum cases included those carrying a diagnosis of "schizoid or inadequate personality." In addition to the mothers whose names were drawn from the psychiatric register, there was a comparison group of mothers who were free of mental illness. Schizophrenia and the spectrum cases constituted 21.5% of the total cohort. Neurotic depression accounted for another 33.3%; personality disorders, for 22.6%; situational reactions, 13.0%; and other neuroses contributed 9.6% of the total group.

Three groups served as contrasting controls to the schizophrenic group, two of which reflected risk for neurotic depression, and personality disorders, plus a no-mental-illness control group. These became the component groups of the longitudinal study. The collection of follow-up data for this study has been under way for 23 years and has continued with subsequent follow-ups carrying the cohort into later adolescence and currently into young adulthood.

Reports from the Rochester investigation (Fisher et al., 1980), focused initially on school-age children, have failed to find differences between children of schizophrenic mothers contrasted with other children whose mothers had received other psychiatric diagnoses. However, the severity of mothers' illnesses and symptom dimensions did prove to be related significantly to competence indicators in the offspring. Further, children whose mothers were *not* mentally ill but who exhibited behavior problems in school appeared to be far less competent than were the high-risk children.

Taking a page from Rutter's earlier study, the Rochester investigators have turned to their case history data to select 10 stressor indicators with a view to cumulating them to study the consequences of such summation for enhancing deficit behaviors in the offspring. The source of this decision has been described in the closing pages of an early monograph authored by Sameroff et al. (1982). The investigators recognized that the offspring of schizophrenic parents could constitute a high-risk sample, not necessarily solely by virtue of maternal diagnosis per se but rather as a resultant of characteristics within the family including "a combination of prolonged emotional disturbance, unstable family organization, poor economic circumstance and low social status that characterizes many of these families" (p. 64).

To quantify the risk potential of the children, Sameroff and his colleagues (1993) selected 10 factors on the assumption that these, when cumulated, would advance the risk status of the offspring. At age 4, and subsequently at age 13 (the age 18 evaluation is currently under way), the research team developed and tested a multiple risk index which was then applied to each of the 152 participating families. These parents have remained research participants, beginning with the mothers' pregnancies, and continuing with the participating offspring present from the very onset of the Rochester study.

The 10 family risk factors used when the children were 4 and 13 years old are detailed in a recent report (Sameroff et al., 1993). These have included (1) minority group status of the family; (2) occupation of the head of household; (3) maternal education; (4) family size; (5) father absence; (6) stressful life events; (7) parental perspectives on attitudes, beliefs, and values that parents held with regard to their child's development; (8) maternal anxiety; (9) maternal mental health; and (10) the affective relationship between parent and child.

These 10 factors are compressed in this presentation. The family attributes are described in greater detail in the investigators' recent articles (Sameroff et al., 1982; Sameroff et al., 1987; Seifer et al., 1992). Two findings are of particular interest: first, the average number of risk factors have ranged from 0 to 9 at 4 years, and 0 to 8 at the 13-year evaluation. The correlation of these composite risk factors over the 9-year span was .77. Second, a general finding of the two temporal measures was the relationship of the cumulative multiple risk scores to the child's IQ. The greater the number of family risks, the lower was the IQ score of the child (see Figure 9.2). The social status factors bore the strongest relationship to the child's IQ, together with the parenting perspective and the maternal health score. Controlling for minority status did not modify the impact of multiple risk on the child's IQ performance. At both ages 4 and 13, multiple risk was related to children's IQ even when the effects of SES and race were controlled. A series of statistical analyses confirmed that the greater the number of risk factors, the poorer the child's developmental out-

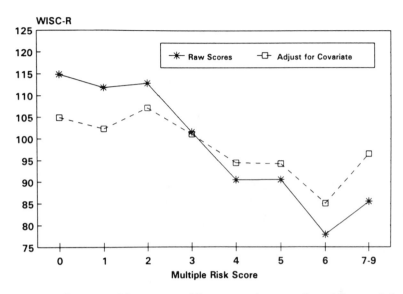

Figure 9.2. Mean 13-year IQ scores, and means adjusted for covariation of SES and race, within multiple-risk groups.

come. This relationship remained steady across the time span of the longitudinal evaluation ($r = .76$). In the authors' words, the children who "had poor family and social environments when they were born, still had them when they were 13, and probably would continue to have them for the foreseeable future" (p. 95). Further, the most important consideration was the *number* of risk factors that cumulated rather than the *types* of risk factors that were evident.

Many questions remain to be answered about the current Rochester study. What portion of the sample included schizophrenic mothers? Were the effects of cumulative risk on IQ similar for this specific subset of families? What is known, beyond the IQ score, of the children who had exposure to a minimal number of risk scores as opposed to those who were subjected to a substantial number of such risk factors?

The study has emphasized IQ as a relevant factor in resilience. As a mere set of test questions, issues may be raised about the overall relevance of intelligence test performance as too simplistic a measure of a construct as complex as resilience. However, there are sufficient reliability and validity data that accompany IQ test performance to accept it as a critical personal attribute that typically bears a strong correlation with school-based competence, peer and teacher judgments, and efficacy in meeting the challenges of childhood and adolescence.

Masten et al. (1988) have demonstrated that higher intelligence in children accompanies stable performance under stress. Further, Kandel et al. (1988) studied four groups of men chosen from a specific Danish birth cohort who differed on intelligence test measures and on subsequent outcomes. The groupings were: (1) those at high risk for subsequent criminality based upon having severely criminal fathers but who gave no evidence of delinquency; (2) a comparison group with a similar pattern of paternal criminality but who engaged in severe delinquent acts; (3) a low-risk group with noncriminal fathers who did not show criminal behavior; and (4) a comparable low-risk group who did demonstrate criminal behavior. The first group exhibited higher mean IQ scores than did the other three groups.

The investigators ascribe these results to the reinforcing power of successful school performance and to the correlated standards of behavior that bring approbation as well as achievements – attributes that stand in opposition to criminality and increase the likelihood of the further acquisition and maintenance of conventional social behaviors. Such patterns, in turn, influence the development of academic and social competence behaviors, generate friendships with other prosocial children, and heighten the probable development of positive modes of coping with frustration and the negative forces that too often accompany poverty (Luthar and Zigler, 1992).

These studies of cumulating risk and protective factors raise a provocative and frequently asked question. Are protective elements simply the converse of the complementary risk factors? Thus, if poor parenting is a risk factor, is good parenting protective? Given the presence of maternal psychiatric disorder as a risk factor, is its absence a protective element?

The answer to the question, while unresolved, seemingly constitutes a simplification of what is required: namely, that the search for both risk and protective factors should extend beyond simplistic opposites. A conservative proposition would suggest that the boundaries of identifiable risk or protective factors in development do not warrant the assumption that opposites alone are the "be all" and "end all" of the search for influencing categories of events and situations that exert powerful effects on adaptive and/or maladaptive behavior. An example may suffice: in traumatic situations a deep religious belief housed in *some* persons appears to play a protective role. However, there are no available systematic data that nonbelievers are at heightened risk when exposed to traumatic events for lacking a religious conviction. The processes generated by dire events may not be actualized by religious belief and disbelief. Other complex elements undoubtedly intrude in predicting responsiveness to trauma.

The predictive power of early competence indicators in development: The case for resilient children under stress and for recovery in schizophrenia

The second unifying theme that ties resilience in childhood to differential outcomes in schizophrenia is found in developmental patterns of early behavioral competencies. For schizophrenia there is the lengthy history that maps the "process–reactive" dimension in psychiatry. The history of that distinction is evident in the writings of the great psychiatrists of the twentieth century. Eugen Bleuler (1924) early formulated the concept of a *reactive psychosis in schizophrenia.* Jaspers (1923), too, a year earlier, provided a summary of three significant factors that accompanied *genuine reactions:* (1) a manifest precipitating factor that bears a close temporal relationship to the reactive state; (2) a meaningful connection that can be found to exist between the contents of the event and the patient's reaction; and (3) the disappearance of the abnormal reaction when the primary event that evoked the reaction had ended or had been attenuated. Jaspers concluded that "reactive abnormalities are therefore a complete contrast to all morbid processes that appear spontaneously" (p. 392, in 1963 translation).

In an early review of the process–reactive dichotomy (Garmezy, 1968, 1970), I commented on Kraepelin's view regarding psychiatric classification schema as one that iterated his viewpoint that the validity of diagnosis was to be determined by outcome. Thus, anticipated outcomes reflected correct diagnoses; an unanticipated outcome reflected an earlier diagnostic error. Further, Kraepelin perceived mental disorders to be either exogenous or endogenous in character. If external events served as precipitants, cure was possible; if such events were not evident, inherent biological-constitutional defects were operative and recovery and cure could not be foreseen. The differentiation, whatever its limitations, was supportive of an endogenous distinction in schizophrenia, and thus a historical tie to the later issue that schizophrenia could be cast into the context of a process–reactive distinction. Meyer (1910), too, commented on this differentiation that existed within the diagnostic entity of schizophrenia. His focus was on the premorbid period and the factors that could shape or undo "life-specified" defects.

But it was Bleuler (1924) who provided a great insight with his observation that dementia praecox was not a single viable disease entity but rather a group of reactions, some of which did not eventuate in deterioration. It was this view that provided a gateway to the study of outcomes including remissions. Such acceptance of the concept of potential recoveries in certain cases led inevitably to the study of premorbid adaptation and the mental status factors and symptoms that could facilitate a differentiation of patients who recovered as opposed to those who deteriorated.

Heterogeneity in the adaptation of schizophrenic patients

Thus, the process–reactive dichotomy became a focus for research in which psychopathologists sought to trace the antecedents that might provide prognostic indices to help in differentiating these two types of patients.

The literature of differentiation of typologies in schizophrenia in time produced a revision of the nomenclature of the disorder. In the 1980 (DSM-III) revision of the Diagnostic and Statistical Manual of Mental Disorders the more adaptive subset of schizophrenic patients were assigned a new designation, termed *schizophreniform* – a differentiation that has been maintained in DSM-III-R (1987) and in DSM-IV (1994). Schizophrenia's diagnostic criteria bear the long-term credentials of bizarre delusions, flat and grossly inappropriate affect, long-term continuous signs of disorder, functional deterioration in work, social relations, and self-care, social isolation and withdrawal, inadequate role functioning, and long-term traditional early signs of the disorder as evidenced in a premorbid personality marked by suspiciousness, introversion, withdrawal, and often eccentricity and impulsivity.

The contrast with *schizophreniform disorder* is striking. Among the favorable prognostic features that accompany this diagnosis are: (1) good premorbid social and occupational functioning; (2) the absence

Table 9.1. *Case-history criteria for differentiating process and reactive schizophrenia from Kantor, Wallner, and Winder*

Process schizophrenia	Reactive schizophrenia
Birth to the fifth year	
a. Early psychological trauma.	a. Good psychological history.
b. Physical illness, severe or long.	b. Good physical health.
c. Odd member of family.	c. Normal member of family.
Fifth year to adolescence	
a. Difficulties at school.	a. Well adjusted at school.
b. Family troubles paralleled with sudden changes in patient's behavior.	b. Domestic troubles unaccompanied by behavior disruptions. Patient had "what it took."
c. Introverted behavior trends and interests.	c. Extroverted behavior trends and interests.
d. History of breakdown of social, physical, mental functioning.	d. History of adequate social, physical, mental functioning.
e. Pathological siblings.	e. Normal siblings.
f. Overprotective or rejecting mother. "Momism."	f. Normal protective, accepting mother.
g. Rejecting father.	g. Accepting father.
Adolescence to adulthood	
a. Lack of heterosexuality.	a. Heterosexual behavior.
b. Insidious, gradual onset of psychosis without pertinent stress.	b. Sudden onset of psychosis; stress present and pertinent; later onset.
c. Physical aggression.	c. Verbal aggression.
d. Poor response to treatment.	d. Good response to treatment.
e. Lengthy stay in hospital.	e. Short course in hospital.
Adulthood	
a. Massive paranoia.	a. Minor paranoid trends.
b. Little capacity for alcohol.	b. Much capacity for alcohol.
c. No manic-depressive component.	c. Presence of manic-depressive component.
d. Failure under adversity.	d. Success despite adversity.
e. Discrepancy between ability and achievement.	e. Harmony between ability and achievement.
f. Awareness of change in self.	f. No sensation of change.
g. Somatic delusions.	g. Absence of somatic delusions.
h. Clash between culture and environment.	h. Harmony between culture and environment.
i. Loss of decency (nudity, public masturbation, etc.).	i. Retention of decency.

of blunted or flat affect; (3) the duration of symptoms of less than six months; and (4) a short-term period for the rapid onset and manifestation of prominent psychotic symptoms that can include confusion and disorientation. Unlike schizophrenia, in the schizophreniform disorder, recovery typically follows and the patient returns to the community and to his or her adaptive role as employee, family member, and friend.

Four decades ago (Kantor et al. 1953), these differentiations were set forth (Table 9.1) distinguishing the dissimilarities between process and reactive conditions that formed their developmental progression from birth to adulthood. Examination of the table makes evident the striking differences in the developmental progression for the two types of patients. These differences have been affirmed in the research of Astrup et al. (1962), Garmezy (1985a), Huston and Pepernik (1958), Kantor and Herron (1966), Kantor et al. (1953), Phillips (1968), Rodnick (1985), Rodnick and Garmezy (1975), and others.

The long-term differentiation between so-called *process* and *reactive* patients has come to be accepted by research investigators and clinicians. In terms of developmental histories, the process group is marked by manifest incompetencies in multiple domains across the life span. But the reactive core group, as many investigators have shown, often provides a strikingly different developmental trajectory marked by early competencies, generally mature role-taking behavior, appropriate interpersonal behavior, and patterns of achievement, sociability, and responsibility. Recent literature reviews have pointed to this interrelatedness of competence, resilience, and psychopathology.

The consistency of description is striking over decades of research. A quarter of a century ago Huston and Pepernik (1958) defined the social and personal history factors that differentiated favorable and unfavorable prognostic indices in schizophrenia. On the favorable side was found upper SES status, good educational history, good occupational history, steady church attendance, marriage marked by a good marital adjustment, a good recent sexual adjustment, stable behavior prior to onset, and under 30 years of age. High IQ and little impairment of abstract thinking were other characteristic positive factors.

The data derived from these early studies were manifestly consistent. In summarizing the status of these two forms of schizophrenia, Zigler and Glick (1986) provided a brief table of the differences that characterized the process and reactive forms of schizophrenia (Table 9.2).

The bifurcation of schizophrenia into true schizophrenia and schizophreniform does not negate the striking predictive power provided by early manifestations of competence. The Phillips Scale of Premorbid Adjustment in Schizophrenia (Phillips, 1953) was an ordinal prognostic rating scale. Initially it was developed through an examination of multiple case histories of schizophrenic patients. In its original form it sought information for rating: (1) premorbid history with special reference to "recent sexual adjustment"; (2) social aspects of sexual life during adolescence and immediately beyond; and (3) social aspects of recent sexual life – 30 years and above. Informa-

Table 9.2. *The process–reactive distinction*

Criterion	Process	Reactive
Premorbid adjustment	Poor; marked sexual, social, and occupational inadequacy	Relatively adequate prepsychotic social, sexual, and occupational adjustment
Onset of disorder	Gradual, with no identifiable precipitating stress	Sudden, with clear-cut precipitating stress
Age of onset	Frequently in late adolescence	Generally later in life
Course and outcome	Deteriorating course, poor prognosis	Good prognosis

tion was also sought of the "history of personal relations" (i.e., friendships, close friends, casual friends, no intimate friendships). These measures involved social competence, work competence, marital status, friendship patterns, closeness versus casual relationships. By comparison, poor premorbid patients provided lengthy histories of incompetence in social relationships, incapacities at work, lack of close friends, and so on.

Aspects of social adaptation in children provide, in part, comparable dimensions of work abilities, social friendships, closeness of ties to others, and the like. In the field of children's adaptation, incapacities in these behavioral spheres often are manifested in externalizing behaviors which do not typically characterize the behavior of children who present internalizing symptoms.

Updated versions of competence measures now appear to show the parallels in behavior and adaptation of stress-resistant or resilient children (Garmezy, 1985b, 1987). Other investigators have provided similar findings.

The longitudinal studies of Jack and Jeanne Block (1980, 1993) reveal the developmental patterns of so-called ego resilients as one of "a long-standing characterological integrity and resourcefulness." As junior high school students these individuals were dependable and productive. They set ambitious goals, their interests were widespread, and their ethics straightforward. They were introspective yet outgoing, sympathetic, warm, and socially perceptive (Block, 1993).

These studies reveal a confluence of important predictors of later positive developmental histories. These include the power of competence behaviors that can help individuals to transcend social class barriers, family risk factors, deprived social conditions, racial and religious discrimination, and the many other slings and arrows so readily released by our contemporary society.

How do such children, adults, patients, and elders exposed to noxious environmental conditions, potential genetic disadvantage, and negative home environments survive and transcend their risk status? Here is a phenomenon the reality of which is evident. The research needed is the search for those mechanisms and processes that underlie the behaviors of at-risk children and adults who despite multiple disadvantages still manage to survive. The reality is evident but the needed longitudinal histories, with prominent exceptions (Werner and Smith, 1982, 1992), are in small supply. What is evident from the literature is that a critical linkage lies in the development of competencies over time. Children at risk give us clues to the critical factors that play a role in normative development and in development beset by numerous traumas. Presumably the nature of gene and environment and the availability of support systems may partially negate the cumulative stressors to which children and adults are so often subjected. The search for the processes and mechanisms that underlie the efforts to survive and to continue to achieve under highly stressful circumstances likely will involve biological, psychological, and sociocultural elements. Children are at risk as a result of numerous deficiencies in their biology, their environments, their familial backgrounds, and the traumas they must endure. The need is for longitudinal studies of adaptive children amid such stressful circumstances. In that matrix of complexities there are many avenues to follow in research. Perhaps the parallels perceived in the active efforts of adult mental patients who transcend their disease status can help to unlock the contemporary mystery of positive adaptations made by children and adults under the most dire conditions.

It is evident that importance must be accorded competence indicators, which appear to serve as protective factors that often transcend the effects of age, social status, familial disturbance, and some disease processes (Anthony and Cohler, 1987; Garmezy and Masten, 1991; Masten et al., 1988; Rathjen and Foreyt, 1980; Strayhorn, 1988; Wine and Smye, 1981). Manifest competence in the domains of work and of social and interpersonal functioning appear to be guideposts to the adaptive efforts of children under stress and (apparently) to the more effective predictions of recovery of adults from severe mental illnesses. If competence can, at least partially, counteract some of the overpowering effects of mental disorder, then efforts to provide training programs in the acquisition and maintenance of such skills will clearly warrant consideration in seeking paths of recovery for the nation's disturbed children and adults.

Various terms have appeared in the literature to summarize the basic construct that reflects these positive outcomes: competence, coherence, ego strength, resilience, stress resistance, and, more recently, personal resourcefulness (Schuldberg, 1993).

If research, over time, conquers the mystery of mental disorders, then the seemingly paradoxical partnership of disorder and resilience may slowly dissolve to be replaced by the search for risk and protective factors and processes that characterize the life-span development of all persons.

New discoveries will replace to-day's concept by others. It is important, however, that we have obtained a general view of the immense and bewildering amount of knowledge of details. And it is hoped that the present concept brings us closer to the patient, enables us to see him as one who has been defeated at some time by the same battle for a harmonious inner life in which we are all engaged, that his fate need not be hopeless and that our therapeutic endeavours are not to be underestimated as "only symptomatic" but correspond to the patient's essential needs. (M. Bleuler, 1986, p. 9)

Acknowledgments

The author acknowledges the support provided over the years by the National Institute of Mental Health, the William T. Grant Foundation, the John D. and Catherine T. MacArthur Foundation, and the University of Minnesota. I am grateful to Drs. Ann S. Masten and Auke Tellegen, research collaborators, for their contributions to the development of themes discussed in this chapter.

References

American Psychiatric Association. 1980. *Diagnostic and Statistical Manual of Mental Disorders DSM-III.* 3d ed. Washington, D.C.: American Psychiatric Association.

American Psychiatric Association. 1987. *Diagnostic and Statistical Manual of Mental Disorders DSM III-R.* 3d ed., rev. Washington, D.C.: American Psychiatric Association.

American Psychiatric Association. 1994. *Diagnostic and Statistical Manual of Mental Disorders DSM-IV,* 4th ed. Washington, D.C.: American Psychiatric Association.

Anthony, E. J., and Cohler, B. J., eds. 1987. *The Invulnerable Child.* New York: Guilford Press.

Astrup, C., Fossum, A., and Holmboe, R. 1962. *Prognosis in Functional Psychoses.* Springfield, Ill.: Charles C. Thomas.

Bastide, R. 1972. *The Sociology of Mental Disorder.* New York: David McKay.

Bleuler, E. 1924. *Textbook of Psychiatry.* New York: Macmillan.

Bleuler, M. 1986. "Introduction and Overview." In *Handbook of Studies on Schizophrenia,* Part I, edited by G. D. Burrows, T. R. Norman, and G. Rubinstein, pp. 1–10. New York: Elsevier.

Block, J. 1993. "Studying Personality the Long Way." In *Studying Lives Through Time,* edited by D. C. Funder, R. D. Parke, C. Tomlinson-Keasey, and K. Widaman, pp. 9–41. Washington, D.C.: American Psychological Association.

Block, J. H., and Block, J. 1980. "The Role of Ego-control and Ego-resiliency in the Organization of Behavior." In *Development of Cognition, Affect, and Social Relations: The Minnesota Symposium on Child Psychology,* vol. *13,* edited by W. A. Collins, pp. 39–101. Hillsdale, N.J.: Lawrence Erlbaum.

Burrows, G. D., Norman, T. R., and Rubinstein, E., eds. 1986. *Handbook of Studies on Schizophrenia.* Part 1: Epidemiology, aetiology, and clinical features, Introduction and Overview by M. Bleuler, pp. 1–10. New York: Elsevier.

Cicchetti, D., ed. 1989. *Rochester Symposium on Developmental Psychopathology,* vol. *1: The Emergence of a Discipline.* Hillsdale, N.J.: Lawrence Erlbaum.

Cicchetti, D., and Toth, S. L., eds. 1991. *Rochester Symposium on Developmental Psychopathology,* vol. *2.: Internalizing and Externalizing Expressions of Dysfunction.* Hillsdale, N.J.: Lawrence Erlbaum.

Cicchetti, D., and Toth, S. L., eds. 1992. *Rochester Symposium on Developmental Psychopathology,* vol. *4.: Developmental Perspectives on Depression.* Rochester, N.Y.: University of Rochester Press.

Dunham, H. W. 1959. *Sociological Theory and Mental Disorder.* Detroit: Wayne State University Press.

Eaton, W. W. 1986. *The Sociology of Mental Disorder.* New York: Praeger.

Eisenberg, L. 1977. "Development as a Unifying Concept in Psychiatry." *British Journal of Psychiatry* 131:225–37.

Fisher, L., Harder, D. W., and Kokes, R. F. 1980. "Child Competence and Psychiatric Risk: Comparisons Based on Diagnosis of Hospitalized Parent." *Journal of Nervous and Mental Disease* 168:338–342.

Garmezy, N. 1968. "Process and Reactive Schizophrenia: Some Conceptions and Issues." *The Role and Methodology of Classification in Psychiatry and Psychopathology*, edited by M. M. Katz, J. O. Cole, and W. E. Barton. Chevy Chase, Md.: U.S. Department of Health, Education, and Welfare.

Garmezy, N. 1970. "Process and Reactive Schizophrenia: Some Conceptions and Issues." *Schizophrenia Bulletin* 2:30–74.

Garmezy, N. 1975. "The Experimental Study of Children Vulnerable to Psychopathology." In *Child Personality and Psychopathology, vol. 2*, edited by A. Davids, pp. 171–216. New York: Wiley.

Garmezy, N. 1978. "Observations on High Risk Research and Premorbid Development in Schizophrenia." In *Nature of Schizophrenia: New Findings and Future Strategies*, edited by L. C. Wynne, R. Cromwell, and S. Matthysse, pp. 460–472. New York: Wiley.

Garmezy, N. 1985a. "Competence and Adaptation in Adult Schizophrenic Patients and Children at Risk." In *The Stanley R. Dean Award Lectures, vol. 2*, edited by R. Cancro and S. R. Dean, pp. 69–112. New York: Medical and Scientific Books: Spectrum Publications.

Garmezy, N. 1985b. "Stress-resistant Children: The Search for Protective Factors." In *Recent Research in Developmental Psychopathology: Journal of Child Psychology and Psychiatry Book Supplement No. 4*, edited by J. E. Stevenson, pp. 213–233. Oxford: Pergamon Press.

Garmezy, N. 1987. "Stress, Competence and Development: Continuities in the Study of Schizophrenic Adults, Children Vulnerable to Psychopathology, and the Search for Stress-resistant Children." *American Journal of Orthopsychiatry* 57:159–174.

Garmezy, N. 1993. "Developmental Psychopathology: Some Historical and Current Perspectives." In *Longitudinal Research on Individual Development*, edited by D. Magnusson and P. Casaer, pp. 95–126. Cambridge University Press.

Garmezy, N., and Masten, A. S. 1991. "The Protective Role of Competence Indicators in Children at Risk." In *Life Span Developmental Psychology: Perspectives on Stress and Coping*, edited by E. M. Cummings, A. L. Greene, and K. H. Karraker, pp. 151–174. Hillsdale, N.J.: Lawrence Erlbaum.

Hans, S. L., and Marcus, J. 1987. "A Process Model for the Development of Schizophrenia." *Psychiatry* 50:361–370.

Hollingshead, A. B., and Redlich, F. C. 1958. *Social Class and Mental Illness*. New York: Wiley.

Hunter, R., and Macalpine, I. 1963. *Three Hundred Years of Psychiatry 1535–1860*. London: Oxford University Press.

Huston, P. E., and Pepernik, M. C. 1958. "Prognosis in Schizophrenia." In *Schizophrenia: A Review of the Syndrome*, edited by L. Bellak, pp. 531–554. New York: Logos Press.

Jaspers, K. 1923. *General Psychopathology.* Chicago: University of Chicago Press.

Kandel, E., Mednick, S. A., Kirkegaard-Sorensen, L., Hutchings, B., Knopf, J., Rosenberg, R., and Schulsinger, F. 1988. "IQ as a Protective Factor for Subjects at High Risk for Antisocial Behavior." *Journal of Consulting and Clinical Psychology* 56:224–226.

Kantor, R. E., and Herron, W. G. 1966. *Reactive and Process Schizophrenia.* Palo Alto, Calif.: Science and Behavior Books.

Kantor, R. E., Wallner, J. M., and Winder, C. L. 1953. "Process and Reactive Schizophrenia." *Journal of Consulting Psychology* 17:157–162.

Kolvin, I., Miller, F.J.W., Fleeting, M., and Kolvin, P. A. 1988. "Risk/Protective Factors for Offending with Particular Reference to Deprivation." In *Studies of Psychosocial Risk: The Power of Longitudinal Data,* edited by M. Rutter, pp. 77–95. Cambridge University Press.

Kraepelin, E. *Dementia Praecox and Paraphrenia.* 1919/1971. Facsimile edition. Huntington, N.Y.: Robert E. Krieger.

Langner, T. S., and Michael, S. T. 1963. *Life Stress and Mental Health.* Glencoe: Free Press.

Lewis, M., and Miller, S. M., eds. 1990. *Handbook of Developmental Psychopathology.* New York: Plenum.

Lief, A. 1948. *The Commonsense Psychiatry of Dr. Adolf Meyer.* New York: McGraw-Hill.

Linton, R. 1956. *Culture and Mental Disorders.* Springfield, Ill.: Charles C. Thomas.

Luthar, S. S. 1993. "Annotation: Methodological and Conceptual Issues in Research on Childhood Resilience." *Journal of Child Psychology and Psychiatry* 34:441–453.

Luthar, S. S., and Zigler, E. 1992. "Intelligence and Social Competence Among High-Risk Adolescents." *Development and Psychopathology* 4:287–299.

Marcus, J., Hans, S. L., Nagler, S., Auerbach, J. G., Mirsky, A. F., and Aubrey, A. 1989. "Review of the NIMH Kibbutz-City Study and the Jerusalem Infant Development Study." *Schizophrenia Bulletin* 13:425–437.

Masten, A. S., Garmezy, N., Tellegen, A., Pellegrini, D. S., Larkin, K., and Larsen, A. 1988. "Competence and Stress in School Children: The Moderating Effects of Individual and Family Qualities." *Journal of Child Psychology and Psychiatry* 29:745–764.

Mednick, S. A., and Schulsinger, F. 1968. "Some Premorbid Characteristics Related to Breakdown in Children with Schizophrenic Mothers." *Journal of Psychiatric Research (Supplement 1)* 6:354–362.

Meyer, A. 1910. "The Dynamic Interpretation of Dementia Praecox." *American Journal of Psychology* 21:385–403.

Phillips, L. 1953. "Case History Data and Prognosis in Schizophrenia." *Journal of Nervous and Mental Disease* 117:515–525.

Phillips, L. 1968. *Human Adaptation and Its Failures.* New York: Academic Press.

Rathjen, D. P., and Foreyt, J., eds. 1980. *Social Competence: Interventions for Children and Adults.* Oxford: Pergamon Press.

Rodnick, E. 1985. "Antecedents and Continuities in Schizophreniform Behavior." In *Research in the Schizophrenic Disorders: The Stanley R. Dean Award Lectures, vol. 2,* pp. 49–67. New York: Spectrum Publications.

Rodnick, E. H., and Garmezy, N. 1975. "An Experimental Approach to the Study of Motivation in Schizophrenia." In *Nebraska Symposium on Motivation,* edited by M. R. Jones, pp. 109–184. Lincoln: University of Nebraska Press.

Rolf, J., Masten, A. S., Cicchetti, D., Nuechterlein, K. H., and Weintraub, S., eds. 1990. *Risk and Protective Factors in the Development of Psychopathology.* Cambridge University Press.

Rutter, M. 1979. "Protective Factors in Children's Response to Stress and Disadvantage." In *Primary Prevention and Psychopathology, vol. 3: Social Competence in Children,* edited by M. W. Kent and J. E. Rolf, pp. 49–74. Hanover, N.H.: University Press of New England.

Rutter, M. 1980. *Developmental Psychiatry.* London: William Heinemann Medical Books.

Sameroff, A. J., Seifer, R., and Zax, M. 1982. "Early Development of Children at Risk for Emotional Disorder." *Monographs of the Society for Research in Child Development (7, Serial No. 199)* 47:1–82.

Sameroff, A. J., Seifer, R., Zax, M., and Barocas, R. 1987. "Early Indicators of Developmental Risk: The Rochester Longitudinal Study." *Schizophrenia Bulletin* 13:383–394.

Sameroff, A. J., Seifer, R., Baldwin, A., and Baldwin, C. 1993. "Stability of Intelligence from Preschool to Adolescence: The Influence of Social and Family Risk Factors." *Child Development* 64:80–97.

Schuldberg, D. 1993. "Personal Resourcefulness: Positive Aspects of Functioning in High-Risk Research." *Psychiatry* 56:137–152.

Seifer, R., Sameroff, A. J., Baldwin, C. P., and Baldwin, A. 1992. "Child and Family Factors that Ameliorate Risk Between 4 and 13 Years of Age." *Journal of the American Academy of Child and Adolescent Psychiatry.*

Srole, L., Langner, T. S., Michael, S. T., Opler, M. K., and Rennie, T.A.C. 1962. *Mental Health in the Metropolis: The Midtown Manhattan Study.* New York: McGraw-Hill.

Sroufe, L. A., and Rutter, M. 1984. "The Domain of Developmental Psychopathology." *Child Development* 55:17–29.

Strayhorn, J. M. 1988. *The Competent Child.* New York: Guilford Press.

Watt, N. F., Anthony, E. J., Wynne, L. C., and Rolf, J. E., eds. 1984. *Children at Risk for Schizophrenia.* Cambridge University Press.

Werner, E. E., and Smith, R. S. 1982. *Vulnerable but Invincible: A Longitudinal Study of Resilient Children and Youth.* New York: McGraw-Hill.

Werner, E. E., and Smith, R. S. 1992. *Overcoming the Odds.* Ithaca, N.Y.: Cornell University Press.

Willis, Thomas. "Two Discourses Concerning the Soul of Brutes Which Is That of the Vital and Sensitive in Man." 1672. Reprinted in Hunter and Macalpine, *Three Hundred Years of Psychiatry 1535–1860* (1963), pp. 187–192. London: Oxford University Press.

Wine, J. D., and Smye, M. D., eds. 1981. *Social Competence.* New York: Guilford Press.

Zigler, E., and Glick, M. 1986. *A Developmental Approach to Adult Psychopathology.* New York: Wiley Interscience.

10

A look at the evolution of developmental models of schizophrenia

L. Erlenmeyer-Kimling

The roots of many current models of the development of schizophrenia can be traced to the theory advanced by Meehl in 1962. In this symposium volume, dedicated to Philip Holzman – whose own work and insights have illuminated our present understanding of schizophrenia so greatly and who attributes his turning toward research in that disorder to his reading the 1962 paper (Holzman, 1990) – it seems especially fitting, therefore, to begin my reflections on some of the features of contemporary developmental models with a look back at their most influential source, Meehl's original model. This is not to say that his model is not still up-to-date and important. Meehl (1989, 1990) has continued to update it and to make alterations as appropriate, based on new information. My task here, though, is to point out some of the conceptual changes and additions that have evolved in thinking about modelling schizophrenia's development, in light of accumulating research findings over the past two or three decades.

Summary of Meehl's model

Only a brief reminder about the essential elements of Meehl's model is in order here, as the theory, with its causal chains leading to the symptoms of schizophrenia, has been summarized many times (e.g., Gottesman and Shields, 1972, 1982; Meehl, 1972a, 1972b, 1989, 1990; Gottesman, 1991). Figure 10.1 is a condensed version of Meehl's diagram (first circulated in 1966 and first published in 1972 [1972b]); the boxes above the horizontal dotted line represent concepts that are not actually shown in Meehl's diagram but that can be inferred from it.

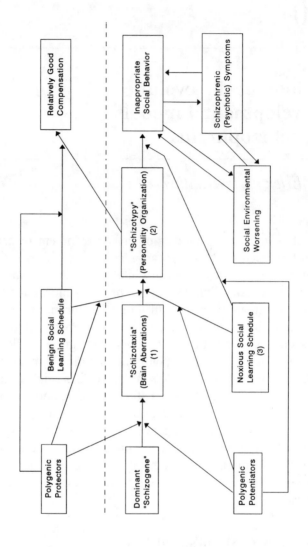

(1) Expression: "Soft" Neurologic and Psychometric Signs, Primary Cognitive Slippage, Aversive Drive

(2) Expression: Secondary Cognitive Slippage, Ambivalence, Social Fear

(3) Mixed Appetitive/Aversive Social Schedule

Figure 10.1. An adaptation and augmented interpretation of Meehl's model.

The starting point was a single dominant "schizogene," which was postulated to be responsible for producing a *schizotaxic brain* – some type of neuronal aberration. The latter was hypothesized to be expressed as "soft" neurological and psychometric signs as well as cognitive slippage and interpersonal aversiveness. In interaction with all *existing* social regimes (but not all theoretically possible ones [Meehl, 1962, 1990]), schizotaxics would develop a schizotypic personality organization, expressed as secondary cognitive slippage, ambivalence, and social fear. (In early, but not later, formulations, Meehl also included anhedonia.) In the presence of other genetically modulated characteristics ("polygenic potentiators"; see below) and noxious social learning conditions (in particular, an inconsistently mixed appetitive–aversive social learning schedule), some schizotypes would then go on to develop clinical schizophrenia. The schizophrenic symptoms would begin as inappropriate behavior, which would trigger a deterioration in the individual's ongoing social environment and a spiralling negative feedback loop between the behavior and the environment. The feedback loop would be further exacerbated and expanded by the emergence of the psychotic symptoms of schizophrenia.

Meehl did emphasize that, depending on the social environment and the polygenic potentiator characteristics, the schizotype could manifest any degree of compensation, from being well compensated, as expressed in "normal" functioning (following the causal pathways above the dotted line in Figure 10.1), to complete clinical decompensation as manifested as schizophrenia. This part of the model and its implications for the later conceptualization of the schizophrenic spectrum, however, were largely neglected by most researchers.

A generic sketch of recent models

Although details and points of emphasis of the developmental models engendered from Meehl's vary considerably, a generic sketch incorporating most of the models can be depicted as in Figure 10.2. Meehl (1972b) called the diagram of his theory one of "minimal complexity," and so, too, is the sketch in Figure 10.2. A more complete plot of the causal pathways would indicate the many levels of steps between the boxes representing gene(s) and brain aberrations. Other concepts included in some models (e.g., nutrition) or pathways in the route to schizophrenia are also omitted in Figure 10.2. Most developmental

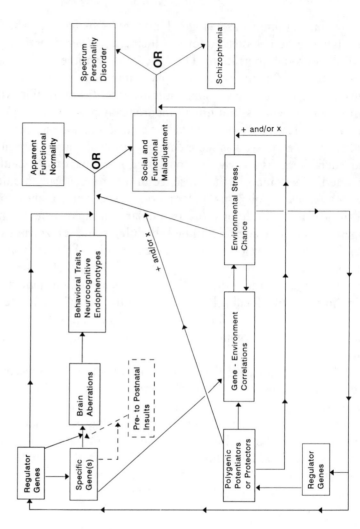

Figure 10.2. A generic scheme of current developmental models of schizophrenia.

models do not explicitly include the idea of gene–environment correlations, but the generic sketch incorporates it as a useful concept that allows for the probability that certain aspects of the environment may be self-selected by given genotypes (or, more precisely, phenotypes), although such selection may not be intentional (c.f. Erlenmeyer-Kimling, 1972; Kendler and Eaves, 1986). For example, the often observed overrepresentation of lower socioeconomic status among schizophrenic patients has prompted researchers to ask whether the main cause is interactional (a social causation hypothesis, in which the stresses of lower social class interact with a genetic susceptibility to produce schizophrenia) or correlational (a social selection hypothesis, in which genetically susceptible individuals, or possibly their schizophrenia-prone forebears, tend to drift downward into or fail to rise out of the lower socioeconomic levels). Recent work in Israel by Dohrenwend and colleagues (Dohrenwend et al., 1992) has mustered compelling support for the correlational (selection) hypothesis, although clearly, once the individual moves downward into the more stressful strata, there are probably resulting interactional effects as well.

In Figure 10.2, the symbol "+ and/or ×" at the intersections of the polygenic potentiators (or protectors) and environmental stress pathways is intended to indicate that these factors may each act directly as main effects and/or that the combination may act as an interaction effect. For disorders such as schizophrenia, interactional feedback loops between genes and environment are probably important. It is possible that, as Singer and Wynne (1965, p. 208, cited in Gottesman and Shields, 1982, p. 169) have commented, ". . . constitutional and experiential influences recombine in each developmental phase to create new biologic and behavioral potentialities which then help to determine the next phase." Obviously, it is not possible to convey in the diagram a sense of how such multifold interactions might influence each successive step in development over time. Gottesman and Shields (1972, 1982) have made an attempt at representing developmental trajectories for individual genotypes (with different genetic liabilities to schizophrenia) interacting with individual histories of psychological stress. Their schematic drawing, however, does not lend itself to a more *generalized* representation of how genetic liability and stress combine across different stages of the life span, just as the generic sketch here doesn't make it possible to predict individual trajectories.

Although it springs from Meehl's (1972b) model, the generic developmental model in Figure 10.2 looks quite different, as comparison with Figure 10.1 shows. I consider here some of the differences and how they have come about through newer emphases and findings in research, starting first with the boxes representing specific genes, potentiators, and environmental stress – basic concepts that are common to both Figures 10.1 and 10.2, though different in detail. Then, without pretending to follow exact historical accuracy, I trace some of the research developments that have altered the way we view the central box (labelled "behavioral traits, neurocognitive endophenotypes" in Figure 10.2) and the possible ensuing "outcomes." Much of the work and thinking about the conceptual boxes representing pre- to postnatal insults, possible neurodevelopmental brain aberrations, and the role of regulatory genes is comparatively new (vis-à-vis that on some of the other conceptual boxes), and some of it is still controversial; I touch on these components of the generic model only toward the end of this chapter.

Specific genetic etiology and potentiators

Many investigators concerned with understanding the etiology and development of schizophrenia now see the susceptibility (or liability) to this disorder as arising from the joint action of several genes (a multilocus theory of transmission), rather than being attributable to a single, low-penetrant "schizogene." The shift in emphasis toward a multilocus theory has come about largely as a result of the repeated demonstration that the cumulative empirical risk figures from a large number of family aggregation and twin studies are more consistent with expectations from multilocus than from monogenic transmission (e.g., Gottesman et al., 1987; McGue and Gottesman, 1989; Risch, 1990). It is to be hoped, however, that the term "multilocus" will prove to be more accurately described as "oligogenic" (involving a few genes) than as "polygenic" (involving many genes), if localization (in DNA) and identification of the function of the genes are near-term goals.

While almost no one takes a strict single locus position toward schizophrenia these days, some investigators have proposed that components of the disorder may act as monogenic traits. For example, Holzman and Matthysse (Matthysse et al., 1986; Holzman et al., 1988; Holzman and Matthysse, 1990) have suggested that inheritance of a latent trait, which is expressed variably as schizophrenia or as bad smooth pursuit visual tracking or both, depending on the particular brain area or areas that are invaded by the disease process (Holzman and Matthysse, 1987; Holzman, 1992), may be under single gene control.

Considerable attention has been paid also to the possibility that schizophrenia may not be one entity but, instead, may be genetically heterogeneous, the behavioral end-product of several different single major loci (SMLs), each acting independently and resulting in phenotypic mimics. The genetic heterogeneity hypothesis appears to be an attractive way to explain the large amount of variability of both clinical phenomena and biological expression seen among schizophrenic patients. (Recently, also, failure of one study to replicate another's apparent linkage results has been taken – without good grounds, as Risch [1990] has pointed out – as evidence for genetic heterogeneity.) There are no firm grounds supporting the genetic heterogeneity hypothesis, however, just as there is no definitive refutation of it.

Polygenes underlying potentiators (or protectors) in Meehl's model and in the generic sketch in Figure 10.2 are not to be confused with those entering into a polygenic complex as the specific etiology for schizophrenia. The potentiators (which include, in Meehl's list: deviant perceptual–cognitive traits; low hedonic capacity and energy level; low or high aggression and sex drive; high social introversion and anxiety level) or protectors (such assets as high IQ, beauty, special talents, etc.) are independent of the susceptibility to schizophrenia, and genes underlying them are not part of the specific etiology for the illness. Although some recent developmental models of schizophrenia do not explicitly contain a role for potentiators in the causal chains leading to clinical outcomes, the idea is important and needs to be retained. There are certain to be gene–environment correlations, as well as interactions, between some of the polygenic potentiators and environment, as indicated in Figure 10.2.

Environmental factors

A second departure from Meehl's original model is in the type of environmental factors postulated in some current developmental models. Whereas Meehl (e.g., 1962, 1972a, 1972b) emphasized a deviant social learning reinforcement schedule in childhood and a schizophrenogenic mother as causes "pushing the schizotype toward schizophrenic decompensation" (Meehl, 1973, p. 141), most of the recent theories no longer give much salience to these ideas. This later deemphasis of early social learning and the pernicious psychological influence of the mother is based largely on the considerable body of research that, first, has failed to demonstrate childhood factors both universally shared by schizophrenics-to-be and specific to them, and, second, has undercut the viability of the schizophrenogenic mother hypothesis (Hirsch and Leff, 1975; Neill, 1990).

At the same time, research in different directions has promoted two other approaches toward environmental factors. One family of hypotheses is concerned with major environmental events occurring pre- or perinatally, which may have direct damaging effects on the brains of preschizophrenic individuals (I refer to such hypotheses later in the chapter). An alternative viewpoint about environmental influences holds that instead of single major events, the cumulative effects of nonspecific, even chance, life stressors are responsible for the development of schizophrenia, in interaction with heredity. Such stressors would include psychological as well as somatic events. A picture of the ways in which many minor, including idiosyncratic, experiences over the life course may link together to form a deleterious environmental whole is aptly described by Gottesman and Shields (1982) for individual cases of genetic vulnerability. In their view of the diathesis-stress theory, specific major events with damaging effects on the brain, such as obstetric complications, would simply be included among the large set of stressors that *can* act jointly with the genetic substrate in a negative way to produce the illness and that *do* so in a fraction of all preschizophrenic cases. Meehl (1990, p. 51), in an update of his theory, has noted that "almost any insult, organic or social, suffices to raise the odds" (of adult decompensation of a schizotype). He has added that "sheer luck" or a "random walk" may play a crucial role in determining the clinical outcome of a person with a genotype predisposing to schizophrenia.*

The center and end of the models: Behavioral traits, neurocognitive endophenotypes; clinical outcomes

Although a role for brain aberrations in the development of schizophrenia is acknowledged in almost all of the models, speculations

---

* See also Chapter 22, by Einar Kringlen, this volume – Eds.

about what such aberrations could be or how they could come about are quite often ignored. Instead, much of the work directed toward modelling has gone straight to a consideration of the ways in which genetic susceptibility may be expressed in premorbid phenotypic characteristics (the center of the diagrams, i.e., the "schizotypy" box in Figure 10.1 and the "behavioral traits, neurocognitive endophenotypes" box in Figure 10.2) and in final clinical outcomes. I do the same here in tracing avenues of change in the models but turn briefly at the end of the chapter to recent work directed toward elucidating deviant processes in the brain.

It is probably fair to say that significant changes in the ways in which the center and outcome parts of the models have come to be viewed began as a result of high-risk research. This new approach, which emerged in the 1960s and early 1970s, initially sought to detect precursors of schizophrenia and to describe the traits and histories of preschizophrenic individuals by prospectively following up at-risk individuals. In the first wave of such studies, the at-risk subjects were uniformly offspring of schizophrenic parents, selected because, as a group, they have greater than average risk of evincing schizophrenia in adulthood and because the advantages of information gained through longitudinal follow-up from young ages seemed to outweigh the burden of the long wait until the expected clinical outcome would appear (e.g., Pearson and Kley, 1957; Fish and Alpert, 1963; Mednick and Schulsinger, 1968; Kallmann et al., 1964; Mednick and McNeil, 1968; Garmezy, 1974). Importantly, in a further departure from previous attempts to characterize premorbid schizophrenia, the high-risk studies took on new dimensions in the goal of depicting the center (schizotypy) box of the developmental models (Figures 10.1 and 10.2). These studies intended not merely to offer descriptions of early subclinical symptoms, but also to identify "harder" behavioral and neurocognitive traits and signs based on laboratory examinations. These traits were thought to be early indicators that could separate out the future schizophrenics from the remainder of the statistically at-risk subjects.

At the beginning of these studies, the expected clinical outcome seemed quite clear to most of the high-risk researchers, who – forgetting Kraepelin's (1919/1971) and Bleuler's (1911/1950) reports of a variety of disturbances in the relatives of their schizophrenic patients or the substantial category of relatives with "questionable" schizophrenia in earlier family studies (e.g., Kallmann, 1938) or Meehl's (1962) emphasis on the range of clinical outcomes that schizotypes could show – seemed to believe that their at-risk subjects would become either manifestly schizophrenic or clinically unremarkable. This split in possible outcomes for members of the high-risk group was, of course, seen differently by investigators with a genetic orientation – who thought of the outcomes chiefly as distinguishing subjects with the schizogene (SML hypothesis), or a sufficient quantity of unfortunate alleles to surpass a liability threshold (polygenic hypothesis), from subjects without such genes – compared with researchers with other theoretical orientations – who thought primarily in terms of environmentally acquired "resilience" versus lack of it.

Then, the outcome expectations began to change. Almost simultaneously with the establishment of most of the high-risk research, the adoption studies directed by Kety, Rosenthal, Wender, and colleagues (1968, 1975) in Denmark and by Heston (1966) in Oregon started bringing forth new evidence addressing the question of the array of clinical outcomes that could be found among the biological relatives of schizophrenic probands. While schizophrenia itself was significantly more frequent in these relatives than in the general population or in controls not related to a schizophrenic proband, other, milder and less functionally debilitating, conditions with schizophrenic-like features were even more common in the relatives. The concept of a spectrum of schizophrenic disorders, which fitted well into genetic transmission theories (e.g., Heston 1970; Gottesman and Shields, 1972), both expanded the outcome end of the developmental models and widened the goal of high-risk research beyond that of looking for the antecedents of frank schizophrenia to that of seeking to predict a range of schizophrenia-related pathological expressions, indicated in Figure 10.2 as the spectrum personality disorders.

Other work starting in the 1970s had much the same orientation as the high-risk research on offspring of schizophrenic parents, but, by focussing on adult subjects, the investigators hoped to avoid the problems of longitudinal follow-up from infancy, childhood, or early adolescence into the schizophrenia risk period many years later. Two approaches were undertaken: one examined adult relatives of schizophrenic probands as the at-risk subjects and the other selected subjects from normal populations based on some characteristic – psychometric (e.g., Chapman et al., 1980; Chapman and Chapman, 1987),*

---

* See also Chapter 14, by Jean P. Chapman and Loren J. Chapman, this volume – Eds.

biochemical (e.g., Buchsbaum et al., 1976), or behavioral (Goldstein et al., 1968) – that allegedly typified a large percentage of schizophrenic patients. The so-called high-risk subjects identified by this second type of approach were then usually examined on other variables of interest in schizophrenia research. Some of this work has been cross-sectional, and, thus, while it has yielded a number of interesting correlations (e.g., Balogh and Merritt, 1985; Chapman and Chapman, 1987; Lenzenweger et al., 1991) and has added to the picture of deviant phenotypic expressions in the adolescent or young adult schizotype, it has not been able to contribute a great deal of information about the relationships of these to later clinical outcomes. Recently, however, the Chapmans (see Chapter 14 and Chapman et al., in press) have reported on a 10-year follow-up of subjects classified earlier as "psychosis-prone" based on psychometric assessments.

Studies examining biobehavioral or other test-assessed traits in adult relatives of schizophrenic probands, however, have contributed evidence for an additional category of outcome that schizotypes may exhibit. This extension of the range of phenotypic expressions among the outcomes was first well documented in work by Philip Holzman and his colleagues (Holzman et al., 1974), who observed that deviance in a behavioral trait (eye tracking) which differentiates many schizophrenic patients from normal controls also occurs in excess among adult relatives, most of whom are not expected to go on to display a diagnosable disorder. Other groups of investigators have since replicated the finding of eye tracking dysfunctions in relatives of schizophrenic probands (e.g., Blackwood et al., 1991; Iacono et al., 1992). Later research by investigators examining deviance in different traits – for example, Wood and Cook (1979) examining visual vigilance performance; Freedman and colleagues (1987) and Siegel et al. (1984) using the event-related potential component P50 to study sensory gating deficits; and Kinney et al. (1986, 1991) studying neurological signs – has yielded similar indications of an outcome category in which schizophrenic-like deviance in a biobehavioral trait is found among adult relatives with no apparent clinical disorders (see box in Figure 10.2). Whether, with closer scrutiny, most of these relatives will be found to be clinically "normal" remains uncertain, though. For example, Steinhauer et al. (1991) have reported that in a small sample of siblings of schizophrenic patients, deficits on an index of attentional sensitivity were limited to those who met criteria for schizotypal personality disorder. Moreover, Freedman et al. (1987) have reported that family members with deficits in sensory gating had significantly higher schizophrenia subscale scores on the Minnesota Multiphasic Personality Inventory (MMPI) than did relatives with normal gating.

In any event, resulting from the research on adult relatives and, to an extent, from the longitudinal follow-up of offspring of schizophrenic parents, the emphasis of high-risk and other family strategies has shifted away from a search focused primarily on the discovery of traits predicting future schizophrenic pathology toward one looking for phenotypic "markers" of susceptibility genes themselves. That is, in recent work, the accent is on finding ways in which the genes may express themselves other than in clinical psychiatric or psychological disturbances. The concept of incomplete penetrance, long invoked in connection with schizophrenia because of discordance in MZ twin pairs, has thus changed from one in which it is assumed that there is *no* phenotypic expression of the gene(s) in some individuals to one involving pleiotropic effects. (Note that while the term "pleiotropy" is traditionally used in connection with the variable expression of a single gene, we might take the license here of also allowing it to mean the variable effects of genes of a polygenic or oligogenic set.)

The criteria for marker research, as well as its potential implications for elucidating the pathophysiological effects of the genes, and for aiding in the pursuit of genetic linkage, have been stated many times and need not be reviewed here. The various trait deviances that have been reported among high-risk offspring and other first-degree relatives of schizophrenic probands, and that thus offer a picture of behavioral and neurocognitive dysfunctions experienced by the schizotype (center boxes in Figures 10.1 and 10.2), also have been reviewed frequently (e.g., Erlenmeyer-Kimling, 1987; Erlenmeyer-Kimling and Cornblatt, 1987a; Syzmanski et al., 1991; Moldin and Erlenmeyer-Kimling, 1993).

These trait anomalies include, besides those mentioned above for adult relatives: attentional and other cognitive disturbances noted from childhood onward (Erlenmeyer-Kimling and Cornblatt, 1987b, 1992; Nuechterlein, 1991; Schreiber et al., 1992; Mirsky et al., 1992) and neuromotor difficulties in infancy and childhood (e.g., reviewed in Marcus et al., 1985, and Fish et al., 1992).* Other less strongly documented (because confined to single reports or small samples or because of contradictions across studies) areas of dysfunction in

---

* See also Chapter 17, by Allan Mirsky, this volume – Eds.

schizophrenics' relatives appear to include: (1) the P300 component of the event-related potential (Saitoh et al., 1984; Blackwood et al., 1991), although deviance in this component appears in our study of off-spring of schizophrenic, affectively ill or normal parents (Erlenmeyer-Kimling and Cornblatt, 1987b) to be unrelated to either schizo-phrenic illness in the parent or type of psychopathology developed by the offspring (Squires-Wheeler et al., 1993), and (2) several psycho-metric or symptom measures observed by midadolescence, namely, thought disorder (Arboleda and Holzman, 1985; Shenton et al., 1989), an index of MMPI items (Moldin et al., 1990), negative symp-toms (Dworkin et al., 1990, 1991), and social incompetence and global maladjustment (Cornblatt and Erlenmeyer-Kimling, 1984; Erlenmeyer-Kimling et al., 1990; Dworkin et al., 1990, 1991; Hans et al., 1992). Anhedonia (measured by the Physical Anhedonia Scale of Chapman and Chapman, 1978b), which also has been reported to be more frequent in relatives of schizophrenic patients than in controls (Katsanis et al., 1990), was not significantly increased in adolescent offspring of schizophrenic parents compared with adolescents with affectively ill or normal parents in the New York High-Risk Project (Erlenmeyer-Kimling et al., 1993). Nevertheless, we found a positive relationship between adolescent anhedonia and a schizophrenia-spectrum type of adult outcome – a social isolation factor (Cornblatt et al., 1992) derived from a personality disorder interview (Loranger et al., 1987) – in the schizophrenia-risk group but not in the other two offspring groups (Erlenmeyer-Kimling et al., 1993).

Do all of these possible markers occur together in the majority of schizotypes? It is unlikely. We know that few, if any, deviant bio-behavioral or psychometric traits are found in 100% of schizophrenic patients, although all of those mentioned above have been observed in substantial percentages of patients. While schizophrenic patients are assumed to have a generalized performance deficit (Chapman and Chapman, 1978a) – meaning that, as a group, they do less well than normals on almost any task – unfortunately, we do not know just how frequently, and in what pattern, dysfunctions in several marker traits co-occur in the same patient, or, conversely, how often patients who do not display deviance with respect to trait A do so on traits B, C, and D. This is because multivariate studies of patients have been rare and, still more rarely, have been reported in a fashion that draws composite pictures of individual patients. The same is true of re-search on offspring and other relatives of schizophrenic probands;

even in those studies, such as our own and several other high-risk projects, that have collected multitrait information results have usually been reported for one marker trait at a time, or, at best, in correlational types of analyses that probably obscure patterns of relationships in different types of subgroups of individuals. Recently initiated research on schizophrenics' relatives (e.g., Katsanis et al., 1990; Blackwood et al., 1991; Grove et al., 1991) may have the potential to clarify more about how biobehavioral markers interrelate with each other both in the patients and in the relatives.

For now, however, the question is how to interpret this plethora of well-established, and some not so well-established, markers. Do they represent pleiotropic effects of one or two major genes, or causally linked or cascading processes deriving from one primary trait-deficit that then leads to others? Are they reflections of dysfunctions in different genes that quantitatively, though probably fungibly, determine what category of clinical outcome will be manifested? Or must we think of genetic heterogeneity, with different genes presenting different pictures of schizotypic traits in the course of development of similar psychopathological outcomes? Note that in this last case, it would still be necessary to invoke pleiotropic effects because of the limited (see above), but nevertheless positive, evidence of correlations among some of the marker traits.

Brain aberrations: Neurodevelopmental approaches and the beginning parts of the models

The last decade has seen an explosion of interest in understanding the role of brain pathology in producing schizophrenia. As I have already noted, much of the research on the development of schizophrenia until recently has concentrated on the center and outcome end of the models. Now, instead of jumping over the beginning parts of the models and treating them, especially the brain, as a black box, newer work is *focussing* there, on early aberrations of the brain: what these are, how they come about, and what their intermediate and long-term behavioral consequences may be.

This clearly is not the place to attempt to review the now vast literature that has accumulated on brain abnormalities seen in schizophrenia or on the several converging lines of evidence that support a neurodevelopmental approach (e.g., Heyman and Murray, 1992) to the understanding of this illness and its variant expressions. Suffice to mention that there is substantial agreement that some type of neuropathologic change of a developmental nature exists in schizophrenia, considerable evidence indicating that brain abnormalities are present prior to onset of overt clinical illness, and further evidence suggesting, in fact, that they can be traced to disturbances in the normal programming of pre- or postnatal neurodevelopment (all reviewed in Bloom, 1993).*

Controversies remain about how early brain abnormalities believed to be associated with later development of schizophrenia may come about. Two possible classes of environmental insults – namely, obstetric complications and prenatal infections – are suggested most prominently in the literature, as either interacting with or substituting for genetic effects. Obstetric complications have been reported in subgroups of preschizophrenic patients or at-risk children in a number of studies reviewed by McNeil (1987), but other studies (Fish, 1984; Crow et al., 1991a; Erlenmeyer-Kimling et al., 1991) have failed to find an association between elevated obstetric complications and later schizophrenia. Moreover, some reviewers of the neuropathology of schizophrenia (Jones and Murray, 1991; Roberts, 1991) have pointed out that these factors could play an etiological role in, at most, only a fraction of future cases of the illness.

Interuterine viral infections, long theorized by some investigators (e.g., Torrey, 1990) to be implicated in schizophrenia, appear to be supported by the epidemiological research of Mednick et al. (1988) and of Murray and colleagues (e.g., Sham et al., 1992). However, other workers (Kendell and Kemp, 1989; Bowler and Torrey, 1990; Crow et al., 1991b; Susser et al., 1993; Erlenmeyer-Kimling et al., 1994) investigating the hypothesized association between prenatal exposure to influenza and later emergence of schizophrenic symptoms have not obtained similar findings. Further, according to Murray's (see Sham et al., 1992) own calculations, the influenza viral exposure would account for a small percentage of increased schizophrenia risk. Bloom (1993) has noted (1) that it is not clear exactly how a virus might produce the kinds of delaying in the timing of neuronal migration and attendant perturbations in brain cell organizations postulated by neurodevelopmental theorists, and (2) that, even without external insults such as viral infections, some genomes might ". . . fail to maintain the expression of one or another of the genes required to complete the process of cortical neuronal migration" (p. 226).

Because overt signs of schizophrenia, especially positive symptoms,

* See also Chapter 6, by Francine Benes, this volume – Eds.

usually do not appear until adolescence or young adulthood, some investigators (e.g., Weinberger, 1987) have postulated that early brain abnormalities remain essentially "quiet" for many years. As I have reviewed above, however, in considering the developmental models' center box and its connections, there is substantial evidence that marker traits may be seen from infancy or young childhood onward in preschizophrenic and other schizotypic individuals. Certainly, that is what we might expect to see from Goldman-Rakic's (1987) tracing of the course of cognitive development following fetal or neonatal damage to cortical circuits. Nevertheless, hypotheses about deficiencies in brain processes normally occurring later in development, closer to the time that schizophrenic symptoms typically appear, have also been offered. Specifically, it has been suggested that synaptic pruning (Feinberg, 1982/1983) or myelination changes (Benes, 1989) that normally take place in adolescence and young adulthood may be faulty in schizophrenia. Benes (1989) has pointed out that even though not appearing until many years later, a failure to show normal increases in myelination could be attributable to the effects of pre- or postnatal lesions. Abnormalities in postpubertal brain changes need not necessarily be attributed to early-occurring lesions, however. The timing of normal changes in myelination and synaptic pruning in adolescence and young adulthood, for example, is evidently controlled by genes programmed to switch on at these later stages of development, just as other genes that are not activated until middle life or later must underlie the many types of maturational and aging changes that take place over the course of the normal life span. (Or perhaps some genes may be designated to turn off, rather than on, over time.) Errors in genes usually activated (or deactivated) in adolescence or young adulthood could thus account for the usual onset of the psychotic symptoms of schizophrenia at that particular time of life, just as errors in later on-switching genes may be implicated in other late-onset disorders – including monogenic ones like Huntington's disease, and more complex disorders like coronary heart disease and diabetes.

Thus, our developmental models of schizophrenia are evolving into ones that build on a large, slowly acquired knowledge-base about the many biobehavioral and clinical expressions of schizophrenia-susceptibility genes, whatever they may be, and, especially, in recent years about the neuroscience of the brain. It is understandable that, thus far, most of the excitement over these new models is engendered by a rapidly unfolding understanding of how steps in the early developmental stages of brain circuitry are programmed and timed, under the control of genetic regulators, to make their essential connections, and how missteps may give rise to a chain of other disruptions in the formation and functioning of developing circuits.* Indeed, it is probably appropriate that future research efforts, for some time to come, be concentrated on the effort to trace schizophrenia and its attendant dysfunctions to the earliest periods of brain development. Nevertheless, the suggestion just mentioned about the possible contribution to brain pathology and psychopathology of late on-switching genes is a reminder that development continues, albeit at a slower pace, under the control of genes that turn on and off at different stages throughout the life span. In the long run, explanations of the development of schizophrenia need to take greater account of the implication of these continuing opportunities for neurodevelopmental changes and continuing potentials for errors at the next step originating from defects in regulatory genes.

Acknowledgments

Work on this paper was supported in part by the Office of Mental Health of the State of New York and a grant, MH-19560, from the National Institute of Mental Health. Irving I. Gottesman provided valuable advice on the two figures. The help of Mimi Simon in the preparation of the manuscript and Sky Pape and Simone Roberts in the preparation of the figures is gratefully acknowledged.

References

Arboleda, C., and P. S. Holzman. 1985. Thought disorder in children at risk for psychosis. *Arch. Gen. Psych.* 42:1004–1013.

Balogh, D. W., and R. D. Merritt. 1985. Susceptibility to Type A back pattern masking among hypothetically psychosis-prone college students. *J. Abn. Psychol.* 94:377–383.

Benes, F. M. 1989. Myelination of cortical-hippocampus relays during late adolescence. *Schiz. Bull.* 15:585–593.

Blackwood, D.H.R., D. M. St. Clair, W. J. Muir, and J. C. Duffy. 1991. Auditory P300 and eye tracking dysfunction in schizophrenic pedigrees. *Arch. Gen. Psych.* 48:899–909.

Bleuler, E. 1950. *Dementia Praecox or the Group of Schizophrenias* (Translated

---

* See Chapter 25, by Steven Matthysse, this volume – Eds.

by J. Zinkin, originally published 1911, Leipzig: Deuticke). New York: International Universities Press.

Bloom, F. E. 1993. Advancing a neurodevelopmental origin for schizophrenia. *Arch. Gen. Psych.* 50:225–227.

Bowler, A. E., and E. F. Torrey. 1990. Influenza and schizophrenia. *Arch. Gen. Psych.* 47:876–877.

Buchsbaum, M. S., R. D. Coursey, and D. L. Murphy. 1976. The biochemical high-risk paradigm: Behavioral and familial correlates of low platelet monoamine oxidase activity. *Science* 194(4262):359–361.

Chapman, L. J., and J. P. Chapman. 1978a. The measurement of differential deficit. *J. Psychiat. Res.* 14:303–311.

Chapman, L. J., and J. P. Chapman. 1978b. *Revised Physical Anhedonia Scale* (unpublished test).

Chapman, L. J., and J. P. Chapman. 1987. The search for symptoms predictive of schizophrenia. *Schiz. Bull.* 13:497–503.

Chapman, L. J., W. S. Edell, and J. P. Chapman. 1980. Physical anhedonia, perceptual aberration, and psychosis proneness. *Schiz. Bull.* 6:639–653.

Chapman, L. J., J. P. Chapman, T. R. Kwapil, M. Eckblad, and M. C. Linser. 1993. Putatively psychosis-prone subjects ten years later. *J. Abn. Psychol.*

Cornblatt, B., and L. Erlenmeyer-Kimling. 1984. Early attentional predictors of adolescent behavioral disturbances in children at risk for schizophrenia. In *Children at Risk for Schizophrenia: A Longitudinal Perspective,* N. F. Watt, E. J. Anthony, L. C. Wynne, and J. E. Rolf, eds., pp. 198–212. Cambridge University Press.

Cornblatt, B. A., M. F. Lenzenweger, R. H. Dworkin, and L. Erlenmeyer-Kimling. 1992. Childhood attentional dysfunctions predict social deficits in unaffected adults at risk for schizophrenia. *Brit. J. Psychiat.* 161 (Suppl. 18):59–64.

Crow, T. J., D. J. Done, C. D. Frith, J. Golding, E. C. Johnstone, and P. M. Shepherd. 1991a. Complications of pregnancy and delivery in relation to psychosis in adult life: A study using the perinatal mortality survey. *Schiz. Res.* 4:253.

Crow, T. J., D. J. Done, and E. C. Johnstone. 1991b. Schizophrenia and influenza. *Lancet* 338:116–118.

Dohrenwend, B., I. Levav, P. E. Shrout, S. Schwartz, G. Naveh, B. G. Link, A.E. Skodol, and A. Staeve. 1992. Socioeconomic status and psychiatric disorders: the causation-selection issue. *Science* 255:946–952.

Dworkin, R. H., G. Bernstein, L. M. Kaplansky, J. D. Lipsitz, A. Rinaldi, S. L. Slater, B. A. Cornblatt, and L. Erlenmeyer-Kimling. 1991. Social competence and positive and negative symptoms: A longitudinal study of children and adolescents at risk for schizophrenia and affective disorder. *Amer. J. Psychiat.* 148:1182–1188.

Dworkin, R. H., S. R. Green, N. E. Small, M. L. Warner, B. A. Cornblatt, and L. Erlenmeyer-Kimling. 1990. Positive and negative symptoms and social competence in adolescents at risk for schizophrenia and affective disorder. *Amer. J. Psychiat.* 147:1234–1236.

Erlenmeyer-Kimling, L. 1972. Gene–environment interactions and the variability of behavior. In *Genetics, Environment and Behavior*, L. Ehrman, G. S. Omenn, and E. Caspari, eds. New York: Academic Press.

Erlenmeyer-Kimling, L. 1987. Biological markers for the liability to schizophrenia. In *Biological Perspectives of Schizophrenia*, H. Helmchen and F. Henn, eds. New York: Wiley.

Erlenmeyer-Kimling, L., and B. Cornblatt. 1987a. High-risk research in schizophrenia: A summary of what has been learned. *J. Psychiat. Res.* 21:401–411.

Erlenmeyer-Kimling, L., and B. Cornblatt. 1987b. The New York High-Risk Project: A follow-up report. *Schiz. Bull.* 13:451–463.

Erlenmeyer-Kimling, L., and B. Cornblatt. 1992. A summary of attentional findings in the New York High-Risk Project. *J. Psychiat. Res.* 26:405–426.

Erlenmeyer-Kimling, L., B. Cornblatt, A. Bassett, S. Moldin, U. Hilldoff-Adamo, and S. Roberts. 1990. High risk children in adolescence and young adulthood: Course of global adjustment. In *Straight and Devious Pathways from Childhood to Adulthood*, L. Robins and M. Rutter, eds., pp. 351–364. Cambridge University Press.

Erlenmeyer-Kimling, L., D. Rock, E. Squires-Wheeler, S. Roberts, and J. Yang. 1991. Early life precursors of psychiatric outcomes in adulthood in subjects at risk for schizophrenia or affective disorders. *Psych. Res.* 39:239–256.

Erlenmeyer-Kimling, L., B. A. Cornblatt, D. Rock, S. Roberts, M. Bell, and A. West. 1993. The New York High-Risk Project: Anhedonia, attentional deviance, and psychopathology. *Schiz. Bull.* 19:141–153.

Erlenmeyer-Kimling, L., Z. Folnegović, V. Hrabak-Žerjavić, B. Borčić, V. Folnegović-Šmalc, and E. Susser. 1994. Schizophrenia and prenatal exposure to the 1957 A2 influenza epidemic in Croatia. *Am. J. Psychiat.* 151:1496–1498.

Feinberg, I. 1982/1983. Schizophrenia: Caused by a fault in programmed synaptic elimination during adolescence? *J. Psychiat. Res.* 17:319–344.

Fish, B. 1984. Characteristics and sequelae of the neurointegrative disorder in infants at risk for schizophrenia: 1952–1982. In *Children at Risk for Schizophrenia: A Longitudinal Perspective*, N. F. Watt, E. J. Anthony, L. C. Wynne, and J. Rolf, eds., pp. 423–439. Cambridge University Press.

Fish, B., and M. Alpert. 1963. Patterns of neurological development in infants born to schizophrenic mothers. In *Recent Advances in Biological Psychiatry, Volume 5*, J. Wortis, ed. New York: Plenum.

Fish, B., J. Marcus, S. Hans, J. Auerbach, and S. Perdue. 1992. Sequelae of a genetic neurointegrative defect in infants at risk for schizophrenia: A review and replication analysis of pandysmaturation in the Jerusalem Study. *Arch. Gen. Psych.* 49:221–235.

Freedman, R., L. E. Adler, G. A. Gerhardt, M. Waldo, N. Baker, G. M. Rose, C. Drebing, H. Nagamoto, P. Bickford-Wimer, and R. Franks. 1987. Neurobiological studies of sensory gating in schizophrenia. *Schiz. Bull.* 13:699–678.

Garmezy, N. 1974. Children at risk: The search for the antecedents of schizophrenia. Part II: Ongoing research programs, issues and intervention. *Schiz. Bull.* 9:55–125.

Goldman-Rakic, P. S. 1987. Development of cortical circuitry and cognitive function. *Child Devel.* 58:601–662.

Goldstein, M. J., L. L. Judd, E. H. Rodnick, A. Alkire, and E. Gould. 1968. A method for studying social influence and coping patterns within families of disturbed adolescence. *J. Nerv. Ment. Dis.* 147:233–251.

Gottesman, I. 1991. *Schizophrenia Genesis: The Origins of Madness.* New York: W. H. Freeman.

Gottesman, I. I., and J. Shields. 1972. *Schizophrenia and Genetics: A Twin Study Vantage Point.* New York: Academic Press.

Gottesman, I. I., and J. Shields. 1982. *Schizophrenia: The Epigenetic Puzzle.* Cambridge University Press.

Gottesman, I. I., P. McGuffin, and A. E. Farmer. 1987. Clinical genetics as clues to the "real" genetics of schizophrenia (A decade of modest gains while playing for time). *Schiz. Bull.* 13:23–47.

Grove, W., B. Lebow, B. Clementz, A. Cerri, C. Medus, and W. Iacono. 1991. Familial prevalence and co-aggregation of schizotypy indicators: A multi-trait family study. *J. Abn. Psychol.* 100:115–121.

Hans, S. L., J. Marcus, L. Henson, J. G. Auerbach, and A. F. Mirsky. 1992. Interpersonal behavior of children at risk for schizophrenia. *Psychiat.* 55:314–335.

Heston, L. L. 1966. Psychiatric disorders in foster home reared children of schizophrenic mothers. *Brit. J. Psychiat.* 112:819–826.

Heston, L. L. 1970. The genetics of schizophrenia and schizoid disease. *Science* 167:248–256.

Heyman, I., and R. M. Murray. 1992. Schizophrenia and neurodevelopment. *J. Royal College of Physicians of London* 26:143–146.

Hirsch, R., and J. P. Leff. 1975. *Abnormalities in the Parents of Schizophrenics.* London: Oxford University Press.

Holzman, P. S. 1990. Comments on Paul Meehl's "Toward an integrated theory of schizotaxia, schizotypy and schizophrenia." *J. Pers. Disorders* 4:100–105.

Holzman, P. S. 1992. Behavioral markers of schizophrenia useful for genetic studies. *J. Psychiat. Res.* 26:427–455.

Holzman, P. S., and S. Matthysse. 1987. Genetic latent structure models: Implications for research on schizophrenia. *Psychol. Med.* 17:271–274.

Holzman, P. S., and S. Matthysse. 1990. The genetics of schizophrenia: A review. *Psychol. Sci.* 1:279–286.

Holzman, P. S., L. R. Proctor, D. L. Levy, N. J. Yasillo, H. Y. Meltzer, and S. W. Hurt. 1974. Eye-tracking dysfunctions in schizophrenic patients and their relatives. *Arch. Gen. Psych.* 31:143–151.

Holzman, P. S., E. Kringlen, S. Matthysse, S. D. Flanagan, R. B. Lipton, G. Cramer, S. Levin, K. Lange, and D. L. Levy. 1988. A single dominant gene can account for eye tracking dysfunctions and schizophrenia in offspring of discordant twins. *J. Psychiat. Res.* 20:57–67.

Iacono, W. G., M. Moreau, M. Beiser, J.A.E. Fleming, and T.-Y. Lin. 1992. Smooth pursuit eye-tracking in first episode psychotic patients and their relatives. *J. Abn. Psychol.* 101:104–116.

Jones, P., and R. M. Murray. 1991. The genetics of schizophrenia is the genetics of neurodevelopment. *Brit. J. Psychiat.* 158:615–623.

Kallmann, F. J. 1938. *The Genetics of Schizophrenia*. New York: J. J. Augustin.

Kallmann, F. J., A. Falek, M. Hurzeler, and L. Erlenmeyer-Kimling. 1964. The developmental aspects of children with two schizophrenic parents. In *Recent Research on Schizophrenia, Psychiatric Research Report No. 19*, P. Solomon and B. C. Glueck, eds. Washington, D.C.: American Psychiatric Association.

Katsanis, J., W. G. Iacono, and M. Beiser. 1990. Anhedonia and perceptual aberration in first-episode psychotic patients and their relatives. *J. Abn. Psychol.* 99:202–206.

Kendell, R. E., and I. W. Kemp. 1989. Maternal influenza in the etiology of schizophrenia. *Arch. Gen. Psych.* 46:878–882.

Kendler, K. S., and L. J. Eaves. 1986. Models for the joint affect of genotype and environments on the liability to psychiatric illness. *Amer. J. Psychiat.* 143:279–289.

Kety, S. S., D. Rosenthal, P. H. Wender, and F. Schulsinger. 1968. The types and prevalence of mental illness in the biological and adoptive families of adopted schizophrenics. In *Transmission of Schizophrenia*, D. Rosenthal and S. S. Kety, eds., pp. 345–362. Oxford: Pergamon Press.

Kety, S. S., D. Rosenthal, P. H. Wender, F. Schulsinger, and B. Jacobsen. 1975. Mental illness in the biological and adoptive families of adopted individuals who have become schizophrenic: A preliminary report based on psychiatric interviews. In *Genetic Research in Psychiatry*, R. R. Fieve, D. Rosenthal, and H. Brill, eds., pp. 147–165. Baltimore: Johns Hopkins University Press.

Kinney, D. K., B. T. Woods, and D. Yurgelun-Todd. 1986. Neurological abnormalities in schizophrenic patients and their families: II. Neurologic and psychiatric findings in relatives. *Arch. Gen. Psych.* 43:665–668.

Kinney, D. K., D. Yurgelun-Todd, and B. T. Woods. 1991. Hard neurologic signs and psychopathology in relatives of schizophrenic patients. *Psych. Res.* 39:45–53.

Kraepelin, E. 1971. *Dementia Praecox and Paraphrenia* (Translated by R. M. Barclay, first published in 1919). New York: Robert E. Krieger.

Lenzenweger, M. F., B. A. Cornblatt, and M. E. Putnick. 1991. Schizotypy and sustained attention. *J. Abn. Psychol.* 100:84–89.

Loranger, A. W., V. L. Susman, J. M. Oldham, and L. M. Russakoff. 1987. The personality disorder examination: A preliminary report. *J. Persy. Disorders* 1:1–13.

Marcus, J., S. L. Hans, S. A. Mednick, R. Schulsinger, and N. Michesen. 1985. Neurological dysfunctioning in offspring of schizophrenics in Israel and Denmark: A replication analysis. *Arch. Gen. Psych.* 42:753–761.

Matthysse, S., P. S. Holzman, and K. Lange. 1986. The genetic transmission of schizophrenia: Application of Mendelian latent structure analysis to eye tracking dysfunctions in schizophrenia and affective disorder. *J. Psychiat. Res.* 20:57–65.

Matthysse, S., D. L. Levy, D. Kinney, D. Deutsh, C. Lajonchere, D. Yurgelun-Todd, B. Woods, and P. S. Holzman. 1992. Gene expression in mental illness: A navigation chart to future progress. *J. Psychiat. Res.* 26:461–473.

McGue, M., and I. I. Gottesman. 1989. Genetic linkage in schizophrenia: Perspectives from genetic epidemiology. *Schiz. Bull.* 15:281–292.

McNeil, T. F. 1987. Perinatal influences in the development of schizophrenia. In *Biological Perspectives of Schizophrenia*, H. Helmchen, and F. A. Henn, eds., pp. 125–138. Chichester: Wiley.

Mednick, S. A., and T. McNeil. 1968. Current methodology in research on the etiology of schizophrenia; Serious difficulties which suggest the use of the high-risk group method. *Psych. Bull.* 70:681–693.

Mednick, S. A., and F. A. Schulsinger. 1968. A preschizophrenic sample. *Acta Psych. Scand.* 40 (Suppl. No. 180):135–139.

Mednick, S. A., R. A. Machon, M. O. Huttenen, and D. Bonnett. 1988. Adult schizophrenia following prenatal exposure to influenza epidemic. *Arch. Gen. Psych.* 45:189–192.

Meehl, P. E. 1962. Schizotaxia, schizotypy, schizophrenia. *Amer. Psychol.* 17:827–838.

Meehl, P. E. 1972a. A critical afterward. In *Schizophrenia and Genetics: A Twin Study Vantage Point*, I. I. Gottesman and J. Shields, eds. New York: Academic Press.

Meehl, P. E. 1972b. Specific genetic etiology, psychodynamics, and therapeutic nihilism. *Int. J. Ment. Health* 1:10–27.

Meehl, P. E. 1973. *Psychodiagnosis: Selected Papers.* Minneapolis: University of Minnesota Press.

Meehl, P. E. 1989. Schizotaxia revisited. *Arch. Gen. Psych.* 46:935–944.

Meehl, P. E. 1990. Toward an integrated theory of schizotaxia, schizotypy and schizophrenia. *J. Persy. Disorders* 4:1–99.

Mirsky, A., S. J. Lochhead, B. P. Jones, S. Kugelmass, D. Walsh, and K. S. Kendler. 1992. On familial factors in the attentional deficit in schizophrenia: A review and report of two new subject samples. *J. Psychiat. Res.* 26:383–403.

Moldin, S. O., and L. Erlenmeyer-Kimling. 1994. Special Issue: Measuring liability to schizophrenia. *Schiz. Bull.* 20.

Moldin, S. O., I. I. Gottesman, L. Erlenmeyer-Kimling, and B. Cornblatt, 1990. Psychometric deviance in offspring at risk for schizophrenia: I. Initial delineation of a distinct subgroup. *Psych. Res.* 32:297–310.

Neill, J. 1990. Whatever became of the schizophrenogenic mother? *Amer. J. Psychiat.* 64:499–505.

Nuechterlein, K. H. 1991. Vigilance in schizophrenia and related disorders. In *Handbook of Schizophrenia, Volume 5: Neuropsychology, Psychophysiology and Information Processing,* S. R. Steinhauer, J. H. Gruzelier, and J. Zubin, eds., pp. 397–433. Amsterdam: Elsevier.

Pearson, J. S., and I. B. Kley. 1957. On the application of genetic expectancies as age-specific base rates in the study of human behavior disorder. *Psych. Bull.* 54:406–420.

Risch, N. 1990. Genetic linkage and complex diseases, with special reference to psychiatric disorders. *Genet. Epid.* 7:3–16.

Roberts, G. W. 1991. Schizophrenia: A neuropathological perspective. *Brit. J. Psychiat.* 158:8–17.

Saitoh, O., S. I. Niwa, K. I. Hiramatsu, T. Kameyama, K. Rymar, and K. Itoh. 1984. Abnormalities in late positive components of event-related potentials may reflect a genetic predisposition to schizophrenia. *Biol. Psychiat.* 19:293–303.

Schreiber, H., G. Stolz-Born, H. Heinrich, H. H. Kornhaber, and J. Born. 1992. Attention cognition and motor perseveration in adolescents at genetic risk for schizophrenia and control subjects. *Psych. Res.* 44:125–140.

Sham, P. C., E. O'Callaghan, N. Takei, G. K. Murray, E. H. Hare, and R. M. Murray. 1992. Schizophrenia following pre-natal exposure to influenza epidemics between 1939 and 1960. *Brit. J. Psychiat.* 160:461–466.

Shenton, M. E., M. R. Solovay, P. S. Holzman, M. Coleman, and H. J. Gale. 1989. Thought disorder in the relatives of psychotic patients. *Arch. Gen. Psych.* 41:897–901.

Siegel, C., M. Waldo, G. Mizner, L. E. Adler, and R. Freedman. 1984.

Deficits in sensory gating in schizophrenic patients and their relatives: Evidence obtained with auditory evoked responses. *Arch. Gen. Psych.* 41:607–612.

Singer, M. T., and L. C. Wynne. 1965. Thought disorder and family relations of schizophrenics. IV. Results and implications. *Arch. Gen. Psych.* 12:201–212.

Squires-Wheeler, E., D. Friedman, A. E. Skodol, and L. Erlenmeyer-Kimling. 1993. A longitudinal study related P3 amplitude to schizophrenia spectrum disorders and to global personality functioning. *Biol. Psychiat.* 33:774–785.

Steinhauer, S. R., J. Zubin, R. Condray, D. B. Shaw, J. L. Peters, and D. P. van Kammen. 1991. Electrophysiological and behavioral signs of attentional disturbance in schizophrenics and their siblings. In: *Schizophrenia Research: Advances in Neuropsychiatry and Psychopharmacology, Volume 1.* C. A. Tamminga and S. C. Schulz, eds., pp. 169–178. New York: Raven.

Susser, E., S. Lin, A. Brown, L. Lumey, L. Erlenmeyer-Kimling. 1994. No increase in schizophrenia after prenatal exposure to influenza. *Am. J. Psychiat.* 151:922–924.

Szymanski, S., J. M. Kane, and J. A. Lieberman. 1991. A selective review of biological markers in schizophrenia. *Schiz. Bull.* 17:99–111.

Torrey, E. F. 1980. *Schizophrenia and Civilization.* New York: Aronson.

Vogel, F., and A. G. Motulsky. 1979. *Human Genetics: Problems and Approaches.* New York: Springer-Verlag.

Weinberger, D. R. 1987. Implications of the normal brain development for the pathogenesis of schizophrenia. *Arch. Gen. Psych.* 44:660–669.

Wood, R. L., and M. Cook. 1989. Attentional deficit in siblings of schizophrenics. *Psychol. Med.* 9:465–467.

11

Developmental theory: Lessons from the study of risk and psychopathology

Dante Cicchetti

Ever since my graduate school years, I have been passionately interested in unraveling the mysteries underlying the relation between normality and pathology, and in reducing the dualisms that exist between the clinical study of and research into childhood and adult high-risk conditions and disorders, between the behavioral and the biological sciences, between developmental psychology and psychopathology, and between basic and applied research. Thus, although no such field of specialization was present at the time, I vowed to commit myself to embarking on a career with these goals in mind. The field of developmental psychopathology has been my chosen pathway in clarifying and pursuing these aims.

Since adopting this philosophy, my goal has been to work toward the formulation of an integrative theory of development that charts the interrelations among the biological, psychological, and social domains across the life course. I have tried to accomplish this by focusing both on clinical and nonclinical populations of children and adults, because I firmly believe that not only must we know how normal development proceeds before we can truly understand psychopathology, but also that in investigating pathology we gain insight into the processes and mechanisms underlying typical forms of ontogenesis (Cicchetti, 1984b, 1990; Rutter, 1986).

In the decade since the publication of the Special Issue on Developmental Psychopathology in *Child Development* (Cicchetti, 1984a), major progress has occurred and developmental psychopathology is now viewed as an emergent scientific discipline (Cicchetti, 1989). Given the recent attention toward and excitement about the developmental psychopathology perspective, it is tempting to view this field as a recent discovery of the past several decades. However, as is often the case with "new" ideas, they have their roots in earlier times (cf. Bronfenbrenner et al., 1986; Cairns, 1983).

In a recent paper, I provided a "back to the future" odyssey of some of the historical forerunners of developmental psychopathology thinking (Cicchetti, 1990). For example, Heinz Werner (1948) believed that the study of atypical populations enables developmentalists to confirm and expand the principles on which their theories are based. As he stated: "A whole series of mental diseases are important to developmental psychology in that they represent the regression, the dissolution, of the higher mental processes, or inhibitions of the genetically advanced levels" (1948, p. 23). Werner further advocated that "the results of psychopathology . . . become valuable in many ways for the general picture of . . . development, just as psychopathology is itself enriched and its methods facilitated by the adoption of the genetic approach" (p. 34). Likewise, Jean Piaget (1975) opined that "developmental psychologists (including myself . . .) are looking forward with great expectation to the emergence of developmental psychopathology as a new discipline" (p. ix) and hoped that "this science will constitute itself on an interdisciplinary basis as wide as possible and on a common language that helps to unify what is precise and generalizable" (p. ix).

In this chapter, I focus on the possible contributions that the study of high-risk conditions and psychopathological disorders can make to elucidating our understanding of theories and principles of normal development. Because many developmental psychopathologists received their training in other disciplines (Cicchetti & Toth, 1991), the term "developmental" connotes different meanings to different people. Therefore, before proceeding with my exposition of how the investigation of atypical populations can inform the study of typical developmental processes, I define the field of developmental psychopathology and specify its central tenets.

Definitional parameters of developmental psychopathology

Developmental psychopathologists are committed primarily to the study of high-risk and disordered populations. Inherent within this framework is a focus on the importance of applying our knowledge of normal development to the study of atypical populations and, likewise, recognition of the value in examining abnormality in order to enhance our understanding of normal processes. Consequently, developmental psychopathologists may be as interested in individuals who are at risk for the development of pathology but who do not manifest it, as they are in individuals who develop an actual disorder (Masten et al., 1990; Sroufe & Rutter, 1984). Thus, developmental psychopathologists also are committed to understanding pathways to competent adaptation despite exposure to conditions of adversity (Cicchetti & Garmezy, 1993; Masten, 1989; Rutter, 1990). A related aspect of the developmental psychopathology perspective involves an interest in the mechanisms and processes that moderate the ultimate outcome of risk factors (Cicchetti & Aber, 1986; Cicchetti & Lynch, 1993; Kopp & Recchia, 1990; Rutter, 1988). The approach suggested by a developmental psychopathology perspective requires a comprehensive assessment of functioning, including multidisciplinary, multidomain, multicontextual measurement strategies (Cicchetti & Manly, 1990; Cicchetti & Wagner, 1990). Finally, while many active theoreticians and researchers in developmental psychopathology have focused their efforts on childhood disorders, I believe that a life-span perspective is necessary because it is only by examining a range of conditions and populations from infancy through adulthood that developmental continuities and discontinuities can be elucidated fully. Developmental psychopathology, considered a "macroparadigm" (Achenbach, 1990), integrates the ontogenetic changes occurring in the behavioral repertoire, including socioemotional, cognitive, linguistic, and representational processes and functions, with developments taking place in neurobiological structures and functions and physiological and neurochemical processes of the brain throughout the life span (Cicchetti, 1990; Institute of Medicine, 1989).

Developmental psychopathologists view disorders of childhood and adulthood from within the broader context of knowledge that has been accrued about normal biological, psychological, and sociological processes. In practice, this requires an understanding of and appreciation for the developmental transformations and reorganizations that occur over time (Cicchetti & Schneider-Rosen, 1986; Sroufe, 1989; Sroufe & Rutter, 1984); an analysis and appropriate weighting of the risk and protective factors and mechanisms operating in the individual and his or her environment across the life span (Cicchetti & Aber, 1986; Cicchetti & Lynch, 1993; Rutter, 1990); the investigation of how emergent functions, competencies, and developmental tasks modify the expression of a disorder or lead to new symptoms and difficulties (Angold & Costello, 1991; Rutter, 1988; Rutter & Garmezy, 1983; Sroufe & Rutter, 1984); and the recognition that a specific stress or underlying mechanism may lead to different behavioral difficulties, at different times in the developmental process and in varied contexts (Cicchetti & Aber, 1986; Cicchetti & Lynch, 1993; Garmezy & Rutter, 1983). As such, individuals will experience the same events differently depending on their level of functioning across all domains of psychological and biological development. Accordingly, various occurrences will have different meanings for an individual depending on both the nature and the timing of his or her experience. The interpretation of the experience, in turn, will affect the adaptation or maladaptation that follows.

Perspectives on the interface between normal and atypical development

Throughout history, prominent theoreticians, researchers, and clinicians have adopted the premise that knowledge about normal and abnormal development is reciprocally informative. Embryologists, neuroscientists, and psychiatrists, as well as clinical, developmental, and experimental psychologists, have emphasized that research on normal and atypical populations must proceed concurrently in order for an integrative theory of development that can account for normal as well as deviant forms of ontogenesis to emerge (Cicchetti, 1990; Hesse & Cicchetti, 1982; Sroufe, 1990; Weiss, 1961; Werner, 1948).

For example, research conducted in embryology has made significant contributions to developmental theory (Fishbein, 1976; Gottlieb, 1983; Sarnat, 1992). It was from their empirical efforts to unravel the mysteries of normal embryological functioning through isolation, defect, and recombination experiments, and the investigation of surgically altered and transplanted embryos, that early embryologists derived the principles of differentiation, of a dynamically active organism, and of a hierarchically integrated system (Waddington, 1966; Weiss, 1969). These three principles form the cornerstone beliefs of most contemporary developmental theories (Cairns, 1983; Gottlieb, 1983; Sroufe, 1979).

Moreover, throughout time experiments conducted on genetic mutations have enhanced our understanding of normal functioning by magnifying the processes involved in normal ontogenesis (see Lawrence, 1992; Plomin et al., 1991; Sarnat, 1992). For example, investigations of inborn errors of metabolism eventuated in the "one gene, one enzyme" hypothesis that is viewed as the major mechanism underlying normal gene action (Beadle & Tatum, 1941). Mutagenesis has evolved into one of the primary strategies in the geneticists' research armamentarium. While investigators initially relied on spontaneously occurring mutations, genetically engineered mutations have been initiated. These mutagenesis experiments are designed to produce specific effects, including causing lesions in a particular gene and impacting upon genes in a biochemical pathway (Lawrence, 1992). It is through the examination of aberrant genetic makeup that the normal functioning of genes can be elucidated.

Similarly, within the neurosciences, progress in molecular cell biology has stemmed from developmental research on normal and abnormal variations in cells (e.g., research on the development of cell specificity, cancer, immunity, etc. [see Darnell et al., 1986]). Likewise, research on the development of the central nervous system has led to an increased comprehension of the processes underlying the diversity and complexity of the mature nervous system. Specifically, one might inquire as to what mechanisms dictate which genes are expressed in particular cell types and what regulates the timing of the genetic expression (see Nowakowski, 1987; Watson et al., 1987). Finally, molecular neurobiological research on developmental disorders of the nervous system (e.g., critical periods in brain development, genetic mutations, disorders of neural tube formation, disorders of neural migration, disorders of myelination, disorders of synapse formation, etc.) has augmented our knowledge of basic molecular neurobiology (Ciaranello et al., 1990; Sarnat, 1992).

Investigations in the field of cognitive neuroscience likewise have revealed that the study of the intellectual impairments that proceed from brain damage provide important clues about the development of normal cognition. For example, Farah's (1990) investigation of visual agnosia – the inability to recognize objects despite the fact that elementary visual functions are unimpaired – reveals how a relatively rare disorder can provide an entree into the manner in which the normal brain might carry out the complex process of vision.

Unfortunately, despite the adherence of developmental psychopathologists to the belief that normal and abnormal ontogenetic processes must be examined concurrently (Cicchetti, 1984b; Sroufe, 1990), most contemporary theory and research in developmental psychopathology have focused on the contributions that normal development can make to advancing our knowledge of psychopathology. Indeed, as I have noted elsewhere, before developmental psychopathology could become a distinct field of inquiry, the science of normal development needed to mature (Cicchetti, 1984b). The proliferation of knowledge about typical psychological and biological development that has occurred during the past several decades has enabled developmental psychopathologists to make compelling progress in their quest to understand the causes, trajectories, and consequences of mental disorder.

For example, research conducted with normal infants and children has led to major advances in our comprehension of the developmental organization of autistic children. Specifically, many of the achievements made in enhancing the understanding of the neurobiological, attentional, cognitive, representational, socioemotional, and social-cognitive aspects of autism are directly attributable to progress in the study of the normal development of these domains and the application of this knowledge to the study of autism (see, e.g., Baron-Cohen et al., 1985; Dawson, 1989; Frith, 1989; Mundy & Sigman, 1989a, 1989b; Rutter & Garmezy, 1983).

Researchers studying the etiology of schizophrenia similarly have focused their energies on attempting to pinpoint what has gone awry in the genetic and epigenetic specification of normal brain development. Advances in our knowledge of the development and maturation of the central nervous system have begun to influence the manner in which many investigators are conceptualizing schizophrenia (see, e.g., Benes, 1991; Feinberg, 1982; Weinberger, 1987).

In view of the contributions that the study of psychopathological and extreme risk conditions have made to theory development and refinement in other disciplines, it is curious that until recently there has been less recognition and acceptance that the examination of high-risk and pathological conditions can affirm, expand, and challenge extant developmental theories. This reluctance to apply knowledge derived from atypical populations to normal developmental theory is even more surprising in view of the historical interest in children who developed in unusual circumstances. Case studies dating to the turn of the nineteenth century of the Wild Boy of Aveyron, a child who was deprived of all contact with his own species, caused scholars to question the unfolding of the developmental process in conditions severely discrepant from more normative childhood experiences (Humphrey & Humphrey, 1932). Examinations of aberrant circumstances such as those endured by the "Wild Boy" shed light on theories of cognitive, linguistic, and social development.

For example, Yamada's (1990) report of the case of Laura, a mentally retarded woman, demonstrates that language can develop and function despite the presence of serious and pervasive intellectual impairments. Moreover, Yamada's work offers supportive evidence for the claim that language is a separate cognitive ability.

In order to elucidate the potential for studies of risk and psychopathology to enhance our theories of normal development, in this chapter I draw upon relevant illustrations from investigations of Down syndrome, maltreated, and mood-disordered populations. I have chosen to focus on these conditions because each occurs with sufficient frequency to warrant research and clinical attention, and because each of these populations constitutes a continuum in terms of the relative contribution to developmental outcome of reproductive (genetic/constitutional) and care-taking (parental/environmental) factors. Moreover, they all possess compelling characteristics that enable us to augment our understanding of normal developmental theory. It is important to emphasize that these populations are by no means the only examples of atypical conditions informing developmental theory (see, for example, Tager-Flusberg, 1994). Moreover, the research studies presented for each condition similarly are nonexhaustive, but rather relevant exemplars.

Illustrations drawn from abnormal populations

Investigations of the determinants of human behavior are greatly hampered by the ethical impossibility of conducting experiments that will compromise the integrity of biological and psychological ontogenetic processes. Along with other developmentalists such as Eric Lenneberg (1967) and Uri Bronfenbrenner (1979), I believe we must direct our attention toward "experiments of nature" like those provided by high-risk conditions and pathological deviations in order to elucidate our understanding of developmental processes and mechanisms. Often, the study of a system in its smoothly operating normal or healthy state does not afford us the opportunity to comprehend the interrelations among its component subsystems. Noam Chomsky (1968) reflected upon this state of affairs when he asserted: "One difficulty in the psychological sciences lies in the familiarity of the phenomena with which they deal. . . . One is inclined to take them for granted as necessary or somehow 'natural.'" Because pathological conditions such as brain damage and growing up in malignant environments enable us to isolate the components of the integrated system, their investigation sheds light on the normal structure of the system and prevents us from falling prey to the problem identified by Chomsky.

The investigation of atypical populations provides a basis for verifying claims of universality of an ontogenetic sequence and for affirming and challenging developmental theory, while simultaneously contributing precision to current theoretical formulations. Similar to genetic research on pathological embryos and to neurobiological and linkage studies of psychopathology, investigations of factors that cause development to go awry can help to inform more normative developmental processes. By studying various samples who manifest disorders and high-risk conditions with different etiologies, it will be possible to discover the processes and structures that are necessary and/or sufficient for achieving the same or different developmental outcomes.

Furthermore, through investigating these outcomes, we will be in a better position to understand the sequencing, structuring, organization of advances, and mechanisms of change in the various psychological and biological domains, as well as their interrelations. The examination of abnormality may enlighten our understanding of the normal ontogenetic course because focusing on the nontypical may be critical for separating elements or domains that usually proceed or occur in tandem (Cicchetti & Sroufe, 1976). The examination of similarities or variations in the psychological and biological deviations that may become manifest in clinical populations with different etiologies underlying their developmental problems will contribute to our current systems of diagnosing and classifying psychopathology (Richters & Cicchetti, 1993) and will facilitate the direction of prevention and intervention strategies (Cicchetti & Toth, 1992b). When syndrome or high-risk condition-specific impairments are discovered, the next step will be to identify and to implement developmentally appropriate interventions that are targeted at ameliorating these difficulties (see Cicchetti & Toth, 1992a). Hence, examinations of psychopathological populations and developmental extremes must be conducted. If we choose simply to ignore or bypass the study of these atypical phenomena, then the eventual result is likely to be the construction of theories that are contradicted by the revelation of critical facts in psychopathology (cf. Cicchetti & Schneider-Rosen, 1984; Lenneberg, 1967). Although caveats and limitations must be considered and noted before generalizing from findings obtained on atypical populations to theories of normal development, I agree with Rutter's (1989) assertion that "there can be no presupposition that normal and abnormal development do, or do not, share the same qualities; rather, there must be a concern empirically to test for similarities and dissimilarities" (p. 26).

Down syndrome

Investigations of children with Down syndrome, the most common organic form of mental retardation, offer many advantages for addressing basic questions about developmental processes. For example, an examination of the postnatal development of individuals with an extra autosomal chromosome may provide a clear test of the hypothesis that abnormal chromosomal material may be used as an independent variable to study behavioral differences. Whereas very few autosomal trisomies are viable, nor do they occur frequently enough to be tested for behavioral phenotypes, Down syndrome is a notable exception. For example, Down syndrome, characterized by the presence of three chromosomes at autosomal pair 21, is diagnosable in utero through amniocentesis and therefore can be assessed and followed very early in the process of development. It possesses a suitable complexity and intactness of phenotypic expression and occurs with sufficient frequency to allow for meaningful developmental analysis (see Cicchetti & Beeghly, 1990).

The delayed and heterogeneous development of individuals with Down syndrome allows for a more precise examination of ontogenetic sequences in various psychological and biological domains and for the assessment of their interrelations at specific periods in ontogenesis. In normally developing children, it is difficult to determine whether mental structures that emerge simultaneously are necessarily or coincidentally linked. However, by studying atypical children such as those with Down syndrome, researchers can discover which structures co-emerge regardless of wide variability in the timing of their emergence, and describe with more confidence sequences of development – that is, which structures are necessary prerequisites for later developing structures.

For instance, the delayed cognitive development of infants with

Down syndrome allows a separation of the early prototypes of what will later be affective expressions from genuine emotional reactions that are dependent on more sophisticated psychological processes. Researchers in developmental psychology had debated for years about whether defensive reactions to the visual information for impending collision were present in newborns (Bower, 1974), or not until the second half-year, when other cognitive advances such as intentionality and causality were present (Yonas et al., 1977). Very young babies with Down syndrome reacted with blinking to imploding visual stimuli at the same rate as normal infants (Cicchetti & Sroufe, 1978). However, youngsters with Down syndrome did not show anticipatory reactions and motoric evasive maneuvers until quite late in infancy, a finding revealing significant delays compared to normal babies. It became clear that two distinct processes were involved in defensive reactions: one reflexive and appearing quite early, the other based on cognitive development and maturation. In this case, the study of disordered development allowed researchers to separate processes not easily distinguished in normal samples.

Likewise, the investigation of the ontogenesis of affect in infants with Down syndrome has important implications for understanding the organization of normal development – in particular, the relationship between affect and cognition (see Hesse & Cicchetti, 1982). Emotions may be regarded as developing ontogenetically earlier than cognition, thereby providing the context within which cognitive development may occur (*cognitive epiphenomenalism*). The emergence of new emotions may be dependent on cognitive advances that must be made before various emotions may be expressed (*emotional epiphenomenalism*). Emotions may develop along a separate pathway from cognitive advances, so that the sequence, rate, and quality of change must be considered distinctly within each domain (*parallelism*). Finally, emotions may emerge in interaction with cognitive advances, thereby suggesting a progression that necessitates a consideration of developmental changes that occur across domains and that exert a reciprocal influence on each other (*interactionism*).

The ontogenesis of laughter in infants with Down syndrome provides a good illustration of the intimate connection that underlies emotional and cognitive development. In previous research with several samples of normal infants, Sroufe and Wunsch (1972) found that changes in laughter were associated with cognitive development. Infants in the first half-year of life laughed primarily in situations that were physically intense or vigorous (e.g., auditory and tactile stimulation). Increasingly during the second half-year, however, infants laughed at progressively more subtle and complex social and visual stimulation, whereas laughter at simple stimuli abated. For example, young babies laughed at being kissed on the stomach, popping sounds of the lips, and bouncing on the knee, whereas only older infants laughed consistently at mother sucking on the baby's bottle, crawling on the floor, or covering her face with a human mask. These findings suggested that later laughter is related to developmental changes in available cognitive schemata (cf. Kagan, 1971).

The question thus arises: Would infants who show atypical cognitive development also show a corresponding lag in their affective development? To address this issue, we conducted a study of infants with Down syndrome to extend and elaborate the reported association between affect and cognition. We reasoned that if affective development is a function of cognitive development and not merely a coincidental co-occurrence of chronological age, then the sequence of affective stages should occur in the same order as that exhibited by normal babies. Because items such as mother hiding behind a mask elicit laughter when normal infants have achieved the appropriate cognitive developmental level (for example, when infants are capable of finding a completely covered object), such affective and cognitive occurrences should also appear concurrently in retarded children, albeit at later ages.

Cicchetti and Sroufe (1978) followed 25 infants with Down syndrome longitudinally between 4 and 24 months of age. Babies were presented with the same laughter items that were administered to normal babies. The items were presented by their mothers twice monthly in their homes. Observers coded the affective reactions of the babies to the stimulus presentations. In addition, cognitive assessments were given to infants by examiners who had no knowledge of the infants' performance on the laughter items.

We found that even though infants with Down syndrome displayed a later onset of laughter, they laughed at these stimulus items in the same order as normal infants – first to intrusive auditory and tactile items, later to the more complex social and visual items. Such an ordering suggests a link between cognitive development and laughter at the more sophisticated items.

Perhaps the most persuasive data on the nature of the relation between affect and cognition were found on the cognitive test results.

The infants with Down syndrome with the highest developmental quotients laughed earliest and laughed at the most social and visual items. Likewise, the babies with Down syndrome who had the lowest cognitive scores, showed the most delayed laughter.

Finally, despite the statistically significant positive correlations that were obtained between affective and cognitive development, factors in addition to cognition accounted for some of the variability in affective growth. Interestingly, even when infants with Down syndrome were matched on mental age with normal babies, the infants with Down syndrome laughed less than would have been expected if cognitive factors were solely responsible for the delay in affect ontogenesis.

These data with retarded babies reveal that affect and cognition, though interrelated, are separate developmental systems (see Izard, 1991). For babies with Down syndrome who vary greatly in their progression through the stages of infancy, affect and cognition interact in a reciprocal fashion. Neither the cognitive nor affective epiphenomenalism positions can explain our findings.

Not surprisingly in view of the opportunities that the study of Down syndrome affords researchers interested in charting the course and mechanisms of ontogenesis, we now possess considerable knowledge about the development of children with Down syndrome (Cicchetti & Beeghly, 1990; Cicchetti & Ganiban, 1990; Nadel, 1988). Investigators generally have found that the development of infants and young children with Down syndrome across various psychological domains follows a developmental course comparable to that of nonhandicapped, normally developing children. Although the pace of development is slower for children with Down syndrome, they demonstrate similar developmental trends, moving from states of low differentiation and simple interactions with the world, to the development of specific abilities, complex integrated thought, articulated concepts of the world, and a vast array of behaviors and schemes for interacting with the world. In this transition, the child ceases to be "stimulus bound," or simply a "reactor" to environmental events. Rather, through their increasing abilities to evaluate and mentally represent their experiences, children with Down syndrome begin to shape their own reactions and to manipulate their environments in an active fashion. Additionally, when developmental level is considered, infants and young children with Down syndrome generally appear to progress through the same stages of development as normally developing children. Development occurs in an orderly fashion, with children from both populations acquiring increasingly more complex skills with on-togenesis.

In terms of the structuring and integration of abilities, infants and young children with Down syndrome demonstrate a coherence and organization in their development that typically parallels that of nor-mally developing nonhandicapped individuals. Underlying changes in the child's ability to evaluate and mentally represent the world are concomitantly reflected in affect, attachment, play, language, and self-systems. Such relationships suggest that their development is highly organized and coherent despite their organic handicap.

To provide an illustration, data from my laboratory revealed that the symbolic play of children with Down syndrome reflected their social knowledge. With development, children with Down syndrome evidenced increasingly differentiated concepts of self and other in their enactive play schemes. In addition, parallel advances were found in their ability to utilize language as a communicative social tool (Beeghly et al., 1990). Likewise, the self-language of children with Down syndrome (e.g., talking about their ongoing activities, using personal pronouns, giving adult directives, describing their internal states, etc. [Kagan, 1981]) was highly related to advances in symbolic and cognitive development (Cicchetti et al., 1990). Interestingly, in-ternal state language occurred significantly more often during sym-bolic play than during other kinds of play both in children with Down syndrome and in their nonhandicapped mental-age counterparts. These results are consistent with Werner and Kaplan's (1963) con-ceptualization that in normal development the process of symboliza-tion becomes increasingly autonomous and that the self becomes more cognizant of its symbolic activities.

Striking parallels between spontaneously occurring symbolic play and expressive language also were observed both in children with Down syndrome and in normally developing children. Specifically, (1) no prelinguistic child engaged in any symbolic play; (2) children in the one-word stage of language development produced only single schemes in symbolic play; (3) children in early Stage I of language development (mean length of utterance [MLU] = 1.01−1.49, Brown, 1973) were beginning to combine simple symbolic schemes during play; and (4) children with more advanced language (i.e., in late Stage I or higher) produced planned, hierarchically integrated symbolic play bouts. Moreover, both MLU and mental age were significantly corre-lated with indices of symbolic play maturity both for children with

Down syndrome and for their cognitively matched nonhandicapped controls. Specifically, the complexity of children's play schemes and true depiction of social roles during pretend play were closely tied to mental age, MLU, and pragmatic skills.

In addition to the associations we found among cognitive, linguistic, and symbolic play domains, developmental asynchronies and dissociations were discovered that may shed light on the process of normal development. For example, despite the fact that children with Down syndrome did not differ significantly from their mental-age (MA) matched normally developing peers on measures of *nonlinguistic* representation, and even though similar patterns of correlations were obtained among play, language, and cognition for both groups of children, the children with Down syndrome did differ from MA-matched comparisons in their performance on *linguistic* measures of representations of self and other. The children with Down syndrome produced significantly less mature self-related language than did their MA-matched nonhandicapped counterparts. Children with Down syndrome used fewer personal pronouns, spoke less about their internal states, in both present and hypothetical contexts, and described their ongoing actions less often (Cicchetti et al., 1990). Thus, the ability to use self-related language is more delayed for children with Down syndrome than one might expect based on their level of cognitive development alone. This again suggests the separateness of developmental domains, specifically cognition and language.

Moreover, children with Down syndrome were significantly delayed in expressive language relative to their level of cognitive development, with syntactic and vocabulary skills developing at a slower pace than pragmatic skills (Beeghly & Cicchetti, 1987). Consequently, when children with Down syndrome are matched with nonhandicapped normally developing children on the basis of developmental level, their syntax and vocabulary are significantly poorer than that of peers.

Because many domains of ontogenesis unfold concurrently in normally developing children, it is very difficult to ascertain the nature of their interrelations (i.e., interdependent or independent). The dissociations between language and cognition in children with Down syndrome provide evidence for existing theoretical claims that cognition is multifaceted (Gardner, 1983; Gazzaniga, 1988; Yamada, 1990) and that language is not reducible to cognitive factors.

As the preceding examples highlight, the study of infants and children with Down syndrome has illuminated our knowledge of normal development. Specifically, research on Down syndrome provides insight into what developmental sequences are logically necessary, what alternate pathways of development are possible, and provides evidence on which factors accounting for mental growth are most important (i.e., biological, socioemotional, cognitive, linguistic, representational). Organically retarded persons are not only "different" from nonretarded persons; they are organized in their own right, and the study of that organization will tell us what ontogenetic processes are common to all persons, normally developing and retarded alike.

Maltreatment

In view of the adverse circumstances in which they are reared, children who have been maltreated serve as yet another atypical population whose study can inform and expand our theories of development. Although maltreatment is a heterogeneous phenomenon, it is unified by an experience of caregiving that does not optimize normal development. Thus, children who have been maltreated are at risk for the emergence of developmental delays and/or anomalies (Cicchetti & Carlson, 1989; Cicchetti & Toth, 1993; Starr & Wolfe, 1991). Through the examination of atypicalities in the developmental process of maltreated children, our theories of development can be enhanced.

An especially powerful example of the effect of maltreatment on the process of ontogenesis and its potential for expanding and informing developmental theory can be gained from a brief case review of "Genie," a child discovered in adolescence after being subjected to a childhood of extreme abuse, neglect, deprivation, and isolation (Curtiss, 1977). Until her discovery at the age of 13-1/2, Genie's environment had consisted of a sparsely furnished room largely devoid of visual, auditory, or tactile stimulation. In addition to severe deprivation and physical abuse, Genie reportedly was never spoken to. Thus, the unfolding of Genie's development after her discovery provided insight into a number of issues of interest to developmentalists. For example, controversies over "critical periods" for language acquisition, the lateralization of language if it is acquired after puberty, and the capacity to form attachment relationships in later years even if socially isolated during childhood could be addressed by observing

Genie's development. Similar to findings of dissociations and asynchronies of language in children with Down syndrome, the language development of Genie, a severely maltreated child, attests to the multifaceted nature of cognition. In a further exposition of how atypicality can inform normal developmental theory, I next draw from relevant research studies of attachment relationships, representational models, and development of self in maltreated children.

By approximately 9 to 12 months of age, normally developing infants have begun to internalize the history of their interactions with their primary caregivers and the caregiving matrix becomes part of a core of emerging inner organization (Cicchetti, 1991). Representational models of these primary relationships are thought to emerge by the end of the first year of life.

During this period, the infant responds to novel situations based on earlier experiences with caregivers. One way in which a caregiver influences an infant's inner world of experiences is by shaping the infant's expectations of the environment. The infant's perceptions of the world as responsive, stable, and secure largely depend on the caregiver's sensitivity to the baby's needs. Thus, the history of interactions between caregivers and their infants is expected to color the child's interpretation of and reaction to events in the world.

The experience of a caretaker as being reliably available and emotionally responsive allows infants to build accessible, responsive representational models of their attachment figure(s), as well as a reciprocal representational model of the self as acceptable in the eyes of the attachment figure(s). Conversely, the psychological unavailability of parents for extended periods of time exerts powerful influences on future expectations regarding the unavailability of attachment figures and on the view of the self as unlovable. The representational models of the self in relation to attachment figures that are formed during this period possess important implications for understanding the infant's subsequent interactions with the broader environment, as well as the course of positive versus maladaptive developmental outcome.

Attachment theory serves as an example of how the examination of maltreated children can play a role in expanding developmental theory. In fact, attachment theory evolved from John Bowlby's (1944) inquiries into the lives of 44 thieves who he found uniformly had suffered early emotional deprivation. Thus, it is even more fitting that almost 50 years since its development, attachment theory has been elaborated upon through the inclusion of atypical populations of infants.

According to attachment theory, adequately nurturing care is necessary if the infant is to use the caregiver as a base of emotional support that increases felt security and fosters exploration of the environment (Bowlby, 1969/1982). Similar to nonhuman primates (Ruppenthal et al., 1976), infants exposed to caregiving adversity have been found to establish attachment relationships. However, the *quality* of the attachment relationships of maltreated children that emerges under conditions of adverse caregiving sheds light on attachment theory conceptualizations derived from normal populations (Crittenden & Ainsworth, 1989; Lynch & Cicchetti, 1991).

The most widely used method for assessing attachment relationships, the Strange Situation (Ainsworth & Wittig, 1969), is a 21-minute laboratory paradigm that presents the infant with a series of stress-producing segments involving separation and reunion with the caregiver and exposure to a nonfamiliar adult. This procedure was developed to activate the infant's attachment system, thereby allowing the quality of the attachment relationship to be assessed. The paradigm was developed on a middle socioeconomic status population and found to yield three primary attachment classifications; one secure (Type B) and two insecure (Type A – anxious avoidant) and (Type C – anxious ambivalent).

As investigators began to assess maltreated and other high-risk infants in the Strange Situation, difficulties classifying the infants with the original system derived from normative populations emerged (Main & Solomon, 1986). After reviewing a group of "unclassifiable" tapes from laboratories from around the country, Main and Solomon (1986) described the difficult-to-classify infants as lacking coherent, organized strategies for dealing with the stress aroused during the Strange Situation. Rather, these infants from high-risk samples evidenced unusual combinations of elements derived from the three primary attachment categories in conjunction with bizarre behaviors in the presence of the caregiver, such as stereotypies, stilling, freezing, dazing, and depressed affect (Main & Solomon, 1990). These children were classified as disorganized/disoriented (Type D). Investigators of high-risk populations have subsequently found that maltreated infants evidence a preponderance of disorganized/disoriented attachment strategies (Carlson et al., 1989).

The modified classification system that emerged in response to the "unclassifiable" infants reflects an empirical advance in capturing the "bizarre" attachments that Bowlby (1969/1982) expected to occur in dysfunctional caregiving environments. Examinations of populations of those experiencing maltreatment can lead to the discovery of new attachment organizations, as well as uncover the various pathways whereby such anomalous attachments occur. Thus, the incorporation of maltreated and high-risk populations into studies of attachment resulted in an affirmation and elaboration of Bowlby's early theoretical formulations.

In exploring the possible mechanisms that may contribute to disorganization and attachment atypicality in maltreated children, the early emergence of fear and the burden that this places on the infant's ability to self-regulate may be one possible contributory factor. Specifically, disorganized attachments are believed to arise when the caregiver, who evolutionarily serves as a secure base, elicits fear in the infant (Main & Hesse, 1990). The work of Gaensbauer (1980, 1982) lends support to this formulation. In his examinations of affect in maltreated infants, Gaensbauer found that, in contrast to the normative emergence of fear at 8–9 months of age, physically abused infants exhibited fear as early as 3–4 months of age (Gaensbauer, 1980, 1982). Thus, it may be the case that maltreatment experiences accelerate the development of the "hard-wiring" of negative affect neural pathways in the brain as well as the emergence of negative emotions. The earlier appearance and consolidation of these negative affects may arise from the interjection of fear into the caregiving experience and predispose abused infants to develop disorganized/disoriented attachments. Furthermore, such findings suggest that caregiving experiences, in addition to biological processes, can impact upon brain functioning.

The representational models that emerge from the caregiving matrix of maltreated children also are informative in examining ways in which multiple models of relationships may be integrated. In this regard, work on child maltreatment can yield insights into notions regarding general versus specific models of relationships (Bretherton, 1987; Lynch & Cicchetti, 1991).

Representational models of specific relationships undoubtedly contain information unique to that relationship. Expectations about how available the other person is, how effective the self is in eliciting contingent responses from that person, attitudes toward and commitment to the relationship, and affective tone may all be incorporated into models of specific relationships. Moreover, these specific models may also contribute information relevant to and part of more generalized models of relationships (see Crittenden, 1990). It is possible, then, that internal representations of the parent–child relationship may provide the child with general information and expectations about other possible social partners and the self in relation to those partners. Because maltreated youngsters typically are insecurely attached to their primary caregivers, the internal representational models of these specific attachment relationships may generalize to new relationships, creating negative expectations of how others will behave and how successful the self is likely to be in relation to others. If maltreated children's models reflect insecurity and fear, then they may enter relationships with new partners with approach–avoidance conflicts that result in maladaptive patterns of relating (see Crittenden & Ainsworth, 1989).

Examinations of maltreated children have revealed substantial concordance in their representational models of relationships with their mothers, peers (e.g., best friend), and teachers (Lynch & Cicchetti 1991; Toth & Cicchetti, in press). In keeping with Bowlby's (1969/1982) theoretical claims, these findings suggest that the importance of the primary attachment figure plays a major role in determining whether or not a generalized or specific model of relationships will be utilized in subsequent interpersonal relationships. A negative model of one important relationship (e.g., one's relationship with the primary caregiver) may be salient enough to cause children to form negative global models of other relationships, even if the nature of their subsequent interactions with these persons is positive.

Studies of story stem narratives elicited from maltreated children in efforts to assess emotional regulation, internal representations of relationships, and moral development serve as yet another example of the value of atypical populations for enhancing developmental theory (Buchsbaum et al., 1992). In the narrative technique, an interviewer begins a story using doll play and then asks the child to complete the story (Buchsbaum et al., 1992). In a recent study, we presented maltreated and nonmaltreated children with a series of stories developed to encourage representations of various themes. Although studies with normative populations certainly have shed light on issues of moral development and representation, findings derived from relatively homogeneous samples of normal children may be unable to address issues such as whether the narratives yield reflections of actual experience, personalized alterations of reality, or a combination of the two strategies. In comparison to nonmaltreated children, the narratives told by maltreated children evidenced more themes of inappropriate aggression, neglect, and sexualized behaviors. Conceptualizations of the self as "bad" and a perception of caregiving figures as unavailable also were more common in the narratives of maltreated children (Bushsbaum et al., 1992). Not only did the representations of aggression that emerged in the narratives of maltreated children far exceed the base rates found in nonatypical populations, but also the intensity of the aggression contained in the narratives of maltreated children enabled us to assess more directly whether the stories were reflections of the children's experiences or were transformations of reality. By providing much greater variability in the content and organization of stories than those provided by normative populations, the use of these narratives with an atypical group of children allowed for the clarification of questions related to event representation that were previously unanswered.

A final example of how the study of maltreated children can enhance our theories of normal development can be obtained from research on the early emergence of self. As the inner representations of maltreated children are carried forward into new contexts, their relationships, as well as their experiences, are likely to be affected. For example, research on the development of self-recognition in maltreated toddlers illuminates the representational models of self that maltreated youngsters form. Although studies reveal that maltreated children are comparable with normal children in recognizing their rouge-marked mirror images, unlike normals, maltreated children are more likely to display neutral or negative affect upon visual self-recognition (Schneider-Rosen & Cicchetti, 1984, 1991). Thus, it appears that biological maturation rather than quality of caregiving is responsible for the appearance of this aspect of self-knowledge (Cicchetti, 1991; Kagan, 1981). However, despite their adequate early self-knowledge, the affective responses of maltreated youngsters suggest that they may feel badly or shameful about themselves, a finding consistent with what would be predicted based on their poor-quality representational models of attachment figures and of the self (Crittenden & Ainsworth, 1989; Lynch & Cicchetti, 1991). As with our exploration of children with Down syndrome, these data reveal that self-development is multifaceted.

Studies of communicative functioning in maltreated children also elucidate the impact of child maltreatment on the emergence of internal state or self-language. Specifically, maltreated children were found to use proportionately fewer internal state words, to attribute their internal states to fewer social agents, and to be more context-bound in their use of self-language than their nonmaltreated peers (Cicchetti & Beeghly, 1987). Interestingly, maltreated children also spoke less about their negative internal emotional states than did nonmaltreated children. Our findings are consistent with those of Crittenden (1988), who discovered that sometime during the second year of life, some maltreated youngsters learn not only to inhibit negative affect but also to display falsely positive affect. These "overbright" expressions are not thought to communicate these children's true feelings but, rather, are conceived as false displays whose purpose is to make the caregiver feel good (cf. Carlson et al., 1989; Main & Solomon, 1990). An additional, and not necessarily mutually exclusive, interpretation of the emotional language data is that the use of negative emotion terms, references to the self, and the self's desires, has provoked responses in the mother that generate anxiety in the child that necessitate regulation and control. Thus, maltreated children, in an attempt to control their anxiety, may modify their language (and perhaps even their thinking) in order to preclude the anxiety engendered by certain aspects of language and discourse in general.

Parallel investigations that examined maltreating mothers' discourse with their infants revealed that these mothers ignored their babies' signals and symptoms of distress, as well as their infants' negative affect, focusing instead on getting them to carry out imperative commands. Taken together, the results of these studies underscore the role that parental socialization plays in the emergence of language and self-development and emphasizes the importance of a benign rearing environment for language and self-development.

Depression

The study of aberrations in biological, affective, cognitive, and interpersonal capacities in depressed persons affords a more complete understanding of how these domains function in the normal course of development. One aspect of emotional development that has captured the attention of developmentalists over the past decade is emotion dysregulation, a prominent component of the mood disorders. As

Marian Radke-Yarrow and Carolyn Zahn-Waxler (1990) have noted, investigators in the field of developmental psychopathology have provided the major impetus for the shift in research on emotions from a predominantly functionalist or adaptive function perspective to one that also endeavors to understand the ontogenesis of dysregulation and maladaptive patterns.

Research on the offspring of parents with unipolar and bipolar mood disorders reveals that these children clearly are adversely affected by exposure to their parents' distressing emotional displays. For example, these youngsters show great difficulty in reestablishing their own emotional equilibrium after they observe expressions of anger between their parents (Cummings et al., 1981). Similarly, when children whose parents have a mood disorder express their own stressful emotions, they are likely to have their bids for comfort ignored or addressed in terms of their parents' own needs. An interesting finding in this regard stems from the work of Zahn-Waxler and Kochanska (1990). These investigators asked mothers to simulate sadness to a pictured child's distress while they were examining photographs with their own child. Depressed mothers were more likely to extend their expressions of sadness and to prolong the elicitation of comfort from their children. The results of these studies on emotional development in the offspring of mood-disordered parents suggest that research on normal populations may have underestimated the importance of parenting in the socialization of affect.

In moving from the effects on child development of having a depressed caregiver to direct examinations of the effects of depression on the individual, research with depressed adults also has been valuable in enhancing developmental theory. Evidence from a variety of lines of research, including work conducted with depressed patients, has contributed to a growing understanding of the role of the cerebral hemispheres in emotional functioning in adults (Davidson, 1991). One important source of information about the neural bases of emotion in adults derives from neuropsychological assessments of patients in whom there is evidence of emotional dysfunction as a result of brain damage, epilepsy, or psychopathology. The conclusions stemming from these studies, as well as from others on patterns of brain activation associated with normal emotional functioning, suggest that key aspects of emotional perception and production are lateralized (Davidson, 1991). For example, patients with left frontal brain damage consistently have been found to manifest a catastrophic depressive reaction, whereas patients with right frontal brain damage evince euphoria and indifference to their condition. Several electroencephalographic (EEG) studies of subjects engaged in normal emotional functioning have identified different patterns of frontal hemispheric activation asymmetries associated with positive versus negative emotions. For the most part, it appears there is relatively less left frontal activation and/or greater right frontal activation during negative emotional states such as sadness, disgust, and fear. This asymmetry is reversed for positive emotions such as happiness and interest (see Davidson, 1984, 1991; Fox & Davidson, 1984; Tucker & Williamson, 1984).

An additional contribution of the study of depression to our understanding of normal ontogenesis stems from the way in which a neuropsychological approach to the study of emotion has elucidated the inextricable links between emotion and cognition. Tucker (1981) has argued that certain types of cognitions and cognitive skills are facilitated or hampered by particular mood states. For example, neuropsychological assessments of adult depressives have revealed a deficit in visuospatial and perceptual skills associated with right posterior cerebral dysfunction that improves with the remission of the depression. Interestingly, EEG studies have revealed that depressed persons who manifest right frontal activation exhibit a corresponding right parietal inhibition of activity. It has been posited that the pattern of frontal activation asymmetries associated with depression may exert an inhibitory effect on the right posterior regions, thereby providing the neural mechanism responsible for the observed cognitive deficits in depression. Clearly, these studies of adult depressives highlight the need to investigate the interconnectivity of the developing substrates of emotional and cognitive functioning for our understanding of depression in childhood. At the same time, because emotional and cognitive dysfunctions of infants and children can be conceptualized and understood as distortions of normal ontogenetic processes, a longitudinal developmental neuropsychological perspective on depression can enhance our knowledge of the nature of the relation among affective, cognitive, and biological systems throughout the normal life course.

Summary

In conclusion, it is commonly assumed that the difficulties associated with understanding the process of development in healthy or normal individuals are heightened with respect to conditions involving risk and psychopathology. Therefore, rather than further exacerbate the challenges of their task by attempting to comprehend development simultaneously in the presence of disease and risk conditions, developmentalists frequently have opted to focus on nonatypical populations. Such a position is based on the erroneous assumption that disease and deviation *necessarily* eventuate in more complicated developmental patterns. Contrary to this position, I believe that risk conditions and pathological processes do not necessarily intensify the complexity of developmental structures and processes.

Rather than compounding the intricacies of development, the study of atypical populations can delineate processes that elucidate the course of ontogenesis more clearly. In fact, atypical populations and pathological conditions do not ordinarily produce behavior that exceeds the level of complexity found in normal populations (cf. Lenneberg, 1967). When extrapolating from abnormal populations with the goal of informing developmental theory, however, it is important that a range of populations and conditions be considered. The study of a single psychopathological or risk process may result in spurious conclusions if generalizations are made based solely on that condition or disorder. However, if we view a given behavioral pattern in the light of an entire spectrum of diseased and disordered modifications, then we may be able to attain significant insight into the processes of development not generally achieved through sole reliance on studies of relatively homogeneous nondisordered populations.

Acknowledgments

My work on this paper was supported by grants from the William T. Grant Foundation, the Prevention Research Branch of NIMH (MH 45027), and the Spunk Fund, Inc.

References

Achenbach, T. (1990). What is "developmental" about developmental psychopathology? In J. Rolf, A. Masten, D. Cicchetti, K. Nuechterlein, and S. Weintraub (Eds.), *Risk and Protective Factors in the Development of Psychopathology* (pp. 29–48). Cambridge University Press.
Ainsworth, M.D.S., & Wittig, B. A. (1969). Attachment and exploratory behavior of one-year-olds in a strange situation. In B. M. Foss (Ed.), *Determinants of Infant Behavior* (Vol. 4, pp. 113–136). London: Methuen.

Angold, A., & Costello, E. J. (1991). Developing a developmental epidemiology. In D. Cicchetti and S. L. Toth (Eds.), *Rochester Symposium on Developmental Psychopathology, Volume 3: Models and Integrations* (pp. 75–96). Rochester, NY: University of Rochester Press.

Baron-Cohen, S., Leslie, A., & Frith, U. (1985). Does the autistic child have a "theory of mind"? *Cognition, 21,* 37–46.

Beadle, G. W., & Tatum, E. L. (1941). Experimental control of developmental reaction. *American Naturalist, 75,* 107–116.

Beeghly, M., & Cicchetti, D. (1987). An organizational approach to symbolic development in children with Down syndrome. *New Directions for Child Development, 36,* 5–29.

Beeghly, M., Weiss-Perry, B., & Cicchetti, D. (1990). Beyond sensorimotor functioning: Early communicative and play development of children with Down Syndrome. In D. Cicchetti and M. Beeghly (Eds.), *Children with Down syndrome: A Developmental Perspective* (pp. 329–368). Cambridge University Press.

Benes, F. (1991). Toward a neurodevelopmental understanding of schizophrenia and other psychiatric disorders. In D. Cicchetti and S. L. Toth (Eds.), *Rochester Symposium on Developmental Psychopathology, Volume 3: Models and Integrations* (pp. 161–184). Rochester, NY: University of Rochester Press.

Bower, T. (1974). *Development in Infancy.* San Francisco: W. H. Freeman.

Bowlby, J. (1944). Forty-four juvenile thieves: Their characters and home life. *International Journal of Psychoanalysis, 25,* 19–52, 107–127.

Bowlby, J. (1969/1982). *Attachment and Loss* (Vol. 1). New York: Basic Books.

Breslin, N. A., & Weinberger, D. R. (1990). Schizophrenia and the normal functional development of the prefrontal cortex. *Development and Psychopathology, 2,* 409–424.

Bretherton, I. (1987). New perspectives on attachment relations: Security, communication, and internal working models. In J. Osofsky (Ed.), *Handbook of Infant Development* (2nd ed., pp. 1061–1100). New York: Wiley.

Bronfenbrenner, U. (1979). *The Ecology of Human Development: Experiments by Nature and Design.* Cambridge, MA: Harvard University Press.

Bronfenbrenner, U., Kessel, F., Kessen, W., & White, S. (1986). Toward a critical social history of developmental psychology: A propaedeutic discussion. *American Psychologist, 41,* 1218–1230.

Brown, R. (1973). *A First Language.* Cambridge, MA: Harvard University Press.

Buchsbaum, H., Toth, S. L., Clyman, R., Cicchetti, D., & Emde, R. (1992). The use of a narrative story stem technique with maltreated children: Implications for theory and practice. *Development and Psychopathology, 4,* 603–625.

Cairns, R. B. (1983). The emergence of developmental psychology. In P. Mussen (Ed.), *Handbook of Child Psychology* (Vol. 1, pp. 41–102). New York: Wiley.

Carlson, V., Cicchetti, D., Barnett, D., & Braunwald, K. (1989). Finding order in disorganization: Lessons from research in maltreated infants' attachments to their caregivers. In D. Cicchetti and V. Carlson (Eds.), *Child Maltreatment: Theory and Research on the Causes and Consequences of Child Abuse and Neglect* (pp. 494–528). Cambridge University Press.

Chomsky, N. (1968). *Language and Mind.* New York: Harcourt Brace Jovanovich.

Ciaranello, R., Wong, D., & Rubenstein, J. (1990). Molecular neurobiology and disorders of brain development. In S. Deutsch, A. Weizman, & R. Weizman (Eds.), *Application of Basic Neuroscience to Child Psychiatry* (pp. 9–32). New York: Plenum.

Cicchetti, D. (Ed.). (1984a). *Developmental Psychopathology.* Chicago: University of Chicago Press.

Cicchetti, D. (1984b). The emergence of developmental psychopathology. *Child Development, 55,* 1–7.

Cicchetti, D. (Ed.). (1989). *Rochester Symposium on Developmental Psychopathology, Volume 1: The Emergence of a Discipline.* Hillsdale, NJ: Lawrence Erlbaum.

Cicchetti, D. (1990). A historical perspective on the discipline of developmental psychopathology. In J. Rolf, A. Masten, D. Cicchetti, K. Nuechterlein, & S. Weintraub (Eds.), *Risk and Protective Factors in the Development of Psychopathology* (pp. 2–28). Cambridge University Press.

Cicchetti, D. (1991). Fractures in the crystal: Developmental psychopathology and the emergence of self. *Developmental Review, 11,* 271–287.

Cicchetti, D., & Aber, J. L. (1986). Early precursors to later depression: An organizational perspective. In L. Lipsitt and C. Rovee-Collier (Eds.), *Advances in Infancy, Vol. 4* (pp. 87–137). Norwood, NJ: Ablex.

Cicchetti, D., & Beeghly, M. (1987). Symbolic development in maltreated youngsters. *New Directions for Child Development, 6,* 5–29.

Cicchetti, D., & Beeghly, M. (Eds.). (1990). *Down Syndrome: A Developmental Perspective.* Cambridge University Press.

Cicchetti, D., & Carlson, V. (Eds.). (1989). *Child Maltreatment: Theory and Research on the Causes and Consequences of Child Abuse and Neglect.* Cambridge University Press.

Cicchetti, D., & Ganiban, J. (1990). The organization and coherence of developmental processes in infants and children with Down syndrome. In R. M. Hodapp, J. A. Burack, E. Zigler (Eds.), *Issues in the Developmental Approach to Mental Retardation* (pp. 169–225). Cambridge University Press.

Cicchetti, D., & Garmezy, N. (Eds.). (1993). Milestones in the development of resilience. Special Issue: *Development and Psychopathology, 5,* (4).

Cicchetti, D., & Lynch, M. (1993). Toward an ecological/transactional model of community violence and child maltreatment: Consequences for children's development. *Psychiatry, 56,* 96–118.

Cicchetti, D., & Manly, J. T. (1990). Problems and solutions to conducting research in maltreating families: An autobiographical perspective. In G. Brody & I. Sigel (Eds.), *Methods of Family Research* (Vol. 2, pp. 87–133). New York: Academic Press.

Cicchetti, D., & Schneider-Rosen, K. (1984). Theoretical and empirical considerations in the investigation of the relationship between affect and cognition in atypical populations of infants: Contributions to the formulation of an integrative theory of development. In C. Izard, J. Kagan, & R. Zajonc (Eds.), *Emotions, Cognition and Behavior* (pp. 366–406). Cambridge University Press.

Cicchetti, D., & Schneider-Rosen, K. (1986). An organizational approach to childhood depression. In M. Rutter, C. Izard, & P. Read (Eds.), *Depression in Young People, Clinical and Developmental Perspectives* (pp. 71–134). New York: Guilford.

Cicchetti, D., & Sroufe, L. A. (1976). The relationship between affective and cognitive development in Down's syndrome infants. *Child Development, 47,* 920–929.

Cicchetti, D., & Sroufe, L. A. (1978). An organizational view of affect: Illustration from the study of Down's syndrome infants. In M. Lewis & L. Rosenblum (Eds.), *The Development of Affect* (pp. 309–350). New York: Plenum.

Cicchetti, D., & Toth, S. L. (1991). The making of a developmental psychopathologist. In J. Cantor, C. Spiker, & L. Lipsitt (Eds.), *Child Behavior and Development: Training for Diversity* (pp. 34–72). Norwood, NJ: Ablex.

Cicchetti, D., & Toth, S. L. (1992a). Special Issue: Developmental approaches to prevention and intervention. *Development and Psychopathology, 4*(4), 489–728.

Cicchetti, D., & Toth, S. L. (1992b). The role of developmental theory in prevention and intervention. *Development and Psychopathology, 4,* 489–493.

Cicchetti, D., & Toth, S. L. (Eds.) (1993). *Child Abuse, Child Development, and Social Policy.* Hillsdale, NJ: Lawrence Erlbaum.

Cicchetti, D., & Wagner, S. (1990). Alternative assessment strategies for the evaluation of infants and toddlers: An organizational perspective. In S. Meisels & J. Shonkoff (Eds.), *Handbook of Early Intervention* (pp. 246–277). Cambridge University Press.

Cicchetti, D., Ganiban, J., & Barnett, D. (1991). Contributions from the study of high risk populations to understanding the development of emotional regulation. In J. Garber & K. Dodge (Eds.), *The Development of Emotion Regulation and Dysregulation* (pp. 15–48). Cambridge University Press.

Cicchetti, D., Beeghly, M., Carlson, V., & Toth, S. (1990). The emergence of the self in atypical populations. In D. Cichetti and M. Beeghly (Eds.), *The Self in Transition: Infancy to Childhood* (pp. 309–344). Chicago: University of Chicago Press.

Crittenden, P. (1988). Relationships at risk. In J. Belsky & T. Nezworski (Eds.), *Clinical Implications of Attachment Theory* (pp. 136–174). Hillsdale, NJ: Lawrence Erlbaum.

Crittenden, P. (1990). Internal representational models of attachment relationships. *Infant Mental Health Journal, 11,* 259–277.

Crittenden, P., & Ainsworth, M. (1989). Attachment and child abuse. In D. Cicchetti & V. Carlson (Eds.), *Child Maltreatment: Theory and Research on the Causes and Consequences of Child Abuse and Neglect* (pp. 432–463). Cambridge University Press.

Cummings, E. M., Zahn-Waxler, C., & Radke-Yarrow, M. (1981). Young children's responses to expressions of anger and affection by others in the family. *Child Development, 52,* 1274–1282.

Curtiss, S. (1977). *Genie: A Psycholinguistic Study of a Modern-Day "Wild Child."* New York: Academic Press.

Darnell, J., Lodish, H., & Baltimore, D. (1986). *Molecular Cell Biology.* New York: W. H. Freeman.

Davidson, R. J. (1984). Affect, cognition, and hemispheric specialization. In C. Izard, J. Kagan, & R. Zajonc (Eds.), *Emotions, Cognition, and Behavior* (pp. 320–365). Cambridge University Press.

Davidson, R. (1991). Cerebral asymmetry and affective disorders: A developmental perspective. In D. Cicchetti & S. L. Toth (Eds.), *Rochester Symposium on Developmental Psychopathology, Volume 2: Internalizing and Externalizing Expressions of Dysfunction* (pp. 123–154). Hillsdale, NJ: Lawrence Erlbaum.

Dawson, G. (Ed.). (1989). *Autism: Nature, Diagnosis, and Treatment.* New York: Guilford Press.

Farah, M. (1990). *Visual Agnosia.* Cambridge, MA: MIT Press.

Feinberg, I. (1982). Schizophrenia: Caused by a fault in programmed synaptic elimination during adolescence? *Journal of Psychiatric Research, 17,* 319–334.

Fishbein, H. (1976). *Evolution, Development, and Children's Learning.* Pacific Palisades, CA: Goodyear.

Fox, N. A., & Davidson, R. J. (1984). Hemispheric substrates of affect. In

N. A. Fox & R. J. Davidson (Eds.), *The Psychobiology of Affective Develop-ment* (pp. 353–381). Hillsdale, NJ: Lawrence Erlbaum.

Frith, U. (1989). *Autism: Explaining the Enigma.* Oxford: Blackwell.

Gaensbauer, T. J. (1980). Anaclitic depression in a three-and-one-half-month old child. *American Journal of Psychiatry, 137,* 841–842.

Gaensbauer, T. J. (1982). The differentiation of discrete affects. *The Psycho-analytic Study of the Child, 37,* 29–66.

Gardner, H. (1983). *Frames of Mind: The Theory of Multiple Intelligences.* New York: Basic Books.

Garmezy, N., & Rutter, M. (Eds.). (1983). *Stress, Coping and Development in Children.* New York: McGraw-Hill.

Gazzaniga, M. (1988). *Mind Matters.* Boston: Houghton Mifflin.

Gottlieb, G. (1983). The psychobiological approach to developmental issues. In P. Mussen (Ed.), *Handbook of Child Psychology* (pp. 1–26). New York: Wiley.

Hesse, P., & Cicchetti, D. (1982). Toward an integrative theory of emotional development. *New Directions for Child Development, 16,* 3–48.

Humphrey, G., & Humphrey, M. (1932). *The Wild Boy of Aveyron.* New York: Appleton-Century-Crofts.

Institute of Medicine (1989). *Research on Children and Adolescents with Mental, Behavioral, And Developmental Disorders.* National Academy Press: Washington, DC.

Izard, C. (1991). *The Psychology of Emotions.* New York: Plenum.

Kagan, J. (1971). *Change and Continuity in Infancy.* New York: Wiley.

Kagan, J. (1981). *The Second Year: The Emergence of Self-Awareness.* Cambridge, MA: Harvard University Press.

Kopp, C., & Recchia, S. (1990). The issues of multiple pathways in the development of handicapped children. In R. Hodapp, J. Burack, & E. Zigler (Eds.), *Issues in the Developmental Approach to Mental Retardation* (pp. 272–293). Cambridge University Press.

Lawrence, P. A. (1992). *The Making of a Fly: The Genetics of Animal Design.* Oxford: Blackwell Scientific Publications.

Lenneberg, E. (1967). *Biological Foundations of Language.* New York: Wiley.

Lynch, M., & Cicchetti, D. (1991). Patterns of relatedness in maltreated and nonmaltreated children: Connections among multiple representational models. *Development and Psychopathology, 3,* 207–226.

Main, M., & Hesse, P. (1990). Lack of resolution of mourning in adulthood and its relationship to infant disorganization: Some speculations re-garding causal mechanisms. In M. Greenberg, D. Cicchetti, & E. M. Cummings (Eds.), *Attachment During the Preschool Years* (pp. 161–182). Chicago: University of Chicago Press.

Main, M., & Solomon, J. (1986). Discovery of a disorganized/disoriented attachment pattern. In T. B. Brazelton & M. W. Yogman (Eds.), *Affective Development in Infancy* (pp. 95–124). Norwood, NJ: Ablex.

Main, M., & Solomon, J. (1990). Procedures for identifying infants as disorganized/disoriented during the Ainsworth Strange Situation. In M. Greenberg, D. Cicchetti, & E. M. Cummings (Eds.), *Attachment During the Preschool Years* (pp. 121–160). Chicago: University of Chicago Press.

Masten, A. (1989). Resilience in development: Implications of the study of successful adaptation for developmental psychopathology. In D. Cicchetti (Ed.), *Rochester Symposium on Developmental Psychopathology, Vol. 1: The Emergence of a Discipline* (pp. 261–294). Hillsdale, NJ: Lawrence Erlbaum.

Masten, A., Best, K., & Garmezy, N. (1990). Resilience and development: Contributions from the study of children who overcome adversity. *Development and Psychopathology, 2,* 425–444.

Mundy, P., & Sigman, M. (1989a). Second thoughts on the nature of autism. *Development and Psychopathology, 1,* 213–217.

Mundy, P., & Sigman, M. (1989b). The theoretical implications of joint-attention deficits in autism. *Development and Psychopathology, 1,* 173–183.

Nadel, L. (Ed.). (1988). *The Psychobiology of Down Syndrome.* Cambridge, MA: MIT Press.

Nowakowski, R. S. (1987). Basic concepts of CNS development. *Child development, 58,* 568–595.

Piaget, J. (1975). Foreword. In E. J. Anthony (Ed.), *Explorations in Child Psychiatry* (pp. vii–ix). New York: Plenum.

Plomin, R., Rende, R., & Rutter, M. (1991). Quantitative genetics and developmental psychopathology. In D. Cicchetti and S. L. Toth (Eds.), *Rochester Symposium on Developmental Psychopathology, Vol. 2: Internalizing and Externalizing Expressions of Dysfunction* (pp. 155–202). Hillsdale, NJ: Lawrence Erlbaum.

Radke-Yarrow, M., & Zahn-Waxler, C. (1990). Research on children with affectively-ill parents: Some considerations for theory and research on normal development. *Development and Psychopathology, 2,* 349–366.

Richters, J., & Cicchetti, D. (1993). Mark Twain meets DSM-III-R: Conduct disorder, development and the concept of harmful dysfunction. *Development and Psychopathology, 5,* 5–29.

Ruppenthal, G. C., Arling, G. L., Harlow, H. F., Sackett, G. P., & Suomi, S. J. (1976). A 10-year perspective of motherless mother monkey behavior. *Journal of Abnormal Psychology, 85,* 341–349.

Rutter, M. (1986). Child psychiatry: The interface between clinical and developmental research. *Psychological Medicine, 16,* 151–169.

Rutter, M. (1988). Epidemiological approaches to developmental psychopathology. *Archives of General Psychiatry, 45,* 486–495.

Rutter, M. (1989). Age as an ambiguous variable in developmental research. *International Journal of Behavioral Development, 12,* 1–34.

Rutter, M. (1990). Psychosocial resilience and protective mechanisms. In J. Rolf, A. S. Masten, D. Cicchetti, K. H. Nuechterlein, & S. Weintraub (Eds.), *Risk and Protective Factors in the Development of Psychopathology* (pp. 181–214). Cambridge University Press.

Rutter, M., & Garmezy, N. (1983). Developmental psychopathology. In E. M. Hetherington (Ed.), *Socialization, Personality and Social Development* (pp. 775–911). New York: Wiley.

Sarnat, H. (1992). *Cerebral Dysgenesis: Embryology and Clinical Expression.* New York: Oxford University Press.

Schneider-Rosen, K., & Cicchetti, D. (1984). The relationship between affect and cognition in maltreated infants: Quality of attachment and the development of visual self-recognition. *Child Development, 55,* 648–658.

Schneider-Rosen, K., & Cicchetti, D. (1991). Early self-knowledge and emotional development: Visual self-recognition and affective reactions to mirror self-image in maltreated and nonmaltreated toddlers. *Developmental Psychology, 27,* 481–488.

Sroufe, L. A. (1979). The coherence of individual development. *American Psychologist, 34,* 834–841.

Sroufe, L. A. (1989). Pathways to adaptation and maladaptation: Psychopathology as developmental deviation. In D. Cicchetti (Ed.), *Rochester Symposium on Developmental Psychopathology, Vol. 1: The Emergence of a Discipline* (pp. 13–40). Hillsdale, NJ: Lawrence Erlbaum.

Sroufe, L. A. (1990). Considering normal and abnormal together: The essence of developmental psychopathology. *Development and Psychopathology, 2,* 335–347.

Sroufe, L. A., & Rutter, M. (1984). The domain of developmental psychopathology. *Child Development, 55,* 17–29.

Sroufe, L. A., & Wunsch, J. (1972). The development of laughter in the first year of life. *Child Development, 43,* 1326–1344.

Starr, R., & Wolfe, D. (Eds.) (1991). *The Effects of Child Abuse and Neglect: Issues and Research.* New York: Guilford.

Tager-Flusberg, H. (Ed.). (1994). *Constraints on Language Acquisition: Studies of Atypical Children.* Hillsdale, NJ: Lawrence Erlbaum.

Toth, S. L., & Cicchetti, D. (in press). Patterns of relatedness and depressive symptomatology in maltreated children. *Journal of Consulting and Clinical Psychology.*

Tucker, D. (1981). Lateral brain function, emotion, and conceptualization. *Psychological Bulletin, 89,* 19–46.

Tucker, D., & Williamson, P. (1984). Asymmetric neural control systems in human self-regulation. *Psychological Review, 91,* 185–215.

Waddington, C. H. (1966). *Principles of Development and Differentiation.* New York: Macmillan.

Watson, J., Hopkins, N., Roberts, J., et al. (1987). *Molecular Biology of the Gene* (4th ed.). Menlo Park, CA: Benjamin/Cummings.

Weinberger, D. R. (1987). Implications of normal brain development for the pathogenesis of schizophrenia. *Archives of General Psychiatry, 44,* 660–669.

Weiss, P. (1961). Deformities as cues to understanding development of form. *Perspectives in Biology and Medicine, 4,* 133–151.

Weiss, P. (1969). The living system: Determinism stratified. In A. Koestler & J. Smythies (Eds.), *Beyond Reductionism* (pp. 3–55). Boston: Beacon Press.

Werner, H. (1948). *Comparative Psychology of Mental Development.* New York: International Universities Press.

Werner, H., & Kaplan, B. (1963). *Symbol Formation: An Organismic-Developmental Approach to Language and the Expression of Thought.* New York: Wiley.

Yamada, J. (1990). *Laura: A Case for the Modularity of Language.* Cambridge, MA: MIT Press.

Yonas, A., Bechtold, A. G., Frankel, D., Gordon, F. R., McRoberts, G., Norcia, A., & Sternfels, S. (1977). Development of sensitivity to information for impending collision. *Perception and Psychophysics, 21,* 97–104.

Zahn-Waxler, C., & Kochanska, G. (1990). The origins of guilt. In R. Thompson (Ed.), *Nebraska Symposium on Motivation, Vol. 36: Socioemotional Development* (pp. 183–258). Lincoln: University of Nebraska Press.

12

The return of the ancients: On temperament and development

Jerome Kagan

Deviant human behavior, like a Halloween mask, creates a state of uncertainty in the viewer because it is a transformation on what is so totally familiar. The apathy of the depressive and the incoherence of the schizophrenic are upsetting and provoke, along with empathy, attempts at explanation derived from the deepest philosophical assumptions of the society. Although the heart of this chapter is a discussion of the relation of contemporary research on temperament to psychopathology, a brief synopsis of Western explanations of psychopathology is relevant for temperamental interpretations have cycled in popularity over the last two millennia.

The student of intellectual history reflexively begins with Plato who, on this issue, regarded abnormal behavior as a sign of failure to understand the moral imperatives of Greek society. Chronic inability to control the moods of envy and hostility, which were serious deviations from Athenian ethical standards, revealed a lapsed soul and a vulnerability to melancholy, mania, or delusions. Aristotle replaced this moral evaluation of symptoms with an empirical and ethically neutral biological description that lasted for almost a thousand years. In the most popular form, elaborated in the second century by Galen, each person possessed a profile of the four humors of blood, phlegm, and yellow and black bile, the bodily analogues of air, water, fire, and earth, which generated a physiological pattern combining a cold–warm and a dry–moist dimension. An excess of blood moved the body toward increased heat and moisture; an excess of black bile moved it toward a cooler and drier state. A perfect balance of these humors led to mental health, but any imbalance was associated with symptoms. The sources of the imbalance were both endogenous and exogenous. The former was the product of the individual's constitution – the

Greek term for temperament – the latter forces included diet and climate. For example, melancholy increased in the fall because the level of black bile rose when the days became dry and cool. A confident, sanguine mood increased in the summer because the blood enhanced the hot and moist components.

Galen's ideas, like the concept of energy, must have a fundamentally attractive feature to human minds. Similar concepts still exist in rural Malay communities (Laderman, 1991). The Malay substituted the inheritance of "inner winds" – called angin – for body humors. These qualities are revealed during trance states; under ordinary conditions neither observers nor the person know the mixture of angin a person possesses. But the Malay temperamental types are slightly different. They retained two of Galen's type – the melancholic and the choleric – but the phlegmatic and sanguine were replaced with two very different categories. The lazy, impulsive, somewhat antisocial gambler has no obvious analogue in Galen's scheme. Nor does the person who combines hedonism, mild exhibitionism, and a concern with cleanliness. It is not clear why the Malay did not posit the sanguine and phlegmatic temperaments that survived in the West to the end of the nineteenth century. George Ladd, a Yale professor who wrote a popular textbook in 1895, assumed the validity of Galen's four types. The absence of the sanguine personality might be because Malay mores favor a gentle, restrained interpersonal style. No one should strive to develop an excessively sociable personality. Those who do, violate community values; perhaps that is why these traits are combined with asocial behavior. The absence of the phlegmatic is more puzzling. A temperament characterized by low energy is supported by observations of infants and young children. Perhaps scholars better acquainted with Malay society will be able to explain this novelty.

These essentially biological interpretations of pathology were replaced during the medieval era with a Christian philosophy that treated mental symptoms as a sign of sin and possession by the devil or witches. Aristotle's temperamental ideas did not return to Europe until after the Enlightenment, when the motivation to expunge metaphysical ideas from scientific explanations became strong. One of the most famous of the constitutional hypotheses of the eighteenth and nineteenth centuries is attributable to Gall (1835) and Spurzheim (1834), who reversed the modern strategy of using knowledge of the brain to explain behavior by using knowledge of behavior to infer the structure of the brain.* This pair of scholars selected variation in skull shape as diagnostic of mood and behavior; their ideas represent to many an outrageous example of constitutional theory. Spurzheim, who consolidated Gall's original ideas, retained the premise of a location for each primary human quality and, reflecting nineteenth-century biases, assigned more space in the cranial cavity to emotions than to intellectual processes. Love was in the cerebellum, aggression in the temporal lobe, and timidity in the upper lateral and posterior parts of the head.

In a book that enjoyed eight editions, Joseph Simms (1887) awarded the shape of the face more diagnostic power than even Paul Ekman or Carroll Izard would have dared. Simms, who acknowledged that both heredity and experience produced a person's facial and bodily form, described five ideal bodily types that were variations of the meso-morph, ectomorph, and endomorph and, like Kretschmer, suggested that there was a link between body type and mental illness. These scholars enjoyed greater acceptance than Gall or Spurzheim because they offered explanatory statements that attempted to relate behavior to physiology, thus making their arguments more palatable. Sheldon (1940) continued this approach in his book on personality and phy-sique. But 1940 was the year the Nazis threatened Europe and the idea that physical qualities were associated with characteristic human behaviors was too close to Hitler's version of Aryan types, and this research stopped abruptly. The suddenness is not surprising for tucked away in Sheldon's book is the dangerous suggestion that the Negro population contains a large number of aggressive mesomorphs while Jews are heavily represented with intellectual ectomorphs. When the Harvard anthropologist Ernest Hooton (1939) suggested that some bodily constitutions were naturally inferior and associated with crimi-nal behavior, the prose had a defensive tone because Hooton was aware of how unpopular this position had become to most Americans.

But at the turn of the century, the professional consensus was that the profiles we call depression, mania, and schizophrenia were due primarily to inherited biological biases. The reason for the indif-ference to early experience, considering its current popularity, re-mains an enigma. Perhaps nineteenth-century commentators believed there was minimal variability in childhood encounters. There is an analogy to infectious diseases. If all the individuals living in a crowded

---

* See also discussion in Chapter 5, by Deborah L. Levy, this volume – Eds.

slum are exposed to the microbe that causes tuberculosis, but only some contract the disease, it is reasonable to conclude that the victims were biologically vulnerable to acquiring the illness.

It is important to appreciate that the primary concern of nineteenth-century physicians was with the serious pathological symptoms of depression, mania, delusions, and dementia and not the ordinary, everyday worries that are endemic to the human condition. It was understood, tacitly, that all adults were anxious over status, money, health, and acceptance – these were characteristic of human nature – hence, these worries were not signs of mental illness.

Freud defined the watershed by making deviant childhood experiences more critical than a deviant constitution. The creative case histories of Hans and Schreber emphasized their unusual families, not their unusual temperaments. Prior to Freud, and for several centuries, most commentators were interested in the small number of individuals with serious pathology rather than the common worries about storms or illness. Freud changed the discourse by providing an experiential basis for fear and anxiety that applied to all. Because everyone was potentially vulnerable to anxiety and guilt over sexual and hostile ideas, Freud implied that anyone could develop a serious phobia. By the late 1930s, psychodynamic explanations of pathology were de rigueur and the ideological barrier between normal and abnormal dissolved. All adults were potentially vulnerable to suicidal depression, schizophrenia, and panic attacks if the environmental contingencies were arranged appropriately. Thomas Szasz even persuaded some that mental disease was a social construction.

Psychoanalytic theories also turned scholars away from conceptualizing categories of persons who were vulnerable to the acquisition of fear or depression, to continuous moods and habits that were established through environmental experiences. "Fearful" and "sad" became adjectives describing a continuum of intensity of affect on which all individuals could be placed. The difference in connotation between a continuous disposition and a qualitative type is captured by comparing the phrase "Reading one grade below expected level" with "Dyslexic," or "Ran a five-minute mile" with "Olympic sprinter." The dyslexic and the Olympic athlete are not just quantitatively different from others; they are qualitatively distinct.

It is not an exaggeration to suggest that the substitution of continuous, acquired psychological processes for inherited biological biases was abetted by the independent historical fact that psychology and sociology were emerging as academic disciplines at the time Freud was promoting his creative ideas. These new sciences would gain in power if mental illness were a product of social conditions and personal encounters rather than biological vulnerabilities.

A second catalyst was the need to rationalize educational efforts with poor, immigrant European children. Liberal scholars favored an egalitarian ethic which assumed that the immigrants and their children were biologically similar to indigenous Yankees. Such an assumption was necessary to defend the efficacy of benevolent therapeutic interventions. This hypothesis became dogma when Pavlov's discoveries were disseminated in the United States by John Watson. The ascent of the social sciences in the academy and the politically based decision to deny all biological variation came together to make Freud's and Watson's arguments eminently reasonable. As a result, the belief that mental illness was primarily experiential in origin dominated textbooks, journals, and popular magazines for almost three-quarters of a century.

The recent return to temperamental ideas is the result of several relatively independent factors. The first is the failure of empirical data to support a strictly experiential interpretation of mental illness. Many studies have tried to correlate variations in home experience with psychological profiles, especially in children. The amount of variance explained is occasionally significant, but always relatively small in magnitude. One major frustration is the frequent fact that siblings living in the same family differ in manifest psychopathology. The growing pessimism was reflected over 10 years ago in a review chapter by Eleanor Maccoby and John Martin (1983) in the *Handbook of Child Psychology*. The authors suggest in the final pages that in most of the studies the relations between aspects of parental functioning and the characteristics of children were small, and they add:

The trends are sufficiently weak, that it is evident that there must be a very large number of exceptions to them. . . . Biologically unrelated children growing up in the same household are shown to be quite unlike. . . . These findings imply strongly that there is very little impact of the physical environment that the parents provide for children and very little impact of parental characteristics that must be essentially the same for all children in a family. . . . Indeed, the implications are either that parental behaviors have no effect, or that the only effective aspects of parenting must vary greatly from one child to another within the same family. (page 82)

The writings of Thomas and Chess (1977) on the significance of temperament, which were bold suggestions to their psychiatric colleagues, also promoted a renewed curiosity about temperament. Finally, the evidence being generated by neuroscientists provided rational bases for speculations as to how inherited differences in physiology and neurochemistry might lead to abnormal profiles. The brain contains more than 150 known chemomodulators, including monoamines, opioids, and hormones, each with a capacity to influence the excitability of specific sites in the central nervous system. Individuals inherit different concentrations of some of these neurochemicals, as well as the density of associated receptors. As a result, it is at least possible to imagine how a child who inherited a high concentration of corticotropin-releasing hormone or norepinephrine might be especially vulnerable to fear. Scientists are appropriately conservative and resist explanations that do not rest on a rationale built of robust facts arranged in a logical argument. The environmental explanation of why a child was excessively fearful had been, until the 1970s, familiar and reasonable; hence, psychologists were reluctant to relinquish it until another equally commanding one was provided.

Neuroscientists were supplying these new arguments and their conclusions were supported by behavioral biologists, who were discovering important intraspecific differences in the behavior of a large number of species. Dogs, mice, rats, cats, wolves, cows, monkeys, and even paradise fish differ, within species, in their tendency to approach or to avoid novelty. South American squirrel monkeys of two different strains, reproductively isolated by only a thousand miles of jungle, vary in their morphology, physiology, and behavior. One of the most extensive studies of the genetic origins of behavior, published more than 20 years ago, showed dramatic variation in the degree of timidity displayed in unfamiliar situations by five different breeds of dogs (Scott and Fuller, 1974). Basenjis, terriers, and shelties were more timid than beagles and cocker spaniels. Even rats from within a single strain bred over many generations vary in both brain biochemistry and associated behavior. Among Wistar rats some display large potentials in the dentate gyrus of the hippocampus following stimulation of the lateral amygdala, while some animals do not. The former animals are protected from ulceration of the stomach following immobilization, while the latter, who did not display potentiation, were more likely to develop ulcers following stress (Hencke, 1990).

Inhibited and uninhibited temperaments

Our laboratory has been studying two members from the much larger set of temperamental categories. We believe Galen would have smiled upon learning of the results to be summarized because the two categories seem to be childhood precursors of melancholic and sanguine adults. The research rests on the hypothesis that the amygdala and its projections to motor, autonomic, cortical, and brain stem targets are important participants in temperamental vulnerability to a state we call *fear of the unfamiliar*. The reader should note the specificity of this state. Unfamiliar people, objects, and situations generate a state that should be differentiated from other members of the fear family, including conditioned fear states, imminent physical harm, and anxiety over possible loss of a resource or love object, rejection, failure, or identification with role models whose characteristics violate community standards.

There is a great deal of evidence to show that the amygdala, especially the central nucleus, participates in a major way in fear states (LeDoux et al., 1988; Kemble et al., 1990; Maier et al., 1993). There are two important areas within the amygdala that are relevant to the prediction of a fearful or fearless profile from behavior displayed during infancy. The projections from the basolateral area of the amygdala to the ventral striatum and ventral pallidum mediate an increase in motor activity to stimulation, primarily flexion and extension of the arms and legs. The projections from the central nucleus of the amygdala to the cingulate cortex, central gray, hypothalamus, and sympathetic nervous system lead to motor spasticity, distress vocalizations, and increase in sympathetic activity, especially increases in heart rate, blood pressure, and pupillary dilation.

The major assumption is that some 4-month-old infants inherit a neurochemical profile that renders the basolateral and central areas either highly excitable or not. High excitability is associated in infancy with frequent motor behavior and irritability to stimulation; low excitability, with infrequent motor behavior and minimal irritability. We assume, further, that the children who will be classed as inhibited in the second year, because they show consistent fear to and avoidance of unfamiliar people, situations, and events, inherit the more excitable amygdala, whereas the uninhibited children, who show the complementary profile of sociability and approach behavior, have a less excitable amygdala. It is not clear whether an excitable amygdala would also predispose a child to other classes of fear or types of anxiety.

We have administered to more than 600 4-month-old infants a battery consisting of dynamic visual, auditory, and olfactory stimuli and have coded the frequency and intensity of motor activity, particularly limb movement, spasticity, and arching of the back, as well as fretting and crying. The battery consists of (1) an initial baseline period in which the mother looks at the child for 1 minute; (2) a tape recording of eight short sentences spoken by a female voice; (3) presentation of colorful moving mobiles consisting of one, four, or seven objects; (4) administration of a dilute butyl alcohol solution on a cotton swab applied to the nose; (5) tape recording of syllables varying in loudness; (6) popping of a balloon; and finally, (7) a second baseline in which the mother looks at the child for a final minute.

About 20% of healthy Caucasian infants from intact middle-class families react to these events, especially to the mobiles, with high levels of motor activity and frequent irritability on about a third of the trials. These children are called *high reactive*. About 35% of the infants show the complementary profile of low motor activity and minimal irritability. These *low reactive* infants are equally attentive, but are relaxed, rarely fret or fuss, and occasionally smile at the stimuli. A third group of 25% shows a pattern of low motor activity, but frequent fretting and crying. A final group of 10% shows a profile of high motor activity, but minimal irritability.

Infants from all four groups were observed at 9, 14, and 21 months in a laboratory battery consisting of a series of unfamiliar situations, including people, objects, and procedures. The child could display one fear on each of the standardized episodes, 17 episodes at 9 and 14 months of age, and 21 episodes at 21 months. Fear was defined narrowly as fretting or crying at an unfamiliar event or reluctance to approach an unfamiliar person or object despite a friendly invitation to do so. The episodes that most often produced a fear score at 14 months were: crying when a pair of puppets appeared on a stage in front of the child accompanied by a tape-recorded nonsense phrase; crying when the examiner assumed a facial frown and spoke a nonsense phrase in a stern voice; reluctance to imitate the examiner, who asked the child to put his or her hand into a cup containing water and red- or black-colored liquid. The most frequent bases for fear at 21 months were: the child stayed close to the mother and refused to play with a set of unfamiliar toys in a small, unfamiliar room, and showed reluctance to approach both a metal robot and a clown despite a friendly invitation to do so.

At every age, the reactive infants showed the highest number of fears; the low reactive infants showed the smallest number of fears. For example, at 14 months, 62% of the high reactive infants displayed high fear (defined as four or more fears), while only 10% showed low fear (defined as no or one fear). By contrast, only 10% of the low reactive infants showed high fear, while 60% showed low fear. The other two groups showed intermediate levels of fear at all ages.

The differences noted at 14 months were preserved through 21 months of age for 275 children from the group of 478 children who were observed at 14 months. The correlation for all children for the fear score from 14 to 21 months was .44 ($p < .0001$). When we combined each child's fear score at both 14 and 21 months, 34% of the high reactive infants showed high fear at both ages, while only 5% showed low fear. Among the low reactive infants, only 6% showed high fear, and 38% showed low fear at both 14 and 21 months (chi square = 36.9 $p < .0001$).

The expected predictive relation between the reactive profile displayed at 4 months, and the pattern of fearful or fearless behavior in the second year, is in accord with the notion that the two groups differ in the excitability of the amygdala and its circuits.

It is also important to note that these two groups differ in other characteristics. For example, high reactive infants smiled and laughed much less often at 9, 14, and 21 months than low reactive infants. In addition, more high reactive infants showed signs of high sympathetic reactivity in cardiac patterns. For example, the children who would be classified as high reactive at 4 months showed higher fetal heart rates during the last few weeks of pregnancy than low reactive infants. In addition, high reactive infants had higher heart rates while sleeping in an erect posture at 2 weeks of age, compared with low reactive infants. There were no differences in resting heart rate between the two groups after 4 months of age; nonetheless, high reactive infants showed larger cardiac accelerations than low reactive infants to mild stress. For example, one of the episodes at 14 months of age involved the administration of a drop of sweet or sour liquid on the infant's tongue. There were no differences in resting heart rate or the magnitude of heart rate increase to the sweet taste. Ninety percent of all children showed larger heart rate accelerations in reaction to the sour than to the sweet taste. But the high reactive children showed larger magnitudes of acceleration to the sour taste (dilute lemon juice) than either the low reactive infants or the majority of infants who belonged to other groups. We interpret this result to mean that the circuit from the amygdala to the sympathetic fibers serving the heart is more excitable in high than in low reactive infants to stimulus events that usually produce large heart rate accelerations.

It also appears that inhibited children are more likely to show EEG activation in right frontal cortical areas, while uninhibited children show greater activation in left frontal areas. Richard Davidson of the University of Wisconsin has found that children selected to be inhibited or uninhibited in the third year of life, using procedures similar to the ones we used in Cambridge, have greater desynchronization of alpha frequencies in the right frontal area, while uninhibited children show greater desynchronization on the left. Nathan Fox of the University of Maryland has found that high reactive infants, who are likely to become inhibited children in the second year, show greater activation on the right side, while low reactive infants, who are likely to become uninhibited children, show greater activation on the left frontal area.

We have found a parallel asymmetry in facial temperature on the forehead. The arterioles serving the face constrict under sympathetic innervation mediated by alpha adrenergic receptors. Because the sympathetic nervous system does not cross, one would expect that if there were greater activity in the right hemisphere, or greater reciprocal neural activity between the right amygdala and the right frontal cortex, high reactive children would be prone to show greater vasoconstriction on the right side, and therefore a cooler right side of the face. Low reactive children should show greater vasoconstriction on the left side and greater cooling on that side. We gathered thermographic images at 21 months on more than 200 children. The high reactive children who also showed a very low frequency of smiling during the assessments at 4, 9, 14, and 21 months were cooler on the right than on the left side of the forehead. The low reactive infants who showed a high frequency of smiling during the laboratory visits showed greater cooling on the left side of the face. Thus, there is a concordance between the EEG data and the asymmetries in facial temperature, and both sets of data are in accord with the popular hypothesis that the right hemisphere participates more fully in dysphoric states than does the left hemisphere (Cutting, 1990).

Our first investigation of these temperamental categories, initiated in 1979, began with groups of children who were selected to be inhibited or uninhibited when they were 21 or 31 months old. We observed these children recently when they were 13 years old. Although there were some changes in behavioral profile from the original selection in the second or third year through 7 years of age, there was much less change from 7 to 13 years. The children who had been selected to be inhibited at 21 or 31 months and who were still shy and minimally spontaneous at 7 years were shy, quiet, and much less affective at age 13 than those selected to be uninhibited who retained their profile through 7 years. Variation in spontaneous smiling with an examiner during the 90-minute laboratory session was an especially sensitive variable. The uninhibited children smiled often, and especially following task failure, while the inhibited children smiled infrequently. It is of interest, therefore, that high reactive children smiled infrequently at 9, 14, and 21 months, while uninhibited children smiled frequently.

These two temperamental categories may be related to several distinct categories of psychopathology. The shy, timid, anxious profile that defines the inhibited child implies that a proportion of these children may be vulnerable to a diagnosis of social phobia or panic in adulthood. We are testing a number of children at 14 and 21 months who have a parent with a diagnosis of panic or agoraphobia. These children show more fears than do average children. More than one-half of the children of panic parents had four or more fears, compared with 30% of a random sample of children from the same ethnic and social class background.

A small proportion of uninhibited children, especially boys, may be vulnerable to conduct disorder and delinquency. This subgroup of low reactive, uninhibited boys who have very low sympathetic reactivity, as evidenced by small pupil size, very low heart rates, and high heart rate variability, appear to experience minimal anxiety over violations of standards. The parents of these boys often complain that they are extremely difficult to socialize and do not respond to punishment. Should such children be raised in environments that are unusually permissive of aggression, it is likely that they, compared with other children, will be vulnerable to a delinquent career. If, however, the family and peer environments are not permissive of asocial behavior, these children should become the spontaneous, extroverted, enthusiastic youngsters who are so popular with adult and peers.

Summary

The return to temperamental ideas following their exile during most of this century is characterized by a great deal more sophistication. We now believe that some temperamental qualities are mediated by differences in neurochemistry. Second, there is a consensus that environmental experiences are necessary to actualize every temperamental bias. The idea of a synthesis of an inherited temperamental vulnerability combined with a particular set of encounters was not explicit in nineteenth-century arguments.

The categories of inhibited and uninhibited refer to an etiological profile and not just to a specific contemporary pattern. The same temperamental bias can lead to an envelope of behaviors that appear different on the surface. Some children classified as inhibited in the second year who are talented and grow up in homes that encourage academic excellence are likely to be productive scholars who will not show psychiatric symptoms. Children who are less successful in school and do not find a domain of compensation may be at greater risk for social phobia, depression, or panic. The most important change in the last 90 years is the idea that the adaptiveness of a temperamental profile depends upon life history, social conditions, and historical moment. This idea is missing in Hippocrates, Galen, and Avicenna. This notion accepts, even expects, changes in behavioral profile over time – what the nineteenth century called character – and entertains the possibility that the underlying physiology may change. This view is more dynamic and less deterministic than the constructions of the ancients.

Acknowledgments

This research was supported in part by a grant from the John D. and Catherine T. MacArthur Foundation and the Leon Lowenstein Foundation.

References

Cutting, J. (1990). *The Right Cerebral Hemisphere and Psychiatric Disorders.* New York: Oxford University Press.

Davidson, R. J. (1988). EEG measures of cerebral asymmetry. *International Journal of Neuroscience,* 39:71–89.

Fox, N. A. (1991). If it's not left, it's right. *American Psychologist,* 46:863–872.

Hencke, P. (1990). Potentiation of inputs from the posterolateral amygdala to the dentate gyrus and resistance to stress ulcer formation in rats. *Physiology and Behavior,* 48:659–664.

Gall, F. J. (1835). *On the Organ of the Moral Qualities and Intellectual Faculties in the Plurality of the Cerebral Organs,* trans. W. Lewis. 6 vols. Boston: Marsh, Copen & Lyon.

Hooton, E. A. (1939). *Crime in the Man.* Cambridge, MA: Harvard University Press.

Kemble, E. D., Blanchard, D. C., & Blanchard, R. J. (1990). Effects of regional amygdaloid lesions on the flight and defensive behavior of wild black rats (rattus rattus). *Physiology and Behavior,* 48:1–5.

Laderman, C. (1991). *Taming the Wind of Desire.* Berkeley: University of California Press.

LeDoux, J., Iwata, J., Cicchetti, P., & Reis, D. J. (1988). Different projections of the central amygdalar nucleus mediate autonomic and behavioral correlates of conditioned fear. *Journal of Neuroscience,* 8:2517–2529.

Maccoby, E. E., and Martin, J. A. (1983). Socialization in the context of the family. In E. M. Hetherington, ed., *Socialization, Personality and Social Development,* vol. 4, pp. 1–101, of P. H. Mussen, ed., *Handbook of Child Psychology.* 4th ed. New York: Wiley.

Maier, S. F., Grehn, R. E., Kalban, B. A., Sutton, L. C., Wiertelak, E. P., & Watkins, L. R. (1993). The role of the amygdala and dorsal raphe nuclei in mediating the behavioral consequences of inescapable shock. *Behavioral Neuroscience,* 107:377–388.

Scott, J. P., and Fuller, J. L. (1974). *Dog Behavior: The Genetic Basis* (first published as *Genetics and the Social Behavior of the Dog* [Chicago: University of Chicago Press, 1965]).

Sheldon, W. H. (1940). *The Varieties of Human Physique.* New York: Harper.

Simms, J. (1887). *Physiognomy Illustrated or Nature's Revelations of Character.* 8th ed. New York: Murray Hill.

Spurzheim, J. G. (1834). *Phrenology.* Boston: Marsh, Copen & Lyon.

Thomas, A., and Chess, S. (1977). *Temperament and Development.* New York: Brunner/Mazel.

Thinking

13

Editor's introduction: Upward toward phenomenology, downward toward physiology

Steven Matthysse

Thought disorder is a defining attribute of schizophrenia – but just what is it that is wrong with schizophrenic thinking? The question requires an answer that goes beyond a set of diagnostic rules, such as those that appear in DSM-IV. Characterizations like these "lead nowhere theoretically," as Roger Brown suggests, because they are not embedded in a rigorous conceptual system. Of course, the expectation that a characterization *can* lead somewhere theoretically remains a hope; a scrambling of neocortical wiring, even a scrambling caused by a single gene, would not necessarily be sufficiently coherent in its manifestations that the road could be followed backward from symptoms to the underlying process. Yet the very "strangeness" of schizophrenic thinking has led generations of investigators to suspect that the phenomenology of schizophrenic thinking, perspicaciously interpreted, will be a clue to the underlying process; in other words, that *something* is wrong with schizophrenic thinking, and we need to find out what that something is. The authors gathered here (and the editor) share that belief.

The richness of Loren and Jean Chapman's account of disordered thinking and perception in psychosis-prone individuals shows how hard it will be to render a convincing account of thought disorder in terms of any more fundamental process. It is not going to be easy for any theory to do justice to phenomena like these:

- ". . . distortions in the perception of one's own body and of the environment"
- "belief in forms of causation that, by conventional standards . . . are regarded as invalid and magical"

- "hearing a hallucinatory outer voice of another person that recites a blow-by-blow commentary on one's behavior"
- belief that other people can read one's mind, or that "the devil gave one feelings or forced one to act"
- "suspicion that another person . . . has stolen one's thoughts" or that "other people hypnotize one through energy that they radiate from their eyes"

The authors in our section have grappled with schizophrenic cognition by designing experiments in which it can be observed under controlled conditions. Brendan Maher has used verbal recall and semantic priming; Allan Mirsky has worked with a battery of attentional tests measuring the factors *focus-execute, sustain, shift,* and *encode;* Brown has pressed into service real-life situations requiring polite behavior [4]. In their several paradigms, these cognitive scientists are not, like the blind men inspecting the elephant, mistaking it for a wall, a rope, or a tree. Rather, it is as if they were observing the elephant when it lifts loads, or feeds, or uses its working memory, or tries to be polite – which is not a bad way to get to know an elephant.

Designing effective experimental conditions under which to observe schizophrenic thought disorder depends, first of all, on what Ann Sereno nicely describes as "parsing cognitive processes." We are not handed in advance any fixed vocabulary with which to describe mental life. The intuitive theoretical terms of "folk psychology" usually turn out to be not sufficiently precise. "When we use the term attention," Sereno asks, "do we mean arousal, vigilance, orienting, search, selection, or shift?"

Having defined a psychological process, the next problem is to design experimental tasks that selectively challenge it. What makes this problem hard is that any realistic task makes demands on many components of behavior. Choice of a task that maximally isolates the process of interest is critical. The delayed-response task, for example, adds a single critical component (delay) to a task, and measures the effect. This "complication" method goes back to Donders in 1868 (see the discussion by Holzman, in Chapter 26 of this volume). It was employed to good effect by Sternberg [14], who was able to isolate four serial stages in a task requiring binary classification of numbers, using the principle that when task factors do not influence the same stages, their effects on reaction time should be additive, whereas if two factors influence a common stage, their effects are likely to be interactive. A task pair isolating the delay component by "complication" and subtraction is much to be preferred to comparing two very different tasks, such as the Wisconsin Card Sorting Task and Raven's Progressive Matrices, if the purpose is to challenge working memory.[1]

Even the relatively interpretable delayed response task can be analyzed into smaller components, as Sohee Park and Gillian O'Driscoll have done (see Chapter 3, this volume):

1. "mental representation of goal or sequence"
2. "maintenance of target representation during the delay period"
3. "inhibition of competing, irrelevant stimuli"
4. "initiation and execution of an appropriate motor response"

One dividend of such careful subdivision is that Park and O'Driscoll are able to separate the working memory component from the response inhibition component, by observing whether the subject corrects his or her errors on subsequent tries. One may worry whether the onion is infinite, but presumably peeling will reach a natural limit when we hit upon task components that correspond to well-defined biological mechanisms. To the extent that we have insight into biological mechanisms, the "parsing" problem is made much easier, as Sereno suggests:

Understanding the biological mechanisms . . . can . . . alter the way cognitive psychology carves up human behavior into processes such as attention and memory.

In practice, however, the problem may have to be tackled in the reverse order: psychological delineation of task components may come before brain mechanisms are known. Indeed, it may be hoped, successful psychological "parsing" will serve to guide neurophysiological investigations.

So difficult is the design of experimental tasks that selectively challenge specific psychological processes, it would be no exaggeration to say that laurels in the field of psychology are won by inventing them. One has to pause in admiration of the techniques used by Maher to measure guidance by context (improvement of recall when words are included in sequences "increasingly approximate to the structure of a sentence") and access to associations (second-order semantic priming, e.g., enhancement of response to the word "stripe" by presentation of the word "lion").

Although schizophrenic thought disorder may provide the inspiration for an experimental paradigm, once abnormal performance of schizophrenic subjects has been demonstrated, the paradigm takes on a life of its own. Each successful laboratory investigation of schizophrenic cognition uncovers phenomena which may, if followed to their neurophysiological roots, be effective in pursuing the biology of schizophrenia. In the same way, eye movement dysfunction has been an important biological and genetic clue, even though it makes no pretense of directly accounting for thought disorder.

Although each laboratory manifestation can be pursued in a "downward" direction, toward brain mechanisms, it may not also be possible to follow it "upward," toward the clinical phenomena of thought disorder. Working memory is an instructive example because, while the finding of *spatial* working memory deficit in schizophrenia has generated valuable neuroanatomical and neurophysiological hypotheses (see Chapter 2, by Patricia Goldman-Rakic), it is not difficult to show through examples that *verbal* working memory deficit cannot, by itself, account for the phenomena of thought disorder. Consider some typical manifestations of thought disorder, as reported in a seminal study by our honoree [13]. In each of these examples, working memory is intact; thinking is not.

1. *Perseveration.* The patient was asked to define several words: [remorse] "Means whenever you're mourning." [sanctuary] "Means cemetery." [matchless] "Is like whenever someone dies and leaves a match behind" (p. 84). Here, working memory is working all too well, but "the associative process seems to be no longer regulated by the original task, but rather by some internal set . . ." (pp. 70–71).

2. *Relationship Verbalization.* This type of thought disorder occurs when the subject continues the story on each Rorschach card, as in "You have the same thing here, except for the pig's being slaughtered . . . now the devil has destroyed the animal and the butterfly" (p. 84).

3. *Looseness.* The patient was asked to explain the proverb "shallow brooks are noisy." "Something that is small can cause a great explosion because . . . it causes a building of sediment . . . the water of a shallow stream wears away the rocks beneath, which causes the rocks beneath, which causes the rocks to move and causes a mudslide" (p. 91). Here the

original stimulus remains in working memory, driving the associative chain, even though the meaning of the proverb has been lost.

For inspiration on the "upward" direction, I opened Johnston and Holzman [13] once again, and turned to the beginning, where a conversation with a schizophrenic young woman is reported.

Patient: I'm responsible for my own motives. I keep my mouth closed and my nose open.

Nurse: Can you say things a bit more clearly . . .

Patient: Just ask my autograph book who was signing it all the time. It's not my fault it's ripped up.

Nurse: I suspect no one else in this room knew what you were talking about.

Patient: I said I could remember when my mother's hair was down her back and she kept cutting it off.

Psychiatrist: I don't know what that means.

Patient: There's been a pass over me. I've been passed over.

If, as Brown showed in the context of polite behavior, schizophrenics are too "Gricean," in this excerpt our speaker is surely not Gricean enough. The *maxim of relation* ("make your contribution relevant") and the *maxim of manner* ("avoid obscurity of expression; avoid ambiguity") could not be more completely violated. On the other hand, as I read the fragment, the patient's communication failure is even more serious than violating conversational maxims. Normal semantic constraints seem to have been "lifted," just as schizophrenic impoliteness indicates the "lifting of a pragmatic system." I count seven semantic incongruities in the excerpt, all the more remarkable because – as the reader can check – there are no syntactic anomalies at all. I realize I am on dangerous ground here, for two reasons: (1) rigorous talk of semantic anomaly should be relative to a formal theory, which I am not attempting to provide; (2) Brown concluded, in his American Psychological Association presidential address just over twenty years ago, that effort to understand schizophrenic language would be more rewarding if it focused, not on semantics, but on "*psychological* implication, principles of affective consistency, principles of attribution, and the common fallacies of logic and of evidence evaluation" [3].

Nevertheless, I see an astonishing degree of semantic anomaly in this fragment.

1. *"I'm responsible for my motives."* Motives are not entities one can take or fail to take responsibility for, the way one can take

responsibility for completing a mission; to declare a motive for an action is already to assign responsibility to the actor.

2. *"I keep my mouth closed and my nose open."* The nose is not something like the eye, that one can keep open; it just is open, by the way it is constructed. "I keep . . . my nose open" could be interpreted metaphorically, as an expression that "induces the hearer . . . to view a thing . . . as being like something else, by applying to the former linguistic expressions which are more normally employed in references to the latter" [7]; but metaphorical interpretation does not give a satisfactory account of the other utterances of this patient.

3. *"Just ask my autograph book . . ."* "Ask" requires a grammatical object qualified as capable of answering.

4. *". . . who was signing it all the time"* contains two anomalies:
   (a) The incompleteness (imperfective aspect) of ". . . was signing," reinforced by the continuity implied by "all the time," is inconsistent with the nature of autograph signing, which consists of discrete events of short duration.
   (b) Because the pronoun "who" occurs in the context of an uninterrupted continuous action, it should refer to one actor or one constant group of actors; but that requirement is also inconsistent with the meaning of an autograph book, which is an object signed, not by one person repeatedly, but by many people once.

5. *". . . she kept cutting it off"*: Similar problem to (4a): an incomplete, continuous action is implied by "kept cutting," which contradicts the discreteness and finality of cutting off one's hair.

6. *"There's been a pass over me . . . I've been passed over."* The only literal interpretation of "a pass over me" is as someone's throwing a football above the speaker's head, whereas "I've been passed over" refers to being slighted or disregarded. Trying to make the first utterance coherent with the second by interpreting it metaphorically seems strained.

I suspect that the relationship between the semantic failure exhibited in this fragment, and the "lifting" of the politeness system observed by Brown, is more than an analogy. In both cases, we are dealing with a *formal system,* a set of more or less restrictive rules that specify a domain of competence. The system is "unbounded in scope, not determined by external stimuli or internal state, not random but coherent and appropriate to situations . . ." [5, p. 36]. Schizophrenia may be a condition in which neuronal structures that make possible performance of several rule-based but "unbounded" cognitive systems are damaged.

The formalization of aspects of intelligent behavior as systems that, by analogy with language, may be called "syntactic" (i.e., domains of competence regulated by rules, but unlimited in possibilities of combination) has made considerable progress, although the depth to which it can successfully be pursued remains an open question. Jackendoff has begun the ambitious project of applying formal linguistic ideas to other domains of competence, such as music and spatial perception. In his view, "the power of the brain is in part a result of having . . . many different 'languages of the mind,' each with its own repertoire of primitive distinctions and its own principles of combination" [12, p. 4].

Hobbs and Moore [11] have assembled projects attempting to formalize commonsense knowledge, covering such intriguing subjects as "naïve physics," "ontology for liquids," temporal reasoning, belief, and metaphor. It is even possible that the different cognitive systems that are impaired in schizophrenia share underlying neural mechanisms. Chomsky [5, p. 48] makes the interesting suggestion that

it is by virtue of the way the cognitive system is embedded in performance systems that the formal properties of expressions are interpreted as rhyme, entailment, and so on . . . embedded in different performance systems in some hypothetical . . . organism, they could serve as instructions for some other activity, say locomotion.

It is plausible that performance in rule-governed domains would be especially vulnerable to damage, because such systems require "global properties of computations of a kind that are known to yield extreme computational complexity" [5, p. 51]. (For a detailed study of computational complexity in linguistics, see [2].) Indeed, as Chomsky has noted, the intractability of language to mechanistic explanation was one of the arguments Descartes advanced in favor of dualism.

[Automata] could never use words, or put together other signs, as we do in order to declare our thoughts to others. For we can certainly conceive of a machine so constructed that it utters words, and even utters words which correspond to bodily actions causing a change in its organs (e.g., if you touch it in one spot it asks what you want of it, if you touch it in another it cries out that you are hurting it, and so on). But it is not conceivable that such a machine should produce different arrangements of words so as to give an appropriately meaningful answer to whatever is said in its presence . . . [8, vol. 1, p. 140].

Whatever other arguments may be advanced for dualism, this argument seems destined to fail. While it is not possible to enter into this question in adequate detail here, it is worth giving a hint of how mechanical systems could underlie domains of competence defined in analogy with formal syntax. For that purpose, let us consider a paper by J. J. Collins and I. Stewart, "Hexapodal gaits and coupled nonlinear oscillator models" [6]. Collins and Stewart study a ring of six oscillators, connected in a circle. They show that the patterns of activity that can occur in the ring are limited to a small number of types, listed in Table 13.1 (reproduced from their paper). "*A*" and "*B*" stand for two distinct waveforms, and expressions like "*A* + 60" mean "waveform *A*, phase-shifted 60°." The allowed patterns do not depend strongly on the internal dynamics of the oscillators; they are determined primarily by symmetry. Think of each row as if it were a "sentence" made up of six "words" (ignore the first column, which is a mathematical label, and the last, which is an interpretation to be discussed in a moment). If the lexicon contained the eight "words"

$$A, A + 60, A + 120, A + 180, A + 240, A + 300,$$
$$B, B + 180$$

and there were no syntactic constraints, 65,536 combinations would be possible. The interactions between the oscillators allow only 18 combinations or, to speak figuratively, the syntactic rules of the circuit allow only 18 grammatical sentences to be formed out of the very large number of word combinations possible.

The "grammatical" reading of the circuit's behavior becomes especially interesting because Collins and Stewart interpret each pattern as the walking movement of an insect, whose six legs (numbered from front to back, with *L* for left and *R* for right) are enumerated at the heads of the columns of Table 13.1. As shown in the last column, some of the allowed patterns correspond to walking movements actually observed in insects: the "pronk" (all limbs extending in synchrony); the "metachronal rhythm" (wave of leg motion from back to front, on alternating sides); and the "tripod" (front and back legs on one side moving together with the middle leg on the other side, alternating with the mirror image pattern).

Although it is not known whether insect gaits are actually con-

Table 13.1. *Patterns of activity in a ring of oscillators*

rep	L_1	L_2	L_3	R_1	R_2	R_3	comments
ϱ_0	A	A	A	A	A	A	pronk
ϱ_1	A	A + 60	A + 120	A + 180	A + 240	A + 300	front-to-rear rhythm
	A	A + 300	A + 240	A + 180	A + 120	A + 60	metachronal rhythm
	A	B	B + 180	A + 180	B + 180	B	
	B	A	B	B + 180	A + 180	B + 180	
	B + 180	B	A	B	B + 180	A + 180	A = A + 180: half period
	B + 180	A	B	A	B + 180	B + 180	A = A + 180: half period
	B + 180	B + 180	B	B	A	B + 180	A = A + 180: half period
ϱ_2	A	A + 120	A + 240	A	A + 120	A + 240	bound-like gait
	A	A + 240	A + 120	A	A + 240	A + 120	
	A	A	B	A	A	B	
	B	A	A	B	A	A	
	A	B	A	A	B	A	
	A	A	B	A	A	B	
	B	A	A	B	A	A	B = B + 180: half period
	A + 180	A	A	A	A	A + 180	B = B + 180: half period
	A	B	A	A	B	A	B = B + 180: half period
ϱ_3	A	A + 180	A	A + 180	A	A + 180	tripod

trolled in the manner suggested by Collins and Stewart, their model illustrates nicely how a mechanical system can embody the syntactic rules of a simple domain of competence. In invertebrates, it is known that a single neural network may be capable of generating several different behaviors, such as reflexive withdrawal and escape swimming. On the basis of experimentally observed functional reconfigurations, Getting [10, p. 199] concludes:

The comparative study of neuronal networks has led to a picture of neural networks as dynamic entities, constrained by their anatomical connectivity but, within these constraints, able to be organized and configured into several operational modes, each depending upon the expression and modulation of the constituent cellular, synaptic, and network building blocks.

What I am proposing is that local neuronal circuits may be replicated in many copies, each copy expressing at any instant of time one of the behaviors consistent with the syntactic constraints imposed by the wiring diagram. At any time, a large number of alternative "syntactically correct" patterns will be available, in parallel, for behavioral selection.[2] This is how, I imagine, a Cartesian machine could "produce different arrangements of words so as to give an appropriately meaningful answer to whatever is said in its presence . . ." Obviously it is a great leap to go from the multifunctional circuits observed in oscillator models and invertebrates to the unbounded but rule-governed nature of human language, and only detailed modeling and experimental work will tell whether the analogy can be turned into a theory.

The word "lifted," which Brown used to describe the nonfunctioning of the expected rule system in the behavior of schizophrenic patients in situations requiring politeness, is particularly appropriate because patients do not always fail. Sometimes a schizophrenic patient will speak in a perfectly normal way, with neither semantic nor pragmatic anomalies, and then, for unknown reasons, revert to a pattern as disturbed as the example we considered earlier. The formal system is "lifted," but not destroyed. It turns out that systems of the kind studied by Collins and Stewart are dependent on correct "tuning" of the connections between the individual units [1]. Neurotransmitter imbalances, which could be present at one moment and not another, might be just the sort of change that would "detune" an array of local neuronal circuits, so that it was no longer capable of implementing its normal syntactic rules. Neuroleptic-induced improvement, conversely, might be understood as the restoration to function of arrays subserving rule-governed domains of competence. The "enhanced ability to discriminate social role differentiation" noted by Spohn after neuroleptic treatment might be an example of this kind of reversible change.

In summary, it seems useful to distinguish between the "upward" and "downward" directions of interpreting experiments on schizophrenic thinking. Any manifestation of disordered thinking under laboratory conditions may be followed "downward," toward neurophysiology, brain chemistry, and genetics. This path, now being followed successfully with smooth pursuit eye movement and working memory, may be a very profitable means to uncover the biology of schizophrenia. On the other hand, the "upward" path, toward the phenomenology of schizophrenic thinking, will only yield to us as we progress in untying the Cartesian knot.

Notes

1. See Chapter 5, by Deborah L. Levy, this volume, for more on the subdivision of tasks.
2. This model resembles Edelman's "theory of neuronal group selection" (TNGS) [9, pp. 82ff.], except that TNGS does not postulate internal constraints on the options presented by neuronal groups.

References

[1] Ashwin, P., G. P. King, and J. W. Swift. 1990. Three identical oscillators with symmetric coupling. *Nonlinearity,* 3:585–601.
[2] Barton, G. E., Jr., R. C. Berwick, and E. S. Ristad. 1987. *Computational Complexity and Natural Language.* Cambridge, MA: MIT Press.
[3] Brown, R. 1973. Schizophrenia, language, and reality. *American Psychologist,* 28:395-403.
[4] Brown, R. 1990. Politeness theory: exemplar and exemplary. In I. Rock, ed., *The Legacy of Solomon Asch: Essays in Cognition and Social Psychology,* pp. 3–38. Hillsdale, NJ: Erlbaum.
[5] Chomsky, N. 1993. *Language and Thought.* Wakefield, RI: Moyer Bell.
[6] Collins, J. J., and I. Stewart. 1993. Hexapodal gaits and coupled nonlinear oscillator models. *Biological Cybernetics,* 68:287–298.
[7] Cruse, D. A. 1986. *Lexical Semantics.* Cambridge University Press, p. 41.
[8] Descartes, R. 1984/1985. *The Philosophical Writings of Descartes,* J. Cottingham, R. Stoothoff, and D. Murdoch, trans. 2 vols. Cambridge University Press.

[9] Edelman, G. M. 1992. *Bright Air, Brilliant Fire: On the Matter of the Mind.* New York: Basic Books.

[10] Getting, P. A. 1989. Emerging principles governing the operation of neural networks. *Annual Review of Neuroscience,* 12:185–204.

[11] Hobbs, J. R., and R. C. Moore, eds. 1985. *Formal Theories of the Commonsense World.* Norwood, NJ: Ablex.

[12] Jackendoff, R. 1992. *Languages of the Mind: Essays on Mental Representation.* Cambridge, MA: MIT Press.

[13] Johnston, M. H., and P. S. Holzman. 1979. *Assessing Schizophrenic Thinking.* San Francisco: Jossey-Bass.

[14] Sternberg, S. 1969. The discovery of processing stages: Extensions of Donders' method. *Acta Psychologica,* 30:276–315.

14

The psychometric assessment of schizophrenia proneness

Jean P. Chapman and Loren J. Chapman

Clinicians have provided rich descriptions of schizophrenia-prone individuals. These descriptions are primarily anecdotal and speculative, but they provide a valuable source of hypotheses for testing in more rigorous research. Both Kraepelin ([1913] 1919) and Bleuler (1924), working from case history information as well as from observations of relatives of schizophrenic patients, described schizophrenia-prone individuals as having deviant but nonpsychotic symptoms. The symptoms were often milder or transient versions of the types of symptoms displayed by psychotic patients. They interpreted these symptoms as early signs of the disorder but reported that only a portion of persons who show these symptoms of schizophrenia proneness actually develop full-fledged schizophrenia.

The construct of schizophrenia proneness

"Schizophrenia proneness" refers to a predisposition or diathesis to schizophrenia. Most researchers in the field guide their work by a diathesis-stress model. Well-known examples include those of Gottesman (1991), and Meehl (1962), and Slater and Cowie (1971). It is usually assumed that the diathesis is genetic, but that assumption is not necessary for the logic of the model. Although there is clearly a strong genetic predisposition to schizophrenia (Gottesman 1991), other contributions to the predisposition could be environmental. The stress component of diathesis-stress is considered to be only environmental, although the concept of environmental stress is broad, and includes much more than interpersonal stress. For example, one variety of environmental stress is the difficulty of coping with the problems of life for a person with a poor genetic endowment, such as genetically weak physique or low intelligence. Environmental stress also includes physical stress, such as anoxia at birth or viral infections in utero.

The principal assumption of the diathesis-stress model is that schizophrenia results from an interaction of environmental stress with a predisposition or proneness. Evidence for the importance of both the diathesis and the stress comes from many sources, but most clearly from the observation that the rate of schizophrenia in monozygotic twins of schizophrenics is about 45% to 50% (Gottesman, 1991). The fact that the rate of the disorder in monozygotic twins of schizophrenics is vastly higher than the roughly 1% in the general population is evidence for a genetic diathesis. The fact that the concordance rate falls short of 100%, the concordance rate expected of a completely genetic disorder, is evidence for the importance of nongenetic, that is, environmental factors.

Even more compelling evidence for the diathesis-stress model comes from the study of the offspring of the nonschizophrenic monozygotic twins of schizophrenics. These offspring become schizophrenic about as often as do the offspring of schizophrenics (Gottesman and Bertelsen, 1989), a finding that can be explained by a genetic diathesis that remains unexpressed in the nonschizophrenic twin but may, nevertheless, be expressed in that twin's offspring.

Our term "schizophrenia-prone" means having the diathesis for schizophrenia. Thus, many schizophrenia-prone persons will never become schizophrenic because they do not undergo sufficient stress to precipitate the disorder. The statement that a person is schizophrenia-prone is only a statement of heightened risk, that is, a prediction that the person is more likely than the average person to become schizophrenic. For example, the strongest available evidence of schizophrenia proneness is that a person has two schizophrenic parents or has a schizophrenic identical twin. Yet only about half of such persons become schizophrenic.

Studies of the nonschizophrenic relatives of schizophrenics

Schizophrenia runs in families and a portion of the relatives of schizophrenics often experience symptoms and problems even when they do not develop schizophrenia. Kraepelin reported, "Not infrequently, one learns further that among the brothers and sisters of the patients are found striking personalities, criminals, queer individuals, prostitutes, suicides, vagrants, wrecked and ruined human beings" (Kraepelin, [1913] 1919, p. 234). Kraepelin interpreted these deviancies as arrested forms of the disorder itself. Bleuler (1924) reported similar observations and made a similar inference.

Two principal descriptions have been offered repeatedly for the relatives of schizophrenics. One is that the relatives include an excess of persons who might be described as uncontrolled and antisocial, and the other is that they are eccentric, schizophrenic-like, and withdrawn.

Uncontrolled and antisocial behavior

Planansky (1972) after reviewing the literature on the characteristics of the family members of schizophrenics, reported that the most consistently reported deviant personality in the schizophrenic family has been "the coarse unfeeling type, usually troublesome, occasionally outright anti-social" (p. 153). Dunaif and Hoch (1955) offered the term "pseudopsychopathic schizophrenia" for the antisocial pattern that often precedes schizophrenia. Heston (1966) found that the adopted-away offspring of schizophrenic mothers not only showed the expected greater frequency of schizophrenia than did control adoptees, but also showed a greater frequency of sociopaths and convicted felons. Eysenck and Eysenck (1976) found the evidence of sociopathy as an indicator of psychosis so compelling that they relied heavily on sociopathic items in constructing their Psychoticism Scale.

Rosenthal (1975) suggested that sociopathic traits in the relatives of schizophrenics may not be evidence of a genetic link of sociopathy to schizophrenia in the usual sense. He found assortative mating of schizophrenic women with men who have sociopathy, a disorder that also has a substantial genetic component. As a result, both disorders are found in the offspring, although sociopathy may not indicate schizophrenia proneness.

Eccentric, schizophrenia-like, and asocial behavior

A commonly studied clinical syndrome in the relatives of schizophrenics is one of schizophrenic-like thinking and behavior. "Schizophrenic-like" means having the characteristics of schizophrenia, but in attenuated form. These people are characterized by "strange" thinking, with a tendency to ignore both reality and logic, by vague speech, and by brief episodes of more severe cognitive distortion that are called "micropsychoses." Many of these people show no deep involvement with anyone. Their behavior often appears strange or eccentric. Yet their symptoms are not so severe or so constantly aberrant that the person is diagnosed as clinically psychotic.

Shields et al. (1975) surveyed the literature looking for reports of withdrawn, schizophrenic-like behavior in the nonschizophrenic monozygotic twins of schizophrenics. They found that interpreting this literature was difficult because of variations among studies in diagnostic practices and in the information reported. However, they found that a substantial portion of the discordant monozygotic twins showed withdrawn, schizophrenic-like adjustment to some degree.

By far, the most influential study of characteristics of schizophrenia-prone persons has been the Danish adoption study (Kety et al., 1968). These investigators studied the biological relatives of schizophrenics who had been adopted away at an early age. These biological relatives showed not only a heightened incidence of clinical schizophrenia, but also a heightened incidence of related disorders that the investigators referred to as "borderline" schizophrenia. Kety et al.'s description of borderline schizophrenia was largely responsible for the DSM-III diagnostic category of schizotypal personality disorder (Spitzer et al., 1979).

Premorbid history of schizophrenic patients

Another body of literature that provides descriptions of schizophrenia-prone individuals consists of studies of premorbid adjustment of schizophrenics. Both James Chapman (1966) and Strauss (1969) have reported that many schizophrenics have shown premorbidly less extreme versions of their later schizophrenic symptoms. It follows that their preschizophrenic symptoms were schizophrenic-like.

Two important early studies of the premorbid history of schizophrenics have reported data from the childhood records of future patients.

Disturbed children who later become schizophrenic

Fleming and Ricks (1970), working at a child guidance clinic, studied the case history records of children who later became schizophrenic. Their report, unlike that of most such studies, provided considerable information about the inner experiences of their subjects. Many of the future schizophrenics were characterized by marked anxiety and by feelings of vulnerability. They also reported occasional hallucinations and delusions, and feelings of estrangement, detachment, and depersonalization, as well as feelings of internal fragmentation and personal dissolution. Many described themselves as crazy. Many reported their senses as blurred or dysfunctional, so that things looked, felt, or tasted wrong or different. Many lacked normal feelings of friendliness and need for sociability with others. As a result, they withdrew from others and, in turn, felt less accepted, less approved of, and less valued by others. A large number of the preschizophrenics, especially those who later became chronic schizophrenics, seemed never to have had any satisfactory emotional relationships with anyone. In summary, the symptoms of these preschizophrenic children closely resembled the symptoms of schizophrenia, although in attenuated form.

The high school adjustment of future schizophrenics

Watt (1974) examined teachers' notes concerning personal adjustment as recorded in the earlier public school records of hospitalized schizophrenic adults and of matched control subjects. This strategy's advantage is that it avoids the bias toward pathology that results from use of subjects who had been seen in a clinical facility. However, its disadvantage is that teachers' notes on personality traits may be less detailed than those of clinical practitioners, and may be limited primarily to behavior rather than inner experience.

Watt found that about half of the future schizophrenics became socially deviant by early adolescence. He found support for both the descriptions of future schizophrenics as antisocial and the descriptions of their being more socially withdrawn. The patterns differed, however, for the two sexes. The boys more often became irritable, aggressive, negativistic and defiant of authority, and emotionally unstable, but not more introverted. In contrast, the girls more often became more compliant, shy, and introverted.

Hoch and Cattell's descriptions of pseudoneurotic schizophrenics

Hoch and Cattell (1959) described a schizophrenic-like syndrome that they called "pseudoneurotic." By this term they meant that the symptoms are not severe enough for the patient to receive a conventional diagnosis of schizophrenia. Their description of pseudoneurotic schizophrenia is especially useful because they and their collaborators (Hoch et al. 1962) provided clear evidence that at least some of the patients whom they diagnosed as pseudoneurotic schizophrenics were at heightened risk for full-fledged schizophrenia. They found in a 10-year follow-up that 20% of their pseudoneurotic schizophrenics had decompensated into schizophrenia as conventionally diagnosed and that half of those 20% had become chronic schizophrenics. Hoch and Cattell (1959) described the pseudoneurotic schizophrenic as characterized by: (1) disorders of thinking and arbitrary reasoning like that of clinical schizophrenia but less extreme in character; (2) disorders of emotional regulation including simultaneous awareness of polar affects, such as love and hate or joy and sorrow, diffuse and pervasive anxiety and bewilderment in coping with it, anhedonia, and suspicion of positive, friendly emotions in others; (3) disruptions of sensorimotor and autonomic functioning, including physical clumsiness, body-image distortions, and psychosomatic symptoms.

Schizotypy as described by Paul Meehl*

In his 1962 presidential address to the American Psychological Association, Meehl suggested that there is a genetic transmission of a predisposition toward schizophrenia and that individuals with this predisposition, whom he called "schizotypes," could be identified by their behavioral traits. Meehl's term, "schizotype," was borrowed from Rado (1953), who offered it as a condensation of "schizophrenic genotype." This term conveys Meehl's emphasis on the genetic basis of the disorder.

Meehl (1962) advanced four core symptoms of schizotypy, namely anhedonia (pleasure deficit), cognitive slippage (mild thought disorder), ambivalence, and interpersonal aversiveness. Meehl suggested that anhedonia is a "quasi-pathognomonic" sign of schizotypy, but later (Meehl 1975, 1990) proposed that anhedonia is not specific to schizotypy and schizophrenia but, rather, plays an important role in neurosis as well. Meehl provided a full description of the schizotype in his manual for diagnosing the condition (Meehl, 1964). He chose not to publish this manual, but it became influential because he

---

* See also the review and analysis of Meehl's framework in Chapter 10, by
  L. Erlenmeyer-Kimling, this volume – Eds.

generously distributed copies to other investigators. In this manual, Meehl described in exquisite clinical detail 25 characteristics of schizotypes, including intense ambivalence, anhedonia, body-image aberrations, chaotic sexuality, cognitive slippage, flat or spotty affectivity, magical ideation, micropsychotic episodes, pan-anxiety, psychosomatic symptoms, soft neurological signs, marked social fear, and preoccupation with suicide.

Meehl believes that the schizotype suffers from a neural integrative defect transmitted by a single dominant gene with incomplete penetrance, and that all persons with that defect who are reared in any of the "existing social reinforcement regimes" show the core symptoms of schizotypy. He suggested that environmental influences, as well as the person's other characteristics, such as anxiety level, physical vigor, and problems concerning hostility, determine the severity of the symptoms that the schizotype will experience as well as whether or not the schizotype will decompensate into schizophrenia.

Meehl described schizophrenia as the extreme end of the continuum of schizotypy. Although some schizotypes decompensate into full-blown schizophrenia, the majority do not. More recently Meehl (1990, 1993) estimated that only about 10% of schizotypes decompensate into clinical schizophrenia. He based this estimate on the observation that about 10% of schizophrenics have a schizophrenic parent, together with his assumption that schizophrenia is transmitted by a single dominant gene with incomplete penetrance. Since his dominant gene model dictates that every schizophrenic must have at least one parent who carries the gene, the other 90% of schizophrenics without a schizophrenic parent must have a parent who has the gene but has not decompensated. Meehl described this estimate as conjectural rather than one that follows unambiguously from the available data.

Approaches to identifying schizophrenia-prone subjects

The most widely used method for identifying schizophrenia-prone individuals is to select relatives of schizophrenics. A disadvantage of this method is that 81% of schizophrenics do not have a schizophrenic parent, sister, or brother (Gottesman, 1991). Many attempts have been made to identify schizophrenia-prone persons by measuring one or another of their characteristics. A number of investigators, including the present writers, have attempted to identify schizophrenia-prone individuals by paper-and-pencil measures. These measures include the Psychoticism Scale (Eysenck and Eysenck, 1976), which primarily measures uncontrolled and antisocial behavior, the Schizoidia Scale (Golden and Meehl, 1979), the Schizotypal Personality Scale (Claridge and Broks, 1984), and the Schizotypal Personality Questionnaire (Raine 1991), all of which primarily measure eccentric, schizophrenic-like, and asocial behavior.

A longitudinal study of psychosis proneness

We have pursued a longitudinal research strategy in an attempt to identify psychosis-prone individuals. Our research began as an attempt to measure schizophrenia proneness. However, based upon early findings (Chapman and Chapman, 1985) and the narrowing of the diagnostic criteria for schizophrenia in DSM-III, we broadened our focus to study psychosis proneness. We employed the following research strategy: (1) develop paper-and-pencil self-report questionnaires for screening schizophrenia-prone subjects; (2) develop an interview rating system for assessing psychotic-like experiences; (3) administer the questionnaires to large groups of college students who are at or near the age range of greatest risk for schizophrenia; (4) select candidate schizophrenia-prone subjects on the basis of scores on the questionnaire; (5) interview the subjects at the time of selection and assess them for psychotic-like experiences; (6) re-evaluate the subjects' functioning at follow-up interviews 10 to 15 years later.

Developing questionnaires for psychosis proneness

We relied on paper-and-pencil, true–false questionnaires that were developed earlier in our laboratory to measure several symptoms or traits of psychosis proneness as described in the clinical literature, especially in the writings of Meehl (1962, 1964) and of Hoch and Cattell (1959). The traits were perceptual aberration (Chapman et al., 1978), that is, psychotic-like distortions in the perception of one's own body and of the environment; physical anhedonia (Chapman et al., 1976), which is a marked deficit in the experience of pleasure; magical ideation (Eckblad and Chapman, 1983), or belief in forms of causation that, by conventional standards of our dominant culture, are regarded as invalid and magical; impulsive nonconformity (Chapman et al., 1984), which is the failure to incorporate societal norms, a lack of empathy for the pain of others, and an unrestrained yielding to impulse and self-gratification; and social anhedonia (Eckblad et al., 1982), which is disinterest and a lack of pleasure from interactions with other people.

The development of these questionnaires followed the method of rational scale development recommended by Jackson (1974) for general use in personality scale development. Several procedures were followed to assure appropriateness of the items, including the development of a formal trait specification to guide item writers. The items were worded to refer to stable experiences and to avoid susceptibility to social desirability and acquiescence response biases. Candidate items were administered to several hundred subjects to ensure high item–scale correlations and to eliminate items that correlated with independent measures of acquiescence and social desirability. The coefficient alpha internal consistency reliabilities of all these scales are in the .80s. The test–retest reliabilities for a 6-week interval are between .75 and .85 (Chapman et al., 1982). The articles cited after each scale provide complete descriptions of each of the questionnaires. Subjects scoring high on these scales have been studied extensively, both in our laboratory and in other laboratories, in order to investigate characteristics that may be consistent with their being psychosis-prone. Miller and Yee (in press) review studies of psychophysiological measures using these subjects, and Edell (in press) reviews studies using other kinds of measures.

The rating scales for psychotic-like experiences

Chapman and Chapman (1980) developed a manual for rating psychotic-like experiences on a continuum of deviancy. This rating system was designed in light of the principle that psychotic-like experiences are often precursors of full-fledged psychosis. Deviant experiences reported by hypothetically psychosis-prone subjects were selected. These experiences seemed to fall on a continuum of deviancy between full-fledged psychosis and normalcy. Consider, for example, the psychotic experience of hearing a hallucinatory outer voice of another person that recites a blow-by-blow commentary on one's behavior as it occurs. This symptom is usually regarded as psychotic and is listed by Kurt Schneider (1959) as a "first-rank" symptom of schizophrenia (a symptom of diagnostic significance). A less deviant hallucinatory experience would be to hear, as an inner voice, another person berating the subject for a half-hour every couple days. We might rate that as markedly psychotic-like. An even less deviant experience, which we would rank close to the normal end of the continuum, would be occasionally to hear an inner voice speaking one's own thoughts, as a voice of conscience, admonishing the subject about his or her behavior. Many of us have similar experiences.

The manual classifies the experiences into six categories and provides an 11-point scoring continuum for each type of experience. The rating values in the manual are medians of values suggested by six prominent clinical investigators of schizophrenia. Scores of 2 to 5 are given for psychotic-like experiences while scores of 6 to 11 are reserved for those of psychotic deviancy. Although this rating scale is designed for both psychotic and psychotic-like experiences, we refer to it in this chapter, for convenience of exposition, as a scale for rating psychotic-like experiences. Rating an experience as psychotic on this scale does not mean that the person is clinically psychotic by DSM-III-R criteria. Instead, it means that the experience is of the severity that is commonly observed in patients who receive such diagnoses. The categories include: (a) Transmission of One's Own Thoughts. An example, with a score of 5, is the suspicion that others were reading one's mind against one's will. A full acceptance of such a belief would receive a score of 8. (b) Passivity Experiences. An example, with a score between 3 and 5 depending on subcultural support, is the belief that the devil gave one feelings or forced one to act. A belief that a person other than God, the devil, an angel, or spirit did so would receive a score of 9. (c) Voice Experiences and Other Auditory Hallucinations. An example, with a score of 8, is hearing an external hallucinatory voice, other than spirits, that speaks intelligible phrases and believing it was produced by others. (d) Thought Withdrawal. An example, with a score of 6, is the suspicion that another person or being, other than God, has stolen one's thoughts. (e) Other Personally Relevant Aberrant Beliefs. An example, with a score of 5, is a tentative acceptance of a delusional belief, such as that other people hypnotize one through energy that they radiate from their eyes. (f) Visual Hallucinations and Other Visual Experiences. An example, with a score of 6, is brief visual hallucinations that occur while wide-awake accompanied by a belief that the events are real. The rating values given in the manual are the median of the values assigned by six expert judges, who showed high agreement (coefficient alpha of .94).

The manual makes some allowance for differences in subcultural and religious background in rating experiences that involve God, the devil, angels, and spirits. An experience is judged as less deviant if it receives some subcultural support from the subject's religion. Nevertheless, this rating system may have some cultural bias in that it was developed using white college students in the Midwest. We do not know if the rating values are suitable for African-American or Hispanic subjects or members of other minority subcultures. Since we have found some variation of scores with race on our psychosis proneness questionnaires, we suspect that the same may be true of some of the rating scales for psychotic-like symptoms.

Ten-year follow-up of subjects deviant on these measures

We tested the predictive validity of our interview ratings of psychotic-like experiences and our questionnaire measures of psychosis proneness in a 10-year follow-up study of an initial group of 534 subjects (Chapman et al., 1994). We interviewed all 534 subjects soon after selecting them and successfully reinterviewed 508 of them at a 10-year follow-up, a 95% success rate. We initially administered our screening questionnaires to approximately 7,800 introductory psychology students from the years 1978 to 1981 and selected subjects for interview on the basis of their scores. While the subjects were administered all five questionnaires, we focus now primarily on the interview findings for two groups. These are subjects who scored deviantly on the Perceptual Aberration (PerAb) and/or Magical Ideation (MagicId) scales ($n = 182$) and control subjects ($n = 153$). (Chapman et al. [in press] provide a complete description of groups selected by the other scales.) Subjects who scored at least 1.96 standard deviation (*SD*) above the mean on PerAb or MagicId were selected as hypothetically psychosis-prone. Because the MagicId Scale and PerAb Scale correlated about .70, subjects with a standard score of at least 1.96 on either of these two scales were combined into a single Perceptual Aberration–Magical Ideation (Per-Mag) group. In addition, we included 14 subjects in the Per-Mag group whose sum of z-scores on PerAb and MagicId totalled 3.0 and above, although they fell short of 1.96 on the two component scales. Our control subjects were selected randomly from a large group of subjects who scored lower than .5 *SD* above the mean on all of the scales.

Subjects were not initially selected on the basis of ratings of psychotic-like experiences, because of the inefficiency of interviewing an unselected sample of subjects. Instead, subjects who had been selected by one of the questionnaires were assessed for psychotic-like experiences during an initial interview.

Initial interviews. Soon after identifying the subjects, we interviewed them using Spitzer and Endicott's (1977) Schedule for Affective Disorders and Schizophrenia-Lifetime Version (SADS-L) with additional questions on psychotic-like experiences and schizotypal symptoms. These additional questions were chosen to correspond directly with items on Chapman and Chapman's (1980) rating scales for psychotic-like experiences. At the initial interview, we found that the Per-Mag subjects were especially deviant on psychotic-like experiences (Chapman et al., 1980). Thirty-four percent scored moderately psychotic-like (score of 4) or higher. At a 25-month follow-up (Chapman and Chapman, 1985), the deviant subjects were diagnosed by DSM-III criteria, primarily using interview information but also using information from hospital records, where appropriate. Three of the hypothetically schizophrenia-prone subjects had become psychotic, but only one of the three was schizophrenic. The other two psychotic subjects included one who had episodes of bipolar disorder with psychotic features and one who had delusional disorder.

Ten-year follow-up evaluation. From 10 to 15 years after initial identification and selection, we reinterviewed 508 of the original 534 subjects. We diagnosed by DSM-III-R criteria, again using interviews and hospital records. We once again used a modified SADS-L interview, but also included portions of Loranger's (1988) Personality Disorder Examination (PDE) interview to assess schizotypal, schizoid and paranoid personality disorder. The PDE contains questions for each DSM-III-R criterion for each personality disorder and yields a clinical diagnosis as well as a dimensional score for each personality disorder. The dimensional score measures the presence of some of the symptoms that are required for a diagnosis of schizotypal personality disorder, and so is useful for describing less disturbed subjects who do not show enough of the symptoms to qualify for the full diagnosis.

We used several criteria for assessing psychosis proneness. The first criterion is, of course, DSM-III-R psychosis. Other criteria, however, reflect psychosis proneness even in the absence of psychosis. These criteria are: (a) reports of psychotic relatives (because of the well-established finding that psychosis runs in families); (b) elevated psychotic-like experiences; and (c) elevated schizotypal, or paranoid, or schizoid dimensional scores. It is commonly reported that psychotic-like experiences and schizotypal, paranoid, or schizoid symptoms tend to be elevated both in persons who later become schizophrenic and in the relatives of schizophrenics (Kendler et al., 1981).

Interviewers and scorers at each evaluation were unaware of the subjects' group membership. We diagnosed psychosis in relatives using information from the subject, but did not attempt differential diagnoses between psychoses.

Psychotic-like experiences at initial interview as a marker of psychosis proneness. We measured each subject's deviancy of psychotic-like experience at the initial interview by his or her single highest (most deviant) psychotic-like experience, choosing a rating of at least moderately psychotic-like (score of 4 or more) as a cutting point for hypothetical psychosis proneness. Of the group with moderately psychotic-like experiences, 9% were found to have a history of psychosis at the 10-year follow-up, while only 1% of the remaining subjects developed psychosis, a significant difference. The higher group also significantly more often reported psychosis in relatives: 15% by those who initially showed moderately psychotic-like experiences, and 8% by the remaining subjects. The subjects rated as moderately psychotic-like at the initial interview also significantly exceeded the remaining subjects on diagnoses of DSM-III-R major depression and of DSM-III-R mania or hypomania.

The PerAb and MagicId scales as markers of psychosis proneness. Ten of the 182 Per-Mag subjects reported DSM-III-R psychosis at the 10-year follow-up, as did 2 of the 153 control subjects, a significant difference. The psychotic subjects were found to suffer from a variety of psychoses, not just schizophrenia. The 10-year Per-Mag subjects included 3 patients with schizophrenia, 3 with bipolar disorder with psychotic features, 1 with delusional disorder, and 3 with psychosis not otherwise specified (NOS). The control subjects included 1 with a diagnosis of schizophrenia and 1 of major depression with psychotic features. The 3 Per-Mag subjects with psychosis NOS displayed fully developed schizophrenic syndromes except for the DSM-III-R criterion of deterioration of functioning. They reported symptoms such as persistent hallucinations, bizarre delusions, thought broadcasting, and passivity experiences as pervasive features of daily living, despite the fact that all three were responsibly employed. For example, one such subject, who maintained a responsible professional position, reported directly experiencing that his thoughts and actions were routinely controlled by an alien force and that he was also able to travel through time. He also experienced auditory and visual hallucinations as well as thought broadcasting. He showed no deterioration of functioning, although his co-workers must have recognized him as unusual.

We asked our subjects about psychosis in relatives and tabulated psychosis in first- or second-degree relatives. One or more such psychotic relatives were reported by 15% of the Per-Mag group as compared to 7% of the control group, a significant difference.

Although mean scores of psychotic-like experiences for both Per-Mag and control subjects were lower at the follow-up interview than at the initial interview, the Per-Mag group differed significantly from the control group on psychotic-like experiences on both occasions. The Per-Mag group also significantly exceeded the control group on the rate of DSM-III-R major depression and on the rate of DSM-III-R mania or hypomania, as well as on schizotypal dimensional score. The groups did not differ, however, on proportion of subjects diagnosed with schizotypal personality disorder, as very few of our subjects qualified for this diagnosis.

We performed a series of hierarchal regression analyses, using the Per-Mag subjects only, in order to evaluate the independent variance contributed by our various predictors. With either the schizotypal dimensional score or psychotic-like experiences as the dependent variable, we found that the only significant independent predictors were psychotic-like experiences from the first interview, MagicId score, Social Anhedonia (SocAnh) score, and presence of psychotic relatives.

Deviant subgroups within the Per-Mag group. The MagicId Scale appeared to be more successful than the PerAb Scale in identifying psychosis-prone subjects. Eight of 10 Per-Mag subjects who became psychotic had scored deviantly (standard scores of 1.96 or above) on MagicId as compared to 4 who were deviant on PerAb. Within the Per-Mag group, subjects who were high on MagicId and, in addition, were above the mean of all the college students tested (above 7) on

SocAnh ($n = 33$) were the most deviant subjects of all. This subgroup had a psychosis rate of 21%, which was considerably higher than that of any other subgroup that we identified in this study.

Combination of Per-Mag group membership with initial psychotic-like experiences. Both initial psychotic-like experiences and membership in the Per-Mag group appear to be effective markers of psychosis proneness. To test our hypothesis that subjects identified as deviant by both measures will be at especially heightened risk, we repeated the analyses for indicators of psychosis proneness using the Per-Mag subjects alone. The Per-Mag subjects with initial moderately psychotic-like experiences showed a 14% incidence of psychosis at follow-up, as compared to only 1% for the Per-Mag subjects with lower scores on psychotic-like experiences, a significant difference. Per-Mag subjects with moderately psychotic-like experiences also differed significantly from other Per-Mag subjects on psychotic-like experiences at follow-up, and on schizotypal dimensional score. The two groups did not differ significantly, however, on reports of psychotic relatives.

Implication of findings

These findings strongly support both the Per-Mag Scale and the interview measure of psychotic-like experiences as indicators of psychosis proneness. Persons scoring high on either measure exceeded control subjects both on clinical psychosis and on other indicators of psychosis proneness.

Both measures offer advantages and disadvantages. The Per-Mag scale is relatively easy to administer. It can be completed in under 30 minutes, administered during mass surveys of large numbers of subjects, and does not require a trained examiner. The psychotic-like symptoms rating scale, however, requires a thorough interview and a trained rater to assess the deviancy of the symptoms. Using the two measures in conjunction appears especially useful for identifying psychosis-prone subjects.

We have often encountered the suggestion that psychotic-like experiences in adolescence are merely a passing developmental phase, or perhaps a transient response to experimentation with drugs or alcohol. This may be true for some persons, as suggested by the finding that psychotic-like experiences of both experimental and control subjects diminished somewhat between the initial and follow-up interviews. In contrast, psychotic-like experiences became more severe between interviews for subjects who became clinically psychotic, as well as for the Mag-SocAnh group (of whom 21% became psychotic). Moreover, the relationship between psychotic-like experiences at the first interview and psychosis at the second interview demonstrates that such experiences are, for many persons, a precursor of far more serious psychopathology.

Although the results show that the scales are useful for identifying psychosis-prone persons, we do not know just how accurate these identifications may be. We do not know the valid-positive and the false-positive rates. We cannot determine these rates by the portion who actually became psychotic by the 10-year follow-up, both because the majority of our psychosis-prone subjects are not expected ever to develop clinical psychosis and because our subjects have not yet passed through all of their age of risk for developing psychosis. Just how much risk remains is difficult to say but we can probably safely infer that the number of psychotics in our sample will eventually be much higher than we have seen thus far.

We must be cautious in interpreting the exceptional deviancy of the MagicId-SocAnh subgroup. Unlike the results for the Per-Mag group and for psychotic-like experiences, the findings of a high rate of psychosis and psychosis-proneness for this subgroup were not hypothesized and may well have capitalized on chance. That is, we tested these relationships for the MagicId-SocAnh subgroup using the same data in which we first observed them. Nevertheless, we would speculate, with the benefit of hindsight, that this pattern of scores makes good sense as a predictor of severe psychopathology. The MagicId Scale asks about many severely psychotic-like symptoms and the SocAnh Scale asks about a trait that most clinical writers on the topic have described as a feature of psychosis-prone subjects. Moreover, social anhedonia would be expected to produce withdrawal from other people, depriving the person of the emotional strength that comes from close relationships as well as of the opportunity to validate ideas and perceptions consensually. This deprivation could increase the likelihood of psychosis in a psychosis-prone person.

We found an unexpectedly high incidence of mood psychoses in our hypothetically schizophrenia-prone subjects. We measured symptoms that were advanced as predictive of schizophrenia by Meehl (1964, 1990, 1993) and by Hoch and Cattell (1959), but we found instead that these symptoms tend to predict psychosis, rather than schizophrenia in particular. Our finding parallels recent research evidence on the correlates of schizotypal symptoms, which also have been widely assumed to reflect a proneness to schizophrenia in particular. The first-degree relatives of mood-disordered patients have been found to show as elevated an incidence of schizotypal symptoms as do the relatives of schizophrenic patients (Silverman et al., 1993; Squires-Wheeler et al., 1988; Squires-Wheeler et al., 1989). Similarly, when the first-degree relatives of schizotypal patients are examined, they show an elevated incidence of mood disorder (Bornstein et al., 1988; Schulz et al., 1986).*

The instruments used in the present study clearly cannot distinguish between proneness to affective psychosis and proneness to schizophrenia and other non-affective psychoses. One screening instrument that might be of use for identifying persons prone to manic disorder is the Hypomania Scale (Eckblad and Chapman, 1986).

Conclusion

The rating system for psychotic-like experiences as well as the Perceptual Aberration Scale and the Magical Ideation Scale are useful for assessing psychosis proneness. Furthermore, predictive power is enhanced by using these instruments together. Both the screening questionnaires and the interview ratings identify psychosis-prone persons by measuring milder, transient forms of the symptoms and problems experienced by psychotic patients. While these psychosis-prone persons have a much higher rate of clinical psychosis than the general population, the majority of such individuals remain compensated. These instruments may be of use in studies of etiological factors in psychosis, as well as in genetic studies. The distinction between proneness to schizophrenia and proneness to other psychoses must be made by other instruments.

Acknowledgments

This research was supported by Research Grant MH-31067 and by a Research Scientist Award to the second author, from the National Institute of Mental Health.

* See also the introduction to the Genetics section, this volume – Eds.

The authors are indebted to Thomas R. Kwapil and Michael B. Miller for helpful comments on the manuscript.

References

Bleuler, E. 1924. *Textbook of psychiatry.* Translated by A. A. Brill. New York: Macmillan.

Bornstein, R. F., D. N. Klein, J. C. Mallon, and J. F. Slater. 1988. Schizotypal personality disorder in an outpatient population: Incidence and clinical characteristics. *Journal of Clinical Psychology,* 44:322–325.

Chapman, James. 1966. The early symptoms of schizophrenia. *British Journal of Psychiatry,* 112:225–251.

Chapman, L. J., and J. P. Chapman. 1980. Scales for rating psychotic and psychotic-like experiences as continua. *Schizophrenia Bulletin,* 6:476–490.

Chapman, L. J., and J. P. Chapman. 1985. Psychosis proneness. In *Controversies in schizophrenia,* ed. M. Alpert. New York: Guilford.

Chapman, L. J., J. P. Chapman, and M. L. Raulin. 1976. Scales for physical and social anhedonia. *Journal of Abnormal Psychology,* 85:374–382.

Chapman, L. J., J. P. Chapman, and M. L. Raulin. 1978. Body-image aberration in schizophrenia. *Journal of Abnormal Psychology,* 87:399–407.

Chapman, L. J., W. S. Edell, and J. P. Chapman. 1980. Physical anhedonia, perceptual aberration, and psychosis proneness. *Schizophrenia Bulletin,* 6:639–653.

Chapman, L. J., J. P. Chapman, T. R. Kwapil, M. Eckblad, and M. C. Zinser. 1994. Putatively psychosis-prone subjects ten years later. *Journal of Abnormal Psychology,* 103:171–183.

Chapman, L. J., J. P. Chapman, and E. N. Miller. 1982. Reliabilities and intercorrelations of eight measures of proneness to psychosis. *Journal of Consulting and Clinical Psychology,* 50:187–195.

Chapman, L. J., J. P. Chapman, J. S. Numbers, W. S. Edell, B. N. Carpenter, and D. Beckfield. 1984. Impulsive nonconformity as a trait contributing to the prediction of psychotic-like and schizotypal symptoms. *Journal of Nervous and Mental Disease,* 172:681–691.

Claridge, G., and P. Broks. 1984. Schizotypy and hemisphere function – I. Theoretical considerations and the measurement of schizotypy. *Personality and Individual Differences,* 5:633–648.

Dunaif, S. L., and P. H. Hoch. 1955. Pseudopsychopathic schizophrenia. In *Psychiatry and the law,* ed. P. H. Hoch and J. Zubin. New York: Grune & Stratton.

Eckblad, M., and L. J. Chapman. 1983. Magical ideation as an indicator of schizotypy. *Journal of Consulting and Clinical Psychology,* 51:215–225.

Eckblad, M., and L. J. Chapman. 1986. Development and validation of a scale for hypomanic personality. *Journal of Abnormal Psychology*, 95:214–222.

Eckblad, M., L. J. Chapman, J. P. Chapman, and M. Mishlove. 1982. [The Revised Social Anhedonia Scale]. Unpublished test (copies available from authors). University of Wisconsin, Madison.

Edell, W. S. In press. The psychometric measurement of schizotypy using the Wisconsin scales of psychosis proneness. In *The behavioral high-risk paradigm in psychopathology*, ed. G. A. Miller. New York: Springer-Verlag.

Eysenck, H. J., and S.G.B. Eysenck. 1976. *Psychoticism as a dimension of personality*. London: Hodder & Stoughton.

Fleming, P., and D. F. Ricks. 1970. Emotions of children before schizophrenia and before character disorder. In *Life history research in psychopathology*, ed. M. Roff and D. Ricks. Minneapolis: University of Minnesota Press.

Golden, R. R., and P. E. Meehl. 1979. Detection of the schizoid taxon with MMPI indicators. *Journal of Abnormal Psychology*, 88:217–233.

Gottesman, I. I. 1991. *Schizophrenia genesis: The origins of madness*. San Francisco: Freeman.

Gottesman, I. I., and A. Bertelsen. 1989. Confirming unexpressed genotypes for schizophrenia: Risks in the offspring of Fischer's Danish identical and fraternal discordant twins. *Archives of General Psychiatry*, 46:867–872.

Heston, L. L. 1966. Psychiatric disorders in foster home reared children of schizophrenic mothers. *British Journal of Psychiatry*, 112:819–825.

Hoch, P. H., and J. P. Cattell. 1959. The diagnosis of pseudoneurotic schizophrenia. *Psychiatric Quarterly*, 33:17–43.

Hoch, P. H., J. P. Cattell, M. O. Strahl, and H. H. Pennes. 1962. The course and outcome of pseudoneurotic schizophrenia. *American Journal of Psychiatry*, 11:106–115.

Jackson, D. N. 1974. *Manual for the Personality Research Form*. Goshen, NY: Research Psychologists Press.

Kendler, K. S., A. M. Gruenberg, and J. S. Strauss. 1981. An independent analysis of the Copenhagen sample of the Danish adoption study of schizophrenia: II. The relationship between schizotypal personality disorder and schizophrenia. *Archives of General Psychiatry*, 38:982–984.

Kety, S. S., D. Rosenthal, P. H. Wender, and F. Schulsinger. 1968. The types and prevalence of mental illness in the biological and adoptive families of adopted schizophrenics. In *The transmission of schizophrenia*, ed. D. Rosenthal and S. S. Kety. New York: Pergamon Press.

Kraepelin, E. [1913] 1919. *Dementia praecox and paraphrenia*. Translated by R. M. Barclay. Edinburgh: E. and S. Livingstone.

Loranger, A. W. 1988. *Personality Disorder Examination (PDE) Manual.* Yonkers, NY: DV Communications.

Meehl, P. E. 1962. Schizotaxia, schizotypy, schizophrenia. *American Psychologist,* 17:827–838.

Meehl, P. E. 1964. *Manual for use with checklist of schizotypic signs.* Unpublished manuscript, University of Minnesota.

Meehl, P. E. 1975. Hedonic capacity: Some conjectures. *Bulletin of the Menninger Clinic,* 39:295–307.

Meehl, P. E. 1990. Toward an integrated theory of schizotaxia, schizotypy, and schizophrenia. *Journal of Personality Disorders,* 4:1–99.

Meehl, P. E. 1993. The origins of some of my conjectures concerning schizophrenia. In *Progress in experimental personality and psychopathology research,* vol. 16, ed. L. J. Chapman, J. P. Chapman, and D. C. Fowles. New York: Springer.

Miller, G. A., and C. M. Yee. In press. Risk for severe psychopathology: Psychometric screening and psychophysiological assessment. In *Advances in psychophysiology, Vol. 5.,* ed. J. R. Jennings, P. K. Ackles, and M.G.H. Coles. London: Jessica Kinglsey.

Planansky, K. 1972. Phenotypic boundaries and genetic specificity in schizophrenia. In *Genetic factors in "schizophrenia,"* ed. A. R. Kaplan. Springfield, IL: Charles C. Thomas.

Rado, S. 1953. Dynamics and classification of disordered behavior. *American Journal of Psychiatry,* 110:406–426.

Raine, A. 1991. The SPQ: A scale for the assessment of schizotypal personality based on DSM-III-R criteria. *Schizophrenia Bulletin,* 17:555–564.

Rosenthal, D. 1975. Discussion: The concept of subschizophrenic disorders. In *Genetic Research in Psychiatry,* ed. R. R. Fieve, D. Rosenthal, and H. Brill. Baltimore: Johns Hopkins University Press.

Schneider, K. 1959. *Clinical psychopathology.* Translated by M. W. Hamilton. New York: Grune & Stratton.

Schulz, P. M., S. C. Schulz, S. C. Goldberg, P. Ettigi, R. J. Resnick, and R. O. Friedel. 1986. Diagnoses of the relatives of schizotypal outpatients. *Journal of Nervous and Mental Disease,* 174:457–463.

Shields, J., L. L. Heston, and I. I. Gottesman. 1975. Schizophrenia and the schizoid: The problem for genetic analysis. In *Genetic Research in Psychiatry,* ed. R. R. Fieve, D. Rosenthal, and H. Brill. Baltimore: Johns Hopkins University Press.

Silverman, J. M., L. J. Siever, T. B. Horvath, E. F. Coccaro, H. Klar, M. Davidson, L. Pinkham, S. H. Apter, R. C. Mohs, and K. L. Davis. 1993. Schizophrenia-related and affective personality disorder traits in relatives of probands with schizophrenia and personality disorders. *American Journal of Psychiatry,* 150:435–442.

Slater, E., and V. Cowie. 1971. The genetics of mental disorders. London: Oxford University Press.

Spitzer, R. L., and J. Endicott. 1977. *Schedule for Affective Disorders and Schizophrenia-Lifetime Version (SADS-L)*. New York: New York State Psychiatric Institute.

Spitzer, R. L., J. Endicott, and M. Gibbon. 1979. Crossing the border into borderline personality and borderline schizophrenia: The development of criteria. *Archives of General Psychiatry*, 36:17–24.

Squires-Wheeler, E., A. E. Skodol, D. Friedman, and L. Erlenmeyer-Kimling. 1988. The specificity of DSM-III schizotypal personality traits. *Psychological Medicine*, 18:757–765.

Squires-Wheeler, E., A. E. Skodal, A. Bassett, and L. Erlenmeyer-Kimling. 1989. DSM-III-R schizotypal personality traits in offspring of schizophrenic disorder, affective disorder, and normal control parents. *Journal of Psychiatric Research*, 23:229–239.

Strauss, J. S. 1969. Hallucinations and delusions as points on continua function. *Archives of General Psychiatry*, 21:581–586.

Watt, N. F. 1974. Childhood and adolescent routes to schizophrenia. In *Life history research in psychopathology: 3*, ed. D. F. Ricks, A. Thomas, and M. Roff. Minneapolis: University of Minnesota Press.

Comments on Jean P. Chapman and Loren J. Chapman's chapter

Philip S. Holzman

"Proneness" can be interpreted either as vulnerability or as being at heightened risk. The two are not synonymous, and using them interchangeably can lead to confusion among conceptual and empirical issues.

"Vulnerability" refers to perceivable, palpable, or measurable variation in structure or function that represents a predisposition to a specific disease process. Examples of vulnerability traits include the absence of the enzyme glucose-6-phosphate dehydrogenase for hemolytic anemia, the presence of hemoglobin S, which leads to the formation of sickle-shaped red blood cells for sickle-cell anemia, a high pepsinogen level for peptic ulcer, and the absence of phenylalanine hydroxylase for phenylketonuria. All of these traits are identifiable prior to the onset of the disease and place the person possessing such traits in a position of being susceptible to the specific disorders, given certain known or as yet unknown environmental conditions. These traits, moreover, are not intrinsically the disease. They represent a necessary but not sufficient condition for the disease to develop.

In contrast, "risk factors" refers to statistical probabilities that some groups of people will become affected by a particular disorder. Thus, being a child of a schizophrenic parent puts that child in a group with a larger statistical risk than the general population runs, although that child may not be at all vulnerable because he or she may not have the specific – but as yet unknown – structural underpinning that predisposes to schizophrenia. Cigarette smoking and obesity, for example, are two risk factors with respect to coronary artery disease. But, in the absence of observable tissue modifications associated with the development of the disease, an obese, three-pack-a-day smoker may live to be 90. Cigarette smoking and obesity are, of course, no advantages, and they are useful indices of behaviors that place people at risk for many disorders.

There are thus many more people at statistical risk for a disorder than are vulnerable, and vulnerable people are more prevalent than those who eventually contract the disorder. One of the novel and incisive aspects of Norman Garmezy's studies of "invulnerable" children, as described in Chapter 9 in this volume, is his empirical demonstration that risk and vulnerability are separable. In a high-risk sample, the Minnesota research group is able to identify those children who possess traits of psychological and social competence that may presage invulnerability to later serious psychiatric disorder.

Acknowledgment

Adapted from: P. S. Holzman. 1982. The Search for a Biological Marker of the Functional Psychoses. In *Preventive Intervention in Schizophrenia: Are we Ready?* M. Goldstein (ed.). Rockville, MD: Department of Health and Human Services.

15

Politeness in schizophrenia

Roger Brown

Twenty years ago I wrote a paper on schizophrenic language (Brown, 1973) saying that in a strict sense of language there is no such thing; that is, there is nothing consistently awry with any of the systems linguistics describes, nothing amiss with phonemics, phonotactics, morphology, or syntax. Of course, there is something wrong or strange about the speech of some schizophrenics some of the time and the strange utterance is easily spotted by either laymen or psychiatrists and such utterances can be reliably rated for degree of "strangeness" from, for instance, odd to bizarre. When we try to say what "strangeness" is, we invoke irrationality, thought disorder, delusion, or failure to test reality. What all such characterizations lack is a systematic definition. They lead nowhere theoretically.

We have recently obtained a hint of evidence that there may be something clearly definable and already systematically described that is startlingly off, even totally missing, from some schizophrenic speech. It is not a system of linguistics, but a system of pragmatics. Linguistics is a theory of sentences in abstraction from context. Pragmatics is a theory of utterances by specified speakers in specified contexts. The pragmatic system of interest is politeness, specifically the universal theory of politeness constructed by Penelope Brown and Stephen Levinson (1987), who are, respectively, an anthropologist and a linguist at Cambridge University. I think this theory is a masterpiece of social science, almost unequaled in scope, rigor, and nuance.

Politeness theory belongs to Speech Act Theory, which was originated by John Austin in *How to Do Things with Words* (1962). Speech Act Theory was a reaction against that version of logical positivism which held that only verifiable propositions had meaning. The "truth conditional" theory of meaning left most discourse about aesthetics, ethics, and politics technically meaningless. Far from viewing this conclusion with dismay, strong-minded theorists like A. J. Ayer (1936) thought it correct and downright delightful.

John Austin's artful counterattack begins with a class of utterances to which verifiability is irrelevant. For instance: "I now pronounce you man and wife" or "I christen this ship the *H.M.S. Pinafore*" (spoken by authorized persons in appropriate circumstances). For such utterances, which Austin called "performatives," questions of truth or falsity simply do not arise. Performatives do not assert anything. It is rather the case that, when the conditions are right ("felicitous"), performatives *do* something. Using performatives as an entering wedge, Austin was ultimately able to show that virtually all utterances, including those to which verifiability applies, have a performative aspect or "illocutionary force."

The Brown–Levinson conception of politeness starts with the fact that some speech acts are intrinsically face-threatening (face-threatening acts or FTAs). For instance, the kind of act we call a "criticism" is a threat to the addressee's *want* to have his public self-image appreciated, approved, and ratified by others. Brown and Levinson call a criticism a threat to positive face. A command or request, on the other hand, threatens the addressee's *want* to be unimpeded, not to be imposed upon, to have his or her prerogatives and territory respected. Brown and Levinson call this a threat to negative face. Politeness is an elaborate auxiliary system of speech acts designed to redress FTAs.

Politeness means putting things in such a way as to take account of the feelings of the other person. That means on the whole being less straightforward and uncomplicated than if you ignored the other's feelings. Polite speech is to be contrasted with maximally efficient speech, which is sometimes called "Gricean," after Paul Grice (1975), who set down the four maxims governing such speech. These are: the Maxim of Quality – "Tell the truth"; the Maxim of Manner – "Be unambiguous"; the Maxim of Quantity – "Say all that is necessary but no more"; and the Maxim of Relation – "Be relevant." Politeness takes more time and effort, but politeness systems are universal in languages and for most of us on most days the work of politeness constitutes a substantial part of the total talking we do. Probably it has always done so everywhere.

Consider the following exchange from *King Lear* between Albany, a duke, and Edgar, passing as a common man:

Edgar: If e'er your Grace had speech with man so poor, Hear me one word.
Albany: Speak. (V, *i*, 38–39)

In Gricean form, without politeness, the exchange would be:

Edgar: Listen.
Albany: Speak.

Edgar's request is a negative FTA, an imposition, and Albany is an addressee of high rank, and so Edgar's speech is complicated for reasons of politeness with four substrategies of negative politeness: "Your Grace" expresses deference; "man so poor" is self-abasing; "one word" minimizes the imposition; and the request is put in a form that does not assume compliance. We have found the speech of a few schizophrenics in test circumstances to be maximally efficient in the Gricean sense, devoid of politeness, essentially: "Listen; Speak."

As an example of the subtle connection between politeness theory and Speech Act Theory, I offer the treatment of conventionalized indirect questions, a form of negative politeness. A request such as "Pass the salt" threatens to impose upon the hearer's freedom, if only in a small way, and when expressed in the straightforward Gricean imperative, the threat is evident. English is rich in circumlocutory alternatives: "Can you reach the salt?"; "Is there any salt down there?"; "We need the salt"; "Would you mind passing the salt?" Functionally these are all requests, but grammatically they are questions or statements. Indirect requests like these turn out to be constructed in a principled way. The simple imperative "Pass the salt" will not accomplish its purpose unless certain contextual principles are satisfied: (1) there should be salt within reach of the hearer; (2) the speaker should genuinely want salt; (3) the hearer should have no fixed objection to passing the salt – and so on. If these circumstances are satisfied, then the world is ready for "Pass the salt" to have its intended effect. The circumstances that constitute a happy environment for imperatives are called "felicity conditions" (Searle, 1975) in Speech Act Theory. Indirect requests that are more polite than the imperative (such as "Can you pass the salt?") all either question a felicity condition or call attention to a felicity condition and in that way satisfy the hearer's negative face by leaving him an "out." It is as if the speaker thought the hearer might not be remiss at all; perhaps there is no salt or perhaps he cannot reach it or has scruples about passing it (Gordon & Lakoff, 1971; Labov & Fanshel, 1977).

If Brown and Levinson left the matter there, the sensitivity of their linguistic intuitions could be faulted because it is obvious that indirect requests like "Can you pass the salt?" are not processed in terms of grammatical form but are understood to be requests even by very young children (Bates, 1976). To answer "Can you pass the salt?" by saying "Yes, I can" is either a joke or a snub. Of course, Brown and Levinson know this and so they call such indirect requests "fully conventionalized," which is to say that frequent use has turned them into functional requests whatever their grammar. However, Brown and Levinson add, the original derivation still has enough semantic life in it to give indirect polite requests like "Would you mind passing the salt?" the feel of a compromise between a selfish wish to have the salt and a face-considerate reluctance to impose. In speech processing terms this means that both the functional meaning and the literal meaning are computed, and Herb Clark and his associates (Clark, 1979; Clark & Lucy, 1975; Clark & Schunk, 1980) have found ways to demonstrate experimentally that this is so. What makes the analysis of polite requests impressive is the fact that they are derived the same way, from felicity conditions, in some languages not related to English – possibly in all (Blum-Kulka, 1982; Fraser, 1978). Brown and Levinson (1978, 1987) have shown that in Tamil and Tzeltal indirect requests are based on felicity conditions as they are in English. Brown and Gilman (1989) have shown that the same is true of polite requests in Early Modern English (1500–1700) as used by Shakespeare. The phrases are now archaic: *I entreat you, I do beseech you, Prithee, If you will give me leave, If it please you.* However, they all either express the sincerity of the speaker's wish or else inquire about the willingness of the hearer to comply and these are both felicity conditions.

Outline of the Brown–Levinson theory

The core of the Brown–Levinson theory of politeness is schematically represented in Figure 15.1. The point of view is that of the speaker. The mental processes modeled are his and they are assumed to be swift and unconscious, though we will generally have to use words that suggest deliberation. The problem the speaker is considering is whether or not to perform some single face-threatening act, and if the decision is to perform it, then how to perform it, in what way. The FTA is addressed to the hearer, and taking account of the feelings of the hearer poses the problem of politeness. The relevant feelings concern positive face and negative face and have already been described.

There are five numbered politeness strategies in Figure 15.1:

1. Do the FTA without redressive action, baldly.
2. Do the FTA on-record with redressive positive politeness.
3. Do the FTA on-record with redressive negative politeness.
4. Do the FTA off-record.
5. Don't do the FTA.

Positive politeness is simply defined as any effort to meet positive face needs. The phrase "Have a good day," renewed daily, is a quintessential act of positive politeness: the speaker wishes for the hearer what the hearer wishes for himself. Brown and Levinson identify and illustrate 15 varieties of positive politeness. These include attending to and showing concern for the other's health, appearance, possessions, etc.; emphasizing in-group identity by using familiar forms of address, a common dialect, slang, ellipsis that works because of shared past experience; seeking areas of agreement (the weather at least); avoiding disagreement on politics, people, but also books, movies, whatever; and giving gifts that may be either material or psychological.

Negative politeness may be defined as any effort to meet negative face wants, and there are 10 subvarieties. Negative face is threatened by an imposition on freedom of action or any challenge to prerogatives or territory, and negative politeness is designed to redress just the specific FTA that creates the occasion for politeness. The most common speech act requiring negative politeness is a request. Subvarieties of negative redress include: not taking compliance for granted, indirection through use of the passive voice or nominalization, expression of deference, and minimization of the imposition.

The principal empirical claim of the theory is that the five strategies (really superstrategies) are ordered as they appear in Figure 15.1 against a scale of lesser to greater estimated risk to face. Figure 15.1 says that when risk is minimal the FTA may be done in a Gricean way which is on-record without redressive action, baldly, and when risk is maximal the theory advises "Don't do the FTA." The three remaining strategies are associated with intermediate risk levels. An on-record strategy is a way of doing the FTA that leaves the speaker's intention unambiguous and so makes the speaker fully accountable. An off-record FTA does not permit an unambiguous assignment of

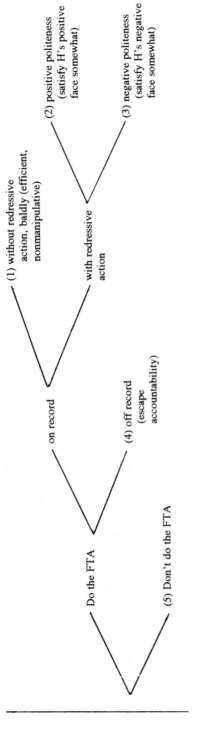

Estimation of
risk of face loss:

Lesser

(1) without redressive
action, baldly (efficient,
nonmanipulative)

on record

with redressive
action

(2) positive politeness
(satisfy H's positive
face somewhat)

(3) negative politeness
(satisfy H's negative
face somewhat)

Do the FTA

(4) off record
(escape
accountability)

(5) Don't do the FTA

Greater

$W_x = D(S,H) + P(H,S) + R_x$

Politeness (like W_x) increases as Distance goes up.

Politeness (like W_x) increases as Power of H over S increases.

Politeness (like W_x) increases as Risk of imposition goes up.

Figure 15.1. Superstrategies of politeness ordered against estimated risk of face loss (the Brown–Levinson [1978, 1987] theory of politeness)

intention to the speaker and so any interpretation made is deniable and the speaker is not accountable.

Politeness theory holds that the selection of the strategies is universally determined by just three variables. Two concern the relationship between speaker and hearer: vertical social distance or "power" (P) and horizontal social distance or "solidarity" (D). These are the same dimensions that Brown and Gilman used in 1960 to describe the semantics of European pronouns of address as typified by the French *tu/vous* distinction, and that have been reported since 1960 to be the dimensions underlying pronominal (and other) address in at least 28 different languages, many of them unrelated.

While power and distance are postulated to be universal determinants of politeness, the personal characteristics that enter into the calculation of power and distance vary both culturally and historically. Race, sex, age, generation, kinship, occupation, religion, and language have all figured prominently, and the "samba clubs" of Rio de Janiero and the "benevolent societies" of New York's Chinatown teach us that almost any personal characteristic can serve in this way. If we looked only at cultural features, externally viewed, we should see a high degree of cultural relativism, but if we look at intracultural meanings in terms of P and D, we see universality or invariance.

Pronouns of address have relational rather than referential meanings and in this way they are like kin terms. Just as it is not a property of a person always to be addressed as *dad* or *son*, so it is not a property of a person always to be addressed as *tu* or *vous;* in both cases the form used varies with a relation, the relation between speaker and addressee. The very important difference between kin terms and pronouns is that the former (unless "extended" or "fictive") serve to relate only some members of a social group with some others, whereas the latter serve to relate each one to each other one and so constitute a fully connected language of relationship. If the dimensions governing such relational forms are universal across languages, then such dimensions would seem to have a privileged fundamental status for the analysis of social life. On present evidence they are universal and, in politeness theory, they are called "power" and "distance," symbolized as, respectively, P and D.

There is a third variable that affects the choice of a politeness strategy and this is the intrinsic extremity of the face-threatening act. In the culture and situation in question, how much does the FTA interfere with self-determination (negative face) and approval (positive face)? The assumption made is that there will be a fairly constant ranking of impositions in terms of expenditures of time, expertise, and goods and also a ranking of threats to positive face in terms of desired attributes like honesty, honor, and generosity. The necessary operations are not all at hand but the idea is clear: asking for a loan of $5 is less of an imposition than asking for a loan of $50; criticizing someone's life work is a greater imposition than criticizing a necktie.

Brown and Levinson combine additively the three variables affecting the selection of a strategy into the formula $W_x = D(S,H) + P(H,S) + R_x$, which in words says the weightiness or riskiness of FTA_x is a function of the social distance between speaker and hearer plus the power of the hearer over the speaker plus the culturally ranked intrinsic threat posed by the FTA. In crude operational terms W should be greater if H is a superordinate than if H is a subordinate; W should be greater if S and H are new acquaintances than if S and H are old friends; and W should be greater if R is a request to borrow a car than if R is a request to borrow a book. Experiments so far have mostly used written scenarios that use two values of one variable while holding the other constant.

We know how riskiness or weightiness is compounded. But what exactly is the relation between weightiness levels and numbered strategies? It might appear to be a kind of stimulus-response prediction (with both stimuli and strategies rank ordered), but that is not what the authors intend. Brown and Levinson (1987) make it very clear that politeness strategies are to be thought of as goal-oriented plans, not simple responses, and they add:

The wonders explored in cognitive psychology, linguistics or artificial intelligence have no counterparts in social theory . . . Here we merely scratch, in a groping way, the surface of one area of interaction, and we wish to draw the attention of social scientists to the richness and complexity of the assumptions and inferences upon the basis of which humans understand and cooperate with one another. (p. 56)

With respect to Figure 15.1, the theory claims universality for the strategies and their ordering and, in the formula, for P, D, and R. What clearly varies by language and culture are the factors figuring in the calculation of the weightiness variables. On the molecular level of substrategies there are occasional structural and functional correspondences that are as pan-linguistic as indirect requests. The more usual case is to find some function like hedging an imposition expressed by a variety of forms – for example, particles, adverbs, pro-sodics, and kinesics – with the formal mix varying by languages.

Examples of positive politeness and negative politeness have al-ready been given, but little has been said about the outlying strategies. The first, "on the record, without redress, baldly," is the maximally efficient Gricean speech introduced as a general contrast to all forms of politeness. Speech becomes Gricean whatever the relation between speaker and hearer in certain circumstances that override all consid-erations of politeness such as extreme urgency ("Fire!" "Stop, thief!" "Help me!") or noisy channels ("I'll call back!" "Fasten seat belts"). The surgeon in the operating theater is an ultimate Gricean with his "Scalpel," "sponge," "retractor," and so is the 18-month-old child with his "cookie," "milk," "doggie." In Figure 15.1, however, Gricean speech is associated with minimal values of P, D, and R, and that seems to be right. Taking off several layers of politeness is one of the comforts of coming home where D is low and so is P.

Off-record speech (strategy no. 4) is called for when there is a high risk but not so much as absolutely to prohibit the FTA. The idea is to communicate your intention with enough ambiguity so that you can-not be held strictly accountable. The Brown–Levinson treatment is elegant. Since the hearer must *interpret* what he hears, must go from what is said to something hinted at, there must be a "trigger" to alert him to do more than the usual amount of interpretive work. What should the trigger be? Some violation, the theory proposes, of the Gricean Maxims of Cooperative Conversation. The speaker must say too little – or too much – must say something not clearly relevant, must be vague or self-contradictory. A trigger is a signal to look for what Speech Act Theory calls an "implicature" or "inference," some-thing implied by what has been said, together with the situation and the personalities involved.

In Act III, Scene iii, of *Othello*, Iago, Othello's ensign, intends to make Othello believe that Desdomona and the honorable Cassio are secret lovers. This is not something he can say given the difference of power and the extremity of the accusation, but it is something he can insinuate, off-record.

Iago: Ha! I like not that. [Ellipsis violating the Maxim of Quantity]
Othello: What dost thou say? [Registering the violation]
Iago: Nothing, my lord or if – I know not what. [Vague, contradictory, and
        elliptical, violating the Maxims of Quality, Quantity, and Manner]
Othello: Was that not Cassio parted from my wife?

Iago: Cassio, my lord? No sure I cannot think it. That he would steal away so guilty like, hearing you coming. [Hint, violating the Maxim of Relevance]

Finally, there is strategy no. 5 – Don't do the FTA, which is the strategy to adopt when the risk of speaking is prohibitively great. One might think it impossible to provide an example since it is necessary to know not only that something was not said but that it was thought and suppressed. Dramatists, however, have ways of representing inner life. Shakespeare, in *Hamlet*, *King Lear*, *Macbeth*, and *Othello*, used the psychological soliloquy. Hamlet in Act I, Scene ii, is asked by his uncle and now stepfather, "How is it that the clouds still hang on you?" and he answers, "Not so, my lord, I am too much in the sun." For an attentive and well-prepared audience, Hamlet's response is off-record. We can infer the meaning: "too much in the royal favor," with a pun on "son." The king makes no response to the speech and it is fair to suppose that it simply seems oddly irrelevant. When Hamlet's mother, the queen, urges "cast thy nighted color off" Hamlet speaks only of the intensity of his grief. From what he says to them, Claudius and Gertrude could not infer his thought:

O, most wicked speed to post
  With such dexterity to incestuous sheets! (I, ii, 156–157)

which is expressed in the soliloquy that immediately follows upon their exit, and which ends:

But break, my heart, for I must hold my tongue. (I, ii, 158)

That is strategy no. 5: Don't do the FTA.

Two emendations

In Figure 15.1 positive politeness and negative politeness are ordered with respect to one another on the scale of face loss, positive being associated with the lesser risk, and are represented as mutually exclusive. Virtually all empirical research (e.g., Brown & Gilman, 1989; Craig et al., 1986; Field, 1991; Holtgraves & Yang, 1992) has found these assumptions to be incorrect. Positive and negative substrategies are routinely combined in the same speech act and so in Figure 15.2 they are not ordered and not represented as mutually exclusive.

While the principal claim of the Brown–Levinson theory concerns the ordering of the five superstrategies, they make a suggestion that has led some investigators to try out an ordering *within* the on-record

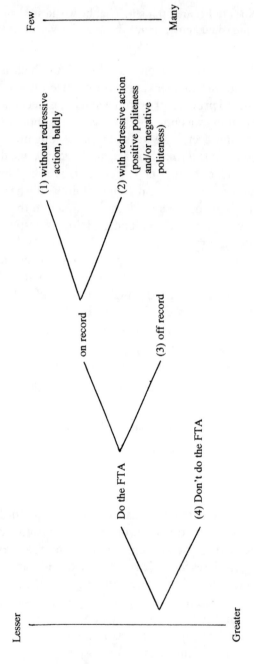

Estimation of
risk of face loss:

Lesser

Greater

Do the FTA

(4) Don't do the FTA

on record

(3) off record

(1) without redressive
action, baldly

(2) with redressive action
(positive politeness
and/or negative
politeness)

Few

Many

$W_x = D(S,H) + P(H,S) + R_x$

Politeness (like W_x) increases as Distance goes up.

Politeness (like W_x) increases as Power of H over S increases.

Politeness (like W_x) increases as Risk of imposition goes up.

Figure 15.2. Superstrategies of politeness ordered against estimated risk of face loss (after Brown & Levinson [1978, 1987] but modified as described in text)

positive–negative superstrategy. "The more *effort* a speaker expends in face-preserving work, the more he will be seen as trying to satisfy H's face wants . . . the greater the number of compatible outputs . . . the more [S] may be judged as trying to at least appear polite" (Brown & Levinson, 1987, p. 143).

If someone says, "Forgive me, sir, you may not recognize me but our children are good friends and so I venture to ask a small favor," the FTA "Can you give me a lift home?" seems more appropriate than "Can you tell me the time?" A politeness windup of some six substrategies, positive and negative, calls for an FTA that is riskier than asking the time. So at least R. Brown and Gilman (1989) reasoned and therefore they scored their on-record positive–negative speech acts by counting distinct substrategies, one point per substrategy, and predicted that the scores would increase with *W* or total face risk. They did so and the results seemed intuitively reasonable. Field (1993) has also scored her data in this way. Figure 15.2, unlike Figure 15.1, represents scoring by number-of-substrategies.

Politeness in three patients

That some schizophrenics are sometimes impolite is hardly interesting. What does interest us is the serendipitous discovery that some schizophrenic persons, just two of six who answered a 24-item instrument designed to test the Brown–Levinson theory, were consistently impolite, almost as impolite as the items permit, on almost all 24 items. One additional subject gave maximally impolite responses: a woman who is not herself schizophrenic, but who has an aunt and a niece who are. To be maximally impolite in our sense is to be maximally efficient or Gricean. The impression these test results gave is that a total pragmatic system has been lifted or that a continuing concern – concern for the feelings of others – has been overlooked, set aside, or foregone. Nothing remotely like this has appeared in the results with the same instrument obtained from 33 normal persons.

The principal assumptions and predictions of the Brown–Levinson theory, as I have described them above, have by now been confirmed by research of many kinds. Most generally and convincingly I think by the doctoral dissertation (Harvard, 1991) of Susan Field.

Dr. Field constructed two forms (48 items) of what she calls a Discourse Completion Task. A representative item is:

Pat is new on the job in a construction company. He wants to take the next two days off to visit his mother out of town. His boss says that he can only take extra time off if he finds someone to do his work. He approaches Clayton, one of the other new carpenters. He doesn't know Clayton very well, but their brief exchanges so far have been friendly.

Pat:_____

Clayton: I can do tomorrow for sure, but I have to check and see if it's O.K. with my wife for me to do a double shift on Thursday.

The respondent is to provide Pat with a speech, in this case a request, and that speech is scored in terms of the 25 strategies the theory provides.

From two schizophrenic patients and the woman who is not schizophrenic but has two relatives who are, we have obtained a very exciting result. The result can be illustrated by the speeches composed in response to the above item by one normal person and two patients.

Normal: "Clayton, I know I'm new on the job and do not know you very well, but I would really appreciate it if I could take a couple of days off and you could fill in for me."

Patient RR: "Could you work in my place for two days?"

Patient PC: "Can you cover for two days?"

The normal response utilizes eight substrategies that make it quite polite. The patient responses utilize either one or no substrategies and so eschew the work of politeness.

The Discourse Completion Task includes as many criticisms – which are threats to positive face – as requests – which threaten negative face. Criticisms are sometimes striking in that almost all normal subjects choose to soften them in similar ways. For example, in item 14, a junior employee has been invited to a cocktail party by his boss, and on being asked to taste and give an opinion on the spicy dip, must tell the boss that it needs more salt. A typical normal response is: "Well, Mr. Niels, it tastes great but it could use a little more salt." Patient RR said: "I think the spicy dip needs more salt" and Patient PC said: "I think it could use some salt." Item 22 similarly involved a senior asking the opinion of a junior – of his daughter's sculpture – and the opinion expressed was required to be negative. A normal response both softens and hedges: "Well, I don't know much about art, sir; it certainly looks quite different." Patient RR does neither: "I think the sculpture has a few faults," and Patient PC is as direct as you can be: "I do not like your daughter's sculpture."

An occasional efficient response unredressed by politeness would not be interesting. What we have found, however, is that some patients, for instance, RR and PC, *invariably,* across all items in the test, fail to use politeness. The result is the same for requests and criticisms; it is the same regardless of relative status of speaker and hearer, familiarity of the two, and extremity of the imposition. What this finding suggests is that politeness in a language is indeed organized as a system like that described by the Brown–Levinson theory since politeness is either present or absent, not in a quantitative piecemeal fashion, but qualitatively as a whole system. Theoretically, the result seems to validate politeness theory.

The first question that must be asked is whether the Gricean patient simply cannot be bothered by the requirements of politeness or, more interestingly, does not see the need or, perhaps, know how to meet it. Our initial approach has been to ask patients who have responded once to the Discourse Completion items to go through them a second time and this time try to make what they say more polite. The results with the first 23 patients are, not surprisingly, complex but they sustain our interest because there are 8 "Gricean" respondents and all these make a "bald" speech more polite only in some stereotyped unchanging fashion: adding "please," changing an imperative to "would you," etc. On the other hand, one patient we have seen outdoes any normal on record with long paragraphs of substrategies. It looks as if we have a lot to learn about politeness in schizophrenia.

References

Austin, John L. 1962/1975. *How to do things with words.* Cambridge, MA: Harvard University Press.

Ayer, Alfred J. 1936. *Language, truth, and logic.* New York: Oxford University Press.

Bates, Elizabeth. 1976. *Language and context: The acquisition of pragmatics.* New York: Academic Press.

Blum-Kulka, Shoshanna. 1982. Learning to say what you mean in a second language: A study of the speech act performance of learners of Hebrew as a second language. *Applied Linguistics* 3:29–59.

Brown, Penelope, & Levinson, Stephen C. 1978. Universals in language usage: Politeness phenomena. In Esther N. Goody (ed.), *Questions and politeness.* Cambridge University Press.

Brown, Penelope, & Levinson, Stephen C. 1987. *Politeness: Some Universals in language usage.* Cambridge University Press.

Brown, Roger. 1973. Schizophrenia, language, and reality. *American Psychologist* 28:395–403.

Brown, Roger, & Gilman, Albert. 1960. The pronouns of power and solidarity. In T. A. Sebeok (ed.), *Style in language.* Cambridge, MA: MIT press and John Wiley.

Brown, Roger, & Gilman, Albert. 1989. Politeness theory and Shakespeare's four major tragedies. *Language in Society.* 18:159–212.

Clark, Herbert H. 1979. Responding to indirect speech acts. *Cognitive Psychology* 11:430–477.

Clark, Herbert H., & Lucy, Peter. 1975. Understanding what is meant from what is said: A study in conversationally conveyed requests. *Journal of Verbal Learning and Verbal Behavior* 14:56–72.

Clark, Herbert H., & Schunk, Dale H. 1980. Polite responses to polite requests. *Cognition* 8:111–143.

Craig, Robert T., Tracy, Karen, & Spisak, Frances. 1986. The discourse of requests: Assessment of a politeness approach. *Human Communication Research* 12:437–468.

Field, Susan E. O. 1991. Upon saying unpleasant things: An experimental investigation of politeness theory. Doctoral dissertation, Harvard University.

Field, Susan E. O. 1993. Upon saying unpleasant things: Politeness in requests and criticisms. Unpublished manuscript, Harvard University.

Fraser, Bruce. 1978. Acquiring social competence in a second language. *RELC Journal* 9:1–26.

Gordon, D., & Lakoff, George. 1971. Conversational postulates. In *Papers from the seventh regional meeting of the Chicago Linguistic Society,* Chicago, pp. 63–84.

Grice, H. Paul. 1975. Logic and conversation. In Peter Cole and Jerry L. Morgan (eds.), *Syntax and semantics, III: Speech acts.* New York: Academic Press.

Holtgraves, Thomas, and Yang, Joong-Nam. 1992. Interpersonal underpinnings of request strategies: General principles and differences due to culture and gender. *Journal of Personality and Social Psychology* 62:246–256.

Labov, William, and Fanshel, David. 1977. *Therapeutic discourse.* New York: Academic Press.

Searle, John R. 1975. The classification of illocutionary acts. *Language in Society* 5:1–24.

Comments on Roger Brown's chapter

Philip S. Holzman

The brusk, blunt responses of schizophrenic patients to Field's "Discourse Completion Task" may at first suggest that these patients are showing the social consequences of the chronic form of their illness, which results in failures in personal and social functioning. Gruenberg called these effects "the Social Breakdown Syndrome" (Gruenberg, 1967), which is a secondary, and purely sociogenic, type of decompensation. It is a result both of the patient's illness and of the responses of those who come into contact with him or her once they detect the dysfunctions; but it is not a necessary expression of the disease itself.

Very quickly, however, one must discard this explanation, because the first-degree relative, who does not have schizophrenia, also shows the same insensitive, blunt, Gricean responses. And, strikingly, the relative demonstrates this callousness on all 24 items, just as the patients did. While we wait for the results of a larger study that can give us reliable distributions of this phenomenon, we can make a few additional observations.

The two patients and the relative engaged in face-threatening acts with no apparent self-consciousness or awareness of their social consequences. On the face of it, then, these people did not seem to understand the intentions or suppositions of the people they were addressing. It is as if their sense of empathy was significantly reduced, to be replaced by a mechanical, flat and devitalized social commerce. We have, of course, previously recognized this feature of chronic schizophrenia in the emotional blunting described by Kraepelin. We recognize in this study, moreover, that this blunting may not be a feature merely of the chronic syndrome, but may be a behavioral characteristic of those with subclinical features of the disorder.

We have many excellent methods to study the cognitive dysfunctions of schizophrenia, but we have hitherto lacked experimental tools to study the affective dysfunctions. This simple test of politeness focuses on a defect in what Gardner (1983) called "personal intelligence" – a quality of intelligence that clinical neurological studies have shown involves circuits linking the limbic system, where older emotional functions are regulated, with the more recent, distinctly human parts of the prefrontal cortex. The study of this apparent social ineptitude, which focuses on politeness behavior, may open the door to the understanding of the elusive disorder of affective regulation in schizophrenia.

References

Gardner, Howard. 1983. *Frames of Mind.* New York: Basic Books.
Gruenberg, Ernest M. 1967. The social breakdown syndrome – some origins. *American Journal of Psychiatry, 123,* 1481–1489.

16

Neuroleptic treatment effects in relation to psychotherapy, social skills training, and social withdrawal in schizophrenics

Herbert E. Spohn

Introduction

There is a substantial literature bearing on the effects of neuroleptics on cognitive or attention/information processing dysfunction (A/IP) in schizophrenics. The focus in most of the studies concerned with these issues has been on the question of whether neuroleptics normalize or impair cognitive functioning. The predominant findings in such studies have been that neuroleptics do not so much impair as they normalize, partially and selectively, cognitive functioning (see Spohn & Strauss, 1989). In a series of studies over the last 15 years, my associates and I have made contributions to this literature. In the present context, however, we seek to consider our findings from a novel perspective. First we review our findings that some forms of thought disorder and A/IP dysfunctions appear to be normalized by neuroleptic treatment. This review will set the stage for the question, What do such findings imply for psychotherapy and rehabilitation programs involving schizophrenic patients and, more generally, what do they imply for how such patients function in the interpersonal environment? The second part of this chapter is, in a sense, a variation on its first and main theme. As already noted, in a series of studies we have identified acute episode dysfunctions which are *normalized* by neuroleptics and dysfunctions evident in both acute episodes and remission which *resist* modification by neuroleptics in both phases. Accordingly, we are in a position to address the question of what the implications of drug treatment resistance or drug treatment sensitivity of a given dysfunction are for its state or trait status.

Neuroleptic normalization and interpersonal functioning

We begin an examination of the implications of normalizing effects of neuroleptics in schizophrenics for interpersonal functioning with a review of our findings regarding the effects of neuroleptics on thought disorder.

The Thought Disorder Index (TDI) developed by Holly Johnston and Philip Holzman (1980) assesses thought disorder reflected in responses on the Rorschach at four levels of severity: minimal, mild, moderate, and severe. Our findings (Spohn et al., 1986) indicate that verbalizations on the Rorschach scored as moderate and severe are reduced, if not altogether eliminated, by neuroleptic treatment in chronic schizophrenics. Minimal and mild thought pathology, however, persist when clinical remission has been attained. At the clinical level these findings imply that delusional and paranoid thought processes as well as conceptual disorganization typically associated with acute episodes are normalized by neuroleptic treatment but that minimally or mildly disabling, residual thought pathology persists in remission.

Does the significantly reduced intrusiveness of *grossly pathological* verbalizations into communication reflect a change in the schizophrenics' discrimination of their own role and that of others in interpersonal discourse? The answer to this question is, perforce, highly speculative since there are virtually no empirical data that bear directly on this issue.

We note that administration of the Rorschach represents an interpersonal situation in which an exchange of information is required. Moreover, most testees are likely to be aware of role differentiation as between themselves and the Rorschach examiner such that the examiner raises questions and the testee is expected to answer them. Also, many testees tend to be guarded in their response to questions because they regard the responses to be a form of self-disclosure and subject to critical evaluation by the examiner.

We suggest that in the Rorschach encounter neuroleptics strengthen the ability of schizophrenics to edit out of the stream of communication ideation that is recognized to be socially inappropriate, irrelevant, or idiosyncratic. If this is a valid inference, it follows further that neuroleptically responsive schizophrenics have gained or regained some appreciation of social norms that govern communication and an understanding of the relation between autistic ideation and conventional discourse. Moreover, the ability to edit out idiosyncratic ideation in the Rorschach testing situation could be taken to imply that schizophrenics have a clearer idea of social role relationships.

An alternative explanation of reduced pathological responses may well be that neuroleptics suppress such ideation. Hence, it needs to be granted that the question as to whether neuroleptic treatment directly reduces autistic ideation or interposes a mediating mechanism which results, indirectly, in reduced severely pathological communication, is an empirical one. To the best of our knowledge, there is no evidence that unequivocally bears on this issue. It is noteworthy, however, that behavior therapists (e.g., Wallace & Boone, 1984) concerned with social skills and social role training tend to prefer to work with patients whose symptoms are improved by neuroleptic treatment. One plausible explanation is that medicated schizophrenics are better able to discriminate and respond appropriately to social roles.

These speculations now set the stage for a discussion of the medication-induced normalization of other A/IP dysfunctions and what such normalization implies for how schizophrenics function in the interpersonal environment. We shall be dealing here with the effects of neuroleptics on vigilance or concentrative attention, as well as on distractibility in schizophrenics.

The relation of drug treatment to performance on the Continuous Performance Test (CPT) (Rosvold et al., 1956), generally regarded as a measure of concentrative attention or vigilance, has been examined in several studies (Orzack et al., 1967; Spohn et al., 1977; Wohlberg & Kornetsky, 1973). Briefly, the CPT requires that subjects pull a lever or press a button whenever a target letter or stimulus identified by prior instruction appears among a series of nontarget letters or stimuli. Unmedicated patients tend to manifest a significantly larger number of errors of omission than do medicated patients and normal controls (Spohn et al., 1977), but schizophrenic patients in a drug-induced remission still show a significantly larger number of errors of omission than normal controls (Wohlberg & Kornetsky, 1973). One may infer from this that vigilance or concentrative attention is enhanced by neuroleptic treatment, but not to the extent of being fully normalized.

Two recent studies (Spohn et al., 1985a; Spohn et al., 1985b) have confirmed findings by Oltmanns et al. (1978): "Antipsychotic medication . . . helps specifically in the alleviation of the disrupting influence of distracting stimuli" (p. 90).

To formulate these findings in somewhat different terms, one might say that neuroleptic treatment is associated with improvement in the ability to discriminate relevant from irrelevant stimuli and with improvement in the ability to maintain, over time, orientation to relevant stimuli. In relating this to neuroleptically enhanced social role and social norm discrimination, we propose that these functions are a specific expression, perceptually, of discrimination of relevant stimuli and that in schizophrenics, insofar as the latter is enhanced by neuroleptic treatment, the former is necessarily enhanced. More generally speaking, we propose that in schizophrenics neuroleptic treatment increases the efficiency of reality testing. Informed by these suppositions, we are now conceptually prepared to raise the question, In what ways does enhanced reality testing influence the course schizophrenics steer in the interpersonal environment?

As pertinent to this issue we cite results obtained by Schooler and Spohn (1982) in an evaluation of the efficacy of a controlled experimental ward program applied to chronic schizophrenics for a 2-year period in the late 1950s. This program was explicitly designed to increase the frequency of interpersonal encounters, an experimental intervention predicated on the hypothesis that social withdrawal in chronic schizophrenics is a by-product of the custodial regimen prevalent in many Veterans Administration and state mental hospitals before the large-scale use of neuroleptic medication. We assumed that by establishing a ward social environment that increased interpersonal encounters and promoted a sense of community, we could peel away the crust of social withdrawal engendered by long-term institutionalization.

Our findings indicated that we had, indeed, succeeded in generating higher levels of social interaction on the experimental ward compared with the period prior to the implementation of the program and compared with levels on a control ward at termination of the program. However, to our surprise and consternation, psychotic symptoms and anxiety were exacerbated in most patients on the experimental ward compared with the period prior to implementation of the program and with the control ward. We were forced to conclude that by eroding the social withdrawal defenses of most patients on the experimental ward, we had exacerbated their schizophrenic psychosis.

A subgroup of patients on the experimental ward showed dramatically different outcome, however. Unlike the majority of the patients on the experimental ward, these patients had received neuroleptic treatment throughout the program. Outcome data for this group showed both statistically significant symptomatic *improvement* as well as *lower* frequency of social interaction.

This finding is interpreted in the context of prior speculations that neuroleptic treatment enhances reality testing. We assume that both medicated and unmedicated patients were strongly motivated to protect and maintain social withdrawal, but that medicated patients were able to do so more effectively. That is, medicated patients, by virtue of clearer apprehension of relevant stimuli (threats to social withdrawal) and by virtue of an enhanced ability to discriminate social role differentiation, perceived ward staff as motivated to encourage social interaction and themselves as the targets of such efforts. Accordingly, medicated patients were enabled to elude staff maneuvers to trap them in interpersonal encounters which threatened their defenses. Unmedicated patients, not equipped to make such discriminations, were less able to avoid staff encounters; their social withdrawal defense was breached with consequent exacerbation of psychotic symptoms.

These speculations also bear on reports by Leff and Vaughn (1985) that, among discharged schizophrenic patients returned to high expressed emotion families, patients who are on neuroleptics are less likely to relapse than unmedicated patients, and, more generally, that asymptomatic schizophrenics require 35 hours per week of withdrawal time to protect against exacerbation of symptoms. We think a case can be made that in medicated patients their enhanced reality testing permits them to elude hostile and critical confrontations, and thus protects, prophylactically, against symptom exacerbation that might lead to relapse and rehospitalization.

We recognize that an alternative explanation of why medicated patients "survive" longer in high expressed emotion families than unmedicated patients is that the former may show less psychotic behavior than their unmedicated counterparts, and may therefore invite fewer hostile invasions of their privacy. The validity of these two alternative hypotheses is an issue that awaits empirical data. We do venture the hypothesis that among the avoidant strategies available to patients whose reality testing has been enhanced, is one of controlling the expression of behaviors recognized as socially inappropriate or likely to invite criticism.

Our speculations regarding neuroleptically enhanced reality testing also have implications for psychotherapy and social skills training. Medicated patients may be better able to perceive appropriate therapy role relationships and may be less prone to misapprehend the significance of patient–therapist interactions. In social skills training, medicated schizophrenics may become capable of role playing as a means for learning to adopt new roles. More generally, successful neuroleptic treatment may set the stage for successful psychosocial treatment. This speculation is indirectly supported by findings (Smith et al., 1980) that in psychiatric patients a combination of psychotherapy and psychopharmacological treatment is more efficacious than either alone. A caveat needs to be advanced, however. The need for personal privacy and for social withdrawal remains undiminished in medicated schizophrenics. Hence, therapists of all persuasions are well advised to maneuver in such a fashion as to not threaten this defense until some degree of therapeutic alliance has been achieved.

Neuroleptic normalization and trait attribution

In the series of investigations that examined neuroleptic effects on thought disorder and A/IP dysfunctions, we have identified not only dysfunctions that are partially normalized, but also dysfunctions that appear to be unaffected by neuroleptic treatment. Such findings permit speculations regarding the state or trait status of A/IP dysfunctions as either drug treatment *sensitive* or drug treatment *resistant*. Stability of A/IP dysfunctions is a commonly applied criterion in terms of which trait status is attributed. That is, dysfunctions manifest during an acute episode as well as in remission are seen as meriting the attribution of trait status. To be sure, stability is not the only criterion in terms of which trait status is attributed. Specificity and aggregation of the dysfunction in biological relatives also play a role in trait status attribution.

There are three forms of dysfunctions which are resistant to normalization by neuroleptic treatment and which, by virtue of the rationale developed above, merit attribution of trait status. They are eye tracking dysfunction (Levy et al., 1993; Spohn et al., 1988), the reaction time crossover effect (Spohn & Coyne 1988), generally regarded as reflecting major set impairment, and skin conductance orienting response (SCOR) nonresponding (Spohn et al., 1989), generally interpreted as representing failure to allocate attention to novel stimuli. Trait attribution, by virtue of the stability criterion, to eye tracking dysfunction (ETD) and the reaction time crossover effect (RTX) is independently confirmed by Holzman et al. (1984) findings and those of De Amicis et al. (1986) that both ETD and RTX aggregate in biological relatives of schizophrenics.

The independence of ETD, RTX, and SCOR from neuroleptic drugs supports their designation as traits. Other dysfunctions such as thought disorder, vigilance, and distractibility are exacerbated in the acute psychotic phase and normalized in remission. Although acute exacerbation of these dysfunctions could be interpreted to mean that they are state-related, and do not merit trait status, such a conclusion is not wholly justified. Normalization by neuroleptic treatment for each of these dysfunctions is incomplete (Wohlberg & Kornetsky 1973; Spohn 1985b; Spohn et al., 1986; Spohn & Strauss 1989). Residual impairment persists in remission. Accordingly, these forms of cognitive impairment merit putative trait status for the same reasons that dysfunctions completely unaffected by neuroleptic treatment deserve this attribution.

A further issue that can be examined in the present context relates to the implications of the *disjunctive effect of neuroleptics* on these two arrays of cognitive impairment. In considering this question, it is instructive to seek to identify what thought disorder, distractibility, and impaired vigilance, on the one hand, and ETD, RTX, and SCOR nonresponding, on the other, have in common. We believe a case can be made that the former reflect generalized impairment in the interpretation of events or stimuli in the external environment, or in the attribution of information value to stimuli. The latter may be seen to share some degree of variance representing impairment in orienting to the perceived occurrence of significant events as well as to perceived change in the environment. It is possible that the disjunctive effect of neuroleptic treatment on thought disorder, etc., and on eye movement, etc., serves to identify groups of traits that reflect two independent forms of cognitive impairment. If these speculations are empirically confirmed, as they are in some of our data, such confirmation would strengthen the case for the use of these two kinds of cognitive traits as alternative phenotypes in genetic studies of schizophrenia.

References

De Amicis, L. A., et al. 1986. Brief communication: Reaction time crossover as a marker of schizophrenia and of higher functioning. *J. Nerv. Ment. Dis.* 174:177–179.

Holzman, P. S., et al. 1984, Pursuit eye movement dysfunctions in schizophrenia. *Arch. Gen. Psychiatry* 41:136–139.

Johnston, M. H., & Holzman, P. S. 1980. *Assessing schizophrenic thinking: A clinical and research instrument for measuring thought disorder.* San Francisco: Jossey-Bass.

Leff, J., & Vaughn, C. 1985. *Expressed emotion in families: Its significance for mental illness.* New York: Guilford Press.

Levy, D. L., et al. 1993. Eye tracking dysfunction and schizophrenia: A critical perspective. *Schizophr. Bull.* 19:461–536.

Oltmanns, T. F., et al. 1978. The effect of anti-psychotic medication and diagnostic criteria on distractibility in schizophrenia. *J. Psychiatr. Res.* 14:81–91.

Orzack, M. H., et al. 1967. The effects of daily administration of carphenazine on attention in the schizophrenic patient. *Psychopharmacology (Berl)* 11:31–38.

Rosvold, H. E., et al. 1956. A continuous performance test of brain damage. *J. Consult. Psychol.* 20:343–350.

Schooler, C., & Spohn, H. E. 1982. Social dysfunction and treatment failure in schizophrenia. *Schizophr. Bull.* 8:85–98.

Smith, M. L., et al. 1980. *The Benefits of Psychotherapy.* Baltimore: Johns Hopkins University Press.

Spohn, H. E., & Coyne, L. 1988. The effect of neuroleptics and tardive dyskinesia on reaction time. Paper presented at the meetings of the Society for Research in Psychopathology, 10–13 November 1988, Cambridge, Massachusetts.

Spohn, H. E., & Strauss, M. E. 1989. Relation of neuroleptic and anticholinergic medication to cognitive functions in schizophrenia. *J. Abnorm. Psychol.* 98:367–380.

Spohn, H. E., Lacoursiere, R. B., et al. 1977. Phenothiazine effects on psychological and psychophysiological dysfunction in chronic schizophrenics. *Arch. Gen. Psychiatry* 34:633–644.

Spohn, H. E., Coyne, L., Lacoursiere, R., et al. 1985a. Relation of neuroleptic dose and tardive dyskinesia to attention, information-processing, and psychophysiology in medicated schizophrenics. *Arch. Gen. Psychiatry* 42:849–859.

Spohn, H. E., Coyne, L., Mittleman, F., et al. 1985b. Effect of neuroleptic treatments on attention, information processing, and thought disorder. *Psychopharmacol. Bull.* 21:582–587.

Spohn, H. E., Coyne, L., Larson, J., et al. 1986. Episodic and residual thought pathology in chronic schizophrenics: Effect of neuroleptics. *Schizophr. Bull.* 12:394–407.

Spohn, H. E., Coyne, L., & Spray, J. 1988. The effect of neuroleptics and tardive dyskinesia on smooth-pursuit eye movement in chronic schizophrenics. *Arch. Gen. Psychiatry* 45:833–840.

Spohn, H. E., Coyne, L., Wilson, J., et al. 1989. Skin-conductance orienting response in chronic schizophrenics: The role of neuroleptics. *J. Abnorm. Psychol.* 98:478–486.

Wallace, C. J., & Boone, S. E. 1984. Cognitive factors in the social skills of schizophrenic patients: Implications for treatment. In W. D. Spaulding & J. K. Cole (eds.), *Theories of schizophrenia & psychosis: Nebraska symposium on motivation, 1983*. Lincoln: University of Nebraska Press, 283–318.

Wohlberg, G. W., & Kornetsky, C. 1973. Sustained attention in remitted schizophrenics. *Arch. Gen. Psychiatry* 23:533–537.

Comments on Herbert E. Spohn's chapter

Philip S. Holzman

This chapter addresses a subtle irony in the treatment of mental disorders: after antipsychotic medication has helped psychotic patients to gain control over some of their cognitive functions, they recognize and understand that they have been and to an extent remain psychologically impaired. Some psychotic patients may then withdraw even further from social commerce. An improvement in one area of functioning seems to bring on, or at least is accompanied by, a worsening in another area. This observation with respect to severe psychological illnesses is not a new one. Sigmund Freud, in his study of depression, noted a similar paradox.

In his paper *Mourning and Melancholia* (1917), Freud wrote that severely depressed people experience a profound impoverishment of their self-respect. Such people reproach themselves for all manner of sins and evil deeds, and they are perplexed about why their friends and family bother with them since they are so debased. Their self-criticism seems to know no bounds. Freud then commented,

It would be . . . fruitless . . . to contradict a patient who brings these accusations against [himself]. He surely must be right in some way and be describing something that is as it seems to him to be. Indeed, we must at once confirm some of his statements without reservation . . . it is merely that he has a keener eye for the truth than other people who are not melancholic. When in his heightened self-criticism he describes himself as petty, egoistic, dishonest, lacking in independence, one whose sole aim has been to hide the weakness of his own nature, it may be, so far as we know, that he has come pretty near to understanding himself; we only wonder why a man has to be ill before he can be accessible to a truth of this kind. For there can be no doubt that if anyone holds and expresses to others an opinion of himself such as this . . . he is ill, whether he is speaking the truth or whether he is being more or less unfair to himself.[1]

Note

1. Freud's insightful commentary on depression became the jumping-off point for a set of studies on reality awareness and depression (Dykman et al., 1989).

References

Dykman, B., Abramson, L., Alloy L., and Hartlage, S. 1989. Processing of ambiguous and unambiguous feedback by depressed and nondepressed college students: Schematic biases and their implications for depressive realism. *Journal of Personality and Social Psychology* 56(3):431–45.

Freud, S. 1957. *The Standard Edition of the Complete Psychological Works*, 14:239–258. London: Hogarth Press.

17

Familial factors in the impairment of attention in schizophrenia: Data from Ireland, Israel, and the District of Columbia

Allan F. Mirsky

I. Introduction and historical note

The observation of impaired attention in schizophrenia was made at least as early as 1919 by Kraepelin (Kraepelin, 1919). He may also have been the first investigator to apply the techniques of the experimental psychology laboratory to patients with major neuropsychiatric disorder. This work is cited by Hoch in a paper referring to Kraepelin's application of Wundt's techniques to the study of psychiatric patients (Hoch, 1896). In *Dementia Praecox*, Kraepelin (1919) noted specifically these characteristics of impaired attention in his schizophrenic patients: "It is quite common for them to lose both inclination and ability on their own initiative to keep their attention fixed for any length of time. It is often difficult to make them attend at all" (p. 6).

Laboratory studies of this behavioral abnormality in patients with schizophrenia came not long after the publication of *Dementia Praecox*, when the group at Worcester State Hospital led by Shakow, Rodnick, and Huston began publishing reports in the 1930s focusing on the attention loss in schizophrenia. The earliest citation appears to be an abstract Shakow published in the *Psychological Bulletin* in 1936, entitled "Mental set in schizophrenia studied in a discrimination reaction setting." This may be the first published report in a psychological journal of impaired attention in schizophrenia.

Over the years, since Shakow's (1936) first report, there have been many literature citations confirming the phenomenon of impaired attention in persons with schizophrenia. This deficit has been measured in a variety of ways, and reviews of this research have appeared in Mirsky and Duncan (1986) and elsewhere. In addition to this research, many publications have been concerned with the assessment of attention in populations at risk for schizophrenia because of their genetic relationship to persons with the disorder. Almost uniformly the finding has been that such "vulnerable" populations (to use Zubin and Spring's [1977] term) are more likely than matched normal or nonschizophrenic psychiatric controls to show impaired attention. Many of these studies have been reviewed by Nuechterlein and Dawson (1984) and, more recently, by Mirsky et al. (1992).

II. The analysis of attention deficits

There have been a number of attempts to capture the precise aspect or aspects of attention that are impaired in persons with schizophrenia and those at risk for the disorder. In addition to Shakow's (1979) concept of "segmental set," these attempts at a more precise characterization of the deficit have also included such explanations as impaired ability to shift attention (Zubin, 1975), deficits in vigilance or sustained attention (reviewed in Mirsky and Duncan, 1986) and impairment in information processing, either at the level of automatic (Frith, 1979) or controlled processing (Callaway and Naghdi, 1982).

The work of these and other authors leads to the view that it is more fruitful to consider attention as a multifactorial or multiple-component process. This multi-component view of attention is in keeping with information processing studies that identify a variety of functions linked to attention such as selectivity, focusing, sustaining concentration or vigilance, switching attention, distractibility, modulating the intensity of attention and attention to memorial processes such as rehearsal, retrieval and coding (e.g., Parasuraman & Davies, 1984; Posner, 1978; Shiffrin, 1988). The model I present here is a preliminary effort to bring a degree of empirical and theoretical order to the confused and confusing, but vitally important area of the study of attention. It substitutes for a rather diffuse and global concept a more manageable group of processes or elements, provides a tentative identification of these elements and some preliminary data concerning their linkage to a putative system or organization of cerebral structures (Mirsky et al., 1991). This will be the subject of sections III–VII of this chapter; following this, there will be a description of research, based on this model, concerned with familial factors in the attention deficit in schizophrenia.

III. The identification of elements of attention

Our initial effort to systematize the assessment of attention stemmed from an attempt to select from a large battery of neuropsychological tests used routinely in our laboratory (Mirsky and Duncan, 1987) smaller batteries targeted at specific problems. We thus chose for further study a group of eight tests that are in common use in neuro-psychological assessment and/or psychological experiments on attention and information processing.

The scores on these tests obtained from two groups of subjects, comprising a total population of 630 persons, were subjected to two independent principal components analyses. The results, virtually identical for the two groups, revealed distinct components of attentional performance, conforming to a multi-element model.

The first factor comprises loadings from four tests of perceptual-motor speed or focusing, including the Digit Symbol Substitution subtest of the Wechsler Adult Intelligence Scale–Revised (WAIS-R) (Wechsler, 1981), the Stroop Test (Stroop, 1935), the Talland Letter Cancellation Test (Talland, 1965), and the Trail Making Test (Reitan and Davidson, 1974). The first factor would thus seem to be composed of two elements: as measured here, it comprises a visual-perceptual ability to scan stimulus material for a target rapidly and efficiently and an ability to make either verbal (Stroop) or skilled manual responses (Digit Symbol, Letter Cancellation, Trail Making) quickly. Hence, the designation *focus-execute* for this factor was an effort to encompass both aspects of the skills tapped by these tasks.

The second factor to emerge has loadings from the measures on a single test – the Wisconsin Card Sorting Test (Grant and Berg, 1948) – and has been labelled *shift*. It appears to reflect the capacity to shift in an adaptive and flexible manner from attending to one aspect or stimulus feature of objects to another aspect.

The third factor has very substantial loadings from the measures derived from the Continuous Performance Test (CPT) (Rosvold et al., 1956). The CPT, like the Mackworth Clock (Mackworth, 1950), is designed to measure the capacity to *sustain* attention, i.e., vigilance. The task requires sustained attention for periods of 7 to 10 min and yields measures of correct responses, commission errors and reaction time. The motor requirement of the CPT is not very demanding, since a response occurring within 700 ms of stimulus onset is scored as correct.

The fourth factor has loadings from two tests involving manipulation of numbers: the Arithmetic and Digit Span subtests of the WAIS-R (Wechsler, 1981). The tests require sequential registration, recall and mental manipulation of numeric information, somewhat diverse processes covered by the term *encode*.

These principal components analyses have been replicated in their essentials by five different groups of investigators on five independent populations of normal and disordered subjects (Kremen et al., 1992; Steinhauer et al., 1991; K. S. Kendler, personal communication; P. D. Harvey, personal communication; and Tatman, 1992). Tatman (1992) has proposed a fifth factor or attentional element; this one is concerned with the *stability* or *reliability* of response occurrence and is assessed by the variance of reaction time on the X and AX tasks of the CPT, and by the commission error score on the AX task. The salience of this attention factor has been demonstrated recently in studies of the children of women whose alcohol consumption during pregnancy was monitored; significant correlations were found between measures of maternal drinking of alcohol and the stability/reliability factor in their 14-year-old offspring (Streissguth et al., 1994).

IV. Localization of the factors of attention within the brain

There is evidence from neuroanatomical, clinical and neuropsychological studies that an attention "system" can be described within the brain (Mirsky et al., 1991) and that different parts of it may have some degree of specialization for different functions. Figure 17.1 summarizes this conception. The structures included within this cerebral model are similar to those included within models proposed earlier by Heilman and co-workers (1983) and by Mesulam (1987). Their models are based upon anatomical data from human clinical cases in which neglect (the inability to respond to stimuli in one half of space) was a symptom, as well as upon some animal lesion studies. Our model, as we show, is also based on human and animal data; however, it differs from previous models in that distinct functions have been proposed for specific cerebral regions. It is thus similar to the models proposed by Pribram and McGuinness (1975) and by Posner and Petersen (1990), which are discussed in section VII.

We believe that the neglect phenomenon (central to the theorizing

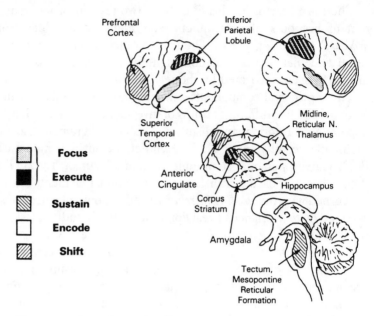

Figure 17.1. Semischematic representation of the proposed brain attention system, with tentative attributions of functional specialization to distinct brain regions (from Mirsky et al., 1991).

of Heilman and of Mesulam) represents an extreme form of deficit and is insufficient to account for the diversity of behavior subsumed under impaired attention. A brief review of the evidence for our model of attention follows.

The sustain element

The tectum and the mesopontine regions of the reticular formation and other structures of the brain stem are depicted in the lower right portion of Figure 17.1. The work of Moruzzi and Magoun (1949) and Lindsley et al. (1949) established these areas as essential to the maintenance of consciousness and to the regulation of levels of arousal. In our view, these structures constitute the basic fundamental, phylogenetically most primitive component of the attention system of the brain. We are strongly influenced in this assertion by the theorizing of MacLean (1990), who has pointed out that the brain of the reptile, although little more than a brain stem and a few ganglia, supports a complex series of behaviors, including many of the attention functions discussed in our model. The notion that the reptile is able to exhibit a rudimentary form of sustained attention is particularly compelling.

A number of other studies could be cited in support of the role of midbrain and brain stem structures in the maintenance of vigilance or sustained attention. Mirsky and Oshima (1973) provided evidence that subcortical aluminum cream lesions in the brain stem of the monkey impair sustained visual attention. Using another technique, Bakay Pragay et al. (1975) demonstrated that subcortical electrical stimulation of the brain stem reticular formation impairs sustained visual attentive behavior in the monkey. Mirsky et al. (1977) showed that electrical stimulation of the brain in regions that produce impairment of sustained attention also produced reduced visual evoked potentials. In all of these studies, a monkey version of the CPT was used so as to increase the likelihood that animal data could be generalized to human clinical data (e.g., Mirsky and Van Buren, 1965). Furthermore, in all of these studies, the findings support the view that mesencephalic brain stem structures are critical for the maintenance of sustained attention. A somewhat modified version of this monkey CPT (i.e., a go/no-go visual attention task) was also used in the successful search for single neural units involved in attention (Bakay Pragay et al., 1978). The following is a brief summary of that work.

Basically, these experiments employed simultaneous measurement of behavior and neuronal firing in trained monkey subjects. Bakay Pragay and co-workers identified cells in the midline thalamus, deep layers of the superior colliculus, tectal and pretectal regions, and pontine and mesencephalic portions of the brain stem that apparently support attention (Bakay Pragay et al., 1978; Ray et al., 1982). These "Type II" cells increased their firing on both go *and* no-go trials of a go/no-go visual discrimination task designed to be analogous to the CPT (Rosvold et al., 1956). Type II cells ceased responding to the task stimuli when they were no longer associated with reinforcement. Moreover, in some instances, Type II cells began firing hundreds of milliseconds before the occurrence of task stimuli – as though in anticipation of the appearance of the reinforced stimuli in this repetitive, predictable task. The firing of these cells was unrelated to the occurrence of eye movements, supporting the view that they are *not* part of a visual orientation or signal detection system (Ray et al., 1982) of the type described by Posner and Petersen (1990). Bakay

Pragay et al. (1987) also found Type II cells in regions of the monkey prefrontal cortex extending from the midprincipal sulcus to the central sulcus, although the frequency with which they were encountered diminished in the more caudal (and thus more purely motor) locations. Type II cells were also identified in the medial prefrontal regions and in the cingulate gyrus. Moreover, Bakay Pragay et al. (1988) also found Type II cells in the inferior parietal lobule (area 7) and the prestriate cortex (area V4). Every region of the monkey brain that has been explored by Bakay Pragay and co-workers on the basis of a presumptive role in attention (i.e., mesopontine brain stem structures, medial thalamus, prefrontal and frontal association cortex, inferior parietal and prestriate cortex) has been found to contain attention-related Type II cells. There are no contradictions between their distribution and the schematic map of the human brain in Figure 17.1.

The emphasis in this section is on the neural substrate of the *sustain* element; Type II cells can sustain task-related firing over hundreds of trials and could thus qualify as the *anlage* of this element. However the characteristics of Type II cells could also be construed as essential to the function of *focusing* on some aspect of the environment: go and no-go stimuli elicit increased firing and remain potent as long as the stimuli are associated with reinforcement. Furthermore, as the task stimuli are dissociated from reinforcement, the cell almost immediately ceases task-related firing; such a rapid disconnection implies the capacity for rapid *shifting* to other aspects of the environment that may hold more promise as reinforcers.

The data are insufficient to conclude that Type II cells have distinct functions in different attention-related areas of the brain (illustrated in Figure 17.1). The prefrontal cells in the Bakay Pragay et al. (1987) study showed great sensitivity in response to changes in task parameters; this finding is consistent with a role for these cells in the *shift* element of attention. However, since these experimental maneuvers were not tried in most of the mesopontine cells (or those in other locations) it is not clear whether this flexibility is unique to cells of the frontal cortex. Other characteristics by which Type II cells differ include the degree of symmetry in firing pattern between go and no go trials, the latency at which the cell fires in "anticipation" of stimulus onset and whether the cell increases or decreases firing in relation to the stimuli. The Type II cell may thus represent a kind of primordial attention cell that, depending on the network in which it is embedded, can support the several functions necessary for attention that are postulated here.

The medial view of the right hemisphere (center of Figure 17.1) depicts the midline thalamic region (and the reticular nuclei), for which a role in attention is supported by the anatomical and physiological studies of Ajmone Marsan (1965) and Jasper and co-workers (Jasper, 1958). The studies of Yingling and Skinner (1975) on the role of the reticular nucleus of the thalamus in modulating visual information also supports the role of thalamic structures in sustained attention. These authors demonstrated that stimulation of this thalamic nucleus could modify the influence of reticular formation effects on visual signals. These brain stem and thalamic structures appear to be essential for the maintenance of vigilance, rather than simply the regulation of levels of arousal (i.e., stages of sleep). This is an extension of the Moruzzi–Magoun–Lindsley concept (which dealt primarily with the role of the reticular formation in arousal) but is certainly compatible with it. The writings of Lindsley (e.g., Lindsley, 1960) are, of course, conducive to the view that within the general state of wakefulness, there exist degrees of behavioral tuning. One of the ways in which this is expressed is in variations in readiness to respond. Readiness to respond (as measured by reaction time and number of correct responses in a visual discrimination task) can be modified by low-intensity stimulation of the reticular formation (Fuster & Uyeda, 1962). Scheibel (1980) has speculated that the brain stem reticular formation and portions of the nonspecific or reticular thalamus act in concert with certain cortical regions to provide the "structurofunctional" basis of awareness.

Our argument that these reticular structures are specific substrates of the sustain element of attention would be stronger if we had more information than that provided by disruptions of performance on a monkey version of the CPT (and other similar data). Animal models of some of the tasks utilized in our attention battery are difficult or impossible to achieve; however, previously, we tried with some success (using drugs rather than lesions) to show differential effects of various classes of drugs on different cognitive-attentive tasks (i.e., match-to-sample vs. CPT) in the monkey (Bakay Pragay et al., 1969).

Some reasonably direct evidence of the effects of brain-stem pathology on the CPT was provided recently by Greenblatt (1986). She found that posterior fossa tumors that compressed the brain stem (and impaired the function of the reticular formation) affected speed of response on a CPT-type task. A correlation of .82 was found between tumor size and reaction time on the CPT. We may add that the specificity of the localization of sustained attention in the brain stem and reticular thalamus is indirectly supported by human clinical studies showing the relative lack of effect of large cortical lesions on the CPT (e.g., Lansdell and Mirsky, 1964).

Nevertheless, despite the difficulties in reaching unequivocal conclusions, we believe that the information presented here supports the view that the element of attention we have labeled "sustain" is particularly dependent upon the brain stem and the thalamic portions of the attention system of Figure 17.1.

The stability/reliability element

Since the identification of this attention element has been relatively recent, there are relatively few data available concerning its possible localization within the "attention system." We might speculate, however, that the brain stem and thalamic structures that support the sustain element also play a major role in support of this function.

The encode element

The hippocampus is presented in phantom on this brain view. The involvement of the hippocampus in attention is suggested by both behavioral and electrophysiological measures (e.g., Blakemore et al., 1972). The classical hippocampal theta rhythm, associated with heightened attention, has been amply characterized (Adey, 1969). We assume from other studies of the neuropsychological role of the hippocampus (Scoville & Milner, 1957; Mishkin, 1978) that it is involved primarily (although possibly not exclusively) in the mnemonic aspects (encode) of attention, as defined by our model. Mishkin (1978) has provided animal data that the amygdala may also be involved in the support of memory functions.

The shift element

The localization of the capacity to shift in the prefrontal cortex is based primarily on the work of Milner (1963). Milner demonstrated that resection of the dorsolateral prefrontal cortex for relief of seizure disorders produces impairment on performance on the WCST. The resection of other cerebral areas (i.e., the anterior temporal lobe) failed to produce the deficit. This test has been used in conjunction with radioactive xenon imaging of cerebral blood flow in schizophrenic patients (Weinberger et al., 1986). The results have led to speculation that the prefrontal areas of those patients are relatively inactive. We have provided supporting evidence for the role of the prefrontal region in supporting the WCST from the intensive neuropsychological study of a psychosurgical patient. She has been unable to learn the WCST despite 38 years of instruction. This person, who was evaluated with both positron emission tomography and computed tomography scans, has little functional tissue anterior to the central fissure – pursuant to two radical prefrontal lobotomies (Mirsky and Rosvold, 1990).

We have included the medial frontal cortex and the anterior cingulate gyrus in the focal representation of the shift element; this is primarily on the basis of our monkey data indicating that "attention" cells are equally well represented in the medial as in the dorsolateral prefrontal regions (Bakay Pragay et al., 1987).

Obviously, more information from the study of human subjects with brain lesions is necessary to establish whether or not the shift function is dependent exclusively upon prefrontal cerebral tissue. In fact, recent findings suggest that the shift element may be supported by other regions of the attention system of the brain (e.g., Corcoran and Upton, 1993).

Another issue concerns whether it is more useful to consider the Shift element of the WCST as a component of an overarching classification of behaviors – that of executive function, rather than that of attention per se. The boundaries between "attention" and "executive function" are rather indistinct; therefore, the decision to consider shift behavior assessed by the WCST as attention appears reasonable. Other empirical (or theoretical) information may suggest the need to revise this view.

The focus-execute element

From the standpoint of neuropsychological tests, impaired attention is usually identified with poor performance on such measures as Digit Symbol Substitution, Cancellation, Stroop and Trail Making; moreover, the loss of ability to focus on specific environmental cues and to respond appropriately to them would seem to constitute a reasonable working definition of neglect, at least in its milder form.

In the neuropsychological domain, studies of the symptom of neglect have led to a neural system view of spatial selective attention. This symptom, described originally by Geschwind and colleagues as a consequence of damage to the right posterior and, most often, parietal cortical regions (Heilman et al., 1983), involves the reported lack of awareness of visual, auditory or somatosensory stimuli from one-half of space. The neglect symptom may also occur following damage to portions of the cingulate gyrus, thalamus and the corpus striatum (Healton et al., 1982). Heilman and co-workers (Heilman et al., 1983) and Mesulam (1987) have linked these findings to the concept of a cortico-limbic-reticular circuit, damage to which underlies the neglect symptom. While it is attractive to think of attention as dependent upon a system (as opposed to a single focus supporting a specific behavior), the behavioral concept of neglect – although a powerful and impressive symptom – seems too narrow to support all that is implied by attention impairment.

Nevertheless, we may turn to the clinical literature on neglect for clues as to where the focus-execute element may be represented in the attention system of the brain. Unfortunately, this does not lead to a specific localization of this element of attention; Heilman et al. (1983) and Mesulam (1987), on the basis of their own observations and the reports of others, have concluded that neglect may follow damage to *any* of the cerebral structures shown in Figure 17.1. The possibility exists, therefore, that the focus-execute element is represented everywhere in the system delineated in Figure 17.1.

However, we would like to propose that the inferior parietal, superior temporal and striatal regions have a special role in the support of these functions. The first two are major multimodal sensory convergence areas of the brain. The posterior parietal cortex, in particular, has connections with sensory, limbic (i.e., cingulate cortex), thalamic and brain stem reticular areas as well as motor regions of the brain (Mesulam, 1987). The multiplicity of these connections, as well as the many reports of neglect following parietal lesions (particularly on the right side) (Heilman et al., 1983), led to the selection of this brain area as the primary cerebral locus of the focus-execute element. The connection of parietal cortex with the corpus striatum, as well as the important modulatory motor role of this nuclear complex, dictate its inclusion in the focus-execute (with possible emphasis on the execute) cerebral support system. Of possible relevance, as well, is the role of the caudate nucleus (a component of the corpus striatum) in support of such behavioral tasks as delayed alternation and delayed response (Battig et al., 1960).

The role of the superior temporal cortex or, more accurately, the superior temporal sulcus, as a multimodal sensory convergence area with a role in focused attention, is supported by the anatomical studies of Pandya and co-workers (e.g., Pandya & Yeterian, 1985). Recent studies of attention-related behavior in patients with complex partial seizures (with foci of abnormal tissue in the temporal lobe) and of similar patients who have undergone anterior temporal lobectomy for relief of seizures, support the view that the anterior temporal lobe is part of the brain system involved in the focus-execute element of attention. Roth et al. (1988) reported that patients with left or right temporal epileptogenic foci have "mild" attentional deficits, as assessed by tests that included (among others) the Stroop, Trail Making, Digit Span and Digit Symbol. Those with right-sided foci had significantly greater deficits on Trails B than the group with left-sided foci. Similarly, Hermann and Wyler (1988) reported that there was a decline in 40% of their measures of attention and concentration in a study of 38 patients who underwent anterior temporal lobectomy. Their attention measures included the Stroop and Trail Making tests. Also of interest in this study was the finding indicating sparing of performance on the WCST (the shift element) after anterior temporal lobe resections. Moreover, Lansdell and Mirsky (1964) had previously reported no impairment on the CPT (the sustain element) following temporal lobe resections.

The pattern of findings in these studies supports the view that performance on tests assessing what we have labeled the focus-execute element of attention (Stroop, Trail Making) is impaired with dysfunction of destruction of temporal lobe tissue. We have, however, insufficient data on these tests to claim that the superior temporal cortex has a different or unique role with respect to attention than the inferior parietal or striatal regions. Nevertheless, since the superior temporal sulcus is not clearly implicated in motor (i.e., execute) functions, we have not included the execute function in the temporal region in Figure 17.1. Another complication in the interpretation of the data of Roth et al. (1988) and Hermann and Wyler (1988) is that patients with complex partial seizures may have, in addition to their temporal cortical abnormalities, abnormal tissue in the amygdala and anterior hippocampus (Penfield and Jasper, 1954). Concurrent involvement of temporal cortex and hippocampus, according to our model, would suggest that two of the elements of attention (focus-execute *and* encode) would be impaired in such patients and that this impairment might increase with anterior temporal lobe resection.

V. The primary constructs within the model

These may be summarized as follows:

a. Attention is a complex process or set of processes. It can be subdivided into a number of distinct functions, including *focus-execute, sustain, stabilize, shift* and *encode.*
b. These functions may be supported by different brain regions, which have become specialized for this purpose but which are nevertheless organized into a system.
c. The system organization allows for shared responsibility for attentional functions, implies that the specialization is not absolute and that some structures may substitute for others in the event of injury.
d. The function of *focusing* on environmental events is shared by superior temporal and inferior parietal cortices as well as by structures that constitute the corpus striatum.
e. The *execution* of responses must depend heavily on the integrity of inferior parietal and corpus striatal regions. (See the discussion in Mesulam, 1987).
f. *Sustaining* a focus on some aspect of the environment is the major responsibility of rostral midbrain structures, including the mesopontine reticular formation and midline and reticular thalamic nuclei. We suspect that the function tentatively labeled as *stabilize* may also be dependent upon midline-thalamic and brain stem structures.
g. The capacity to *shift* from one salient aspect of the environment to another is supported by the prefrontal cortex, including the anterior cingulate gyrus, and possibly by other cerebral regions as well.
h. *Encoding* of stimuli is dependent upon the hippocampus and amygdala.
i. Damage or dysfunction in one of these brain regions can lead to circumscribed or specific deficits in a particular attention function.

It seems reasonable to propose that the brain structures presented in Figure 17.1 could be construed to form a system; anatomical connections among the various areas have been well described (e.g., Jones and Peters, 1986). Considerable evidence indicates that performance on different tests of attention may be impaired selectively by different brain lesions. This implies that distinct elements of attention (*focus-execute, sustain, stabilize, shift, encode*) are supported by distinct brain regions (Figure 17.1). It should be noted at the outset that this effort of assigning functional specialization of components of attention to different brain regions is not meant to be absolute, and it is likely that some brain regions share more than one attentional function.

VI. Relation to models of attention stemming from cognitive psychology

As noted earlier, in recent years cognitive psychologists have become interested in the problem of attention, and insightful and original analyses and models have been contributed by Kahnemann (1973), Posner (1978), Shiffrin and Schneider (1977), Parasuraman and Davies (1984) and others.

The complexities of some of the models proposed by cognitive psychologists are beyond our current knowledge of the correspondence between structure and function in the brain. Moreover, it would be premature to attempt to achieve a complete synthesis of the neuropsychological and the cognitive approaches to attention and attention disorder. Nevertheless, there are some basic principles stemming from cognitive psychology that can guide the development of a neuropsychologically based model of attention. These are: (a) attention (or to use the more inclusive term, information processing) is not a unitary phenomenon but comprises a series of elements or stages. The notion of stages suggests that information processing occurs in sequential fashion. For the most part, we are unable at this point to speculate about information-processing stages within a neuropsychological context, because we simply do not have sufficient information. However, the notion of individual components or elements of attention is one that we have attempted to apply in the present model. (b) Another insight the cognitive psychologists have provided is the contrast between automatic and controlled processing (Shiffrin & Schneider, 1977; Posner, 1978). Each of these has different characteristics and different demands upon the information-processing system. (c) Also useful is the notion that attention is not an inexhaustible resource; allocations of this limited resource have to be made in part on the basis of the supply available to the individual and in part on the basis of motivational criteria.

What can be said about the relationship between the present model and the insights from cognitive psychology and information processing? The principle of attentional stages or *elements* has obviously been central to the development of this model. The elements identified here could ultimately be arranged into a sequential model. The other most direct application, conceivably, is to the concept of attention as a limited resource; thus, as lesions, disease, or "functional" disorders (e.g., petit mal epilepsy, schizophrenia) damage one or more parts of the attention system, there may be impairment of specific elements of attention; however, there may also simply be less of the total attentional resource available to allocate to various demands. Nevertheless, to the extent that the remaining, intact portions of the system can substitute for the lesioned portions, the capacity for at least some attention remains, despite the loss of considerable amounts of tissue.

It is unclear as to how to relate the concept of automatic versus controlled aspects of information processing to the present model. The qualities of automatic information processing, namely, that it occurs without conscious awareness and is not capacity limited, do not seem readily assignable to any specific part of this system. There are two possibilities: one is that automatic processing involves a low demand on the system, but that it is a system characteristic rather than one dependent on a specific element, such as are proposed here. The second possibility, as suggested by Nuechterlein et al. (1983), is that vigilance tasks that require detection of highly practiced stimulus material can occur virtually automatically. This would be compatible with classifying the *sustain* aspects of the model as concerned with automatic processing. More demanding vigilance tasks would, however, be classified as controlled processing. In terms of the present discussion, the balance of the attention system (i.e., elements concerned with *focusing, execution, stabilizing* and *shifting*) is necessary for controlled information processing.

VII. Relation to other neural models of attention

We have noted the similarity between the brain components implicated in the present model and those in the models proposed by

Heilman and co-workers (Heilman et al., 1983) and by Mesulam (1987); the latter two conceptions are essentially identical. A major difference between those models and the present one has to do with the degree to which differentiated functions are assigned to different brain regions. This is a key feature of our model. We have also suggested that those models may be of value primarily in relation to the focus-execute element; this aspect of attention seems to capture the essence of the neglect syndrome, the primary datum with which these models are concerned. A detailed comparison of our model with all other current models of the cerebral basis of attention is beyond the scope of this chapter; however, a brief synopsis of the differences between this model and two other current conceptions of how the brain supports attention may be instructive. We shall discuss the models of Pribram and McGuinness (1975) and of Posner and Petersen (1990), both of which assign different functional roles to different parts of the system.

Pribram and McGuinness (1975) proposed arousal, activation and effort as essential factors or elements in the control of attention. Arousal, according to these authors, is more or less defined by the orienting response to sensory input, which is generated by a "core system of neurons . . . from the spinal cord through the brainstem reticular formation, including hypothalamic sites. . ." (Pribram and McGuinness, 1975, p. 123). In their conception, this is the core, or possibly, primordial attention system which mediates the action of an effective external stimulus. Forebrain control over this system is exerted by the amygdala and portions of the frontal cortex, which regulate arousal (a phasic or short-lasting effect), and by the basal ganglia, which regulate activation (a tonic or long-lasting effect). The system which coordinates arousal and activation is centered in the hippocampus.

Although the structures discussed by Pribram and McGuinness are included within the system we have proposed, the assignment of functional specialization differs from theirs. We would include arousal and activation within the sustain element; in addition, effort is a concept with which our model does not deal, although we have recognized the eventual necessity of discussing automatic versus effortful *processing*. Pribram and McGuinness do not deal with this issue either. These differences aside, the present model is more concerned with an articulation of clinical neurobehavioral issues. This might be expected in view of the fact that the database which gave rise to the present model, i.e., neuropsychological data from neuropsychiatric patients, differs considerably from the primarily animal research orientation of Pribram and McGuinness. Moreover, the information accumulated during nearly two decades of research since 1975 (particularly, but not limited to, the functions of parietal and temporal cortices) would require an update of their treatment.

This latter observation does not apply, however, to the conception proposed by Posner and Petersen (1990). Their model is based upon a consideration of "three major functions that have been prominent in cognitive accounts of attention . . . (a) orienting to sensory events; (b) detecting signals for focal (conscious) processing; and (c) maintaining a vigilant or alert state" (Posner and Petersen, 1990, p. 26). These authors suggest, further, that the attention system of the human brain is made up of two major loci. One of these is a posterior attention system that lies in the dorsal visual pathway, and has its primary cortical projection area in V_1, extending into the parietal lobe. This system has the responsibility for the process of orienting. (Note the difference in the treatment of orienting by these authors and by Pribram and McGuinness.) The second major locus is the anterior attention system, which seems to be headquartered in the anterior cingulate gyrus and supplementary motor cortex (both of which are midline frontal lobe structures). This system has the responsibility for signal detection. The function of alertness (or maintaining vigilance) is not quite so clearly defined anatomically by these authors, but the structures involved seem to constitute, at a minimum, the norepinephrine innervation system, extending from the locus coeruleus of the brain stem rostrally to the posterior attention system, particularly of the right hemisphere.

There is at least a correspondence between some of the structures constituting the Posner–Petersen model and those included within the one proposed here (i.e., prefrontal cortex, parietal cortex, selected brain stem structures). There is clearly not total agreement between the two models as to the definition of the essential elements of attention; nevertheless, there appears to be considerable overlap in conception between what we have referred to as *focus-execute* and as *sustain,* and the Posner–Petersen elements of *orient-detect* and *maintaining vigilance.* (The combining of the two elements of orienting and detection into one is our proposal, and not that of Posner and Petersen.) There is a difference in the neural basis proposed for shift behavior. Posner and Petersen link this to the superior colliculus and surrounding structures, and therefore to their posterior attention system. In our model, based on the WCST, this behavior is linked to the dorsolateral prefrontal cortex. The difference is obviously a function of whether shifting is defined in terms of movement of the eyes (Posner and Petersen) or the shifting of sorting concepts (the present model).

The differences among the models notwithstanding, there is a fundamental similarity in the assignment of what we have referred to as *sustain,* that which Posner and Petersen have called *maintaining vigilance* and Pribram and McGuinness' *core arousal;* structures in the brain stem and medial thalamus support this attentional function.

From this brief review of two other models of an attention system in the brain it would appear that the nature of the neuropsychological model of attention that is created depends upon the behavioral data that are used to generate it. Since all these conceptions deal with fundamentally the same database, there is a fair degree of communality among them. The differences seem to be a function of the part of the database that particular authors have chosen to emphasize.

VIII. The application of the model to the study of schizophrenia

We have applied this model of attention, derived from principal components analysis, to the study of three groups of patients with schizophrenia. In each case, first-degree relatives and appropriate control groups were studied as well. Comparisons within and among samples constitute the next section of the chapter.

The Irish sample

Availability of a sample of persons from Ireland allowed us to study a population of English-speaking schizophrenic persons and their first-degree relatives of largely Celtic origin, who reside in a rural area (County Roscommon) characterized by large family sizes, high rates of cooperation, and the availability of well-established psychiatric case registers. A preliminary report of that study was published (Mirsky et al., 1992). The number of subjects in that sample included 16 schizophrenic patients (as diagnosed by the Structural Clinical Interview for DSM-III-R (SCID)) (Spitzer et al., 1987); 30 relatives of schizophrenics; and 37 normal control subjects. (Since that publication, additional subjects have been tested – increasing the ns, respectively, to 23, 39 and 43. Some preliminary results of the analysis of the larger sample have been added to the text.) Most of the schizophrenic patients and a few of the other subjects were on some form of psycho-active medication(s) at the time of testing. No effort has been made to control for possible behavioral effects of the drugs in this report.

The Israeli–NIMH sample

The Israeli sample is a unique population of subjects that has been followed since 1966 when they were an average of 11 years of age. As originally constituted, the subject population consisted of two groups of 25 vulnerable or high-risk (index) subjects (at high risk because they had a parent with schizophrenia). Half of each group was raised by their own parents and half by professional child-care workers (*metapelet*) in the communal child-rearing setting of kibbutzim in Isra-el. Two groups of 25 matched control subjects were also studied, each chosen from the same classroom or kibbutz from which an index case was selected, but whose parents had no psychiatric diagnoses (Nagler, 1985; Nagler and Mirsky, 1985). The total sample, comprising four cells, was thus 100 persons. Prior work has shown that the index cases had lower scores on a number of attention tests than the controls and that the poorest scores were achieved by the kibbutz-index cases (Mirsky et al., 1985). This finding was probably related to the fact that, when examined at age 26, the largest number of schizophrenia spectrum ($n = 6$) and affective spectrum ($n = 9$) diagnoses were found among the 23 kibbutz-index cases. There was a total of 16 DSM-III-R diagnoses in the kibbutz-index cell as compared with 7 among the 23 cases in the parent-reared-index cell. This included 3 schizophrenia spectrum and 1 affective spectrum diagnoses. (A total of 4 diagnoses, including 1 affective spectrum and no schizophrenia spectrum cases, was seen in the combined group of 44 controls.) In the diagnostic follow-up conducted when the probands were in their early to mid-30s (discussed below), 14 additional affective spectrum cases were found, distributed throughout the four cells in the study (Ingraham et al., 1995).

The same battery of attention tests given to our Irish sample was administered to 63 of the Israeli subjects: 32 index cases ("relatives") and 31 controls. We augmented this sample by adding test scores of

31 additional control subjects from our NIMH population and, for purposes of comparison, the scores of a group of 17 schizophrenic patients that had been studied at NIMH. These patients were matched fairly closely to the relatives and the controls in terms of age and educational level. All subjects were administered the Schedule for Affective Disorders and Schizophrenia-Lifetime version (Spitzer and Endicott, 1978/1979) in either Hebrew (Israeli subjects) or English.

The Washington, D.C., sample

This group of subjects comprised 23 persons with schizophrenia, 21 first-degree relatives of persons with schizophrenia and 48 normal controls matched as closely as possible to the schizophrenic patients. All subjects were recruited from newspaper advertisements and notices in publications sponsored by patient support groups.

The majority were from the metropolitan Washington, D.C., area, although some were recruited from Philadelphia, Pennsylvania. All subjects were administered the Computerized Psychiatric Diagnosis–$_{TM}$(C-DIS) (Blouin, 1985), and the diagnosis of schizophrenia was confirmed in all cases. The same battery of attention tests given to the Irish subjects was given in the D.C. sample.

Hypotheses

In this work, we made use of the factor-analyzed tests described above. We also assessed the sensitivity of different versions of the CPT in the Irish and D.C. samples. Performance on this test has been shown consistently to be impaired in vulnerable persons (Cornblatt and Erlenmeyer-Kimling, 1985; Herman et al., 1977).

We predicted that the first-degree relatives would demonstrate attentional impairment, but to a lesser extent than the probands. Moreover, our hypothesis was that while performance on all tests might be impaired in the schizophrenic subjects, different tests might vary in their sensitivity to the disorder. We also wished to see whether we could confirm and extend the work of Stammeyer (1961), Wohlberg and Kornetsky (1973) and Nuechterlein (1983) indicating that versions of the CPT that require more effortful processing show increased sensitivity to the attentional dysfunction in schizophrenia.

Table 17.1. Demographic characteristics of the three subject samples

Sample	Group	n	Age [a]	Sex (Males/Females)	Educational Level [a]
Irish	Schizophrenics	16	45 (12.0)	10/6	10 (1.7)
	Relatives	30	47 (12.5)	16/14	10 (2.3)
	Controls	37	47 (13.3)	18/19	11 (2.5)
Israeli-NIMH	Schizophrenics [b]	17	29 (8.8)	8/9	14 (2.3)
	Relatives	32	32 (1.6)	14/18	14 (1.8)
	Controls [c]	62	32 (3.8)	24/38	15 (1.9)
D. C.	Schizophrenics	23	37 (8.9)	12/11	14 (2.2)
	Relatives	21	53 (17.5)	8/13	17 (2.1)
	Controls	48	39 (12.7)	21/27	16 (1.9)

[a] Standard deviation in parentheses.
[b] From NIMH.
[c] 31 Controls were from NIMH.

Demographic information

Descriptive information concerning the persons in the three samples of subjects is summarized in Table 17.1. There is a greater range in the age and educational level of the Irish cohort than the Israeli and D.C. cohorts, primarily because the Israeli subjects were selected to be about the same age (11) when the longitudinal study began. In contrast, the Irish subjects were chosen simply on the basis of being related to schizophrenic probands born after the year 1930 (Kendler et al., 1993), and the D.C. subjects on the basis of their response to advertisements.

Test procedures

All subjects were administered the battery of eight standard neuro-psychological tests of attention described above. In addition to the standard X and AX versions of the CPT, the Irish and D.C. samples were also administered a degraded version of the X task, similar to one described by Nuechterlein (1983). The choice of degraded stimulus parameters was such that normal controls could achieve a performance level of approximately 80% correct responses – in contrast with near-perfect scores on the standard X and AX tasks. An auditory version of the CPT X task was also administered to the subjects in the Irish and D.C. samples. The auditory task required a response to the highest tone of a random series of three tones differing in pitch (i.e., 640, 1,000 and 1,600 Hz). The auditory task was intended to be comparable in difficulty level to the visual task, although in these samples of control subjects it was, in fact, significantly more difficult than the visual X task but easier than the visual degraded X task.

Results

Comparisons within samples

The typical result found with all three samples is that the schizophrenic patients performed most poorly on the attention tests, the controls performed best, and the relatives, whether or not they had a psychiatric diagnosis, performed at an intermediate level. These results are summarized in Figure 17.2. The similarity in the pattern of results among the groups of subjects across the three samples is striking. In order to facilitate comparisons among the different elements in this figure, the mean standard or z score of the tests comprising a particular element is presented. Thus, the *encode* element is the mean of the z scores for the Arithmetic and Digit Span subtests (scaled scores). The *focus-execute* element is the mean z score for the Digit Symbol Substitution Test (scaled score), the Trail Making Test (mean of parts A and B), the Talland Letter Cancellation Test (mean of six scores) and/or the Stroop Test (mean score on the word, color and incongruous color/word tasks). (The Stroop Test was not administered to the Irish sample (see below) and the Talland Letter Cancellation Test not administered to the Israeli sample (see below)). The *sustain* element is the mean of the six z scores for the CPT X and AX tasks (percentage of correct responses, percent-

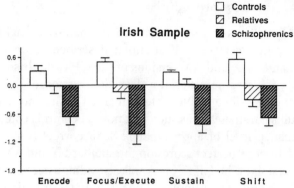
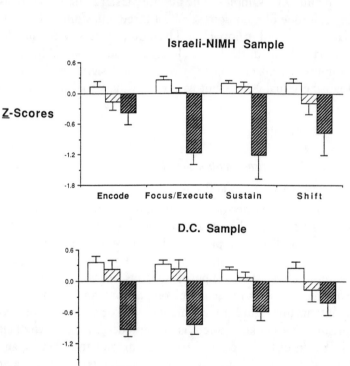

Figure 17.2. Mean *z* scores on the four attention elements for the controls, relatives and schizophrenics in the Irish sample (top), the Israeli-NIMH sample (middle) and the D.C. sample (bottom).

age of errors of commission and mean reaction time for each task). Finally, the *shift* element is the mean of the three standard scores derived from the Wisconsin Card Sorting Test (WCST) (number of categories attained, total errors and percentage of correct responses).

The decision to weight the test scores equally in computing the mean z score for each element was based on the fact that in several of the original principal component analyses from which the elements were derived (e.g., Table VII in Mirsky et al., 1991), there was little evidence to suggest much variability among the factor loadings. For example, for the *encode* element in the initial adult sample, the rotated factor loadings for the Digit Span and Arithmetic Tests were, respectively, .78 and .80. Similarly, for the *focus-execute* element, the rotated factor loadings for the Digit Symbol Substitution and Talland Letter Cancellation Tests were, respectively, .88 and .83. For the *shift* element, the rotated factor loadings for the number of correct responses and number of categories obtained on the WCST were, respectively, .92 and .93. We elected, therefore, not to weight the loadings differentially in the mean z-score computations. However, such a differential weighting might prove more appropriate in the derivation of mean z-scores for other subject samples.

Although not presented here, results virtually identical to those presented in Figure 17.2 for the Israeli-NIMH and D.C. samples were obtained when the analysis was restricted to the scores of only those relatives and controls who were free of any psychiatric diagnosis, as determined by either the SCID, SADS-L (Hebrew or English version) or C-DIS (Mirsky et al., 1992). (*Note:* A different result was seen subsequently in the Irish sample, based on the augmentation of the original cohort of 83 by the additional 22 cases. It was possible to divide the group of Irish relatives into two groups, one with and the other without a DSM-III-R diagnosis. Relatives with a diagnosis had scores similar to the group of schizophrenics; relatives without a diagnosis had scores similar to the combined group of controls. The controls with and without diagnoses did not differ on these tests (Mirsky et al., in press).)

Table 17.2 summarizes the p values for the main effect of diagnostic group obtained from the analysis of variance of each attention element depicted in Figure 17.2 for the total Irish, Israeli and D.C. cohorts. Overall, the best discrimination among groups is provided by the *focus-execute* and *sustain* elements, although all of the elements are quite discriminating for the Irish cohort.

Table 17.2. *Results of statistical analyses:*
Comparisons among groups
on attention elements

Sample	Element	p value
Irish	Encode Focus/Execute Sustain Shift	.0005 .0001 .0001 .0001
Israeli- NIMH	Encode Focus/Execute Sustain Shift	.08 .0001 .0001 .004
D.C.	Encode Focus/Execute Sustain Shift	.0001 .0001 .0001 .02

Additional statistical comparisons (not presented here), using co-variance analysis to control for the overall intellectual level of the Irish schizophrenic subjects, suggested that some of the component tests within the *sustain* and *focus-execute* elements provide better separation among groups than the element as a whole. Tests from these elements (i.e., some versions of the CPT, trail making, letter cancellation) may therefore provide useful clues in future work designed to look for genetic linkage in schizophrenia.

Contrasting CPT tasks – The Irish and D.C. samples

Figure 17.3 summarizes the mean percentage of correct responses for the three groups of subjects in the Irish and D.C. samples on the four versions of the CPT: the visual X, AX and degraded tasks, and the auditory X task. Figure 17.4 presents the percentage of errors of commission for the three groups on the four tasks. The general trend in results in the two samples is quite similar. The data suggest that increases in effortfulness of the CPT task (proceeding from X to AX, from AX to X degraded, and from a visual to an auditory task) tend to be associated with poorer performance, particularly among the schizophrenic subjects. The sharp increase in errors of commission

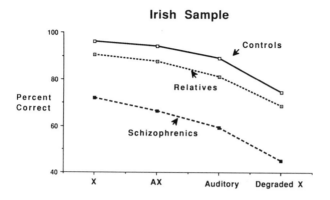

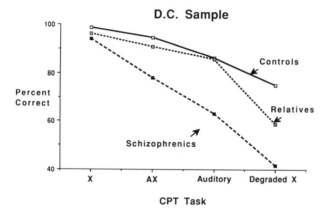

CPT Task

Figure 17.3. Mean percentage of correct responses for the three groups of Irish subjects (top) and the three groups of D.C. subjects (bottom) on four versions of the CPT. The scores for 1 of the 16 Irish schizophrenic patients and 4 of the 30 Irish relatives who could not perform the degraded X task are not included in the means. Scores for 6 of the Irish schizophrenics and 7 of the Irish relatives who could not perform the auditory task were also excluded from the means. All 37 Irish controls were able to perform the degraded X and auditory tasks.

(Figure 17.4) shown by the schizophrenics on the auditory task is especially marked.

Although the graph of percentage of correct responses (Figure 17.3) suggests that the degraded X task was the most difficult for the Irish schizophrenic patients, this was, in fact, not the case. Of the 16

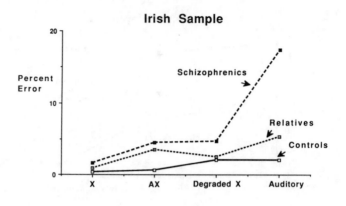

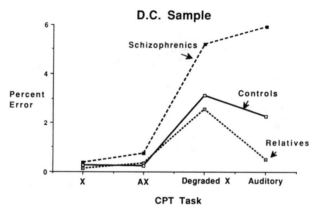

CPT Task

Figure 17.4. Mean percentage of commission errors for the three groups of Irish subjects (top) and the three groups of D.C. subjects (bottom) on four versions of the CPT. No scores were entered for the Irish schizophrenic patients and the Irish relatives who were unable to perform the degraded X or the auditory CPT tasks.

schizophrenics, 7 were unable to do the auditory CPT. Had their performance been counted as zero percent correct, the mean percentage correct for the auditory task in Figure 17.3 would have been much lower. Repeated measures analyses of variance performed on the data shown in Figures 17.3 and 17.4 revealed that for both samples there were highly significant ($p < .0001$) main effects of group and task for both measures. The interaction of group and task was statistically significant at $p < .0001$ for percentage correct for the

D.C. sample and at $p < .0001$ for percentage errors for the Irish sample.

The lower scores of the D.C. relatives than the controls, seen in Figure 17.4 (lower graph), are likely a chance occurrence. In general, there appeared to be a substantially lower level of impairment in the D.C. sample of schizophrenics and first-degree relatives than that seen in the Irish schizophrenic subjects and first-degree relatives. This is apparent in the scale of the Y-axis (i.e., percent error) of Figure 17.4, and is discussed below.

The results of these analyses thus support the view that some versions of the CPT (and in particular the auditory and degraded versions) may be more sensitive in discriminating among schizophrenics, their relatives and controls.

Comparisons among samples to cultural and socioeconomic factors

We are very much interested in the differences among samples. Thus, the standard scores presented in Figure 17.2 have concealed, to some extent, the fact that there was striking variation in the level of performance on some of the attention tests among the Israeli–NIMH, D.C. and Irish cohorts. The among-sample differences are illustrated by comparing the Y-axes for the Irish and D.C. samples in Figure 17.4: the range of errors is three times as large for the Irish as for the D.C. sample. The variability in performance levels among the cohorts is seen clearly in the raw scores, samples of which are presented in Figures 17.5–17.8. These indicate that although the gradient of performance was usually maintained across groups within a population (i.e., controls > relatives > schizophrenics), the absolute scores of the three populations could differ in a striking and statistically significant manner. Figures 17.5, 17.6, and 17.7 present, respectively, the mean scores on the Digit Symbol Substitution Test, the Trail Making Test and WCST for each group in the Israeli-NIMH, D.C. and Irish samples. The mean performance level of the D.C. and "Israeli" *schizophrenic* subjects on the Digit Symbol Substitution Test, the Trail Making Test and Wisconsin Card Sorting Test is about the same as that of the Irish *controls*.

More detailed analyses of these findings are presented elsewhere (Mirsky et al., in press; Mirsky et al., 1995). In general, however, the schizophrenic group differed from the control subjects across the three samples at high levels of statistical significance (usually at $p <$

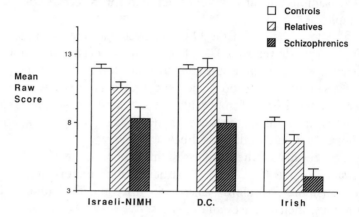

Figure 17.5. Mean (and standard error) of the raw (age-scaled) scores on the Digit Symbol Substitution Test for the three groups of subjects in the Israeli–NIMH, D.C. and Irish samples.

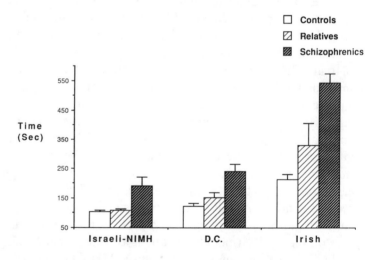

Figure 17.6. Mean (and standard error) of the raw time scores on the Trail Making Test (2 × score on Trails A + score on Trails B) for the three groups of subjects in the Israeli–NIMH, D.C. and Irish samples.

.01). There were few statistically significant differences between the Israeli first-degree relatives and the combined group of NIMH and Israeli controls; however (as noted above), the Irish first-degree relatives without diagnoses performed similarly to the controls, whereas

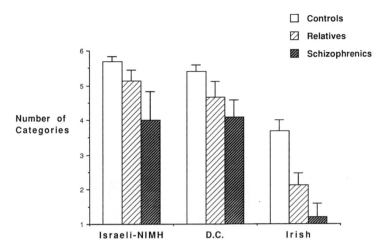

Figure 17.7. Mean (and standard error) for number of categories achieved on the Wisconsin Card Sorting Test for the three groups of subjects in the Israeli–NIMH, D.C. and Irish samples.

relatives with DSM-III-R diagnoses tended to perform like the schizophrenic patients. Most of the diagnoses in the relatives were affective disorder or alcohol dependence/abuse (Mirsky et al., in press).

The question arises as to how to interpret the low scores seen in the Irish sample and, in particular, the schizophrenic subjects. The poor scores of the Irish schizophrenic subjects may be a reflection of increased severity of the disorder in this population; other factors, for the Irish cohort as a whole, may be the age of the subjects or the relatively limited educational background of this rural sample. In the patients, age is confounded with years of identified illness; in the group of Irish schizophrenics, this period was in excess of 20 years. Age and educational level (and their interaction) seem the likely explanation for the differences among the respective groups of relatives and controls. However, age per se probably does not account for the poor scores of the Irish subjects, since there was no correlation of test scores and age in either the probands or the nondisordered controls (these data will be reported elsewhere). Duration of illness and its consequences (Chapman et al., 1976) and the relatively modest education of the subjects (leading to unfamiliarity with cognitive tasks and assessment procedures) cannot be ruled out as contributing to the low scores obtained by the Irish schizophrenics in this study. Education

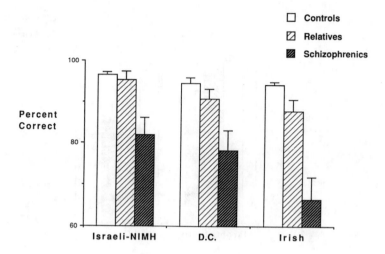

Figure 17.8. Mean (and standard error) of the percentage of correct responses on the CPT AX task for the three groups of subjects in the Israeli–NIHM, D.C. and Irish samples.

and related socioeconomic factors are thus probably responsible for the poorer performance of the nonpatient Irish groups.

Results such as these suggest caution in the interpretation of the absolute scores of these tests and remind us that the sociocultural and educational milieu from which test subjects are recruited may influence their scores. The low scores of these rural Irish subjects on the WCST are of particular interest, in view of the fact that by age 10, the majority of a group of U.S. schoolchildren are able to achieve six categories on this test (Chelune and Baer, 1986; Fey, 1951). These findings are reminiscent of the results obtained by Luria (as reported by Cole, 1990) in his studies during the 1930s of problem-solving behavior in members of rural populations in Central Asia. These subjects had great difficulty in solving the Russian cognitive puzzles brought to them by Luria.

In contrast to the findings in the Irish cohort with the WCST and other attention tests, the scores on the CPT (Figure 17.8) tend to be very similar for comparable subjects in the three samples. The performance of the control subjects, the relatives and the schizophrenic subjects was more similar between samples than it was within samples. This result suggests that tests such as the CPT may be more useful (or more robust) in cross-national or cross-socioeconomic investigations of schizophrenia (and possibly, other neuropsychiatric disorders) than measures that appear to be strongly influenced by the education, background and/or cultural milieu of the subjects.

Comment

We assessed attention in three independent samples of subjects, each of which comprised persons with schizophrenia, first-degree relatives of such persons and age- and education-matched control subjects. We found deficits in attention in the schizophrenic subjects, as compared with the respective control groups; such deficits were also present in the first-degree relatives of schizophrenics, but to a lesser extent. In the Irish sample, the relatives and schizophrenic subjects were from the same families; this was not the case in the Israeli–NIMH or D.C. samples. Nevertheless, the same general pattern of results was found. Although the deficit seen in the first-degree relatives in the D.C. and Israeli samples was not affected appreciably by the presence of a diagnosis, this was not the case in the Irish sample. In contrast, in those Irish relatives with diagnoses, the deficit tended to be exacerbated.

Other investigations, although primarily of the *offspring* of schizophrenics, have shown poorer attention in the first-degree relatives of schizophrenic probands (reviewed in Mirsky et al., 1992). Data recently reported by Steinhauer et al. (1991) on the siblings of schizophrenics seem to support our finding as well.

These data and those of Steinhauer et al. (1991) may be unique in that the first-degree relatives were of approximately the same age and educational level as the schizophrenic probands. In the present study, this was true of the Irish and Israeli–NIMH samples. In both Steinhauer's sample and our samples, the probands were closely matched to the controls.

Our data support the view that the attention elements we have identified as *focus-execute* and *sustain* are more powerful discriminators of impaired attention in schizophrenia than are *encode* or *shift*.

Figure 17.1 depicts the attention support system in the brain (Mirsky et al., 1991). Of particular relevance to this discussion are the proposed cerebral support mechanisms underlying the *focus-execute* and *sustain* elements. We have reviewed evidence (Mirsky et al., 1991) that the *focus-execute* element of attention is supported by cerebral structures in the superior temporal and parietal cortical regions, as well as the basal ganglia. In contrast, the *sustain* element is supported, according to that analysis, by portions of the midline thalamus and upper brain stem reticular formation. The possible implication of the present findings is that the brain regions supporting these attentional elements may be involved in the pathophysiology of schizophrenia. The findings of Shenton and numerous others (reviewed in Shenton, Chapter 4, this volume) implicate damage in the superior temporal gyrus in patients with schizophrenia. The results of three recent studies (Erwin et al., 1991; Harell et al., 1986; Karson et al., 1991) point to the possible role of damage to regions of the midline thalamus and reticular formation of the brain stem, as well, in the pathophysiology of schizophrenia.

Our D.C. and Irish sample data confirm earlier findings that the performance of schizophrenic patients relative to control subjects becomes more impaired as the effortfulness of the task is increased (Stammeyer, 1961; Wohlberg and Kornetsky, 1973). The visual AX task, slightly more difficult than the visual X for the control subjects and relatives, appeared to be substantially more difficult for the schizophrenics; this was also true for the degraded visual and auditory CPT tasks. The four versions of the CPT may be ranked in terms of effortfulness as follows: visual X, visual AX, visual degraded X and auditory tasks. This would apply to the Irish sample and, to a more limited extent, the D.C. sample.

The enhanced deficit seen in the schizophrenics on the auditory task is supported by other recent findings. Duncan (1988, 1990; Duncan et al., 1987) has reported lower amplitude of the *auditory* P300 component (an endogenous component of the event-related brain potential that indexes attention) in schizophrenic patients as compared with controls; in contrast, the *visual* P300 component differs much less between patients and controls. In Chapter 4 of this volume Shenton presents evidence that the auditory P300 reduction may be most clearly seen in the left temporal lobe region.

A possibly related finding is that of Mussgay and Hertwig (1990), who reported that schizophrenic patients perform more poorly on auditory than on visual versions of the CPT. Additional studies are clearly needed to confirm these findings in schizophrenic patients and to help us understand them.

Nevertheless, we may speculate that the pathophysiological sources of this auditory information processing deficit are related in part to the peculiar vulnerability of the inferior colliculus, a major component of the brain stem auditory processing system. As described by

Kety (1962) in a classic study, the inferior colliculus has the highest metabolic requirement of any portion of the brain and is therefore especially vulnerable to asphyxic insult (Reivich et al., 1969). Such insult has long been known to accompany prolonged and difficult labor – frequently noted in the perinatal period of life in persons who later develop schizophrenia (Mednick, 1970; Mednick et al., 1989). The work of Ranck and Windle with a guinea pig model (Ranck and Windle, 1959; Windle et al., 1944) and the later work of Myers (1969, 1971) with a monkey model emphasized the potentially devastating effect of an asphyxic insult on the integrity of the inferior colliculus at the time of full term. Myers also showed that asphyxia occurring in midpregnancy could be the cause of damage to the inferior colliculus. Therefore, the fact of a normal delivery does not preclude the possibility that injury to the fetal inferior colliculus may have occurred earlier in gestation.

Also of considerable interest is the fact that an additional, extremely vulnerable target of perinatal asphyxia is the superior olive, another brain stem structure important for auditory information processing (Mirsky et al., 1979; Yakovlev and Lecours, 1967). Therefore, a mechanism exists that could account for early injury to brain stem auditory structures in schizophrenic persons; this mechanism could contribute to impaired auditory information processing in this disorder. There have also been reports of delayed or altered brain stem auditory evoked responses in schizophrenia (Buchsbaum et al., 1984; Pfefferbaum et al., 1980), a finding that supports the view of impaired auditory processing in such patients.

To this series of reports of auditory dysfunction should be added the recent findings of Shenton and co-workers (as discussed above), pointing to abnormalities in the left superior temporal gyrus and related structures in schizophrenics. This cortical region is part of a system with major responsibility for the processing of auditory-verbal information (Shenton, Chapter 4, this volume). These findings dovetail well with our findings of impaired auditory attention in schizophrenics; together they underline the potential importance of auditory dysfunction in understanding the pathophysiology of the disorder.

IX. Conclusion

The present study has provided some clues from the study of attentional behavior that may be useful in future genetic linkage studies in schizophrenia. Impairment in certain elements of attention may be markers of *vulnerability* to schizophrenia (i.e., these deficits are found in persons from families of patients with schizophrenia) as well as being features of the disorder itself. Therefore, these deficits in attention are candidates for trait markers of schizophrenia and are presumably inherited along with other parts of the schizophrenic diathesis. We cannot exclude entirely the possibility that these deficits in attention, seen in the relatives, are due to a common environment shared with the schizophrenic persons. Such influence seems to be relatively weaker than the genetic influence, however, as illustrated in studies of twins reared apart (Gottesman, 1991) and adopted-away offspring of schizophrenic persons (Kety, 1988; Kety et al., 1968; Rosenthal et al., 1971). The inference that attentional skills are inherited traits receives other support from research with nonclinical populations (Kendler et al., 1991).

The assessment of discrete aspects or elements of attention may thus prove to be a powerful tool in concurrent study of behavioral and genetic factors in schizophrenia.

Acknowledgments

Thanks are due to the many persons who contributed inspiration, ideas, data and effort to this work, including Connie C. Duncan, Marie Elliott, Bryan J. Fantie, Teresa Hebron, Barbara P. Jones, Kenneth S. Kendler, Mary H. Kosmidis, Sol Kugelmass, Janet E. Tatman, and Susan L. Yardley.

References

Adey, W. R. (1969) Spectral analysis of EEG data from animals and man during alerting, orienting and discriminative responses. In *Attention and Neurophysiology: An International Conference* (ed. C. R. Evans, and T. B. Mulholland), pp. 194–229. London: Butterworth.

Ajmone Marsan, C. (1965) The thalamus. Data on its functional anatomy and on some aspects of the thalamo-cortical integration. *Archives Italiennes de Biologie 103*, 847–882.

Bakay Pragay, E., Mirsky, A. F., and Abplanalp, J. M. (1969) The effects of chlorpromazine and secobarbital on matching from sample and discrimination tasks in monkeys. *Psychopharmacologia 7*, 128–138.

Bakay Pragay, E., Mirsky, A. F., Fullerton, B. C., Oshima, H. I., and Arnold, S. W. (1975) Effect of electrical stimulation of the brain on visually controlled (attentive) behavior in the *Macaca mulatta*. *Experimental Neurology 49*, 203–220.

Bakay Pragay, E., Mirsky, A. F., Ray, C. L., Turner, D. F., and Mirsky, C. V.

(1978) Neuronal activity in the brain stem reticular formation during performance of a "go-no go" visual attention task in the monkey. *Experimental Neurology 60.*

Bakay Pragay, E., Mirsky, A. F., and Nakamura, R. K. (1987) Attention-related unit activity in the frontal association cortex during a go/no-go visual discrimination task. *Experimental Neurology 96*, 481–500.

Bakay Pragay, E., Mirsky, A. F., and Nakamura, F. K. (1988) Attention-related activity in the inferior-parietal and prestriate cortex of the monkey during a go/no-go visual discrimination task. Unpublished manuscript.

Battig, K., Rosvold, H. E., and Mishkin, M. (1960) comparison of the effects of frontal and caudate lesions on delayed response and alternation in monkeys. *Journal of Comparative & Physiological Psychology 53*, 400–404.

Blakemore, C., Iversen, S. D., and Zangwill, O. L. (1972) Brain functions. *Annual Review of Psychology 23.*

Blouin, A. (1985) Computerized Psychiatric Diagnosis. (Based on NIMH Diagnostic Interview Schedule developed by Robbins, L. and Helzer, J.) Department of Psychiatry, Ottawa Civic Hospital. Ontario.

Buchsbaum, M. S., Mirsky, A. F., DeLisi, L. E., Morihisa, J., Karson, C. N., Mendelson, W. B., King, A. C., Johnson, J., and Kessler, R. (1984) The Genain quadruplets: Electrophysiological, positron emission, and X-Ray tomographic studies. *Psychiatry Research 13*, 95–108.

Callaway, E., and Naghdi, S. (1982) An information processing model for schizophrenia. *Archives of General Psychiatry 39*, 339–347.

Chapman, L. J., Chapman, J. P., and Raulin, M. L. (1976) Scales for physical and social anhedonia. *Journal of Abnormal Psychology 85*, 374–382.

Chelune, G. J., and Baer, R. A. (1986) Developmental norms for the Wisconsin Card Sorting Test. *Journal of Clinical and Experimental Neuropsychology 8*, 219–228.

Cole, M. (1990) Alexandr Romanovich Luria: Cultural psychologist. In *Contemporary Neuropsychology and the Legacy of Luria* (ed. E. Goldberg), pp. 11–28. Hillsdale, NJ: Erlbaum.

Corcoran, R., and Upton, D. (1993) A role for the hippocampus in card sorting? *Cortex 29*, 293–304.

Cornblatt, B., and Erlenmeyer-Kimling, L. (1985) Global attentional deviance as a marker of risk for schizophrenia: Specificity and predictive validity. *Journal of Abnormal Psychology 4*, 470–486.

Duncan, C. C. (1988) Event-related brain potentials: A window on information processing in schizophrenia. *Schizophrenia Bulletin 14*, 199–203.

Duncan, C. C. (1990) Current issues in the application of P300 to research on schizophrenia. In *Schizophrenia: Concepts, Vulnerability, and Intervention* (ed. E. R. Straube and K. Hahlweg), pp. 117–134. New York: Springer-Verlag.

Duncan, C. C., Perlstein, W. M., and Morihisa, J. M. (1987) The P300 metric in schizophrenia: Effects of probability and modality. In *Current Trends in Event-related Potential Research* (EEG Supplement 40) (ed. R. Johnson, Jr., J. W. Rohrbaugh, and R. Parasuraman), pp. 670–674. Amsterdam: Elsevier.

Erwin, R. J., Mawhinney-Hee, M., Gur, R. C., and Gur, R. E. (1991) Midlatency auditory evoked responses in schizophrenia. *Biological Psychiatry 30*, 430–442.

Fey, E. T. (1951) The performance of young schizophrenics and young normals on the Wisconsin Card Sorting Test. *Journal of Consulting Psychology 15*, 311–319.

Frith, C. D. (1979) Consciousness, information processing and schizophrenia. *British Journal of Psychiatry 134*, 225–235.

Fuster, J. M., and Uyeda, A. (1962) Facilitation of tachistoscopic performance by stimulation of midbrain tegmental points in the monkey. *Experimental Neurology 6*, 384–406.

Gottesman, I. I. (1990). *Schizophrenia Genesis*. New York: Freeman.

Grant, D. A., and Berg, E. A. (1948) A behavioral analysis of degree of reinforcement and ease of shifting two new responses in a Weigl-type card sorting problem. *Journal of Experimental Psychology 38*, 404–411.

Greenblatt, R. M. (1986) The effects of brain stem compression on attention and memory (doctoral dissertation, City University of New York, 1986). *Dissertation Abstracts International 47*, 1301B.

Harell, M., Englender, M., Demer, M., Kinhi, R., and Zohar, M. (1986). Auditory brain stem responses in schizophrenic patients. *Laryngoscope 96*, 908–910.

Healton, E. B., Navarro, C., Bressman, S., and Brust, J.C.M. (1982) Subcortical neglect. *Neurology 32*, 776–778.

Heilman, R. M., Watson, R. T., Valenstein, E., and Damasio, A. R. (1983) Location of lesions in neglect. In *Localization in Neuropsychology* (ed. A. Kertez), pp. 319–331. New York: Academic Press.

Hermann, B. P., and Wyler, A. R. (1988) Neuropsychological outcome of anterior temporal lobectomy. *Journal of Epilepsy 1*, 35–45.

Herman, J., Mirsky, A. F., Ricks, N., and Gallant, D. (1977) Behavioral and electrographic measures of attention in children at risk for schizophrenia. *Journal of Abnormal Psychology 86*, 27–33.

Hoch, A. (1896, January) Kraepelin on psychological experimentation in psychiatry. *American Journal of Insanity*, 1–10.

Ingraham, L. J., Kugelmass, S., Frenkel, E., Nathan, M., and Mirsky, A. F. (1995) Twenty-five-year followup of the Israeli high risk study: Current and lifetime psychopathology. *Schizophrenia Bulletin 21*, 183–192.

Jasper, H. H. (1958) Recent advances in our understanding of ascending activities of the reticular system. In *Reticular Formation of the Brain* (ed. H. H. Jasper), pp. 319–331. Boston: Little, Brown.

Jones, E. G., and Peters, A. E. (Eds.) (1986) *Cerebral Cortex: Sensory-Motor Areas and Aspects of Cortical Connectivity.* New York: Plenum.

Kahnemann, D. (1973) *Attention and Effort.* Englewood Cliffs, NJ: Prentice-Hall.

Karson, C. N., Garcia-Rill, E., Griffin, W. S., Mrak, R., Husain, M., and Casanova, M. (1991) The brainstem reticular formation in schizophrenia. *Biological Psychiatry 29,* 90A.

Kendler, K. S., Ochs, A. L., Gorman, A. M., Hewitt, J. K., Ross, D. E., and Mirsky, A. F. (1991) The structure of schizotypy: A pilot multitrait twin study. *Psychiatry Research 36,* 19–36.

Kendler, K. S., McGuire, M., Gruenberg, A. M., O'Hare, A., Spellman, M., Walsh, D. (1993) The Roscommon Family Study: 1. Methods, diagnosis of probands and risk of schizophrenia in relatives. *Archives of General Psychiatry 50,* 527–540.

Kety, S. S. (1962) Regional neurochemistry and its application to brain function. In *Frontiers in Brain Research* (ed. J. D. French), pp. 97–120. New York: Columbia University Press.

Kety, S. S. (1988) Schizophrenic illness in the families of schizophrenic adoptees: Findings from the Danish National Sample. *Schizophrenia Bulletin 14,* 217–222.

Kety, S. S., Rosenthal, D., Wender, P. H., and Schulsinger, F. (1968) The types and prevalence of mental illness in the biological and adoptive families of adopted schizophrenics. In *The Transmission of Schizophrenia* (ed. D. Rosenthal and S. S. Kety), pp. 345–362. Oxford: Pergamon Press.

Kraepelin, E. (1919) *Dementia praecox and paraphrenia* (trans. R. M. Barclay). New York: Robert E. Krieger.

Kremen, W. S., Seidman, L. J., Faraone, S. V., Pepple, J. R., and Tsuang, M. T. (1992) Attention/information-processing factors in psychotic disorders: Replication and extension of recent neuropsychological findings. *Journal of Nervous and Mental Disease 180,* 89–93.

Lansdell, H., and Mirsky, A. F. (1964) Attention in focal and centrencephalic epilepsy. *Experimental Neurology 9.*

Lindsley, D. B. (1960) Attention, consciousness, sleep and wakefulness. In *Handbook of Psychology* (ed. J. Field, H. W. Magoun, and V. E. Hall), pp. 1553–1593. Washington, DC: American Psychological Society.

Lindsley, D. B., Bowden, J. W., and Magoun, H. W. (1949) Effect upon the EEG of acute injury to the brain stem activating system. *Electroencephalography and Clinical Neurophysiology 1,* 475–486.

Mackworth, N. H. (1950) Researches on the measurement of human performance. Medical Research Council Special Report (No. 268). London: HMSO.

MacLean, P. D. (1990) *The Triune Brain in Evolution: Role in Paleocerebral Functions.* New York: Plenum Press.

Mednick, S. A. (1970) Breakdown in individuals at high risk for schizophrenia: Possible predispositional factors. *Mental Hygiene 54,* 50.

Mednick, S. A., Machon, R. A., and Huttunen, M. O. (1989) Disturbances of fetal neural development and adult schizophrenia. In *Schizophrenia: Scientific Progress* (ed. S. C. Schulz and C. A. Tamminga), pp. 69–77. New York: Oxford University Press.

Mesulam, M. M. (1987) Attention, confusional states and neglect. In *Principles of Behavioral Neurology* (ed. M. M. Mesulam), pp. 125–168. Philadelphia: Davis.

Milner, B. (1963) Effects of different brain lesions on card sorting. *Archives of Neurology 9.*

Mirsky, A. F. (1988) Behavioral and psychophysiological effects of petit mal epilepsy in the light of a neuropsychologically based theory of attention. In *Elements of Petit Mal Epilepsy* (ed. M. S. Myslobodsky and A. F. Mirsky), pp. 311–340. New York: Peter Lang.

Mirsky, A. F. (1989) The neuropsychology of attention. Elements of a complex behavior. In *Integrating Theory and Practice in Clinical Psychology* (ed. E. Perecman), pp. 75–91. Hillsdale, NJ: Erlbaum.

Mirsky, A. F., and Duncan, C. C. (1986) Etiology and expression of schizophrenia: Neurobiological and psychosocial factors. *Annual Review of Psychology 37,* 291–319.

Mirsky, A. F., and Duncan, C. C. (1987) An introduction to modern techniques of clinical neuropsychology. *Research Paradigms in Psychosomatic Medicine* (ed. G. A. Fava and T. N. Wise), pp. 167–184. Basel: Karger.

Mirsky, A. F., and Rosvold, H. E. (1990) The case of Carolyn Wilson – a thirty-eight year followup of a schizophrenic patient with two prefrontal lobotomies. In *Contemporary Neuropsychology and the Legacy of Luria* (ed. E. Goldberg), pp. 51–75. Hillsdale, NJ: Erlbaum.

Mirsky, A. F., Bakay Pragay, E., and Harris, S. (1977) Evoked potential correlates of stimulation-induced impairment of attention in Macaca mulatta. *Experimental Neurology 57.*

Mirsky, A. F., Orren, M. M., Stanton, L., Fullerton, B. C., and Harris, S. (1979) Auditory evoked potentials and auditory behavior following prenatal and perinatal asphyxia in rhesus monkeys. *Developmental Psychobiology 12,* 369–379.

Mirsky, A. F., Silberman, E. K., Latz, A., and Nagler, S. (1985) Adult outcomes of high-risk children: Differential effects of town and kibbutz rearing. *Schizophrenia Bulletin 11,* 150–154.

Mirsky, A. F., Anthony, B. J., Duncan, C. C., Ahearn, M. B., and Kellam, S. G. (1991) Analysis of the elements of attention: A neuropsychological approach. *Neuropsychology Review 2*, 109–145.

Mirsky, A. F., and Van Buren, J. M. (1965) On the nature of the "absence" in centrencephalic epilepsy: A study of some behavioral, electroencephalic and autonomic factors. *Electroencephalography and Clinical Neurophysiology 18*, 334–348.

Mirsky, A. F., and Oshima, H. I. (1973) Effect of subcortical aluminum cream lesions in attentive behavior and the electroencephalogram in monkeys. *Experimental Neurology 39*, 1–18.

Mirsky, A. F., Lochhead, S. J., Jones, B. P., Kugelmass, S., Walsh, D., and Kendler, K. S. (1992) On familial factors in the attentional deficit in schizophrenia: A review and report of two new subject samples. *Journal of Psychiatric Research 26*, no. 4, 383–403.

Mirsky, A. F., Ingraham, L. J., and Kugelmass, S. (1995) Neuropsychological assessment of attention and its pathology in the Israeli cohort. *Schizophrenia Bulletin 21*, 193–204.

Mirsky, A. F., Yardley, S. L., Jones, B. P., Walsh, D., and Kendler, K. S. (In press) Analysis of the attention deficit in schizophrenia – a study of patients and their relatives in Ireland.

Mishkin, M. (1978) Memory in monkeys severely impaired by combined but not separate removal of the amygdala and hippocampus. *Nature 273*.

Moruzzi, G., and Magoun, H. W. (1949) Brain stem reticular formation and activation of the EEG. *Electroencephalography and Clinical Neurophysiology 1*.

Mussgay, L., and Hertwig, R. (1990) Signal detection indices in schizophrenics on a visual, auditory, and bimodal continuous performance test. *Schizophrenia Research 3*, 303–310.

Myers, R. E. (1969) The clinical and pathological effects of asphyxiation in the fetal rhesus monkey. In *Diagnosis and Treatment of Fetal Disorders* (ed. K. Adamsons), pp. 226–249. New York: Springer-Verlag.

Myers, R. E. (1971) Brain damage induced by umbilical cord compression at different gestational ages in monkeys. In *Second Conference on Experimental Medicine and Surgery in Primates* (ed. E. I. Goldsmith and J. Moor-Jankowski), pp. 394–425. New York: S. Karger.

Nagler, S. (1985) Overall design and methodology of the Israeli high-risk study. *Schizophrenia Bulletin 11*, 31–37.

Nagler, S., and Mirsky, A. F. (1985) Introduction: The Israeli High-Risk Study. *Schizophrenia Bulletin 11*, 19–29.

Nuechterlein, K. H. (1983) Signal detection in vigilance tasks and behavioral attributes among offspring of schizophrenic mothers and among hyperactive children. *Journal of Abnormal Psychology 92*, 4–28.

Nuechterlein, K. H., and Dawson, M. E. (1984) Information processing and attentional function in the developmental course of schizophrenic disorders. *Schizophrenia Bulletin 10*, 160–203.

Nuechterlein, K. H., Parasuraman, R., and Qiyuan, J. (1983) Visual sustained attention: Image degradation produces rapid sensitivity decrement over time. *Science 220*, 327–329.

Pandya, D. N., and Yeterian, E. H. (1985) Architecture and connection of cortical association areas. In *Cerebral Cortex: Association and Auditory Cortices: Vol. 4* (ed. A. Peters and E. G. Jones), pp. 3–61. New York: Plenum.

Parasuraman, R., and Davies, D. R. (1984) *Varieties of Attention.* Orlando, FL: Academic Press.

Penfield, W., and Jasper, H. H. (1954) *Epilepsy and the Functional Anatomy of the Human Brain.* Boston: Little, Brown.

Pfefferbaum, A., Horvath, T. B., Roth, W. T., Tinklenberg, J. R., and Kopell, B. S. (1980) Auditory brain stem and cortical evoked potentials in schizophrenia. *Biological Psychiatry 15*, 209–223.

Posner, M. I. (1978) *Chronometric Explorations of Mind.* Hillsdale, NJ: Erlbaum.

Posner, M. I., and Petersen, S. E. (1990) The attention system of the human brain. *Annual Review of Neuroscience 13*, 25–42.

Pribram, K. H., and McGuiness, D. (1975) Arousal, activation, and effort in the control of attention. *Psychological Review 2*.

Ranck, J. B., and Windle, W. F. (1959) Brain damage in the monkey, macaca mulatta by asphyxia neonatorum. *Experimental Neurology 1*, 130–154.

Ray, C. L., Mirsky, A. F., and Bakay Pragay, E. (1982) Functional analysis of attention-related unit activity in the reticular formation of the monkey. *Experimental Neurology 77*, 544–562.

Reitan, R. M., and Davidson, L. A. (1974) *Clinical Neuropsychology: Current Status and Applications.* Washington, DC: V. H. Winston and Sons.

Reivich, M. O., Jehle, J., and Sokoloff, L. (1969) Measurement of regional cerebral blood flow with antipyrine-14C in awake cats. *Journal of Applied Physiology 27*, 296–300.

Rosenthal, D., Wender, P. H., Kety, S. S., Welner, J., and Schulsinger, F. (1971) The adopted-away offspring of schizophrenics. *American Journal of Psychiatry 128*, 307–311.

Rosvold, H. E., Mirsky, A. F., Sarason, I., Bransome, E. D., Jr., and Beck, L. H. (1956) A continuous performance test of brain damage. *Journal of Consulting Psychology 20*, 343–350.

Roth, B. E., Connell, R. E., Faught, R. E., and Adams, B. (1988) Attention deficits in patients with complex partial seizures. *Epilepsia 29*, 693.

Scheibel, A. B. (1980) Anatomical and physiological substrates of arousal: A view from the bridge. In *The Reticular Formation Revisited* (ed. J. A. Hobson, and M.A.B. Brazier), pp. 55–60. New York: Raven Press.

Scoville, W. B., and Milner, B. (1957) Loss of recent memory after bilateral hippocampal lesions. *Journal of Neurology, Neurosurgery and Psychiatry* 20, 11–21.

Shakow, D. (1936) Mental set in schizophrenia studied in a discrimination reaction setting. *Psychological Bulletin 33*, 795–796.

Shakow, D. (1979) *Adaptation in Schizophrenia: The Theory of Segmental Set.* New York: Wiley.

Shiffrin, R. M. (1988) Attention. In *Stevens' Handbook of Experimental Psychology*, 2nd ed. (ed. R. C. Atkinson, R. J. Herrnstein, G. Lindzey, and R. D. Luce), pp. 739–812. New York: Wiley.

Shiffrin, R. M., and Schneider, W. (1977) Controlled and automatic human information processing. II: Perceptual learning, automatic attending, and a general theory. *Psychological Review 84*, 127–190.

Spitzer, R. L., and Endicott, J. (1978/1979) Schedule for Affective Disorders and Schizophrenia-Lifetime Version (SADS-L). New York: New York State Psychiatric Institute.

Spitzer, R. L., Williams, J. B., and Gibbon, J. (1987) Structured Clinical Interview for DSM-III-R Patient Version (SCID-P, 4/1/87). New York: New York State Psychiatric Institute.

Stammeyer, E. C. (1961) The effects of distraction on performance in schizophrenic, psychoneurotic, and normal individuals. Doctoral dissertation. Catholic University, Washington, D.C.

Steinhauer, S. R., Zubin, J., Condray, R., Shaw, D. B., Peters, J. L., and Van Kammen, D. P. (1991) Electrophysiological and behavioral signs of attentional disturbance in schizophrenics and their siblings. In *Advances in Neuropsychiatry and Psychopharmacology. Volume 1* (ed. C. A. Tamminga and C. Schultz), pp. 169–178. New York: Raven Press.

Streissguth, A. P., Sampson, P. D., Carmichael Olson, H., Bookstein, F. L., Barr, H. M., Scott, M., Feldman, J., & Mirsky, A. F. (1994) Maternal drinking during pregnancy: Attention and short-term memory in 14-year-old offspring – A longitudinal prospective study. *Alcoholism: Clinical and Experimental Research 18*, 202–218.

Stroop, J. R. (1935) Studies of interference in serial verbal reactions. *Journal of Experimental Psychology 18*, 643–662.

Talland, G. A. (1965) *Deranged memory.* Academic Press, New York.

Tatman, J. E. (1992) Elements of attention and concentration in normal aging adults: Locus of decline. Master's thesis, The American University, Washington, D.C.

Wechsler, D. (1981) *Wechsler Adult Intelligence Scale-Revised.* Psychological Corporation, New York.

Weinberger, D. R., Berman, K. F., and Zec, R. F. (1986) Physiological dysfunction of dorsolateral prefrontal cortex in schizophrenia. 1: Regional cerebral blood flow (rCBF) evidence. *Archives of General Psychiatry 43*, 114–125.

Windle, W. F., Becker, R. F., and Weil, A. (1944) Alterations in brain structure after asphyxiation at birth. An experimental study in the guinea pig. *Journal of Neuropathology and Experimental Neurology 3*, 224–228.

Wohlberg, G. W., and Kornetsky, C. (1973) Sustained attention in remitted schizophrenics. *Archives of General Psychiatry 28*, 533–537.

Yakovlev, P. I., and Lecours, A.-R. (1967) The myelogenetic cycles of regional maturation of the brain. In *Regional Development of the Brain in Early Life* (ed. A. Minkowski), pp. 3–70. Oxford: Blackwell Scientific Publications.

Yingling, C. D., and Skinner, J. E. (1975) Regulation of unit activity in nucleus reticularis thalami by the mesencephalic reticular formation and the frontal granular cortex. *Electroencephalography and Clinical Neurophysiology 39*, 635–642.

Zubin, J. (1975) Problem of attention in schizophrenia. In *Experimental Approaches to Psychopathology* (ed. M. L. Keitzman, S. Sutton, and J. Zubin), pp. 139–166. New York: Academic Press.

Zubin, J., and Spring, B. (1977) Vulnerability: A new view of schizophrenia. *Journal of Abnormal Psychology 86*, 103–126.

18

Parsing cognitive processes: Psychopathological and neurophysiological constraints

Anne Sereno

The concept of attention is most intriguing since, at first glance, it appears impossible to study. Somehow it seems more feasible to examine and determine the basic structure of perceptual or mnemonic processes – establishing parameters such as perceptual thresholds and memory capacities. It is unsettling to learn that a slight attentional change, for example in the instructions of a task, can radically change these so-called parameters of the system. That is, telling a subject *where* a target is likely to appear, or *what* target is likely to appear, might determine whether or not the subject will be able to detect, discriminate, or even remember the target.*

The relation between attention and eye movements

The relation between eye movements and attention has been discussed for over a century, but usually in the context of *dissociating* attention from eye movements. In 1890, William James in *The Principles of Psychology* noted that "we may attend to an object on the periphery of the visual field and yet not accommodate the eye for it" (p. 413). He further elaborated by referring to Helmholtz, who, according to James, "states the fact so strikingly that I will quote his observations in full" (p. 414). The quote from Helmholtz begins with the description of an experiment, and concludes,

then, our attention is quite independent of the position and accommodation of the eyes, and of any known alteration in these organs, and free to direct itself by a conscious and voluntary effort upon any selected portion of a dark and undifferenced field of view. This is one of the most important observa-

* See glossary at end of this chapter for definitions of technical terms – Eds.

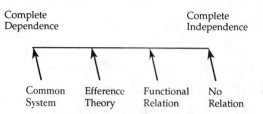

Figure 18.1. Logical relationships between overt and covert orienting of attention (adapted from Posner, 1980).

tions for a future theory of attention. (Helmholtz, *Physiologische Optik*, quoted in *The Principles of Psychology*, p. 414)

James, however, also commented that

no object, lying in the marginal portions of the field of vision can catch our attention without at the same time 'catching our eye' – that is, fatally provoking such movements of rotation and accommodation as will focus its image on the fovea, or point of greatest sensibility. Practice, however, enables us, *with effort*, to attend to a marginal object whilst keeping the eye immovable. (p. 413)

This striking ability to allocate attention to different parts of the visual field while maintaining fixation has dominated the theories of researchers interested in the relation between attentional movements and eye movements. Posner (1980) outlined four possible relations between eye movements and attention ranging from complete dependence to complete independence (see Figure 18.1). He argued that the attention and eye movement systems cannot be one and the same because attention can be shifted with the eyes fixed. A less restrictive view of the relation between eye movements and attention has been labeled *efference theory* (Posner, 1980) or *oculomotor readiness theory* (Klein, 1980). This view proposes that attentional shifts are eye movement programmings. Posner (1980) and Klein (1980) argued against this view, contending that there seemed to be no relation between shifts of attention and a readiness to move the eyes. Neither Posner nor Klein proposed, however, that eye movements are unrelated to attention. Posner (1980) concluded that the relation is a functional one. That is, attention and eye movements are both summoned by important peripheral events and thus have a close functional relationship but no intrinsic physiological relationship.

Much of the research examining the relation between attention and eye movements in the past few decades has emphasized the *differences* between these two forms of orienting; nevertheless, this same research also documents a close relation between the two systems. Many studies have reported a facilitation in processing for items in a location to which a saccade is about to be made (Bryden, 1961; Crovitz & Daves, 1962; Jonides, 1976; Rayner et al., 1978). Rayner et al. (1978) presented subjects with two stimuli (one on each side of the fixation point). One of the stimuli was a word and the other a random letter string. Subjects were instructed to look to the left or right stimulus on a given block of trials. During the eye movement, the extrafoveal random letter string was replaced on the screen so that the target word was the same in both locations. Subjects were unaware of any change in the display and were instructed to name the word that was the target of their eye movement as quickly as possible. Rayner et al. found that an extrafoveal preview of a word in the location to which the eyes were about to move facilitated naming latency over having an incorrect preview, whereas a preview in a location opposite to that in which the eyes were about to move provided no facilitation in naming latency. The Rayner et al. (1978) results suggest that, prior to the eye movement, useful information is acquired from the position to which the eyes are about to move. In addition, the results indicate that little information is acquired from an extrafoveal location which is in the opposite direction from that in which the eyes are about to move. The most common explanation for these findings is that there is a covert shift of attention (to the target location) that precedes this next eye movement.

Although many findings seem to suggest a consistent relation between an attentional shift and an eye movement, there are several studies that show either mixed or negative results. Using a threshold detection task, Remington (1980) performed a series of experiments examining the relation between eye movements and attention. Subjects were instructed to make an eye movement to a target presented 10° randomly to the left or to the right of fixation. Following the presentation of the target (but in some cases before the eye movement), a 3 msec probe stimulus was presented in one of four possible positions (on 50% of the trials) and subjects were required to report whether the probe stimulus was present or absent. Before, during, and after the saccade, probes were more often detected if they occurred in the same position as the eye movement target. In another experiment, he used a central cue (i.e., an arrow) to initiate the saccade. In this experiment he found that the cued position showed no advantage in probe detection until after the eye movement was completed. Remington concluded that a peripheral stimulus summons both attention and an eye movement, whereas when saccades are directed by a central cue, there is no advance allocation of attention to the destination of the eye movement. Thus, he claimed, in the absence of a peripheral stimulus, a saccade does not involve the allocation of attention to the target position.

In a dual task paradigm, Klein (1980) tested (1) whether preparing to make an eye movement to a particular location would facilitate the detection of events presented there (similar question as Remington, 1980), and (2) whether attending to a location would facilitate making an eye movement to that position. He reported no evidence for either of these effects. However, he noted that the dual-task blocks in both experiments were very difficult for the subjects. Although he did not see this as a problem, some have argued that the results may not be replicable under more normal conditions. Furthermore, in both experiments subjects had to distinguish an asterisk from the brightening of a dot in peripheral vision, before they would know whether to make an eye movement or press a key, respectively. This detail of the design would seem to undermine an assumption of the first experiment: it was assumed that given that subjects knew where to make the eye movement (e.g., always to the left), they would prepare it ahead of time. However, since the subjects needed to discriminate a peripheral event that could occur on either side of the fixation before knowing whether to make an eye movement, it is not clear that they could program the eye movement ahead of time.

A series of experiments by Shepherd et al. (1986) suggests a close relation between attention and eye movements and directly challenges Remington's (1980) and Klein's (1980) findings. Shepherd et al. (1986) used a central arrow cue as a signal to make a saccade and as a cue to indicate the likely location of a probe stimulus requiring a manual response. The probe stimulus onset could occur before, during, or after the saccade. They found that the detection of the probe at the eye movement target location was facilitated long before the eye movement began, even though saccades were directed by a central cue rather than elicited by a peripheral stimulus. This finding, they suggest, indicates that making a voluntary saccade necessarily involves an allocation of attention to the target position. In addition, they found that a probe stimulus shortened saccadic latency if it appeared in the eye movement target location and lengthened saccadic latency if it appeared at a location different from the eye movement target location. They conclude that the results suggest a reciprocal relationship between eye movements and spatial attention: attention to a peripheral position is facilitated by preparing to make a saccade to that position, and saccade latency is reduced by attention to the eye movement target location. They do also note an asymmetry in the relation between attentional shifts and eye movements: that is, it is possible to shift the focus of attention without moving the eyes, but it is not possible to make eye movements without also moving the focus of attention. They do not assign this asymmetry, however, any special role in defining the relation between, or rather distinguishing between, attentional movements and eye movements.

Klein et al. (1992) carefully point out that the original experiments (Klein, 1980) do not apply to exogenous orienting (peripheral cue/target), where there may be a tight linkage between attention and saccade execution. In addition, they concede that there may also be a linkage between attention and endogenous saccade execution (cf. Bryden, 1961; Crovitz and Daves, 1962; Rayner et al., 1978; Shepherd et al., 1986). However, they maintain that attention is not linked to endogenously generated saccade programming. In his 1980 paper, Klein argues that the onset of a stimulus may attract both the eye movement system and attentional mechanisms without any causal relationship between the two systems being implied. Thus, one may have "tight linkage" with no relationship between the two systems. He later adds, however, that the linkage between the eye movement and attention systems may be a reflexive one that is not under cognitive control. Thus, an eye movement necessitates an attentional shift, whereas cognitive preparation to look does not. This situation was addressed by Rafal et al. (1989), who showed that cognitive preparation to make a saccade can cause an attentional shift because under some conditions it results in inhibition of return (a phenomenon tightly coupled to an exogenous attentional shift).

Rafal et al. (1989) discuss saccade preparation and its role in the phenomenon of inhibition of return. Their goal is to determine how neural systems responsible for attention are integrated with eye movement systems. They begin with the fact that a visual signal or cue that is eccentric to fixation has a biphasic effect both on the covert orienting of attention and on eye movements. Initially, the cue summons attention automatically and facilitates detection of stimuli at the location of the signal (Posner et al., 1982). The cue also biases midbrain oculomotor centers to prepare a saccade toward it (Posner & Cohen, 1980). These facilitating effects are followed by an inhibition (inhibition of return), which slows detection at the cued location and induces a bias against making a saccade toward it (Posner & Cohen, 1984; Maylor, 1985; Maylor & Hockey, 1985; Posner et al., 1985; Tassinari et al., 1987).

Whereas inhibition of return appears after covert shifts of attention summoned by an eccentric (or exogenous) visual signal, it does not usually occur with endogenously activated shifts in attention (e.g., using symbolic cues, such as an arrow at the fixation point). The explanation for the different effects of exogenous and endogenous orienting of attention on inhibition of return was clarified in an elegant paradigm by Rafal et al. (1989). They showed that it was possible to activate inhibition of return to an endogenous signal merely by priming the oculomotor system to prepare a saccade. The results suggest that inhibition of return does not arise either from sensory exogenous processes alone (since it occurs after endogenous cueing that involves saccade preparation) or from covert orienting of attention alone (since it does not occur after endogenous cueing without saccade preparation), but rather from activation of the oculomotor system. Thus, exogenous signals (i.e., peripheral signals) automatically begin saccade preparation and hence produce inhibition of return, whereas endogenous signals will produce inhibition of return only under circumstances that induce saccade preparation.

Although Klein concluded that endogenous orienting is not involved in saccade programming, the Rafal et al. findings only provide evidence that endogenous orienting is not automatically or directly involved in reflexive saccade programming, but can affect it under certain conditions (as evidenced by inhibition of return after preparing but not executing a voluntary eye movement). Endogenous attention may not be involved as closely (or in a facilitatory manner) in the exogenous or reflexive eye movement programming system (examined in Rafal et al., 1989) as in the endogenous or voluntary eye movement programming system.

A model of the relation between attention and eye movements

One finds apparent contradictions in the literature as to whether attention facilitates or inhibits an eye movement. For example, Fischer and colleagues claim that in order to make an eye movement, attention needs to be disengaged from its current focus (Fischer & Breitmeyer, 1987). They observed that attention directed to the target position provides no advantage when an eye movement to a peripheral target is required. On the other hand, Shepherd and colleagues, as noted above, obtained evidence that saccade latencies are shortened if a probe stimulus appears at the target position. That is, attention to the target position reduces saccade latency. There are important differences among experiments in how attention is cued and how the eye movement is made. These differences may have led to the different findings.

Some of the differences have been addressed and most clearly described by Klein and colleagues (1992). They highlight two important distinctions: (1) whether or not an eye movement accompanies or follows the attentional shift, and (2) whether or not there is an abrupt peripheral onset in the position of the object to be attended. The first distinction is usually labelled overt versus covert orienting (that is, for eye movements versus attentional movements). The second distinction is often labelled exogenous versus endogenous or, equivalently, reflexive versus voluntary orienting (that is, for a peripheral onset cue versus a central or cognitive cue). In this chapter, the terms "reflexive" and "voluntary" are used preferentially. Despite differences in paradigms that may be the cause for the different findings, the question remains: Is visuospatial selective attention related to saccadic eye movements? And, if so, how?

It can be argued that spatial selective attention *is* related to saccadic eye movements. The following schematic model (adapted from Sereno, 1992) suggests how they may be related (see Figure 18.2). The model serves two functions: First, it makes explicit the proposed relation between visuospatial attention and saccadic eye movements. Second, specific hypotheses can be generated from the model about the interactions and influences between visuospatial selective attention and saccadic eye movements not only for normal subjects, but also for subject populations with dysfunctions involving regions of the brain important for orienting.

A few principal features of the model deserve brief discussion. A variety of evidence suggests a model where there are two basic orienting systems (i.e., subcortical for reflexive and cortical for voluntary). The cortical system tonically inhibits the subcortical system (via the caudate and substantia nigra; Illing & Graybiel, 1985; Hikosaka & Wurtz, 1989), and although there is also a direct phasic excitatory projection from the cortical to the subcortical system (Lynch & Gray-

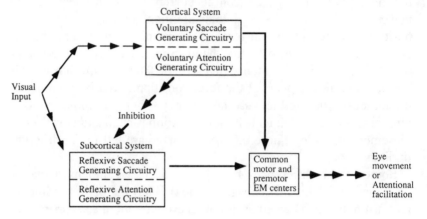

Figure 18.2. Model of orienting systems.

biel, 1983; Illing & Graybiel, 1985; Segraves & Goldberg, 1987), inhibition represents the primary relation between the cortical and subcortical systems at both a cellular and a behavioral level of organization (Guitton et al., 1985; Hikosaka & Wurtz, 1985; Schiller et al., 1987). By decreasing the inhibition and/or increasing the excitation, the cortical system can act through the subcortical system.

The model also proposes that within each system (cortical and subcortical), attention is conceived as a subthreshold activity of an eye movement center. In order for a saccade to be executed, a super-threshold attentional activation in the target position is required. Such a scenario would explain the asymmetry so often observed with attention and eye movements: i.e., you need attention to get an eye movement, but you can have attentional changes (subthreshold activations) without ever having an eye movement. The model suggests a fairly explicit structure for spatial selective attention. Some of the evidence that forms the basis for this model is reviewed below.

Physiological localization

Reflexive attention and the superior colliculus

In 1980, Posner argued that the relation between attention and saccadic eye movements was a functional one; that is, attention and eye movements are both summoned by important peripheral events and thus have a close functional but no intrinsic physiological relationship. Perhaps the best supported finding to emerge from neural considerations, however, is the idea that the superior colliculus and related eye movement brainstem structures play a role in reflexive or exogenous attention.

This picture began emerging when Posner et al. (1982) examined attention and eye movements in progressive supranuclear palsy patients with midbrain degeneration (involving the superior colliculus, pretectum, periaqueductal gray, and mesencephalic raphe). Although these patients were able to orient attention in directions to which they could not move their eyes voluntarily (findings supportive of a merely functional relation between the two systems), covert orienting was delayed in directions in which eye movements were most affected. In fact, whereas covert orienting was quite rapid in the direction of unimpaired eye movements (as reflected by an advantage for the cued position beginning around 50 ms after cue onset), there was no evidence for covert orienting in the impaired direction until 1,000 ms after the cue. Although they concluded that only the latency of covert orienting seemed to be affected, we now know, as more detailed evidence concerning the time course of facilitation following a peripheral cue (as well as a central or symbolic cue) has accumulated (e.g., Nakayama & Mackeben, 1989), that it is unlikely that the advantage that occurred at 1,000 ms after cue onset was due to a delayed *reflexive* shift of attention. This suggests that reflexive attention and reflexive saccadic eye movements were similarly impaired across direction.

Some evidence also suggests that inhibition of return, a phenomenon intimately associated with reflexive orienting, is mediated by a midbrain mechanism involving the superior colliculus. Posner et al. (1985) demonstrated that neurologic patients with progressive supranuclear palsy involving peritectal degeneration had a deficit of inhibition of return in the same directions in which eye movements were most severely impaired. In addition, Rafal et al. (1989) showed a temporal hemifield dominance under monocular viewing conditions for inhibition of return; they suggested that it may be mediated by the retino-tectal pathway or midbrain pathways.

Early neurophysiological work suggested that the superior colliculus and related brainstem structures play a role only in overt orienting (i.e., that accompanied by an eye movement), whereas the posterior parietal cortex plays a unique role in covert shifts of attention (Wurtz & Mohler, 1976; Wurtz et al., 1980; Bushnell et al., 1981;

Wurtz et al., 1984). A fixating monkey was trained to release a bar when a peripheral receptive field stimulus dimmed (spatial attention condition), but not when the fixation point dimmed (baseline cell response condition). Cells in posterior parietal cortex showed an enhanced response even when no eye movement to the receptive field stimulus occurred, indicating independence of attention and eye movements. For cells in the superior colliculus, a most dramatic enhanced response occurred when the monkey responded with a saccade to the receptive field stimulus. Although these studies are often cited as evidence against the superior colliculus's playing a role in covert orienting, caution is warranted for two reasons. First, the task could be considered a *voluntary* or *endogenous* attention paradigm; thus, these studies suggest that the superior colliculus does not play an important role in *voluntary* covert orienting. Second, recent findings suggest that there *is* modulation of cell response in the superior colliculus that is specific to voluntary covert orienting, beginning about 300 ms after the cue (Glimcher & Sparks, 1992). It is likely that this cell modulation in the superior colliculus is not the site for the *generation* of such a signal (in a related task, modulation of cell response in prefrontal cortex begins about 250 ms after the cue; Goldman-Rakic et al., 1990). Rather, the effects of voluntary covert orienting detected in the cell response of the superior colliculus may instead be viewed as a spillover of the voluntary covert orienting signal generated in other brain areas such as prefrontal or parietal cortex. In sum, much evidence suggests that the superior colliculus and other closely related brainstem oculomotor structures play an integral role in the generation of reflexive or exogenous attention.

Voluntary attention and prefrontal cortex

In the cognitive literature, many quite different paradigms have been employed to elicit voluntary or endogenous attention. It is therefore difficult to suggest a neural substrate of voluntary attention since it is difficult to define strictly what one is seeking. A general description may be to look for a signal in the brain that is not directly dependent in either space or time on a sensory signal, or, perhaps, a signal that can be maintained for a relatively long period following a sensory cue. Most reports showing attentional modulation of cell response have demonstrated stimulus selective attentional effects rather than spatial selective effects. Detailed studies have documented changes in cell response in area V4 and in inferotemporal cortex (IT) that are dependent on what stimulus properties the monkey is searching for (see, e.g., Fuster & Jervey, 1982, for cell modulation dependent on color; and Haenny et al., 1988 and Maunsell et al., 1991, for cell modulation dependent on orientation). The task most often used in these studies has been a match-to-sample (MTS) task. In a MTS task, the monkey is briefly presented a sample stimulus and, after a brief delay, a test stimulus. If the test stimulus matches the sample, the monkey responds (e.g., by releasing a response bar).

Moran and Desimone's 1985 *Science* paper, purportedly showing that attenuation of irrelevant information in neurons in monkey visual cortex can be based purely on spatial location, is often cited as providing evidence for a *spatially* selective attentional mechanism in temporal cortex. Their task, however, was a modified match-to-sample task where successful performance required the monkey to attend to the *color* or *orientation* of the sample. Thus, it remains to be demonstrated whether the effects in question can be obtained independently of *stimulus* selective effects (see Sereno, 1990). Such stimulus selective effects (e.g., color or orientation selective effects), as mentioned above, have already been demonstrated to occur in MTS tasks in temporal cortex.

At first glance, the modulation of cells in posterior parietal cortex, as discussed above, appears to be the clearest neurophysiological correlate for voluntary or endogenous spatial selective attention (e.g., Wurtz et al., 1984). A related task, perhaps, is a spatial delayed-response task. In this task the monkey must maintain fixation on a central point, during which time a visual target flashes briefly in the periphery. After a delay, the fixation point is extinguished, which signals the monkey to make a saccade to the location where the target previously appeared. Delay-period modulation of cell response in this task has been reported in several different areas, including the principal sulcus (Funahashi et al., 1989), the frontal eye fields (Bruce & Goldberg, 1985), the posterior parietal cortex (Gnadt & Andersen, 1988), the basal ganglia (Hikosaka & Wurtz, 1983; Hikosaka et al., 1989), the premotor and motor cortex (Tanji et al., 1980; Tanji & Kurata, 1985), and the hippocampus (Watanabe & Niki, 1985). The usual interpretation of this activity proposes that these cells are involved in maintaining an image of the location of the target in spatial working memory (Goldman-Rakic, 1987). It is perhaps the striking demonstrations, beginning with Jacobsen (1936), of prefrontal cortex damage producing a profound and selective deficit in spatial delayed response tasks that most strongly suggest that the prefrontal cortex, compared to other areas, plays a particularly crucial role in spatial working memory. The fact that one may describe the activity of some neurons as a "transient spatial memory" process or as a "sustained spatial attention" process suggests that this distinction in terminology may no longer serve a useful purpose (see Conclusion, this chapter).

Schizophrenia and orienting

In view of the present model, schizophrenic patients are an interesting population to investigate for several reasons. First of all, one of the most commonly cited deficits in schizophrenia has been an attentional deficit (McGhie & Chapman, 1961). In addition, there is a long history of reports of eye movement problems in schizophrenia, starting with Diefendorf and Dodge (1908) and rediscovered and advanced by Holzman and colleagues (for a review, see Holzman, 1985). And, finally, over the years, many studies have suggested that there is a prefrontal cortex dysfunction in schizophrenia (for reviews, see Levin, 1984a; Levin, 1984b; Goldman-Rakic, 1987).

If schizophrenia involves a dysfunction of prefrontal cortex, according to the model, this dysfunction would lead to two behavioral changes. First, schizophrenic patients would show deficits in the voluntary system: that is, on an antisaccade task (see Figure 18.3, panel A), schizophrenic patients would have longer reaction times (RTs) and make more errors, and on a voluntary attention task schizophrenic patients would not show as much attentional facilitation as would normal subjects. Second, there would also be a disinhibition or enhancement of the reflexive or exogenous system: that is, in a gap paradigm schizophrenic patients would show a greater benefit than normal subjects and, on a reflexive attention task, schizophrenic patients would show greater attentional facilitation than normal subjects. In a gap paradigm, the fixation point is extinguished before the target appears; hence, there is a brief temporal gap before the target onset which allows the subject to make express saccades (i.e., saccades with very short latency, typically 100–150 msec).

Early findings by Holzman and colleagues showed that although smooth pursuit was impaired in many schizophrenic patients, these same patients showed intact smooth eye movements during vestibulo-ocular reflex (VOR) or optokinetic nystagmus (OKN) (Levy et al.,

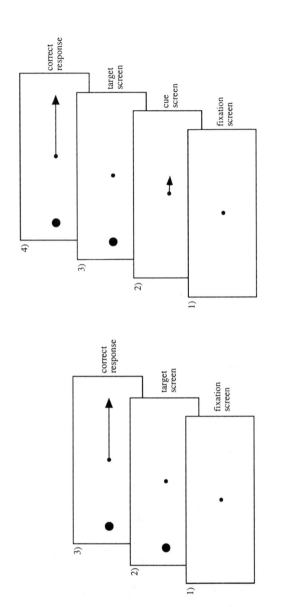

Figure 18.3. Schematic of an anti-saccade task (Panel A) and an anti-saccade task with a voluntary attentional cue that is always valid (Panel B). In an anti-saccade task, subjects are instructed to make an eye movement in the direction opposite to the target when the target appears. When there is a voluntary attentional cue, subjects know ahead of time where they need to make the upcoming eye movement, but must wait for the target to appear at some random interval after fixation. The attentional cue shortens saccade latency in an antisaccade task.

1978; Latham et al., 1981; Levin et al., 1982). This suggested that the subcortical pathways responsible for generating smooth eye movements were intact and that the disruption had to be occurring at a higher level in the brain. More recent studies demonstrate that a prefrontal lesion can result in a disruption of both saccades and smooth pursuit eye movements (Bruce et al., 1985; Lynch, 1987; Schiller et al., 1987; MacAvoy et al., 1991). Hence, abnormal smooth pursuit tracking may be a marker of a prefrontal dysfunction. If this is so, it is perhaps the patients with abnormal tracking who will show the following pattern of performance across the voluntary and reflexive tasks of eye movements and attention: deficit performance on voluntary saccadic eye movements and voluntary attention, and disinhibited or enhanced performance on reflexive saccadic eye movements and reflexive attention.

Voluntary and reflexive saccadic eye movements

In a study of these issues, supportive evidence was found for such a pattern (Sereno, 1991). On an antisaccade task, the *voluntary* eye movement task, schizophrenic patients showed *greater difficulty* than normal subjects. When schizophrenic patients were divided into two groups based on their ability at tracking a moving target, schizophrenic patients with abnormal tracking were significantly worse on the antisaccade task compared with schizophrenic patients whose tracking was normal (Sereno & Holzman, 1991; Sereno & Holzman, 1995). On the gap task, a *reflexive* eye movement task, schizophrenic patients showed *greater benefit* than normal subjects. Further, schizophrenic patients with abnormal tracking were significantly better than schizophrenic patients with normal tracking on the gap task (Sereno & Holzman, 1991; Sereno & Holzman, 1993a).

It remains debatable whether humans (as opposed to monkeys) really show a separate population of express saccades or whether there is just a shift in the distribution of saccade latencies toward smaller values (see Wenban-Smith & Findlay, 1991). The original experiments did not elicit many saccades with short latencies, making it difficult to make a comparison of the *number* of express saccades across subject groups. Preliminary results from some experiments in progress, however, do show greater numbers of short latency saccades and support the original findings (Sereno & Holzman, 1993b). Schizophrenic patients show significantly more express saccades than do normal subjects, not only in a gap paradigm, but also in an overlap paradigm, where Fischer and others (e.g., Fischer & Breitmeyer, 1987) have demonstrated that it is very difficult for normal subjects to make express saccades under this condition.

Influence of voluntary attention on saccadic eye movements

Another prediction of the model is that voluntary attention will facilitate a voluntary saccadic eye movement, whereas it will inhibit a reflexive saccadic eye movement. This second prediction is counterintuitive in that it suggests that when subjects know where the target will appear, this knowledge (voluntary spatial attention) will *slow them down* or cause them to make a sluggish saccade to the target. In order to engage voluntary spatial selective attention, an arrow was presented at the fixation point indicating the proper direction required for the upcoming eye movement (see Figures 18.3 and 18.4 for the voluntary and reflexive eye movement tasks respectively). This arrow cue was always valid. There was a variable interval between this cue and the upcoming target to prevent anticipations. Subjects had to wait until the target appeared before making a saccade. If they made a saccade away from the fixation point before the target appeared, the trial would abort and be presented again later. When the target appeared, subjects were instructed to make a correct saccade as quickly as possible. Correct saccades were saccades of a specific amplitude in the same direction as the arrow. For the antisaccade task (voluntary eye movement task), a correct response was a saccade to the opposite field of the target, whereas for the reflexive saccade task, it was a saccade to the target.

Preliminary findings suggest that voluntary attention *facilitates* a *voluntary* eye movement (Sereno, 1993). That is, subjects have shorter saccadic latencies on an antisaccade task when they are given the arrow cue compared with the same task without the arrow cue. Further, these findings demonstrate that voluntary attention *inhibits* a *reflexive* eye movement. That is, subjects have longer saccadic latencies on a reflexive saccade task when they are given the arrow cue compared with the same task without the arrow cue. This is true both for normal subjects and for schizophrenic patients. There is, however, an additional prediction of the model: that schizophrenic patients should show less attentional facilitation in the voluntary eye movement task and less attentional inhibition in the reflexive eye movement task.

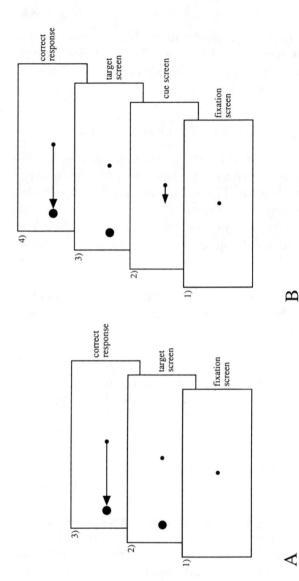

Figure 18.4. Schematic of a reflexive saccade (overlap) task (Panel A) and a reflexive saccade task with a voluntary attentional cue that is always valid (Panel B). In a reflexive saccade task, subjects are instructed to make an eye movement to the target when the target appears. When there is a voluntary attentional cue, subjects know ahead of time where they need to make the upcoming eye movement, but must wait for the target to appear at some random interval after fixation. The attentional cue lengthens saccade latency in a reflexive saccade task.

Although preliminary findings agree qualitatively with this hypothesis, this interaction was not statistically significant in a small sample.

Voluntary and reflexive attention

On a voluntary attention task, schizophrenic patients showed a *reduced* attentional benefit compared with normal subjects. On a reflexive attention task, schizophrenic patients showed a *greater* or *enhanced* attentional benefit compared to normal subjects (Sereno & Holzman, 1992; Sereno & Holzman, submitted).

In summary, schizophrenic patients show impaired performance on voluntary eye movement and voluntary attention tasks. On the other hand, schizophrenic patients show enhanced or disinhibited performance on reflexive eye movement and reflexive attention tasks. In addition, within the schizophrenic group itself, the abnormal trackers were significantly *worse* on the voluntary eye movement task and significantly *better* on the reflexive eye movement task compared with schizophrenic patients with normal tracking.

Conclusions

The present findings seem directly related not only to the neurophysiological findings of Funahashi et al. (1989), who used a spatial delayed working memory task, but also to the detailed studies with both infant monkeys and human infants in the developmental literature (for a review, see Diamond, 1990). Specifically, the similarity between a spatial working memory task and a selective visual attention task seems clear if, in a spatial delayed working memory task, one thinks of the first stimulus as a cue. During the interval in a spatial working memory task, while cells in prefrontal cortex are firing, the animal is holding on to a spatial position to which it will eventually make a saccade. But as Goldman-Rakic noted (see Chapter 2, this volume), a large percentage of these cells do not fire during the response (eye movement), but only during the delay, as if their function is to hold that position on line. This, it can be argued, is similar to what occurs on a task of spatial selective attention, where subjects must hold information on line about a particular location in the visual field where the target is most likely to appear. And, indeed, in recent positron emission tomography (PET) findings, Petersen and col-

leagues reported prefrontal activation during a voluntary spatial selective attention task (Petersen et al., 1991).

This brings us to a problem that one often sees between disciplines,
or even research programs: the findings in one field become inacces-
sible to another field because the issues become bogged down in
terminology. As we attempt to bridge the gap between fields such as
experimental psychology and neuroscience, one can foresee two fundamental changes. First, we may be able to tie separate processes
together: for example, to see how what some researchers label *spatial
selective attention* may involve the same neurophysiological underpinnings as what others call *spatial working memory;* or, to realize that
there may be *more* than superficial similarities between attentional
shifts and saccadic eye movements. Second, we may be able to break
down cognitive processes, such as attention, into more physiologically
realistic processes. Over the years, it has become clear in the cognitive
literature that "attention" is not a very precise or unambiguous term.
When we use the term "attention," do we mean arousal, vigilance,
orienting, search, selection, or shift? Quite different neurophysiological mechanisms are probably involved in these different aspects of
attention.

Even within a given literature, such as the visual selective attention
literature, there may be important distinctions that are not carefully
observed – distinctions grounded in separate physiological mechanisms. One such distinction can be made between selective attention
to an object's *properties* (such as color, form, or direction of movement)
versus selective attention to an object's *location.* Careful manipulation
of attention to object properties separately from attention to spatial
location has rarely been performed in either physiological or psychological experiments (cf. the discussion of Moran & Desimone, 1985,
above). For recent experiments attempting to distinguish between
feature and spatial attention, see Sereno and Maunsell, 1995 (cf. also
Chapter 2 by Goldman-Rakic, this volume).

In 1982, Ungerleider and Mishkin proposed that visual processing
proceeds along two anatomically segregated streams of processing in
cerebral cortex: a ventral pathway and a dorsal pathway. Each pathway
comprises a different series of cortical visual areas and supports distinct types of functions. The ventral stream includes areas of temporal
cortex and is involved in form analysis and object recognition (the
"what" pathway), whereas the dorsal stream includes areas of parietal
cortex and is important for vision related to spatial relations (the

"where" pathway; Maunsell & Newsome, 1987). This distinction between object and spatial properties may also be an important distinction in understanding the mechanisms of attentional effects. Attentional modulation of cell response, like sensory processing, may perhaps show anatomically segregated effects. That is, modulation of cell response arising from attention to object properties (e.g., color or orientation) may occur in the later stages of the ventral pathway (e.g., areas V4 and inferotemporal cortex), whereas modulation of cell response that is due to attention to spatial location may occur in the later stages of the dorsal pathway (e.g., area 7a and the lateral inferior parietal area).

One important step toward understanding the brain mechanisms of attention will be to determine whether attention to object properties and attention to spatial location are anatomically segregated. The parietal and temporal pathways in visual cortex interact (Felleman & Van Essen, 1991; Ferrera et al., 1992) and both project to prefrontal regions (e.g., area 46 and area 10, respectively). Higher stages of processing in prefrontal cortex are particularly likely sites of convergence for information from the two pathways. There is little existing neurophysiological data that addresses the question of interactions between different types of attention. For example, one interesting avenue for research, currently under investigation by the author, is to explore the degree of segregation of the effects of *stimulus selective* versus *spatially selective* attention in cortical neurons using single unit recording techniques in behaving rhesus monkeys performing these visual attention tasks. With careful experimental design, both tasks can be constructed so that they present the same visual stimuli and require the same response. Under these conditions, one can dissociate at the cellular level the effects of the two forms of attention on cell response. Several areas, including temporal, parietal, and prefrontal cortices, and superior colliculus, can be examined. Exploring the role of these separate areas in different aspects of attention may provide a clue to where these different processes may be occurring in the brain. Both prefrontal and temporal cortical areas have been implicated in the pathophysiology of schizophrenia. A closer examination of the physiological basis of different aspects of attention as described here may provide researchers in schizophrenia with clues about what aspects of voluntary attention are affected in schizophrenia and what areas of the brain may be involved in the disruption of such processes. Distinctions between behaviors that are grounded in physiologically distinct mechanisms, such as might be the case for spatial and object property selective attention, are important to any understanding of behavior.

Cognitive neuroscience really represents just a *reawakening* of interest in the biological basis of cognitive functions. And just as neuroscience can guide and inform experiments in psychopathology, psychopathology can reveal potentially instructive dissociations of behavior that provide a clue about how the brain functions. Discoveries about how the brain functions at both the cellular and system levels will be as important as cognitive experiments in determining the structure of cognitive processes and how they occur. Understanding the biological mechanisms, in some cases, can do more than just guide experimental psychology – it can also alter the way cognitive psychology carves up human behavior into processes such as attention or memory. Changes in our conceptions of behavior that come about either by collapsing across what were once separate and distinct entities (such as visuospatial selective attention and visual working memory) or by creating distinctions (such as attention to spatial location and attention to object properties) will be crucial for a reparsing of cognitive processes.

Glossary

endogenous:	voluntary, internally generated, willful; frequently prompted by a symbolic cue
exogenous:	reflexive, externally prompted, automatic; prompted by the onset of a stimulus in the position where the attention/gaze is to be moved
saccade execution:	the process of actually performing an eye movement
saccade programming:	the processes involved in determining exactly where and how the eye will move, before the actual saccade
peripheral onset cue:	a sudden onset cue in the position where attention/gaze is to be moved; used in exogenous attention/eye movement tasks
central cue:	a cue located at the point of fixation, usually of a symbolic nature (e.g., an arrow)

	and indicating the likely position of an upcoming target; used in endogenous attention/eye movement tasks
overt orienting:	a shift in the location of gaze
covert orienting:	a shift in the location of attention
antisaccade task:	a voluntary eye movement task, requiring a subject to make an eye movement away from a target appearing in the periphery
reflexive saccade task:	a task requiring the subject to make an eye movement to a target in the periphery immediately after the target appears
overlap task:	a saccade task in which the fixation point remains present after the onset of the target
gap task:	a saccade task with a brief gap (usually 200 ms) between the offset of the fixation point and the onset of the target
express saccade:	a very short latency reflexive saccade; such saccades are more frequent in a gap task
dual-task experiment:	each trial requires the subject to perform two tasks at the same time; e.g., making an eye movement to a target and simultaneously detecting whether or not there is a small change in luminance in the visual field.

References

Bruce, C. J., and Goldberg, M. E. (1985). Primate frontal eye fields. I. Single neurons discharging before saccades. *Journal of Neurophysiology*, *53*, 603–635.

Bruce, C. J., Goldberg, M. E., Bushnell, M. C., and Stanton, G. B. (1985). primate frontal eye fields. II. Physiological and anatomical correlates of electrically evoked eye movements. *Journal of Neurophysiology*, *54*, 714–734.

Bryden, M. P. (1961). The role of post-exposural eye movements in tachistoscopic perception. *Canadian Journal of Psychology*, *15*, 220–225.

Bushnell, M. C., Goldberg, M. E., and Robinson, D. L. (1981). Behavioral enhancement of visual responses in monkey cerebral cortex. I. Modulation in posterior pariental cortex related to selective visual attention. *Journal of Neurophysiology*, *46*, 755–772.

Crovitz, H. F., and Daves, W. (1962). Tendencies to eye movement and perceptual accuracy. *Journal of Experimental Psychology*, *63*, 495–498.

Diamond, A. (1990). The development and neural bases of memory functions as indexed by the Ab and delayed response tasks in human infants and infant monkeys. In A. Diamond (ed.), *The Development and Neural Bases of Higher Cognitive Functions*, pp. 267–317. New York: New York Academy of Sciences.

Diefendorf, A. R., and Dodge, R. (1908). An experimental study of the ocular reactions of the insane from photographic records. *Brain*, *31*, 451–489.

Felleman, D. J., and Van Essen, D. C. (1991). Distributed hierarchical processing in the primate cerebral cortex. *Cerebral Cortex*, *1*, 1–47.

Ferrera, V. P., Nealey, T. A., and Maunsell, J.H.R. (1992). Mixed parvocellular and magnocellular geniculate signals in visual area V4. *Nature*, *358*, 756–758.

Fischer, B., and Breitmeyer, B. (1987). Mechanisms of visual attention revealed by saccadic eye movements. *Neuropsychologia*, *25*, 73–83.

Funahashi, S., Bruce, C. J., and Goldman-Rakic, P. S. (1989). Mnemonic coding of visual space in the monkey's dorsolateral prefrontal cortex. *Journal of Neurophysiology*, *61*, 331–349.

Fuster, J. M., and Jervey, J. P. (1982). Neuronal firing in the inferotemporal cortex of the monkey in a visual memory task. *Journal of Neuroscience*, *2*, 361–375.

Glimcher, P. W., and Sparks, D. L. (1992). Movement selection in advance of action in the superior colliculus. *Nature*, *355*, 542–545.

Gnadt, J. W., and Andersen, R. A. (1988). Memory related motor planning activity in posterior parietal cortex of macaque. *Experimental Brain Research*, *70*, 216–220.

Goldman-Rakic, P. S. (1987). Circuitry of primate prefrontal cortex and regulation of behavior by representational memory. In F. Plum and V. Mountcastle (eds.), *Handbook of Physiology: Higher Cortical Function, Volume V*, pp. 373–417. Washington, D.C.: American Physiological Society.

Goldman-Rakic, P. S., Funahashi, S., Bruce, C. J. (1990). Neocortical Memory Circuits. In *Cold Spring Harbor Symposia on Quantitative Biology, Volume LV*, pp. 1025–1038. New York: Cold Spring Harbor Laboratory Press.

Guitton, D., Buchtel, H. A., and Douglas, R. M. (1985). Frontal lobe lesions in man cause difficulties in suppressing reflexive glances and in generating goal-directed saccades. *Experimental Brain Research*, *58*, 455–472.

Haenny, P. E., Maunsell, J.H.R., and Schiller, P. H. (1988). State dependent activity in monkey visual cortex. II. Retinal and extraretinal factors in V4. *Experimental Brain Research, 69,* 245–260.

Hikosaka, O., and Wurtz, R. H. (1983). Visual oculomotor functions of monkey substantia nigra pars reticulata. III. Memory-contingent visual and saccade responses. *Journal of Neurophysiology, 49,* 1268–1284.

Hikosaka, O., and Wurtz, R. H. (1985). Modification of saccadic eye movements by GABA-related substances. I. Effect of muscimol and bicuculline in monkey superior colliculus. *Journal of Neurophysiology, 53,* 266–291.

Hikosaka, O., and Wurtz, R. H. (1989). The basal ganglia. In R. H. Wurtz and M. E. Goldberg (eds.), *The Neurobiology of Saccadic Eye Movements,* pp. 257–281. New York: Elsevier.

Holzman, P. S. (1985). Eye movement dysfunctions and psychosis. *International Review of Neurobiology, 27,* 179–205.

Illing, R.-B., and Graybiel, A. M. (1985). Convergence of afferents from frontal cortex and substantia nigra onto acetyl-cholinesterase-rich patches of the cat's superior colliculus. *Neuroscience, 14,* 445–482.

Jacobsen, C. F. (1936). Studies of cerebral functions in primates: I. The functions of the frontal association areas in monkeys. *Comparative Psychology Monographs, 13,* 3–60.

James, W. (1890). *The Principles of Psychology.* Cambridge, MA: Harvard University Press, 1983 edition.

Jonides, J. (1981). Voluntary versus automatic control over the mind's eye's movement. In J. Long and A. Baddeley (eds.), *Attention and Performance IX.* Hillsdale, NJ: Erlbaum.

Klein, R. M. (1980). Does oculomotor readiness mediate cognitive control of attention? In Nickerson (ed.), *Attention and Performance VIII.* Hillsdale, NJ: Erlbaum.

Klein, R., Kingstone, A., and Pontefract, A. (1992). Orienting of visual attention. In K. Rayner (ed.), *Eye Movements and Visual Cognition.* New York: Springer-Verlag.

Latham, C., Holzman, P., Manschreck, T. C., and Tole, J. (1981). Optokinetic nystagmus and pursuit eye movements in schizophrenia. *Archives of General Psychiatry, 38,* 997–1003.

Levin, S. (1984a). Frontal lobe dysfunctions in schizophrenia – I. Eye movement impairments. *Journal of Psychiatric Research, 18,* 27–55.

Levin, S. (1984b). Frontal lobe dysfunctions in schizophrenia – II. Impairments of psychological and brain functions. *Journal of Psychiatric Research, 18,* 57–72.

Levin, S., Jones, A., Stark, L., Merrin, E. L., and Holzman, P. S. (1982a). Identification of abnormal patterns in eye movements of schizophrenic patients. *Archives of General Psychology, 39,* 1125–1130.

Levy, D. L., Holzman, P. S., and Proctor, L. R. (1978). Vestibular responses in schizophrenia. *Archives of General Psychiatry, 35,* 972–981.

Lynch, J. C. (1987). Frontal eye field lesions in monkeys disrupt visual pursuit. *Experimental Brain Research, 68,* 437–441.

Lynch, J. C., and Graybiel, A. M. (1983). Comparison of afferents traced to the superior colliculus from the frontal eye fields and from two subregions of area 7 of the rhesus monkey. *Neuroscience Abstracts, 220.5,* 750.

MacAvoy, M. G., Gottlieb, J. P., and Bruce, C. J. (1991). Smooth-pursuit eye movement representation in the primate frontal eye field. *Cerebral Cortex, 1,* 95–102.

Maunsell, J.H.R., and Newsome, W. T. (1987). *Annual Review of Neuroscience, 10,* 363–401.

Maunsell, J.H.R., Sclar, G., Nealey, T. A., and DePriest, D. D. (1991). Extraretinal representations in area V4 in the macaque monkey. *Visual Neuroscience, 7,* 561–573.

Maylor, E. A. (1985). Facilitatory and inhibitory components of orienting in visual space. In M. I. Posner and O.S.M. Marin (eds.), *Mechanisms of Attention: Attention and Performance XI,* pp. 189–204. Hillsdale, NJ: Erlbaum.

Maylor, E. A., and Hockey, R. (1985). Inhibitory component of externally-controlled covert orienting in visual space. *Journal Experimental Psychology: Human Perception and Performance, 11,* 777–787.

McGhie, A., and Chapman, J. (1961). Disorders of attention and perception in early schizophrenia. *British Journal of Medical Psychology, 34,* 103–116.

Moran, J., and Desimone, R. (1985). Selective attention gates visual processing in the extrastriate cortex. *Science, 229,* 782–784.

Nakayama, K., and Mackeben, M. (1989). Sustained and transient components of focal visual attention. *Vision Research, 29,* 1631–1647.

Petersen, S. E., Corbetta, M., Shulman, G. L., and Miezin, F. M. (1991). Frontal activation during shifts of visual spatial attention: A PET study. *Society for Neuroscience Abstracts, 17,* 1210.

Posner, M. I. (1980). Orienting of attention. *Quarterly Journal of Experimental Psychology, 32,* 3–25.

Posner, M. I., and Cohen, Y. (1980). Attention and the control of movements. In G. E. Stelmach and J. Requin (eds.), *Tutorials in Motor Behavior,* pp. 243–258. Amsterdam: North Holland.

Posner, M. I., and Cohen, Y. (1984). Components of visual orienting. In H. Bouma and D. G. Bouwhuis (eds.), *Attention and Performance X,* pp. 531–556. Hillsdale, NJ: Erlbaum.

Posner, M. I., Cohen, Y., and Rafal, R. D. (1982). Neural systems control of spatial orienting. *Philosophical Transactions of the Royal Society of London B, 298,* 187–198.

Posner, M. I., Rafal, R. D., Choate, L. S., and Vaughn, L. (1985). Inhibition of return: Neural basis and function. *Cognitive Neuropsychology, 2*, 211–228.

Rafal, R. D., Calabresi, P. A., Brennan, C. W., and Sciolto, T. K. (1989). Saccade preparation inhibits reorienting to recently attended locations. *Journal of Experimental Psychology: Human Perception and Performance, 15*, 673–685.

Rayner, K., McConkie, G. W., and Ehrlich, S. (1978). Eye movements and integrating information across fixations. *Journal of Experimental Psychology: Human Perception and Performance, 4*, 529–544.

Remington, R. W. (1980). Attention and saccadic eye movements. *Journal of Experimental Psychology: Human Perception and Performance, 6*, 726–744.

Schiller, P. H., Sandell, J. H., and Maunsell, J.H.R. (1987). The effect of frontal eye field and superior colliculus lesions on saccadic latencies in the Rhesus monkey. *Journal of Neurophysiology, 57*, 1033–1049.

Segraves, M. A., and Goldberg, M. E. (1987). Functional properties of corticotectal neurons in the monkey's frontal eye field. *Journal of Neurophysiology, 58*, 1387–1419.

Sereno, A. B. (1990). Commentary on Moran and Desimone's "spotlight" in V4. Manuscript, Harvard University.

Sereno, A. B. (1991). Attention and eye movements in schizophrenic, affective disorder, and normal subjects. Doctoral dissertation, Harvard University.

Sereno, A. B. (1992). Programming saccades: The role of attention. In K. Rayner (ed.), *Eye Movements and Visual Cognition: Scene Perception and Reading*. New York: Springer-Verlag.

Sereno, A. B. (1993). Voluntary attention facilitates voluntary saccades but inhibits reflexive saccades. *Investigative Ophthalmology and Visual Science, 34*, 1290.

Sereno, A. B., and Holzman, P. S. (1991). Express and antisaccades in schizophrenic, affective disorder, and normal control subjects. *Society for Neuroscience Abstracts, 17*, 858.

Sereno, A. B., and Holzman, P. S. (1992). Exogenous and endogenous attention in schizophrenic, affective disorder, and normal control subjects. *Investigative Ophthalmology and Visual Science, 33*, 1264.

Sereno, A. B., and Holzman, P. S. (1993a). Express saccades and smooth pursuit eye movement function in schizophrenic, affective disorder, and normal control subjects. *Journal of Cognitive Neuroscience, 5*, 303–316.

Sereno, A. B., and Holzman, P. S. (1993b). Eye movements and spatial selective attention in schizophrenia. *Schizophrenia Research*.

Sereno, A. B., and Holzman, P. S. (1995). Antisaccades and smooth pursuit eye movements in schizophrenia. *Biological Psychiatry, 37*, 394–401.

Sereno, A. B., and Holzman, P. S. (submitted). Spatial selective attention in schizophrenic, affective disorder, and normal subjects.

Sereno, A. B., and Maunsell, J.H.R. (1995). Spatial and shape selective sensory and attentional effects in neurons in the macaque lateral intraparietal cortex (LIP). *Investigative Ophthalmology and Visual Science, 36,* 5692.

Shepherd, M., Findlay, J. M., Hockey, R. J. (1986). The relationship between eye movements and spatial attention. *Quarterly Journal of Experimental Psychology, 38A,* 475–491.

Tanji, J., and Kurata, K. (1985). Contrasting neuronal activity in supplementary and precentral motor cortex of monkeys. I. Responses to instruction determining motor responses to forthcoming signals of different modalities. *Journal of Neurophysiology, 53,* 129–141.

Tanji, J., Tanuguchi, K., and Saga, T. (1980). The supplementary motor area: Neuronal response to motor instructions. *Journal of Neurophysiology, 43,* 60–68.

Tassinari, G., Aglioti, S., Chelazzi, L., Marzi, C. A., and Berlucchi, G. (1987). Distribution in the visual field of the costs of voluntarily allocated attention and of the inhibitory after-effects of covert orienting. *Neuropsychologia, 25,* 55–71.

Ungerleider, L. G., and Mishkin, M. (1982). Two cortical visual systems. In D. J. Ingle, R.J.W. Mansfield, M. S. Goodale (eds.), *The Analysis of Visual Behavior,* pp. 549–586. Cambridge, MA: MIT Press.

Watanabe, T., and Niki, H. (1985). Hippocampal unit activity and delayed response in the monkey. *Brain Research, 325,* 241–254.

Wenban-Smith, M. G., and Findlay, J. M. (1991). Express saccades: Is there a separate population in humans? *Experimental Brain Research, 87,* 218–222.

Wurtz, R. H., and Mohler, C. W. (1976). Enhancement of visual responses in monkey striate cortex and frontal eye fields. *Journal of Neurophysiology, 39,* 766–772.

Wurtz, R. H., Goldberg, M. E., and Robinson, D. L. (1980). Behavioral modulation of visual responses in the monkey: Stimulus selection for attention and movement. *Progress in Psychobiology and Physiological Psychology, 9,* 43–83.

Wurtz, R. H., and Richmond, B. J., and Newsome, W. T. (1984). Modulation of cortical visual processing by attention, perception, and movement. In G. Edelman, W. Gall, and W. Cowan (eds.), *Dynamic Aspects of Neocortical Function,* pp. 195–217. New York: Wiley.

19

Cognitive psychopathology in schizophrenia: Explorations in language, memory, associations, and movements

Brendan A. Maher

The central goal of the work that is reported in this chapter has been to arrive at an understanding of the pathology/ies that underlie the manifest cognitive disorders in schizophrenia. A satisfactory understanding – still a great way off – would ultimately encompass an unbroken chain of links from the manifest clinical symptomatology, through a fine-grain account of the functional anomalies of psychological processes such as memory, associational activation, attentional deployment, language plan formation, and so on, to the neuropsychological processes that produce these anomalies, and thence to the physical, biochemical, and genetic events that control the neuropsychology. In this volume, different investigators work at different interfaces in this explanatory sequence. Our work has been primarily at the interface between the manifest clinical phenomena – the symptoms – and the operation of basic psychological processes involved in information processing, i.e., language and thought, and memory.

This work has been done mostly at the Massachusetts General Hospital, the Erich Lindemann Center in Boston, the New Hampshire Hospital in Concord, plus, in recent years, the Psychiatrische Universitätsklinik at Heidelberg. Many people have worked with us, as students and colleagues. In most cases they have collaborated in our own planned research; in others we have collaborated with work primarily developed and managed by distinguished colleagues in other institutions. Before turning to an account of the research, we think it may be helpful to consider first certain important issues of methodology.

Methodological issues in psychopathology

1. The multiple possible independent causes of manifestly similar behavior

Any particular sample of human behavior may arise from one of several different causes. A sequence of disrupted speech may arise as an unavoidable consequence of particular kinds of neuropathology, as a time-limited consequence of the disruptive effect of strong emotion, as an adaptive strategy to deter others from social contact, and so forth. The belief that one is being spied upon by the FBI may arise as a delusional explanation of strange experiences, or as a veridical description of an uncommon but real event. There is no need to belabor the issue with additional examples; the important point is that much research into psychopathology necessarily begins with the observation of manifest behavior, with consequences and not with causes. To the extent that we hope to establish the etiology of a particular syndrome, we are therefore faced with the always dubious requirement of arguing backward from consequences to causes.

This problem is exacerbated when we are content to categorize the manifest behavior in relatively gross terms. In principle it is entirely possible that the detailed presentation of a delusional belief by a patient differs from the detailed presentation of what is essentially the same belief by an individual to whom the highly implausible thing is actually happening. Distinctions between superficially similar manifest phenomena require the kind of fine-grain microanalysis of differences in detail that have been found to be essential in scientific classification across other disciplines. Whenever we can detect these detailed differences within a single gross category, and relate them to differences in the specific etiologies that underlie them, we will succeed in reducing the constraints that multiple causation has created so far. Which brings us to the next item.

2. On the value of counting wherever possible

There is no doubt that the development of structured clinical interviews for the assessment of pathology has been a significant step forward in measurement. Certainly it has made possible the selection of groups of patients for research who are diagnostically more homogeneous than was the case when global diagnostic decisions were made on the basis of less systematic clinical impression. Nevertheless, when a clinician assigns a rating to a response made to a structured interview, there is obviously a large element of fallible human judgment involved. More important than that, the sensitivity of rating scales is limited; their limited sensitivity sets a low ceiling on our capacity to detect the fine-grain differences essential to significant further progress in psychopathological research.

Many variables that are currently rated lend themselves to direct counting. In our own work we have turned to the use of counting whenever possible, with interesting results. Examples will follow later in this chapter.

3. Relationships between organismic variables are not always linear

Dealing as we often do with relationships between variables that we can only measure but not manipulate, our process of inference adopts the logic of correlations. For reasons more lodged in habitual than rational choice, the common tendency is to turn to the simple linear regression as the model most likely to reflect the association between two variables. Sometimes this proves to offer a good fit to the scattergram of data points. Where it does not do so, we often ignore the possibility that the underlying relationship is curvilinear, even though we are familiar with the curvilinearity of relationships in many other adaptive functions, such as learning, adaptation thresholds, motivation and performance, and the like.

4. The concept of deficit

It may be helpful to consider as a general working principle that organisms, human and otherwise, rarely do "nothing" in response to the situations in which they find themselves. They may not do, however, what the observer regards as the correct thing to do, and what may appear to be normally the most effective thing to do. When this happens it is tempting to classify what we observe as an instance of a *deficit* or *lack* of capacity to make the normal response. Unfortunately, while this is a valid inference as stated, this kind of classification tends to distract us from observing what the individual *actually does do* – an observation that might otherwise have provided a clue to the nature of the active pathological process that determined the "wrong" response.* By making this point we are, of course, simply rephrasing the position enunciated by J. Hughlings Jackson when he pointed out that the disordered behavior seen in cases of severe central nervous system (CNS) damage is produced by the undamaged lower centers.

A good example of this problem is found in the classification of the language utterances of a patient as exhibiting "poverty of content," "derailment," or "incoherence." The very choice of a term such as "incoherent" tells us we have noticed something that is *lacking* in the utterance, i.e., "coherence," but it does not tell us what was present in the utterance. In one of our own studies, for example (Maher et al., 1987), we found that the counted repetitions of words and phrases in samples of speech in schizophrenic patients significantly correlated with rated levels of Derailment, Understandability, and Poverty of Content as assessed in the Schedule for Affective Disorders and Schizophrenia (SADS) in the same patients at a different time. What the patients were not doing was showing a richness of content; what the patients *were* doing, at least in part, was repeating and perseverating in speech. This observation leads us to become interested in the positive determinants of repetition and perseveration, which seems to us a more manageable definition of the research problem than does the question of "Where did the content go?"

However, as the Chapmans (1973) have tellingly pointed out, patients in psychopathological research may show deficits in a wider range of tasks for reasons that do not necessarily provide direct clues as to their underlying pathology. Problems of diminished motivation, medication, general energy level, and the like all have the potential to impair performance. Because of this, hypotheses that predict patients will fail to equal control groups in the performance of a specific task are quite likely to receive misleading support from the data. There are several technical solutions to the research design problem that this creates. One of them is to employ tasks in which the putative psychopathology should lead to superior performance. If it is confirmed that the performance of the psychopathological group is superior to controls, the methodological difficulties surrounding deficit predictions are alleviated, even if not entirely eliminated.

---

* See also Chapter 5, by Deborah L. Levy, this volume – Eds.

5. The heterogeneity of schizophrenia

There has been general, if sometimes, tacit, acceptance over many decades that the syndrome patterns that lead to a diagnosis of schizophrenia are the surface manifestations of a set of subtypes. Each of these subtypes shares some features in common with the others, a circumstance that gives rise to the use of a single term, "schizophrenia," to refer to them. It is not clear what these subtypes are. That is to say, we do not yet have satisfactory models of these types, encompassing etiology, pathology (both neurological and psychological), clinical syndrome, responses to therapies, and prognosis. Many attempts have been made to ascribe typologies to the available data. Dimensional classification, such as the positive–negative symptom axis, the process–reactive axis, the chronic–acute distinction, and so on have demonstrated some utility in accounting for some of the heterogeneity in the clinical pictures and the laboratory data that have been accumulated over time. Nonetheless, a convincing typology eludes us still. From a methodological point of view, this constitutes at least a nuisance and at best a major challenge to the investigator.

The nuisance lies in the fact that samples of schizophrenic patients, no matter how homogeneous they may appear to be in those manifest aspects that can be measured, are still likely to be somewhat heterogeneous in those matters that are not manifest, such as etiology, neuropathology, and so forth. Heterogeneity of pathology means that when we establish significant differences between schizophrenic patients and other comparison samples on a theoretically important variable, the number of nonconforming cases in the schizophrenic sample is not likely to be trivial. Correlations are often more modest than we would like them to be; differences between means may reach satisfactory levels of significance and yet the distributions around them overlap disturbingly. While some of this is doubtless due to the imperfections of our measurement techniques, some is certainly due to the essential heterogeneity of the populations from which we draw our samples. Given this, we may perhaps regard significant but modest correlations not necessarily as evidence that we are looking at an intrinsically trivial finding, but as an impetus to delineate more sharply the boundaries of the heterogeneity underlying the manifest behavior.

6. States and traits

Pathological behavior frequently undergoes episodic changes in severity and composition, sufficient at times to warrant discharge from care or to return to care after previous discharge. This is because some symptoms are in the nature of states that fluctuate over time, while others are more permanent traits. The only reliable way to distinguish between these two alternatives is to use the method of test–retest stability. While it is routinely accepted that this be done with formal psychometric tests, such as those of intelligence, this has been much less often the case with measures developed specifically for psychiatric populations. The method of group comparisons, made cross-sectionally at single time periods, establishes differences between some aspect of the behavior of a group of patients and that of controls; it cannot establish that the obtained differences are stable, and will be found again in the same sample if the comparison is made sometime later. Because of this, we can never be sure that a failure to replicate a previous study is due to some methodological flaw in the original, or reflects the fact that the behavior under scrutiny is state-like, and hence difficult to replicate on demand.

With these methodological considerations in mind, we now turn to an account of some of the research we have done, and some of the directions we are currently pursuing.

Research studies

1. Language and thought disorder in schizophrenia

The question of the quantitative description and the development of a model of language disturbances in schizophrenia has been a central topic of interest for more than 25 years. A series of studies, beginning with an original investigation by Maher et al. (1966) on that topic, has been summarized elsewhere (cf. Maher, 1972, 1983), and need not be repeated here. We have continued to pursue this general topic with a series of studies intended to provide a basis for the quantitative description and analysis of language utterance in schizophrenia. In these studies we have found that the division of schizophrenic samples into those with current thought disorder (TD) as defined by the SADS interview versus those without current thought disorder

(NTD) identifies significant differences in the measured features of language in several variables. Thought disorder is defined in the studies reported in this chapter by the attainment of a rated score of 3 or higher in one or more of the four SADS categories, *Incoherence, Loosening of Associations, Illogical Thinking,* and *Poverty of Content of Speech.* From these studies, the following general conclusions emerge.

a) Repetition. The spoken utterances of schizophrenic patients, when compared with those of normal controls or affectively disordered patients, are characterized by various kinds of repetition. These include the sequential repetition of single words, two-word phrases, three-word phrases, as well as the nonsequential repetition of words throughout a passage of utterance. Examples from the files include: "I think I'll put on my hat, my hat, my hat" (Maher et al., 1966, p. 786); "What is this there, what is this, what is this" (Bleuler, 1950, p. 187). When we compare TD schizophrenic patients with NTD patients, the high levels of repetition are found to be concentrated in the TD group. The details of the method and a review of the individual studies can be found in Maher et al. (1987).

b) Object chaining. In an original study of schizophrenic written utterances, we observed that there was a significant tendency for TD schizophrenic patients to chain object nouns, i.e., write sentences with more object nouns than subject nouns (Maher et al., 1966). An example of this phenomenon is: "I am still at the University of Berlin, the University of Moscow, the University of Paris, Oxford . . ." (Maher, 1983).

This finding was replicated in additional samples within the original study itself, and has now been replicated, using spoken rather than written utterances (Manschreck et al., 1991a). Using the transcribed utterances of 12 TD and 10 NTD schizophrenics, and 10 normal controls, we replicated the prior study. Ratio of objects to subjects was correlated with Cloze score assessment of the predictability of these utterances (rho. = .53, $p < .001$). The ratio was not, however, significantly correlated with measures of repetition, suggesting that object chaining and repetitiousness contribute independently to the clinical judgment of thought disorder. This, in turn, suggests that the investigation of the correlates and determinants of these two measures may have promise in elucidating the various and heterogeneous cognitive pathologies that are found in schizophrenia. They also demonstrate the value of counting rather than rating as a method for the analysis of symptomatic behavior.

c) Pause patterns. It has often been observed that the timing and rhythms of speech utterances by schizophrenic patients differ from those of normal speakers. A comprehensive model of pausing in normal speech has been provided by Beattie and Butterworth (1979). Among other factors, they established that longer than usual pauses precede: (a) a word of low predictability in the context in which it is uttered even when the word itself has high-frequency use in English, and (b) words of low frequency, regardless of context. The current interpretation of these effects is that the pauses occurring before low-frequency words reflect lexical search time, while those occurring before words of low predictability are governed by the pragmatic limitations of the local context. As the general trend in our findings is that schizophrenic patients do not behave in ways that are guided by relevant contexts, we examined the pause patterns of four TD and four NTD schizophrenics (Maher et al., 1983). Our findings were that NTD patients showed the same pause patterns as do normals, while TD patients exhibited only the word-frequency effect, the relationship between pause length and contextual probability having disappeared.

Spitzer et al. (1993a) examined the relative length of pauses before nouns. Word frequencies were defined by the actual frequency of use by the speaker rather than from large-scale population norms for word frequency. This definition essentially selects words that are similar in character to the unpredictable class of words defined in the earlier study. With this method, normals showed the expected effect – longer pauses before saying infrequent words than before frequent words, but schizophrenics did not. In this investigation, the schizophrenic patients were not divided into TD and NTD groups. Hence, such differences as might have existed between these subsets of patients probably served to diminish the difference between patients and normals. The investigators suggest that their data are consistent with the hypothesis that the infrequent (i.e., unpredictable) words spoken by schizophrenics occur as uncontrolled intrusions rather than as a result of an intention to use them – and hence no lexical decision is involved. It is clear that the determinants of pausing in schizophrenic patients are complex, and that the pauses may reflect factors that are typically absent in normal speech – such as associational intrusion and the like. The findings are fundamentally consistent with those reported by Maher et al. (1983).

2. *Verbal memory*

Some psychopathologists have suggested that the language defects in schizophrenia may be a result of impaired verbal memory, whether of storage or retrieval. We have looked at certain aspects of this.

a) Context. Many studies of normal memory for verbal material have indicated that the degree of contextual organization inherent in the material has a powerful effect on the efficiency of retrieval for recall. On the basis of preliminary studies in our own laboratory we have settled on the use of a derivative of the method pioneered by Miller and Selfridge (1950). In this procedure, the subject listens to a sequence of lists of words. In the minimum context condition, the list consists of unrelated equal-frequency words. Three other lists contain words of similar frequency but that have an increasing degree of context, i.e., they are in sequences increasingly approximate to the structure of a sentence. Immediately after hearing each list (which is given in random order), the subject is asked to recall as many as possible of the words heard. The total of items correctly recalled in each list constitutes the measure of memory. In normal subjects, recall scores increase systematically as a function of the degree of context. This effect is very reliable and has been established across various languages (French, by Taylor and Moray, 1960; Hindi, by Sharma and Sen, 1977; Danish, by Maher and Skovengaard, 1988). Our investigations of context-aided memory in schizophrenics indicate that TD schizophrenics do as well as NTD and normal controls in recalling simple word lists but, unlike the others, TD patients do not improve their performance with context (Maher et al., 1980). This finding is in line with many other studies reporting failure of schizophrenics to profit from context in memory tasks.

In a very recent preliminary study we have been able to look at the relationship of total volume of the frontal area of the brain as a proportion of total volume of the brain, as determined by magnetic resonance imaging (MRI) scan, and the capacity to gain from context, in a sample of 18 schizophrenics (Maher et al., 1994). The results of this preliminary study indicate that capacity to improve recall under conditions of increasing context is significantly related to frontal proportional volume, the age-partialled correlation between frontal volume and recall being .062 (NS) for zero context, which is consistent with the hypothesis that frontal lobe volume did not affect memory for unrelated words. Age-partialled correlations calculated on the other lists, in which there is a systematic increase in order of context, were as follows: second-order $r = +.482$ $(p = .04)$; third-order $r = +0.67$ $(p = .001)$; fourth-order $r = +.604$ $(p = .006)$. This seems to us to be a promising initial finding, and to increase confidence that this measure of context memory may be generally useful. Given the importance of contextual control in maintaining the coherence of language utterance, evidence of impaired ability to utilize context in thought-disordered schizophrenic patients is consistent with what we already know about their manifest disorders of language. The implication of frontal brain involvement points to the possible locus of neuropathology in schizophrenia (an implication that has already been drawn by many other psychopathologists on the basis of a range of evidence),* and as a possible focal locus for the language aspects of the schizophrenic syndrome.

b) Primacy and recency. Grossberg (1982) has proposed that primacy effects in recall (the greater recall of items placed earliest in the list to be recalled) require attentional efficiency in order that limited capacity higher-order processes can chunk items into units that facilitate recall. The general hypothesis is that the formation of single units from groups of stimulus items that have been presented sequentially requires that they be held in short-term memory as a unit, or "chunk," long enough to be combined. He proposes that poor attentional efficiency impairs this process. Diminished or absent primacy effects in schizophrenia have been reported by other investigators (Oltmanns, 1978; Frame and Oltmanns, 1982), and one study reports decreased primacy in children at risk for schizophrenia (Harvey et al., 1981). With these findings in mind, and noting our own findings of impaired capacity for TD schizophrenics to profit from the inherent "chunkiness" of high-context verbal material, we investigated groups of 20 patients each with schizophrenia, affective disorder, and normal controls (Manschreck et al., 1991b). Primacy and recency scores were derived from the recall material elicited by the Miller–Selfridge tech-

---

* See Chapter 2, by Patricia Goldman-Rakic, this volume – Eds.

nique. The findings of this study were as follows. Schizophrenic patients showed impaired primacy but no impairment of recency – a finding that replicates the studies of other investigators just cited. Schizophrenics who showed some improvement in recall with high-context lists, did so mainly in the recency segment (the last 5 of the 20 words) of the list. Schizophrenic patients exhibiting repetitiousness in spontaneous speech, showed most marked impairment of primacy under all conditions; the correlation between low primacy and low variability in speech was .54, $p < .05$. Low primacy also correlated with impaired ability to profit from context, $r = .44$, $p < .03$. The general pattern of these relationships is that low primacy, low capacity to respond to context, and repetitiousness in speech go together.

3. Associational processes

From the model of language disturbance that developed from that work, clear importance attached to the disruptive role of associational processes in the language and thought of these patients. Sentences appear to be most vulnerable to associational intrusions at breakpoints in the units of an utterance, typically but crudely identified with the points at which syntax markers such as commas and periods are placed in written utterance. Accepting the reliability of this observation for the moment, we turn to the associational process itself. Word association responses to lists of stimulus words are readily elicited in normal subjects, but rarely if ever intrude disruptively into sentences in which one of these stimulus words happens to be employed. This suggests that either (a) the associations are very briefly activated but then immediately inhibited, or (b) the formation of the plan of an utterance brings into action a general inhibition of associations, an inhibition that is not present in the special circumstances and instructions employed in the standard word-association test, or (c) the activation of associational networks in schizophrenic patients is more vigorous and long-lasting, i.e., spreads across a wider network of relatively remote associations and is slower to decay to a normal state of nonactivation. Whatever the model we adopt, the prediction is that schizophrenic patients will respond more quickly and reliably than non-schizophrenics in tasks that require access to associations. As this prediction is one of superior performance and not of deficit, it is less vulnerable to the problems that arise with deficit predictions.

The task we have employed to examine associational processes in this way is the *lexical decision* or *semantic priming* procedure, used widely in the study of normal cognitive functions. The patient is presented with a stimulus word on a computer screen (the prime), and this is followed by a second string of letters (the target), which may or may not be a word. When the target appears, the subject presses one of two keys, indicating whether the target is a word or a nonword. Where the target is a word, it may be related to the prime by being a common direct association to it (e.g., doctor – nurse), a clang association (tailor – sailor), or an indirect association (lion – *tiger* – stripe, where lion is the prime and stripe the target, the implicit mediating link not being shown). The measures of interest are the speed and accuracy of the recognition response. A major independent variable in this technique is the time interval between target and prime, as programmed in milliseconds. Very brief intervals (less than 500 msec) are regarded as tapping automatic cognitive processes, while longer intervals permit the operation of controlled or strategic cognitive processes by the subject.

Our studies with this procedure indicate that TD schizophrenic patients showed significantly greater gains in performance in identifying associated targets compared to nonassociated targets than did normal controls and affective and NTD schizophrenics (Maher et al., 1987; Manschreck et al., 1988). This topic has been investigated further by Spitzer and his associates at Heidelberg. Spitzer et al. (1994b) report findings from an investigation of 70 schizophrenic patients, with 124 normal controls. The results can be summarized as follows:

1. The expected larger semantic priming effect in schizophrenic patients than in normal controls was found and was specifically related to the presence of thought disorder.
2. The effect was not an artifact of general slowness of response in these patients. The overall reaction time (RT) of the TD patients was not different from that of NTD.
3. The effect was robust, occurring at three prime-target intervals (200 msec 400 msec 700 msec).
4. At short prime-target intervals, normal subjects have slower responses to clang (rhyming) associations as compared to nonrhyming words, indicating an inhibition effect in this condition; TD schizophrenics do not exhibit this inhibition at the shortest interval, i.e., in what is most clearly the automatic.

5. In a small pilot study currently ongoing, 11 of these patients have been tested twice, first during the acute phase of the illness and later during improvement. In this latter phase, semantic priming decreases toward normal levels, and inhibition of clang associations is restored. This, of course, suggests that high levels of associational activity found in schizophrenia are state rather than trait in nature.

In the second study by Spitzer et al. (1993b), 32 schizophrenics and 32 normal controls were presented with the semantic priming task, including an indirect association condition. Indirect priming was found in both groups when the prime-target interval was large (700 msec), but was found only in schizophrenics at a short, automatic-level interval of 200 msec. This is consistent with the hypothesis that network activation is more widespread in schizophrenic patients than in normals and occurs very rapidly when a stimulus word is activated.

One advantage of this approach is that the hypothesis predicts *superior* performance by schizophrenics. The faster reaction time cannot plausibly be interpreted as an artifact of general deficit, and thus avoids some of the methodological ambiguities that surround deficit-produced artifacts.

Finally, we turn to studies of semantic priming in normal subjects, wakened from REM sleep, i.e., when dreaming, a state commonly supposed to be one in which associational processes are unusually active. Spitzer et al. (1991) reported a pilot study of four normal subjects, each of whom spent two nights in a sleep laboratory, and who performed lexical decision tasks before going to sleep, on being awakened from REM sleep, and on being awakened from Non-REM sleep. Sleep states were determined by polygraph. In this small sample, priming under the REM condition was greater than in the waking condition ($p = .0646$). Performance in NREM was below that in the REM condition, but not significantly so. In the REM there were no errors of recognition; in the other two conditions there were equal and small error rates (4.2%). This pilot study has been replicated by Spitzer et al. (1994a) with 10 subjects, on two nights each, with the same results as those obtained in the pilot study.

4. Motor performance

Studies of the language and thought of psychotic populations always run the risk of "discovering" the presence of manifest behavioral features that were, in fact, essential to the diagnosis that had defined the patient in the first place. It is true that the quantitative measurement of these features is an advance upon the use of the kind of clinical impression of them that influenced the original diagnosis; indeed, this quantification is an essential step to conducting adequately scientific research into the underlying pathology. However, the ultimate relevance of the measurement of the clinically manifest aspects of pathology depends upon establishing correlations between them and other systems, neuropsychological, behavioral, and so on, in ways that provide a comprehensive model of the entire pathological process from etiology to outcome.

One promising direction in which this strategy may be pursued is in the area of motor behavior. Motor components of schizophrenic behavior have been observed and described clinically over many decades (e.g., Bleuler, 1911/1950; Kraepelin, 1919; King, 1975; Manschreck, 1983). These have included the motor stereotypies, the various postural and movement anomalies in catatonia, and so forth. However, there have been many obstacles to the systematic study of motor behavior, chief among them being the lack of reliable systems measurement. This, in turn, has been a function of the difficulties that beset the definition of a unit of motor activity. Language can be conveniently segmented into words, phrases, syllables, sentences, and so on, each conveniently divided by spaces or pauses. Spontaneous motor activity, on the other hand, does not present itself in a manner in which meaningful units are intuitively clear.

In a series of studies, we have sought to establish the relationship between anomalies of language and anomalies of motor behavior. Our approach has involved the use of structured clinical assessment techniques as well as the development and application of laboratory measures. In an early study (Manschreck et al., 1981) we looked at relationship of verbal repetitiousness to motor behavior as assessed by a series of scales, side effects of medication being assessed by the Abnormal Involuntary Movement Scale (AIMS) (National Institute of Mental Health, 1974) and the Targeting of Abnormal Kinetic Effects (TAKE) of Wojcik et al. (1980). Groups of TD and NTD schizophrenics, unipolar affectives, and normal controls were employed. With adjustment for medication effects by regression, the mean total motor disruption score of TD schizophrenics was significantly higher than that of NTD schizophrenics or either of the other two groups. Within the group of schizophrenic patients we were able to compare medicated and drug-free patients, and found that the relationship between thought disorder and abnormal motor behavior was unaffected by medication. Variability (i.e., low repetitiousness scores) of speech correlated highly negatively with motor anomaly scores ($r = -.59, p < .001$, df. 32) in all of the psychiatric subjects together, and $-.58$ ($p < .01$, df. 20) in the group of schizophrenics taken separately. The most frequent clinical forms of motor anomaly were clumsiness, stereotypies, manneristic responses, and motor blocking.

In later studies we have employed a motor tapping synchrony task, in which the patient is asked to synchronize tapping responses to the sound of a computer-generated series of clicks. Accuracy scores include the mean interval of the patient's actual tapping (compared to the true interval of the computer stimulus) and variability of the patient's response as defined by the standard deviation around the response mean interval. An ideal score would consist of a zero standard deviation, and a mean that corresponds exactly to that of the stimulus series. With this technique we have obtained results that indicate a relationship between the tapping measure and clinical measures of motor anomaly, i.e., the synchrony test appears to have a valid relationship to the clinical phenomenon. In subsequent studies (e.g., Manschreck et al., 1985) we found that a group of 21 schizophrenics did not differ from other groups in their ability to produce a mean response interval similar to that of the stimulus series, but did differ very significantly in the standard deviation around that mean. An examination of the synchrony performance of a subset of 12 nonmedicated schizophrenics indicated that the nonmedicated patients were no better than the medicated, and at one interval (40 beats per minute) were significantly worse, suggesting that medication was not responsible for the poor performance of the medicated subset. Analysis of the nonmedicated patients produced significant correlations between the standard deviation and the following negative symptoms: blunted affect as measured by the Brief Psychiatric Rating Scale (BPRS) (Overall and Gorham, 1962) 0.59; emotional withdrawal (BPRS) 0.62; refusal to speak, as assessed by the Nurses Observation Scale for Inpatient Examination (NOSIE) (Honigfeld and Klett, 1965) 0.65.

A fuller account of our early motor investigations is to be found in Manschreck (1983) and in Maher et al. (1987). The development of this research topic is currently in progress. We have become interested in the possibility of developing a simpler measure of clumsiness and tremor than has hitherto been available. In a very recent study by Blyler et al. (1992) we have employed a simple line-drawing task, wherein the patient is asked to draw a series of four straight lines, each one obliquely across a 2-inch square. Two are drawn from left to right, and two from right to left. One of each of these sets is done with the right hand and the other set with the left hand. The lines are then scanned optically into a computer. Here the scan converts each line to x and y numerical coordinates and calculates the simple regression line for those points. The root mean square then becomes the measure of departure from a true straight line. Preliminary tests with this technique indicate that it can be used very reliably to differentiate the use of the self-defined preferred and nonpreferred hand. The magnitude of the difference between the performance of the two hands may have promise as a measure of relative cerebral dominance in patients. We have looked at a set of data from 49 schizophrenics and 31 controls. Schizophrenic performance was significantly worse overall ($p = .01$) than the controls. It also appears that the relative performance of left-handed and right-handed schizophrenic patients does not simply mirror that of normals. The data suggest that the relative dominance of left-handed schizophrenics is much smaller than in right-handed schizophrenics. This is clearly a preliminary approach to the measurement of this kind of motor performance, but appears to have the advantage of initial validity and requires a very small amount of time or effort to obtain from patients.

Summary

The studies described in this chapter point to the importance of the study of impairment of contextual control in schizophrenic pathology, the role of failure of inhibition of associations in overriding contextual control, and the importance of extending our observations of cognitive anomalies to include their connection with motor symptoms.

Acknowledgments

The studies reported here have been conducted over many years with my colleague and close collaborator, Theo C. Manschreck, currently Professor of Psychiatry at Brown University Medical School, and in recent years, Manfred Spitzer of the University Psychiatric Clinic at Heidelberg.

References

Beattie, G. W., and Butterworth, B. L. (1979) Contextual probability and word frequency as determinants of pauses and errors in spontaneous speech. *Language and Speech, 22,* 201–211.

Bleuler, E. (1950) *Dementia Praecox or the Group of Schizophrenias.* New York: International Universities Press. (Originally published 1911)

Blyler, C. R., Maher, B. A., Brooks, A., and Manschreck, T. C. (1992) A new method to assess motor disorder and handedness in schizophrenia. Unpublished manuscript.

Chapman, L. J., and Chapman, J. P. (1973) *Disordered Thought in Schizophrenia.* New York: Appleton-Century Crofts.

Frame, C., and Oltmanns, T. F. (1982) Serial recall by schizophrenic and affective patients during and after psychotic episodes. *Journal of Abnormal Psychology, 91,* 311–318.

Grossberg, S. (1982) *Studies of Mind and Brain.* Boston: Reidel.

Harvey, P., Winter, K., Weintraub, S., and Neale, J. M. (1981) Distractibility in children vulnerable to psychopathology. *Journal of Abnormal Psychology, 90,* 298–304.

Honigfeld, G., and Klett, C. J. (1965) The Nurses Observation Scale for Inpatient Observation. *Journal of Clinical Psychology, 21,* 65–71.

King, H. E. (1975) Psychomotor correlates of behavior disorder. In M. L. Kietzman, S. Sutton, and J. Zubin (Eds.), *Experimental Approaches to Psychopathology.* Orlando, FL: Academic Press.

Kraepelin, E. (1919) *Dementia Praecox.* (trans. E. Barclay and W. Barclay). Edinburgh: Livingston.

Maher, B. A. (1972) The language of schizophrenia: A review and interpretation. *British Journal of Psychiatry, 120,* 1–17.

Maher, B. A. (1983) Towards a tentative theory of schizophrenic utterance. *Progress in Experimental Personality Research,* vol. 12. New York: Academic Press, pp. 1–51.

Maher, B. A., Manschreck, T. C., Hoover, T. M., and Weisstein, C. C. (1987) Thought disorder and measured features of language production in schizophrenia. In P. D. Harvey and E. F. Walker (Eds.), *Positive and Negative Symptoms of Psychosis.* Hillsdale, NJ: Erlbaum, pp. 195–215.

Maher, B. A., and Skovengaard, J. (1988) Contextual constraint: A Danish language replication of Miller–Selfridge with methodological improvements. *Scandinavian Journal of Psychology, 29,* 194–199.

Maher, B. A., McKean, K. O., and McLaughlin, B. (1966) Studies in psychotic language. In P. J. Stone, D. C. Dunphy, M. S. Smith, and D. M. Ogilvie (Eds.), *The General Inquirer: A Computer Approach to Content Analysis.* Cambridge, MA: MIT Press, pp. 469–503.

Maher, B. A., Manschreck, T. C., and Rucklos, M. E. (1980) Contextual constraint and the recall of verbal material in schizophrenia: The effect of thought disorder. *British Journal of Psychiatry, 137,* 69–73.

Maher, B. A., Manschreck, T. C., and Molino, M.A.C. (1983) Redundancy, pause distributions and thought disorder in schizophrenia. *Language and Speech, 26,* 191–199.

Maher, B. A., Manschreck, T. C., Woods, B., Yurgelun-Todd, D., and Tsuang, M. (1995). Frontal brain volume and context effects in short-term recall in schizophrenia. *Biological Psychiatry, 37,* 144–150.

Manschreck, T. C. (1983) Psychopathology of motor behavior in schizophrenia. In *Progress in Experimental Personality Research,* vol. 12. New York: Academic Press.

Manschreck, T. C., Maher, B. A., and Ader, D. N. (1981) Formal thought disorder, the type-token ratio, and disturbed voluntary motor movement in schizophrenia. *British Journal of Psychiatry, 139,* 7–15.

Manschreck, T. C., Maher, B. A., Waller, N. G., Ames, D., and Latham, C. A. (1985) Deficient motor synchrony in schizophrenic disorders: Clinical correlates. *Biological Psychiatry, 20,* 990–1002.

Manschreck, T. C., Maher, B. A., Milavetz, J. J., Ames, D., Weisstein, C. C., and Schneyer, M. L. (1988) Semantic priming in thought-disordered schizophrenics. *Schizophrenia Research, 1,* 61–66.

Manschreck, T. C., Maher, B. A., Celada, M., Schneyer, M., and Fernandez, R. (1991a). Object chaining and thought disorder in schizophrenic speech. *Psychological Medicine, 21,* 443–446.

Manschreck, T. C., Maher, B. A., Rosenthal, J. E., and Berner, J. (1991b) Reduced primacy and related features in schizophrenia. *Schizophrenia Research, 5,* 35–41.

Miller, G., and Selfridge, J. (1950) Verbal context and the recall of meaningful material. *American Journal of Psychology, 63,* 176–185.

National Institute of Mental Health. (1974) *Abnormal Involuntary Movement Scale (AIMS).* U.S. Public Health Service Publication No. MH-9-17. Washington, DC: U.S. Government Printing Office.

Oltmanns, T. F. (1978) Selective attention in schizophrenic and manic psychosis: The effect of distraction on information processing. *Journal of Abnormal Psychology, 87,* 212–225.

Overall, J. E., and Gorham, D. R. (1962) The Brief Psychiatric Rating Scale. *Psychological Record, 10,* 799–812.

Sharma, N. K., and Sen, A. (1977) Effect of verbal context on communication in Hindi. *Indian Journal of Psychology, 7,* 240–249.

Spitzer, M. (1993) Assoziative Netzwerke, formal Denkstörungen und Schizophrenie. Zur experimentellen Psychopathologie sprachabhängiger Denkprozesse. *Nervenarzt, 64,* 147–159.

Spitzer, M., Mamelak, A., Stickgold, R., Williams, J., Koutstaal, W., Rittenhouse, C., Maher, B., and Hobson, J. (1991) Semantic priming in a lexical decision task on awakenings from REM sleep. *Sleep Research, 20,* 131.

Spitzer, M., Beuckers, J., Maier, S., and Hermle, L. (1993a) Contextual insensitivity in schizophrenic patients is due to semantic network pathology: Evidence from spontaneous pauses in speech.

Spitzer, M., Braun, U., Maier, S., Hermle, L., and Maher, B. A. (1993b) Indirect semantic priming in schizophrenia. *Schizophrenia Research, 11,* 71–80.

Spitzer, M., Walder, S., and Clarenbach, P. (1994a) Semantische Bahnung im REM-Schlaf. In K. Meier-Ewert and E. Rüther (Eds.), *Shlafmedizin, S.* Stuttgart: Gustav Fischer, pp. 168–178.

Spitzer, M., Weisker, I., Maier, S., Hermle, L., and Maher, B. A. (1994b) Semantic and phonological priming in schizophrenia. *Journal of Abnormal Psychology, 103,* 485–494.

Taylor, A., and Moray, N. (1960) Statistical approximation to English and French. *Language and Speech, 3,* 7–40.

Wojcik, J., Gelenberg, A., LaBrie, R. A., and Berg, M. (1980) Prevalence of tardive dyskinesia in an outpatient population. *Comprehensive Psychiatry, 21,* 370–379.

Genetics

20

Editors' introduction: Contemporary issues in the genetics of psychopathological disorders

---

Deborah L. Levy, Steven Matthysse, and Philip S. Holzman

For many years empirical research supported the genetic independence of schizophrenia and the affective disorders. Morbid risk for schizophrenia was found to be significantly elevated among relatives of schizophrenics, but not among relatives of affective disorder patients. Moreover, morbid risk for affective disorders was found to be heightened among relatives of patients with affective disorders, but not among relatives of schizophrenics. Twin studies also yielded concordance rates in monozygotic (MZ) and dizygotic (DZ) twins that were consistent with a genetic etiology for each disorder, but not with a genetic relation between the two disorders.

More recent work indicates that both the magnitude of the risk and the specificity of familial liability for schizophrenia were probably overestimated in early studies. These changes are largely a function of refinements in methodology that include: (1) blind diagnostic evaluations of family members, (2) diagnostic data that are now almost routinely based on personal interviews, (3) inclusion of psychiatric and normal control groups, (4) use of standardized diagnostic interviews, (5) use of population-based as well as hospitalized samples, and (6) the availability of operationalized diagnostic criteria, which tend to restrict rather than broaden the boundaries of a disorder. For similar reasons concordance rates in early twin studies may have been inflated (Gottesman and Shields, 1972).

Neither this reduction in morbid risk for schizophrenia in relatives of schizophrenics nor the reduced specificity of familial aggregation for schizophrenia lessens the role of genetic liability, however. This is because the range of psychiatric disorders that show a familial relation to schizophrenia has expanded, due in large part to the use of nar-

455

rower diagnostic criteria for schizophrenia and more clearly operationalized criteria for all psychiatric disorders. Thus, disorders that were once labelled as schizophrenia now receive a variety of labels in addition to schizophrenia. Consequently, morbid risk for several disorders, including but not limited to schizophrenia, is increased in individuals who are biologically related to schizophrenics, and morbid risk for schizophrenia is increased in relatives of individuals with these other disorders. Such variable expression of a clinical phenotype is not uncommon in disorders with a homogeneous genetic basis, as discussed below. Growing understanding of the nature of the familiality of psychiatric disorders is largely responsible for the emerging awareness of the heterogeneous clinical manifestations of genetic liability for schizophrenia.

1. The clinical phenotype: Which psychiatric disorders are cofamilial manifestations of increased liability?

1.1 Schizophrenia

Schizophrenia is a familial disorder. Numerous studies have documented the familial aggregation of schizophrenia among relatives of schizophrenics (Scharfetter and Nusperli, 1980; Tsuang et al., 1980; Guze et al., 1983; Kendler and Gruenberg, 1984; Baron et al., 1985; Frangos et al., 1985; Kendler et al., 1985a, 1993, 1994; Gershon et al., 1988; Maier et al., 1990). Although a few family studies have failed to confirm this finding (Pope et al., 1982; Abrams and Taylor, 1983; Coryell and Zimmerman, 1988), there are several possible reasons for the discrepancies. These include small samples (which limit power to detect group differences when the base rates for the disorders under study are low), diagnoses based on data other than personal interviews (which lower sensitivity, especially for schizotypal signs like affective blunting, interpersonal aloofness, behavioral oddness), and possibly, sampling variation (Kendler, 1988).

The familial aggregation of schizophrenia suggests that genetic factors play an important role in the etiology of the disorder. Shared environment can, of course, account for the increased morbid risk for schizophrenia among relatives of schizophrenics, but in addition to twin studies (Kringlen, 1967; Gottesman and Shields, 1972), adoption studies (Heston, 1966; Rosenthal et al., 1971; Kety et al., 1975; see Chapter 21, by Seymour Kety, this volume) support genetic liability as a key determinant in the development of severe psychopathology.

1.2 Other psychotic disorders

The enhanced risk of relatives of schizophrenics is not restricted to schizophrenia alone. Other clinical disorders also aggregate among these family members. Prominent among them is schizoaffective disorder (Scharfetter and Nusperli, 1980; Baron et al., 1982; Kendler and Gruenberg, 1984; Kendler et al., 1985b, 1986; Gershon et al., 1988; Maier et al., 1990). Delusional disorder, schizophreniform disorder, atypical psychosis and nonaffective psychosis also show a familial relationship to schizophrenia (Guze et al., 1983; Kendler et al., 1985b, 1986; Farmer et al., 1987), but there are exceptions to this pattern (Kendler and Hays, 1981; Kendler et al., 1981c, 1985a).

These family data indicating that schizophrenia is not the only clinical expression of liability are also consistent with the results of some twin studies. Farmer et al. (1987) found that the highest MZ/DZ concordance ratios were obtained when atypical psychosis, major affective disorder with psychotic features and mood-incongruent delusions, and schizotypal personality disorder (SPD) were considered along with schizophrenia.*

1.3 Affective disorders

The familial relation between the affective disorders and schizophrenia remains the most controversial – and complicated – issue in understanding conflicting data from family studies. Many studies have found no increased liability for affective disorders among relatives of schizophrenics (Kendler et al., 1982, 1985a, 1985b, 1994; Kendler and Gruenberg, 1984; Guze et al., 1983; Frangos et al., 1985), and consistent with this negative result, no increased risk for schizophrenia among relatives of patients with affective illness (Frangos et al., 1983; Weissman et al., 1984).

There is, however, substantial evidence that the risk for some forms of affective disorder may have been underestimated among relatives of schizophrenics. Significantly increased rates of affective disorder,

---

* See also comment by Philip S. Holzman and Steven Matthysse on Chapter 22, by Einar Kringlen, this volume – Eds.

particularly psychotic affective disorders and bipolar disorder, have been reported among relatives of schizophrenics (Tsuang et al., 1980; Gershon et al., 1988; Crow, 1990; Maier et al., 1990; Kendler et al., 1993). Conversely, the risk for schizophrenia is elevated among relatives of patients with psychotic affective illness (Coryell et al., 1984, 1985; Kendler et al., 1993) and the relatives of manic patients (Tsuang et al., 1980).

Data on familial risk in relatives of schizoaffective patients, who have some symptoms associated with schizophrenia, and some associated with affective illness (e.g., depression, mania) are similarly inconsistent. Although some studies have shown an increased rate of both schizophrenia and affective psychosis in relatives of patients with schizoaffective disorder, not all findings have been uniform in this regard (Scharfetter and Nusperli, 1980; Baron et al., 1982; Gershon et al., 1988; Pope et al., 1988; Kendler et al., 1993). Results vary not only with respect to which kinds of affective illness aggregate among relatives of schizophrenics and schizoaffectives, but also whether subtyping of schizoaffective disorder (e.g., mainly schizophrenic or mainly affective, manic or depressed) clarifies whether and how these disorders are familially related.

There are several possible reasons for inconsistent findings on the familial relation between schizophrenia and affective disorders.

1.3.1. The boundaries between schizophrenia and the affective disorders are equivocal, even with the more clearly delineated criteria currently in use – *International Classification of Diseases,* 9th edition (ICD-9) and *Diagnostic and Statistical Manual –* 3rd edition, revised (DSM-III-R) and now the fourth edition (DSM-IV). Of the patients who received a hospital diagnosis of schizophrenia in a recent epidemiologic study (Kendler et al., 1993) 24% (68/282) met "best-estimate" DSM-III-R criteria for a major affective disorder, other nonaffective nonschizophrenic disorder, or no disorder. Indeed, only 57% of the patients who were diagnosed as schizophrenic by hospital psychiatrists met DSM-III-R criteria for schizophrenia or schizoaffective disorder. Similarly, 17% (16/93) of the patients who received hospital diagnoses of affective disorders were judged independently to meet DSM-III-R criteria for schizophrenia, SPD, or a nonaffective psychosis (Kendler et al., 1993). Thus, the degree of certainty attached to any cross-sectional clinical evaluation is imperfect, even with explicit diagnostic criteria.

1.3.2. Most family studies use a diagnostic hierarchy to handle co-morbidity for several Axis I disorders and/or Axis I and Axis II disorders, even though hierarchical diagnosis makes little sense in the context of genetic studies. Disorders that are thought to be related to schizophrenia are ranked higher in the hierarchy and are mutually exclusive of disorders that are ranked lower in the hierarchy. In the recent Kendler et al. (1993) study, for example, SPD preempts both psychotic and nonpsychotic affective illness because it ranks higher in the hierarchy. Thus, individuals with both SPD and an affective disorder are counted only in the morbid risk estimates for SPD. Risk for major affective disorder is therefore underestimated, because it includes only individuals with no disorder higher in the hierarchy, including the nonpsychotic category of schizotypal personality disorder.

The magnitude of the effect of this hierarchy on morbid risk estimates for affective illness depends on the frequency of its comorbidity with SPD. And since SPD is expected to be more frequent among relatives of schizophrenics than among relatives of controls, the effect of the hierarchy on morbid risk estimates for affective illness will not be uniform in both groups. In the Kendler et al. study, the hierarchy did not obscure the detection of elevated risk for psychotic affective illness in relatives of schizophrenics, although it may have reduced the magnitude of that elevated risk. The impact of the hierarchy on morbid risk for nonpsychotic major depression could also be a factor in the low rates of nonpsychotic affective illness in relatives of schizophrenics, but again the frequency of comorbidity with SPD is a critical and unknown variable.

In another recent family study, Parnas et al. (1993) used a similar hierarchy, but reported both "hierarchical" and "nonhierarchical" lifetime DSM-III-R diagnoses. Comparing prevalence data from the hierarchical and nonhierarchical figures provides a good illustration of the potential for *selectively biased* underestimates when hierarchical diagnoses are used. The rate of major depression more than doubled in adult offspring of schizophrenics when not precluded by other diagnoses higher in the hierarchy, including schizotypy, but changed very little in offspring of controls. High comorbidity for major depression and schizotypy is known. Siever et al. (1990), for example, reported that 65.4% of patients with schizotypal personality disorder met Research Diagnostic Criteria for a lifetime diagnosis of major depression, and 53.9% of these subjects met criteria for current major depression. Thus, the familiality of major depression among relatives of schizophrenics may vary depending on whether schizotypy is assessed, the structure of the diagnostic hierarchy, and, as discussed below, diagnostic practices in distinguishing between schizotypal signs and symptoms and depression.

1.3.3. Differential diagnostic sensitivity affects recurrence risk estimates. Is there an oversensitivity to affective disorders in studies that find "unexpectedly" high rates of major depression or affective illness among relatives of schizophrenics? Are low rates of affective disorder a reflection of diagnostic insensitivity? Are signs and symptoms that some investigators consider schizotypal (e.g., social isolation, blunted affect, anhedonia) interpreted by other investigators as depressive? For major depression, in particular, which is relatively common in the general population (Blazer et al., 1994; Kessler et al., 1994), differing thresholds for attributing significance to symptoms can result in marked variability in morbid risk. Although diagnostic criteria are more operationalized than ever before, diagnosis continues to involve many subjective judgments, which can have a significant impact on rates of different disorders.

Variability in results across studies can reflect differences in the populations from which patient or family samples are drawn, but this is an incomplete explanation; the systematic causes of the variation need to be explored. A similar point was made by Smith and Iacono (1986) when they showed that the varying results regarding lateral ventricular enlargement in schizophrenics had more to do with ventricle size of the controls than with ventricle size of the schizophrenics.

Comparing the results of two recent studies, each of which used "best-estimate" DSM-III-R diagnostic criteria, provides some interesting contrasts that implicate diagnostic practices at least as much as population differences in rates of disorders. Overall features of the results are similar in that both studies described significant elevations in risk for schizophrenia among first-degree relatives of schizophrenics, compared with relatives of normal controls. Yet there are also striking disparities. The prevalence of psychotic affective illness was significantly elevated among relatives of schizophrenics in the Kendler et al. (1993) study, yet there was not even a single case in 311 high-risk or low-risk adult offspring in the Parnas et al. (1993) study. Morbid risk for schizophrenia differed by a factor of almost 3 in relatives of schizophrenics in the two studies (6.5% in the Kendler et al., 1993, study; 17.1% in the Parnas et al., 1993, study) and by a factor of almost 6 in relatives of controls (0.5% vs. 2.9%). None of the offspring was schizophrenic in the Kendler et al. study, in contrast to 16.1% in the Parnas study. Indeed, 43% of the offspring in the Parnas et al. study had a schizophrenia spectrum disorder. Ironically, the Kendler et al. (1993) study reported a substantially higher risk for schizophrenia in relatives of schizophrenics than did many other recent family studies, yet the figures are quite low when compared with those reported by Parnas et al. (1993). Although features of the sampling and design (chronicity of the mothers' illnesses, longitudinal follow-up of offspring) are undoubtedly factors in the higher rates reported by Parnas et al. (1993), such large differences raise the question of site-specific diagnostic practices in applying the same diagnostic criteria.

Other considerations relevant to differences in diagnostic practices are the issues of control groups and blindness. Morbid risk for schizophrenia may be found to be higher in relatives of schizophrenics than in relatives of psychotic affective disorder patients, but without a normal control group it is impossible to determine whether both groups of relatives have elevated morbid risks but differ in the magnitude of increased risk, or whether an increase is specific to one group of relatives. Scharfetter and Nusperli (1980), for example, reported an increased risk for schizophrenia, but not for affective psychosis, among relatives of schizophrenics. This conclusion was based on a risk for schizophrenia of about 10%, and a lower risk of 4% for affective psychosis, in first-degree relatives of schizophrenics. Although 4% is less than 10%, whether either number is higher than the base rate in the normal population cannot be determined without psychiatric data on a control population. Comparison data on normal samples studied by other investigators do not circumvent the interpretive ambiguity, because we do not know what risk for schizophrenia and affective illness the same investigators might have found in the normal population. Control groups make possible estimation of relative diagnostic sensitivity. Exclusion of a "normal control" group also makes it impossible for interviews to be "blind," because every subject is known to be either a patient proband or a relative of a patient proband. The awareness that everyone is related to a psychiatric proband can predispose toward diagnostic false positives and undermine comparative estimates of sensitivity.

1.3.4. Not all investigators distinguish between psychotic and non-psychotic forms of affective illness. Thus, when there are different patterns of familial aggregation between the two, as in the Kendler et al. (1993) study, it is hard to compare the results with those of studies that lump all affective disorders or all major depressive disorders into one category. The category "affective illness" is used in some studies, but bipolar disorder and major depression are used in others. Sometimes major depression with and without psychotic features is distinguished, sometimes single and recurrent episodes are distinguished, and sometimes schizoaffective disorder is subtyped. Until there is a consistent orientation to the ways affective disorders and affective features are characterized, the kinds of inconsistencies summarized above will be difficult to resolve.

1.4 Nonpsychotic disorders

The greater risk for psychiatric illness among relatives of schizophrenics is not limited to the psychotic disorders discussed above. Schizotypal and paranoid personality disorder seem to show a familial link to schizophrenia. These disorders are significantly more prevalent among relatives of schizophrenics than among relatives of controls (Kety et al., 1975; Kendler et al., 1981b, 1994; Baron et al., 1983; Gunderson et al., 1983; Kendler and Gruenberg, 1984; Dorfman et al., 1993), and schizoid personality disorder may be as well (Kety et al., 1968; Bleuler, 1978; Lowing et al., 1983; Frangos et al., 1985; Dorfman et al., 1993).

Some recent work suggests that schizotypal personality traits are not specific to relatives of schizophrenics. Squires-Wheeler et al. (1988, 1989) found these traits to be as prevalent among offspring of affective disorder patients as among offspring of schizophrenic patients. Kendler (1985), however, has pointed out that only a subset of the signs and symptoms of SPD may distinguish biological relatives of schizophrenics. If only the "attenuated negative" symptoms and signs of SPD (e.g., social isolation, odd speech, poor rapport, and aloof affect) distinguish relatives of schizophrenics from relatives of controls, use of categorical diagnoses will underdetect individuals with distinctively aberrant traits and obscure patterns of specificity. Consistent with this orientation, perceptual aberrations, which can be considered an attenuated positive schizotypal symptom, may actually be more common among relatives of controls (Katsanis et al., 1990).

Not only may only selected schizotypal signs and symptoms be specific to relatives of schizophrenics, but the interaction of these signs and symptoms with other clinical features may also influence patterns of familial aggregation. The results of a study by Silverman et al. (1993) suggest that schizotypal traits that occur in the *absence* of affective symptoms, i.e., "pure" schizotypal features, show greater specificity to relatives of schizophrenics than does a combination of schizotypal and affective symptoms. Using the family history method, Silverman et al. (1993) assessed schizotypal and affective traits in relatives of schizophrenics and relatives of individuals with: (1) SPD; (2) borderline personality disorder; (3) mixed schizotypal-borderline features; and (4) other personality disorders. They found that the relatives of schizophrenics had a significantly increased prevalence of "pure" schizotypal traits (social isolation, eccentricity, suspiciousness, and/or odd speech, but *no* features of chronic affective lability) compared with relatives of individuals with borderline and other personality disorders. The findings in relatives of schizotypal individuals were similar to those of relatives of schizophrenics, but the pattern was not as strong. The combination of schizotypal *and* affective traits, in contrast, was significantly more frequent in relatives of individuals with borderline personality disorder and the relatives of individuals with mixed schizotypal-borderline features than in relatives of schizophrenics or relatives of individuals with SPD. Thus, only schizotypy without coexisting affective symptomatology was specific to relatives of schizophrenics.

1.5 Reciprocity

The discussion above has summarized the evidence showing enhanced liability for certain disorders other than schizophrenia in relatives of schizophrenics. The converse is true as well: the relatives of patients with the nonschizophrenic illnesses that aggregate among relatives of schizophrenics also have an increased risk for schizophrenia. The familial predisposition to schizophrenia is significantly elevated among relatives of patients with schizoaffective disorder, nonaffective psychoses, and psychotic affective illness (Scharfetter and Nusperli, 1980; Tsuang, 1991; Maier et al., 1992). The risk for schizophrenia is also significantly increased in relatives of individuals with schizotypal personality disorder (Battaglia et al., 1991; Kendler et al., 1993) or with psychometrically defined schizotypy (Lenzenweger and Loranger, 1989; see Chapter 14, by Chapman and Chapman, this volume), but not all studies confirm this association (Torgersen, 1983; Gunderson et al., 1983; Baron et al., 1985; Schulz et al., 1986). Severity of illness of the schizotypal patients may be a factor in the varying results. In the Kendler et al. (1993) study, for example, the 16 SPD probands had not only been hospitalized, but 69% of them had been diagnosed as schizophrenic by hospital psychiatrists. These schizotypal subjects may be more severely ill than other clinical samples of schizotypal subjects or a community-based sample of schizotypes.

1.6 Specific or generalized predisposition

The range of disorders for which relatives of schizophrenics have an increased risk could suggest that the familial predisposition is for all psychiatric disorders, rather than for a certain cluster of specific illnesses. This, however, is not the case. Neither relatives of schizophrenics, nor relatives of individuals with the psychotic and non-psychotic conditions that show a familial relation to schizophrenia, have a generalized increase in risk for all psychiatric disorders. Increased risk for schizophrenia and schizophrenia-related illnesses occurs primarily in relatives of psychiatric patients with psychotic disorders. Relatives of patients with *nonpsychotic* affective disorders are at no greater risk for these disorders than the general population (Kendler et al., 1993, 1994). Nor does there appear to be a familial relation between schizophrenia and anxiety disorders (Kendler et al., 1981a, 1985b, 1994). Rather, relatives of schizophrenics show a predisposition to a number of psychotic conditions, including affective disorders with certain clinical features, and to specific kinds of nonpsychotic conditions and traits that have long been linked to schizophrenia. Schizophrenia is therefore one of several possible clinical outcomes of enhanced liability.

2. Pleiotropy

It may seem inappropriate or inaccurate to refer to genetic liability for "schizophrenia" when this liability includes increased risk for disorders with other diagnostic labels. Wide variability in clinical phenotype is well documented even in diseases whose precise genetic mutation is known, however. Some examples of pleiotropy involving nonpsychiatric disorders are described below to help clarify the point: the behavioral expression of the same gene can vary widely in clinical manifestations, severity, and penetrance, even among members of the same family with the *same* mutation. All members of the family with the mutation are affected, but not all affected individuals have identical symptoms, an identical clinical course, or the same age of onset. All members of the family do not necessarily have the same disease, however, because once a particular disease process starts, it may involve self-reinforcing mechanisms that set it apart as a distinct entity. Thus, it is useful to retain the distinction between schizophrenia and schizophrenia-related disorders.

Psychiatry has found it difficult to incorporate fully the concept of pleiotropy into thinking about the genetics of major psychiatric illness, perhaps because its historical reliance on descriptive phenomenology is so closely tied to clusters of symptoms and clinical course as distinctive features of different diseases. This orientation stands in sharp contrast to an intrinsic feature of pleiotropy: *the varying manifestations of a gene need not involve even ostensibly similar kinds of traits.* It therefore appears harder to believe that the same genetic mutation can result in brittle bones that are easily fractured *or* blue sclerae, as is the case for Type I osteogenesis imperfecta (Tenni et al., 1991), because they seem so dissimilar, than it is to believe that mutations in the same gene can result in muscle degeneration of varying severity, as is the case for Duchenne and Becker muscular dystrophy (Worton and Thompson, 1988). Analogously, the possibility that schizotypal signs and symptoms may be attenuated expressions of the same gene that causes schizophrenia seems somehow more reasonable than that the same mutation may cause depression or mania. This is probably because features of schizotypy like perceptual aberrations, odd beliefs, and illusions can be readily viewed as milder but phenomenologically similar variants of hallucinations and delusions. Nor do blunted affect and interpersonal aloofness seem far removed from affective flattening and social withdrawal. The familial relation between schizophrenia and other psychotic illnesses (e.g., affective illness, unspecified functional psychosis, delusional disorder, schizoaffective disorder) also seems less unsettling, because one can at least point to the common feature of psychosis as a way of conceptually integrating the nature of familial liability.

Pleiotropy does not require a conceptual explanation at the level of symptom expression. It is at the molecular level that the "explanation" occurs, both for manifestly similar and manifestly very different kinds of traits. It is thus erroneous to assume that because it makes more sense conceptually for psychotic affective illness to be an alternative expression of the schizophrenia gene than for nonpsychotic affective illness, that it is somehow more likely to be correct. Psychiatry's long experience in appreciating the difference between latent and manifest meanings of behavior and dreams is, ironically, quite relevant to the distinction between the latent, or genotypic, level of explanation, and the manifest, or phenotypic, level of explanation.

The "logic" at the molecular level can be observed indirectly, by identifying traits that are genetically related to schizophrenia and that are more prevalent among relatives of schizophrenics than schizophrenia is (Matthysse and Parnas, 1992). This approach explicitly recognizes behaviors or traits as potentially meaningful at the molecular level regardless of their apparent similarity or cohesiveness at the behavioral level. Seemingly dissimilar behaviors, such as abnormal pursuit eye movements, thought disorder, minor physical anomalies, and frontal lobe deficits are all examples of behaviors that not only aggregate in schizophrenics, but are also more prevalent among relatives of schizophrenics than is schizophrenia (Matthysse et al., 1992). How these traits are genetically related to schizophrenia is not yet fully understood, but their phenotypic dissimilarity does not lessen their potential significance as alternative expressions of the schizophrenia genotype any more than phenotypic resemblances would enhance it. A single autosomal dominant gene can, for example, account for many of the features of the familial distribution of schizophrenia and eye tracking dysfunction in offspring of twins discordant for schizophrenia (Holzman et al., 1988).

3. Implications for the future of genetic studies of schizophrenia

Recent advances in understanding the mechanisms of genetic diseases underscore the importance of not letting apparent inconsistencies in risk ratios among classes of relatives, low MZ twin concordances, or patterns of familial aggregation that do not fit standard models stifle the exploration of fresh approaches to the genetics of schizophrenia. It is true that recurrence risks for schizophrenia are low, especially compared with those found in single gene Mendelian disorders. They are certainly too low for conventional linkage studies to have a high probability of success in most families (Matthysse and Parnas, 1992). It is also true that few schizophrenics have an ill parent. Nevertheless, the risk to first-degree relatives of schizophrenics is much higher than that found in the general population. In a recent epidemiologic study, for example, the risk of schizophrenia in first-degree relatives of schizophrenics was 13 times greater than in relatives of controls (Kendler et al., 1993). Yet morbid risk was only 6.5%. Concordance rates in MZ twins and risk to the offspring of dual matings are too high to be accounted for by a single gene, and they are too low to be explained by purely polygenic transmission or classic Mendelian inheritance (Matthysse and Kidd, 1976, 1978). The fact that morbid risks for schizophrenia are equivalently elevated in the offspring of the sick and well members of discordant MZ twin pairs (Gottesman and Bertelsen, 1989) strongly suggests that a transmissible genetic component can be present in individuals who have no symptoms.

It would be easy to retreat from the complexity of the data by postulating unspecified polygenic effects or environmental interactions. Unfortunately, no one has been able to identify an environmental factor with demonstrable explanatory power. This may reflect lack of knowledge about what to measure and how to measure it, rather than the absence of environmental effects. Yet, it leaves us with the terms "diathesis–stress," which amount to a vague, nonspecific description of unknown stressors or unidentified aspects of individual experience (see Chapter 10 by Erlenmeyer-Kimling, and Chapter 14, by Chapman and Chapman, this volume) to compensate for the imperfect fit between complex patterns of recurrence risk and simple models of single gene transmission.

The many recent successes in cloning disease genes (e.g., Huntington's disease, cystic fibrosis, muscular dystrophy) tempt psychiatric investigators to pursue linkage studies despite the many hurdles to be overcome. So far the results have been disappointing and it is difficult not to feel uneasy about the consistent failure to replicate every report of linkage, even in so-called high-density families (Kennedy et al., 1988; Sherrington et al., 1988). Adopting the hypothesis of polygenic transmission would account for these failures (McGue et al., 1983), but many genes with small effects would preclude linkage analysis and the data do not demand such a drastic interpretation. There are two more hopeful strategies, which are presented briefly below. They are: (1) linkage studies of a multidimensional phenotype, and (2) capitalizing on the potential relevance of newly identified mutational mechanisms.

3.1 Linkage studies of a multidimensional schizophrenia phenotype

Linkage studies of a multidimensional schizophrenia phenotype have been proposed by Matthysse and Parnas (1992). Even though a single gene probably does not cause schizophrenia, linkage analysis may be able to locate individual contributory genes. Those authors demonstrate through simulation studies that conventional linkage analyses of a clinical phenotype alone are *unlikely to detect linkage that is actually present.* When viewed from this vantage point, the many disconfirmations of linkage between schizophrenia and a region on chromosome 5 become the expected outcome of low power rather than a disappointing surprise.

As an alternative, Matthysse and Parnas (1992) suggest that linkage analysis has greater power if the definition of "affectedness" is made multidimensional, including clinical and nonclinical phenotypes that are genetically related to schizophrenia and that are more prevalent among relatives of schizophrenics than schizophrenia is. These phenotypes are not simply incorporated into the delineation of schizophrenia, broadening the definition of affectedness, but each aspect of the syndrome is included with its own genotype-dependent probability of occurrence. This approach explicitly recognizes pleiotropy in gene expression, and it is less likely than linkage studies restricted to clinical phenotypes to misclassify individuals with the genotype as unaffected simply because they are not clinically ill. The pool of informative families would potentially include all nuclear and extended families, not merely those atypical families with unusually high numbers of schizophrenics.

3.2 New kinds of mutations

Recent work on cystic fibrosis, Huntington's disease, prion diseases, and developmental disorders of genetic origin has identified new kinds of mutations that are implicated in unusual patterns of symptom expression, disease severity, and inheritance within families.

3.2.1. Amplification of trinucleotide repeats. Until their identification a few years ago these triplet expansions were unrecognized as mutations, yet since their discovery this mutation format is now known to be centrally involved in a number of human diseases: fragile X syndrome, myotonic dystrophy, spinal and bulbar muscular atrophy (Kennedy's disease), and Huntington's disease. In some cases, such as Huntington's disease and Kennedy's disease, the triplet expansions seem to be located in coding regions of the gene, but in other diseases, such as fragile X syndrome and myotonic dystrophy, the trinucleotide repeats occur in untranslated regions. The consequences of triplet expansions are also not uniform; they may change protein structure, alter mRNA stability, or preclude gene expression. The length of the amplified triplet is related to severity and age of onset. In some diseases, the number of repeats tends to be unstable and to increase across generations, giving a plausible explanation of anticipation effects (tendency for earlier ages of onset and/or increased disease severity in successive generations). Evidence favoring anticipation effects in bipolar disorder (McInnis et al., 1993) and against anticipation effects in schizophrenia (Asherson et al., 1994) has recently been reported.

3.2.2. Double point mutations. Identical mutations at the same locus can produce completely different clinical syndromes, depending on which of several frequent and typically inconsequential polymorphisms occurs elsewhere in the same gene. Such "opportunistic" polymorphisms were recently shown to modify the phenotypic expression of the same mutation in the prion protein gene as well as disease severity, age of onset, and extent of central nervous system involvement. Both Fatal Familial Insomnia and a variant of Creutzfeldt-Jakob disease are caused by the identical mutation in codon 178. When methionine is present at position 129, the combination results in Fatal Familial Insomnia, but when valine is present at position 129, the combination results in a subtype of Creutzfeldt-Jakob disease (Goldfarb et al., 1992).

3.2.3. Imprinting. Genetic imprinting refers to one kind of gene inactivation, or phenotype *suppression*. Mendelian transmission of the gene or allele occurs, but because the expression of the imprinted gene is inhibited, the pattern of Mendelian inheritance is obscured. For reasons not yet fully understood, some genes seem to be more prone to imprinting than others, but both normal and disease genes can be imprinted.

The key feature of imprinting is that *parental sex*, not parental affectedness or offspring sex, determines whether the transmitted gene is expressed or inactivated in offspring who inherit it. Thus, an identical gene can be transmitted by either parent, but the expression of the gene will not be identical if the copy of the gene from each parent is imprinted differently. Paternal imprinting inactivates genes transmitted by the father; maternal imprinting inactivates genes transmitted by the mother. Ordinarily, imprinting effects are not passed from generation to generation; they depend on the sex of the most recently transmitting parent.

Children of either sex who inherit an imprinted disease gene will not manifest the disease, or they will be only mildly affected. In the case of a paternally imprinted gene, the children of carrier sons who inherit the gene will also not show the trait, but the children of carrier daughters who inherit the gene will express the phenotype, even though the carrier daughters themselves do not. Unaffected females with affected fathers and affected offspring of either sex are indicators of paternal imprinting, and unaffected males with affected mothers and affected offspring of either sex are indicators of maternal imprinting (Hall, 1990). Asherson et al. (1994) found no evidence of imprinting in relation to schizophrenia, but their analyses were restricted to a comparison of ages of onset in the offspring of affected male and female parents.

Neither trinucleotide expansions, nor double point mutations, nor imprinting may be involved in the diverse traits that are familially related to schizophrenia. Yet they are useful as illustrations of variations in qualitative manifestations of a gene defect, and they may have possible relevance. These novel mechanisms provide opportunities to reexamine the statistical data on patterns of familial aggregation in schizophrenia for relationships that have not been considered in the past. The association of accelerated age of onset and increased illness severity in successive generations with trinucleotide expansions underscores the usefulness of examining family data for evidence of anticipation effects, and for looking for trinucleotide repeats in appropriate pedigrees. Modification in number of triplet repeats is a conceivable mechanism for the variation in severity between schizotypy and schizophrenia, and even for the coaggregation of major depression and schizophrenia in some families. Imprinting mechanisms are dependent on the sex of the *parent*, requiring a shift away from the traditional emphasis on sex dependence of offspring. Imprinting also changes the rationale for calculating morbid risk estimates in different classes of relatives, because the clinical status and sex of first- and second-degree relatives are essential for determining whether the offspring of siblings of one sex are preferentially affected. Double point mutations highlight one mechanism whereby different behavioral outcomes can result from a single gene defect. Double point mutations are a conceivable mechanism for the coaggregation of schizophrenia and major affective disorder in some families but not others, and even potentially for the cofamiliality of traits like eye tracking dysfunction, thought disorder, and schizophrenia.

References

Abrams, R., and M. A. Taylor. 1983. The genetics of schizophrenia: A reassessment using modern criteria. *American Journal of Psychiatry* 140:171–175.

Asherson, P., C. Walsh, J. Williams, M. Sargeant, C. Taylor, A. Clements, M. Gill, M. Owen, and P. McGuffin. 1994. Imprinting and anticipation. Are they relevant to genetic studies of schizophrenia? *British Journal of Psychiatry* 164:619–624.

Baron, M., R. Gruen, L. Asnis, and J. Kane. 1982. Schizoaffective illness, schizophrenia, and affective disorders: Morbidity risk and genetic transmission. *Acta Psychiatrica Scandinavica* 65:253–262.

Baron, M., R. Gruen, L. Asnis, and J. Kane. 1983. Familial relatedness of schizophrenia and schizotypal states. *American Journal of Psychiatry* 140:1437–1442.

Baron, M., R. Gruen, J. D. Rainer, J. Kane, L. Asnis, and S. Lord. 1985. A family study of schizophrenic and normal control probands: Implications for the spectrum concept of schizophrenia. *American Journal of Psychiatry* 142:447–455.

Battaglia, M., M. Gasperini, G. Sciuto, P. Scherillo, G. Diaferia, and L. Bellodi. 1991. Psychiatric disorders in the families of schizotypal subjects. *Schizophrenia Bulletin* 17:659–668.

Blazer, D. G., R. C. Kessler, K. A. McGonagle, and M. S. Swartz. 1994. The prevalence and distribution of major depression in a national community sample: The national comorbidity study. *American Journal of Psychiatry* 151:979–986.

Bleuler, M. 1978. *The Schizophrenic Disorders.* New Haven: Yale University Press.

Coryell, W., and M. Zimmerman. 1988. The heritability of schizophrenia and schizoaffective disorder. *Archives of General Psychiatry* 45:323–327.

Coryell, W., M. T. Tsuang, and J. McDaniel. 1984. Psychotic features in major depressions: Is mood congruence important? *Journal of Affective Disorders* 7:227–236.

Coryell, W., J. Endicott, M. Keller, and N. C. Andreasen. 1985. Phenomenology and family history in DSM-III psychotic depression. *Journal of Affective Disorders* 9:13–18.

Crow, T. J. 1990. Nature of the genetic contribution to psychotic illness – a continuum viewpoint. *Acta Psychiatrica Scandinavica* 81:401–408.

Dorfman, A., G. Shields, and L. E. DeLisi. 1993. DSM-III-R personality disorders in parents of schizophrenic patients. *American Journal of Medical Genetics (Neuropsychiatric Genetics)* 48:60–62.

Farmer, A. E., P. McGuffin, and I. I. Gottesman. 1987. Twin concordance for DSM-III schizophrenia. *Archives of General Psychiatry* 44:634–641.

Frangos, E., G. Athanassenas, S. Tsitourides, P. Psilolignos, and N. Katsanou. 1983. Psychotic depressive disorder. A separate entity? *Journal of Affective Disorders* 5:259–265.

Frangos, E., G. Athanassenas, T. Tsitourides, N. Katsanou, and P. Alexandrakou. 1985. Prevalence of DSM-III schizophrenia among the first-degree relatives of schizophrenic probands. *Acta Psychiatrica Scandinavica* 72:382–386.

Gershon, E. S., L. E. DeLisi, J. Hamovit, J. I. Nurnberger, M. E. Maxwell, J. Schreiber, D. Dauphinais, C. W. Dingman, and J. J. Guroff. 1988. A controlled family study of chronic psychoses. *Archives of General Psychiatry* 45:328–336.

Goldfarb, L. G., R. B. Petersen, M. Tabaton, P. Brown, A. C. LeBlanc, P. Montagna, P. Cortelli, J. Julien, C. Vital, W. W. Pendelbury, M. Haltia, P. R. Wills, J. J. Hauw, P. E. McKeever, L. Monari, B. Schrank, G. D. Swergold, L. Autilio-Gambetti, D. C. Gajdusek, W. Lugaresi, P., and Gambetti. 1992. Fatal familial insomnia and familial Creutzfeldt-Jakob disease: Disease phenotype determined by a DNA polymorphism. *Science* 258:806–808.

Gottesman, I. I., and A. Bertelsen. 1989. Confirming unexpressed genotypes for schizophrenia. *Archives of General Psychiatry* 46:867–872.

Gottesman, I. I., and J. Shields. 1972. *Schizophrenia and Genetics.* New York: Academic Press.

Gunderson, J. G., L. J. Siever, and E. Spaulding. 1983. The search for a schizotype. *Archives of General Psychiatry* 40:15–22.

Guze, S. B., C. R. Cloninger, R. L. Martin, and P. J. Clayton. 1983. A follow-up and family study of schizophrenia. *Archives of General Psychiatry* 40:1273–1276.

Hall, J. 1990. Genomic imprinting. Review and relevance to human diseases. *American Journal of Human Genetics* 46:857–873.

Heston, L. L. 1966. Psychiatric disorders in foster home reared children of schizophrenic mothers. *British Journal of Psychiatry* 112:819–825.

Holzman, P. S., E. Kringlen, S. Matthysse, S. D. Flanagan, R. B. Lipton, G. Cramer, S. Levin, K. Lange, and D. L. Levy. 1988. A single dominant gene can account for eye tracking dysfunctions and schizophrenia in offspring of discordant twins. *Archives of General Psychiatry* 45:641–647.

Katsanis, J., W. G. Iacono, and M. Beiser. 1990. Anhedonia and perceptual aberrations in first-episode psychotic patients and their relatives. *Journal of Abnormal Psychology* 99:202–206.

Kendler, K. S. 1985. Diagnostic approaches to schizotypal personality disorder: A historical perspective. *Schizophrenia Bulletin* 11:538–553.

Kendler, K. S. 1988. Familial aggregation of schizophrenia and schizophrenia spectrum disorders. *Archives of General Psychiatry* 45:377–383.

Kendler, K. S., and A. M. Gruenberg. 1984. An independent analysis of the Copenhagen sample of the Danish adoption study of schizophrenia. VI. The relationship between psychiatric disorders as defined by DSM-III in the relatives and adoptees. *Archives of General Psychiatry* 41:555–564.

Kendler, K. S., and P. Hays. 1981. Paranoid psychosis (delusional disorder) and schizophrenia: A family history study. *Archives of General Psychiatry* 38:547–551.

Kendler, K. S., A. M. Gruenberg, and J. S. Strauss. 1981a. An independent analysis of the Copenhagen sample of the Danish adoption study of schizophrenia. I. The relationship between anxiety disorder and schizophrenia. *Archives of General Psychiatry* 38:973–977.

Kendler, K. S., A. M. Gruenberg, and J. S. Strauss. 1981b. An independent analysis of the Copenhagen sample of the Danish adoption study of schizophrenia. II. The relationship between schizotypal personality disorder and schizophrenia. *Archives of General Psychiatry* 38:982–984.

Kendler, K. S., A. M. Gruenberg, and J. S. Strauss. 1981c. An independent analysis of the Copenhagen sample of the Danish adoption study of schizophrenia. III. The relationship between paranoid psychosis (delusional disorder) and the schizophrenia spectrum disorders. *Archives of General Psychiatry* 38:985–987.

Kendler, K. S., A. M. Gruenberg, and J. S. Strauss. 1982. An independent analysis of the Copenhagen sample of the Danish adoption study of schizophrenia. IV. The relationship between major depressive disorder and schizophrenia. *Archives of General Psychiatry* 39:639–642.

Kendler, K. S., C. C. Masterson, and K. L. Davis. 1985a. Psychiatric illness in first-degree relatives of patients with paranoid psychosis, schizophrenia and medical illness. *British Journal of Psychiatry* 147:524–531.

Kendler, K. S., A. M. Gruenberg, and M. T. Tsuang. 1985b. Psychiatric illness in first-degree relatives of schizophrenic and surgical control patients. *Archives of General Psychiatry* 42:770–779.

Kendler, K. S., A. M. Gruenberg, and M. T. Tsuang. 1986. A DSM-III family study of nonschizophrenic psychotic disorders. *American Journal of Psychiatry* 143:1098–1105.

Kendler, K. S., M. McGuire, A. M. Gruenberg, A. O'Hare, M. Spellman, and D. Walsh. 1993. The Roscommon family study. I. Methods, diagnosis of probands and risk of schizophrenia in relatives. *Archives of General Psychiatry* 50:527–540.

Kendler, K. S., A. M. Gruenberg, and D. K. Kinney. 1994. Independent diagnoses of adoptees and relatives as defined by DSM-III in the provincial and national samples of the Danish adoption study of schizophrenia. *Archives of General Psychiatry* 51:456–468.

Kennedy, J. L., L. A. Giuffra, H. W. Moises, L. L. Cavalli-Sforza, A. J. Pakstis, J. R. Kidd, C. M. Castiglione, B. Sjogren, L. Wetterberg, and K. K. Kidd. 1988. Evidence against linkage of schizophrenia to markers on chromosome 5 in a northern Swedish pedigree. *Nature* 336:167–170.

Kessler, R. C., K. A. McGonagle, S. Zhao, C. B. Nelson, M. Hughes, S. Eshleman, H.-U. Wittchen, and K. S. Kendler. 1994. Lifetime and 12-month prevalence of DSM-III-R psychiatric disorders in the United States. *Archives of General Psychiatry* 51:8–19.

Kety, S. S., D. Rosenthal, P. H. Wender, and F. Schulsinger. 1968. "The types and prevalence of mental illness in the biological and adoptive families of adoptive schizophrenics." In *The Transmission of Schizophrenia*, edited by D. Rosenthal and S. S. Kety, 345–362. Oxford: Pergamon.

Kety, S. S., D. Rosenthal, P. H. Wender, F. Schulsinger, and B. Jacobsen. 1975. "Mental illness in the biological and adoptive families of adopted individuals who have become schizophrenic: A preliminary report based on psychiatric interviews." In *Genetic Research in Psychiatry*, edited by R. Fieve, D. Rosenthal, and H. Brill, 147–165. Baltimore: Johns Hopkins University Press.

Kringlen, E. 1967. *Heredity and Environment in the Functional Psychoses*. Oslo: Universitetsforlaget.

Lenzenweger, M. F., and A. W. Loranger. 1989. Detection of familial schizophrenia using a psychometric measure of schizotypy. *Archives of General Psychiatry* 46:902–907.

Lowing, P. A., A. F. Mirsky, and R. Pereira. 1983. The inheritance of schizophrenia spectrum disorders: A reanalysis of the Danish adoptee study data. *American Journal of Psychiatry* 140:1167–1171.

Maier, W., J. Hallmeyer, and D. Lichterman. 1990. "Morbid risks in relatives of affective, schizoaffective, and schizophrenic patients – Results of a family study." In *Affective and Schizoaffective Disorders*, edited by A. Marneros and M. T. Tsuang, 201–207. Berlin: Springer-Verlag.

Maier, W., D. Lichterman, J. Minges, R. Heun, J. Hallmeyer, and O. Benkert. 1992. Schizoaffective disorder and affective disorders with mood-incongruent psychotic features: Keep separate or combine? Evidence from a family study. *American Journal of Psychiatry* 149:1666–1673.

Matthysse, S., and K. K. Kidd. 1976. Estimating the genetic contribution to schizophrenia. *American Journal of Psychiatry* 133:185–191.

Matthysse, S., and K. K. Kidd. 1978. The value of dual mating data in estimating genetic parameters. *Annals of Human Genetics* 41:477–480.

Matthysse, S., and Parnas. 1992. Extending the phenotype of schizophrenia: Implications for linkage analysis. *Journal of Psychiatric Research* 26:329–344.

Matthysse, S., D. L. Levy, D. Kinney, C. Deutsch, C. Lajonchere, D. Yurgelun-Todd, B. Woods, and P. S. Holzman. 1992. Gene expression in mental illness: A navigation chart to future progress. *Journal of Psychiatric Research* 26:461–473.

McGue, M., I. I. Gottesman, and D. C. Rao. 1983. The transmission of schizophrenia under a multifactorial threshold model. *American Journal of Human Genetics* 35:1161–1178.

McInnis, M. G., F. J. McMahon, G. A. Chase, S. G. Simpson, C. A. Ross, J. R. DePaulo. 1993. Anticipation in bipolar affective disorder. *American Journal of Human Genetics* 53:385–390.

Parnas, J., T. D. Cannon, B. Jacobsen, H. Schulsinger, F. Schulsinger, and S. A. Mednick. 1993. Lifetime DSM-III-R diagnostic outcomes in the offspring of schizophrenic mothers. *Archives of General Psychiatry* 50:707–714.

Pope, H. G., J. M. Jonas, B. M. Cohen, and J. F. Lipinski. 1982. Failure to find evidence of schizophrenia in first-degree relatives of schizophrenic probands. *American Journal of Psychiatry* 139:826–828.

Pope, H. G., B. M. Cohen, J. F. Lipinski, and D. Yurgelun-Todd. 1988. DSM-III criteria for affective disorders and schizophrenia: A preliminary appraisal using family interview findings. *Psychiatry & Psychobiology* 3:159–169.

Rosenthal, D., P. H. Wender, S. S. Kety, J. Welner, and F. Schulsinger. 1971. The adopted-away offspring of schizophrenics. *American Journal of Psychiatry* 128:307–311.

Scharfetter, C., and M. Nusperli. 1980. The group of schizophrenias, schizoaffective psychoses, and affective disorders. *Schizophrenia Bulletin* 6:586–591.

Schulz, P. M., S. C. Schulz, S. C. Goldberg, F. Ettigi, R. J. Resnick, and R. O. Friedel. 1986. Diagnoses of the relatives of schizotypal outpatients. *Journal of Nervous and Mental Disease* 174:457–463.

Sherrington, R., J. Brynjolfsson, H. Petursson, M. Potter, K. Dudleston, B. Barraclough, J. Wasmuth, M. Dobbs, and H. Gurling. 1988. Localization of a susceptibility locus for schizophrenia on chromosome 5. *Nature* 336:164–167.

Siever, L. J., R. Keefe, D. P. Bernstein, E. F. Coccaro, H. M. Klar, Z. Zemishlany, A. E. Peterson, M. Davidson, T. Mahon, T. Horvath, and R. Mohs. 1990. Eye tracking impairment in clinically identified patients with schizotypal personality disorder. *American Journal of Psychiatry* 147:740–745.

Silverman, J., L. J. Siever, T. R. Horvath, E. F. Coccaro, H. Klar, M. Davidson, L. Pinkham, S. H. Apter, R. C. Mohs, and K. L. Davis. 1993. Schizophrenia-related and affective personality disorder traits in relatives of probands with schizophrenia and personality disorders. *American Journal of Psychiatry* 150:435–442.

Smith, G. N., and W. G. Iacono. 1986. Lateral ventricular size in schizophrenia and choice of control group. *Lancet* 1:1450.

Squires-Wheeler, E., A. E. Skodol, D. Friedman, and L. Erlenmeyer-Kimling. 1988. The specificity of DSM-III schizotypal personality traits. *Psychological Medicine* 18:757–765.

Squires-Wheeler, E., A. E. Skodol, A. Bassett, and L. Erlenmeyer-Kimling. 1989. DSM-III-R schizotypal personality traits in offspring of schizophrenic disorder, affective disorder, and normal control patients. *Journal of Psychiatric Research* 23:229–239.

Tenni, R., P. Biglino, K. Dyne, A. Rossi, M. Filocamo, F. Pendola, P. Brunelli, P. Buttitta, C. Borrone, and G. Cetta. 1991. Phenotypic variability and abnormal Type I collagen unstable at body temperature in a family with mild dominant osteogenesis imperfecta. *Journal of Inherited Metabolic Disease* 14:189–201.

Torgersen, S. 1983. Genetic and nosologic aspects of schizotypal and borderline personality disorders. *Archives of General Psychiatry* 41:546–554.

Tsuang, M. T. 1991. Morbidity risks of schizophrenia and affective disorders among first-degree relatives of patients with schizoaffective disorders. *British Journal of Psychiatry* 158:165–170.

Tsuang, M. T., G. Winokur, and R. R. Crowe. 1980. Morbidity risks of schizophrenia and affective disorders among first degree relatives of patients with schizophrenia, mania, depression and surgical conditions. *British Journal of Psychiatry* 137:497–504.

Weissman, M. M., E. S. Gershon, K. K. Kidd, B. A. Prusoff, J. F. Leckman, E. Dibble, J. Hamovit, W. D. Thompson, and D. L. Pauls. 1984. Psychiatric disorders in the relatives of probands with affective disorders. *Archives of General Psychiatry* 41:13–21.

Worton, R. G., and M. W. Thompson. 1988. Genetics of Duchenne muscular dystrophy. *Annual Review of Genetics* 22:601–629.

21

Genetic and environmental factors in the etiology of schizophrenia

Seymour S. Kety

The causes of the major psychiatric disorders such as schizophrenia, manic depressive illness, and the dementias of senility still elude us despite burgeoning research in the neural and behavioral sciences over the past few decades. Equally obscure are the roots of serious behavioral disturbances such as suicide, sociopathy, and substance abuse. All of these are tragic, all costly to the individual, to the family, and to society. These problems are found among all races and nations, and in many societies account for a major fraction of the costs of health care and the loss of human potential. It is there that schizophrenia is the most serious of the mental disorders.

Genetic factors in the etiology of schizophrenia

The well-known observation that the major psychoses, schizophrenia and manic-depressive illness, tend to show a familial distribution has led many investigators to assume the importance of hereditary factors in their etiology. Although others have attempted to explain that phenomenon in terms of familial rearing and acculturation, the role of heredity has been reinforced, not only by studies on twins but by recent studies employing adoption to separate the genetic and environmental influences. In addition, the latter studies have opened the way to new research aimed at the identity of etiologically important genes. Molecular genetic techniques are being used, without notable success to date, in a search for linkage between given mental disorders and chromosomal regions in pedigrees with multiple instances of the disorder.*

* See Chapter 24, by Kenneth K. Kidd, this volume – Eds.

Mental illnesses in general do not follow clear Mendelian patterns of transmission, and several possible reasons have been offered. Etiologic heterogeneity is perhaps the one most often invoked. Some believe that as much as 50% of schizophrenia could be sporadic, resulting from environmental factors with negligible genetic contribution. Even those forms with significant genetic load need not necessarily represent a single monogenic mode of transmission, and it has been maintained that the genetic contribution may be polygenic. Similar etiological factors may not always express themselves as similar mental disturbances, and there are those who argue that schizophrenia and manic-depressive illness represent different manifestations of the same disorder. Psychiatric nosology is largely phenomenological, diagnosis is imprecise, rarely based on objective and pathognomonic criteria, and the same genetic deviance may have a variety of alternative expressions by virtue of the complexities of the brain.

Evaluation of genetic contributions has been the object of several different types of approach:

1. Study of pedigrees. The probability of a hereditary vulnerability to schizophrenia was recognized by Kraepelin and Bleuler, who first described the syndrome, and was supported by them on its tendency to cluster in families. That tendency has been consistently observed and quantified in well-controlled studies which made an exhaustive search for mental illness in the families. Because the prevalence of a psychiatric syndrome in any population depends on how broadly or narrowly it is defined, the morbidity rates for schizophrenia vary with the investigator and the diagnostic criteria employed, which vary in turn with time and place. European studies which used classical criteria have found lifetime risks for schizophrenia of approximately 12% in children and 9% in siblings of schizophrenic patients compared with roughly 0.8% in the general population. Second-degree relatives have approximately half the morbid risk of siblings, and the prevalence in parents is found to be much lower than that in offspring, probably by virtue of selective factors operating against parenthood in schizophrenic individuals. Recent family studies find somewhat lower prevalences of the disorder (Kendler & Tsuang, 1988). This may reflect a diminishing incidence of schizophrenia generally, as some believe, or merely a more narrow definition of the disorder.

Familial transmission, however, may result from genetic or environmental factors, or most likely from both. Thus it does not constitute proof for any degree of genetic transmission unless the shared environment can be shown to have a negligible effect. Carefully controlled adoption studies have done this in the case of schizophrenia so that the familial clustering of the disorder supports genetic transmission (Kety et al., 1968, 1995; Kety & Ingraham, 1992) and can be used to examine many genetic questions.

2. Concordance in twins. A high concordance for a disorder in monozygotic (MZ) twins, with a significantly lower concordance in dizygotic (DZ) twins comparable to that in siblings, has constituted presumptive evidence for a genetic contribution. This is based on the assumption that MZ and DZ twins differ only in their degree of genetic overlap while the environment is constant. However, MZ twins share many more psychosocial and biological influences than DZ twins and these environmental influences may play an etiologic role.

The concordance for schizophrenia in monozygotic twins has been found to lie between 40% and 50% in the best controlled studies, while the concordance in dizygotic twins is no higher than that in siblings (Plomin et al., 1990). This certainly supports the operation of genetic factors, but supports even better the importance of nongenetic or environmental factors. A disorder which was entirely genetic would have a 100% concordance in monozygotic twins.

3. The study of adopted individuals and their biological and adoptive families offers a means of disentangling genetic and family-associated environmental variables since adoptees share their genetic endowment with one family and their environment with another. Selective placement and the transfer of information between the two families, if these occurred to a significant extent, could diminish the completeness of the separation of the two types of influence. These sources of bias are recognized and evaluated in most well-designed studies and have been found to be negligible, and in some types of studies, irrelevant.

My colleagues and I have been engaged in several controlled studies that examined the incidence of schizophrenia in the biological and adoptive relatives of schizophrenic adoptees (Kety et al., 1968, 1975, 1994), and each has found that schizophrenia is concentrated in their biological families rather than in their adoptive relatives. Two separate studies, in Copenhagen and in the rest of Denmark, examined the biological and adoptive relatives of schizophrenic and control adoptees, finding a highly significant increase in the prevalence of both chronic and latent schizophrenia in those who were related genet-

Table 21.1. *Diagnoses in the relatives of chronic schizophrenic index probands and controls in the national sample of adoptees*

RELATIVES	SCHIZOID PERSONALITY	LATENT SCHIZOPHRENIA	CHRONIC SCHIZOPHRENIA	TOTAL RELATIVES
Biological, of 46 chronic schizophrenic Adoptees	12 4.4%	27 9.8% 0.00003*	14 5.1% 0.0008*	275
Biological, of 49 Control Adoptees	13 5.1%	4 1.6%	1 0.4%	253
Adoptive, of 46 chronic Schizophrenic Adoptees	0	2 1.8%	0	111
Adoptive, of 49 Control Adoptees	0	2 1.6%	0	124

* Fisher exact 1 tailed p for biological index vs control relatives
Source: From Kety & Ingraham (1992)

ically to adoptees who had developed classical chronic schizophrenia. These diagnoses were made blindly from extensive psychiatric interviews and were based on the descriptions of Kraepelin and Bleuler for dementia praecox or schizophrenia, respectively, and for the milder syndrome with some of the features of schizophrenia that Bleuler called "latent schizophrenia." In DSM-III and DSM-III-R (the most recent versions of the diagnostic manual of the American Psychiatric Association) "schizotypal personality disorder" is comparable to our diagnosis of latent schizophrenia from which it was largely derived (Spitzer et al., 1979).

A finding of considerable significance in both the Copenhagen Sample and that from the rest of Denmark (the Provincial Sample) is the apparent genetic specificity shown by the classical syndrome of schizophrenia as it was originally described by Kraepelin and Bleuler, and which was observed almost exclusively in the biological relatives of such adoptees (Table 21.1).

The only other syndrome in the original "schizophrenia spectrum" of disorders that we have found to be significantly concentrated in the biological relatives of classical schizophrenic adoptees is latent schizophrenia (Kety et al., 1975; Table 21.1). This was confirmed in a replication on the same subjects using the DSM-III diagnosis of schizotypal personality disorder (Kendler et al., 1981), which is not surprising considering its derivation from latent schizophrenia. Adoptees with latent schizophrenia were also found to have some biological relatives with classical schizophrenia, which is consistent with findings in one but not all studies on natural families (Battaglia et al., 1991). So-called acute schizophrenia has not been found to be associated with schizophrenia in our studies, providing no support for the Schneiderian notion that positive symptoms alone constitute schizophrenia (Kety, 1980).

On this point Bleuler was very specific:

Hallucinations and delusions are partial phenomena of the most varied diseases. Their presence is often helpful in making the diagnosis of a psychosis, but not in diagnosing the presence of schizophrenia. (Bleuler, 1911, p. 204)

Naturally nothing is gained thereby except another symptomatological picture which is then called a disease and which, moreover, is misleadingly defined by the same terms as the qualitatively and quantitatively quite different Kraepelinian concept. (p. 278)

In the case of latent schizophrenia, however, Bleuler was convinced he had identified a milder form of schizophrenia that had a familial relationship to it. Our results confirm this and indicate further that the relationship is genetic.

The results of recent applications of molecular genetic techniques to schizophrenia have been inconclusive. This may be attributed in part to the looseness of the diagnostic categories that were used and the genetic heterogeneity of the phenotypes.

The application of molecular genetic techniques in other branches of medicine including neurology has been successful in localizing the genetic defect on a particular chromosome in the case of a number of diseases. It has not yet occurred for the major psychoses. It is possible that more rigorous diagnoses and their use in renewed search for linkages with more homogeneous subsyndromes, using improved molecular and statistical strategies now available, may lead to greater success.

Environmental etiological influences

Evidence that genetic factors are important in etiology does not argue against the existence of significant or essential environmental influences. A number of these have been suggested; some are supported by empirical evidence, although no single environmental factor has been shown to play an essential role in the etiology of some segment of schizophrenia or manic depressive illness.

Because environmental factors have been the focus of much attention and conviction, there is reason to examine current hypotheses relating to the possible role of specific environmental influences. Although major roles for parental characteristics and rearing have been widely blamed for the development of schizophrenia, no well-controlled evidence substantiates the premise, and children born of a schizophrenic parent but reared by other agents free of mental illness have an undiminished incidence of schizophrenia.

The risk for schizophrenia in genetically vulnerable children is relatively insensitive to parental rearing. Heston (1966) found no significant difference in the prevalence of schizophrenia or other psychopathology between children at high genetic risk for schizophrenia reared by foster families and those brought up in foundling institutions. On the other hand, Parnas et al. (1985) in a study of offspring of schizophrenic mothers found the presence of schizophrenia among them to be related not only to genetic loading but also to institutionalization during the first five years of life, suggesting a contributory etiologic role for institutionalization, although other explanations are possible. Higgins (1966, 1976) studied 50 young adults, all born of schizophrenic mothers, half of whom had been reared by their mothers, the other half, separated from their mothers early in life and reared by agents without a history of psychiatric illness. Four chronic schizophrenics were found in each group and other types of psychopathology were no higher in the group reared by their schizophrenic mothers. Wender and associates (1974) studied individuals born of normal biological parents but reared by adoptive parents with severe psychopathology or psychosis. No increased risk for schizophrenia spectrum disorders was found among them.

The biological and adoptive siblings of schizophrenic adoptees offer some means of examining the relative influence of genetic and rearing factors on the risk for schizophrenia. If rearing factors were significant influences, one would expect the adoptive siblings of schizophrenic adoptees, reared by the same parents, to show some increase in risk, whereas the biological siblings reared in a different family should show a diminished risk. This prediction is not borne out. An extensive study in Iceland found 8 schizophrenics reared in foster families. These had 20 biological siblings reared apart from them, of whom 6 became schizophrenic, and 28 foster siblings reared with them of whom none became schizophrenic (Karlsson, 1966). In the Provincial Sample of our Danish Adoption Study, there were 29 chronic schizophrenic probands reared in adoptive families, of whom none of their foster siblings became schizophrenic, although 6 of their 24 biological siblings, reared apart from them, developed chronic or latent schizophrenia (Kety et al., 1994).

Birth injury, viral infection during gestation, dietary factors, auto-immune processes, and developmental mishaps have been the basis of plausible etiological hypotheses supported by provocative and often compelling evidence. The twofold higher prevalence of schizophrenia in the lower socioeconomic classes of large cities has suggested an etiological role for some of the environmental stresses that exist to a greater extent in the lower socioeconomic classes. Although the downward drift of educational, social, and occupational competence which tends to occur in many of the affected individuals accounts for much of the concentration (Goldberg and Morrison, 1963; Wender et al., 1973), external factors would be expected to participate. A large number of social and psychological stressors pertaining to status, role perception, values, and child-rearing practices are associated with poverty. These have provided a number of etiological hypotheses pertinent to schizophrenia, although none have received definitive support.

Certain biological hazards associated with lower social class should also be considered. To the extent that perinatal injuries, malnutrition, and infection may operate in the etiology of schizophrenia, their impact would be exaggerated in the lower socioeconomic class of large cities. Several infectious diseases, especially those of viral origin, occur significantly more frequently in lower socioeconomic classes. Some of these, like cytomegalovirus, are known to be congenitally transmitted and may be latent in the central nervous system, eventually giving rise to deafness or mental retardation (Hanshaw et al., 1976). Although an involvement of cytomegalovirus in schizophrenia has not been found, a number of influenza epidemics have been found to be associated with a significant increase in the births of individuals who later became schizophrenic (Murray, 1992). Cohorts whose mothers were exposed to Asian flu in the second trimester of pregnancy showed a greater risk for schizophrenia (Mednick et al., 1988). This is reminiscent of the influenza epidemic after World War

I, which produced many cases of Parkinson's disorder but was also found by Karl Menninger (1928) to be followed sometimes by schizophrenia.

Knight (1982) has advanced arguments that autoimmune processes operate in some forms of schizophrenia as they are now known to operate in myasthenia gravis, diabetes, or Graves' disease, disorders which share with schizophrenia a juvenile grace period, a monozygotic concordance rate of 30–50%, and a disparity in age of onset between members of such pairs. It is interesting that the lymphocytes and other cells of the immune system may be very different even in monozygotic twins, which could bring the concordance rate in them well below 100% for an autoimmune disorder. There is evidence that some strains of influenza virus may induce autoimmune changes in the brain (Laing et al., 1989), an opportunity for an etiological role in a segment of schizophrenia.

There are some perinatal stresses other than viral that may operate etiologically in schizophrenia. McNeil and Kaij (1978) found a significantly higher number of obstetrical complications attending the birth of subjects who eventually became schizophrenic; this was confirmed in an independent study by Jacobsen and Kinney (1980), and by two recent studies in England (Murray et al., 1992).

Thus, schizophrenia continues to pose a number of unanswered questions. Although the evidence is good for the operation of both genetic and environmental factors, no genetic locus has been identified, and the mode of genetic transmission remains enigmatic, although the latent trait model proposed by Matthysse et al. (1986) is capable of accounting for the distribution of eye tracking dysfunction and schizophrenia in the offspring of MZ twins (Holzman et al., 1988) and much of the distribution in families. Numerous environmental influences which could play etiological roles have been suggested and encouraging support has been acquired for some of them, although none has been established or achieved wide acceptance. Simplistic notions regarding gene expression on the activity of particular neurotransmitters have given way to a recognition of the many embryonic and developmental processes that must intervene between genetic change and a clinical phenotype (Erlenmeyer-Kimling et al., 1992).*

In sharp contrast to the absence of cerebral structural or functional

---

* See also Chapter 10, by L. Erlenmeyer-Kimling, this volume – Eds.

abnormalities only 20 years ago, there are reasonably well-defined morphological, metabolic, and physiological changes, demonstrable by new and older techniques, and although no one among them is pathognomonic, each opens the way to further investigation and knowledge. Neuropsychological functions, made definable by quantitative techniques, are showing some of the characteristics of "genetic markers" (Holzman, 1992). Smooth pursuit eye tracking (Holzman, 1985) and continuous performance (Mirsky et al., 1992) are among the challenges which show a familial disturbance. At the clinical level, much of the confounding accretions to classical schizophrenia which developed over the objections of Kraepelin and Bleuler are being stripped away, permitting the classical syndrome to emerge, if not suffused with new light, at least with many of the former shadows better illuminated.

Note

This chapter was formulated while the author was a Fellow at the Study and Conference Center of the Rockefeller Foundation in Bellagio, Italy.

References

Battaglia, M., Gasperini, M., Sciuto, G., Scherillo, P., Diaferia, G., and Bellodi, L. 1991. Psychiatric disorders in the families of schizotypal subjects. *Schizophrenia Bulletin* 17:659–668.

Bleuler, E. 1911/1950. *Dementia Praecox, or the Group of Schizophrenias.* Translation by J. Zinkin. Monograph Series on Schizophrenia, No. 1. New York: International Universities Press.

Erlenmeyer-Kimling, L., Cantoni, G. L., and Kety, S. S. (eds.). 1992. Genetics and gene expression in mental illness. *Journal of Psychiatric Research* 26:221–470.

Goldberg, E. M., and Morrison, S. L. 1963. Schizophrenia and social class. *British Journal of Psychiatry* 109:785–802.

Hanshaw, J. B., Scheiner, A. P., Moxley, A. W., Gaev, L., Abel, V., and Scheiner, B. 1976. School failure and deafness after 'silent' congenital cytomegalovirus infection. *New England Journal of Medicine* 295:468–470.

Heston, L. L. 1966. Psychiatric disorders in foster home reared children of schizophrenic mothers. *British Journal of Psychiatry* 112:819–825.

Higgins, J. Effects of child rearing by schizophrenic mothers. 1966. *Journal of Psychiatric Research* 4:153–167.

Higgins, J. 1976. Effects of child rearing by schizophrenic mothers: A follow-up. *Journal of Psychiatric Research* 13:1–9.

Holzman, P. S. 1985. Eye movement dysfunction and psychosis. *International Review of Neurobiology* 27:179–205.

Holzman, P. S. 1992. Behavioral markers of schizophrenia useful for genetic studies. *Journal of Psychiatric Research* 26:427–448.

Holzman, P. S., Kringlen, E., Matthysse, S., et al. 1988. A single dominant gene can account for eye tracking dysfunction and schizophrenia in offspring of discordant twins. *Arch. Gen. Psychiatry* 45:641–647.

Jacobsen, B., and Kinney, D. K. Perinatal complications in adopted and nonadopted schizophrenics and their controls: Preliminary results. *Acta Psychiatr. Scand.* (Suppl.), 285:337–346.

Karlsson, J. L. 1966. *The Biological Basis of Schizophrenia*, Springfield, IL: C. C. Thomas.

Kendler, K. S., Gruenberg, A. M., and Strauss, J. S. 1981. An independent analysis of the Copenhagen sample of the Danish adoption study of schizophrenia, II: The relationship between schizotypal personality disorder and schizophrenia. *Arch. Gen. Psychiatry* 38:982–984.

Kendler, K. S., and Tsuang, M. T. 1988. Outcome and familial psychopathology in schizophrenia. *Arch. Gen. Psychiatry* 45:338–346.

Kety, S. S. 1980. The 52nd Maudsley Lecture. The syndrome of schizophrenia: Unresolved problems and opportunities for research. *British Journal of Psychiatry* 136:421–436.

Kety, S. S., and Ingraham, L. J. 1992. Genetic transmission and improved diagnosis of schizophrenia from pedigrees of adoptees. *Journal of Psychiatric Research* 26:247–255.

Kety, S. S., Rosenthal, D., Wender, P. H., and Schulsinger, F. 1968. The types and prevalence of mental illness in the biological and adoptive families of adopted schizophrenics. In D. Rosenthal and S. S. Kety (eds.), *The Transmission of Schizophrenia.* Oxford: Pergamon Press, pp. 345–362.

Kety, S. S., Rosenthal, D., Wender, P. H., Schulsinger, F., and Jacobsen, B. 1975. Mental illness in the biological and adoptive families of adoptive individuals who have become schizophrenic: A preliminary report based on psychiatric interviews. In R. R. Fieve, D. Rosenthal, and H. Brill (eds.), *Genetic Research in Psychiatry.* Baltimore: Johns Hopkins University Press, pp. 147–165.

Kety, S. S., Wender, P. H., Jacobsen, B., Ingraham, L. J., Jansson, L., Faber, B., and Kinney, D. 1994. Mental illness in the biological and adoptive relatives of schizophrenic adoptees: Replication of the Copenhagen Study in the rest of Denmark. *Arch. Gen. Psychiatry* 51:442–455.

Knight, J. G. 1982. Dopamine-receptor-stimulating autoantibodies: A possible cause of schizophrenia. *Lancet* ii:1073–1076.

Laing, P., Knight, J. G., Hill, J. M., Harris, A. G., Oxford, J. S., Newman, R., Webster, R. G., Markwell, M.A.K., Paul, S. M., and Pert, C. B. 1989. Influenza viruses induce autoantibodies to a brain-specific 37-KDa protein in rabbits. *Proceedings of the National Academy of Sciences USA* 86:1998–2002.

Matthysse, S., Holzman, P. S., and Lange, K. 1986. The genetic transmission of schizophrenia: Application of Mendelian latent structure analysis to eye tracking dysfunctions in schizophrenia and affective disorder. *Journal of Psychiatric Research* 20:57–65.

McNeil, T. F., and Kaij, L. 1978. Obstetric factors in the development of schizophrenia. In L. C. Wynne, R. L. Cromwell, and S. Matthysse (eds.), *The Nature of Schizophrenia.* New York: Wiley, pp. 401–429.

Mednick, S., Machon, R. A., and Huttunen, M. O. 1988. Adult schizophrenia following prenatal exposure to an influenza epidemic. *Arch. Gen. Psychiatry* 45:189–192.

Menninger, K. 1928. The schizophrenic syndrome as a product of acute infectious disease. *Archives of Neurology and Psychiatry* 20:464–481.

Mirsky, A. F., Lochhead, S. J., Jones, B. P., Kugelmass, S., Walsh, D., and Kendler, K. S. 1982. On familial factors in the attentional deficit in schizophrenia: A review and report of two new subject samples. *Journal of Psychiatric Research* 26:383–404.

Murray, R. M. 1992. A neurodevelopmental approach to the classification of schizophrenia. *Schizophrenia Bulletin* 18:319–332.

Murray, R. M., Jones, P., O'Callaghan, E., Takei, N., and Sham, P. 1992. Genes, viruses, and neurodevelopmental schizophrenia. *Journal of Psychiatric Research* 26:225–236.

Parnas, J., Teasdale, T. W., and Schulsinger, H. 1985. Institutional rearing and diagnostic outcome in children of schizophrenic mothers. A prospective high-risk study. *Arch. Gen. Psychiatry* 42:762–769.

Plomin, R., DeFries, J. C., and McClearn, G. E. 1990. *Behavioral Genetics.* New York: W. H. Freeman, pp. 334–340.

Spitzer, R. L., Endicott, J., and Gibbon, M. 1979. Crossing the border into borderline personality and borderline schizophrenia. The development of criteria. *Arch. Gen. Psychiatry* 36:17–24.

Wender, P. H., Rosenthal, D., Kety, S. S., Schulsinger, F., and Welner, J. 1973. Social class and psychopathology in adoptees. *Arch. Gen. Psychiatry* 28:318–325.

Wender, P. H., Rosenthal, D., Kety, S. S., Schulsinger, F., and Welner, J. 1974. Cross-fostering: A research strategy for clarifying the role of genetic and experiential factors in the etiology of schizophrenia. *Arch. Gen. Psychiatry* 30:121–128.

22

Problems and paradoxes in research on the etiology of schizophrenia

Einar Kringlen

Our knowledge concerning schizophrenia has increased during the last decades. Nevertheless, a number of fundamental questions are still unresolved. Data from twin and adoption studies make it certain that there are both genetic and environmental components of the development of schizophrenia. However, the natures of the genetic and of the environmental contributions are, so far, not clear.

During the 1960s, ideas about psychosocial causation in schizophrenia were rife. Since then, empirical research has not been able to document with certainty any specific etiologic social factors. In contrast, during the last 15 years neuroscientific research has put the brain back in schizophrenia research. A number of new empirical findings have emerged. It is sufficient to mention the work on eye tracking by Holzman and co-workers, and the recent observations obtained through new imaging techniques, described in Chapter 4, by Martha Shenton, this volume. However, we still do not know how specific these deviations are, nor do we know their origin and etiological meaning. Thus it is also difficult, at the present stage, to incorporate the various empirical findings in one theoretical model. I am therefore afraid that I shall pose more questions than I shall provide answers.

We should keep in mind some of the fundamental problems and paradoxes in research on the etiology of schizophrenia. First, we are confronted with uncertainty regarding the clinical boundaries of schizophrenia. It makes, of course, a large difference whether one considers the "spectrum disorders," such as paranoid, schizotypal and schizoid personality, as part of the schizophrenia concept. In that case schizophrenia becomes a rather common disorder. If, on the other hand, one adheres to a strict clinical concept, then schizophrenia will stand out as a relatively rare illness. Related to the problem of clinical boundaries in schizophrenia, we also have the problem of the biological distinctiveness of schizophrenia and severe affective disorder. Second, how can one explain that 30–40% of monozygotic (MZ) co-twins of schizophrenics are clinically normal (Kringlen, 1986)? And how can one explain that 65–70% of the offspring of two schizophrenics show a nonschizophrenic picture (Rosenthal, 1966; Kringlen, 1978)? These facts tend to be neglected by research workers in the field today.

Distinct entities?

Previous European research tended to support the Kraepelinian view that schizophrenia and severe affective disorder are biologically distinct entities. Nevertheless, in the older literature, one also encounters some coaggregation or overlapping between the syndromes. There are, however, several problems inherent in this research, problems that relate to sampling and clinical diagnostic practice. First of all, investigators have frequently started with samples of clear-cut schizophrenic or manic-depressive cases, leaving doubtful cases out. Second, even recent studies have employed "samples of convenience," i.e., chronically hospitalized patients who might not be representative of the psychotic population at large. Third, diagnoses have not always been blind with respect to the diagnosis of the proband, and in addition have often been based on clinical impressions rather than on operationally defined criteria. In several cases, the diagnostic evaluation has been built upon circular reasoning, by using family incidence of the illness as supportive of the diagnosis.

Some studies performed during the last decade, employing rigorous methodology, operationalized diagnostic criteria, personal interviews of relatives, and blind diagnoses, have supported the view that there is a familial relationship between schizophrenia and severe affective disorder (Gershon et al., 1988; Maier et al., 1990). In a study from a rural county in the west of Ireland, the risk of schizophrenia was observed to be significantly higher, not only in first-degree relatives of probands with schizophrenia, but also in relatives of probands with schizoaffective, schizotypal and nonaffective psychosis diagnoses, compared with relatives of controls (Kendler et al., 1992). Thus, several reports in recent years speak against a specific disposition toward "narrow" schizophrenia. Nor do we find support for the theory that being liable to schizophrenia means being liable to all mental illnesses. On the contrary, the findings point in the direction of predisposition to the development of psychosis, since the risk of schizophrenia was considerably higher in relatives of all the proband groups with nonschizophrenic psychotic disturbance. In contrast to Torgersen (1984), Kendler et al. (1992) also reported an increased risk of schizophrenia in the relatives of probands with schizotypal disorder. However, this finding might be due to skewed sampling, since these probands had been hospitalized, and most schizotypal individuals will never be hospitalized. Other studies also show that schizotypal personality disorder is related to schizophrenia. Whether this relationship is of a genetic nature is still unclear (Kringlen & Cramer, 1989; Onstad et al., 1991).

In conclusion, the notion of schizophrenia and affective disorder as distinct syndromes remains debatable; recent studies suggest some familial relationship between schizophrenia and severe forms of affective disorder. By broadening the concept of schizophrenia, one might in fact return to the old German notion of *Einheitspsychose.* Could it be that there is only one functional psychosis, wherein schizophrenia and severe manic-depressive illness are different variations of the same underlying disturbance? Could it be that there is a genetic liability to psychosis in general, and that environmental factors determine the type of illness? If one accepts the premise that schizophrenia is a heterogeneous syndrome, there are also several other possibilities. Have we perhaps to start afresh, throwing away our present classification system, which has its uses for clinical work, but might limit etiological research?

Unraveling the effect of genes and environment

Familial clustering is, of course, no proof of heredity. If genetic factors are at work, a tendency to familial clustering would be self-evident. However, if a common disease is environmentally determined, one would also expect some clustering, because family members experience a more similar environment than unrelated subjects. The old question regarding nature versus nurture is outdated. Today we know that the phenotype is the result of both environment and genotype. The confusion that genotype or environment could be the exclusive cause of a phenotype has, however, persisted into modern genetics through the concept of "phenocopy," which is supposed to be an environmentally caused phenotypic deviation, similar in form to one that is genetically caused. In fact, both mutant and phenocopy result from interactions of gene and milieu.

Twin research is based on the existence of two types of twins – monozygotic (MZ) and dizygotic (DZ). MZ twins are identical from a genetic point of view, whereas DZ twins share, on the average, 50% of their genes. By comparing MZ and DZ pairs with respect to different diseases, one may obtain a picture of the relative contributions of heredity and environment. In all recent twin studies of schizophrenia, the concordance figures for MZ twins are considerably higher than for DZ twins. While twin studies provide strong evidence that schizophrenia is a genetically determined disorder, the discordance of 60–70% in MZ twins (Table 22.1) suggests that environmental factors are also powerful. Torrey (1992) reviewed the twin literature on schizophrenia, and concluded that the genetic contribution to schizophrenia is considerably overestimated in the American literature today. Torrey chose to analyse pairwise rather than probandwise rates, and arrived at values below 30% for concordance in MZ twins. McGue (1992), however, defended probandwise estimation in preference to the pairwise method, and maintained that the probandwise method may be more sound for estimating heritability. The MZ/DZ ratio is approximately 2.79 (probandwise), or 3.40 (pairwise), also consistent with the importance of genetic factors.

In adoption studies, it is theoretically possible to separate genes from environment. Basically, two methods have been employed. In the adoptees study, one examines the adopted-away offspring of parents affected by a certain disorder. A higher prevalence of the disorder among adoptees born to affected parents, compared with controls, indicates that genetic factors are important. In the adoptees' relatives study, on the other hand, one starts with adoptees known to be disturbed, and then investigates their biological and adoptive families. Comparison of prevalence rates among the relatives of biological index and control families permits one to estimate the influence of genetic factors, while comparison of prevalence rates among the relatives of rearing index and control families permits one to estimate the influence of environmental factors. Although these studies – as do all studies on human subjects – have methodological problems (Kringlen, 1991), it is fair to say that adoption studies corroborate the twin studies with regard to the etiology of schizophrenia (Rosenthal et al., 1968; Kety et al., 1975; Rosenthal et al., 1975; Kety et al., 1978).

Table 22.1. *Twin concordance rates for schizophrenia in studies based upon nation twin registers*

STUDY	MZ		DZ	
	PAIRWISE IN PERCENT	PROBANDWISE IN PERCENT	PAIRWISE IN PERCENT	PROBANDWISE IN PERCENT
TIENARI 1963	15 (3/20)	26 (6/23)	7 (3/42)	13 (6/45)
KRINGLEN 1967	31 (14/45)	46 (26/57)	7 (6/90)	13 (12/96)
FISCHER 1973	24 (5/21)	36 (9/25)	10 (4/41)	18 (8/45)
TOTAL	26 (22/86)	39 (41/105)	8 (13/173)	14 (26/186)

ADOPTED FROM TORREY ET AL (1994)

Together, twin and adoption studies have established the importance of genetic factors in schizophrenia. The findings from the Finnish adoption study by Tienari et al. (1991) have been interpreted as suggesting that, at least in some schizophrenics, there is a strong interaction of genetic and rearing factors, i.e., that individuals with a genetic liability may be particularly vulnerable to a noxious family environment.

Genetic transmission

It was discovered, early in the history of psychiatric genetics, that the major psychoses did not follow a simple mode of genetic transmission. It is clear that classical Mendelian single major locus models cannot adequately explain all the empirical observations. Of the offspring of two schizophrenic parents 60% to 70% are nonschizophrenic, an important fact that does not support such models (Kringlen, 1978). The apparent constancy of the prevalence of schizophrenia in the population, despite the reduced reproduction rate in schizophrenia, is also difficult to explain by single major locus models. Some reports at the end of the 1980s suggested a significant fall in first admissions of schizophrenia over the past three decades in the U.K., Denmark and New Zealand. A closer scrutiny of the recent literature shows, however, that while there is a trend toward diminishing incidence of hospitalized cases, there is no proof of real decline in the illness rate (Jablensky, 1992).

A strict polygenic model proposes that the cumulative effect of genes at many loci may explain the pattern of transmission. Indeed, the existence of different degrees of severity of schizophrenia may be more easily explained by differences in the number of loci responsible than by a single major locus model, although single-gene disorders with variable expression are known (e.g., neurofibromatosis). The most popular model today is the multifactorial model, which postulates that schizophrenia results from a combination of genetic transmission and environmental influences. The multifactorial model is often employed in studying traits such as hypertension, diabetes mellitus, intelligence, height and weight. The model proposes that all individuals have some genetic liability to the disorder, and when the sum of genetic and environmental factors crosses a threshold, the syndrome emerges. This model interprets the schizophrenia spectrum disorders as a subthreshold condition.

Other possibilities are also at hand. Schizophrenia might be a heterogeneous group of illnesses. In some cases a single gene model might explain the disorder; in other cases there might be a polygenic disposition; and in still other cases the illness might be mainly environmentally determined. However, it has never been possible to separate types of schizophrenia that conform to these three models, except that twin research has indicated that nonparanoid schizophrenia appears "more genetic" than paranoid schizophrenia (Kringlen, 1967; Onstad et al., 1991). In this connection it is also of interest to note that the risk in first-degree relatives of schizophrenic patients varies from 2% to 7% across studies, which could mean that schizophrenia in some regions is more a family disease, and in other regions is more determined by individual risk factors.

Defining the phenotype

As we have failed to identify any specific biological marker or any consistent structural or physiological abnormality in schizophrenic patients, the only defining characteristic available is the syndrome itself. But how should we define the schizophrenic syndrome? It is often said that the main problem in psychiatric diagnosis is unreliability. That is wrong. A criterion-based diagnostic system such as DSM-III-R or ICD-10 has made reliability, i.e., agreement between clinicians, feasible. The central problem, however, remains validity. How true or how meaningful are our diagnostic classifications? Do our clinical diagnoses reflect some underlying subtraits? Or, in general terms, do our phenotypes reflect some underlying genotype? Before we can expect to obtain results from linkage studies, answers to these questions are mandatory.

Some researchers have attempted to arrive at a valid classification by comparing various definitions of the disorder to obtain the highest MZ/DZ concordance ratio. Gottesman & Shields (1972) observed that neither too broad nor too narrow a concept of schizophrenia provided a phenotypic definition that was the "most genetic." Farmer et al. (1992) found that the highest MZ/DZ concordance ratio was achieved when schizotypal personality, affective disorder with mood incongruent psychosis, and atypical psychosis were included together with typical schizophrenia as the phenotype. Similarly, Onstad et al. (1991) observed that by adding schizoaffective disorder, delusional disorder and atypical psychosis to typical schizophrenia, the MZ con-

Table 22.2. *Psychopathology in co-twins of schizophrenic MZ twins in population-based studies (Percentages)*

DIAGNOSIS OF CO-TWIN	FISCHER N = 21	KRINGLEN N = 45	TIENARI N = 17	TOTAL N = 83
SCHIZOPHRENIA	24	31	18	27
OTHER NON-AFFECTIVE PSYCHOSIS, BORDERLINE OR SCHIZOID	39	9	18	15
NEUROTIC-LIKE PATHOLOGY	5	29	6	18
CLINICAL NORMALITY	43	31	59	40

BASED UPON STUDIES BY FISCHER (1973), KRINGLEN (1967), TIENARI (1963). FISCHER'S TWINS WERE RELATIVELY OLD, THUS SEVERAL TWINS WERE NOT PERSONALLY INVESTIGATED. TIENARI STUDIED ONLY MALE TWINS. OF THE 10 NORMAL CO-TWINS SIX WERE RATED "HEALTHY INTROVERTS".

cordance was increased to a maximum, while the DZ concordance remained practically unchanged. However, the MZ/DZ concordance ratio has some methodological problems: first of all because the ratio is base-rate sensitive, i.e., it varies as a function of the population risk and, second, because the standard error of this ratio of ratios (MZ/DZ) can be quite large (Kendler, 1989).

Normal co-twins of MZ schizophrenics

In all modern twin studies of schizophrenia, considerable disparity in the clinical pictures of MZ pairs has been reported. The most remarkable finding is the high prevalence of normal co-twins. Based on the studies of Essen-Möller (1941), Slater & Shields (1953), Tienari (1963), Kringlen (1967), Gottesman & Shields (1972) and Fischer (1973), 32% of the co-twins of MZ schizophrenics were schizophrenic, 17% were possible schizophrenics or borderline, 21% were afflicted with neurotic disorders, while 30% were clinically normal. In the three earlier Nordic population-based studies, as many as 40% were classified as normal (Table 22.2).

It is of interest that different subtypes of schizophrenia seem to be more or less randomly paired in the twins. A normal co-twin might be paired with either a paranoid or a nonparanoid type of schizophrenia. Furthermore, a normal co-twin might be paired not only with a moderately severe case, but even with an extremely deteriorated partner.

The fact that schizophrenic MZ twins are paired with clinically normal co-twins in 30–40% of the cases is remarkable, from both a genetic and an environmental point of view. If the genes play a significant role, one would expect to observe, if not identical clinical syndromes, at least some deviance in the schizophrenic direction in the co-twin, such as schizotypal, schizoid or paranoid personality. On the other hand, if environmental factors such as family conflicts predispose to schizophrenia, one would expect that both twins in an MZ pair would be affected in one way or another, since MZ twins are of the same sex and age. Even if the attachment of the twins to their parents might vary, how can two twins with similar genotype develop in such opposite extremes, one being schizophrenic, the other clinically normal?

Developmental and environmental factors

One of the main problems in the study of environmental factors in schizophrenia is that no one has been able to identify the schizophrenic genotype, nor is there any agreed-upon specific biological marker. Little is known about developmental differences between MZ twins discordant for schizophrenia, or about influences that may force a vulnerable individual away from a more or less normal personality toward psychosis.

Long ago, it was observed that approximately half of those suffering from schizophrenia showed deviant traits before the outbreak of illness. Watt et al. (1970) reported that preschizophrenic boys tended to display unusual aggression and were often considered as "disagreeable." Girls who later developed the disorder were described as overinhibited. In line with clinical experience, Watt concluded that at least a decade prior to the first hospitalization, approximately half of the preschizophrenic group manifested some maladjustment. Roff et al. (1976) observed that poor peer relations and social isolation were common in children who later developed schizophrenia. These studies do not tell us whether the early social deviancies are causal factors in themselves, or simply signs of the unfolding illness. In addition, one problem in such studies is the retrospective nature of the data. The individual becomes a subject of the study only after developing

Table 22.3. *Number of offspring in samples of schizophrenic high-risk groups, psychiatric controls, and normal controls*

INVESTIGATOR	HIGH-RISK	PSYCHIATRIC CONTROLS	NORMAL CONTROLS
MCNEIL, KAIJ (1987)	11	53	97
SAMEROFF ET AL (1987)	29	98	57
GOODMAN (1987)	71	36	38
ERLENMEYER-KIMLING (1987)	59	40	91
WEINTRAUB (1987)	80	288	176

the illness. Therefore great hopes were attached to the many prospective longitudinal high-risk studies embarked upon in the 1960s and the 1970s.

High-risk studies

High-risk samples, usually studies of offspring of schizophrenic mothers, have been followed prospectively, but regrettably with meager results. Reviews by Walker and Emory (1983) and Erlenmeyer-Kimling (1987) concluded that the high-risk data with regard to schizophrenia were inconsistent. It is not difficult to agree with these authors. The limited results are probably due to several factors, related to sampling, controls, variation in investigated variables, and absence of sustained follow-up. For instance, the large-scale pioneering study by Mednick and Schulsinger (1968) had only normal controls, not controls with other diagnoses. Furthermore, it is difficult to generalize from these studies, because only a small proportion of schizophrenics actually have a schizophrenic parent. In addition, the unusual environmental interaction may produce children with atypical characteristics. However, there are findings of interest that should be touched upon. Obviously, my review will be selective (Table 22.3).

McNeil (1988), in his thorough review, reported that obstetric complications had been found in many samples of schizophrenic patients, but that there was no consistent pattern. It is therefore interesting to note that high-risk studies, where not only normal but also psychiatric controls have been included, have generally found just as many obstetric complications in children of depressive mothers as in children of schizophrenic mothers (Sameroff et al., 1987). Sameroff et al., who studied 29 high-risk offspring of schizophrenic mothers, had 75 normal mothers as controls, but also 98 mothers with psychiatric diagnoses other than schizophrenia. Among the mental illness measures, severity and chronicity of maternal disturbance were better predictors of risk in offspring than were specific diagnoses; and social status was a more powerful risk factor than any of the mental illness measures. With respect to diagnosis, it was not the schizophrenic mothers whose infants had the worst obstetrical status and were least well functioning after birth, but the depressed ones.

These findings are supported by the study of Goodman (1987), who also included psychiatric controls in addition to normal controls. Seventy-one offspring of schizophrenic parents were compared with 36 psychiatric controls, mostly offspring of depressive mothers, and 38 offspring of normal mothers. In this sample from Atlanta, consisting mainly of black, low-income and single mothers, the findings showed that both schizophrenic and depressive mothers were less emotionally involved than normal controls. Schizophrenic mothers produced a less favorable environment for their children, with less play, less learning, and less emotional and verbal contact, although it is not known whether these factors actually mediated the high risk for schizophrenia in the children. The findings of this study are in line with McNeil & Kaij's (1987) conclusion, that the impact of maternal psychiatric disturbances on pregnancy and birth complications is indirect. They suggest that the lack of competence typical for sick women might be the mechanism that connects the psychopathology of the mother with increased birth complications. Only a small subgroup of children were deviant neurologically; the majority were normal. There were no relationships between the mother's diagnosis and neurological findings in the child, although the majority of the offspring of depressive mothers had low birth weight and size.

In the Israeli high-risk study (Nagler & Mirsky, 1985; Marcus et al., 1987), a number of neurological "soft signs" were found in children at risk between 8 and 14 years of age. There are interesting findings in the Israeli high-risk study that are not easy to explain. Both the high-risk and the low-risk sample had been divided into two equal groups. One group was reared in one of a number of kibbutzim throughout Israel, and the other group was parent-reared in the city of Jerusalem. In the control sample, practically no psychopathology was observed by age 25. However, by comparing offspring reared in kibbutzim with those reared in the city, remarkable differences were found. In the kibbutz group there were considerably more cases of schizophrenia and schizophrenia spectrum disorders, as well as major and minor affective disorders, compared with the city group. Could it be that the closely knit kibbutz society made it difficult to avoid the stigma of mental disorder, since all the members of the community would know that a child had a mentally disturbed parent, whereas that fact might be easier to hide in the city? Or are there other environmental factors that are associated with kibbutz life, that interact with a hypothetical genetic disposition? Theoretically, the results might also have to do with assortative mating, but there was no information about the spouse.

One of the promising studies is the Stony Brook high-risk project (Weintraub, 1987). This sample was large, in fact the largest high-risk project extant – besides the 80 high-risk offspring from schizophrenic parents, there were 155 children of unipolar parents, 134 children of bipolar parents, and 176 children of normal controls. Considerably more children of parents with psychiatric illnesses showed mental disturbances. However, no special diagnosis was predominant: 35% of the offspring of schizophrenics, 30% of the offspring of unipolar parents and 25% of the offspring of bipolar parents were mentally disturbed, compared with 10% of the offspring of controls. Aggression, combined with social withdrawal, appeared to be associated with risk for schizophrenia. The most common diagnosis in children of schizophrenic parents was borderline or other personality disturbance, whereas affective mental disorder was most frequent in children born to unipolar and bipolar parents. Adjustment disorder and anxiety were most common in offspring of normal controls. According to this study, children of schizophrenic parents also showed deficits in the ability to maintain attention and ignore irrelevant input, as well as cognitive slippage. For example, a listener might have difficulties discerning what some children with a schizophrenic parent were talking about. There was considerable longitudinal stability with regard to attentional, cognitive and social impairments in the high-risk group.

With regard to family function, greater marital discord was observed in marriages where one spouse was schizophrenic than in marriages of normal controls, but no significant difference was found between the schizophrenics and the affectively ill group. Often the atmosphere in the schizophrenic family was heavy and cheerless. The feeling level was cold and restricted, and conflict and tension were high.

Taking these studies together, one is struck by the enormous breadth in social deviance shown by schizophrenics' offspring. Some have acting-out problems, others are withdrawn; still others show attentional or cognitive deficits. The overall pattern is that offspring with a schizophrenic parent, as well as offspring with an affectively ill parent, show multiple and extensive cognitive and social impairments. The fact that there was considerable overlap in the problems of offspring whose parents manifested different mental disorders could mean that high-risk children are merely responding to their parents' illness and hospitalization. Or, from a genetic point of view, it might be that schizophrenic and affective disorders are not entirely distinct disturbances.

Finally, it is important to note that although many research workers have considered genetic factors to constitute the basis of increased risk, in studies such as those reviewed, the risk is only an empirical or statistical relationship. Children with a mentally ill parent are subject to a number of nongenetic influences, including birth complications, disruption in the family due to parental quarreling, hospitalization or divorce, and interaction with a disturbed parent. As Zubin & Spring (1977) point out, the concept of vulnerability makes no assumptions about its cause, but only posits that a cause exists.

Discordance in MZ twins

The findings from nearly all recent large-scale twin studies show that birth order, difficulties during birth, birth weight, physical strength in early childhood, and psychomotor development during the first years of life are not related to adult schizophrenia. (The exception is one twin study by Pollin et al. (1966), not based on a population sample, which found that the schizophrenic members of discordant MZ pairs were lighter at birth.)

On the other hand, recent studies of schizophrenic patients have shown that, in some cases, there are structural brain differences between discordant MZ twins. In a computerized tomography (CT) study of 12 MZ pairs clinically discordant for schizophrenia, Reveley et al. (1982) observed that the schizophrenic twin had larger ventricles than the healthy co-twin. These findings are corroborated by more than 30 controlled CT studies of non-twin schizophrenic patients. In a magnetic resonance imaging (MRI) study of 15 MZ pairs discordant for schizophrenia, the schizophrenic twin, in contrast to the healthy co-twin, had enlargement of the brain ventricles and reduced size of part of the hippocampus (Suddath et al., 1990). Several, although not all, recent MRI studies in schizophrenia have reported evidence for reduced size of temporal cortex, amygdalae, hippocampus and the frontal region. These differences are presumably of a nongenetic nature, since they occur in only one of the MZ twins in the pair. However, there is no explanation as to why these differences occur. Illness in pregnancy, birth complications or an interaction between genetic and environmental organic factors are possible explanations.

A similar situation is encountered with regard to physiology. Significant differences in regional cerebral blood flow between affected and unaffected MZ twins were observed during a neuropsychological test of problem solving and abstract reasoning (Wisconsin Card Sorting Test), but only in the prefrontal cortex (Berman et al., 1992). These observations strengthen the assertion that metabolic hypofrontality is characteristic of schizophrenia (Buchsbaum et al., 1992).

There is neither a genetic nor an environmental explanation for these MZ differences. In general, MZ twins share the same familial conditions. Thus, one might expect only subtle differences in the environmental conditions experienced by the discordant twins. Several twin investigators have noted that the twin who was more dependent, submissive and "nervous" was the one more likely to become schizophrenic. However, this does not clarify whether such submissiveness is the result of an already psychobiologically weakened system, an early symptom of mental illness or an independent causal factor.

By studying the life histories of MZ twins discordant for schizophrenia, one gets in general the impression of a dismal and conflictual family atmosphere. It is hard, however, to detect any consistent pattern with regard to differential rearing and parental attachment, except that the dominant twin seemed more often to have been able to avoid the schizophrenic development (Kringlen, 1967, vol. 2). In a study of the offspring of two psychotic parents, in some cases it seemed that the normal offspring had been able to avoid being enmeshed by the sick parents, in contrast to the disturbed siblings (Kringlen, 1978). In the case of one affected parent, Mosher et al. (1971) reported that the schizophrenic members of MZ discordant pairs were more attached to the disturbed parent. Perhaps identification with the more deviant parent might predispose to psychopathology.

General viewpoint

Both twin and adoption studies show that genes contribute to the etiology of schizophrenia. However, views differ with regard to the magnitude of the genetic contribution. Nor do we know what is inherited, or how specific the genetic liability is. Most likely we should conceive of the genetic disposition as providing a potential for deviant response patterns in perception and cognition. Some have entertained the view that ego weakness or a tendency to develop schizotypal personality or borderline schizophrenia is inherited. Strong evidence for such a view is, however, lacking.

During the last decade, a neurodevelopmental theory of schizophrenia has prevailed (Waddington, 1993). This hypothesis points toward very early events that disrupt the development of fundamental brain structures and functions in utero. Speculation along these lines stems, in part, from reports that birth complications increase the susceptibility to schizophrenia, and that patients with schizophrenia are more likely than others to have been born during the winter or early spring months, at which time (in the northern hemisphere) there is a higher risk of maternal influenza. There are also epidemiological reports of an association between maternal exposure to influenza during midpregnancy, and an increased rate of schizophrenia (Mednick et al., 1988). McNeil (1988), in a thorough review, reported that obstetric complications have been found in many samples of schizophrenic patients, and might be related to the development of schizophrenia, although the pattern is not consistent. On the other hand, Done et al. (1991), in a systematic study of individuals born in 1958 and later admitted to psychiatric hospitals with schizophrenia, observed that these individuals were not more likely to have been exposed to any of the factors connected with perinatal death than the 16,000 subjects who did not suffer from the illness. The same study did not find evidence for the "second trimester" hypothesis. Thus, the notion that birth injury and second trimester influenza play a central role in the causation of schizophrenia seems unlikely. In any case, these factors cannot account for more than 5–10% of the overall risk.

Neither genes, viruses, nor drugs are sufficient to produce a schizophrenic episode; the symptoms must be acquired by social learning and human interaction. According to one hypothesis, the family is an important etiological agent in the transmission of schizophrenia, through faulty communication patterns and internal conflicts (Wynne et al., 1977; Goldstein et al., 1987). Compared with controls, parents of schizophrenic patients more often fail to share a focus of attention, to take the perspective of the other, or to communicate clearly and accurately. However, it is not certain whether the parental deficits precede, accompany, or follow the onset of psychosis in the offspring.

Since the MZ discordance in schizophrenia is considerable, and since one might surmise that the familial factors operate more or less similarly in both twins during childhood, social factors operating in adolescence after partial separation of the twins might have been underestimated. We know much more about infant development than about adolescent development. Could superficially trivial social factors in adolescence be responsible for a vicious circle that finally gets out of control? One might call this process the "St. Matthew effect": "For whosoever hath, to him shall be given and he shall have more abundance: but whosoever hath not, from him shall be taken away even that he hath." In psychiatry, one is often impressed by the way some patients have been massively strained by extreme psychopathology, an unhappy marriage, dismal economic success, and poor housing. However, that does not necessarily mean that the original cause of deviant development was a major one. As the historian A.J.P. Taylor says with reference to the outbreak of World War I, it is hard for human beings to conceive that important events often have trivial causes. However, a minor event may start the process, or an unfortunate choice may, in the next round, lead to other unfortunate choices, finally bringing the individual to a disastrous outcome.

In monozygotic twins, one may observe the paradoxical situation that two individuals with the same genetic makeup develop in quite different directions. One twin may develop schizophrenia, and the co-twin may be clinically normal; one twin may become a criminal, the other, a successful businessman; one twin may develop peptic ulcer, the co-twin, depression. The contrary may also be observed.

One twin may have had a dismal childhood, but for various reasons may have been brought into healthy development. If one returns to the twins' childhood, only minor differences might be observed, and no signs that predict later development. Something, however, has happened during their life course, perhaps during early adult life, that had a snowball effect. The possible reinforcement processes are evident whenever one considers a series of choices in social situations where every new event is influenced by previous choices. The normally law-abiding individual starts, for instance, to "borrow" cash from the till in a critical situation, with the intention of paying back the money quickly. However, because of economic troubles, this resolution turns out to be difficult, and he is tempted to borrow more. Each time he exceeds the moral threshold, the feeling of guilt is reduced. Or consider, for instance, the puritanical person who gradually develops a taste for the high life. One barrier after the other falls down. Finally he also begins to look at himself in a new way. In fact, his personality has changed.

Similar developmental processes might be observed on the macrolevel. For instance, the economic bases of a provincial area begin to deteriorate. People start moving away to other regions, and it becomes difficult for those who are left to sustain a viable environment. During the next phase, the school is closed down, the shopkeeper shuts his shop, and finally the central authorities decide to close down the railway. In the end one is left with a disintegrated area, mainly inhabited by older people. A vicious circle of self-reinforcing negative processes has killed the local community.

Each organism has biological processes determined by its genetic equipment. One cannot jump over a biological phase. The genes decide if an organism is to develop into a rose or a pink carnation, into a human being or an animal. Similar processes are not observed in social life. Reinforcing social processes express, in a way, another logic. Even though the concept of reinforcing processes implies a reservation with regard to causal models in psychiatry, this does not mean that the social sciences, including psychiatry, are indeterministic. Nor does it mean that social life is based upon conscious choices.

If a schizophrenic outcome is the result of a sequence of reinforcing social processes acting on a vulnerable genotype, it may become conceptually impossible to assign quantitative values to each individual event. Thus, we might say that hunting for causes for schizophrenia in early development should be given lower priority. That does not mean that one should build one's theory on an indeterministic view. Rather, it might be useful to apply a sequential model, and study the reinforcement process in social change, remembering that small differences in the initial phase can lead to massive differences at a later stage. It is just as important to study the process over time as to hunt for special causative factors. Therefore, longitudinal studies are paramount, and prospective studies are mandatory in order to demonstrate causal relationships.

References

Berman, K. F., Torrey, E. F., et al. (1992). Regional cerebral blood flow in monozygotic twins discordant and concordant for schizophrenia. *Arch. Gen. Psychiatry* 49:927–934.

Buchsbaum, M. S., Maier, R. J., Potkin, S. G., et al. (1992). Frontostriatal disorder of cerebral metabolism in never-medicated schizophrenics. *Arch. Gen. Psychiatry* 49:935–942.

Done, D. J., Johnstone, E. C., & Frith, C. D. (1991). Complications of pregnancy and delivery in relation to psychosis in adult life: Data from the British perinatal mortality survey sample. *Br. Med. J.* 302:1576–1580.

Erlenmeyer-Kimling, L. (1987). High-risk research in schizophrenia: A summary of what has been learned. *J. Psychiatr. Res.* 21:401–411.

Essen-Möller, E. (1941). Twin research and psychiatry. *Acta Psychiatr. Scand.* 39:65–77.

Farmer, A. E., McGuffin, P., Haven, I., et al. (1992). Schizophrenia, how far can we go in defining the phenotype? In P. McGuffin and R. Murray (eds.), *The new genetics of mental illness*. Oxford: Heinemann.

Fischer, M. (1973). Genetic and environmental factors in schizophrenia. *Acta Psychiatr. Scand.*, Suppl. 238:158.

Fish, B., Marcus, J., Sydney, L. H., et al. (1992). Infants at risk for schizophrenia: Sequelae of a genetic neurointegrative defect. *Arch. Gen. Psychiatry* 49:221–235.

Gershon, E. S., Delisi, L. E., Hamovit, J., et al. (1988). A controlled family study of chronic psychoses. *Arch. Gen. Psychiatry* 45:328–336.

Goldstein, M. J., & Strachan, A. M. (1987). The family and schizophrenia. In T. Jacob (ed.), *Family interaction and psychopathology*. New York: Plenum, pp. 481–508.

Goodman, S. (1987). Emory University Project on children of disturbed parents. *Schiz. Bull.* 13:411–424.

Gottesmann, I. I., & Shields, J. (1972). *Schizophrenia and genetics: A twin study vantage point*. New York: Academic Press.

506   *Einar Kringlen*

Hartmann, E., Milofsky, E., Vaillant, G., Oldfield, M., Falke, R., & Ducey, C. (1984). Vulnerability to schizophrenia. *Arch. Gen. Psychiatry* 41:1050–1056.

Jablensky, A. (1993). The epidemiology of schizophrenia. *Current Opinion in Psychiatry* 6:43–52.

Kendler, K. S. (1989). Limitations of the ratio of concordance rates in monozygotic and dizogotic twins (letter). *Arch. Gen. Psychiatry* 46:477–478.

Kendler, K. S., McGuire, M., Gruenberg, A. M., et al. (1992). The Roscommon family study: I: Methods, diagnosis of probands and risk of schizophrenia in relatives. *Arch. Gen. Psychiatry* 49:106–110.

Kety, S. S., Rosenthal, D., Wender, P. H., & Schulsinger, F. (1975). Mental illness in the biological and adoptive families of adoptive individuals who have become schizophrenic. In R. R. Fieve, D. Rosenthal, & H. Brill (eds.). *Genetic research in psychiatry.* Baltimore: Johns Hopkins University Press, pp. 111–120.

Kety, S. S., Rosenthal, D., Wender, P. H., Schulsinger, F., & Jacosen, B. (1978). The biological and adoptive families of adopted individuals who became schizophrenic: Prevalence of mental illness and other characteristics. In L. C. Wynne, R. L. Cromwell, & S. Mathysse (eds.). *The nature of schizophrenia.* New York: Wiley, pp. 25–37.

Kringlen, E. (1967). Heredity and environment in the functional psychoses, vols. 1 and 2. Oslo: Universitetsforlaget (London: Heineman, vol. 2: case histories).

Kringlen, E. (1978). Adult offspring of two psychotic parents with special reference to schizophrenia. In L. C. Wynne, R. L. Cromwell, & S. Matthysse (eds.), *The nature of schizophrenia.* New York: Wiley.

Kringlen, E. (1986). Status of twin research in functional psychoses. *Psychopathology* 19:85–92.

Kringlen, E. (1991). Adoption studies in functional psychosis. *Eur. Arch. Psychiatry Clin. Neurosci.* 240:307–313.

Kringlen, E., & Cramer, G. (1989). Offspring of monozygotic twins discordant for schizophrenia. *Arch. Gen. Psychiatry* 46:873–877.

Lewis, S. W. (1992). Sex and schizophrenia: Vivre la difference. *Br. J. Psychiatry* 161:445–450.

Maier, W., Hallmayer, J., Minges, J., & Lichtermann, D. (1990). Affective and schizoaffective disorders: Similarities and differences. In A. Marneros & M. T. Tsuang (eds.), *Morbid risks in relatives of affective, schizoaffective and schizophrenic patients – results of a family study.* New York: Springer Verlag, pp. 201–207.

Marcus, J., Hans, S. L., Nagler, S., Aurbach, J. G., Mirsky, A. F., & Aubrey, A. 1987. Review of the NIMH Israeli kibbutz–city study and the Jerusalem infant development study. *Schiz. Bull.* 13:425–438.

McGue, M. (1992). When assessing twin concordance, use the probandwise not the pairwise rate. *Schiz. Bull.* 18:171–176.

McNeil, T. F. (1988). Obstetric factors and perinatal injuries. In M. T. Tsuang & J. C. Simpson (eds.), *Handbook of schizophrenia: Nosology, epidemiology and genetics.* New York: Elsevier Science Publishers, vol. 3, pp. 319–344.

McNeil, T. F., & Kaij, L. (1987). Swedish high-risk study: Sample characteristics at age 6. *Schiz. Bull.* 13:373–382.

Mednick, S. A., & Schulsinger, F. (1968). Some premorbid characteristics related to breakdowns in children with schizophrenic mothers. In D. Rosenthal & S. S. Kety (eds.), *The transmission of schizophrenia.* New York: Pergamon Press.

Mednick, S. A., Machon, R. A., Huttunen, M. D., & Bonnet, D. (1988). Adult schizophrenia following prenatal exposure to an influenza epidemic. *Arch. Gen. Psychiatry* 45:189–192.

Mosher, L. R., Pollin, W., & Stabenau, J. R. (1971). Families with identical twins discordant for schizophrenia: Some relationships between identification, thinking styles, psychopathology and dominance-submissiveness. *Br. J. Psychiatry* 118:29–42.

Nagler, S., & Mirsky, A. F. (1985). The Israeli high-risk study. *Schiz. Bull.* 11:19–29.

Onstad, S., Skre, J., Torgersen, S., & Kringlen, E. (1991). Twin concordance for DSM-III-R schizophrenia. *Acta Psychiatr. Scand.* 83:395–401.

Pollin, W., Stabenau, J. R., Mosher, L., & Tupin, J. (1966). Life history differences in identical twins discordant for schizophrenia. *Am. J. Orthopsychiatry* 36:492–509.

Reveley, A. M., Reveley, M. A., Clifford, C. A., et al. (1982). Cerebral ventricular size in twins discordant for schizophrenia. *Lancet* 1:540–541.

Roff, J. D., Knight, R., & Wertheim, E. (1976). A factor-analytic study of childhood symptoms antecedent to schizophrenia. *J. Abnorm. Psychol.* 85:543–549.

Rosenthal, D. (1966). The offspring of schizophrenic couples. *J. Psychiat. Res.* 4:169–188.

Rosenthal, D., Wender, P. H., Kety, S. S., Schulsinger, F., Welner, J., & Østergaard, L. (1968). Schizophrenic offspring reared in adoptive homes. In D. Rosenthal & S. S. Kety (eds.), *The transmission of schizophrenia.* New York: Pergamon Press, pp. 377–392.

Rosenthal, D., Wender, P. H., Kety, S. S., Schulsinger, F., Welner, J., & Riedker, B. (1975). Parent–child relationships and psychopathological disorder in the child. *Arch. Gen. Psychiatry* 32:466–476.

Sameroff, A., Seifer, R., Zax, M., & Barocus, R. (1987). Early indicators of developmental risk: Rochester Longitudinal Study. *Schiz. Bull.* 13:383–394.

Slater, E., & Shields, J. (1953). Psychotic and neurotic illnesses in twins. London: Her Majesty's Stationery Office.

Suddath, R. I., Christison, G. W., & Torrey, E. F. (1990). Anatomical abnormalities in the brains of monozygotic twins discordant for schizophrenia. *New Eng. J. Med.* 322:789–794.

Tienari, P. (1963). Psychiatric illnesses in identical twins. *Acta Psychiatr. Scand.*, Suppl. 171.

Tienari, P. (1991). Genes, family environment or interaction. Findings from an adoption study. In E. Kringlen, N. J. Lavik, & S. Torgersen (eds.), *Etiology of mental disorder.* Oslo: Department of Psychiatry, University of Oslo, pp. 33–49.

Torgersen, S. (1984). Genetic and nosological aspects of schizotypal and borderline personality disorders: A twin study. *Arch. Gen. Psychiatry* 41:546–554.

Torrey, E. F. (1992). Are we overestimating the genetic contribution to schizophrenia? *Schizophr. Bull.* 18:159–170.

Torrey, E. F., Bowler, A. E., Taylor, E., & Gottesman, I. I. (1994). *Schizophrenia and manic-depressive disorder. The biological roots of mental illness as revealed by the landmark study of identical twins.* New York: Basic Books.

Waddington, J. L. (1993). Schizophrenia: Developmental neuroscience and pathobiology. *Lancet* 341:531–536.

Walker, E., & Emeroy, E. (1983). Infants at risk for psychopathology: Offspring of schizophrenic parents. *Child Dev.* 54:1269–1285.

Watt, N. F., Stolorow, R. D., Ludensky, A. W., et al. (1970). School adjustment and behavior of children hospitalized for schizophrenia. *Am. J. Orthopsychiatry* 40:637–657.

Weinberger, D. R., Berman, K. F., Suddath, R., et al. (1992). Evidence of dysfunction of a prefrontal-limbic network in schizophrenia: A magnetic resonance imaging and regional cerebral blood flow study of discordant monozygotic twins. *Am. J. Psychiatry* 49:522–530.

Weintraub, S. (1987). Risk factors in schizophrenia: The Stony Brook High Risk Project. *Schizophr. Bull.* 13:439–450.

Wynne, L. C., Singer, M. T., Bartko, J. J., & Toohey, M. L. (1977). Schizophrenics and their families: Research on parental communication. In M. Tanner (ed.), *Developments in psychiatric research.* London: Hodder & Stoughton.

Zubin, J., & Spring, B. (1977). Vulnerability – A new view of schizophrenia. *J. Abn. Psychology* 96:103–126.

Comments on Einar Kringlen's chapter

Philip S. Holzman and Steven Matthysse

The ratio of monozygotic to dizygotic twin concordances (MZ/DZ) has been used, as Professor Kringlen indicates, as a way of defining the phenotype of schizophrenia (see also Introduction to the Genetics section). Essentially, the idea is that whatever definition has the highest MZ/DZ ratio is the "most genetic." One can also look at the MZ/DZ ratio in a different light. Polygenic or oligogenic factors tend to elevate the MZ/DZ ratio, whereas it is expected to be close to 2 for a dominant trait caused by a single gene [2, 3]. It may be that, if a certain phenotypic definition of schizophrenia yields an MZ/DZ ratio close to 2, that phenotype is most plausibly attributed to a single gene. Other phenotypic definitions with higher MZ/DZ ratios would perhaps be associated with multigenic or polygenic factors. An analysis of this kind requires that the probands be diagnosed with the same criteria, broad or narrow, that are used for the co-twins.

The study of Farmer et al. [1] provides data that may be interpreted in this way. Rediagnosing the 62 probands from the Maudsley series according to DSM-III criteria, Farmer et al. found an MZ/DZ ratio of 5.01 for schizophrenia, consistent with the action of multiple genes, but the ratio decreased progressively as the criteria were broadened, reaching a value of 3.23 when schizophreniform disorder, paranoia and schizoaffective disorder were included. One possible interpretation is that there is a major gene that predisposes to a broad phenotype including schizophreniform disorder, paranoia and schizoaffective disorder as well as schizophrenia, and there are additional genes that enter into the determination of which specific syndrome in this class is the outcome.

With further broadening (including all the probands in the Maudsley sample with any Axis I DSM-III diagnosis – 27 of the 28 probands from the MZ pairs, and all 34 probands from the DZ pairs) – the MZ/DZ ratio fell even further, to 2.39. Granted that the probands were originally ascertained by either being diagnosed schizophrenic (although not by DSM III criteria) or being suspected of having schizophrenia, this broadest group included several patients with DSM-III nonpsychotic affective diagnoses, so it seems to be stretching a point to use this lowest MZ/DZ ratio, 2.39, as an indicator of a still more "pure" major locus. Relative to polygenic or oligogenic traits, both monogenicity and environmental influences (if not specifically shared by MZ twins) will lower the MZ/DZ ratio, so one cannot push the reasoning too far. Nevertheless, it might be a mistake to choose one's phenotypic definition of schizophrenia as the one with the highest MZ/DZ ratio, in the hope of obtaining the "most genetic" trait, if the eventual goal is isolation of contributing major loci through linkage analysis.

References

[1] Farmer, A. E., McGuffin, P., and Gottesman, I. I. (1987). Twin concordance for DSM-III schizophrenia. *Archives of General Psychiatry, 44,* 634–641.
[2] Matthysse, S., and Kidd, K. K. (1976). Estimating the genetic contribution to schizophrenia. *Am. J. Psychiatry, 133* 185–191.
[3] Risch, N. (1990). Linkage strategies for genetically complex traits: I. Multilocus models. *American Journal of Human Genetics 46,* 222–228.

23

Epistemological issues in psychiatric research

Josef Parnas

Introduction

Matthysse and Parnas (1992) demonstrated that studies which only investigate overt schizophrenia as the informative phenotype are bound to result in failures to detect linkage, even if linkage is present. We suggested the use of the spectrum concept of schizophrenia and of putative extraclinical measures, such as eye tracking disorder, in order to enhance the likelihood of detecting existing linkage. The question is how to delimit the range of phenotypes which may be informative in genetic studies of schizophrenia. Many researchers, including the author (Parnas et al., 1993), subscribe to the diathesis-stress model of schizophrenic etiology (e.g., Meehl, 1962, 1989), elegantly formulated by Minkowski (1927) half a century ago:

The notion of schizophrenia, as a mental disease, can be decomposed into two factors, of different order: first, the schizoidia, which is a constitutional factor, highly specific, and temporally enduring through the individual life; and, second, a noxious factor, of an evolutional nature, and which has the ability to determine a morbid mental process. This latter factor has, for itself, no definite taint, it is of a more unspecific nature, and the clinical picture to which it will lead will depend upon the ground on which it will act. It will transform schizoidia into a *specific morbid process*, into *schizophrenia*. (pp. 50–51, my translation, my emphasis).

It follows from Minkowski's statement that subclinical "trait" features, which he called "schizoidia" and which tend to be more permanent than psychotic "state" symptoms, constitute a relevant phenotype to be investigated in a genetic study. According to all models of transmission of schizophrenia, we should encounter in any population individuals who are genetically disposed to schizophrenia but who exhibit only subclinical features of the illness. Such traits are likely to be more proximate to the underlying pathophysiological processes than overt psychotic symptoms (Parnas & Bovet, 1991; Parnas & Bovet, in press). The task of research is therefore to include phenotypes more subtle than overt schizophrenia.

That, however, requires finesse and sophistication, which are simply lacking in current psychopathology (van Praag, 1992). There prevails, instead, a naive quest for "objectivity," in that diagnostic instruments, diagnostic practices, and diagnostic criteria cater to an objective approach. Reciprocally, such diagnostic practices consolidate their tacit and rarely questioned conceptual bias.

The claim of this paper is that psychopathology is in a state of *epistemological crisis* which contributes to slow progress in the etiological research in schizophrenia. A mixture of interrelated theoretical and ideological elements constitutes this postulated crisis of psychopathology:

1. There is exaggerated quest for reliability. Reliability is viewed as a necessary but not a sufficient condition for validity, or as a first step on the ladder toward the truth. This is a simplification. Reliability is very easy to achieve. The decision rule to classify all people as normal would attain this end (Faust & Miner, 1986). This example shows that reliability is empty when it is a primary goal, not combined with some idea about matters worth measuring reliably. Very often methodological "purity" takes today precedence over theoretical meaningfulness. This quest has acquired the character of methodological fetishism, where the direction of research is dictated neither by theory nor by the subject of inquiry, but by the methods that guarantee the reliable reproduction of data (Kozulin, 1990).

2. This exaggerated concern with reliability is reflected in the creation of prematurely closed and simple diagnostic classification systems, and of psychometric instruments solely compatible to these preexisting systems. In such a situation it is impossible to explore other, not predefined areas of interest because diagnostic systems and instruments reinforce each other in a spiral of increasing simplicity and closure. This results in premature abandonment of potentially important discoveries and ideas. Even though diagnostic criteria and psychometric instruments are officially announced as provisional, they become elevated de facto to the status of the ultimate, almost metaphysical, truth, through editorial, publishing, and funding policies.

3. The prevalent psychopathological practice is to count only crude psychopathological observables by means of highly structured interviews, often performed by nonclinicians. The so-called unreliable items are simply removed from the diagnostic criteria (Flaum et al., 1991). An entire range of phenomena is thereby dismissed from the presently "authorized" diagnostic framework.

4. Symptoms are reductionistically considered as unrelated products of a focally dysfunctional brain machine without phenomenological theorizing about the nature of psychiatric disorders, especially about the relationships between the symptomatological components of disorders (in the line exemplified by Bleuler [1911]). This lack of phenomenological theorizing seems to be related to a radical disjunction between clinical work and research. Clinicians rarely participate in research and they rarely consider research as particularly helpful in clinical work. Researchers, on the other hand, expect insights from post hoc statistical analyses, as it is evident in the currently proliferating studies on "comorbidity" which are not guided by any conceptual framework. This situation corresponds to the expectation of scientific progress in infectious medicine from factor analysis of coughs and sneezes (Cromwell, 1984).

These and other problems relate to the absence of critical reflection on theoretical (philosophical) foundations of our discipline. More specifically, these problems relate to an epistemological crisis in contemporary psychiatry. In this presentation, critical points will be raised, with only few constructive concluding suggestions. A radical, pragmatically useful reconstruction of the prevailing epistemology is perhaps an overambitious project, which is only dimly arising on the philosophical horizon (e.g., Rorty, 1980; Maturana and Varela, 1988; Putnam, 1989).

The paradigms of knowledge

Epistemological approaches to the study of the human mind can be depicted as a circle comprising several, intertwined elements (Figure 23.1).

Acquisition of knowledge undergoes an ontogenetic change. Irrespective of the degree of sophistication of our inborn equipment, we increase and modify our capacity to acquire knowledge during our ontogeny. In the Western world there is a long-lasting tradition of distinguishing between affective and cognitive domains, both consid-

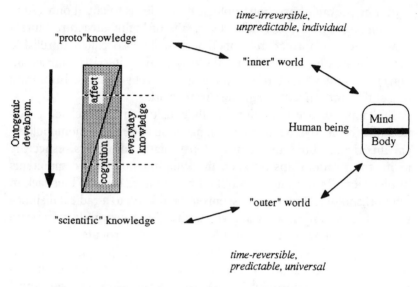

Figure 23.1. Knowledge within Newtonian epistemology

ered to be involved in the process of knowledge acquisition. It is generally acknowledged that affective domain is dominating at the beginning of life with subsequent relative increase of cognitive processes which are only fully developed by the end of adolescence. The primary type of knowledge, strongly linked to affective elements, may be designated as "protoknowledge." The scientific knowledge in this paradigm is the ultimate and ideal achievement of rational, cognitive processes. Knowledge which we use in our everyday interactions with the world occupies a more or less large intermediate span between protoknowledge and scientific knowledge. In the traditional "Newtonian" paradigm, scientific knowledge is best fit to address the "outer" world. The less animate the object of inquiry, the more appropriate is the scientific approach based on ideal objects comprising stones and planetary bodies, or, with decreasing ideality, plants, animals, and the human body. The field which is supposed to constitute the realm of scientific knowledge is ideally describable in mathematical equations, which are universally valid and allow prediction as well as retrodiction, and therefore consider phenomena as time-reversible.

At another level of phenomena, it is generally believed that our own "inner" world (our subjectivity), is of a different nature. It is time-irreversible, largely individual and nonpredictable. Each person lives in the conviction that his own unique, inner mental life-history cannot be exhausted by scientifically deterministic description, or through what is considered as scientific knowledge. Every individual is also convinced that a similar limitation applies to other human beings. Every human being consists of body and mind. The mind–body problem originates here with the most elaborate distinction formalized by Descartes. Mind–body represents a meeting point of two, apparently distinct, realms of reality. At the time of Descartes, the mind–body barrier was complete and the domain of the spiritual was left to the divine forces. Psychology and psychopathology anchored in the traditional Newtonian science paradigm are unable to address the issue of subjectivity, and consequently attempts are made to "move" parts of the human mind through the mind–body barrier into the "outer" sphere in order to make them suitable for scientific apprehension. Basically, human mind is therefore left out of the traditional scientific approach. Such a Newtonian approach is intimately reflected in the adherence to logical empiricism in psychopathology.

Logical empiricism in psychiatry

The designation "logical empiricism" (or logical positivism) stems from the combination of preoccupation with logic in the Vienna circle (and in the later work of analytic philosophers) with positivist assumption that observation of natural phenomena is the only valid source of knowledge. Logical positivists were interested in the issue of meaning: they considered something to be meaningful if, and only if, it either is verifiable empirically – i.e., ultimately by (not necessarily direct) observation through the senses – or is a tautology of logics or mathematics. Verification is often impossible to attain, so it is sometimes required in principle, not in practice. Logical empiricism relies on the following epistemological principles: (1) Methodological monism, which claims the unity of method amid the diversity of subject matters. (2) The postulate that exact sciences (physics and mathematics) set a methodological ideal or standard which measures the degree of development or perfection of all other sciences. (3) An insistence on scientific, i.e., "causal explanation," which consists in the subsumption of individual cases under hypothetically assumed general "laws of nature" (including human nature). In this context priority is given to "prediction" ("explanation") rather than to "understanding" (Wright, 1971). The explicit introduction of logical empiricism in psychiatry came at the moment of crisis of psychiatric diagnosis. American psychiatry was initially dominated by the school of Adolf Meyer (1913), which discarded diagnostic classification and instead emphasized the uniqueness of the individual. Around World War II, psychiatry became rapidly dominated by psychoanalysis, which was likewise uninterested in diagnostic classification. This domination had a devastating impact on diagnostic practices and standards. The results of the U.S.–U.K. diagnostic project (Cooper et al., 1972) demonstrated alarming differences between diagnostic practices of British and American psychiatrists and constituted the decisive impetus toward making diagnostic definitions reliable and consensual. In his address to the APA, Hempel (1965) presented basic ideas of logical empiricism. He insisted on rigorous definitions of terms as a necessary precondition of scientific endeavor. Ideally, terms should be operational, because only operational criteria are unambiguous and therefore scientifically useful. Operational definitions of scientific terms aim at "objectivity" of knowledge, "in the sense of being intersubjectively certifiable, independently of individual opinion or preference." Operational definition assures therefore the link between the concept and reality.

An operational definition of a term is conceived as a rule to the effect that the term is to apply to a particular case if the performance of specified operations in that case yields a certain characteristic result. (Hempel, 1965, p. 123).

One can, for instance, define the term "ice" as a certain volume of water which turns into a solid state under specified thermic and barometric conditions. Hempel knew, however, that in the domain of psychopathology, there was no possibility of applying "operations." In the second half of his APA lecture, he therefore allowed that a term may be called operational if it was rigorously and unambiguously defined. Scientific definitions according to Hempel derive from "meaning analysis" (which refers to the semantics on which scientists agree upon a term) and from "empirical analysis" (which refers to necessary and sufficient criteria of a term's application). Truly scientific concepts derive from "empirical import" and have a character of universal (etiologically based) causal laws from which a prediction concerning each individual case can be made (Schwartz & Wiggins, 1986).

Some philosophical issues

The *Zeitgeist* in psychopathology is connected to these tenets of logical empiricism. These tenets are, however, not unproblematic for psychopathology. The philosophical and epistemic problems can be grouped in the following overlapping issues: (1) The issue of language and meaning; (2) the scientific status of induction; and (3) the problem of the apprehension of the Other.

1. Language and meaning

The philosophical position of logical empiricism concerning meaning and language is summarized in the following assumptions:

A. Every word the speaker uses is associated in his mind with a certain mental representation. B. Two words are synonymous (i.e., have the same meaning) when they are associated with the same mental representation by the speakers who use those words. C. The mental representation determines what the word refers to. (Putnam, 1991, p. 19).

This simple scheme, developed by Aristotle, relies on the following foundation of a spoken (or written) meaning: the object in the "real," external world or the idea in the "spiritual" world gives rise to (constitutes or founds) our "internal" concept of it (i.e., it results in a "mental representation") which in turn becomes converted into a sign (word) which is a symbol of such representation. Language consists of a series of signs whose meaning is guaranteed (or founded) by their correspondence or reference to representations and therefore ultimately to objects in the world.

Words are symbols or signs of affections or impression of the soul (i.e. representations of objects); written words are the signs of words spoken. As writing, so also is speech not the same for all races of men. But the mental affections themselves, of which these words are primarily signs, are the same for the whole of mankind, as are also the objects of which those affections are representations or likenesses, images, copies. (Aristoteles, *De interpretatione*, I).

If one adopts such a view of meaning and language the issue of definitional, operational terms is entirely unproblematic. Meaning of a concept or a category is stabilized and fixed by its representation-mediated foundation upon reality. Categories have clear-cut boundaries and their membership depends on shared features, which are jointly sufficient and singly necessary to define the category in question. This view is *the* cornerstone of objectivist–empirist perspective on meaning and cognition and has deep roots in the Western history of thinking. We bypass the problems of empirical and ontological status of the concept of mental representation, because it is irrelevant in our context. What is, however, relevant is the question of a simple and fixed correspondence between the meaning of a word and its object determinant or, to phrase it differently, of the criteria of a category membership. What is relevant here is the relation between the signified (meaning) and signifying (sign) (*signifié* and *signifiant*). The "linguistic turn" in philosophy was initiated by the revolutionary contribution of Saussure (1922) in the science of linguistics. He pointed out that a relation or a tie between the signified and the signifying is basically syntagmatic. This means that such correspondence is dependent on sequential relations between signifiers or, phrased more simply, dependent on the location of a signifier among all other signifiers. An independent, philosophically anchored critique of the Aristotelian view of meaning was conducted by Wittgenstein in a series of his late publications. Wittgenstein pointed out that one cannot divorce verbal signs from systems to which they belong. His insistence on praxis-bound meaning is epitomized in the famous statement that "the *use* of a word in the language is its meaning. Grammar (i.e., shared community rules) describes the use of words in the language" (Wittgenstein, 1974, § 23). Wittgenstein (1958) (and Saussure) insisted upon *community interpretation* as fixing and determining meaning:

Is what we call "obeying a rule" something that it would be possible for only *one* man to do, and to do only *once* in his life? . . . To obey a rule, to make a report, to give an order, to play a game of chess, are *customs* (uses, institutions). (§ 199).

Wittgenstein's major aim was to rid us of the prejudice that our concepts must have rigid limits. He maintained that it is an absurd requirement that every possible application of a concept can be determined in advance. There is room for indeterminacy and *no form of definition* is secure against this inherent condition. Wittgenstein believed that specification of necessary and sufficient criteria for a definition is very often unattainable:

There is nothing identifiably common to the states of affairs for which we use a word. There is only a number of overlapping resemblances. Our concepts are enormous families with various resemblances. (Ambrose, 1979, § 96).

Recently, Putnam (1991) presented a similar critique of the Aristotelian views on meaning and representation:

None of the methods of representation [e.g., signs, words, definitions] that we know about has the property that representations intrinsically refer to whatever it is that they are used to refer to. All of the representations we know about have an association with their referent which is contingent, and capable of changing as the culture changes or as the world changes . . . Meaning is interactional. The environment itself plays a role in determining what a speaker's words, or a community's words, refer to. (pp. 21–22, 36).

There is growing empirical evidence from the domains of psychology, anthropology, linguistics, and other sciences which supports these original philosophical intuitions that human categorization does not respect objectivist criteria (for an exhaustive review, see Lakoff, 1987).

There exists, of course, a possibility of creating a pure and artificial language, where signified and signifier are unambiguously linked to each other by convention. We find examples of such a language in the domain of physics and mathematics.

The language and terms of psychopathology are far removed from the conditions of physics and mathematics. The language and definitions of psychopathology operate in the realm of human experience and cannot always be fixed in advance. The terminology that we use is a part of a larger, culturally and experientially determined context. An instructive example of these problems is the DSM-III-R (APA, 1987) "operational" definition of delusion. Delusion is the core subject matter in psychopathology. Whereas classical psychopathologists were acutely aware of the difficulties inherent in any attempt at a *formal* definition of a delusion ("No one has yet discovered a way of defining a delusion without invoking the aid of an underlying pathological process"; Schmidt, 1940), the operational approach, as in the DSM-III-R, does not hesitate:

A false personal belief based on incorrect inference about external reality and firmly sustained in spite of what almost everyone believes *and* in spite of what constitutes incontrovertible proof or evidence to the contrary (italics added).

As M. Spitzer (1991) demonstrated, this definition is both internally inconsistent and, in most cases, simply wrong. Usually, we cannot (and do not) disprove a delusion as empirically false or impossible; sometimes a delusional statement is true and not personal, and finally, some delusional ideas do not arise on the basis of incorrect inferences about external reality.

Each of the formal criteria of delusion so far reported in psychiatric literature (Oltmanns, 1988), considered separately, is insufficiently operational. For instance, a criterion "the belief is not shared by others" would be contradicted in cases of *folie-à-deux*. To improve operationality, each of the criteria should be accompanied by a set of subcriteria, which in turn should be more precisely defined. Such a process will inevitably result in an infinite regress of Russian nesting dolls. *We can therefore designate a given statement as delusional only within a specific context, encompassing the patient's and the clinician's experience* (Bovet and Parnas, 1993).

The philosophical inconsistency of the DSM-III-R approach is apparent in the two reterents to truth: one is ontologically autonomous (i.e., "external") reality, and the other is the appeal to intersubjectivity ("what almost everyone believes"). Following this definition, it would be impossible to decide whether Galileo was deluded or not, both at his historical period and today.

The point of this critique is *not* that we abandon striving for clear definitions, but that we remain aware of the limitations of such a striving and do not pretend that our science can be (or even should be) as rigorous as physics or mathematics. Such aspiration only leads to confusion.

2. *"Underestimation" of induction*

Induction, in its widest sense, refers to any rational process, where from premises about some things of a certain kind a conclusion is drawn about some or all of the remaining things of that kind (arriving at "universals" from "particulars"). Induction remains a matter of philosophical dispute (at least since Hume there exists a so-called problem of induction). It is a trivial fact that humans rely on inductive reasoning; what is unclear is the philosophical justification of such a process (which can be reduced to the problem of how prediction about future events can derive from past observations). The *pragmatic* inductive approach admits that induction cannot indeed be validated, in the sense of being shown to be likely to work, but it can be rationally justified as a practical policy because every alternative is less rational; the claim is that induction is likely to work if any method is. Since Popper (1963), there has been a dramatic devaluation of inductive reasoning. It seems to me that this deemphasis is based on a fundamental misunderstanding or ignorance of Popper's ideas. Popper claimed that scientific inquiry was definable only if one was able to deduce from a more general scientific theory a particular aspect of such theory, which was (in conjunction with the theory from which it was derived) potentially refutable. It is clear that Popper did not consider inductive reasoning as being worthless in the acquisition of knowledge.

In psychiatric research, devaluation of inductive reasoning is visible in the absence of clinical material in research publications and in a general mistrust of "clinical experience" (this term has acquired a derogatory connotation). With the elimination of clinical material came elimination of phenomenological reasoning and thus of potentially useful (refutable) conceptualizations concerning the nature of psychiatric observables. Phenomenological descriptions were mainly generated by German-speaking psychopathologists, whose endeavors are, even today, among the best available.

That case studies are not unscientific is illustrated by progress in neuropsychology achieved by Luria's (1966) examination of single cases exposed to brain damage or by the work of Piaget (1955) in developmental psychology. We also know from a meticulous description of a single case by Gaupp and Wollenberg (1914), that cases of delusional disorder (i.e., "paranoia") do not necessarily progress into a schizophrenic deterioration (i.e., "dementia") as was originally supposed by Kraepelin.

Diagnostic categories and concepts do not arise out of the blue but derive from *prototypical case descriptions*. "Prototypic categories are organized around prototypical examples (the best examples of the concept) with less prototypical examples forming a continuum away from these central cases" (Livesley, 1985). Prototypical cases cannot, by definition, be generalized as true or false (e.g., a sparrow is more prototypical of a bird than a penguin, but all of its own characteristics cannot be generalized to the generic class of birds), and empirical work is necessary to assess the sensitivity and specificity of singular features which derive from the prototype.

The historical background of contemporary definition of the schizophrenia spectrum disorder is extremely informative with respect to how prototypical notions guide development of more systematic diagnostic categories. The primary data concerning the schizophrenia spectrum, on which many empirical–statistical investigations have been subsequently performed, stem from the Danish–American adoption studies (Kety et al., 1978). However, the *original selection* of which data were worth collecting depended upon investigators' acquaintance with classic psychiatric literature (with its prototypical descriptions and theorizing) and the researchers' (especially the interviewer's) clinical experience and prototypical notions of "what schizophrenia is." This history is forgotten today and many psychiatrists have the impression that the schizophrenia spectrum concept was invented on the basis of some sophisticated, "controlled" design.

The concepts of schizophrenia and schizophrenia spectrum, in the absence of external validation, have to rely on a dynamic exchange between prototypical conceptualizations and empirical validations.

3. The problem of the apprehension of the Other

In a methodological manifesto, Alpert (1985) stated:

There is a pervasive feeling in psychiatry that clinically important phenomena reside primarily in the intrapsychic experience of our patients, and that access to this experience depends on subjective report. In regard to the functional psychoses, this is not so. Most of the phenomena that are important in the evaluation of schizophrenic patients resides in the signs, not the symptoms, of the disorder. . . . The point of my emphasis on the prevalence of signs in the characterization of schizophrenia refers to that distinction between signs and symptoms, which contrasts their objective and subjective origin. Signs are objective, observable and, at least potentially, are accessible to measurements. . . . For example, central to decisions as to whether a patient is showing signs of mania or retarded depression or type 2 schizophrenia, is the patient's speech rate. But speech rates are never measured. An internist who reported bradycardia without noting the pulse rate . . . would not be viewed favourably. To my knowledge, no clinician has ever reported the rate of speech of a patient described as showing disturbance in speech productivity. The operations for making such measurements are straightforward and the explanation of the lack of interest in this direction seems most directly attributable to a charismatic view of psychiatric diagnosis.

Alpert's appeal for a disjunction between "objective" signs (behavior) and "subjective" symptoms (experience) and his suggestion to disregard symptoms (as somehow "charismatic") are logical and necessary consequences of operationalistic epistemology in psychopathology (see Figure 23.1). The explicit and more often tacit acceptance of such disjunction is at the very root of the so-called problem of other minds which has always haunted empiricism. The problem of other minds as traditionally understood is that of justifying claims to know of the states of minds other than one's own. This "problem" arises from the combination of the Cartesian dualism (that mind and body are logically distinct) with the empirical claim that knowledge can be justified only by an appeal to "sensory data." This combination produces the problem of other minds in the following way: one does not have any strictly sensory contact with other minds. A natural place to look for sensory evidence of other minds is other bodies. But statements about other minds cannot be validly inferred from claims about other bodies. We arrive at a fundamental asymmetry between certainty about our personal state of mind and uncertainty about other people's states of mind.

Analytic philosophy and phenomenology challenge the Cartesian root of the problem. They argue that mind and body are *abstractions* from the more fundamental concept "person" (analytic philosophy); or that the problem arises from another kind of abstraction: personal experience is an abstraction from the *more primary intersubjective experience* (phenomenology). Both analytic philosophy and phenomenology claim that the acquisition of mental concepts happens through their application to other people, and this application to others is a prerequisite of any application of them to oneself. In other words, mental concepts do not arise from our own subjective, inner privacy; rather, they are from the very beginning codependent on and anchored in social interactions (Stern, in press). Phenomenology insists on two interrelated aspects of the comprehension of another person: the primacy of intersubjectivity and the unique status of the body in framing all human experience.

Merleau-Ponty (1945) proposes that personal experience presupposes the cultural and social world where subjects interrelate and communicate. We are constrained in our communicative possibilities by the natural and the cultural world. Both are shared, experienced as intertwined and as self-evident. Objects in the cultural world (language is a primary "cultural object") are artefacts intended by people for people. The behavior patterns deposited in these cultural objects reflect an "anonymous subject": "In the cultural object, I feel the close presence of others beneath a veil of anonymity. *Someone* uses the pipe for smoking, the spoon for eating, the bell for summoning"

(Merleau-Ponty, 1945, p. 348). According to Merleau-Ponty, the reasoning by inference postulated by empiristic thought in explaining human communication (the other, when using the artefact, is doing the same thing that one does oneself when one uses that artefact) does not explain "the anonymous subject." In fact, the reverse is true. In other words, if one perceives others as doing the same thing as oneself, such perception presupposes understanding an anonymous subject: to "read" actions as the same whoever does them is precisely to experience the anonymous subject. According to Merleau-Ponty (1945), one's experience of other bodies is an integral part of one's experience of other subjects: "I must be the exterior that I present to others, and the body of the other must be the other himself" (p. xii). One experiences other bodies as like one's own, as being an animate organism. "The body over there, which is . . . apprehended as an animate organism, must have derived this sense by *an apperceptive transfer* from my animate organism" (Husserl, 1931, p. 110, my emphasis). This apperceptive transfer (*ap*-perception means here *self*-perception) *is not an inference, not an appeal to analogical reasoning.*

For Husserl and Merleau-Ponty, the human body is the medium which subtends all our cognition of the world. Human body is privileged by being intrinsically perceiving-*and*-perceived. When I touch a part of my body, I cannot distinguish the aspect of touching from the aspect of being touched. *I live always simultaneously as an object and as a subject.* Recognition of the other person as being inhabited by a consciousness similar to mine is intimately linked to my experience of my bodily involvement in the world. My body-image is my image of myself. As image it is the object; as myself, it is the subject I am. For the body to function as a ground of human self-identity it must be both the object and the subject simultaneously. In order to grasp the thing, I must see my hand as object, live through it as subject, and tacitly *identify the two aspects.* This tacit identification subtends the corporeal schema (which is called the "lived body").[1] The comprehension of the other is based on what Merleau-Ponty calls "transfer of the corporeal schema":

I can perceive, across the visual image of the other, that the other is an organism, that that organism is inhabited by a "psyche," because the visual image of the other is interpreted by the notion I myself have of my body and thus appears as the visible envelopment of another "corporeal schema." . . . In perceiving the other, my body and his are coupled, resulting in a sort of action which pairs them. This conduct which I am able only to see, I live somehow from a distance, I make it mine; I recover it or comprehend it. Reciprocally, I know that the gestures I make myself can be the objects of an other's intentions. It is this transfer of my intention to the other's body, and of his intentions to my own, my alienation of the other and his alienation of me that makes possible the perception of others. (Merleau-Ponty, 1960, p. 118).

Perceiving another as like oneself involves perceiving a body as displaying a state of consciousness and a consciousness *visible in that body*. For example, our clinical perception of a perplexed schizophrenic, inspecting his empty and incapable hands, is a perception of his behavior *as well as* of his experiencing, or better, "it is a perception of his phenomenological experience, of which behavior is just the *place*, and psychological experience just the *manner*" (Tatossian, 1979, p. 47).

Merleau-Ponty would not have been surprised by a recent discovery that humans possess specific neural network subsystems for categorizations of *animate* objects (Hart & Gordon, 1992). There is a rapidly growing evidence from developmental psychology ("biodynamics") that the infant's bodily involvement in the world fundamentally structures and frames his cognitive capacities (Lockman & Thelen, 1993), including his perception of other persons (Stern, in press).

Proponents of objectivist–empiristic thought (e.g., Alpert, 1985) are bound to conceive consciousness as "inner," hidden states and processes, divorced from the body's inherent expressivity, and solely understandable by the inferential cognitive processes (where "sensory data" are "processed").

The nature of clinical observation: Typification processes

Another problem in Alpert's (1985) call for quantification of the clinical process is a belief that quantification itself solves the diagnostic dilemmas. To pursue Alpert's analogy further: if an internist just reported the rate of the patient's bradycardia, such a report would be, by itself, devoid of any diagnostic meaning were it not embedded in some context, for example, whether the patient is a trained athlete, or is asleep, or is taking some drugs. In psychopathology, a single, accurate report on the speech rate would not make any sense if contextual aspects of the situation (e.g., the content of speech) were not accounted for. If we were given the command to "quantify all aspects of the context," the task would be absurd. Were we to comply with the position of the "unbiased observer," we would have to enumerate all aspects of the situation and therefore by necessity fail (it would correspond to the instruction "observe carefully and write down every fact you see" [Weimer, 1979]).

In order to describe the clinical process, we have to examine briefly a few essential aspects of any perception. What happens in a trivial, everyday perception? When we recognize something moving as a man or as a bus, a place we enter as an office or as a shop, we do not proceed by becoming successively aware of disconnected single features which lead us to infer the class to which the moving object or the place belongs. We have a global and contextual perception of some salient features of the object and of their mutual relationships, which allows us to categorize it in a given class. This process is called *typification*, which is an intrinsic, largely automatic, preconceptual activity of consciousness, originally described by Husserl (1900). Typification is "seeing as . . . or understanding as . . ." (Hanson, 1965). Typification is related to Weber's (1949) notion of "ideal types" and to Wittgenstein's (1958) notion of "family resemblance." It has been recently introduced in psychiatry by Cantor et al. (1980) and Schwartz and Wiggins (1987a, 1987b). Prototypical features of a category are organized around central and best-fitting examples of that category: a sparrow, having wings and being able to fly, is more prototypical of birds than a penguin. Family resemblance extends typification beyond single features, into a network of crisscrossing analogies. In Wittgenstein's example of family resemblance, the category of "games" relies not on any single shared feature, but on such a network of analogies. In the framework of family resemblance, certain objects remain more typical of a category than other objects with a fading gradient of typicality from the central cases toward the border of a category. Typification processes in the acquisition of knowledge undergo ontogenetic changes (Vygotsky, 1934). From early childhood to adolescence, the role of affective components in typification decreases. In our typifications, "everyday" concepts become increasingly modified by "scientific" concepts. Everyday concepts emerge spontaneously from reflections on immediate, everyday experiences; they are experientially rich, but unsystematic and highly contextual. Scientific concepts, on the other hand, are defined by Vygotsky as concepts which do not necessarily relate to scientific issues – they may represent historical, linguistic, or practical knowledge – but their organization is "scientific," in the sense of formal, logical, and more decontextualized structures. As an example, a child would perhaps originally misclassify a bat as a bird, but will stop doing so after acquiring some zoological concepts. Empirical evidence strongly suggests that human cognition operates with prototype effects in concept formation (Lakoff, 1987).

In the clinical encounter with a patient it is impossible not to rely on the process of typification because this process naturally imposes itself. For the purpose of exposition, typification in the domain of schizophrenia can be decomposed into three *circularly interrelated* aspects: (1) the global apprehension of the Other, (2) the *recognition* and classification of a morbid experience, and (3) the comprehension of immediate and temporal links between components of psychopathology.

When we meet an individual in a clinical situation, we immediately and contextually apprehend to what extent he exhibits central features of a "normal" relatedness between humans. There are no operational criteria of normal relatedness, and for such a judgment we rely on our everyday preconceptual apprehension of the Other. If the individual violates such tacitly accepted standards, laypeople would simply classify him as mentally abnormal. A psychiatrist, through his professional skills, performs additional typification, and tentatively classifies the person as being withdrawn or suspicious or disinhibited, and this tentative categorization will guide his further approach but will perhaps become modified by additional exploration. The person is perhaps considered as matching a certain psychopathological prototype, such as schizophrenia or affective illness. This global typification is closely dependent on affective components. Psychiatric typifications comply, however, with a "critical attitude" and remain open to disconfirmation, preventing types from becoming stereotypes. The next component, which is the recognition and classification of a morbid experience, was described by Jaspers (1923) as *"Vergegenwärtigung,"* which literally means "the action of letting someone state his experience in the present context" (sometimes translated as "presentification"). It is clear from reading Jaspers that he meant by that recognition of certain invariant features of morbid experience in the sense of Husserl's (1900) "essence." This identification of the invariant and necessary features of the experience is arrived at by an imaginative process on the part of the psychiatrist. We may consider the process of "presentification" as consisting of the allocation of an experience within its context to a certain typical category of morbid experience. *Morbid experience is, however, always embodied in a particular individual,* which implies that the same experience is described through various phrases or designations by different patients, or that the same phrase in different patients refers to different experiences. In addition, many subpsychotic and psychotic experiences cannot be expressed in propositional terms (i.e., clear descriptive sentences) because these experiences belong to the nonpropositional, preconceptual domain. To use an example from a normal, common experience:

> . . . my present sense of being balanced upright in space at this moment is surely a nonpropositional awareness that I have, even though all my efforts to communicate its reality to you will involve propositional structures. So, while we must use propositional language to describe these dimensions of experience and understanding, we must not mistake our mode of description for the thing described. (Johnson, 1987; p. 4).

Morbid experiences on a preconceptual level, e.g., certain disturbances of volition, cognition, or self-identity, can be expressed by a patient only through a use of some metaphorical statement, to which the clinician must be potentially attuned in order to perform a correct typification.

Therefore, typification can only be successful if the features of the psychiatrist's prototypes are sufficiently enriched through a dialectic between clinical experience and theoretical training. To use Vygotsky's terms, *psychiatric typification involves an interplay between "everyday" concepts and "scientific" concepts.* A good example of such an interplay is the area of transitivistic experiences in schizophrenia (permeability of ego boundaries, e.g., thought diffusion, influence phenomena, and ideas about external control). Clinicians vaguely sense some specificity of such complaints; the theoretical concept of the "disturbance of the experiencing I" ("*Ich-Störungen,*" M. Spitzer, 1988) assists recognition of the specific nature of such complaints, and typification of them not as a product of delusional thinking, but as metaphors used by the patient to describe an, essentially undescribable, experience of the dissolution of his self. Typification has to take into account the context of the patient's expressions. It has to take into consideration both synchronic and diachronic relations between elements of the patient's experience and therefore involves some sort of sense-giving activity. It is my opinion that the disregard of schizophrenic symptomatology's meaning is possible only if one of the following propositions is fulfilled: either that schizophrenics, unlike other human beings, do not have a teleologically oriented activity, or that schizophrenics' symptomatology is completely disconnected from the rest of their activity and experiencing. This is not the place to discuss the relation between "understanding" and "explanation" (Wright, 1971); what I refer to is a certain comprehension of the patient's experiences with respect to their *meaning*. Schizophrenic overt symptomatology is multifarious and it is impossible to apprehend all its range without grouping symptoms into broader classes, like dysfunctions of "ego boundaries" or of "logical association" (Mortimer, 1992). It is hoped that symptom classes correlate with distinct etiologies, and such classifications represent the so-called symptom-based approach in etiological research (Altman and Jobbe, 1992). So far, not much has been gained from this approach, which is exactly what Bleuler (1917) anticipated:

. . . we have to look for the genetic component of schizophrenia [*Erbschizose*]. That component is linked to the visible component [*Sichtschizose*] through a long causal chain, and this chain is complicated by the action of numerous internal and external factors. No wonder that we fail in disclosing the genetic unit [*Erbeinheit*] if we start from the other end of the chain, from the visible component. (My translation).

One reason why such an approach has not been particularly successful is that symptoms are usually considered in a mechanistic way, without necessary theorizing about their phenomenological interconnectedness and without any ideas about the underlying processes (Weiss, 1989), such as the nature of vulnerability.

It might be argued that typification and the use of "everyday" concepts or "proto" knowledge in the *clinical* apprehension of schizophrenia is only a provisional stage, before we get better quantitative instruments and measures allowing a "scientific" apprehension. This is not so, and the reason is illustrated below through a brief exposition of a phenomenological approach to schizophrenic vulnerability.

Another approach to vulnerability

Bleuler (1911) considered autistic tendencies as the fundamental trait feature of the schizophrenia spectrum disorders, but neither Bleuler nor anybody else was able to define autism *through a purely descriptive approach*. Most continental European psychiatrists believe that there are specific features of the clinical picture of the schizophrenia spectrum disorders, but this specificity has proved to be elusive to a descriptive approach. Rümke (1959), in his discussion of the diagnostic value of the Kraepelinian fundamental symptoms, put it in this way:

If the symptoms are taken in the literary sense . . . , these criteria are totally insufficient. But when we add to each of these symptoms the words "a very characteristic," it is clear what Kraepelin meant. It is, however, impossible so far to describe this "very characteristic" property. Properly speaking, these words "a very characteristic" ought to be replaced by "a schizophrenic." To do so would seem to be a scientific absurdity. And yet this is not the case, for every examiner with great experience of genuine schizophrenia knows very precisely what this word "schizophrenic" refers to. (p. 304; translation slightly modified).

Autism, from a phenomenological perspective, is not a symptom but a *phenomenon*, which shows itself in the intersubjective space and refers to a fundamentally altered existential pattern. Recognition of such a change is what, sometimes, enables clinicians immediately to apprehend a given clinical picture as being typical for schizophrenia.

Studying phenomena such as autism is important for at least three reasons. First, it may allow a better comprehension of vulnerability with subsequent, conceptually guided, empirical investigations into its nature, including clinical boundaries of the disorder. Second, such an approach may help to identify individuals at risk of schizophrenia. Third, studying vulnerability may enhance identification of *specific* aspects of overt schizophrenic symptomatology. For instance, it has been proposed (Bovet and Parnas, 1993) that certain features of schizophrenic delusions reflect a particular way of relating to the world exhibited already premorbidly as vulnerability traits. Such an approach enables us to regard delusions not only within the mechanistic metaphor of a factory production line where symptoms are defective products, but also as a way of negotiating an adjustment between the vulnerable individual and his world (Parnas and Bovet, in press).

Autism can be viewed as a defective preconceptual attunement to the world, that is, in an existential pattern transgressing "common sense" aspects of human behavior (Blankenburg, 1971; Parnas and Bovet, 1991; Bovet and Parnas, 1993).

The concept of "common sense" in the history of philosophical thought, as summarized by Gadamer (1960), contains the following, *interrelated connotations*:

(a) An elementary cognitive-perceptual capacity [*sensus communis*], underlying and integrating the specific perceptual modalities, (b) the notion of "practical reason" as opposed to abstract, purely conceptual capacities, (c) an emphasis on *l'esprit de finesse* as opposed to one-sided rational attitude [*l'esprit géométrique*], (d) an emphasis on the probable and the evident [*verisimile*] rather than the true, (e) the notion of renewed adaptation to new and unexpected situations with the ability of "intuitive" grasping of the circumstances in their infinite variety, (f) a sense of proportion, i.e., the ability to distinguish between the proper and the improper, which is more than a mere practical shrewdness and thus presupposes moral elements, (g) a link to intersubjectivity, because common sense is both *founding* and *founded by* communally shared network of perspectives on the world, (h) the notion of social sense [*le sens social*], which governs our relations with other people, whereas specific perceptual modalities relate us to objects and a notion of *savoir vivre* with wit and humor as indispensable for social discourse.

In short, commonsense ability refers not to the storage of propositional knowledge but, rather, to the background cognitive capacities of "*how*" which modulate and adaptively shape all our specific cognitive and affective capacities (Searle, 1992).

Common sense is not an "area of expertise," but a general, that is, domain-independent, capacity that has to do with fluidity in representation of concepts, an ability to sift what is important from what is not, an ability to find unanticipated analogical similarities between totally different concepts. (Hofstadter, 1985, p. 640).

Commonsense capacities are no longer only a matter of philosophical curiosity but represent a crucial topic in cognitive sciences (Hofstadter, 1985; Clark, 1989; Searle, 1992) and modern anthropology (Bourdieu, 1980). In fact, the inability of classic cognitivism (which views the mind as a digital computer analogue) to account for commonsense capacities, provided a decisive impetus for the revival of alternative, "connectionist" models of the brain, where consciousness and intentionality are seen as emergent properties of large resonating ensembles of neuronal networks.

Clearly, common sense cannot be predefined or operationalized because it is "knowing how to negotiate our way through a world that is not fixed and pregiven but that is continually shaped by the types of actions in which we engage" (Varela et al., 1991).

A proper approach to the study of fundamental features of schizo-phrenic vulnerability must therefore incorporate phenomenological notions of common sense and intersubjectivity, with their epistemic consequences. Identification of autistic features requires from us typ-ification processes which cannot be operationalized. The same may be said of the identification of many other morbid experiences in the domain of psychopathology. It is likely that classical psychiatrists, reversing the actual stages of their discoveries, presented these expe-riences as aggregations of symptoms and second-order inferences, whereas, in fact, these discoveries were the fruit of original typifica-tions; that is clearly the case for Bleuler's (1911) conceptualization of schizophrenia.

The recognition of typification as a fundamental component of psychopathological investigation should not prevent us from perform-ing systematic empirical studies on single aspects derived from the domain of typifications. The reverse is frequently true today: empiri-cal studies are conducted without any underlying conceptual frame-work.

Conclusions

1. There is an urgent need to "repotentiate" clinical–phenomeno-logical observation and reasoning, because they are our primary tools on which meaningful research is dependent. The quest is therefore not to abandon empirical observations, but to amplify empirical re-sults by recognizing that studying human experience must take into account specific epistemic aspects of such endeavor.

These aspects cannot be accommodated within a rigid logical-empiristic paradigm. Specifically the development and the conduct of the psychiatric research interview should be guided by the central problem in the interpretation of interviews, namely, the relationship between discourse and meaning (Mishler, 1986). Unreflective striving for reliability and illusory precision leads only to proliferation of pseu-do results with no real progress.

2. Research in psychopathology should not rely only on mere symptom descriptions but should encompass phenomenological–anthropological aspects. The phenomenological notion of "having a world" implies a specific human situatedness in the world and its enaction. The description of a "schizophrenic world" is then legiti-

mate, not simply as a distorted copy of the real world, but as a particular way of being-in-the-world, which can be analyzed in these terms, rather than defined a priori by its nonreality (Tatossian, 1979). Investigation and description of the basic structures of such being-in-the-world may generate important hypotheses for empirical research. These hypotheses may pertain to the nature and clinical boundaries of vulnerability, progression from vulnerability to overt symptomatology, and issues of onset-triggering, course, treatment, and rehabilitation. For instance, a potentially fruitful empirical exploration of autistic vulnerability could involve studying deficient cross-modality of perceptual abilities or deficient autosynchrony in bodily expressivity and their links to more specific cognitive disturbances such as formal thought disorder or propensity to the development of delusions.

Conceptualizing fundamental features of the schizophrenia spectrum disorder in terms of defective commonsense attunement or weak intersubjective anchoring may prove to be crucial to construct validity, as it was conceived in the original definitions of schizophrenia (Bleuler, 1911; Minkowski, 1927).

3. There is a need to reconsider causal processes in a non-mechanistic way. The need for a non-Newtonian epistemology within natural sciences such as physics and chemistry has been felt since the beginning of the century. Such a new epistemology has arrived (e.g., Prigogine & Stengers, 1979), with a theory of "deterministic chaos" (complexity theories) which has modified the notion of causality. The term "deterministic chaos" refers to nonlinear processes, where the evolution of the entire system is unpredictable, even though the underlying interactions among the system's components remain deterministic. In this new epistemology oppositions between predictable and unpredictable, universal and individual, inner and outer, are considered no longer as fundamentally qualitatively distinct, but as complementary phenomena locally applicable within our universe. In the domain of cognition, a similar epistemology is being introduced (Maturana & Varela, 1980, 1988; Varela et al., 1991). Cognitive science drifts away from the idea of mind as an input–output device that processes information toward the idea of mind as an emergent and autonomous network with self-organizing properties ("connectionism"), in which changes are triggered, but not specified, by external or internal perturbations. Viewing schizophrenia from a connectionist perspective involves a shift of attention from localized brain dysfunc-

tions responsible for abnormal mental products, to increasing focus on defective integration of the interplay between brain functions. This is an old idea in schizophrenia research:

Expressions like "discordance" (Chaslin), "intrapsychic ataxia" (Stransky), "intrapsychic dysharmony" (Urstein), "loss of inner unity" (Kraepelin), "dissociation" (Claude and Levy-Valensi), "schizophrenia" (Bleuler) point to the idea that it is not this or that function which is disturbed, but much more their cohesion, their harmonious interplay, in its globality. To make use of an image, the essential disorder does not alter one or many faculties, whatever be their order in the hierarchy of functions, but resides between them, in the "interstitial space." (Minkowski, 1926, p. 12; my translation).

Note

1. German language distinguishes between "lived body" or body-subject (*der Leib*) and physical, objective body (*der Körper*). Respective terms in French are *le corps phénoménal* and *le corps objectif.*

References

Alpert, M. (1985). The signs and symptoms of schizophrenia. *Comprehensive Psychiatry 26*, 103–112.

Altman, E., & Jobe, T. H. (1992). Phenomenology of psychosis. *Current Opinion in Psychiatry 5*, 33–37.

Ambrose, A. (1979). *Wittgenstein's Lectures, Cambridge 1932–1935.* Oxford: Basil Blackwell.

American Psychiatric Association. (1987). Diagnostic and Statistical Manual of Mental Disorders. 3rd ed., revised (DSM-III-R). Washington, DC: American Psychiatric Association.

Blankenburg, W. (1971). *Der Verlust der natürlichen Selbstverständlichkeit. Ein Beitrag zur Psychopathologie symptomarmer Schizophrenien.* Stuttgart: Enke.

Bleuler, E. (1911). Dementia Praecox oder Gruppe der Schizophrenien. In G. Aschaffenburg (ed.), *Handbuch der Psychiatrie.* Spezieller Teil, 4. Abteilung, 1. Hälfte. Leipzig: Deuticke. Translated by J. Zinkin (1950) as *Dementia Praecox or the Group of Schizophrenias.* New York: International University Press.

Bleuler, E. (1917). Mendelismus bei Psychosen, speziell bei der Schizophrenie. *Schweizerische Archiv für Neurologie und Psychiatrie 1*, 19–40.

Bourdieu, P. (1980). *Le sens pratique.* Paris: Les Editions de Minuit.

Bovet, P., & Parnas, J. (1993). Schizophrenic delusions: A phenomenological approach. *Schizophrenia Bulletin 19*, 579–597.

Cantor, N., Smith, E. E., & French, R. (1980). Psychiatric diagnosis as prototype categorization. *Journal of Abnormal Psychology 89*, 181–193.

Clark, A. (1989). *Microcognition: Philosophy, Cognitive Science, and Parallel Distributed Processing*. Cambridge, MA: MIT Press.

Cooper, J. E., Kendell, R. E., Gurland, B. J., Sharpe, L., Copeland, J.R.M., & Simon, R. (1972). *Psychiatric Diagnosis in New York and London*. London: Oxford University Press.

Cromwell, R. L. (1984). Preemptive thinking and schizophrenia research. In W. D. Spaulding & J. K. Cole (eds.), *Theories of Schizophrenia and Psychosis*. Lincoln: University of Nebraska Press, pp. 1–46.

Faust, D., & Miner, R. A. (1986). The empiricist and his new clothes: DSM-III in perspective. *American Journal of Psychiatry 143*, 962–967.

Flaum, M., Arndt, S., Andreasen, N. C. (1991). The reliability of "bizarre" delusions. *Comprehensive Psychiatry 32*, 59–65.

Fodor, J. A. (1983). *The Modularity of Mind*. Cambridge, MA: MIT Press.

Gadamer, H. G. (1960). *Wahrheit und Methode: Grundzüge einer philosophischen Hermeneutik*. Tübingen: J.C.B. Mohr.

Gaupp, R., & Wollenberg, R. (1914). *Zur Psychologie des Massenmords Hauptlehrer Wagner von Degerloch*. Berlin: Springer.

Hanson, N. R. (1965). *The Patterns of Discovery: An Inquiry into the Conceptual Foundations of Science*. Cambridge University Press.

Hart, J., & Gordon, B. (1992). Neural subsystems for object knowledge. *Nature 359*, 60–64.

Hempel, C. G. (1965). *Aspects of Scientific Explanation and Other Essays in the Philosophy of Science*. New York: Free Press.

Hofstadter, D. (1985). *Metamagical Themas: Questing for the Essence of Mind and Pattern*. Harmondsworth: Penguin.

Husserl, E. (1900). *Logische Untersuchungen*. Halle: Niemeyer. Translated by J. N. Findlay (1970) as *Logical Investigations*. London: Routledge & Kegan Paul.

Husserl, E. (1931). *Cartesianische Meditationen*. The Hague: Nijhoff (ed. S. Strasser: *Husserliana* I). Translated by D. Cairns (1973) as *Cartesian Meditations*. The Hague: Nijhoff, 1973.

Jaspers, K. (1923). *Allgemeine Psychopathologie*. 3rd ed. Berlin: Springer.

Johnson, M. (1987). *The Body in the Mind. The Bodily Basis of Meaning, Imagination, and Reason*. Chicago: University of Chicago Press.

Kety, S. S., Rosenthal, D., Wender, P. H., Schulsinger, F., & Jacobsen, B. (1978). The biologic and adoptive families of adopted individuals who became schizophrenic: Prevalence of mental illness and other characteristics. In L. C. Wynne, R. Cromwell, & S. Matthysse (eds.), *The Nature of Schizophrenia*. New York: Wiley, pp. 28–37.

Kozulin, A. (1990). *Vygotsky's Psychology. A Biography of Ideas*. New York: Harvester & Wheatsheaf.

Lakoff, G. (1987). *Women, Fire, and Dangerous Things. What Categories Reveal About the Mind.* Chicago: University of Chicago Press.

Livesley, W. J. (1985). The classification of personality disorder: 1. The choice of category concept. *Canadian Journal of Psychiatry 30,* 353–358.

Lockman, J. J., & Thelen, E. (1993). Developmental biodynamics: Brain, body, behavior connections. *Child Development 64,* 953–959.

Luria, A. R. (1966). *Higher Cortical Functions in Man.* New York: Basic Books.

Matthysse, S., & Parnas, J. (1992). Extending the phenotype of schizophrenia: Implications for linkage analysis. *Journal of Psychiatric Research 26,* 329–344.

Maturana, H. R., & Varela, F. J. (1980). *Autopoiesis and Cognition. The Realization of the Living.* Boston: D. Reidel.

Maturana, H. R., & Varela, F. J. (1988). *The Tree of Knowledge. The Biological Roots of Human Understanding.* Boston: Shambala.

Meehl, P. E. (1962). Schizotaxia, schizotypy, schizophrenia. *American Psychologist 17,* 827–838.

Meehl, P. E. (1989). Schizotaxia revisited. *Archives of General Psychiatry 46,* 935–944.

Merleau-Ponty, M. (1945). *Phénoménologie de la perception.* Paris: Gallimard. Translated by C. Smith (1962) as *Phenomenology of Perception.* London: Routledge & Kegan Paul.

Merleau-Ponty, M. (1960). Les relations avec autrui chez l'enfant. Paris: Cours de Sorbonne. Translated by W. Cobb as The child's relations with others. In J. M. Edie (ed.), (1964), *The Primacy of Perception.* Evanston, IL: Northwestern University Press.

Meyer, A. (1913). *Modern Textbook of Nervous and Mental Diseases.* New York: White & Jellife.

Minkowski, E. (1926). *La notion de perte du contact vital avec la réalité et ses applications en psychopathologie.* Paris: Jouve.

Minkowski, E. (1927). *La schizophrénie. Psychopathologie des schizoïdes et des schizophrènes.* Paris: Payot.

Mishler, E. G. (1986). *Research Interviewing. Context and Narrative.* Cambridge, MA: Harvard University Press.

Mortimer, A. (1992). Phenomenology. Its place in schizophrenia research. *British Journal of Psychiatry 161,* 293–297.

Oltmanns, T. F. (1988). Approaches to the definition and study of delusions. In: T. F. Oltmanns & B. A. Maher (eds.), *Delusional Beliefs.* New York: Wiley, pp. 3–11.

Parnas, J., & Bovet, P. (1991). Autism in schizophrenia revisited. *Comprehensive Psychiatry 32,* 7–21.

Parnas, J., & Bovet, P. In press. Negative/positive symptoms of schizophrenia. Clinical and conceptual issues. *Nordic Journal of Psychiatry.*

Parnas, J., Cannon, T., Jacobsen, B., Schulsinger, H., Schulsinger, F., & Mednick, S. A. (1993). Life-time DSM-IIIR diagnostic outcomes in offspring of schizophrenic mothers: The results from the Copenhagen High Risk Study. *Archives of General Psychiatry 50*, 707–714.

Piaget, J. (1955). *The Child's Construction of Reality.* London: Routledge & Kegan Paul.

Popper, K. (1963). *Conjectures and Refutations.* London: Routledge & Kegan Paul.

Prigogine, I., & Stengers, I. (1979). *La Nouvelle Alliance. Métamorphose de la Science.* Paris: Gallimard. Updated and published in 1964 as *Order Out of Chaos. Man's New Dialogue with Nature.* New York: Bantam, 1984.

Putnam, H. (1991). *Representation and Reality.* Cambridge, MA: MIT Press.

Rorty, R. (1980). *Philosophy and the Mirror of Nature.* Princeton: Princeton University Press.

Rümke, H. C. (1959): Die klinische Differenzierung innerhalb der Gruppe der Schizophrenien. In H. C. Rümke, *Eine blühende Psychiatrie in Gefahr. Ausgewählte Vorträge und Aufsätze,* W. von Baeyer (ed.). Berlin, Springer, pp. 203–211. Translated by W. A. Stoll (1959) as "The clinical differentiation within the group of schizophrenias." In W. A. Stoll (ed.), *Proceedings of the Second International Congress for Psychiatry.* Zürich: Füssli, pp. 302–310.

Saussure, F. (1922). *Cours de linguistique générale.* Paris: Payot. Translated by R. Harris (1983) as *Course in General Linguistics.* Peru, IL: Open Court.

Schmidt, G. (1940). Der Wahn im deutschsprachigen Schrifttum der letzten 25 Jahre (1914–1939). *Zentralblatt für die gesamte Neurologie und Psychiatrie 97*, 113–143.

Schwartz, M. A., & Wiggins, O. P. (1986). Logical empiricism and psychiatric classification. *Comprehensive Psychiatry 27*, 101–114.

Schwartz, M. A. & Wiggins, O. P. (1987a). Scientific and humanistic medicine. A theory of clinical methods. In K. L. White (ed.), *The Task of Medicine. Dialogue at Wickenburg.* Menlo Park, CA: The Henry J. Kaiser Family Foundation, pp. 130–163.

Schwartz, M. A., & Wiggins, O. P. (1987b). Diagnosis and ideal types: A contribution to psychiatric classification. *Comprehensive Psychiatry 28*, 277–291.

Searle, J. R. (1992). *The Rediscovery of the Mind.* Cambridge, MA: MIT Press.

Spitzer, M. (1988). Ichstörungen: In search of a theory. In M. Spitzer, F. A. Uehlein, & G. Oepen (eds.), *Psychopathology and Philosophy.* Berlin: Springer, pp. 167–183.

Spitzer, M. (1991). On defining delusions. *Comprehensive Psychiatry 31*, 377–397.

Stern, D. N. In press. One way to build a clinically relevant baby. *Infant Mental Health Journal.*

Tatossian, A. (1979). *Phénoménologie des psychoses.* Paris: Masson.

Van Praag, H. M. (1992). Reconquest of the subjective. Against the waning of psychiatric diagnosing. *British Journal of Psychiatry, 160,* 266–271.

Varela, F. J., Thompson, E., & Rosch, E. (1991). *The Embodied Mind. Cognitive Science and Human Experience.* Cambridge, MA: MIT Press.

Vygotsky, L. S. (1934/1962). *Thought and Language.* Cambridge, MA: MIT Press.

Weber, M. (1949). *The Methodology of Social Sciences.* New York: Free Press.

Weimer, W. B. (1979). *Notes on the Methodology of Scientific Research.* Hillsdale, NJ: Lawrence Erlbaum.

Weiss, K. M. (1989). Advantages of abandoning symptom-based diagnostic systems of research in schizophrenia. *American Journal of Orthopsychiatry 59,* 324–330.

Wittgenstein, L. (1958). *Philosophical Investigations.* Translated by G.E.M. Anscombe. Oxford: Oxford University Press.

Wittgenstein, L. (1974). *Philosophical Grammar.* Translated by A. Kenny. Oxford: Basil Blackwell.

Wright, H. G. (1971). *Explanation and Understanding.* Ithaca, NY: Cornell University Press.

24

Searching for major genes
for schizophrenia

Kenneth K. Kidd

1. Introduction

Few today would contest that genes are implicated in the etiology of schizophrenia, but general agreement ends at that broad conclusion. The extent of the genetic influence, the mode of genetic transmission, and the identification of specific etiologically relevant genes are still uncertain and are all areas of active research. Holzman and Matthysse (1990) have recently reviewed the genetics of schizophrenia with a perspective that reflects concerns that should be incorporated in research studies on schizophrenia. Others have also recently reviewed the genetics of schizophrenia (e.g., Diehl and Kendler, 1989; McGue and Gottesman, 1989; Gelernter and Kidd, 1990; Gottesman, 1991). Briefly, genetic studies have evolved from studies designed to show that genes are involved to studies designed to illuminate how genes and environment interact in the etiology of schizophrenia (see Figures 24.1 and 24.2). Unfortunately, the studies based on distribution of illness among relatives of schizophrenics, although giving results consistent with a substantial genetic component to etiology, have failed to provide definitive evidence of what the genetic factors are. As the diverse genetic hypotheses have become more sophisticated, it is either impossible to discriminate among them or any apparent discrimination is based on some assumption that, however plausible, remains unproven. For example, Risch (1990) concludes that genetic variation at a single locus cannot explain the recurrence risks observed in various classes of relatives. He is correct, but the extrapolation to the conclusion that no form of schizophrenia is caused by genetic variation at a single locus requires the assumption that schizophrenia is etiologically homogeneous. That assumption seems improbable and is certainly unproven.

A research strategy that is quite "popular" today is genetic linkage, a strategy long used in a variety of experimental organisms but largely inapplicable to humans until it was made efficient by the large number of DNA polymorphisms discovered in the last decade. There are two primary ways in which the genetic linkage paradigm can be used in psychiatric research. Both have many elaborations and variations. The first approach starts with "candidate" genes, which produce substances that might be etiologically important. For example, many interesting and relevant gene products are currently undetectable in living individuals. How can one determine the amount of POMC (pro-opio-melano-cortin) synthesized in the brain of a living individual? How would one measure quantities of beta nerve growth factor in a patient? How can one look at neuropeptide Y? With current methods none of these gene products can be measured directly in a living individual since the relevant tissues cannot be assayed. Even with advances in magnetic resonance imaging (MRI) spectroscopy these may never be directly measurable because each is produced in minute amounts. However, with genetic linkage paradigms we can look at whether or not any genetic variation in or around a specific gene of interest – the "candidate" gene – is relevant to the etiology of a specific neuropsychiatric disorder. We can test whether POMC is related to manic-depressive illness; the evidence is that it is not (Feder et al., 1985; Kidd et al., unpublished). The genetic linkage paradigm also allows us to examine whole chunks of chromosomes in the same way that Gusella et al. (1983) searched for and found the location for the gene for Huntington's disease (cf. also Kidd and Gusella, 1985; Huntington's Disease Collaborative Research Group, 1993). This genetic linkage approach does not require a specific candidate gene; any DNA polymorphism, whether it occurs in a functional gene or a segment of DNA of unknown function (anonymous DNA), can serve as a genetic marker for all genes close by on the same chromosome. Since there are now genetic markers virtually everywhere in the genome, this approach is sometimes referred to as genome scanning: one starts by scanning the genome by linkage to find what part of which chromosome is linked to the illness. Then the task shifts to trying to identify what specific gene in the identified region is responsible for the disorder being studied, in our case, schizophrenia. Though it took nearly a decade for Huntington's disease, that second phase eventually led to identification of the causative gene itself (Huntington's Disease Collaborative Research Group, 1993). The term *positional cloning* is used to refer to the cloning of a disease or trait locus using the position of the locus, determined through genetic linkage studies, as the primary tool to identify the specific DNA of the gene. The term is used to contrast this more indirect approach with more direct cloning strategies based on known function or gene product (e.g., Collins, 1992).

The prospect of finding genetic linkage has rejuvenated the field of psychiatric genetics for a variety of reasons. The discovery of linkage for a psychiatric disorder would provide unequivocal evidence for genetic transmission and also demonstrate that a major locus is involved in the etiology of that specific disorder. Even before the loci themselves are identified, existence of linkage to a region of the genome can clarify the mode of inheritance by use of informative markers spanning the region. The specific linkage found would also provide both an aid in identifying the relevant gene product and an approach to understanding the biology of the disease process. In addition, nosology can be clarified by exploitation of linkage (e.g., the genetic case-control paradigms of Kidd (1985; 1987) – discussed below – and perhaps models such as the latent trait models of Matthysse et al. (1986)). Thus, it is worth noting that discovery of a linkage to a chromosomal region represents a powerful advance even before the critical gene in the region is identified. However, linkage studies for a complex neuropsychiatric disorder are not simple, as recently discussed by Giuffra and Kidd (1990). Moreover, the experiences of the past several years have emphasized the difficulties in using a genetic linkage approach to identify major genes causing neuropsychiatric disorders (Kidd, 1991a, 1991b). Despite these difficulties, genetic linkage still offers one of the most powerful approaches to identifying loci contributing to disease causation.

As an example of the value of simply mapping a gene, Figures 24.1 and 24.2 illustrate schematically two types of genetic case-control studies that become possible once a linked marker is confirmed. Figure 24.1 illustrates a design that focuses on identifying the underlying biological difference associated with having the susceptible genotype. Figure 24.2 illustrates an approach designed to identify the other factors, both biological (including genetic) and environmental (in the broadest sense), that interact with inherited susceptibility. Both types of genetic case-control studies can be done in the same family

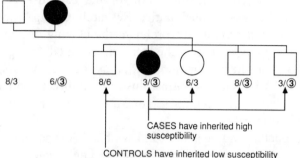

Figure 24.1. Genetic Case-Control Paradigm Number 1: High vs. Low Inherited Susceptibility. In this genetic case-control paradigm the linked marker identifies the children who have inherited high susceptibility and those who have not. The genotype of each individual is given by arbitrary allele symbols: 8, 6, 3. The assumption is that high susceptibility to illness is inherited in this family on the same chromosome and closely linked to the particular 3 allele that is circled. Darkened symbols represented affected individuals. By comparing those with high susceptibility with those with low susceptibility, researchers can look for the fundamental underlying disorder without the confounding of factors that determine the expression of that susceptibility as actual illness. Obviously, comparing affected individuals with unaffected individuals gives a much weaker ability to resolve the nature of susceptibility because we know that the unaffected relatives are a mixture of those with nonmanifesting susceptibility and those who have no inherited susceptibility.

material used to demonstrate linkage since they use different information in those families.

2. The theory and methodology of linkage studies

Several recent papers have reviewed the fundamental biology and statistics in human linkage studies with an emphasis on psychiatric disorders (Diehl and Kendler, 1989; Giuffra and Kidd, 1990). Here we emphasize the way a linkage study is actually carried out, the lessons we have learned from the initial efforts, and, finally, the way the methodology is now evolving.

How is linkage detected?

Genetic linkage between a disorder and a marker locus is detected by finding a concordance when comparing (1) the inferred pattern of transmission of the alleles at the hypothetical disease susceptibility

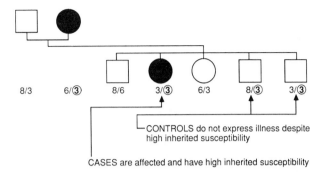

8/3   6/③   8/6   3/③   6/3   8/③   3/③

CONTROLS do not express illness despite high inherited susceptibility

CASES are affected and have high inherited susceptibility

Figure 24.2. Genetic Case-Control Paradigm Number 2: Affected vs. Unaffected Among Individuals with High Inherited Susceptibilities. In this genetic case-control paradigm the linked marker identifies those who have inherited high susceptibility, allowing researchers to examine the differences between those who are affected and those who are unaffected. This paradigm focuses attention on identifying what other factors, be they biological, psychosocial, or environmental, are involved in determining which individuals with high susceptibility are affected, and which individuals with, in fact, that same inherited high susceptibility are unaffected. The relevant factors may have no influence on individuals who have not inherited high susceptibility and so will be difficult to identify unless the study can control for the genetic susceptibility.

locus with (2) the inferred pattern of transmission of alleles at a known marker locus. More specifically, statistical methods commonly used in linkage analysis compare two hypotheses: whether the phenotypes in the pedigree (both trait and marker) can be better explained (a) by assuming linkage when inferring patterns of segregation (i.e., patterns of transmission of alleles) at the hypothesized trait locus and at the marker locus or (b) by assuming that alleles at the trait locus and alleles at the marker locus are transmitted independently ("segregate" independently). Note that one infers transmission patterns for both a hypothetical trait locus (or in some models "loci") *and* the marker locus (or group of closely linked marker loci). In linkage studies of psychiatric disorders the main source of uncertainty is usually the inability to infer any clear pattern of transmission of the hypothetical disease susceptibility allele. Factors which contribute to this uncertainty are the complexity of pedigree structure, the absence of clear Mendelian inheritance of the disease, the low density of illness in the kindreds, and the complexity of diagnosis coupled with nosologic uncertainty. However, another kind of uncertainty frequently arises but has often been overlooked: the inability to know exactly how the genetic marker locus is segregating, especially if the marker has only two alleles. Thus, there are two kinds of uncertainty, compounding the difficulties.

At this stage of research on most neuropsychiatric disorders, and especially schizophrenia, there is hope, but no certainty, that we can resolve some of the uncertainty surrounding the disease susceptibility locus. However, we do know that we definitely can improve the prospects for finding linkage by minimizing the uncertainty associated with the markers: A linkage study is more powerful when we have very high precision in our inference of the inheritance patterns through the family of every segment of every chromosome. The factors that influence such precision for any specific chromosomal segment are the levels of heterozygosity (i.e., the frequency of individuals who have two distinguishable alleles) for markers in the region, the number of clearly resolvable alleles at each marker, and the distances between the markers.

The importance of highly informative markers is shown by a power simulation study done by S. Matthysse and J. Parnas (1992). The study examined both the question of improved inference of the segregation pattern at the trait locus and improved inference of the segregation pattern at the marker locus. With the original type of DNA markers – restriction fragment length polymorphisms (RFLPs) – there are usually only two alleles and heterozygosity is necessarily no greater than 50%. However, even assuming four alleles, the simulation showed there may not be sufficient power to identify a major locus for schizophrenia in obtainable samples of families even with improved inference of the segregation at the trait locus. However, another simulation assumed markers with many alleles and very high heterozygosity; that simulation found sufficient power to warrant carrying out linkage studies. Thus, for schizophrenia at least, more informative markers not only are desirable but appear to be essential. Fortunately, new molecular technology has revealed a class of highly polymorphic markers that precisely meets this need.

The evolution of the linkage map of the human genome

A review of the ongoing dramatic developments in assembling the human genetic map using DNA polymorphisms gives a perspective on past difficulties and future possibilities. The first DNA polymorphism was discovered in 1978 (Kan and Dozy, 1978). By 1981 there were only 24 known DNA polymorphisms that could be used as marker loci in genetic linkage studies (Skolnick and Francke, 1982). While that number seems small from today's perspective, this number was already the equivalent of all the classical markers, such as the blood groups, serum proteins, red cell enzymes, etc., in terms of informativeness for human linkage studies. Thus, within 3 short years DNA methodology had doubled the repertoire of markers that had accumulated over the previous 80 years. It was already clear in 1981, moreover, that many more DNA polymorphisms would be found and that eventually genetic linkage could be used to scrutinize the entire human genome in order to find disease genes (Botstein et al., 1980). That prediction has been realized through a nearly exponential increase in the number of DNA polymorphisms that have been discovered, mapped, and cataloged during the 1980s (see Kidd 1991c, for review). In the most recent published summary (Williamson et al., 1991) there were nearly 3,000 mapped and cataloged DNA polymorphisms. The total now exceeds 5,000 and dozens more appear in the literature every month. The number of additional polymorphic loci that have been identified and mapped, but not yet cataloged, is believed to total many hundreds. These DNA polymorphisms are distributed across the genome and provide a powerful resource for genetic linkage mapping of genes for genetic diseases. In late 1992 two groups independently produced comprehensive genetic maps, each involving more than 1,000 markers spanning the entire human genome (NIH/CEPH Collaborative Mapping Group, 1992; and Weissenbach et al., 1992). Since very few of the markers were common to both studies, the integration of the two maps (now under way) will yield an even denser and more refined map of the human genome.

The dramatic successes of positional cloning for simple Mendelian disorders underscore our motivation for applying this approach to schizophrenia. Many laboratories recognize the power of this "new" tool and are now involved in using genetic linkage with DNA markers to find a gene for schizophrenia. Given all the effort and the strong motivation, why then have we not found the gene (a gene) for schizophrenia? The following section discusses the special problems of this approach for a complex disorder like schizophrenia.

3. Applying positional cloning to schizophrenia

There are several requirements for positional cloning to be successful: adequate markers, sufficient family material for linkage studies, valid nosology of the disorder, thorough diagnostic evaluation of all family members being studied, and good genetic models. As noted above, there would appear to be adequate linkage markers currently available. There are also more than sufficient families if all of schizophrenia were to have a single etiology. The requirements are not so well met when we get to the area of valid nosology. Even "thorough diagnostic evaluations" may not be adequate if the etiologically discriminatory "signs" are not assessed because their relevance is not recognized. These are important research areas, but ones that geneticists are not optimally trained to pursue. Geneticists are prepared, however, to work on eliminating ambiguity in exactly how the genetic material really was transmitted in the families so we can say precisely whether or not any two family members share a segment of the genome identical by descent.

RFLPs, the now "classical" type of DNA polymorphism, are not sufficiently polymorphic nor as yet sufficiently dense in most parts of the genome to allow unambiguous determination of how all segments of all chromosomes are segregating in a large multigenerational family. The first class of highly polymorphic markers to be discovered was composed of loci that had some relatively short DNA sequence (usually less than about 100 bp) which was repeated many times in a tandem array. These loci were polymorphic for the precise number of copies and hence were called VNTRs, the acronym for Variable Number of Tandem Repeats. VNTRs have long (> 9 bp) repeat units (Jeffreys et al., 1985; Nakamura et al., 1987). Such loci have been shown to have a relatively nonrandom distribution through the genome leaving large regions with no known markers of this type. Moreover, in large multigenerational families in which critical connecting individuals are missing, the most polymorphic of the VNTRs are largely unusable, especially when typed using the same basic technique used for RFLPs (Southern blotting, named after E. Southern, who invented it). Technical difficulties do not allow the alleles to be measured precisely and such measurement error manifesting independently on several individuals will prevent alleles from being unambiguously assigned throughout large pedigrees. Recently, typing of some VNTR systems using the polymerase chain reaction (PCR; see the next section for a description of the technique) has overcome the difficulty in resolving and identifying alleles (Boerwinkle et al., 1989; Ludwig et al., 1987; Budowle, 1991; Jeffreys et al., 1991), but the sparse, irregular distribution through the genome remains a problem. The general solution to the problem, however, has become obvi-

---

Single Copy DNA Sequence Flanking a STRP at the DRD2 Locus

. . . CCGAGTGGGCTGGGGTAGGCGGAGGGGTTGCT

GTGATGAGCTGTGTCCTTGGTAGGATGGGAAATGA

AGAGTCTAGCTCCTGGCAGGAGCACGTTTCTCATA ⟶

CACACATGCACACAGGCACACACACACACACACAC

ACACACACACACATGAACGCACCGTCCTCCCCCCT ⟵

CCCCACGTAACACCCATTCACACACAGGCACA . . .

Figure 24.3. DNA Sequence Encompassing the Short Tandem Repeat Polymorphism at the DRD2 Locus. This sequence of just over 200 base pairs (only one strand is shown) is located in a noncoding, intervening region of the gene. The repeat region is underlined with a dotted line and the polymorphism results because different chromosomes in the population can have a different number of repeats of the dinucleotide CA. The rest of the sequence shown is unique single copy DNA; the unique flanking sequences used for PCR amplification to type the STR polymorphism are underlined with arrows. (Based on the work of Hauge et al. (1991) and additional unpublished sequence.)

ous in the past few years: short tandem repeat (STR) loci typed by PCR (Litt and Luty, 1989; Weber and May, 1989; Weber, 1990a; Edwards et al., 1991; Weissenbach et al., 1992). These abundantly distributed polymorphisms are also referred to as microsatellite loci and as simple sequence repeat polymorphisms (SSRPs).

Short tandem repeat polymorphisms (STRPs) – The markers of the 1990s

Though composed of only four "letters" – A, C, G, and T representing the four nucleotides that are chained together to make our genome – most of the DNA we have is "single copy," by which geneticists mean that any stretch of 20 to 30 nucleotides is a combination that occurs only once in the entire sequence of about 3×10^9 nucleotides that constitute our genome. Much of the sequence in Figure 24.3 illustrates such single copy sequence. There are also some sections of the genome composed of hundreds to thousands of tandem repeats of a particular sequence. For example, the centromeric regions of all chromosomes have this type of DNA, sometimes reaching a total length of more than 5×10^6 base pairs made up of (nearly) identical repeat units of only 150 base pairs (Willard, 1992). There are other sequences that occur in nearly identical form in thousands of copies, but scattered in a seemingly random way throughout the genome. However, most of our genome is single copy DNA. The functional genes are mostly single copy but much of the single copy sequence occurs in the DNA between genes and in the noncoding intervening sequences within genes. The short tandem repeats are one category of repetitive DNA that occurs in several subtypes and at thousands of sites throughout the genome. Each of these repeats occurs at a position uniquely definable by the single copy sequences on either side. A specific STR locus may have a few to a few dozen tandemly repeated copies of a short sequence of nucleotides, two to five nucleotides being most common. Of the dinucleotide STRs, the repeats of "CA" are most common. Figure 24.3 shows a sequence at the gene that codes for the dopamine D2 receptor (DRD2 locus) with this pair of nucleotides, CA, repeated many times. Sequences that have more than 12 to 15 or so copies of the "CA" sequence tend to be polymorphic: different chromosomes in the population have the sequence repeated a different number of times; four or five different lengths occur commonly (Weber and May, 1989). Although the differences arose by some sort of mutation process, they have no known functional significance and are transmitted quite faithfully from parent to child. These STR loci represent normal inherited genetic variation.

A revolution in molecular biology has been brought about by the polymerase chain reaction. PCR allows a specific short segment of DNA (generally less than 2,000 to 3,000 nucleotides long) to be amplified (replicated) in the test tube if there are known unique sequences of 20–30 nucleotides at either end. This is ideally suited for the STR loci because, while there are thousands of loci with a poly-CA stretch, each occurs in a position uniquely defined along a chromosome by the flanking single copy sequences. Figure 24.3 shows the unique flanking sequences used for PCR of the "CA" polymorphism at DRD2.

Though the loci with variable numbers of repeats of the "CA" dinucleotide constitute the largest single class of STR loci, the typing

Tyrosine Hydroxylase

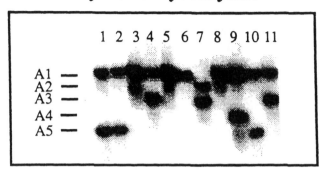

Figure 24.4. Typings for an STR at TH. This scan of an autoradiogram shows the typing of a tetranucleotide repeat in the TH locus (Edwards et al., 1991) on 11 individuals from the Swedish kindred (see section 4 of this chapter). Five of the seven reported alleles were observed in this kindred.

of an STR locus is better illustrated by a locus with a tetranucleotide repeat because the resolution of alleles is technically easier. Figure 24.4 illustrates the results of PCR amplification of a region adjacent to the tyrosine hydroxylase (TH) locus near the tip of the short arm of chromosome 11. The two chromosomes of most individuals have a different number of repeats of the sequence AATG (cf. Edwards et al., 1991) so that when the amplified product of the PCR reaction is separated by size on a gel, two bands (corresponding to two different alleles) occur, the upper (larger) band has more repeats, the lower (smaller) band has fewer repeats. The different alleles in the population form a ladder of sizes, each differing from the next by four nucleotides.

At the Eleventh Human Gene Mapping Workshop (HGM11, August 1991) there were 294 mapped autosomal STR polymorphisms cataloged (Williamson et al., 1991). Weissenbach and colleagues (1992) published a map including many additional STR polymorphisms and many different research groups have each published one or two to dozens of additional STR polymorphisms. Many more are known to have been discovered but not yet published. Estimates are that a multiallelic STR polymorphism exists every few dozen kilobases throughout the genome (Weber, 1990a, 1990b; Edwards et al., 1991). Though STR polymorphisms generally have fewer alleles than the VNTR polymorphisms (which have longer repeat units), the very large number of STR loci and their apparently "uniform" distribution throughout the genome make them excellent markers. Though alleles differ by as little as two base pairs in length, discrete alleles can be readily detected and, for much of the genome, there are already multiple closely spaced STR polymorphisms. At the rate new STR polymorphisms are being identified and characterized, there will certainly be enough within the next year or two to cover nearly the entire autosomal genome at a density of greater than one such marker locus every 5 centimorgans (the measure of genetic distance – the entire human genome is estimated to be about 3,500 to 4,000 centimorgans in length).

4. Genetic linkage studies already under way demonstrate need for better markers

In our laboratory at Yale we are currently studying three psychiatric diseases, Gilles de la Tourette syndrome (TS), bipolar affective disorder, and schizophrenia. The differences in the relative complexity of the pedigrees and the expression of the diseases are evident in the different percentages of the genome which we have been able to examine with definite results for each of these diseases – all definitive results thus far are exclusions. For example, we have searched for linkage in four Tourette syndrome kindreds with DNA samples on over 300 individuals. The pedigree structures of these families are relatively simple with DNA samples available on a large number of the individuals in the pedigree. The expression of the disease is relatively direct with the disease being expressed in some branches through four generations. Several groups are part of a collaborative effort to study these families, and collectively we have typed more than 300 markers on these families, and have excluded over 80% of the genome for the disease (Pakstis et al., 1991a, and subsequent unpublished results). In contrast, in the search for linkage in schizophrenia we have studied a large Swedish kindred in which DNA has been collected on 80 individuals, 29 of whom have been diagnosed as having schizophrenia. The transmission of the disease in this family is not always direct, or obvious. For example, in one particular branch the disease is expressed in an uncle and his nephews but not in the parent. In collaboration with two other groups (Moises et al., 1991; Hallmayer et al., 1992; Barr et al., 1993, 1994), we have analyzed the typings of 144 markers, yet have only excluded 9% of the genome. Therefore, while we have typed in the schizophrenia families over one-third of the number of markers that have been typed in the Tourette families, we have been able to exclude schizophrenia from about one-ninth of the amount of the genome as for Tourette syndrome. Of intermediate complexity between the studies of schizophrenia and Tourette syndrome is the linkage analysis of bipolar affective disorder based on an Old Order Amish kindred. The portion of the Old Order Amish kindred on which we have accumulated the most data contains 99 individuals with diagnoses available on 90 of the persons; 24 are affected and 66 are not affected. We have now screened nearly 200 segregating loci for linkage and have excluded a major gene for the disorder from 25% of the genome (Pakstis et al., 1991b).

We have concluded on the basis of this empiric demonstration (Barr and Kidd, 1991) that much more informative markers are *required* for linkage studies in some of these families and would certainly benefit the studies of others; the simulation studies discussed above lead to the same conclusion. The STR polymorphisms should now meet that need.

Two positive examples further demonstrate the significance of using STRs. Figure 24.4 illustrates the STR polymorphism at the TH locus in 11 individuals from the Swedish schizophrenia kindred. Previous haplotyping of this interesting locus with two good RFLPs was uninformative for linkage in the Swedish kindred; this new marker by itself yields a statistically significant exclusion, clearly demonstrating the greatly increased power attainable with STRs over even haplotypes of RFLPs. Another strong example of the value of STR-based polymorphisms comes from our work in screening for Tourette syndrome. We recently reanalyzed a large TS kindred (the TSC Canadian kindred) for linkage with all of our accumulated genetic marker loci because diagnoses were updated by clinicians during the past year. In particular, about a dozen of the younger individuals in the kindred started expressing the disorder during the last year. One of a number of regions showing modest (though statistically not significant) linkage to TS was near the TH locus on the short arm of chromosome 11. The indication of linkage approached significance in the TSC Canadian kindred with the combination of RFLP systems already typed for TH, although there was a strange combination of sex-specific recombination frequencies for linkage that suggested the "finding" might be spurious; nonetheless, it could not be ignored. Typings with the STR for TH in the TSC Canadian kindred revealed five alleles. When analyzed for linkage with the previously typed TH haplotype in the same family, the TH polymorphisms were shown (with strong statistical significance) to be linked at zero percent recombination, confirming the identity and location of the STR polymorphism. Linkage analysis between the TH STR and TS now results in a statistically significant exclusion of linkage at the same recombination map position where a positive indication of linkage had been found previously and even stronger exclusion for close linkage in both sexes. This reinforces the interpretation that the moderately positive finding had been a statistical fluke made possible by incomplete inference of precisely how the TH locus was transmitted through the pedigree. The new STR data make the TSC Canadian kindred consistent with the negative results for TH in other TS families.

One final example illustrates the value of these highly polymorphic markers. Using an unusual repeat polymorphism at the dopamine-D4-receptor (DRD4) locus (Lichter et al., 1993), we have shown that no major locus genetic model for schizophrenia is compatible with a locus being near DRD4 in the family we studied. We did this by finding that two cousins, both of whom were severely affected and presumably had inherited some causative gene(s) from one of their common grandparents, had completely different alleles at DRD4.

An expectation for the future is that within the next couple of years some positive linkage finding for a major neuropsychiatric disorder (maybe even schizophrenia) will be confirmed in sufficient families to be believable. Several avenues of research will then be pursued. With the molecular tools currently available and being developed, the gene responsible is likely to be identified within a very few years. In the meantime, the markers already available will allow genetic case-control studies (cf. Figures 24.1 and 24.2) to be pursued to clarify the specific phenotype associated with that genetic form of the disorder and possibly identify relevant nongenetic factors. Thus, finding a linkage for a major neuropsychiatric disorder will facilitate improved understanding of both its cause (etiology) and result (disorder). The power of modern molecular genetic techniques offers one of the most hopeful developments for the eventual understanding of schizophrenia and the ability to help those who are affected.

References

Barr, C. L., and K. K. Kidd. 1991. New molecular techniques for genetic linkage studies. In *Biological Psychiatry* (ed. G. Racagni, N. Brunello, T. Fukuda), vol. 2, pp. 468–451. Amsterdam: Exerpta Medica.

Barr, C. L., J. L. Kennedy, J. B. Lichter, H.H.M. Van Tol, L. Wetterberg, K. J. Livak, and K. K. Kidd. 1993. Alleles at the Dopamine D4 receptor locus do not contribute to the genetic susceptibility to schizophrenia in a large Swedish kindred. *American Journal of Medical Genetics (Neuropsychiatric Genetics)* 48:218–222.

Barr, C. L., J. L. Kennedy, A. J. Pakstis, L. Wetterberg, B. Sjogren, L. Bierut, C. Wadelius, J. Wahlstrom, J. Galernter, J. Hallmayer, H. Moises, L. L. Cavalli-Sforza, and K. K. Kidd. 1994. Progress in a genome scan for linkage in schizophrenia in a large Swedish kindred. *American Journal of Medical Genetics (Neuropsychiatric Genetics)* 54:51–58.

Boerwinkle, E., W. Xiong, E. Fourest, and L. Chan. 1989. Rapid typing of tandemly repeated hypervariable loci by the polymerase chain reaction: Application to the apolipoprotein B 3′ hypervariable region. *Proc. Natl. Acad. Sci. USA* 86:212–216.

Botstein, D., R. L. White, M. Skolnick, and R. W. Davis. 1980. Construction of a genetic linkage map in man using restriction fragment length polymorphisms. *American Journal of Human Genetics* 32:314–331.

Budowle, B. 1991. AMPFLPS – Genetic markers for forensic identification. In Proceedings of the International Seminar on the Forensic Applications of PCR Technology, FBI Academy, Quantico, VA, May. *Crime Lab Digest.*

Collins, F. S. 1992. Positional cloning: Let's not call it reverse anymore. *Nature Genetics* 1:3–6.

Diehl, S. R., and K. S. Kendler. 1989. Strategies for linkage studies of schizophrenia: Pedigrees, DNA markers, and statistical analyses. *Schizophrenia Bulletin* 15:403–419.

Edwards, A., A. Civitello, H. A. Hammond, and C. T. Caskey. 1991. DNA typing and genetic mapping with trimeric and tetrameric tandem repeats. *American Journal of Human Genetics* 49:746–756.

Feder, J., H.M.D. Gurling, J. Darby, and L. L. Cavalli-Sforza. 1985. DNA restriction fragment analysis of the proopiomelanocortin gene in schizophrenia and bipolar disorders. *American Journal of Human Genetics* 37:286–294.

Gelernter, J., and K. K. Kidd. 1990. The current status of linkage studies in schizophrenia. In *Brain and Behavior* (ed. P. McHugh and V. A. McKusick), pp. 137–152. New York: Raven Press.

Giuffra, L. A., and K. K. Kidd. 1990. Linkage analysis in psychiatry. *International Review of Psychiatry* 1:231–242.

Gottesman, I. I. 1991. *Schizophrenia Genesis: The Origins of Madness* (eds. R. C. Atkinson, G. Lindzey, and R. F. Thompson) New York: W. H. Freeman.

Gusella, J. F., N. S. Wexler, P. M. Conneally, S. L. Naylor, M. A. Anderson, R. E. Tanzi, P. C. Watkins, K. Ottina, M. R. Wallace, A. Y. Sakaguchi,

A. B. Young, I. Shoulson, E. Bonilla, and J. B. Martin. 1983. A polymorphic DNA marker genetically linked to Huntington's disease. *Nature* 306:234–238.

Hallmayer, J., J. L. Kennedy, L. Wetterberg, B. Sjogren, K. K. Kidd, L. L. Cavalli-Sforza. 1992. Exclusion of linkage between the serotonin 5HT$_2$-receptor and schizophrenia in a large Swedish kindred. *Archives of General Psychiatry* 49:216–219.

Hauge, X. Y., D. K. Grandy, J. H. Eubanks, G. A. Evans, O. Civelli, and M. Litt. 1991. Detection and characterization of additional DNA polymorphisms in the dopamine D2 receptor gene. *Genomics* 10:527–530.

Holzman, P. S., and S. Matthysse, 1990. The genetics of schizophrenia: A review. *Psychological Science* 1:279–286.

Huntington's Disease Collaborative Research Group. 1993. A novel gene containing a trinucleotide repeat that is expanded and unstable on Huntington's disease chromosomes. *Cell* 72:971–983.

Jeffreys, A. J., V. Wilson, and S. L. Thein. 1985. Hypervariable "minisatellite" regions in human DNA. *Nature* 314:67–73.

Jeffreys, A. J., A. MacLeod, K. Tamaki, D. L. Neil, and D. G. Monckton. 1991. Minisatellite repeat coding as a digital approach to DNA typing. *Nature* 354:204–209.

Kan, Y. W., and A. M. Dozy. 1978. Polymorphism of DNA sequence adjacent to human β-globin structural gene: Relationship to sickle mutation. *Proc. Natl. Acad. Sci.* 75:5631–5635.

Kidd, K. K. 1985. New genetic strategies for studying psychiatric disorders. In *Genetic Aspects of Human Behavior* (eds. T. Sakai and T. Tsuboi), pp. 235–246. Tokyo: Igaku-Shoin.

Kidd, K. K. 1987. Genetic research on affective disorders: Current problems and future direction. In *Affective Disorders: Recent Research and Related Developments* (ed. S. M. Channabasavanna and Saleem A. Shah), pp. 79–91. Bangalore: National Institute of Mental Health and Neuro Sciences.

Kidd, K. K. 1991a. Trials and tribulations in the search for genes causing neuropsychiatric disorders. *Social Biology* 38:163–178.

Kidd, K. K. 1991b. The complexities of linkage studies for neuropsychiatric disorders (ed. J. Mendlewicz and H. Hippius), pp. 61–69. New York: Springer-Verlag.

Kidd, K. K. 1991c. Progress towards completing the human linkage map. *Current Opinion in Genetics and Development* 1:99–105.

Kidd, K. K., and J. Gusella. 1985. Report of the committee on the genetic constitution of chromosomes 3 and 4. Human Gene Mapping Workshop 8. *Cytogenetics and Cell Genetics* 40:107–127.

Lichter, J. B., C. L. Barr, J. L. Kennedy, H.H.M. VanTol, K. K. Kidd, and

K. J. Livak. 1993. A hypervariable segment in the human dopamine receptor D4 (DRD4) gene. *Human Molecular Genetics* 2:767–773.

Litt, M., and J. A. Luty. 1989. A hypervariable microsatellite revealed by in vitro amplification of a dinucleotide repeat within the cardiac muscle actin gene. *American Journal Human Genetics* 44:397–401.

Ludwig, E. H., B. D. Blackhart, V. R. Pierotti, L. Caiati, C. Fortier, T. Knott, J. Scott, R. W. Mahley, B. Levy-Wilson, and B. J. McCarthy. 1987. DNA sequence of the human Apolipoprotein B gene. *DNA* 6:363–372.

Matthysse, S., and Parnas, J. 1992. Extending the phenotype of schizophrenia: Implications for linkage analysis. *Journal of Psychiatric Research* 26:329–344.

Matthysse, S., P. S. Holzman, and K. Lange. 1986. The genetic transmission of schizophrenia: application of Mendelian latent structure analysis to eye tracking dysfunction in schizophrenia and affective disorder. *Journal of Psychiatric Research* 20:57–67.

McGue, M., and I. I. Gottesman, 1989. Genetic linkage in schizophrenia: Perspectives from genetic epidemiology. *Schizophrenia Bulletin* 15:453–464.

Moises, H. W., J. Gelernter, L. A. Giuffra, V. Zarcone, L. Wetterberg, O. Civelli, K. K. Kidd, and L. L. Cavalli-Sforza. 1991. No linkage between D_2 dopamine receptor gene region and schizophrenia. *Archives of General Psychiatry* 48:643–647.

Nakamura, Y., M. Leppert, P. O'Connell, R. Wolff, T. Holm, M. Culver, C. Martin, E. Fujimoto, M. Hoff, E. Kumlin, and R. White. 1987. Variable number of tandem repeat (VNTR) markers for human gene mapping. *Science* 235:1616–1622.

NIH/CEPH Collaborative Mapping Group. 1992. A comprehensive genetic linkage map of the human genome. *Science* 258:67–86.

Pakstis, A. J., P. Heutink, D. L. Pauls, R. Kurlan, B.J.M. van de Wetering, J. F. Leckman, L. A. Sandkuyl, J. R. Kidd, G. J. Breedveld, C. M. Castiglione, J. Weber, R. S. Sparkes, D. J. Cohen, K. K. Kidd, and B. A. Oostra. 1991a. Progress in the search for genetic linkage with Tourette Syndrome: An exclusion map covering more than 50% of the Genome. *American Journal of Human Genetics* 48:281–294.

Pakstis, A. J., J. R. Kidd, C. M. Castiglione, and K. K. Kidd. 1991b. Status of the search for a major genetic locus for affective disorder in the Old Order Amish. *Human Genetics* 87:475–483.

Risch, N. 1990. Linkage strategies for genetically complex traits. I. Multilocus models. *American Journal of Human Genetics* 46:222–228.

Skolnick, M. H., and U. Francke. 1982. Report of the committee on human gene mapping by recombinant DNA techniques. *Cytogenetics and Cell Genetics* 32:194–204.

556   *Kenneth K. Kidd*

Weber, J. L. 1990a. Human DNA polymorphisms and methods of analysis. *Current Opinion in Biotechnology* 1:166–171.

Weber, J. L. 1990b. Informativeness of human (dC-dA)n-(dC-dT)n polymorphisms. *Genomics* 7:524–530.

Weber, J. L., and P. E. May. 1989. Abundant class of human DNA polymorphisms which can be typed using the polymerase chain reaction. *American Journal of Human Genetics* 44:388–396.

Weissenbach, J., G. Gyapay, C. Dib, A. Vignal, J. Morissette, P. Millasseau, G. Vaysseix, and M. Lathrop. 1992. A second-generation linkage map of the human genome. *Nature* 359:794–800.

Willard, H. F. 1992. Centromeres – primary constrictions are primarily complicated. *Human Molecular Genetics* 9:667–668.

Williamson, R., A. Bowcock, K. Kidd, P. Pearson, J. Schmidtke, P. Ceverha, M. Chipperfield, D. N. Cooper, C. Coutelle, J. Hewitt, K. Klinger, K. Langley, J. Beckmann, M. Tolley, and B. Maidak. 1991. Report of the DNA committee and catalogues of cloned and mapped genes, markers formatted for PCR and DNA polymorphisms. *Cytogenetics and Cell Genetics* 58:1190–1832.

25

The *Drosophila* eye and the genetics of schizophrenia

Steven Matthysse

1 Cognitive processing defects in schizophrenia

I would like to indulge in a little pole-vaulting across phyla, from *Drosophila* to schizophrenia. This familiar academic sport is usually played by the sellers of animal models, rather than the buyers; but as I work on schizophrenia and not on *Drosophila*, one unique feature of this exercise is that it will be from a buyer's point of view.

It seems to me (and many others) that schizophrenia is best understood as a failure of some aspects of what cognitive psychologists call automatic processing: the background of cognitive activity, carried out without awareness, that supports and facilitates conscious, effortful thought [32]. The existence of efficient cognitive preprocessing mechanisms is suggested by the ease and naturalness of thinking in normal people, despite the complex requirements thinking must meet to function competently. Our thought is able to navigate between Holzman's 20 categories of thought disorder [15, pp. 69–70]. Our memory can take advantage of context and predictability of word sequences, as Brendan Maher has observed (Chapter 19, this volume). Our language must conform to rules of syntax, semantics, logic and pragmatics. Nevertheless, ordinary thinking and speaking demand no special concentration and take hardly any time. We do not calculate before we speak, nor do we form our thoughts by a process of trial and error; we do not have to sift through a mixture of logical and illogical, grammatical and ungrammatical thoughts. There is not even any sign that as children we were clumsy in our thinking, but have practiced the skill to the point where it has become automatic [20]. As Roger Brown shows, children's utterances spontaneously obey rules of form appropriate to their age [4].

In schizophrenia, some aspects of this preconditioning of thought are lost. In one of the better known studies showing this effect [26], schizophrenics and controls were given the task of counting lines, in the presence of irrelevant geometrical grouping. Normal performance deteriorated as grouping became more distracting, whereas schizophrenic performance did not, and actually became better than normal under severe irrelevant grouping conditions. In this clever experiment, the automatic tendency of normal people to group objects before counting caused them to be less efficient at the task than schizophrenics.*

Schizophrenic patients in the early stages try to regain control over their thinking, but eventually they fail; there comes a point, as Bleuler said (quoted by Norman Garmezy, Chapter 9, this volume), "where the patient gives up his attempts to adapt his inner contradictory life to reality." The substitution of conscious effort for processes normally carried out without awareness accounts, in part, for the slowness and poor performance of schizophrenic patients on nearly all psychological tests, a trait that the Chapmans named "generalized deficit" [8].

1.1 Local neuronal circuits

It is a leap, but a small one, to assume that cognitive preprocessing is carried out in genetically programmed local neuronal circuits, like the networks, discovered by Patricia Goldman-Rakic, that retain target locations and features "out of sight, in mind" (Chapter 2, this volume). Although the concept has much older antecedents [28], the term "local neuronal circuit" was introduced at a 1973 Work Session of the Neurosciences Research Program: "local circuits can be defined as any portion of the neuron (or neurons) that . . . functions as an independent integrative unit" [27, p. 300].

Szentágothai's reconstruction of a hypothetical cortical column (Figure 25.1) is a beautiful example. Not all local circuits may be arranged as regularly in space as they are within cortical columns; the concept of a local circuit depends on logical connectivity, not on spatial relationships.

The idea that local neuronal circuits are involved in schizophrenia

---

* For additional examples and discussion of failures of cognitive processing in schizophrenia, see the introduction to the "Thinking" section of this volume – Eds.

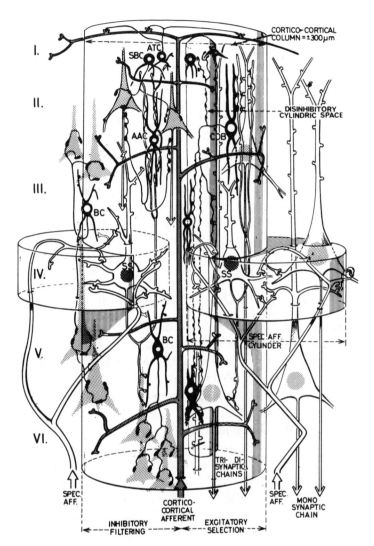

Figure 25.1. ATC = axonal tuft cell; SBC = small basket cell; AAC = chandelier cell; CDB = double bouquet cell; BC =basket cell; SS = spiny stellate cell. The pyramidal cells are unlabeled. From Szentágothai [33, Fig. 14]

is certainly not new. In the Work Session cited, Pasko Rakic suggested that

neuropsychiatric conditions in apparently morphologically "normal" brains might . . . be caused by a disarrangement or dysfunction of local circuits that cannot be detected by methods presently applicable to man. [27, p. 297]

The idea continues to attract interest among students of schizophrenia. In this volume, Francine Benes presents direct histological evidence that local circuits may be miswired in schizophrenia, in particular that there may be a defect in GABAergic inhibition of pyramidal cells (see Chapter 6). If, as Allan Mirsky suggests (see Chapter 17), many regions of the brain are neuropathologically implicated in schizophrenia, it still may be that the disease is caused by a wiring defect in a single circuit plan, widely used throughout the brain, and adapted to different functions in different regions.

My purpose is not to discuss the pros and cons of the local circuit hypothesis, but to draw out its implications for genetics. If the defects in cognitive processing in schizophrenia can be traced to failure of local neuronal circuits, what would we expect the genetic transmission of schizophrenia to be like? What are the implications of a local circuit model for Philip Holzman's enterprise?

2 Genetics of *Drosophila* ommatidia

The *Drosophila* eye is a microcosm where essential features of the genetic control of wiring of local circuits can be observed. Through elegant experiments, a detailed step-by-step description has emerged in the last few years. I do not think it is too great a leap to apply this model to the vertebrate brain, even though the local circuits of mammalian central nervous systems do not form a "neurocrystalline lattice" [29] like the *Drosophila* eye. The model of embryonic determination that we shall see emerge from studies of the *Drosophila* eye does not critically depend on its geometrically regular organization. The same type of developmental sequence may occur in cell populations disposed irregularly in space, as long as cells are able to maintain processes in contact with their appropriate partners.

2.1 The process of self-organization

Drosophila ommatidia assemble themselves through a chain of progressive determination, mediated by cell-to-cell contacts. According to the currently accepted model,

cells read the identities of the cells they contact in order to determine their fate . . . Once a cell has been directed to its fate it will then express signals peculiar to its type that contribute to the determination of cells that it subsequently contacts. [35, p. 186].

Assembly begins in the "morphogenetic furrow," sweeping across the eye imaginal disk. One new ommatidial column appears every two hours. Since the furrow is advancing with time, it is possible to see all the stages of the assembly in a single section (Figure 25.2). Initially, "preclusters" of 6–7 cells form. The first cell to differentiate is the progenitor of photoreceptor R8; then the cells that will become R2 and R5. R3 and R4 are added; R1 and R6 next; and finally R7. The whole sequence takes about 24 hours, each cell requiring about 4 hours from the time it receives its morphogenetic cues from its neighbors to the time it is ready to identify itself to subsequently differentiating cells, as a cue to their fate determination [30]. At the end of this process, the photoreceptor cells are grouped in pairs (R1/R6, R2/R5, R3/R4) about an axis defined by R7 and R8 (Figure 25.3).

2.2 Mutants

At least one mutant is known corresponding to each stage of ommatidial development. These mutations affect the ability of cells to signal and respond to each other about their developmental fates.

2.2.1 Ellipse. The "Ellipse" gene on chromosome 2, originally named for the shape of the mutant eye, is now known as $Egfr^E$ because the gene product is a homologue of human epidermal growth factor receptor (capital first letters indicate dominant mutations; small first letters indicate recessive). In the homozygote, only 10% of the normal number of preclusters form, but those that do form differentiate normally (Figure 25.4). The fact that, despite the disarray of the eye as a whole, individual preclusters differentiate correctly is one piece of evidence for the model of sequential determination by local interactions.

2.2.2 Notch. The *Notch (N)* mutation on the X chromosome is, in a sense, a converse to $Egfr^E$. Instead of a paucity of preclusters, in *Notch* there is a "bulging lawn of photoreceptors" [5, p. 1101] along the morphogenetic furrow (Figure 25.5). In these experiments, a temperature sensitive allele of the *Notch* gene was used (N^{ts1}), so that a decrease in *Notch* gene product could be induced at will by elevating the temperature. The increase in number of preclusters is caused by a decrease in *Notch* expression. Individual ommatidia also contain an

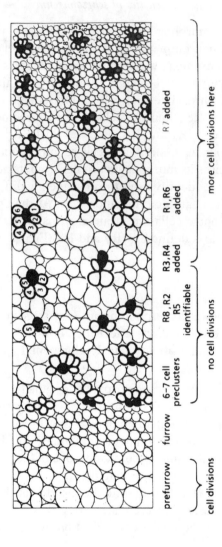

Figure 25.2. The morphogenetic furrow sweeps from right to left, leaving behind photoreceptor clusters in sequential stages of development (at the right are the most fully developed clusters). From Lawrence [17, Fig. 8.6b]

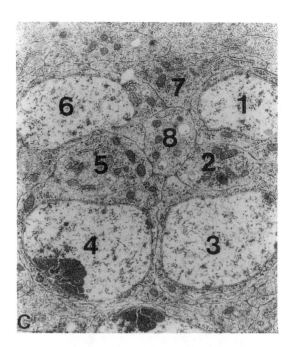

Figure 25.3. Symmetrical arrangement of a mature photoreceptor cluster. From Tomlinson [35, Fig. 2C] Reprinted with permission from the Company of Biologists Ltd.

increased number of photoreceptors; in Figure 25.6 the temperature-pulsed ommatidium has 14, instead of the usual 8.

The formation of preclusters seems to be a two-step process. The first step is the spacing of ommatidia precursors at regular intervals behind the morphogenetic furrow. The regular distance between precursors may be maintained by a diffusible inhibitor, synthesized in the preclusters already laid down [35]. The second step in precluster formation is thought to be competition between precursors, leaving only one to be selected for further development into an ommatidium.

The precursor-competition process, called "lateral inhibition" by Lawrence [17, p. 167], is generally defective in *Notch*⁻ embryos. Figure 25.7 illustrates *Notch* function in epidermal sense organ (bristle) formation. Working through the effects of the temperature-sensitive *Notch* mutant in this case is very instructive. Column A represents normal development. Of all the cells that are capable of becoming bristle precursors, the *Notch* gene product restricts those

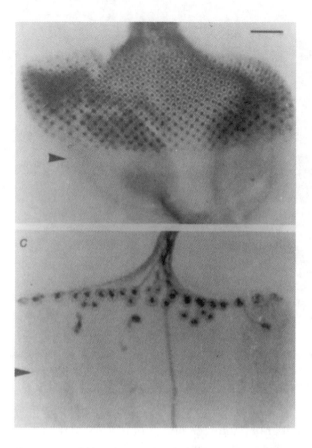

Figure 25.4. Only a few ommatidia differentiate in *Egfr^E* (c) compared to wildtype (a). Arrow points to the morphogenetic furrow. From Baker and Rubin [1, Fig. 2 a/c]. Reprinted with permission from Macmillan Magazines Ltd., copyright 1989.

that actually express this capacity to a few (second level, shown dividing). *Notch* also restricts the fate of becoming a sensory neuron to one of the four precursors within each bristle (third level), the others being left to form cuticular shafts and sockets (fourth level). Column B represents the effects of an early temperature pulse (white section of vertical bar) destroying the "lateral inhibition" of bristle precursors, so that bristles form everywhere. The restoration of *Notch* function at later stages, when the temperature pulse is over, permits normal differentiation within each bristle. Only one of the component cells actually becomes a sensory neuron. Column C represents the effects

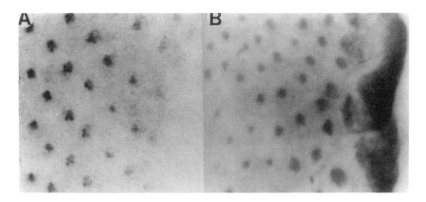

Figure 25.5. Ommatidial clusters in wildtype (A) contrasted with N^{ts1} (B) eye imaginal disks (morphogenetic furrow is on the right). From Cagan and Ready [5, Fig. 3].

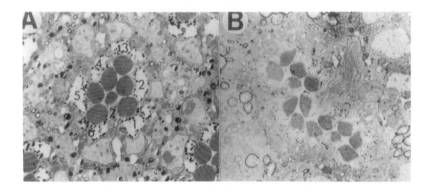

Figure 25.6. Number of photoreceptors in individual N^{ts1} clusters (B) may greatly exceed wildtype (A). From Cagan and Ready [5, Fig. 5 A/B].

of a later heat pulse. In this case, bristle precursors are suitably restricted, but *all* the cells within each of the selected clusters become sensory neurons ("lateral inhibition" failing within the cluster); no accessory cuticular parts form.

2.2.3 rough. [1] In the chromosome 3 mutant called *rough (ro)*, the first cell to develop (R8) is determined normally. The mutation operates at the next step of the morphogenetic chain. *rough* gene product is required only in R2/R5 for normal ommatidia to form [35]. In *ro⁻*, the R2/R5 pair differentiates, but biochemically the cells are not

A   B   C

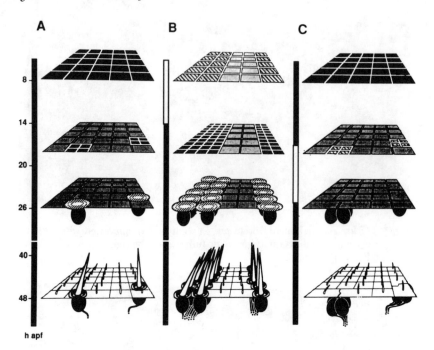

h apf

Figure 25.7. Bristle development in normal (A), early temperature-pulsed (B), and late temperature-pulsed (C) larvae. See text. From Hartenstein and Posakony [10, Fig. 10].

normal; they express antigens that should be found only in R3/R4 and R1/R6 [11]. The R3/R4 precursors, next in the chain, do not differentiate properly, and subsequent steps are scrambled. R2/R5 apparently cannot send the R3/R4 precursors the necessary signals to begin their differentiation, and these cells are unable to carry on the signal sequence in their turn [35].

2.2.4 seven up. Conversely, as *rough* gene product is needed in R2/R5 in order to send the signals for R3/R4 to differentiate correctly, R3/R4 need the *seven up (svp)* gene product (chromosome 3) in order to respond to them. Without it, their development goes astray and they take on morphological and biochemical characteristics of R7 [24].

2.2.5 sevenless. At the end of the chain of photoreceptor development is R7. In the *sevenless (sev)* mutant, on the X chromosome, R7 does

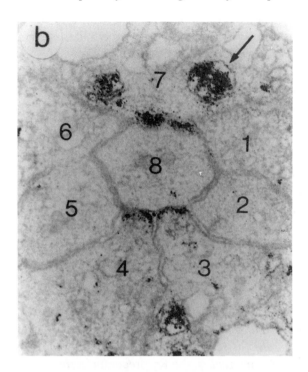

Figure 25.8. Localization of *sevenless* antibody at junction between R8 and its neighbors R3, R4, and R7. From Tomlinson et al. [34, Fig. 3b]. Copyright Cell Press.

not differentiate into a photoreceptor as it should, but into a lens-secreting cell. In genetic mosaics, *sevenless* R7 precursors never become photoreceptors, even if their neighbors are wildtype; conversely, wildtype R7 precursors are able to develop into normal R7 cells, even if their neighbors are *sevenless*. These experiments indicate that the *sevenless* gene product is required for reception of the cues needed to turn the R7 precursor into a photoreceptor, rather than for sending the signal [35].

The *sevenless* antigen is expressed in R3/R4 as well as R7, and in each of these cells it is restricted to the points on the membrane where they contact R8 (Figure 25.8). This pattern of localization suggests that the *sevenless* gene product interacts with a ligand in R8. Binding to this ligand might be a developmental signal to which the R7 precursor cell responds. If that were the case, it would be necessary to explain why the signal – although sent by R8 to all three photoreceptor precursors that contact it (R3, R4, R7) – is only active in transforming the R7 precursor. Presumably other cell contacts of R7, not shared by R3 and R4, account for its selective response [34]. The logic of fate selection may require information about all the neighbors of a cell, not just one.

2.2.6 bride of sevenless. The *sevenless* gene has a functional partner with the charming name *bride of sevenless (boss)* (although it is a bride, it does not live on the same chromosome as *sevenless,* but on chromosome 3). Although *boss* gene product is required for the development of R7, not R8, it is expressed in R8, not R7. These observations suggest that *boss* may be part of the system in R8 responsible for sending the developmental signal to the R7 precursor that causes it to differentiate into R7. Consistent with this hypothesis, *sevenless*-expressing cells have been shown to internalize the *boss* antigen, whereas *sevenless*⁻ R7 precursors do not. In cell culture, *boss*- and *sevenless*-expressing cells aggregate [16].

2.2.7 seven in absentia. seven in absentia (sina) is a gene on chromosome 3 which, like *sevenless,* is required in order that R7 precursors differentiate properly. As in *sevenless,* the R7 precursor in *sina*⁻ becomes an accessory cell rather than a photoreceptor; in addition, one or two other photoreceptor cells are missing. Little is known yet about the function of *sina,* except that, through analysis of genetic mosaics, it is clear that *sina* is like *sevenless* and not like *boss,* in that its gene product is required in the R7 precursor, rather than its neighbors [6].

2.3 Pleiotropy and secondary effects

Several of the genes in the ommatidium developmental pathway are also active in the formation of other organs, and mutant alleles frequently have pleiotropic effects. Some are mild (*Egfr*^{E} has an abnormality in wing veination [1]), while some are severe (*svp* is lethal, even in the heterozygous state). In *sina,* sensory bristles are frequently missing, although the location and extent of loss is variable. Behavior tends to be lethargic, and coordination is subnormal [6]. *Notch* has many alleles with differing phenotypic effects [18, pp. 492–499]. It gets its name from a relatively minor phenotype shared by many alleles, a notched wing. Its actions have in common the failure to restrict expression of potential developmental outcomes to a small

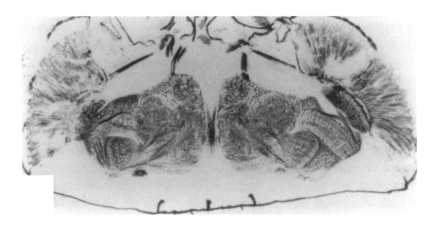

Figure 25.9. Rough gynandromorph. Eye genotype determines normal or disorganized phenotype of the optic lobe on the same side. From Meyerowitz and Kankel [22, Fig. 10B].

number of precursors, as we have seen in ommatidial and bristle development.

The morphological effects of photoreceptor mutations can be much more widespread than the region where the gene product is expressed. It is possible, for example, to construct *rough* gynandromorphs where one eye is mutant and one is wildtype, while both optic lobes are wildtype; or, conversely, where both eyes are wildtype, while one optic lobe is mutant and the other is wildtype. The optic lobe receiving input fibers from the *rough* eye becomes badly disorganized, even if the lobe itself is genetically normal, as shown in Figure 25.9. On the other hand, optic lobes connected to wildtype eyes look normal, even if the lobes are derived from the *rough* genotype. The disorganization in the brain appears to be secondary to the malformation of the eye.

3 Implications for the genetics of schizophrenia

Let us review the argument so far, and draw out its implications for schizophrenia. We reasoned that schizophrenia may be understood as a selective defect in automatic aspects of cognitive processing (section 1), and suggested that such deficits may be attributed to failures of local neuronal circuits (section 1.1). We turned to the *Drosophila* eye as a model system for local circuit development, and saw that its morphogenesis is a sequential process of fate determination, mediated by cell-to-cell contacts (section 2.1). We reviewed mutations affecting ommatidial development, and noted that each mutation interferes with a specific aspect of fate determination, primarily with the sending of, or response to, intercellular signals (section 2.2).

In the *Drosophila* eye, the concepts of polygenic inheritance have no application. Genetic control of ommatidial development is a logical process, no more additive than the steps of a computer program, or the rules of a formal grammar. If schizophrenia does turn out to be caused by an error in local neuronal circuit assembly, we may expect single locus effects to be critical, just as in *Drosophila* there are mutations that interfere in highly specific ways with the sending and receiving of morphogenetic signals. Any one mutation is enough to scramble the circuit.[2] The extensive secondary effects of local circuit mutations in *Drosophila* (e.g., *rough*, section 2.3) warn us that additional genetic or environmental factors might be involved in going from a local circuit mutation to a schizophrenic outcome. Nevertheless we would be off to a good start, if we had a catalog of mutations affecting local circuit assembly in humans, as we do in *Drosophila*. In section 5 we discuss ways of constructing such a catalog, but first let us gather what insights we can from the ways local circuit mutations have been discovered in *Drosophila*.

4 Detecting local circuit mutations in *Drosophila*

4.1 Importance of an adequate stimulus

One lesson that can be learned from *Drosophila* is the importance of an *adequate stimulus* to detect behavioral effects of mutations in circuit assembly. Consider *sevenless*, for example. The ordinary visual and visual-motor behavior of this mutant shows no obvious defects. Nevertheless, an ingenious device, invented by Seymour Benzer [2] for isolating flies with abnormal phototaxis (inspired by "countercurrent fractionation" in physical chemistry), demonstrated that *sev* homozygotes are more attracted to green-blue light (480 nm) than to near-ultraviolet (350 nm), whereas the opposite is true for wildtype. A modern version of the fractionator is shown in Figure 25.10. Out of 17,000 flies screened, 141 were observed to prefer green-blue light consistently. Among the behaviorally selected flies, seven different alleles of the *sevenless* gene were found, as well as mutants in several other genes [9].

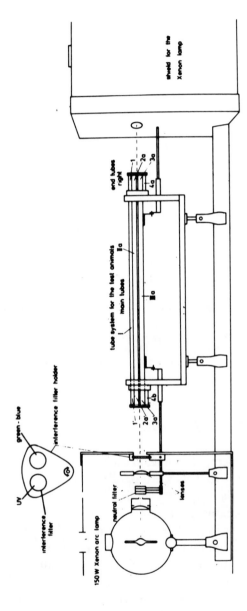

Figure 25.10. Flies with strong relative phototaxis to one of the two stimuli end up in the collecting tubes with the highest numbers, whereas flies with weak preferences are fractionated into intermediate tubes. From Gerresheim [9, Fig. 1a].

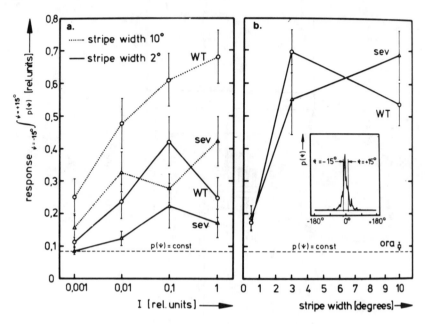

Figure 25.11. Orientation to a stripe by wildtype (WT) and *sevenless* (*sev*): (a) under low light conditions, as a function of intensity; (b) under high intensity conditions, as a function of stripe width. From Heisenberg and Buchner [12, Fig. 4].

4.2 Visual tracking in Drosophila

4.2.1 sevenless. The problem, of course, in carrying out tracking experiments with *Drosophila* is that flies are hard to study while they are flying. In order to simulate tracking of visual objects in flight, Reichardt designed an apparatus in which the fly is held motionless (suspended from a vertical wire), while the yaw torque the fly spontaneously produces is amplified and fed to a motor generating countervailing angular rotation of his visual environment [31]. In other words, the fly is held still, but he can make his visual world rotate. The insert in Figure 25.11 is an orientation histogram of the *sevenless* mutant. It represents the probability $p(\psi)$ of finding the fly at each angle ψ away from a stripe in his visual environment. At high light intensity (b), orientation is normal, but in the low light condition (a), the integrated probability of finding the *sev* fly within 15° of the target is reduced [12].

4.2.2 optomotor-blind. The optomotor deficits of *sev* are mild, but the X chromosome neurological mutant *optomotor-blind (omb)* has profound deficits in large-field tracking. Yaw, pitch and roll responses are all diminished to rotating stripes (Figure 25.12). Tracking by *omb* while walking on a surface shows the same abnormality. In this clever experiment the fly, while suspended, is allowed to walk on a styrofoam ball floating in a stream of air [13].

When *omb* is tested in the orientation paradigm used for *sev,* described above, its behavior at first appears normal. If the stripe is behind the fly when first presented, however, *omb* does not orient to it, in contrast to wildtype flies. Only when the target starts moving front-to-back in the *omb* fly's frontal visual field does it have an orienting effect [14, p. 131]. This is another example of the importance of an adequate behavioral stimulus to reveal mutations. The tracking defect in *omb* has consequences for reproductive fitness. Because the *omb* male does not orient properly to the female's movements, courtship duration is shorter, and mating success is lower [36].

A paradigm closer to human smooth pursuit tracking has been devised by adding an external sinusoidally oscillating voltage to the motor driving the visual surround. The normal fly is able, through compensating yaw torque, to maintain the visual panorama stationary, as shown in Figure 25.13a. If a wildtype fly is now put into a conflict situation, where a single stripe moves relative to a background texture, he manages simultaneously to orient both to the stripe and to the background, by holding the background fixed in his visual field with smooth exertions of torque, while making saccades to keep track of the oscillations of the stripe (Figure 25.13b). The mutant *omb*, having defective large-field responses, does not orient to the background texture, so there is no conflict; he simply stabilizes the stripe, as if the texture were not present [14, pp. 169–171].

5 Detecting local circuit mutations in man

5.1 Selection through psychological task outliers

In principle, the same process can be used to screen for possible local circuit assembly mutations in humans that was described for the isolation of *sevenless* in *Drosophila* (section 4.1). If psychological tasks have not, so far, turned out to be good sources of single gene effects, the reason may simply be that we have painted behavior with too

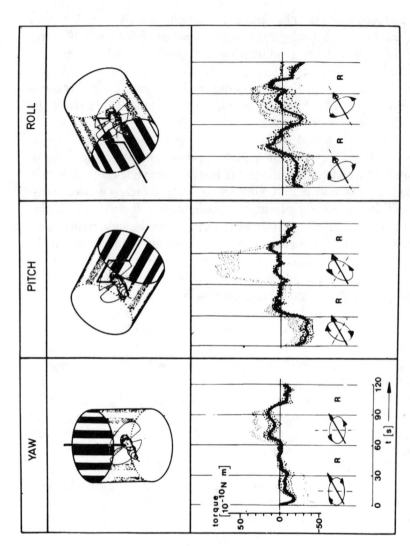

Figure 25.12. Responses of *omb*, with larger wildtype response indicated by dotted lines. From Blondeau and Heisenberg [3; Fig. 5].

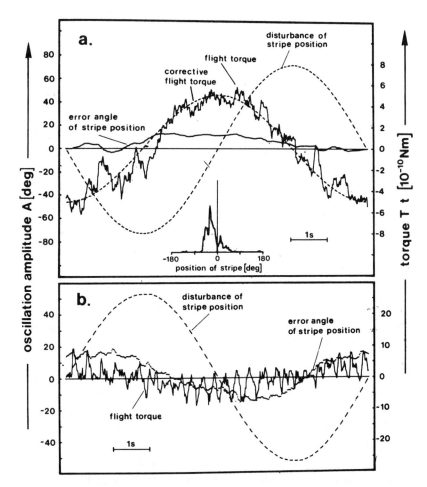

Figure 25.13. Effect of a sinusoidal displacement on torque and fixation accuracy (see text). From Heisenberg and Wolf [14, Fig. 92].

broad a brush. Since overall performance measures reflect the operation of many factors, it is only to be expected that they are polygenic. To find single gene effects, we need to look in detail at the components of behavior that lie beneath overall performance. Recall that in the *omb* mutant, the abnormality in orienting to a stripe only appears if the stripe is presented in a specific way, posteriorly or in back-to-front motion (section 4.2.2).

The measurement of individual factors of attention by Mirsky's laboratory (focus and execute; sustain; shift; encode) is a first step in the direction of subdividing global behavioral traits into components that are more likely to be related to single genes [23].* Probably a few more steps of subdivision will be needed, before attentional behavior can be used as an "adequate stimulus" to isolate individual genes.

As an illustration of the level of detail that may be necessary, I shall describe a recent study by Cavanagh of attentional effects on motion perception. Motion perception is an attractive area for studies of the genetics of local neuronal circuits, because of the wealth of anatomical and physiological information available [19, 21, 25]. In Cavanagh's study [7], a sinusoidal luminance grating and a sinusoidal color grating were superimposed (each was arranged in a ring, like a 45 rpm record), and the two gratings were rotated in opposite directions. For some values of the luminance contrast, the overall perceived motion was in the direction of the luminance grating, but if the subject attended to the color bars, they could be tracked going the opposite direction to the overall motion. One can imagine the experimenter discovering, perhaps unintentionally, that some subjects were outliers, with much stronger or weaker attentional effects on motion perception than the general population. The next step would be segregation analysis in the families of the deviant subjects, to find out whether the anomaly was associated with a major gene.

If a gene were identified, whether it acted on development of local neuronal circuits would remain an open question, but one potentially answerable by known experimental methods. Just as in *Drosophila*, the localization of antibodies to the *sevenless* gene product in the third instar larva (Figure 25.14) provides evidence that the *sevenless* gene acts in the morphogenetic furrow of the eye imaginal disk, histological techniques might be able to narrow down the site of action.

5.2 Selection through ill relatives

The number of subjects required is perhaps the greatest obstacle to mutant selection through psychological task outliers, as described in section 5.1. The screening of 17,000 flies in the phototaxis reversal experiment outlined in section 4.1 must give us pause, although the recovery rate of mutants in this experiment, .8%, was reasonably high.[3]

Fortunately, in human beings a second selection process is available

---

* See also Chapter 17, by Allan F. Mirsky, this volume – Eds.

Figure 25.14. Staining of eye imaginal disk by *sevenless* antisera. Arrow indicates the morphogenetic furrow. From Tomlinson et al. [34, Fig. 1b]. Copyright Cell Press.

to us: *selection through ill relatives.* Cavalli-Sforza once made the memorable observation that "humans are the only organisms where the mutants walk into your office." Selection through ill relatives rests on the pleiotropic and secondary effects of developmentally active genes (section 2.3). Consider the following set of conditions, which is probably a common scenario:

1. There is an unidentified mutation that impairs performance on a psychological task.
2. Impaired task performance may have many other causes.
3. The mutant allele frequency is low in the general population.
4. Through pleiotropic or secondary effects, the mutation also substantially increases the risk for a specific disease.

If this set of conditions obtains, selection of mutants by being on the alert for outliers and examining their families, as described in section 5.1, would be an arduous (although theoretically possible) task. Deviant task performance in the well first-degree relatives of patients with the disease would select the mutant allele more efficiently. Selection through ill relatives has the additional social value that it identifies mutations relevant to a disease. Philip Holzman's successful application of this strategy, to define a major gene that affects smooth pursuit and increases the risk for schizophrenia, is well known.

The view from the *Drosophila* eye shows us that if schizophrenia is a selective disorder of automatic cognitive processing caused by failure of local neuronal circuits, and if the morphogenesis of *Drosophila* photoreceptors is a good model for local circuit wiring in the human brain, then the Holzman strategy is right on target. The road may be long, but there is good reason to believe that it is the right road. So we say to Philip Holzman at mid-career, *ut cogitas persequaris:* as you think, may you pursue.

Notes

1. Genes referred to in lowercase type are recessive.
2. Lineage restriction (cell division leading to daughter cells with inequivalent developmental potentialities) is by no means ruled out as an additional mechanism in the development of local neuronal circuits [37]. Individual gene effects would, presumably, be just as critical in lineage restriction mechanisms as they are in inductive signalling.
3. The mating success of college sophomores has increased significantly since my days in college, but is is still not anywhere near *Drosophila*!

References

[1] Baker, N. E., and Rubin, G. M. (1989) Effect on eye development of dominant mutations in *Drosophila* homologue of the EGF receptor. *Nature 340*, 150–153.
[2] Benzer, S. (1967) Behavioral mutants of Drosophila, isolated by counter-current distribution. *Proceedings of the National Academy of Sciences U.S.A. 58*, 1112–1119.
[3] Blondeau, J., and Heisenberg, M. (1982) The three-dimensional optomotor torque system of *Drosophila melanogaster:* Studies on wildtype and the mutant optomotor-blind[H31]. *Journal of Comparative Physiology 145*, 321–329.
[4] Brown, R. (1973) *A First Language: The Early Stages*. Cambridge, MA: Harvard University Press.
[5] Cagan, R. L., and Ready, D. F. (1989) *Notch* is required for successive cell decisions in the developing *Drosophila* retina. *Genes and Development 3*, 1099–1112.
[6] Carthew, R. W., and Rubin, G. M. (1990) *seven in absentia*, a gene required for specification of R7 cell fate in the *Drosophila* eye. *Cell 63*, 561–577.

[7] Cavanagh, P. (1992) Attention-based motion perception. *Science 257,* 1563–1565.

[8] Chapman, L. J., and Chapman, J. P. (1973) Problems in the measurement of cognitive deficit. *Psychological Bulletin 79,* 380–385.

[9] Gerresheim, F. (1988) Isolation of *Drosophila melanogaster* mutants with a wavelength-specific alteration in their phototactic response. *Behavior Genetics 18,* 227–246.

[10] Hartenstein, V., and Posakony, J. W. (1990) A dual function of the *Notch* gene in *Drosophila* sensillum development. *Developmental Biology 142,* 13–30.

[11] Heberlein, U., Mlodzik, M., and Rubin, G. M. (1991) Cell-fate determination in the developing *Drosophila* eye: Role of the *rough* gene. *Development 112,* 703–712.

[12] Heisenberg, M., and Buchner, E. (1977) The role of retinula cell types in visual behavior of *Drosophila melanogaster. Journal of Comparative Physiology A117,* 127–162.

[13] Heisenberg, M., Wonneberger, R., and Wolf, R. (1978) optomotor-blind[H31] – a *Drosophila* mutant of the lobula plate giant neurons. *Journal of Comparative Physiology A124,* 287–296.

[14] Heisenberg, M., and Wolf, R. (1984) *Vision in* Drosophila: *Genetics of Microbehavior.* Berlin: Springer-Verlag.

[15] Johnston, M. H., and Holzman, P. S. (1979) *Assessing Schizophrenic Thinking: A Clinical and Research Instrument for Measuring Thought Disorder.* San Francisco: Jossey-Bass.

[16] Krämer, H., Cagan, R. L., and Zipursky, S. L. (1991) Interaction of *bride of sevenless* membrane-bound ligand and the *sevenless* tyrosine-kinase receptor. *Nature 352,* 207–212.

[17] Lawrence, P. (1992) *The Making of a Fly.* London: Blackwell Scientific.

[18] Lindsley, D. L., and Zimm, G. G. (1992) *The Genome of* Drosophila Melanogaster. San Diego: Academic Press.

[19] Livingstone, M. S., and Hubel, D. H. (1987) Psychophysical evidence for separate channels for the perception of form, color, movement, and depth. *Journal of Neuroscience 7,* 3416–3468.

[20] Matthysse, S. (1990) Why thinking is easy. In *Philosophy and Psychopathology,* M. Spitzer and B. A. Maher, eds., pp. 178–186. New York: Springer-Verlag.

[21] Maunsell, J.H.R., and Newsome, W. T. (1987) Visual processing in monkey extrastriate cortex. *Annual Review of Neuroscience 10,* 363–401.

[22] Meyerowitz, E. M., and Kankel, D. R. (1978) A genetic analysis of visual system development in *Drosophila melanogaster. Developmental Biology 62,* 112–142.

[23] Mirsky, A. F., Anthony, B. J., Duncan, C. C., Ahearn, M. B., and Kellam, S. G. (1991) Analysis of the elements of attention: A neuropsychological approach. *Neuropsychology Review 2,* 109–145.

[24] Mlodzik, M., Hiromi, Y., Weber, U., Goodman, C. S., and Rubin, G. M. (1990) The *Drosophila seven-up* gene, a member of the steroid receptor gene superfamily, controls photoreceptor cell fates. *Cell 60,* 211–24.

[25] Nakayama, K. (1985) Biological image motion processing: A review. *Vision Research 25,* 625–660.

[26] Place, E.J.S., and Gilmore, G. C. (1980) Perceptual organization in schizophrenia. *Journal of Abnormal Psychology 89,* 409–418.

[27] Rakic, P., ed. (1975) Local circuit neurons. *Neurosciences Research Program Bulletin 13,* 291–446.

[28] Ramón y Cajal, S. (1899) Conexión general de los elementos nerviosos. *La Medicina Práctica.*

[29] Ready, D. F., Hanson, T. E., and Benzer, S. (1976) Development of the *Drosophila* retina, a neurocrystalline lattice. *Developmental Biology 53,* 217–240.

[30] Ready, D. F. (1989). A multifaceted approach to neural development. *Trends in Neurosciences 12,* 102–110.

[31] Reichardt, W. (1973) Musterinduzierte Flugorientierung: Verhaltens-Versuche an der Fliege Musca domestica. *Naturwissenschaften 60,* 122–138.

[32] Schneider, W., and Shiffrin, R. M. (1977) Controlled and automatic human information processing: I. Detection, search, and attention. *Psychological Review 84,* 1–66.

[33] Szentágothai, J. (1983) The modular architectonic principle of neural centers. *Reviews of Physiology, Biochemistry, and Pharmacology 98,* 11–61.

[34] Tomlinson, A., Bowtell, D.D.L., Hafen, E., and Rubin, G. M. (1987) Localization of the *sevenless* protein, a putative receptor for positional information, in the eye imaginal disc of *Drosophila. Cell 51,* 143–150.

[35] Tomlinson, A. (1988) Cellular interactions in the developing *Drosophila* eye. *Development 104,* 183–193.

[36] Tompkins, L., Gross, A. C., Hall, J. C., Gailey, D. A., and Siegel, R. W. (1982) The role of female movement in the sexual behavior of *Drosophila melanogaster. Behavior Genetics 12,* 295–307.

[37] Williams, R. W., and Goldowitz, D. (1992) Lineage versus environment in embryonic retina: A revisionist perspective. *Trends in Neurosciences 15,* 368–373.

Response and reflections

26

Reflections on the developing science of psychopathology

Philip S. Holzman

"O, Wonder!
How many goodly creatures are there here!
How beauteous mankind is! O brave new world
That has such people in't!"
    Miranda, in *The Tempest*, Act V, Scene i

To paraphrase the awestruck Miranda, at the conclusion of *The Tempest*, "O brave new world, that has such insights in 't." How magically different is the contemporary landscape of this evolving science of psychopathology from the one I came upon in 1946 when I began my graduate training. And yet, to pull another quotation from that last great play of Shakespeare's, "What's past is prologue." It therefore may be instructive to cast a backward eye to that earlier period not only to savor the extraordinary leaps we have made, but also to temper a bit the celebration of our successes by grasping whatever lessons there are to be learned from our history.

It has been observed by Boring (1950), a particularly astute commentator on the history of psychological science, that new theories (and I will add new discoveries or sciences) do not flash upon the scene already formed. In almost every case of a new good idea, it is possible to trace its roots to earlier ideas. Such historical precedence does not detract one bit from the merit of the new idea, but it does pose the question of why that new idea blossomed now and not earlier. While historical precedence does presume that the idea is not completely original, as it at first may have seemed, it does not presume that the idea is more correct now than it was then. Indeed, the idea may be wrong, but the net worth of the new ideas or new discoveries is not to be found in either their originality or their correctness, but in their heuristic effect, their power to press scientists on to new discoveries and new generalizations.

In the following pages, I look back in time to reflect on some of what we knew about psychopathology then, what we thought we knew, and what we wished we knew. I then survey some of what we know now and how we got there. In this survey, which I acknowledge is a very selective one, I comment on what conditions made real progress possible. I also note some areas of ambiguity that reflect misunderstandings, probable errors, and misrenderings in our contemporary work, which, ironically, in our successes we may have been blinded to, but which, in our less successful days, we habitually took care to avoid, as cautious and careful if not spectacular scientists.

What we knew then: Grand theory: Kraepelin, Bleuler, Freud, and the Gestaltists

In the mid-1940s, just after the conclusion of World War II, psychology was at a fork in the road it was travelling on. The discipline was coming to the end of the era of the great systematists and was about to enter the era of accelerated experimentation. Although based on observation and insight and even some experimentation, the great systematists produced some formulations that went beyond the scope of their empirical data. But all good theorists stretch their visions beyond what most of us can see. Validation and modification must follow, but that work is usually relegated to others. I include among the great systematic advances the work of Emil Kraepelin (1896, 1919), who believed that schizophrenia (dementia praecox) was a disorder that is distinguishable from manic-depressive illness. The basis of this distinction was to be discerned in the course of the illnesses: cyclic in the case of manic-depressive illness, but continuously and insidiously worsening (or at best stable) in the case of schizophrenia. True, Kraepelin allowed for exceptions, but his description of the natural history of these two illnesses guided most clinicians. I include Eugen Bleuler in this group of systematic observers because he attempted to specify the fundamental symptoms of schizophrenia as well as to mark boundaries of the illness. His demarcation, however, resulted in a widening of the concept of schizophrenia to include nonpsychotic forms. Although his broader view is probably correct, it gave license to unwary diagnosticians, particularly in the United States, to label almost any psychosis "schizophrenia."

Sigmund Freud was a dominant presence at this time. Although he died in 1939, his influence continued to grow, particularly in American psychiatric circles. In the 1940s and 1950s, for example, it could be asserted that one could not be appointed to the chair of a department of psychiatry in a medical school unless one was a trained psychoanalyst. Freud's influence on psychology and psychiatry was felt particularly in a broad emphasis on both unconscious psychological processes and the importance attributed to sexual and aggressive motives, which previously had not been considered in psychological studies. Psychoanalysis placed a heavy emphasis on internal psychological conflicts – between wishes and internalized societal demands, for example – as decisive factors in neurotic symptom formation. A concern with the irrational balanced the scientific rationalism of the mid-twentieth century. One result of this emphasis was the proposition that internal conflicts, whose origins were in very early childhood, played a causal role in psychoses. A vigorous challenge to this proposition had to wait several decades. It can, however, be said with some justification, that in this area we knew little and presumed much.

Grand theory was no less present in psychology than it was in psychiatry. Gestalt psychology, whose leaders were Max Wertheimer, Wolfgang Kohler, Kurt Koffka, and Kurt Lewin, exerted much influence on several centers of academic psychology. This influence was particularly strong at the schools I attended, The College of the City of New York and the University of Kansas, through the articulate disciples of the early Gestalt psychologists, among whom were Fritz Heider, Martin Scheerer, Isidor Chein, and Raymond Wheeler. The whole was, of course, more than the sum of its parts – the Gestaltists' slogan, which was a rallying cry in reaction against the elementalism in associationistic psychology and the "psychology without mind" of radical behaviorism. For the most part, the Gestalt theoretical perspectives were just that: perspectives with a few experimental endeavors.[1]

What we knew then: Techniques of measurement

At the middle of the twentieth century, we were not without facts. Much psychological information had been accumulated from the nineteenth- and early-twentieth-century laboratories of psychology. Fechner's law, formulated in 1860 from the earlier experiments of E. H. Weber, was one of the few regularities we had in psychology; it was a centerpiece of most experimental psychology courses, since it presented a mathematical formulation of a relation between stimulus and sensation, between what is out there and what is within us. It was important because it held out possibilities for measuring ideas, intentions, feelings, and other psychological phenomena with the same precision that physicists measure mass, force, and wavelength.

The measurement of sensation depended upon the use of new methods of experimentation, which are still used today: the method of limits, of constant stimuli, of average error, and of successive comparison. In envy as well as in imitation of physics, these techniques of measurement are called *psychophysical methods*. We used these methods in many small, circumscribed studies, but, in my opinion, they contributed very little toward compiling a cumulative body of knowledge of human behavior, particularly of psychopathological behavior. There was very little ordering of these data or attempts to understand relations among them. In this area, we knew many facts, but presumed very little.

Of equal prominence, then, was the reaction time technique. Essentially perfected by Frans Cornelis Donders in the 1860s from methods that had been used for at least 50 years, the technique made it possible to measure the time between a physical event and a person's response. Although originally undertaken to discover the temporal course of events that intervened between a stimulus (which could be made incrementally more complex) and a response, it later became the cornerstone of a branch of measurement called *mental chronometry*, which enjoyed great visibility up to the 1950s, and then faded until seized upon more recently by the emerging discipline of cognitive psychology as an objective way to study the components of complex thought processes like attention (cf. Posner, 1978).

The measurement of intelligence, begun by the French physician Alfred Binet in 1905, presented a clear developmental view of psychological functioning: intelligent behaviors unfold and develop, and different categories of behaviors have their own epigenetic timetable. This perspective is clearly psychobiological. The invention of the intelligence test, and particularly the modifications introduced by David Wechsler in 1939, made it possible to compare the effects of trauma and illness on the several psychological functions that made up the total test score, or IQ. Thus, if one could understand or "think through" the principal psychological functions underlying each subscale (such as information, arithmetic, vocabulary, digit span, similarities, etc.), one could infer which functions were impaired and which were spared in some illnesses. This task David Rapaport (Rapaport et al., 1946/1960) undertook to accomplish by combining clinical sophistication with a psychological understanding of the various tasks used in Wechsler's intelligence test.

What we knew then: Personality dynamics

The study of personality occupied the center of psychology in the 1940s and 1950s. Those psychologists who set out to investigate personality were chiefly concerned with charting individual differences and consistencies in a variety of behaviors including large units, such as modes of expressing aggression, and comparatively simple units such as the size of just noticeable differences in size perception. If "style is the person," then a specification of the principal dimensions of style could claim a major role in psychological studies of the person. William Stern stated this proposition succinctly: "*Keine Gestalt ohne Gestalter,*" whose literal translation, "no shape without a shaper," can be restated as "all of our acts bear the imprint of our individuality." But finding the proper units for personality study proved to be an elusive task, and at least in this instance and at this time nature could not be carved at its joints because there was not a good map – nor is there one even now – of the gross anatomy of personality to guide the carver. Yet, several studies were able to demonstrate consistencies over time of some behaviors like characteristic styles of judging similarities (Gardner et al., 1959), and the extent to which one is influenced by context (Witkin et al., 1981). It was also possible to show then that motives and drives, including appetitive drives like thirst, did not preempt adaptive behavior (Klein, 1970), a reassuring outcome for the rationalists among us, but a bit upsetting for the literal (and incorrect) translators of Freudian drive theory.

The emphasis on personality consistency influenced a small but articulate number of psychopathologists and clinicians who recognized that diseases and illnesses happen to people, no two of whom are alike, and that people who contract the same illness do not thereby become alike. There was no reason, according to this view, to expect that all schizophrenic patients, any more than all arthritic or pneumonia patients, should show the same personality shifts or the same impairments of cognitive functions to exactly the same extent. This view made it possible to discern the existence of different patterns of dysfunction in incipient, acute, chronic, and remitted psychotic patients. One consequence of this insight was the recognition that the study of psychopathology cannot rely exclusively on the statistical method of comparing mean differences between groups (since there may be much heterogeneity in the pathological group under study), nor can it assume linearity in the distribution of the variables measured. But these insights did not find their way into the experimental laboratory and therefore they were lost to further empirical investigation. Even today, this essentially clinical view may not be fully appreciated by many investigators who expect that differences between people with different diseases should be uniform and captured by the inspection of mean differences. This clinical view is, however, a part of the rationale that underlies the Mendelian latent structure model of schizophrenia (cf. Matthysse et al., 1986), which emphasizes that a disease like schizophrenia may have a single genotype which, although highly penetrant, is expressed in a variety of phenotypes.

What we thought we knew then

Optimism about most endeavors was high during the period prior to the 1960s. After having triumphed over Hitler and the Japanese empire, many Americans believed there was very little that they could not do if they but stubbornly tried. This bullish outlook also influenced approaches to the treatment of mental disorders. For example, Karl Menninger, a distinguished psychiatrist who, with his brother William, in the early 1920s, established a successful mental hospital in America's heartland, Topeka, Kansas, wrote that patients can emerge from treatment "weller than well."[2] This midwestern optimism permeated much of the therapeutic endeavors at a time when, in truth, treatment efforts had very few tools and very few genuine successes. Psychotherapy was the major treatment intervention. At that time, it bore the unmistakable influence of Freudian psychoanalysis in its emphasis on uncovering unconscious conflicts, which were assumed to be decisively pathogenic. It was employed for almost every mental disorder, including schizophrenia, sociopathy, major depressions, irritable bowel syndrome, infertility, and peptic ulcer. Some patients, however, did get well, and when they did, psychotherapy was given the credit. When some patients did not get well, there were many rationalizations, and most of them were without foundation. Although psychotic illnesses were occasionally treated with psychotherapy, electroconvulsive treatments (ECT) and insulin coma were the usual treatments during acute phases of a psychosis.

The somatic treatments were administered mainly in state and other public hospitals and were considered by some commentators to be second class and inferior to the expressive psychotherapy offered to the more affluent patients. It is an ironic commentary on those times that these somatic treatments, particularly ECT for the severely depressed, proved to be much more effective than the lengthy and expensive expressive psychotherapy offered to wealthier patients in private mental hospitals.

This was also a desperate period when almost anything was tried, including various mutilations, to bring about an end to psychotic illness. Prefrontal lobotomy, tooth extractions, hysterectomies, and adrenalectomies were among the so-called therapeutic procedures introduced. Perhaps the most cautionary example of what we thought we knew is the case of prefrontal lobotomy. The advocacy of this useless yet permanently damaging invasive intervention was recognized by the award of the Nobel prize for medicine in 1949.[3]

The emphasis on psychotherapy reflected a particular view of mental disorders that was promulgated by Karl Menninger, namely, that there is but one mental disorder, and the varied forms of illnesses reflected differences not in kind, but in severity (see Menninger, *The Vital Balance*). Madness and neuroses of different types were thought to be on a continuum of organized to disorganized modes of adaptation. Here, too, there was no empirical evidence for the view of mental illness as one disorder, but it did serve as a rationale for delivering only one kind of therapy: one illness, therefore one therapy. It is consequently not surprising that any psychosis unaccompanied by an obvious brain lesion (anatomic or chemical) was called *schizophrenia*, and the Kraepelinian separation of manic-depressive illness from schizophrenia, although not forgotten, was essentially ignored.

During World War II, there were a significant number of psychiatric casualties. It was reasonable to conclude that these casualties were reactions to the stresses of military activities, including combat experiences. The diagnostic scheme put into use during the war by William C. Menninger, then a brigadier general in charge of the psychiatric branch of the Army Medical Corps, emphasized this "reactive" view of mental illness. In 1946, following the war's end, the American Psychiatric Association canonized this view in the second edition of its *Diagnostic and Statistical Manual*. Most psychiatric conditions were labeled *reactions*, such as "Schizophrenic Reaction, of such and such a type"; or "Reactive Depression"; or "Obsessive Compulsive Reaction." The explicit view of reaction types seen among World War II combat casualties became the implicit view of civilian psychiatric disorders: they were regarded as responses to a hostile, sometimes tyrannous, environment.

This view fit well with a prewar outlook that sometimes confused equality of potential with equality of opportunity (see also Chapter 8 by Sheldon White, this volume). During the 1930s, in response to the racist dogma of the Nazis, and also to the absurd excesses of the eugenics movement (cf. Kevles, 1985), there was a distinct aversion to considering the role of genetic factors in behavior. The work of Otto Klineberg, for example, exposed most of the errors in the studies that imputed genetic factors to ethnic differences in intelligence test scores; Klineberg (1935) attributed such differences to experiential factors, most of which reflected restricted training and education opportunities. Klineberg's point, while correct in its criticism of the extant commentary on the data for considering only genetic explanations, made it politically difficult to address a number of characteristics of behavior invariant over time, many of which reflect the unfolding of development, which, in turn, require genetic considerations.[4]

What we wished we knew then

The optimism of psychiatry not only reflected the American *Zeitgeist* after World War II, it expressed the pride of medical science in some astonishing earlier successes in the conquest of two particularly nasty diseases, pellagra and syphilis, which were once considered to be mental illnesses because of accompanying psychotic symptoms. When pellagra was found to be a nutritional disease caused by a dietary deficiency of niacin, a B vitamin, and syphilis was found to be a result of a venereal infection by a spirochete that responded to an arsenic compound, both diseases became treatable. The examples of pellagra and syphilis were a constant inspiration to those who were searching to cure mental disorders. We wished we could find the magic bullet for schizophrenia, depression, and crippling obsessive compulsive disorder, just as Paul Ehrlich had found the magic bullet for syphilis.

Careful phenomenological and psychological test experience convinced many observers that psychotic disorders, particularly schizophrenia, could not be on a continuum with neurotic conditions. The language misusages and thought tangles that characterize schizophrenia simply cannot be reflections of internal psychological conflicts.[5] Nature is far too complex and sturdy for the problems in adaptation, which all of us face most of the time, to wreak such havoc on man's thinking apparatus, the brain, and its product, the mind. In the 1950s there was a definite tilt toward searching for central nervous system referents of thought disorders, perhaps inspired by Penfield and Jasper's description of the revivification of earlier but long forgotten experiences by direct electrical stimulation of parts of the temporal lobe.

There began to appear a trickle of studies on thought processes that took seriously the clinical appearance of attentional dysfunction in schizophrenia. But we wished that we had the conceptual tools to study the vagaries of cognition during psychosis. We wished we could understand the relation between the psychological functions scrutinized by psychology and of brain areas that were necessary for these functions.[6] It was in the area of brain dysfunctions that the search for such relations received its prod, as, indeed, has been the case from the time of the Civil War. It is a tragic and unfortunate fact that during war many medical advances occur. For it was in the setting of the Russo-Japanese War of 1904–1905 that the discovery and identification of the primary visual cortex occurred. Japanese soldiers with penetrating head wounds had lost some vision, but regained consciousness so that they could cooperate with a medical examination. These examinations led to the accurate mapping of the striate cortex (Glickstein and Whitteridge, 1987). It is well known by clinical investigators that when an apparatus functions well and smoothly, and the integration of its parts occurs seamlessly, the identification and study of those parts become problematic because they fail to call attention to their complexity.

We were not prescient enough then to wish for a tool that would permit us to observe the brain while performing mental functions. Nor were we bold enough to imagine that someday the genetic code for mental diseases would be possible to decipher. But the discovery of the double helix structure of DNA now permits progress toward the goal of understanding the genetic factors in mental disorders, and the discovery of methods to image the structure and functioning of the brain now opens new vistas to the creative and visionary scientists.

What we know now

The times were always appropriate for scientists to measure mental processes and thereby to understand them. In the past, however, we were limited by the absence of appropriate tools. It is not that psychopathologists know so much more now than we knew then, nor are we any more correct or original now. We can, however, speed up our calculations with the computer; we can watch the brain at work with our new imaging techniques; we can harness compounds to ablate areas of the brain without permanently mutilating them; we can make use of Donder's chronometric method for reducing the complexity of mental activities; we can record with once unimagined speed the action of organs like the eye. And these technological advances bring us dazzling new knowledge, some of which is reported in this book. It is clear that new technologies have cleared the path for us. This book contains only a sample of the complex information obtained in the past decade.

The way to this brave new world has been prepared for us by the seminal figures of the past, of whom I will mention only five: Frans Cornelis Donders, Gustav Theodor Fechner, Wilhelm Wundt, William James, and Sigmund Freud.

Fechner, trained in physics and medicine, tried to bring the exactness of physics into the life sciences. This he succeeded in doing by his discovery that sensation increases arithmetically with a geometric increase in the stimulus. That is, our awareness of increases in stimulus intensity is related to the level of sensation we are experiencing. This formulation led to a series of experiments which he himself performed, and in this work he gave mathematical precision to Weber's earlier work on "just noticeable differences."[7]

Donders, a Dutch physiologist, tried to solve the problem of measuring the speed of nerve conduction, begun by Hermann von Helmholtz, who was deterred in this search by the presence of large individual differences. In the 1860s, Donders undertook to discover the events that intervened between a stimulus and a motor response, and developed the reaction time method for this purpose.

Wilhelm Wundt, who in 1879 founded the first laboratory of psychology in Leipzig, emphasized that all of psychological activity was approachable as an organismic process that must be studied with both psychological and physiological methods.

William James, probably the most influential American psychologist of the early part of this century, in spite of an antipathy to experimental methods, gave much space in his monumental *Principles of Psychology* to the experimental work done by Helmholtz, Wundt, and other German empiricists. But one of his greatest contributions was a parsing of the elements of consciousness, particularly of attention, which stands today as an extraordinary achievement and a guide to contemporary cognitive studies.

Sigmund Freud entered the area of psychopathology from neurology, and his earliest attempts in this area were devoted to constructing a brain model of psychological functioning that would explain such diverse acts as dreaming, lying, remembering, perceiving, and attending.

But knowledge could not advance as dramatically as it has since the 1960s without the innovations and discoveries in the biological sciences, which opened up an era of expanding knowledge about brain and behavior relations. Up until this time, the insights of Donders, Fechner, Wundt, Freud, and James could be carried hardly any further either by them or their followers. I attribute the rapid advances in the study of psychopathology to the confluence of several events, which resulted in new technologies that made further advances possible.

The first of these is the discovery in 1944, by Seymour Kety, of a method to measure precisely the circulation of the blood in the brain. This advance permitted the measurement of metabolic activity of the brain while performing various behavioral tasks, as is now being done with positron emission tomography (PET). Another discovery was the physics of magnetic resonance, which led to hitherto unparalleled clarity in producing images of the living brain, and now to the echo planar version of this technique, which permits the functional imaging of PET as well as the structural imaging of MRI.

The second is the introduction of the phenothiazines into the treatment of psychosis, which led to the intensive study of neural receptor and transmitter dynamics in major mental illnesses and the role these receptors and transmitters play in behavior.

The third is Watson and Crick's discovery of the double helix structure of DNA, which led to the revolution in molecular biology and opened up the possibility of discovering the genetic etiology of many diseases, including some severe mental diseases.

The fourth factor is the continued but increasingly sophisticated study of brain anatomical mapping and localization, aided by new electronic and computer techniques. Some of the yield is vividly described in the work of Francine Benes (Chapter 6) and Patricia Goldman-Rakic (Chapter 2) in this book.

The fifth is the advent, beginning in the late 1960s, of the precise measurement of cognitive processes, and the ability to partition mental functions, such as attention, into finer units.

Without these five advances, the psychobiological revolution in psychopathology might not have taken place. Some readers may wish to substitute items from their own list, but I believe those additions would not differ much from mine. What is noteworthy about this list of advances is that they all emerged from basic research rather than from a project that targeted a specific goal, such as a cure for a particular disease. This is the way of science. Basic studies, while less dramatic than targeted disease-oriented studies, can yield a bigger and more lasting return on the investment of time, work, and money. Peter Medawar wrote that one should invest in applied science for quick returns, but in pure science (basic science, as I have used the term here) for capital appreciation.

A major difference, however, between "then" and "now" lies in the place of overarching theory. Today the emphasis is on research, the experimental manipulation of variables, and the amassing of new facts. Where once we stood at the crossroads of theory and empirical investigation, today experimentation in our field commands the resources of research money and journal space, while theoretical excursions, especially those that Chein (1973) called *metatheoretical*, are all but forgotten. The broad theories that dominated the past play a very minor role in contemporary research efforts. And contemporary research is quite indifferent to the previously dominant theories, such as psychoanalysis and Gestalt psychology. In most respects, this new accent is refreshing, since we can more easily adjudicate the validity of a fact than a theory. Today, with the rapidity of replication studies, the half-life of an experimentally derived *fact* can be measured in months, in contrast to the suspended animation of such data then. Theories, however, are hardly ever discarded because of infirming factual evidence.

What we don't know we don't know

In one respect the fading influence of grand theory has been a significant loss to our scientific endeavors. It is important to recognize that grand theories or metatheories, like psychoanalysis, do not present specific predictions that could confirm or disconfirm the theories. One of the errors in some psychoanalytic discourse resides in the view that specific predictions from the grand theory could validate Freudian propositions. These propositions, however, were never stated in forms that were capable of rigorous validation, and therefore data amassed from neither the clinical encounter nor the laboratory had any effect on the theory. In the words of George Klein, psychoanalytic metatheory was "a one-way street" in which the theory guided the observation, but there was no possibility for observation to correct the theory (Klein, 1976).

But grand scientific theories present a view of the subject matter – in the case of psychopathology, a view of man – to which experimental endeavors are quite indifferent. Most of the time this indifference makes no difference. Experimentation and measurement go on regardless of any overarching theory. Yet, in our more reflective moments, some of us feel a need for guidance by a view that helps us to know what is required to complete a proper study of a subject matter, lest we lose sight of what is important to include in its study. Thus, psychoanalysis focused on issues of thought processes outside of awareness, now being addressed by cognitive scientists in studies of "implicit memory," and it emphasized the centrality of specific motives such as sex, aggression, self-preservation, and self-regard in organized and disorganized behavior. In most psychopathological research we have no psychological periodic table to guide us toward what is missing in our experimental efforts. Accumulation of sheer numbers of facts does not make a science, any more than does the old Sears, Roebuck catalogue, crammed as it was with very interesting facts. Nor does the physicist hunger after bare numbers. It is the ordering of those facts and numbers and their relation to each other that give them meaning. Such is the guidance provided by grand theory, which now, I say sadly, has lost its mandate. Most of us do not even mourn its loss, perhaps because we had never developed a lasting attachment to it.

The danger, in these metatheories, of course, is that they can become dogmas and thereby permit their promulgators to drop a shroud of obfuscation over reason and unbiased observation. It has been so with Marxism and, at times, with psychoanalysis. But it need not be so, if the balance between guidance by metatheory and accretion of knowledge by experimentation is observed.

There is yet another danger that comes from explicitly shunning metatheory, especially in the area of psychopathology: the danger of adopting an implicit metatheory that is not of one's choosing, and without realizing it. In this regard, some experimentalists embrace a specific view of man, perhaps in contradiction to their own observations, and surely without explicitly intending it. I have in mind some who study psychotic phenomena hoping to localize their *essence* in one or another area of the brain (see Deborah Levy's critique in Chapter 5, this volume). These efforts reveal the experimenters' representation of man as a reflexive, impotent reactor whose behavior is an outcome of two interacting forces: those intrinsic to his makeup (genes, temperament, central nervous system structures) and environmental constraints. Chein (1973) has commented that there is an alternative view that regards the person as doing something to the world about him, injecting himself into the causal behavioral chain. In this view, behavior is not reducible to physiological or physical laws. But neither is behavior incompatible with those laws.

There is an area of experimental psychopathology that has been nurtured almost not at all by the great advances in neurobiology. I refer to the personality disorders, which, in the lexicon of the contemporary diagnostic compendium, are grouped under Axis II disorders. These so-called personality disorders demand a perspective quite different from that used to study the Axis I disorders, most of which can justifiably claim to be diseases. That is, when studying disorders such as schizophrenia and bipolar illness there is little doubt that one is observing powerful forces within a person that recruit and distort functions to their own ends. Such distortions are not hard to spot, although their relations to each other and their origins present problems, as do such factors in any disease. The strategies used to explore these disorders are time-honored, and we celebrate many of them in this volume.

With the personality disorders, however, we face a different quality of behavior. What shall we call a person who is strikingly egocentric, who evades anxiety at every opportunity, who solicits affection and assistance from people with minimal return, whose capacity for tenderness, sympathy, and empathy is weak, and even when over-demonstrative betrays a basic coldness? Such people may be called "narcissistic personality disorders," which implies that this constellation can be viewed as a disease. But in all instances?

What shall we call persons who are pervasively suspicious, and are

litigiously overcautious, whose lives are built around proof and coun-
terproof, evidence, and inference? They are labeled "paranoid personality disorders," but does this constellation constitute a disease
entity?

What of the person who constantly flouts legal or social rules and
who shows a noteworthy indifference to his own antisocial acts; whose
perspective of time seems defective and who has only a flimsy capacity
to delay impulses; whose thinking shows poor integrating ability; and
who constantly looks for situations that induce thrills? Such a person
is labeled "antisocial personality disorder."

These three examples – there are others – are unrelated to any of
the Axis I disorders, and do not appear to run in families of schizophrenic or bipolar patients with any greater frequency than in the
general population, although there may be familial aggregation of
disorders such as antisocial personality disorder. The vagueness of
these syndromes is even more striking than that of the Axis I disorders. Where is the demarcation that sets off a person who is a careful
accountant, suspicious of most business transactions, or a shrewd
detective who follows every lead, from a person who would be labeled
a paranoid personality disorder?[8]

It appears that the strategies adopted for the study of diseases will
not work for the study of these personality exaggerations. The emphasis in these "conditions" is on individual differences in personality
traits, and on the regularities or principles that lend meaning to the
differences. That is, the individual differences in behaviors can be
construed as instances of the principles. The dimensions to be studied are how a person comes to grips with reality constraints, what the
quality of thinking is, how problems are solved, how information is
stored, how affect is modulated. We thus deal here not with disease
states but with action styles. These styles call up the problem of
continuity between the normal and pathological as a quantitative issue, whereas qualitative distinctions preempt attention in the psychoses.

We shall not advance further in our understanding of these so-
called disorders unless we understand that laws of persons rather than
of diseases must be studied. Kagan's (Chapter 12, this volume) research on behavioral inhibition and shyness provides a fine example of
a productive exploration into this area. It examines special trait-like
behaviors like shyness, reduces them to manageable units, tests their
individual consistencies over time, and looks at the biological corre-

lates of these consistencies. But correlates must designate more than relationships or covariations. They must point to critical organizing features, to neural networks, and back again to models of total functioning.

Where do we think we are?

I now climb out on a tree limb, hoping I do not fall to the ground ignominiously. We think we know a number of things about mental disorders that we used to be uncertain about, and I will try to list them.

1. We are now rather certain that the environment is not the tyrannous villain who provides the necessary and sufficient causes of major mental illnesses like schizophrenia. Most will agree that the person cannot be such a passive and plastic pawn, for then all of us born to live nasty, brutish, and short lives in this Hobbesian world would then become mad. And no one has yet been able to specify the environmental conditions, whether they are familial, infectious, or otherwise noxious, that will produce a schizophrenia or a mania.

2. We, as treaters of mental disorders, are no longer as sanguine as we were about the power of our therapeutic ministrations. The era of inflated expectations was a salutary change from the therapeutic nihilism of the eighteenth and nineteenth centuries. Now, however, most of us would agree that psychotherapy alone for the major psychoses is not an efficacious treatment. In my opinion, in our role as psychotherapists, we are guardians who convey *care,* rather than treaters who deliver *cure.* The introduction into psychiatry of psychotropic medications like the phenothiazines, the tricyclics, and lithium have surely alleviated much of the suffering of mental illnesses.[9] For the schizophrenias and even for many manias, the medications still do not cure. We need both the chemical compounds and the caring presence of the healer to convey hope and to "minister to a mind diseased."[10] We have been tempered by our experiences, made cautious by our failures, but made increasingly adventurous by our real progress.

3. We no longer quibble about whether genes play a role in schizophrenia and bipolar disease. We are no longer diverted by the specious issue of assigning weights to genetic and environmental factors in mental disease. We have seen evidence from the twin and adoption studies that schizophrenia and manic-depressive illness run in families and that rearing experience cannot explain the prevalence data

amassed by study after study.[11] Efforts to find chromosomal linkage and to specify appropriate models of transmission preempt the debate now.

4. I firmly believe that a program of *experimental reductionism* is required for discovering the essence of the behavioral abnormalities in such disorders as schizophrenia. I am not advocating that we disavow the reality of psychological events by a rush to translate them into physical events, and thereby to consider the psychological events as nothing but the physical ones. That is a vain and misguided exercise. By experimental reductionism I denote an attempt to discover the smallest number of elements or units that make up a behavior and that can explain how the more complex behaviors work. Such experimental reductionism sparks progress. Watson and Crick's discovery of the double helix structure of DNA represents a colossal triumph of such reductionism. Here the reductionist assertion is that living organisms from the simplest to the most complex can be explained as the outcome of a simple inherited design coded of four bases arranged as triads. Although they cause the organism, they must not be mistaken for the organism, any more than the function of attention should be mistaken for neural firing in a specific brain area.

As for research in psychopathology, we are not content, for example, with the mere demonstration that attention is disordered in schizophrenia. Kraepelin had noted that fact in the first edition of his textbook (Kraepelin, 1896). But attention is a complex term. It refers to many kinds of behaviors, such as paying attention, sustaining attention, looking expectantly for a specific thing, moving attention from one thing to another, an automatic process as well as a deliberate, consciously intended one, to list only a few. The work described by Anne Sereno in Chapter 18 of this volume illustrates experimental reductionism at work in finding that automatic, exogenous attention, the kind that clicks in very quickly – faster than 100 milliseconds after something "attracts attention" – is relatively unimpaired in schizophrenic patients; whereas endogenous, sustained attention, which clicks in after about 200 milliseconds, slightly later than the exogenous type, is quite impaired.

It is a similar progression with respect to memory in schizophrenia. No one has claimed that long-term memory is impaired in schizophrenia, but up to this time it has not been possible to discover if very short-term memory is impaired. Indeed, the distinction between short- and long-term memory storage is a relatively recent one.

Short-term memory, however, is difficult to study apart from the attention required to consolidate something before it can be moved from perception to short-term memory. The studies reported by Park and O'Driscoll (Chapter 3, this volume) show the operation of spatial working memory in humans by modifying a paradigm employed by Goldman-Rakic in monkeys. They report that spatial working memory is impaired significantly in schizophrenics, but not verbally mediated spatial memory or the spatial orientation that requires no working memory. These experiments illustrate the power of experimental reductionism to pinpoint a specific deficit in a class of patients, and in that way move us closer to understanding the basic processes represented by the pathology. Deborah L. Levy and Steven Matthysse (Chapters 2 and 25, this volume) have described this effort as a parsing process that chunks behavior into smaller units whose lawfulness can then be understood more clearly. Physicists use the term "coarse graining" to describe a similar method that searches for essential details of a process. They focus on increasingly simpler entities and then stop when the reductive process no longer yields useful information. In psychopathology, too, we can reach a level at which the successive parsing has reached its limit and the phenomenon of interest is lost, just as in the progressive enlargement of a photograph one reaches a point where only the grain but not the object becomes the image.

There is, moreover, a danger in this brave new world of experimentation and rational dissection of behaviors. It is easy to forget that in this experimental odyssey we started from a concern about the behavior of patients whose conditions have been classified as schizophrenic or manic, or as something else. The urge to understand their behavior is the motive for these studies. It may often happen that we stray far from the clinical picture that we wish to understand. At times this is no cause for alarm, as when studies of basic processes (chemical, physiological, genetic, anatomic) need to go off on their own in order to be able to inform us later about the disease process. Basic research must occasionally touch base with clinical problems and clinical issues must be informed by basic research.

There are times, however, when researchers do lose touch with the clinical phenomenon that began their study. In their efforts at coarse graining, they try to reduce some part of psychotic phenomena to the simpler processes they have been studying, and in this effort they may exemplify a simpleminded and erroneous reductionism that would have us believe that the psychotic phenomena are "nothing more" than those simpler processes.[12] For example, if one studies thought disorder in schizophrenia, one must be intimately acquainted with the myriad ways that thought disorder is displayed. Or if one studies concept formation, one must know how conceptual thinking gets derailed. It is a category error to place the location of these dysfunctions in a specific neuroanatomic area. Although it may be quite true, for example, that Brodmann's area 46 is *necessary* for spatial working memory to occur, it is not true that a defect in area 46 is the location of spatial working memory performance. More is required to be known, as in a network that reaches beyond the localized neuroanatomy itself (cf. Levy, Chapter 5, this volume).

A related error is the use of tests, developed and validated for a specific purpose in one special context, but applied in a different context and then interpreted as yielding information about the new and different context. For example, the Wisconsin Card Sort Test (WCST) was constructed to test frontal lobe functions in patients with diagnosable lesions of the prefrontal area. The WCST is then used to observe the performance of schizophrenic patients, and, finding impairments, investigators conclude that prefrontal functions are impaired in schizophrenics. They even may point to PET data that show diminished blood flow in the prefrontal area while patients perform the WCST. But there is no way in such a study to know if blood flow was diminished because the patients were unable to do the test, able to do the test but unwilling to do it, or if the patients were unable to do the test because blood flow was diminished in the prefrontal area. I sound here a warning against too facile jumping of levels, and against assuming that entire behavioral operations are located in any single brain area.

A final reflection

A collection of essays such as this present book looks simultaneously forward and backward in time. The authors who have contributed to this book span several decades in their ages and therefore they bring with them perspectives on their own subject matter that must reflect their own developing tradition. In our excitement with our shining present and promising future, and with the sea change of our field into something rich, and strange, and miraculous, we may forget our links with the past. At times we may then claim too much and appear a bit too puffed up by pride in our new and undeniably spectacular discoveries. Together with our soaring aspirations and highmindedness there are unmistakable elements of self-deception and a tendency to overreach in the way we present our work. It has always been so. To recognize that, along with our genuine and inspiring advances to loftier levels of knowledge, requires self-reflection, wisdom, and a sense of humor. It enables us to savor the truly astonishing accomplishments of the science of psychopathology, which we have been privileged to witness and to take part in, and to say with Miranda, "O, wonder!"

Notes

1. But see Kurt Koffka, *Principles of Gestalt Psychology* (1935), for a compendium of empirical studies that addressed the concerns of Gestalt Psychology.

2. "And what does psychiatry offer toward the alleviation of the dreadful predicament? Should we be hesitant to contribute to world thinking what we know of human nature? Is one of our colleagues wrong to suggest that perhaps it is 'not an extravagant speculation that mental hospitals will be a nucleus of future progress in man's understanding of man . . .'

   "We psychiatrists are familiar with this in another setting, that of clinical practice. Not infrequently we observe that a patient who is in a phase of recovery from what may have been a rather long illness shows continued improvement, past the point of his former 'normal' state of existence. He not only gets well, to use the vernacular; he gets as well as he was, and then he continues to improve still further. He increases his productivity, he expands his life and its horizons. He develops new talents, new powers, new effectiveness. He becomes, one might say, 'weller than well.'" (Menninger et al., 1963, p. 406).

3. The 1949 Nobel Prize in Physiology or Medicine was divided equally between Walter Hess for his discovery of the functional organization of the diencephalon, and Antonio Moniz "for his discovery of the therapeutic value of leukotomy in certain psychoses."

4. Compare Chapter 12, by Jerome Kagan, and Chapter 9, by Norman Garmezy, this volume. Kagan's introduction of temperament to explain individual consistencies in behavioral inhibition invokes genetic factors as a heuristic proposition. Garmezy, as a genetic agnostic, focuses on the learned or unlearned resilience of some children who carry with them many risk factors for subsequent psychopathology. Chapter 8 carefully examines the radical misuse of observations of childhood to advance political purposes.

5. See Chapter 15, by Roger Brown, this volume, which explores in schizophrenia the fractures in verbal behavior implicated in social interactions as politeness, and shows the possible rich yields in the imbrication of cognitive and social psychological functions.

6. In this volume, Chapter 4, by Martha E. Shenton, presents a novel view of the relations of brain function in specific areas to *dysfunctions* in psychological symptoms such as formal thought disorder.

7. Sigmund Freud acknowledged Fechner's influence on his theory of dreaming. He wrote, ". . . the great Fechner puts forward the idea that *the scene of action of dreams is different from that of waking ideational life.* This is the only hypothesis that makes the special peculiarities of dream-life intelligible." The citation is to Fechner's *Principles of Psychophysics,* and refers to the idea that the way cognitive processes function varies with state of consciousness.

8. Cf. the approach of Chapter 14, by Jean P. Chapman and Loren J. Chapman, this volume, to the preclinical aspects of schizotypy.

9. See Chapter 16, by Herbert E. Spohn, this volume, for an analysis of some of the psychological and social effects of these compounds.

10. *Macbeth,* Act V, Scene iv.
    Macbeth: Cure her of that.
    > Canst thou not minister to a mind diseas'd,
    > Pluck from the memory a rooted sorrow,
    > Raze out the written troubles of the brain,
    > And with some sweet oblivious antidote
    > Cleanse the stuff'd bosom of that perilous stuff
    > Which weighs upon the heart?
    Doctor: Therein the patient
    > Must minister to himself.

11. But see, as examples only, Gottesman & Shields (1972) for a review of the twin data, and Kety et al. (1994) for a report of a large adoption study. See, in this volume, Chapter 24 for Kenneth K. Kidd's exposition of contemporary molecular genetic methods used in the service of research in psychopathology, and Chapter 21, by Seymour S. Kety, on the pioneering behavior genetic studies that paved the way for linkage studies of mental disorders.

12. There is a clear difference between acknowledging the necessity of structures for the integrity of a set of functions and insisting that the function – the emergent behavior – resides in the structure. For example, Hippocrates taught that ". . . from nothing else but the brain come joy, despondency, and lamentation . . . and by this [organ] . . . we acquire wisdom and knowledge, and see and hear . . . By this same organ we become mad and delirious." But Sir Francis Crick's reading of this Hippocratic dictum (1994) is simplistically reductive and fails to grasp the essential issue of the emergent nature of behavior. He writes, "You, your joys and your sorrows, your memories and your ambitions, your

sense of personal identity and free will, are in fact *no more* [italics added] than the behavior of a vast assembly of nerve cells and their associated molecules."

References

American Psychiatric Association. 1968. *Diagnostic and Statistical Manual of Mental Disorders* (2nd ed.). Washington, DC.

Bleuler, E. *Dementia Praecox or the Group of Schizophrenias.* 1911/1950. New York: International Universities Press.

Boring, E. G. 1950. *A History of Experimental Psychology* (2nd ed.). New York: Appleton.

Chein, I. 1972. *The Science of Behavior and the Image of Man.* New York: Basic Books.

Crick, F. J. *The Astonishing Hypothesis.* 1994. New York: Scribner.

Fechner, G. T. 1860/1966. *Elemente der Psychophysik.* (English translation by H. E. Adler; D. H. Howes and E. G. Boring, eds.). New York: Holt, Rinehart & Winston.

Gardner, R. W., Holzman, P. S., Klein, G. S., Linton, H., and Spence, D. P. 1959. *Cognitive Control.* Monograph 4 in *Psychological Issues.* New York: International Universities Press.

Glickstein, M., and Whitteridge, D. 1987. Tatsui Inouye and the mapping of the human cerebral cortex. *Trends in Neurosciences* 10:300–353.

Gottesman, I. I., and Shields, J. 1972. *Schizophrenia and Genetics: A Twin Study Vantage Point.* New York: Academic Press.

Kety, S. S., Wender, P. H., Jacobsen, B., and Ingraham, L. J. 1994. Mental illness in the biological and adoptive relatives of schizophrenic adoptees: Replication of the Copenhagen study in the rest of Denmark. *Archives of General Psychiatry* 51:442–455.

Kevles, D. J. 1985. *In the Name of Eugenics: Genetics and the Uses of Human Heredity.* New York: Knopf, 1985.

Klein, G. S. Two theories or one. 1976. In *Psychoanalytic Theory: An Exploration of Essentials.* New York: International Universities Press, pp. 41–71.

Klein, G. S. 1970. *Perception, Motives, and Personality.* New York: Alfred A. Knopf.

Klineberg, O. 1935. *Race Differences.* New York: Harper.

Koffka, K. 1935. *Principles of Gestalt Psychology.* New York: Harcourt, Brace.

Kraepelin, E. *Psychiatrie, ein Lehrbuch für Studierend und Ärzte.* 1896. 5th ed. Leipzig: Barth.

Matthysse, S., Holzman, P. S., and Lange, K. 1986. The genetic transmission of schizophrenia: Application of Mendelian latent structure analysis to eye tracking dysfunctions in schizophrenia and affective disorder. *Journal of Psychiatric Research* 20:57–65.

Menninger, K., Mayman, M., and Pruyser, P. 1963. *The Vital Balance.* New York: Viking.

Penfield, W., and Jasper, H. H. 1954. *Epilepsy and the Functional Anatomy of the Human Brain.* Boston: Little, Brown.

Posner, M. *Chronometric Explorations of Mind.* 1978. Hillsdale, NJ: Lawrence Erlbaum.

Rapaport, D., Gill, M. M., and Schafer, R. 1946/1968. *Diagnostic Psychological Testing* (rev. ed., Robert R. Holt, ed). New York: International Universities Press.

Stern, W. *General Psychology from the Personalistic Standpoint.* 1938. (H. D. Spoerl, trans.). New York: Macmillan.

Witkin, H. A., and Goodenough, D. R. 1981. *Cognitive Styles: Essence and Origin.* In *Psychological Issues.* Monograph 51. New York: International Universities Press.

Author index

Subject index